The
ECONOMICS
of
DEVELOPING
COUNTRIES
Second Edition

E. Wayne Nafziger

Kansas State University

PRENTICE HALL, Englewood Cliffs, NJ 07632

The author and publisher kindly acknowledge permission to reprint from the following:

John W. Sewell, Stuart K. Tucker, and contributors, *Growth, Exports, and Jobs in a Changing World Economy: Agenda, 1988*, 1988. Published by permission of Transactions Publishers, from *Growth, Exports & Jobs in a Changing World Economy*, by John W. Sewell et al. Copyright © 1988 by Overseas Development Council.

Vito Tanzi, "Quantitative Characteristics of the Tax Systems of Developing Countries," in David Newbery and Nicholas Stern, eds, *The Theory of Taxation for Developing Countries*, 1987. From *The Theory Of Taxation For Developing Countries* edited by David Newbery and Nicholas Stern. Copyright © 1987 by The International Bank for Reconstruction and Development/The World Bank. Reprinted by permission of Oxford University Press, Inc.

To Lorene, Lloyd, and the memory of Mary

Editorial/production supervision and
  interior design: *Patrick Reynolds*
Cover design: *Karen Stephens*
Manufacturing buyer: *Pete Havens*

ISBN 0-13-223660-5

Prentice-Hall International (UK) Limited, *London*
Prentice-Hall of Australia Pty. Limited, *Sydney*
Prentice-Hall Canada Inc., *Toronto*
Prentice-Hall Hispanoamericana, S.A., *Mexico*
Prentice-Hall of India Private Limited, *New Delhi*
Prentice-Hall of Japan, Inc., *Tokyo*
Simon & Schuster Asia Pte. Ltd., *Singapore*
Editora Prentice-Hall do Brasil, Ltda., *Rio de Janeiro*

CONTENTS

PART II   FACTORS OF GROWTH

PART III DOMESTIC RESOURCE POLICIES

PART IV   THE INTERNATIONAL ECONOMICS OF DEVELOPMENT

PART V   DEVELOPMENT STRATEGIES

PREFACE

The growth in real income per person in the third-world nations of Latin America, Asia, and Africa, more than threefold (2.9 percent yearly) since 1950, is unprecedented and more rapid than that of developed countries in any comparable period before 1950. This growth warrants optimism, particularly in Taiwan, South Korea, Singapore, Malaysia, Thailand, Indonesia, Hong Kong, China, Brazil, and other fast-growing Pacific Rim and Middle East countries. The tragedy however is that sub-Saharan Africa, encountering growing misery and degradation from 1965 to 1990, has not shared in these gains. The sub-Sahara is not only vulnerable to the external price shocks and debt crises that destabilized the global economy in the 1970s and 1980s, but the area is also plagued by increasing food deficits, growing rural poverty, urban congestion, overvalued currencies, loss-ridden state-owned enterprises, and inefficient, highly protected, import substitution industry. The problems of Bagladesh, Nepal, Kampuchea, and Burma are as severe as Africa's.

This text focuses on real world problems—from those of newly industrializing countries, such as Taiwan and South Korea, to those of the slow-growing sub-Sahara—rather than abstract growth models. The response by reviewers, instructors, students, and practitioners in the United States, Canada, Europe, Japan, Australia, New Zealand, and the developing world to this stress in the book's first edition is gratifying. This edition continues previous themes, such as the origins of modern growth, problems measuring growth, and analyses of socialist economies (especially China), and presents an even-handed treatment of contrasting economic systems and ideologies; an integration of social, political, and economic issues; and emphases on poverty, inequality, and unemployment; with economic policies and planning discussed throughout the book.

This edition's major changes reflect recent literature or readers' suggestions. I expanded the international economics of development to three chapters, including a new Chapter 17 on the international debt problem, which examines its origins, its impact on developed and developing countries, indicators of debt, the effect of capital flight, the World Bank and International Monetary Fund proposals to resolve the debt crisis, and debt and income distribution. I also added sections on exchange-rate regimes, the floating exchange-rate system, dual exchange rates, real interest and exchange rates, the Eurocurrency market, structural adjustment loans, petroleum-exporting countries' policies, Dutch disease, export commodity concentration ratios, antiexport biases, factor proportions and trade, the product cycle model and the boomerang effect, regional integration, special economic zones, and a UN study on terms of trade, and, I expanded material on aid effectiveness and multinational corporate benefits and costs.

Another new chapter (Chapter 20) looks at state-owned enterprises, the performance of public and private sectors, and privatization, while other chapters analyze indigenization, financial repression and liberalization, the *dirigiste* debate, and why political elites reject the market. I discuss, also, the informal sector, criticisms of the Harris–Todaro model, Simon's population optimism, religion and population policy, and Islamic banking. New analyses on education and technology consist of cognitive skills and worker earnings, education and parental income, the cost of technical knowledge, and technological leadership. Chapter 12 provides more illustrations of how to do benefit-cost analysis.

Other new sections are comparison resistant services in national income accounts and female poverty. Further comparative development material includes South Africa's apartheid economy, sub-Saharan Africa's economic problems, Afro-Asian socialism, newly industrializing countries (South Korea, Taiwan, Hong Kong, and Singapore), Chinese-Indian comparisons of food productivity growth, China's economic reforms, market socialism and worker-managed socialism, the Soviet Union's perestroika or economic restructuring, Soviet and Japanese development models, Japanese and U.S. foreign investment patterns, and the industrial strategy of Japan's Ministry of International Trade and Industry.

The order of chapters changes so the basic facts of economic development and growth (Chapter 3) precede a profile of developing countries (Chapter 4), while theories (Chapter 5) come before Chapters 6 and 7 on poverty, inequality, and agricultural transformation. Furthermore, I have updated tables, figures, and the chapter-end guides to readings.

ACKNOWLEDGMENTS

I am indebted to numerous colleagues and students in the developed and developing world for helping shape my ideas about development economics. I especially benefited from the comments and criticisms of Professors John Adams, Edgar S. Bagley, Thomas W. Bonsor, Antonio Bos, Martin Bronfenbrenner, Wayne Davis, David Edmonds, Patrick J. Gormely, Roy Grohs, Ichirou Inukai, Paul Koch, James Ragan, James Rhodes, Gordon Smith, Meredith Smith, Shanti Tangri, Roger Trenary, Rodney Wilson, Mahmood Yousefi, and Maurice Ballabon. J. Ay from the Food and Agriculture Organization of the United Nations was kind enough to compile Table 7-2 for the book. Edward Minges, Margaret Grosh, Brent Jacques, Stephanie Young, Karen McCulloh, and Carolyn Welfield provided research and proofreading assistance, and Thomas Mettille helped in cover design. Bill Webber, Whitney Blake, Kathleen Dorman, Patrick Reynolds, Jan Nichol, Diane Cupra, and others at Prentice Hall contributed their professionalism to the book. Elfrieda, Brian, and Kevin Nafziger not only assisted in the project, but tolerated inconveniences and assumed responsibilities to leave me more time for writing. Although I am grateful to all who helped, I am solely responsible for any drawbacks in the book.

  I am also grateful to the following for permission to reproduce copyrighted materials: Basil Blackwell Ltd for tables from Celso Furtado, *Economic Development in Latin America* and David Morawetz, "Employment Implications of Industry in Developing Countries," *Economic Journal* 84 (September 1974); the United States Department of Agriculture for graph from *World Indices of Agricultural and Food Production, 1950–86;* Hyperion Press, Inc. for a quote from Maurice Dobb, *Capitalist Enterprise and Social Progress;* the Canadian Tax Foundation for table from David B. Perry, "International Tax Comparisons," in the Fiscal Figures feature *Canadian Tax Journal* 28 (January–February 1980): 91; The East-West Center for table from E. Wayne Nafziger, *Class, Caste, and Entrepreneurship,* University Press of Hawaii; Pergamon Press and author Karsten Laurson for table from "The Integrated Programme for Commodities," *World Development* 8 (April 1978); the International Labor Organization for chart from *Profiles of Rural Poverty* and table from Jacques Lecaillon, Felix Paukert, Christian Morrisson, and Dimitri Germidis, *Income Distribution and Economic Development: An Analytical Survey;* Mrs. Simon Kuznets for Simon Kuznets', "Levels and Variability of Rates of Growth," *Economic Development and Cultural Change* 5 (October 1956); the University of Chicago Press for graph and table from Margaret E. Grosh and E. Wayne Nafziger, "The Computation of World Income Distribution," *Economic Development and*

Cultural Change 34 (January 1986); the Federal Reserve Bank of Kansas City for figures from Mark Drabenstott, Alan Barkema, and David Henneberry, "The Latin American Debt Problem and U.S. Agriculture," *Economic Review,* July/August 1988; North-Holland Publishing Co. and authors Montek S. Ahluwalia, Nicholas G. Carter, and Hollis B. Chenery for tables from "Growth and Poverty in Developng Countries," *Journal of Development Economics* 6 (September 1979); the *Economic Record* for table from M. L. Parker, "An Inter-industry Approach to Planning in Papua New Guinea," September 1974; the International Food Policy Research Institute for table from Leonardo A. Paulino, *Food in the Third World: Past Trends and Projections to 2000,* June 1986; Joginder S. Uppal for table from *Economic Development in South Asia;* the United Nations for quote from Economic Commission for Africa, "ECA and Africa's Development, 1983–2008"; Addis Ababa for 1983 figure from *Demographic Yearbook, 1976,* and table from the *National Account Statistics: Main Aggregates and Detailed Tables, 1985;* the Food and Agriculture Organization of the United Nations for table from Appendix I on page 91 of *The Fourth World Food Survey, 1977;* the International Monetary Fund for tables from *Government Finance Statistics Yearbook, 1984, International Financial Statistics Yearbook, 1981, IMF Survey,* November 30, 1987, and July 25, 1988, *World Economic Outlook,* October 1988, and R.P. Short, "The Role of Public Enterprises: An International Statistical Comparison," May 17, 1983; and Population Reference Bureau, Inc. for tables and graphs from the *1987* and *1988 World Population Data Sheets;* Robert Repetto, "Population, Resources, Environment: An Uncertain Future," *Population Bulletin,* Vol. 42, No. 4 (July 1987); Carl Haub, "Understanding Population Projections," *Population Bulletin,* Vol. 42, No. 2 (December 1987); Madgda McHale and John McHale, "World of Children," *Population Bulletin,* Vol. 33, No. 6 (January 1979); and Thomas W. Merrick, "World Population in Transition," *Population Bulletin,* Vol. 41, No. 2 (April 1986). Thanks to The Economist for graph from *The Economist* (November 7, 1987) copyright 1987 The Economist Newspaper Limited. Reprinted with permission. We are grateful to Macmillan Publishing Company for material from *Entrepreneurship and Economic Development,* Peter Kilby, Editor, Copyright 1971 by The Free Press, a Division of Macmillian, Inc. Reprinted by permission of the publisher. We also acknowledge the World Bank's permission for tables and graphs from the annual *World Development Reports 1979–1988* (New York: Oxford University Press); the *World Debt Tables: External Debt of Developing Countries,* 1988; the *World Bank Atlas; World Tables 1980* (Baltimore: Johns Hopkins University Press, 1980); Michael A. Cohen, "Cities in Developing Countries, 1975–2000," *Finance and Development* (March 1976); Hollis B. Chenery and Moises Synquin, *Patterns of Development, 1950–1970* (New York: Oxford University Press); Hollis Chenery, Montek S. Ahluwalia, C. L. G. Bell, John H. Duloy, and Richard Jolly, *Redistribution with Growth* (London: Oxford University Press); and David Morawetz, *Twenty-five Years of Economic Development, 1950 to 1975* (Baltimore: Johns Hopkins University Press, 1977); and Lyn Squire, *Employment Policy in Developing Countries: A Survey of Issues and Evidence* (New York: Oxford University Press, 1981), pp. 44–45. I have made every effort to trace copyright owners, but in a few cases this was impossible. I apologize to any author or publisher on whose rights I may have unwittingly infringed.

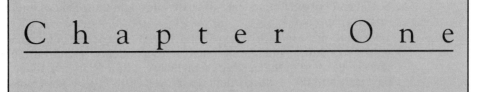

INTRODUCTION

NATURE AND SCOPE OF THE TEXT

This book is an introduction to the economics of development in less developed countries of Asia, Africa, and Latin America. It is suitable for economics majors and students from other disciplines.

The book differs from many other development textbooks,

1. Unlike most texts, it discusses why modern economic growth originated in the West; gives reasons for Soviet and Japanese growth; and explains different growth rates among developing countries, including the success of the newly industrializing countries—especially South Korea and Taiwan.
2. The book illustrates concepts from all major third-world regions (Latin America, Asia, and Africa), with a special emphasis on sub-Saharan Africa's food and economic crisis.
3. Instead of stressing abstract models of aggregate economic growth, it emphasizes poverty, inequality, unemployment, and deficiencies in food, clothing, housing, education, and health of people in less developed countries.
4. Rather than being isolated in a separate chapter, employment and income distribution are discussed along with development throughout the book.
5. Problems of measuring economic growth are stressed along with adjusting income for purchasing power.

6. Social and political factors are discussed throughout instead of limited to one or two chapters.

7. Economic performance is explained in the context of both domestic and global economies, and international interdependence is stressed. Three chapters are devoted to the balance of payments, aid, foreign investment, technology transfer, the external debt crisis, structural adjustment, international trade, exchange-rate policies, regional economic integration, and the demand for a new international economic order.

8. The text analyzes views opposed to prevailing Western economic thought. Two of these views are the dependency theory, which explains the underdevelopment of the third world in terms of the economic and political domination of the industrialized world; and Neo-Marxism, which sees international class conflict as a struggle by workers and peasants in the developing world against their own political elite, who are in alliance with the elite of the developed world. Only by carefully considering these perspectives can the reader understand third-world economic ideologies, political discontent, and demands for a change in the international economic order. I try to present a balanced view of Neo-Marxism and the dependence theory—neither attributing these views to a "devil theory of history" nor using them to explain the distributional effects of international trade as unequivocally unfavorable to developing countries.

9. I try to provide a more detailed and balanced discussion of developing socialist countries, such as China, Yugoslavia, and Cuba. I analyze centralized and market–socialist systems but go beyond the frequently uncritical enthusiasm for market reforms and the reflex condemnation of centralized socialism.

10. The discussion on development planning is integrated with other chapters, emphasizing that antipoverty programs, family planning, agricultural research and extension, employment policies, education, local technology, savings, investment project analysis, monetary and fiscal policies, entrepreneurial development programs, and international trade and capital flows are included in economic planning. I analyze the *dirigiste* debate (largely on the role of government) and discuss privatization in a new chapter on state-owned enterprises.

ORGANIZATION OF THE TEXT

The book is organized into four parts. The first seven chapters focus on concepts, basic facts, and theories of economic development. Chapters 8–13 examine the role of production factors and technology in economic development. Chapters 14 and 15 discuss policies that might mobilize domestic resources, while Chapters 16–18 include the international economics of development. Chapter 19 looks at planning for economic development, and Chapter 20 analyzes public enterprises.

Sections presenting terms to review, questions to discuss, and guides to readings can be found at the end of each chapter. Highlighted terms are defined or identified on pages designated in boldface in the Subject Index. While the guides to readings provide bibliographical help for each chapter's topic, the Name and Author Index indicates in boldface the page on which each bibliographical item is first cited in full.

HOW THE OTHER TWO-THIRDS LIVE

Development economics focuses primarily on the poorest two-thirds of the world's population. These poor are the vast majority, but not all, of the population of developing countries. Many of them are inadequately fed and housed, in poor health, and illiterate. A careful estimate of international protein and calorie distribution indicates that about 1.5 billion of the world's 5.2 billion people are undernourished.[1] Most Americans and Canadians have never seen poverty like that in most of Africa, Asia, and Latin America.

If you have an average income in the United States and Canada, you are among the richest 10 percent of the world's population. The economic concerns of this 10 percent are in stark contrast to those of the majority of people on this planet. The majority see the American with average income as incredibly rich, perhaps as an average American views the Mellons or Rockefellers. Income inequality is even greater for the world as a whole than for countries having high income concentration, such as South Africa and Honduras. To see these contrasts more clearly, let us briefly compare living conditions in one low-income country to those in the United States and Canada.

An average intact family in the United States and Canada, the Smiths, a family of four, has an annual income of $35,000. They live in a comfortable apartment or suburban home with three bedrooms, a living room, kitchen, and numerous electrical appliances and consumer goods. Their three meals a day include coffee from Brazil, tinned fruit from the Philippines, and bananas from Ecuador.

The Smith children are in good health and have an average life expectancy of 76 years. Both parents received a secondary education, and the children can be expected to finish high school and possibly go to a university. Their jobs, even where these require physical work, will probably be relieved by modern machinery and technology. But though the Smiths seem to have a reasonably good life, they may experience stress, frustration, boredom, insecurity, and a lack of meaning and control over their lives. Their air may be dirty, water polluted, and roads congested. Some of these problems may even result from economic progress. Nevertheless millions of less fortunate people throughout the world would be happy with even a portion of the Smiths' material affluence.

The family of Balayya, a farm laborer in India, has a life far different from the Smiths'. Though work, family structure, food, housing, clothing, and recreational patterns vary widely in the developing world, Balayya's family illustrates the relative poverty of a majority of the world's population. Balayya, his wife, Kamani, and their four children, ranging in age from 3 to 12 years, have a combined annual income of $500 to $700, most of which consists of goods produced rather than money earned. Under a complex division of labor, the family receives consumption shares from the patron (or landlord) in return for agricultural work—plowing, transplanting, threshing, stacking, and so on.

The rice-based daily meal, the one-room mud house thatched with palm leaves, and the crudely stitched clothing are produced locally. The house has no electricity, clean water, or latrine. Kamani fetches the day's water supply from the

---

[1] This figure is based on an update of estimates by Shlomo Reutlinger and Marcelo Selowsky, *Malnutrition and Poverty: Magnitude and Policy Options* (Baltimore: Johns Hopkins University Press, 1976).

village well, a kilometer away. Although there is much illness, the nearest doctor, nurse, or midwife is 50 kilometers away, serving affluent city dwellers. Average life expectancy is 54 years. Few villagers can afford the bus that twice daily connects a neighboring village to the city, 40 kilometers away. The family's world is circumscribed by the distance a person can walk in a day.

Neither Balayya nor Kamani can read or write. One of their children attended school regularly for 3 years but dropped out before completing primary school. The child will probably not return to school.

Despite inadequate food, Balayya and the two sons over 7 years old toil hard under the blazing sun, aided by only a few simple tools. During the peak season of planting, transplanting, and harvesting, the work is from sunrise to sunset. Kamani, with help from a 6-year-old daughter, spends most of her long working day in the courtyard near the house. Games, visiting, gossip, storytelling, music, dancing, plays, worship, religious fairs and festivals, weddings, and funerals provide respite from the daily struggle for survival.

Balayya has no savings. Like his father before him, he will be perpetually in debt to the landlord for expenditures, not only for occasional emergencies, but also for the proper marriages of daughters in the family.

The common stereotype is that peasant, agricultural societies have populations with roughly uniform poverty, a generally false view. Although many third-world villagers are poor, a number are better off. A tiny middle and upper class even exists. Accordingly, Sridhar, Balayya's landlord, together with his extended family—his wife, two unmarried children, two married sons, their wives, and their children—is relatively prosperous. The family, whose annual income is $3500, lives in a five- to six-room, brick house with a tile roof and a large courtyard. Their two daily meals consist of a variety of meats as well as seasonal fruits and vegetables.[2] Machine-stitched clothes are acquired from the local tailor, the village bazaar (open-air marketplace), or on monthly bus trips to the city. The house has electric lights and fans. Servants shop for food, cook, clean, carry water, and tend the lawn and garden. Sridhar and his sons and grandchildren have completed primary school. Some of the grandsons, and occasionally a granddaughter, will complete secondary school, or even graduate from the university.

Congestion, squalor, destitution, and insecurity characterize the lives of the unemployed, underemployed, and marginally employed in large Indian cities such as Calcutta, Bombay, and Delhi—more so than for the rural, landless worker. In the central city, people literally live in the street, where they eat, wash, defecate, and sleep on or near the pavement.[3] During the monsoon season, they huddle under the overhanging roofs of nearby commercial establishments. Others with menial jobs live in crowded, blighted huts and tenement houses that make up urban shantytowns. In contrast the family whose major income earner is steadily employed as an assembly line worker in a large company or as a government clerk may live in a small house or apartment. Upper-income professionals, civil servants, and business people usually live in large houses of five to six rooms. Although they have fewer electrical appliances than the Smiths, they achieve some of the same material comfort by hiring servants.

Social institutions and lifestyles vary greatly among third-world countries.

---

[2] Some Indian castes prohibit eating meat for religious reasons.

[3] See N. Vijay Jagannathan and Animsesh Halder, "Income–Housing Linkages: A Case Study of Pavement Dwellers in Calcutta," *Economic and Political Weekly* 23 (June 4, 1988): 1175–78.

Nevertheless, most low-income countries have income inequality and poverty rates as high as India's. Even the poorest Americans are better off than most of the people in India and other low-income countries.

CRITICAL QUESTIONS IN DEVELOPMENT ECONOMICS

An introduction to development economics should help you gain a better understanding of a number of critical questions relating to the economics of the developing world. The following list is a sample of twenty such questions. Each is numbered to correspond to the chapter where it is primarily discussed.

1. How do the poorest two-thirds of the world live?
2. What is the meaning of economic development and economic growth?
3. How have developing countries performed economically since World War II?
4. What are the major characteristics of developing countries?
5. What are the major theories of economic development?
6. Has economic growth in the third world improved the living conditions of its poor?
7. How can poverty be reduced in the rural areas of low-income countries?
8. Is the lack of natural resources a major limitation to the economic development of poor countries?
9. What effect does population growth have on economic development and income equality?
10. Why is there so much unemployment in developing countries?
11. What factors affect labor skills in the third world?
12. What criteria should be used to allocate capital between alternative projects?
13. What factors contribute to successful entrepreneurial activity in developing countries?
14. How can a country increase its rate of capital formation?
15. What monetary and fiscal policies should a country use to achieve economic development with price stability?
16. How can less-developed countries (LDCs) improve their balance of payments position?
17. What policies can ease the debt crisis in many developing countries?
18. Should developing countries use tariffs to protect local industry?
19. Should developing countries rely on market decisions or state planning in allocating resources?
20. Should LDCs privatize state-owned enterprises or use other policies to improve their performance?

LIMITATIONS OF STANDARD ECONOMIC THEORY

These questions are only some of those to be explored. The answers may be more complex than you think. When analyzing the developing countries, rigid adherence to standard economic theory creates problems. Unlike developed countries, developing economies frequently do *not* have a mobile and highly educated labor force, commercial farmers with sizable land holdings, large numbers of responsive entrepreneurs, a favorable climate for enterprise, a high level of technical knowledge, local ownership of industry, heavy reliance on direct taxes for revenue, a large number of export commodities, an average income substantially above subsistence, a well-developed capital market, and a high savings rate. The problems of developing economies are often unique. You may have to unlearn much when studying their economies. As a leading development economist, Dudley Seers, suggests, "The abler the student has been in absorbing the current doctrine, the more difficult the process of adaptation" to a study of the third world.[4] Although this is probably overstated, you must set aside your preconceptions and keep your mind open to other approaches and concepts in analyzing a world different, in many ways, from the United States, Canada, and Western Europe

---

QUESTIONS TO DISCUSS

1. What do you hope to gain from a course in economic development (besides a good grade)?

2. Why is studying economics so central to understanding the problems of developing countries?

3. What impact might rapid economic development have on the lifestyle of Balayya's family? Calcutta's marginally employed?

4. Would you expect the development goal for the Indian poor to be a lifestyle like that of the Smiths?

5. Why are economic theories about developing countries different from those based on Western experience? What assumptions are involved in each case?

6. Give an example of how rigid adherence to Western economic theory may hinder understanding the developing world.

GUIDE TO READINGS

H. W. Arndt, *Economic Development: The History of an Idea* (Chicago: University of Chicago Press, 1987), traces the history of thought about economic development as a policy objective. Seers (note 4) is the focus of discussion by Kurt Martin and John Knapp, eds., *The Teaching of Development Economics* (Chicago: Aldine, 1967), the proceedings of a conference on teaching and learning development economics. In *International Development Review* 11 (December 1969): 1–16, Seers examines "The Meaning of Development," reprinted in David Lehmann, ed., *Development Theory: Four Critical Studies* (London: Frank Cass, 1979), with critical essays on development theory by Seers, E. Wayne Nafziger, Donal Cruise O'Brien, and Henry Bernstein. Deepak Lal, *The Poverty of "Development Economics"*

[4] Dudley Seers, "The Limitations of the Special Case," *Bulletin of the Oxford Institute of Economics and Statistics* 25 (May 1963): 77–98.

(Cambridge, Mass.: Harvard University Press, 1985), criticizes Seers's emphasis on government involvement in LDCs (see Chapter 19).

The February 1986 issue of *World Development* 14 is devoted to a review of the methodology of development economics. Paul Streeten discusses development theories in "A Problem to Every Solution," *Finance and Development* 22 (June 1985): 16–21.

Nobel laureate Gunnar Myrdal discusses the role of values and biases in development economics in *The Challenge of World Poverty: A World Antipoverty Program in Outline* (New York: Vintage Books, 1970), pp. 3–29.

Jagannathan's and Halder's survey (note 3) of the life and work of pavement dwellers in Calcutta is excellent.

THE MEANING AND MEASUREMENT OF ECONOMIC DEVELOPMENT

SCOPE OF THE CHAPTER

This chapter introduces and evaluates terms and measures needed to discuss international differences in material well-being. We include the following:

1. The meaning of economic growth and economic development.
2. The classification of rich and poor countries.
3. The distortion in comparing income per head between rich and poor countries.
4. Adjustments to income figures for purchasing power.
5. Alternative measures and concepts of the level of economic development besides income per head.
6. The problems of alternative measures.
7. The costs and benefits of economic development.

GROWTH AND DEVELOPMENT

A major goal of poor countries is economic development or economic growth. The two terms are not identical. Growth may be necessary but not sufficient for development. **Economic growth** refers to increases in a country's production or income per capita (Box 2-1). Production is usually measured by **gross national product** (GNP), an economy's total output of goods and services. **Economic development** refers to

---

Box 2-1

Assume that in 1989, GNP for India is Rs. (rupees) 3735 billion and its population 830 million, so that **GNP per capita** is Rs. 4500. The GNP in 1990, Rs. 4270 billion, must be divided by the **GNP price deflator,** 1.10 (corresponding to an annual inflation rate of 10 percent) to give a GNP of Rs. 3882 billion at constant (1989) prices. This figure divided by the population in 1990, 845.75 million, nets a GNP per capita of Rs. 4590. **Real economic growth** (growth in real GNP per capita) from 1989 to 1990 is (if expressed in 1989 constant prices)

$$\frac{4590-4500}{4500} = 2.0 \text{ percent}$$

Cross-national comparisons of economic growth rates (1989–90) by such organizations as the World Bank might be calculated in the following manner. The GNP figures in 1989 and 1990 are converted into U.S. dollars at the average exchange rate for the year. Thus 1990 GNP is adjusted for U.S. inflation between 1989 and 1990, rather than Indian inflation. The GNP is divided by population in the middle of the year to determine GNP per capita for each year. From this computation, we obtain a growth rate in GNP per capita in India that can be compared to growth rates in other countries.

Thus at an exchange rate of Rs. 14 = \$1, India's GNP of Rs. 3735 billion is \$266.8 billion for 1989, and Rs 4270 billion is \$305.0 billion for 1990. If U.S. inflation is 9 percent in 1990, GNP in constant (1989) prices is \$279.8 billion. Estimated GNP per capita is \$321.4 in 1989, and \$330.8 in 1990, a growth rate of 2.9 percent per year.

---

economic growth accompanied by changes in output distribution and economic structure. These changes may include an improvement in the material well-being of the poorer half of the population; a decline in agriculture's share of GNP and a corresponding increase in the GNP share of manufacturing, finance, construction, and government administration; an increase in the education and skills of the labor force; and substantial technical advances originating within the country. As with children, growth involves a stress on quantitative measures (height or GNP), whereas development draws attention to changes in capacities (such as physical coordination and learning ability, or the economy's ability to adapt to shifts in tastes and technology).

The pendulum has swung between growth and development.[1] A major shift came near the end of the UN's first development decade (1960–70), which had stressed economic growth in poor countries. Because the benefits of growth did not often spread to the poorer half of the population, disillusionment with the decade's progress was widespread, even though economic growth exceeded the UN target. In 1969, Dudley Seers signaled this shift by asking the following questions about a country's development:

---

[1] Immediately after World War II, scholars and third-world governments were concerned with wider objectives than simply growth. However Nobel laureate W. Arthur Lewis set the tone for the late 1950s and 1960s when he noted that "our subject matter is growth, and not distribution." *The Theory of Economic Growth* (Homewood, Ill.: Richard D. Irwin, 1955), p. 9.

What has been happening to poverty? What has been happening to unemployment? What has been happening to inequality? If all three of these have become less severe, then beyond doubt this has been a period of development for the country concerned. If one or two of these central problems have been growing worse, especially if all three have, it would be strange to call the result "development," even if per capita income has soared.[2]

In 1972, Robert McNamara, then World Bank president, declared that despite the relatively rapid economic growth of developing countries, the world remains one

in which hundreds of millions of people are not only poor in statistical terms but are faced with day to day privations that degrade human dignity to levels which no statistics can adequately describe. . . . Two-thirds of the children [who live beyond five years of age] have their physical and mental growth stunted by malnutrition. There are 100 million more adult illiterates than there were twenty years ago. Education and employment are scarce, squalor and stagnation common.[3]

Despite past growth, the Economic Commission for Africa's (ECA's) 1983 twenty-fifth anniversary projection of past trends to 2008 envisions the following nightmare of explosive population growth pressing on physical resources and social services:

The socio-economic conditions would be characterized by a degradation of the very essence of human dignity. The rural population, which would have to survive on intolerable toil, will face an almost disastrous situation of land scarcity whereby whole families would have to subsist on a mere hectare of land. Poverty would reach unimaginable dimensions, since rural incomes would become almost negligible relative to the cost of physical goods and services.

The conditions in the urban centers would also worsen with more shanty towns, more congested roads, more beggars and more delinquents. The level of the unemployed searching desperately for the means to survive would imply increased crime rates and misery. But, alongside the misery, there would continue to be those very few who, unashamedly, would demonstrate an even higher degree of conspicuous consumption. These very few would continue to demand that the national department stores be filled with imports of luxury goods even if spare parts for essential production units cannot be procured for lack of foreign exchange.[4]

The ECA described Africa's economic situation in 1984 as the worst since the Great Depression, and Africa as "the very sick child of the international economy." Recognizing this, the UN devoted its thirteenth special session in 1986 to develop a

[2] Dudley Seers, "The Meaning of Development," *International Development Review* 11 (December 1969): 3–4.

[3] Robert S. McNamara, address to the UN Conference on Trade and Development, Santiago, Chile, April 14, 1972 (Washington, D.C.: World Bank, 1972), pp.2–3.

[4] Economic Commission for Africa, "ECA and Africa's Development, 1983–2008," Addis Ababa, 1983, pp. 93–94.

strategy to safeguard Africa's economic survival.[5] Thus growth can take place without development.

Economic development can refer not only to the *rate* of change in economic well-being, but also to its *level*. Between 1870 and 1986, Japan had a rapid rate of economic development. Its real (inflation-adjusted) growth rate in GNP per capita was 3.5 percent per year, and there was substantial technical innovation, improved income distribution, and a decline in the share of the labor force in agriculture. On the other hand, Japan has a high level of economic development—its 1986 per capita GNP, $12,840, placed it among the ten richest countries in the world (Table 2-1). Other measures indicate most Japanese are well fed and housed, in good health, and well educated. Only a relative few are poor. This book will use both meanings of economic development.

CLASSIFICATION OF COUNTRIES

When the serious study of development economics began in the late 1940s and early 1950s, it was common to think of rich and poor countries as separated by a wide gulf. The rich included Western Europe, the United States, Canada, Australia, New Zealand, and Japan; and the poor, Asia, Africa, and Latin America.

The boundary between rich and poor countries, overly simple then, has become even more blurred in the 1990s. Today an increasing number of the high- and upper-middle-income countries are non-Western, and the fastest-growing countries are not necessarily the ones with the highest per capita GNP. Those countries considered poor in 1950 grew at about the same rate as rich countries during the subsequent three decades (see Chapter 3). A few of the poor countries in 1950, such as Brazil, Taiwan, Turkey, South Korea, Malaysia, and Thailand, and several countries that later became major oil exporters, grew so much more rapidly than some higher-income countries in 1950 (Ireland and New Zealand, for example) that the GNP per capita of the countries of the world now forms a continuum rather than a dichotomy (see Figure 2-1).[6]

Several GNP per capita rankings shifted substantially between 1950 and 1986. Among seventy present-day Afro-Asian and Latin American LDCs listed in both GNP per capita rankings for 1950 in a World Bank study and for 1986 in Table 2-1, Venezuela fell from first to fourth, Uruguay from second to tenth, and Argentina from third to seventh, being overpassed by war-affected Japan (now one of the richest eight countries in the world), Taiwan (which rose from thirty-fifth to third), and South Korea, which vaulted from forty-fifth to sixth. Another Latin American nation, Chile, fell from from fifth to eighteenth; Peru, from eleventh to twenty-third;

[5] Economic Commission for Africa, *Survey of Economic and Social Conditions in Africa, 1983–1984,* E/ECA/CM 11/16, Addis Ababa, 1985, p. 3; and UN General Assembly, *Programme of Action for African Economic Recovery and Development, 1986–1990* (New York, 1986).

[6] Graduating from developing to developed country is not merely of academic interest, since international agencies such as the General Agreements on Tariffs and Trade (GATT), that set rules for international trade expect reciprocity among developed countries in trade agreements but extend preferential treatment to developing countries. K. A. Koekkoek, "The Integration of Developing Countries in the GATT System," *World Development* (August 1988): 947–57.

TABLE 2-1 Selected Indicators of Development

Country	Population (millions) mid-1986	GNP per Capita 1986 ($)	Average Annual Growth Rate of GNP per Capita 1965–86 (percent)	Life Expectancy at Birth 1985 (years)	Infant Mortality per 1000 Live Births 1985	Adult Literacy Rate 1985 (percent)	POLI[a]	Energy Consumption per Capita 1986 (kilograms of coal equivalent)
Low-income countries	2,493.0 t	270 w	3.1 w	60 w	71 w	55 w	60 w	314 w
China and India	1,835.4 t	300 w	3.7 w	63 w	58 w	58 w	64 w	394 w
Other low income	657.6 t	200 w	0.5 w	52 w	108 w	44 w	51 w	86 w
*Chad	5.1	110		45	138	26	34	
*Ethiopia	43.5	120	0	45	168	8	25	21
*Bhutan	1.3	150		44	133	5	26	
*Burkina Faso	8.1	150	1.3	45	144	13	29	18
*Nepal	17.0	150	1.9	47	133	26	36	23
*Bangladesh	103.2	160	0.4	51	123	33	43	46
*Malawi	7.4	160	0.4	45	156	41	37	43
Zaïre	31.7	160	-2.2	51	102	61	55	73
Cambodia	..	170		46	145	75	50	60
*Mali	7.6	180	1.1	46	174	17	28	23
Burma	38.0	200	2.3	59	66	78	71	76
Mozambique	14.2	210		47	123	38	41	86
Viet Nam (CP)	63.3	210		65	49	84	80	87
Madagascar	10.6	230	-1.7	52	109	68	57	40
*Uganda	15.2	230	-2.6	49	108	57	51	26
*Burundi	4.8	240	1.8	48	118	34	41	21

*Tanzania	23.0	250	-0.3	52	110	85	63	35
*Togo	3.1	250	0.2	51	97	41	48	52
*Niger	6.6	260	-2.2	44	140	14	28	42
*Benin	4.2	270	0.2	49	115	26	40	46
*Somalia	5.5	280	-0.3	46	152	12	29	82
*Central African Rep.	2.7	290	-0.6	49	137	41	43	30
India	781.4	290	1.8	56	89	44	55	208
*Rwanda	6.2	290	1.5	48	12	47	45	42
*Afghanistan	14.2	300		38	187	24	21	71
China (CP)	1,054.0	300	5.1	69	35	69	71	532
Kenya	21.2	300	1.9	54	91	59	58	100
Zambia	6.9	300	-1.7	52	84	76	62	381
*Sierra Leone	3.8	310	0.2	40	175	29	26	77
*Sudan	22.6	320	-0.2	48	112	31	41	58
*Guinea	6.3	330		40	153	28	28	59
*Haiti	6.1	330	0.6	54	123	38	48	50
Pakistan	99.2	350	2.4	51	115	30	43	205
*Lesotho	1.6	370	5.6	54	106	74	61	:
Ghana	13.2	390	-1.7	53	94	53	56	131
Sri Lanka	16.1	400	2.9	70	36	87	87	139
*Mauritania	1.8	420	-0.3	47	132	17	33	114
*Senegal	6.8	420	-0.6	47	137	28	36	116
*Laos PDR	3.7	440		45	151	84	85	37
Middle-income countries	1367.8	1,270	2.6	62	67	73	73	907
Liberia	2.3	460	-1.4	50	127	35	43	166
*Yemen PDR		470		46	145	42	39	714
Indonesia	166.4	490	4.6	55	96	74	63	213
*Yemen Arab Rep.	8.2	550	4.7	45	154	14	28	102
Philippines	57.3	560	1.9	63	48	86	79	180

TABLE 2-1 Continued

Country	Population (millions) mid-1986	GNP per Capita 1986 ($)	Average Annual Growth Rate of GNP per Capita 1965–86 (percent)	Life Expectancy at Birth 1985 (years)	Infant Mortality per 1000 Live Births 1985	Adult Literacy Rate 1985 (percent)	PQLI[a]	Energy Consumption per Capita 1986 (kilograms of coal equivalent)
Morocco	22.5	590	1.9	59	90	33	54	246
Bolivia	6.6	600	−0.4	53	117	74	59	255
Zimbabwe	8.7	620	1.2	57	77	74	67	517
Nigeria	103.1	640	1.9	50	109	43	47	134
Dominican Rep.	6.6	710	2.5	64	70	77	75	337
Papua New Guinea	3.4	720	0.5	52	68	45	54	244
Ivory Coast	10.7	730	1.2	52	105	43	60	175
Honduras	4.5	740	0.3	62	76	59	67	192
Egypt	49.7	760	3.1	61	93	45	60	577
Nicaragua	3.4	760	3.1	59	69	88	74	259
Thailand	52.6	810	4.0	64	43	91	82	325
El Salvador	4.9	820	−0.3	64	65	72	74	216
Angola	9.0	840		44	143	41	37	202
*Botswana	1.1	840	8.8	57	71	71	66	430
Jamaica	2.4	840	−1.4	73	20	92	92	844
Mongolia (CP)	2.0	850		63	49	90	80	1195
Cuba (CP)	10.2	860		77	16	96	98	1086
Cameroon	10.5	910	3.9	55	89	56	58	142
Albania (CP)	3.0	920		70	43	75	82	1664
Guatemala	8.2	930	1.4	60	65	56	64	171

Country							
Congo, People's Rep.	2.0	990	3.6	58	77	63	64	225
Paraguay	3.8	1,000	3.6	66	43	88	83	224
Peru	19.8	1,090	0.1	59	94	85	71	478
Turkey	51.5	1,100	2.7	64	84	74	73	750
Tunisia	7.3	1,140	3.8	63	78	54	66	499
Ecuador	9.6	1,160	3.5	66	67	82	79	575
Mauritius	1.0	1,200	3.0	66	25	83	83	378
Colombia	29.0	1,230	2.8	65	48	88	82	728
Korea, Dem. Rep. (CP)	20.9	1,290		68	27	85	85	2174
Chile	12.2	1,320	−0.2	70	22	97	91	812
Costa Rica	2.6	1,480	1.6	74	19	94	94	565
Jordan	3.6	1,540	5.5	65	49	75	77	767
Syrian, Arab Rep	10.8	1,570	3.7	64	54	60	71	914
Brazil	138.4	1,810	4.3	65	67	78	77	830
Malaysia	16.1	1,830	4.3	68	28	73	81	762
South Africa	32.3	1,850	0.4	55	78	76	66	2470
Mexico	80.2	1,860	2.6	67	50	90	84	1235
Uruguay	3.0	1,900	1.4	72	29	94	91	742
Iraq	45.6	1,970		61	73	47	62	734
Hungary (CP)	10.6	2,020	3.9	71	20	98	93	2985
Poland (CP)	37.5	2,070		72	19	98	94	3369
Lebanon	3.3	2,190		66	44	77	79	846
Portugal	10.2	2,250	3.2	74	19	85	91	1284
Yugoslavia	23.3	2,300	3.9	72	27	92	91	2041
Panama	2.2	2,330	2.4	72	25	88	90	653
Argentina	31.0	2,350	0.2	70	34	96	90	1427
Korea, Rep. of	41.5	2,370	6.7	69	27	92	88	1408
Algeria	22.4	2,590	3.5	61	81	50	62	1034
Venezuela	17.8	2,920	0.4	70	37	87	87	2502
Gabon	1.0	3,080	1.9	51	108	62	54	1141

TABLE 2-1 Continued

Country	Population (millions) mid-1986	GNP per Capita 1986 ($)	Average Annual Growth Rate of GNP per Capita 1965–86 (percent)	Life Expectancy at Birth 1985 (years)	Infant Mortality per 1000 Live Births 1985	Adult Literacy Rate 1985 (percent)	PQLI[a]	Energy Consumption per Capita 1986 (kilograms of coal equivalent)
Taiwan	19.6	3,580	6.5	73	7	92	94	2127
Greece	10.0	3,680	3.3	75	14	98	97	1932
Iran, Islamic Rep.	45.6	3,690		60	111	51	59	958
Spain	38.7	4,860	2.9	77	10	95	98	1928
Oman	1.3	4,980	5.0	54	10	30	46	2146
Ireland	3.6	5,070	1.7	74	10	99	96	2436
Trinidad and Tobago	1.2	5,360	1.6	69	22	96	90	4778
Romania (CP)	22.9	5,470		72	24	93	91	3405
High-income oil exporters	19.1	6,740	1.8	63	61	39	62	3313
Libya	3.9	6,050		60	90	66	66	2259
Saudi Arabia	12.0	6,950	4.0	62	61	24	56	3336
Kuwait	1.8	13,890	−0.6	72	22	70	84	4080
United Arab Emirates	1.4	14,680		70	35	48	74	5086
High-income countries	1033.5	11,510	2.5	74	15	99	96	5,041
Israel	4.3	6,210	2.6	75	14	95	96	1,944
Bulgaria (CP)	9.0	6,620		71	16	95	92	4,590
Hong Kong	5.4	6,910	6.2	76	9	88	95	1,260
Singapore	2.6	7,410	7.6	73	9	86	91	1,851
New Zealand	3.3	7,460	1.5	74	11	99	96	4,127

USSR (CP)	281.1	7,470		70	29	99	91	4,949
Italy	57.2	8,550	2.6	77	12	97	98	2,539
Czechoslovakia (CP)	15.5	8,680		70	15	99	93	4,845
U.K.	56.7	8,870	1.7	75	9	99	97	3,802
Belgium	9.9	9,230	2.7	75	11	99	97	4,809
Austria	7.6	9,990	3.3	74	11	98	96	3,400
Netherlands	14.6	10,020	1.9	77	8	99	99	5,201
France	55.4	10,720	2.8	78	8	99	100	3,640
German, Dem. Rep. (CP)	16.6	10,820		72	10	99	94	5,915
Australia	16.0	11,920	1.7	78	9	99	100	4,710
Germany, Fed. Rep.	60.9	12,080	2.5	75	10	99	97	4,464
Finland	4.9	12,160	3.2	76	6	99	99	5,475
Denmark	5.1	12,600	1.9	75	7	99	98	3,821
Japan	121.5	12,840	4.3	77	6	99	99	3,186
Sweden	8.4	13,160	1.6	77	6	99	99	6,374
Canada	25.6	14,120	2.6	76	8	99	98	8,945
Norway	4.2	15,400	3.4	77	8	99	99	8,803
U.S.	241.6	17,480	1.6	76	11	99	98	7,193
Switzerland	6.5	17,680	1.4	77	8	99	99	4,052

Region	Population (millions) mid-1986	GNP per Capita 1986 ($)	Average Annual Growth Rate of GNP per Capita 1965–86 (percent)	Life Expectancy at Birth 1985 (years)	Infant Mortality per 1000 Live Births (1985)	Adult Literacy Rate 1985 (percent)	PQLI[a]	Energy Consumption per Capita 1986 (kilograms of coal equivalent)
South Asia	1018	282	1.7	55	95	42	53	187
China, People's Rep. of	1054	300	5.1	69	35	69	71	532
Sub-Saharan Africa	424	370	0.9	51	116	43	46	231
Southeast Asia	347	532	3.7	55	74	78	71	193
Latin America	394	1,709	2.6	67	59	85	94	1181
East Asia	89	2,573	6.6	70	22	90	89	3903
Middle East	222	3,412	2.9	57	81	69	60	748
Developing countries	3,861	624	2.9	61	70	61	65	524
High-income oil exporters	19	11,250	3.2	63	61	39	62	3313
Developed countries	699	13,360	2.5	76	10	99	98	6919
Socialist countries	322	7,677		70	27	99	91	1098

Note: Sub-Saharan Africa does not include South or Arab Africa; East Asia includes high-income Hong Kong, but not Japan; Southeast Asia includes the Philippines and high-income Singapore. Developing countries comprise low- and middle-income countries; developed countries, the high-income countries (except Israel, Hong Kong, Singapore, and those centrally planned); socialist includes only centrally planned high-income countries.

[a]The PQLI, a measure of economic well-being, was based on average life expectancy at age one, infant mortality, and literacy.

Methods for GNP per capita: GNP in national currency units was expressed first in weighted average prices for the base period 1984 to 1986, converted into dollars at GNP-weighted average exchange rate for the period, and adjusted for U.S. inflation. The resulting estimate of GNP was then divided by the population in mid-1986.

CP=centrally planned economy; * =least-developed countries; t=total; w=weighted average

Sources: World Bank, *World Development Report, 1988* (New York: Oxford University Press, 1988), pp. 222–23, 240–41; and John W. Sewell, Stuart K. Tucker, and contributors for the Overseas Development Council, *Growth, Exports, and Jobs in a Changing Economy: Agenda, 1988* (New Brunswick, N.J.: Transaction Books, 1988), pp. 246–57. Author's estimates for GNP growth rate for Taiwan and GNP per capita for Taiwan, Afghanistan, Chad, Guinea, Dem. Cambodia, Laos PDR, Viet Nam, Lebanon, Islamic Rep. of Iran, Iraq, Romania, Libya, Albania, Angola, Bulgaria, Cuba, Czechoslovakia, German Dem. Rep., Dem. Rep. of Korea, Mongolia, and the USSR.

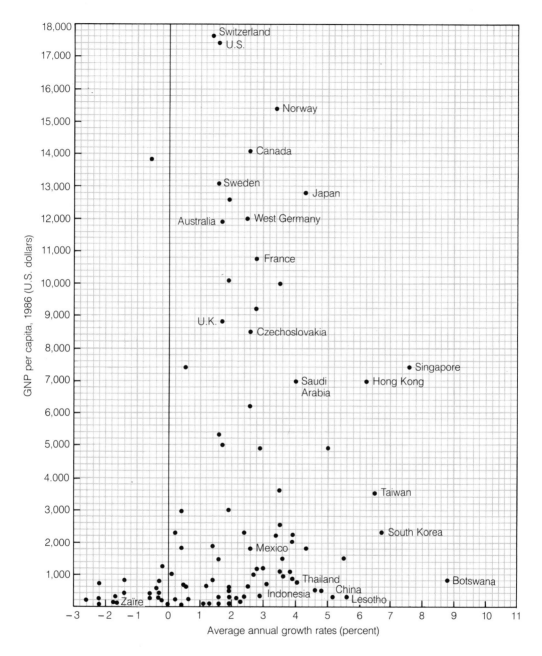

FIGURE 2-1 Income Levels, 1986, and Growth Rates, 1965–86 Rankings of countries by GNP per capita form a continuum rather than a dichotomy. Furthermore except for Japan, Hong Kong, and Singapore, the high-income countries were not the fastest growing ones.

and Bolivia from thirty-first to thirty-ninth. In Africa, Morocco, engaged in conflict with Algeria over the Spanish Sahara and with local labor unions over social policy, declined from seventeenth to forty-second; Zambia, with rapidly falling relative world copper export prices after the mid-1970s, fell from twenty-second to fiftieth; and Ghana, with chronic cedi overvaluation and low farm prices that discouraged export expansion, dropped from a two-way tie for fifteenth and sixteenth to forty-eighth. During this period, Ghana was overpassed by Korea, Taiwan, the Ivory Coast, Nigeria, Malaysia, Turkey, Colombia, and Indonesia, as well as the Cameroon, which rose from fifty-first to twenty-eighth, and Thailand, which rose from forty-ninth to thirty-third.[7]

One classification of development levels used by the World Bank divides countries into three groups on the basis of per capita GNP. In 1986, these categories were low-income countries (less than $450), middle-income countries ($450–$6000), and high-income countries (more than $6000) (see Table 2-1). Each year the boundary between categories rises with inflation, but few countries shifted categories between 1974 and 1986.

Sometimes the high-income countries are designated as developed countries (DCs) and middle- and low-income countries as developing, underdeveloped, or less-developed countries. *Underdeveloped* was the term commonly used in the 1950s and 1960s, but it has since lost favor. Perhaps all countries are underdeveloped relative to their maximum potential. However, the term *underdeveloped,* like *less developed,* has declined in use recently, not because it is inaccurate, but because officials in international agencies consider it offensive. And the term *developing countries* appears to be a euphemism when applied to Bangladesh and parts of sub-Saharan Africa that grew (and developed) very little, if at all, in the 1960s, 1970s, and 1980s. Nevertheless, this book uses the latter term as it is widely understood within the world community to refer to countries with low and middle GNP per capita.

The 127 Afro-Asian and Latin American members of the **United Nations Conference on Trade and Development (UNCTAD)** are often referred to as the **third world,** a term originating in the early post–World War II decade.[8] By refusing to ally themselves with either the United States or the Soviet Union, nonaligned nations forged a third political unit in the UN. Today the term need not imply nonalignment but distinguishes UNCTAD countries from the **first world,** or capitalist countries, where capital and land are owned by individuals; and the **second world,** socialist, or centrally directed countries, where the government owns the means of production. (Contrary to Western usage, the second world describes its economic system as **socialism** rather than communism. In Marxian terminology, communism refers to a later stage of development when distribution is according to needs, money is absent, and the state withers away.) Even a mixed economy, such as that of Great Britain, having government economic planning and limited public ownership of industry (especially under Labor party control) is classified in the first world. Developing socialist countries, such as China, Mongolia, North Korea, Viet Nam, and Cuba, overlap the second and third worlds.

---

[7] Rankings from 1950 were computed from David Morawetz, *Twenty-five Years of Economic Development, 1950 to 1975* (Baltimore: Johns Hopkins Press for the World Bank, 1977), pp. 77–79.

[8] The purpose of UNCTAD, a permanent organization first convened in 1964, is to enhance the position of LDCs in the world economy.

Economic interests vary substantially between and within the following types of third-world countries: (1) the four **high-income oil exporters;** (2) the six **newly industrializing countries (NICs);** (3) the forty one poorest countries, designated as **least developed countries** and starred in Table 2-1; and (4) seventy six other developing countries. (Thirteen of the less populous least developed countries and eight other third-world countries are *not* included in Table 2-1.)

The high-income oil exporters are Libya, Saudi Arabia, Kuwait, and the United Arab Emirates. Iran and Iraq were dropped from this category after the oil output disruptions during the 1979 Iranian revolution and the 1980–88 Iraqi–Iranian war. Two other important members of the oil cartel—the **Organization of Petroleum Exporting Countries,** or **OPEC**—Nigeria and Indonesia, are lower-middle-income countries, because with populations over 100 million, most foreign exchange is spent on basic import requirements, such as machinery, equipment, food, and raw materials.

South Korea, Taiwan, Hong Kong, and Singapore (and sometimes Mexico, Brazil, and others) are included among the NICs. These relatively advanced LDCs have been growing rapidly and are industrially diversified.[9]

In 1971, the United Nations designated twenty-five countries with a low per capita income, low share of manufacturing in gross product, and low literacy rates as least developed. A number of countries asked to be so designated, hoping to obtain economic assistance, especially from the United Nations. Since then the list has grown to forty-one, overlapping greatly with the low-income countries in Table 2-1. Most least developed countries, however, are small. Most UN supporters of this program feared that DCs would treat the proposal seriously only if the number of countries were clearly limited. Thus populous countries, such as India, Pakistan, and Burma, were not included.[10]

During the mid and late 1970s, major aid recipients, such as Bangladesh and Zaïre, were interested in the expansion of official loan facilities, especially to finance increased oil prices. Their attempts to improve financing were directed at OPEC countries in Africa and Asia. The NICs, which rely heavily on manufactured exports, have been more interested in general preferences by DCs for LDC manufacturers than in the primary commodity stabilization agreements sought by Uganda, Burma, Sri Lanka, and Honduras.

Nevertheless, OPEC countries have maintained an alliance with oil-importing, developing countries on a broad range of economic and political issues in international forums. In the 1980s, many OPEC countries and oil-importing LDCs shared a concern with debt relief and reorganization. Additionally most OPEC countries, despite their high per capita GNP, face problems common to most of the developing world—high illiteracy, high infant mortality, and dependence on imported technology.

[9] John W. Sewell, Stuart K. Tucker, and contributors, *Growth, Exports, and Jobs in a Changing World Economy: Agenda, 1988* (New Brunswick, N.J.: Transaction Books, 1988), p. 204, also include Argentina, India, China, Portugal, South Africa, Turkey, and Yugoslavia.

[10] Michael P. Blackwell, "From G-5 to G-77: International Forums for Discussion of Economic Issues," *Finance and Development* 23 (September 1986): 40–41.

For criticism of the UN method of identifying least developed countries, see Perry Selwyn, "The Least-Developed Countries as a Special Case," *World Development* 2, nos. 4 and 5 (April–May 1974): 35–42.

Thus in 1974 to 1975, OPEC countries joined with other members of UNCTAD in the successful adoption by the UN General Assembly of a declaration on principles and programs to reduce the adverse impact of the **international economic order** on LDC development. This order includes all economic relations and institutions, both formal and informal, that link people living in different nations. These economic institutions include international agencies that lend capital, provide short-term credit, and administer international trade rules. Economic relations include bilateral and multilateral trade, aid, banking services, currency rates, capital movements, and technological transfers.

DISTORTIONS IN COMPARING DEVELOPED AND DEVELOPING COUNTRIES' GNP

According to Table 2-1, per capita GNP varies greatly between countries. For example, compare the GNP per capita of India and the United States. The 1986 U.S. GNP per capita of $17,480 is over sixty times that of India's $290. Could an Indian actually survive for one year on less than the weekly income of an average American? In reality income differences between developed and developing countries are very much overstated.

One difference is that developed countries are located in predominantly temperate zones, and LDCs are primarily in the tropics. In temperate areas like the northern United States, heating, insulation, and warmer clothing merely offset the disadvantages of cold weather and add to GNP without increasing satisfaction.

Apart from this discrepancy, *the major sources of error and imprecision in comparing GNP figures for developed and developing countries are as follows:*

1. GNP is understated for developing countries, since a greater proportion of their goods and services are produced within the home by family members for their own use, rather than for sale in the marketplace. Much of the productive activity of the peasant is considered an integral part of family and village life, not an economic transaction. The economic contribution of the housewife who grinds the flour, bakes the bread, and cares for the clothes may not be measured in GNP in poor countries, but the same services *when purchased* are included in a rich country's GNP. In addition, subsistence farmer investments in soil improvements and the cultivation of virgin land are invariably understated in national income accounts. Although a shift from subsistence to commercial production may be slow enough to be dismissed in a country's GNP for 3 to 5 years, it is an important distortion for longer run or intercountry comparisons.

    In some ways, distortions in income differences between the poor country and rich country are analogous to those between the United States in the nineteenth and twentieth centuries. Although estimates indicate U.S. real per capita income for 1860 was one-eleventh what it was in 1990, adjustments would indicate a figure closer to one-fifth. Great-great-grandfather grew his fruits and vegetables, raised dairy cattle for milk and sheep for wool, and gathered and chopped firewood. Great-great–grandmother processed the food, prepared the meals, and sewed quilts and clothes for the family. But few of these activities added to national product. Today their great-great-grandchild purchases milk, fruits, and vegetables at the supermarket, buys meals at restaurants, and pays heating bills—all items that contribute to national product. Moreover, our great-great-grandparents' grain output, when estimated, was valued at farm-gate price, excluding the family's food processing. Statistics show U.S. cereal product consumption increased by 24 percent from 1889 to 1919, even though it decreased 33.5 percent if you impute the value of economic processes at home, like milling, grinding, and baking.[11] Part of today's increased GNP per capita (over that of our great-great-grandparents) occurs because a larger percentage of consumption enters the market and is measured in national income.

2. GNP is overstated for developed counties, since a number of items included in their national incomes are intermediate goods, reflecting the costs of producing or guarding income. The Western executive's business suits and commuting costs should probably be considered means of increasing production rather than final consumer goods and services, just as expenditures on smog eradication and water purification that add to national income are really costs of urbanization and economic growth. Furthermore, part of defense spending is a cost of guarding higher incomes, and not for national power and prestige.

3. The exchange rate used to convert GNP in local currency units into U.S. dollars, if market clearing, is based on the relative prices of internationally traded goods. *However, GNP is understated for developing countries because many of their cheap, labor-intensive, unstandardized goods and services have no impact on the exchange rate, since they are not traded.* Many of the necessities of life are very low priced in dollar terms. In 1986, for example, rice—the staple in the diet of an Indian villager—cost 1 rupee (about 8 U.S. cents) per capita per day. Also services in India tend to be inexpensive. Thus 1986 annual salaries for elementary teachers were about one-tenth as high as those in the United States—a case that surely overstates differences in the quality of instruction.

4. GNP is overstated for countries (usually developing and socialist countries) where the price of foreign exchange is less than a market-clearing price. This overstatement can result from import barriers, restrictions on access to foreign currency, export subsidies, or state trading. Suppose that in 1986 India's central bank had allowed the exchange rate to reach its free market rate, Rs. 26 = $1, rather than the official, controlled rate of Rs. 13 = $1. Then the GNP per capita figure of Rs 3770 would have been $145 ($3770 divided by 26) rather than $290 ($3770 divided by 13). On balance other adjustments outweigh this effect, so that income differences between rich and poor countries tend to be overstated.

COMPARISON RESISTANT SERVICES

Comparison resistant services, like health care, education, and government administration, which comprise more than 10 percent of most countries' expenditure, distort cross-national, but not necessarily DC–LDC, GNP comparisons. People do

[11] Dan Usher, *The Price Mechanism and the Meaning of National Income Statistics* (Oxford: Clarendon Press, 1968), p. 15; and Simon S. Kuznets, *Economic Growth of Nations: Total Output and Production Structure* (Cambridge, Mass.: Harvard University Press, 1971), pp. 10–14.

not buy a clearly defined quantity of university education, crime prevention, health maintenance, and forest management as they do food and clothing. The usual ways of measuring service output are unsatisfactory: by labor input cost or to use productivity differences for a standardized service (for example, a tonsillectomy) as representative of general differences (for example, in medicine).[12]

THE KRAVIS PURCHASING-POWER ADJUSTMENT

Studies have tried to estimate cross-national distortion in income per capita. The International Comparative Project of the UN Statistical Office and the University of Pennsylvania converts a country's GNP in local currency into international dollars (I$) by measuring the country's purchasing power relative to all other countries rather than using the exchange rate. Penn researchers Irving B. Kravis, Alan Heston, and Robert Summers (since 1984, Summers and Heston) compute the **Kravis purchasing-power adjustment or exchange-rate deviation index** (**ERD**) as the ratio of real GNP per capita (measured in I$) to exchange-rate-converted GNP per capita (measured in U.S. dollars). The Penn economists use a series of simultaneous equations to solve the purchasing-power parity for sixty (thirty four in the 1970s) benchmark countries and world average prices for 365 detailed commodities and services, and a shortcut estimating equation to find the purchasing power parity of seventy nonbenchmark countries by computing real (purchasing-power-adjusted) GNP per capita as a function of nominal GNP per capita, steel production per capita, telephone use, motor vehicles, and other variables.

Essentially you compare income per capita more directly if you estimate the value that goods and services produced in one country would have in another. That is, you determine the output of India's goods and services (wheat cakes, sitars, brass tables, and so forth) at the dollar prices these would have in the United States and then compare India's income per capita in dollars to that of the United States. Next calculate U.S. income per capita on the basis of rupee prices (of milkshakes, computers, rock-and-roll records, and so forth) and compare it with India's. The ratio of GNP per capita in India to that in the United States is high in dollar prices and low in rupee prices. Finally, since the dollar price and rupee price ratios differ substantially, you geometrically average the two figures.

The UN–Penn estimates indicate ERD adjustments of 1.85 for Africa, 1.51 for Asia, 1.48 for Latin America, and 0.99 for Europe. The figure for Africa means

---

[12] Irving Kravis, "Comparative Studies of National Income and Prices," *Journal of Economic Literature* 22 (March 1984): 1–57.

There are additional distortions in using GNP to measure welfare that affect comparisons, but not those between DCs and LDCs. Per capita GNP figures do not consider differences in average work week and average leisure between two countries. In addition GNP measures all activity generated through the market whether the activity is productive, unproductive, or destructive. An outbreak of influenza leading to greater drug sales increases GNP, although absence of the disease, by decreasing pharmaceutical consumption, reduces GNP. Likewise durable buildings decrease future GNP because they reduce future construction demand. Wars or earthquakes may increase GNP, since they lead to reconstruction. Furthermore during war, as tanks and bombers go up in smoke, the effective demand for new production may increase. Kimon Valaskakis and Iris Martin, "Economic Indicators and the GPID: An Attempt to Bring Economics Back into the Church without Losing the Faith," (Tokyo: United Nations University, 1980).

that its purchasing-power adjusted (I$) GDP is 1.85 times its GDP converted into U.S. dollars at the existing exchange rate.

The Kravis coefficient of 3.67 for India indicates that its per capita income is not one-sixtieth but one-sixteenth that of the United States. The U.S. per capita expenditure on food is almost eleven times what it is in India, but only six times as much with adjustments in purchasing power. For such staples as bread, rice, and cereals, U.S. per capita consumption is twice that of India, but only 1.5 times as much with the adjustment.[13]

By and large, the greater the difference in per capita income between two countries, the greater the correlation for purchasing power. Chapter 6 indicates that worldwide income inequality is reduced considerably when the gross product in developing countries is adjusted for purchasing power.

A BETTER MEASURE OF ECONOMIC DEVELOPMENT?

But even with the more precise UN–Penn figures, using income as a measure of development is a weak tool, and efforts have been made to replace GNP per capita with a more reliable measure—usually an index of several economic and social variables.

The Physical Quality of Life Index (PQLI)

One alternative measure of welfare is the **PQLI**, which summarizes a great deal of social performance in a single composite index combining three indicators—literacy, life expectancy, and infant mortality (see headings and footnote to Table 2-1). The latter two variables represent the effects of nutrition, public health, income, and the general environment. For example, infant mortality reflects the availability of clean water, the condition of the home environment, and the mother's health. Literacy is a measure of well-being as well as a requirement for a country's economic development.[14]

Critics of this measure stress a close correlation between the three PQLI indicators and the composite index and GNP per capita. Nevertheless, figures on PQLI (between the most unfavorable performance in 1950, valued at 0, and the

---

[13] Irving Kravis, "Comparative Studies of National Income and Prices," *Journal of Economic Literature* 22 (March 1984), 1–57; Robert Summers and Alan Heston, "A New Set of International Comparisons of Real Product and Price Levels Estimates for 130 Countries, 1950–1985," *Review of Income and Wealth* 34 (March 1988): 1–25; Robert Summers and Alan Heston, "Improved International Comparisons of Real Product and its Composition: 1950–1980," *Review of Income and Wealth* 30 (June 1984): 207–62; Irving B. Kravis, "The Three Faces of the International Comparison Project," *World Bank Research Observer* 1 (January 1986): 3–26; Irving Kravis, Alan Heston, and Robert Summers, *United Nations International Comparison Project: Phase II; International Comparisons of Real Product and Purchasing Power* (Baltimore: Johns Hopkins University Press, 1978); and Irving Kravis, Alan Heston, and Robert Summers, "Real GDP per Capita for More than One Hundred Countries," *Economic Journal* 88 (June 1978): 215–42; and Irving Kravis, Alan Heston, and Robert Summers, *World Product and Income: International Comparisons of Real Gross Product* (Baltimore: John Hopkins University Press, 1983).

[14] Martin M. McLaughlin and the Staff of the Overseas Development Council, *The United States and World Development: Agenda, 1979* (New York: Praeger, 1979), pp.129–33.

most favorable figure, 100, expected by the year 2000) reveal exceptions to the correlation (see Table 2-1). For instance, China's life expectancy and infant mortality rates, matching those of the United States in 1940, were achieved at a per capita income of $300. On the other hand, a relatively high per capita does not necessarily reflect widespread well-being, as in the case of such affluent oil countries as Saudi Arabia, Libya, and Oman.

Moreover the development of South Africa's white-ruled **apartheid** (racially separate and discriminatory) economy is explained more adequately by PQLI (66) and its components than GNP per capita, comparable to that of Mexico, Malaysia, and Brazil, with PQLIs, respectively, of 84, 81, and 77. The GNP per capita of black South Africans (1986) is $590, not much more than the $530 for Africa as a whole. Yet this low income for 23.3 million blacks (as well as $1580 for 2.4 million Asians and $1270 for 1.1 million of mixed race) appalls the world community when compared to the $7400 income per capita for the 5.5 million white South Africans, almost as high as Britain's $8870. Life expectancy, an indicator of health, was 55 in South Africa compared to 68 in Malaysia, 67 in Mexico, and 65 in Brazil. But life expectancy was only 46 for black South Africans, 55 for Asians and mixed races, and 66 for whites, 52 for Africa generally, and 74 for DCs.[15]

The PQLI and other indices of social welfare help us make comparisons between capitalist and socialist countries that are difficult to make when using per capita GNP figures. For example, the Soviet Union and most other socialist countries measure agriculture, manufacturing, mining, construction, transport, and trade, but not public administration, education, health, social welfare, finance, defense, and so forth, in their income (material product). Thus in addition to adjusting for common distortions in international income comparisons, national income statisticians must adjust for a lack of market prices and the nonevaluation of services in socialist countries.

In 1986, the high-income socialist countries, East Germany, Czechoslovakia, the Soviet Union, and Bulgaria, had an overall GNP per capita of $7670, less than three-fifths the figure of $13,250 for the twenty high-income capitalist and mixed countries (see Table 2-1). However, East Germany had a PQLI of 94, Czechoslovakia 93, Bulgaria 92, and the Soviet Union 91, figures that compare favorably with the United States (98), West Germany, the United Kingdom (97), and Austria (96).

Five middle-income socialist countries compared favorably with capitalist and mixed countries of similar income levels on PQLI scores. Poland (94) and Hungary (93) have scores comparable to Portugal (91) and Argentina (90); Cuba (98) is slightly higher than Jamaica (92) and much higher than El Salvador (74) and Guatemala (64); however, Romania (91) is lower than Israel (96) and Ireland (96).

A similar study by Yugoslav economist Branko Hôrvat showed that socialist countries ranked much higher on social welfare indicators (life expectancy, educational enrollment rates, and health services) than on per capita GNP, while the reverse was true for capitalist countries. On the other hand, welfare states, such as the Scandinavian countries, the United Kingdom, New Zealand, Israel,

---

[15] E. Wayne Nafziger, *Inequality in Africa: Political Elites, Proletariat, Peasants, and the Poor* (Cambridge: Cambridge University Press, 1988), p. 18; and Jacques Lecaillon, Felix Paukert, Christian Morrisson, and Dimitri Germidis, *Income Distribution and Economic Development* (Geneva: International Labor Office, 1984), p. 46.

and Austria, ranked about the same on social welfare measures as on per capita income.[16]

However PQLI indicators are of limited use in distinguishing levels of development beyond middle-income countries. All three PQLI variables—life expectancy, literacy, and infant mortality—are highly related to per capita income *until* nutrition, health, and education reach certain high levels, then the value of the variables levels off. These indicators have asymptotic limits reflecting biological and physical maxima.[17] Thus all high-income countries have infant mortality rates below 16 per 1000 (except the USSR, 29, whose rate rose during the 1980s), literacy rates of 97 percent or above (except Bulgaria, with 95 percent), and a life expectancy of 70–78 years (see Table 2-1).

Clearly some socialist countries have a high level of social welfare (especially in health, medical care, and education) that is understated by per capita GNP figures. And at this high level, the use of additional economic and social indicators is essential if we are to have a reliable view of differences in well-being between countries.

PROBLEMS WITH ALTERNATIVE MEASURES

There are difficulties with the Kravis purchasing-power adjustment and PQLI not encountered with standard per capita GNP data. Scaling and weighting a composite index, as with PQLI, present a problem, since there is no clear conceptual rationale for giving the core indicators equal weights. Furthermore, alternative measures to GNP require additional time and expense to acquire and also present administrative problems. As a result, they are less up to date and not so easily interpreted as standard income data. The Kravis adjustment, with its detailed prices for a large number of commodities, requires much extra time and effort, whereas the PQLI requires only a little. But the Kravis index is probably easier to interpret than the PQLI. However the Kravis index and even the PQLI do not alter the rankings of countries greatly from per capita income figures. Thus this book most frequently uses income data based on conversions between currencies by means of exchange rates. However you should remember that these data exaggerate per capita income differentials.

WEIGHTED INDICES FOR GNP GROWTH

So far we have concentrated on measures of levels of development rather than on rates of growth. Although changes in both PQLI and Kravis per capita GNP data can be expressed as growth rates, measuring growth in the Kravis figures over time is difficult, and PQLI, although available for both 1960 and the late 1970s, can be readily acquired for only a limited number of countries. Furthermore interpreting the PQLI growth rate, called the **disparity reduction rate,** is difficult—especially when countries are pressing near the physical maximum for the indicators.

[16] Branko Hôrvat, "Welfare of the Common Man in Various Countries," *World Development* 2, no. 7 (July 1974): 29–39.

[17] Norman L. Hicks and Paul Streeten, "Indicators of Development: The Search for a Basic Needs Yardstick," *World Development* 7 (June 1979): 572–75.

So too the growth rate of GNP can be a misleading indicator of development, since GNP growth is heavily weighted by the income shares of the rich. A given growth rate for the rich has much more impact on total growth than the same growth rate for the poor. In Thailand, a country with moderate income inequality, the upper 50 percent of income recipients receive about 80 percent ($32 billion) and the lower 50 percent about 20 percent ($8 billion) of the GNP of $40 million. A growth of 10 percent ($3.2 billion) in income for the top-half results in 8-percent total growth, but a 10-percent income growth for the bottom-half ($0.8 billion) is only 2-percent aggregate growth. Yet the 10-percent growth for the lower-half does far more to reduce poverty than the same growth for the upper-half.

We can illustrate the superior weight of the rich in output growth two ways: (1) as above, the same growth for the rich as the poor has much more effect on total growth; and (2) a given dollar increase in GNP raises the income of the poor by a higher percentage than for the rich.

When GNP growth is the index of performance, it is assumed that a $160 million additional income has the same effect on social welfare regardless of the recipients' income class. But in Thailand, you can increase GNP by $1.6 billion (a 4-percent overall growth on $40 billion) either through a 5-percent growth for the top 50 percent or a 20-percent increase for the bottom 50 percent.

One alternative to this measure of GNP growth is to give equal weight to a 1-percent increase in income for any member of society. In the previous example, the 10-percent income growth for the lower 50 percent, although a smaller absolute increase, would be given greater weight than the same rate for the upper 50 percent, since the former growth affects a poorer segment of the population. Another alternative is a **poverty-weighted index** in which a higher weight is given a 1-percent income growth for low-income groups than for high-income groups.

Table 2-2 shows the difference in annual growth in welfare based on three different weighting systems: (1) GNP weights for each income quintile (top, second, third, fourth, and bottom 20 percent of the population); (2) equal weights for each quintile; and (3) poverty weights of 0.6 for the lowest 40 percent, 0.3 for the next 40 percent, and 0.1 for the top 20 percent. In Panama, Brazil, Mexico, and Venezuela, where income distribution worsened, performance is worse when measured by weighted indices than by GNP growth. In Colombia, El Salvador, Sri Lanka, and Taiwan, where income distribution improved, the weighted indices are higher than GNP growth. In Korea, the Philippines, Yugoslavia, Peru, and India, where income distribution remained largely unchanged, weighted indices do not alter GNP growth greatly.[18]

Is poverty-weighted growth superior to GNP-weighted growth in assessing development attainment? Maximizing poverty-weighted growth may generate too little saving, as in Sri Lanka of the 1960s (Chapter 6), since the rich have a higher propensity to save than the poor (Chapter 14).

Although the different weighting systems reflect different value premises, economists usually choose GNP weights because of convenience and easy interpretation. Given present data, it is easier to discuss poverty reduction by using both GNP per capita and income distribution data than to calculate poverty-weighted growth.

[18] Montek S. Ahluwalia and Hollis Chenery, "The Economic Framework," in Hollis Chenery, Montek S. Ahluwalia, C. L. G. Bell, John H. Duloy, and Richard Jolly, eds., *Redistribution with Growth* (London: Oxford University Press, 1974), pp. 38–42.

TABLE 2-2 Income Equality and Growth

Country	Period	I. Income Growth			II. Annual Increase in Welfare		
		Upper 20 Percent	Middle 40 Percent	Lowest 40 Percent	(A) GNP Weights	(B) Equal Weights	(C) Poverty Weights
Korea	1964–70	10.6	7.8	9.3	9.3	9.0	9.0
Panama	1960–69	8.8	9.2	3.2	8.2	6.7	5.6
Brazil	1960–70	8.4	4.8	5.2	6.9	5.7	5.4
Mexico	1963–69	8.0	7.0	6.6	7.6	7.0	6.9
Taiwan	1953–61	4.5	9.1	12.1	6.8	9.4	10.4
Venezuela	1962–70	7.9	4.1	3.7	6.4	4.7	4.2
Colombia	1964–70	5.6	7.3	7.0	6.2	6.8	7.0
El Salvador	1961–69	4.1	10.5	5.3	6.2	7.1	6.7
Philippines	1961–71	4.9	6.4	5.0	5.4	5.5	5.4
Peru	1961–71	4.7	7.5	3.2	5.4	5.2	4.6
Sri Lanka	1963–70	3.1	6.2	8.3	5.0	6.4	7.2
Yugoslavia	1963–68	4.9	5.0	4.3	4.8	4.7	4.6
India	1954–64	5.1	3.9	3.9	4.5	4.1	4.0

Note: Equal weights imply a weight of 0.2 for the upper 20 percent, 0.4 for the middle 40 percent, and 0.4 for the lowest 40 percent, while poverty weights are calculated giving weights of 0.1, 0.3, and 0.6, respectively.

Source: Hollis Chenery, Montek S. Ahluwalia, C. L. G. Bell, John H. Duloy, and Richard Jolly, eds., *Redistribution with Growth* (London: Oxford University Press, 1974), p. 42.

"BASIC-NEEDS" ATTAINMENT

The relatively rapid growth in per capita GNP of LDCs since the 1950s has had only a limited effect in reducing poverty (see Chapter 6). Partly in reaction, there has been widespread disillusionment with the emphasis on per capita GNP growth in the 1970s and 1980s. Strategies that rely on raising productivity in developing countries are thought to be inadequate *without* programs that directly focus on meeting the basic needs of the poorest 40–50 percent of the population—the **basic-needs approach.** This direct attack is needed, it is argued, because of the continuing serious maldistribution of incomes; because consumers, lacking knowledge about health and nutrition, often make inefficient or unwise choices in this area; because public services must meet many basic needs, such as sanitation and water supplies; and because it is difficult to find investments and policies that uniformly increase the incomes of the poor.

Measures

The basic-needs approach shifts attention from maximizing output to minimizing poverty. The stress is not only on *how much* is being produced, but also on *what* is being produced, in *what ways,* for *whom,* and *with what impact.*

Basic needs include adequate nutrition, primary education, health, sanitation, water supply, and housing. What are possible indicators of these basic needs? Two economic consultants with the World Bank identify the following as a preliminary set of indicators:[19]

— Food: Calorie supply per head, or calorie supply as a percent of requirements; protein
— Education: Literacy rates, primary enrollment (as a percent of the population aged 5–14)
— Health: Life expectancy at birth
— Sanitation: Infant mortality (per thousand births), percent of the population with access to sanitation facilities
— Water supply: Infant mortality (per thousand births), percent of the population with access to potable water
— Housing: None (since existing measures, such as people per room, do not satisfactorily indicate the quality of housing)

Each of these indicators (such as calorie supply) should be supplemented by data on distribution by income class.

Infant mortality is a good indication of the availability of sanitation and clean water facilities, since infants are susceptible to waterborne diseases. Furthermore, data of infant mortality are generally more readily available than data on access to water.

---

[19] Norman L. Hicks and Paul Streeten, "Indicators of Development: The Search for a Basic Needs Yardstick," *World Development* 7 (June 1979): 567–80.

Growth and "Basic Needs"

High basic-needs attainment is positively related to the rate of growth of per capita GNP, since increased life expectancy and literacy, together with reduced infant mortality, are associated with greater worker health and productivity. Furthermore, rapid output growth usually reduces poverty.[20] Thus GNP per head remains an important figure. But we must also look at some indicators of the composition and beneficiaries of GNP. Basic-needs data supplement GNP data but do not replace them. And as the earlier South African example indicates, we must go beyond national averages to get basic-needs measures by income class, ethnic group, region, and other subgroups (see Chapter 6 for a discussion of inequality).

Is the Satisfaction of Basic Needs a Human Right?

The U.S. founders, shaped by the scientific and intellectual activity of the Enlightenment, wrote in the Declaration of Independence: "We hold these truths to be self-evident, that all men are created equal; that they are endowed by their Creator with certain unalienable rights." The UN Universal Declaration of Human Rights goes beyond such civil and political rights as a fair trial, universal adult vote, and freedom from torture to include the rights of employment, minimum wages, collective bargaining, social security, health and medical care, free primary education, and other socioeconomic rights. In fact for many in the third world, the fulfillment of economic needs precedes a concern with political liberties.[21] In Africa there is a saying, "Human rights begin with breakfast"; and a beggar in one of Bertolt Brecht's operas sings, "First we must eat, then comes morality."

Some LDCs may have to reallocate resources from consumer goods for the well-off to basic necessities for the whole population. However even with substantial redistribution, resources are too scarce to attain these social and economic rights for the masses in most low-income countries. Consider the right of free primary education. Most LDCs have less than one-twentieth the per capita GNP of the United States, 1.5 times the population share aged 5–15 (see Chapter 9), and greater shortages of qualified teachers, all of which means a much greater share of GNP would have to be devoted to education to attain the same primary enrollment rates as in the United States. Far less income would be left over for achieving other objectives, such as adequate nutrition, housing, and sanitation. Furthermore, primary school graduates in Africa and Asia migrate to the towns, adding to the unemployed and the disaffected. A carefully selective and phased educational pro-

---

[20] Norman L. Hicks, "Growth versus Basic Needs: Is There a Trade-Off?" *World Development* 7 (November/December 1979): 985–94.

[21] The Marxist economic historian Eugene D. Genovese suggests that in the early nineteenth century slaves in the southern United States fared as well materially as a substantial portion of the workers and peasants in Western Europe and better materially than Russian, Hungarian, Polish, and Italian peasants during the same period; and that the slaves were better off than even most of the population in LDCs today (from Eugene D. Genovese, *Roll, Jordan, Roll: The World the Slaves Made* [New York: Pantheon Books, 1974]). Furthermore, literacy, life expectancy, and infant survival were probably as high among southern slaves as Eastern European peasants. Who was better off—the southern slave or the Polish peasant? Who is better off today—the landless laborer in democratic India or the more prosperous farm worker under North Korea's dictatorship? The tradeoff of political freedom for economic welfare varies from person to person.

gram, including adult literacy programs, can often be more economical, and do more for basic needs, than an immediate attempt at universal primary education.

Setting up Western labor standards and minimum wages in labor-abundant LDCs is not always sensible. With a labor force growth of 2–3 percent per year, imitating labor standards from rich countries in LDCs may create a relatively privileged, regularly employed labor force and aggravate social inequality, unemployment, and poverty. Economic rights must consider the scarcity of available resources and the necessity of choice.[22]

LIBERATION VERSUS DEVELOPMENT

Some leftists, including Latin American Roman Catholic radicals, French Marxists, and scholars sympathetic to China's Cultural Revolution (1966–76), reject economic growth tied to dependence on Western-type techniques, capital, institutions, and elite consumer goods. These scholars believe that the LDCs should control their own economic and political destiny and free themselves from domination by Western capitalist countries and their elitist allies in the third world. According to them, the models for genuine development are not such countries as South Korea and Taiwan, since no fundamental changes in class relationships, social system, and distribution of wealth and power have taken place despite rapid economic growth and industrialization. Indeed, these countries are said to have repressive political regimes overly dependent on the support of the United States.

These leftist scholars consider Tanzania, Cuba, and Maoist China to be examples of economic and social success. The People's Republic of China, under Chairman Mao Zedong until 1976, is said to have abolished mass starvation, overthrown feudalism, uprooted elitism, and created a new Communist, motivated to serve the people. Cuba decreased income inequality, increased employment security, and virtually abolished illiteracy while ending its dependence on the United States. Tanzania is admired because of its rejection of the mass-consumption model, its emphasis on self-reliance in education, and the rejection of foreign aid that might create an elite class. These countries are viewed as stressing indigenous economic and political autonomy, the holistic development of human beings, the fulfillment of human creativity, and selfless serving of the masses rather than individual incentives and the production of material goods.[23]

What is the actual achievement of these three countries in these areas in recent years? Although Cuba, since the victory of Castro's revolution in 1959, has provided greater economic security and met most of the basic needs of the bulk of its population, average consumption levels have been low and discontent substantial among the former bourgeoisie. Since 1974, Tanzania has forced substantial portions of the rural population into planned village communities, whose initial emphasis was on traditional cooperation of communal agricultural production. However, this scheme of *ujamaa* villages has been spoiled by ineffective govern-

[22] Paul Streeten, "Basic Needs and Human Rights," *World Development* 8 (February 1980): 107–11.

[23] Denis Goulet, " 'Development' . . . or Liberation," *International Development Review* 13, no. 3 (September 1971): 6–10; and John W. Gurley, "Maoist Economic Development: The New Man in the New China," *Review of Radical Political Economics* 2, no. 4 (Winter 1970): 26–38.

ment and party officials and the influence of rich peasants. During China's Cultural Revolution, psychological pressures, public humiliations, beatings, and forced migrations were widespread. Before, during, and after this political upheaval, China had mass deference toward the elite, major income gaps between urban and rural populations, and repression of dissent. Today the Chinese government is repudiating much of the Cultural Revolution's emphasis on national self-reliance, noneconomic (moral) incentives, and central price fixing and is stressing an individual responsibility system, limited price reform, and assistance from capitalist countries. As for Taiwan and South Korea, post–World War II land reform has led to income inequalities among the lowest in Asia and lower than in China.[24]

Despite the spotty results in Cuba and elsewhere, Liberationists have succeeded in pointing out the insufficiency of conventional measures of welfare and the importance of local control in providing economic experience and political self-esteem. However the countries they choose as examples fall far short of the model of liberation they espouse. In fact an observer may be hard put to pinpoint in what way the masses in these countries are more liberated than in such countries as South Korea and Taiwan which are described as Fascist.

The Liberationists' strongest criticism is directed toward Western economists who consider capitalist and mixed-capitalist Latin American countries such as Brazil and Colombia, as models for development. They admit, to be sure, that these two countries, as indeed Latin America as a whole, have substantially higher per capita GNPs than India, China, Indonesia, and most of Asia. However, if Latin American economic growth, including Brazil's recent industrial miracle, is regarded as development, Liberationists reject it: Latin America has greater land and income concentration than either Asia or Africa and a higher proportion of the population in poverty than countries with similar levels of income per head. The Liberationists point out that Brazil's rapid growth in the 1960s, 1970s, and 1980s resulted in *increased* income inequality. Furthermore extreme poverty and malnutrition were more widespread in Brazil during this period than in China, even though its per capita GNP was only one-seventh of Brazil's.

The Liberationists are not really criticizing development but rather growth policies disguised as development. Including income distribution and local economic control in the definition of development would be a better approach than abandoning the concept of development. For in the 1980s and early 1990s, even the leaders of China, Tanzania, and Cuba seem to be replacing the language of liberation with that of development.[25]

SMALL IS BEAUTIFUL

Mahatma Gandhi, nonviolent politician and leader of India's nationalist movement for 25 years prior to its independence in 1947, was an early advocate of small-scale development in the third world. He emphasized that harmony with nature, reduc-

---

[24] Nick Eberstadt, "China: How Much Success?" *New York Review of Books,* 26 (May 3, 1979): 38–44; Shail Jain, *Size Distribution of Income* (Baltimore: Johns Hopkins University Press, 1975); and Peter L. Berger, *Pyramids of Sacrifice: Political Ethics and Social Change* (Garden City, N.Y.: Anchor, 1976), pp. 151–82.

[25] Clarence Zuvekas, Jr., *Economic Development: An Introduction* (New York: St. Martin's, 1979), p. 26.

tion of material wants, village economic development, handicraft production, de-centralized decision making, and labor-intensive, indigenous technology were not just more efficient, but more humane. For him, humane *means* for development were as important as appropriate *ends*.

Gandhi's vision has inspired many followers, including the late E. F Schu-macher, ironically an economist who was head of planning for the nationalized coal industry in Britain. His goal was to develop methods and machines cheap enough to be accessible to virtually everyone and to leave ample room for human creativity. For him, there was no place for machines that concentrate power in a few hands and contribute to soul-destroying, meaningless, monotonous work.

Schumacher believed that productive activity needs to be judged holistically, including its social, aesthetic, moral, or political meanings as well as its economic ends. The primary functions of work are to give people a chance to use their faculties, join with other people in a common task, and produce essential goods and services.[26]

Schumacher stressed that LDCs need techniques appropriate to their culture, abundant labor, and scarce capital and these might frequently involve simple labor-intensive production methods that have become economically unfeasible to DCs. These technologies are intermediate between Western capital-intensive processes and the LDCs' traditional instruments. Yet intermediate technology may not be suitable where (1) an industry requires virtually unalterable factor proportions; (2) modifying existing technologies is expensive; (3) capital-intensive technology re-duces skilled labor requirements; and (4) factor prices are distorted (see Chapter 12).

ARE ECONOMIC GROWTH AND DEVELOPMENT WORTHWHILE?

Economic development and growth have their costs and benefits.[27] Economic growth widens the range of human choice, but this may not necessarily increase happiness. Both Gandhi and Schumacher stress that happiness is dependent on the relationship between wants and resources. You may become more satisfied, not only by having more wants met, but perhaps also by renouncing certain material goods. Wealth may make you less happy if it increases wants more than resources. Furthermore, acquisitive and achievement-oriented societies may be more likely to give rise to individual frustration and mental anguish. Moreover, the mobility and fluidity frequently associated with rapidly growing economies may be accompanied by rootlessness and alienation.

Benefits

What distinguishes people from animals is people's greater control over their envi-ronment and greater freedom of choice, not that they are happier. Control over one's environment is arguably as important a goal as happiness, and in order to achieve it, economic growth is greatly to be desired. Growth decreases famine,

---

[26] E. F. Schumacher, *Small Is Beautiful—Economics as If People Mattered* (New York: Harper & Row, 1973).

[27] Much of the material in this section is from W. Arthur Lewis, *The Theory of Economic Growth* (Homewood, Ill.: Richard D. Irwin, 1955), pp. 420–35.

starvation, infant mortality, and death; gives us greater leisure; can enhance art, music, and philosophy; and gives us the resources to be humanitarian. Economic growth may be especially beneficial to societies where political aspirations exceed resources, since it may forestall what might otherwise prove to be unbearable social tension. Without growth the desires of one group can be met only at the expense of others. Finally, economic growth can assist newly independent countries in mobilizing resources to increase national power.

Costs

Growth has its price. One cost may be the acquisitiveness, materialism, and dissatisfaction with one's present state associated with a society's economic struggles. Second, the mobility, impersonality, and emphasis on self-reliance associated with economic growth may destabilize the extended family system, indeed the prevailing social structure. Third, economic growth, with its dependence on rationalism and the scientific method for innovation and technical change, is frequently a threat to religious and social authority. Fourth, economic growth usually requires greater job specialization, which may be accompanied by greater impersonality, more drab and monotonous tasks, more discipline, and a loss of craftsmanship. Fifth, as such critics as Herbert Marcuse charge, in an advanced industrial society, all institutions and individuals, including artists, tend to be shaped to the needs of economic growth.[28]

Additionally the larger organizational units concomitant with economic growth are more likely to lead to bureaucratization, impersonality, communication problems, and the use of force to keep people in line. Economic growth and the growth of large-scale organization are associated with an increased demand for manufactured products and services and the growth of towns, which may be accompanied by rootlessness, environmental blight, and unhealthy living conditions. Even though the change in values and social structure may eventually lead to a new, dynamic equilibrium considered superior to the old static equilibrium, the transition may produce some very painful problems. Moreover the political transformation necessary for rapid economic growth may lead to greater centralization, authoritarianism and coercion, and greater social disruption.

Rising Expectations

Yet in the face of increasing expectations, few societies choose stagnation or retardation. Increasingly the LDC poor are aware of the opulent lifestyle of rich countries and the elite. They have noticed the radios, automobiles, houses, and dinner parties of the affluent; they have seen the way the elite escape the drudgery of backbreaking work and the uncertain existence of a life of poverty; they have been exposed to new ideas and values; and they are restless to attain a part of the wealth they observe.

Increasingly as literacy rates rise, the previously inarticulate and unorganized masses are demanding that the political elite make a serious commitment to a better way of life for all. These demands in some cases have proved embarrassing and threatening to the elite, since the broad economic growth the lower classes expect requires much political and economic transformation.

[28] Herbert Marcuse, *One-Dimensional Man* (Boston: Beacon Press, 1966).

However even if a population is seriously committed to economic growth, its attainment is not likely to be pursued at all costs. All societies have to consider other goals that conflict with the maximization of economic growth. For example, because it wants its own citizens in high-level positions, a developing country may promote local control of manufacturing that reduces growth in the short run. The question is, What will be the tradeoff between the goal of rapid economic growth and such noneconomic goals as achieving an orderly and stable society, preserving traditional values and culture, and promoting political autonomy?

SUMMARY

1. Economic growth is an increase in a country's per capita output. Economic development is economic growth leading to an improvement in the economic welfare of the poorest segment of the population, a decrease in agriculture's share of output, an increase in the educational level of the labor force, and indigenous technological change.
2. Even though it is common to classify countries as high-income (developed countries), middle-, and low-income countries (developing countries), rankings by measures of the level of economic welfare form a continuum rather than a dichotomy.
3. The third world of Africa, Asia, and Latin America is very diverse, ranging from the least developed countries with a low per capita income and little industrialization to the high-income oil exporters and newly industrializing countries.
4. Per capita GNP is an imperfect measure of average economic welfare in a country. For example, social indicators suggest that Mexico has done better in meeting the basic needs of the majority of its people than South Africa, which has roughly the same average income level.
5. The GNP of the LDCs is understated relative to that of the West because LDCs have a higher portion of output sold outside the marketplace, a smaller share of intermediate goods in their GNP, and a large percentage of labor-intensive, unstandardized goods having no impact on the exchange rate.
6. The per capita GNP of LDCs *relative* to the United States increases by one and one-half to four times when adjustments are made for purchasing power.
7. Disadvantages of the PQLI as an alternative measure of average material well-being are its insufficient conceptual rationale for scaling and weighting, the extra time and expense required for its formulation, the lack of current figures, and difficulty in interpreting it.
8. Since GNP is heavily weighted by the income shares of the rich, its growth can be a misleading indicator of development. Alternative measures of growth are those giving equal weights to a 1-percent increase in income for any member of society, or those giving higher weights to a 1-percent income growth for lower income groups than for higher income groups.
9. Economists who emphasize basic needs stress providing food, housing, health, sanitation, water, and basic education in LDCs, especially for low-

income groups. However, despite the view that these needs are rights, resources may be too limited in LDCs to guarantee their fulfillment.

10. Some leftists wish to substitute the goal of liberation, or freedom from external economic and political control, for that of economic development, which they understand as implying economic growth dependent on Western techniques, capital, institutions, and consumer goods. However, the countries they choose as examples (China, Cuba, and Tanzania) fall far short of the model of liberation they espouse. Furthermore the Liberationists are not really criticizing development but growth policies disguised as development.

11. Is economic growth worthwhile? People increase their happiness, not only by having more wants met, but also by renouncing certain material goods. However economic growth gives us more control over our environment and greater freedom of choice. Yet the LDCs, faced with rising expectations, may not have the option of a no-growth society.

TERMS TO REVIEW

- economic growth
- GNP
- economic development
- GNP per capita
- GNP price deflator
- real economic growth
- first world
- second world
- third world
- socialism
- high-income oil exporters
- newly industrializing countries (NICs)

- capital-surplus oil countries
- least developed countries
- United Nations Conference on Trade and Development (UNCTAD)
- Organization of Petroleum Exporting Countries (OPEC)
- international economic order
- comparison-resistant services

- Kravis purchasing-power adjustment (exchange-rate deviation index, or ERD)
- Physical Quality of Life Index (PQLI)
- disparity reduction rate
- poverty-weighted index
- basic needs approach
- apartheid

QUESTIONS TO DISCUSS

1. Is economic growth possible without economic development? Economic development without economic growth?

2. What do you consider the most urgent goal for LDCs to attain by the year 2010? Why is this goal important? What policy changes should LDCs undertake to increase the probability of attaining this goal?

3. Give an example of a LDC that you think has had an especially good development record in the past two decades. Why did you choose this LDC?

4. List three or four countries that have moved significantly upward or downward in the GNP per capita rankings in the last two decades. What factors have contributed to their movements?

5. How useful are generalizations about the third or developing world? Indicate ways of subclassifying the third world.

6. According to the *World Development Report, 1988*, Canada's 1986 GNP per capita ($14,120) was about forty seven times higher than Kenya (with $300). Can we surmise that the average economic well-being in Canada was about forty, seven times the average economic well-being in Kenya?

7. Nigeria's 1986 GNP per capita was $640, two to three times that of Tanzania's $250. What other assessments of socioeconomic welfare (other than GNP per capita in U.S. dollars at the prevailing exchange rates) could be used in comparing Nigeria and Tanzania? What are some of the advantages and disadvantages of these alternative assessments?

8. Compare basic needs attainment, the PQLI, and the Kravis adjustment of GNP for purchasing power to GNP per capita in U.S. dollars at existing exchange rates as measures of economic well-being.

9. In what ways might conventional basic-needs measures be inadequate in assessing the material welfare of the poorest 20 percent of a developing country's population?

10. Are economic welfare and political freedom complementary or competing goals?

11. Choose a country, for example, your own or one you know well. What have been the major costs and benefits of economic growth in this country?

GUIDE TO READINGS

The annual *World Development Report* by the World Bank (see the sources to Table 2-1) is not only the best up-to-date source for basic economic data on LDCs, but also contains a good dicussion of current development issues. The Overseas Development Council's (ODC's) annual *Agenda* volume on the United States and developing nations (see Table 2-1), has a useful statistical annex on basic economic data, including information on international trade, investment, aid, debt, and PQLI. In addition the ODC's 1979 (note 14) and 1980 volumes have a discussion of PQLI and basic needs. Other useful data sources are the annual *World Economic Survey* by the Department of International Economic and Social Affairs of the United Nations, the annual *World Economic Outlook* by the International Monetary Fund, and UN regional economic commissions, such as the ECA (notes 4 and 5).

Usher's and Kuznet's books (note 11) have good discussions of errors in cross-national income comparisons. Leading sources on adjusting national product for purchasing power are listed in notes 12 (first source) and 13. Weighted indices for GNP growth are discussed in Chenery et al., *Redistribution with Growth* (note 18).

There are useful articles on the concept of liberation by Goulet and Gurley (note 23). The classic discussion of the costs and benefits of economic growth appears in the appendix of Lewis's *Theory of Economic Growth* (note 1). On basic needs see notes 19 and 20.

Chapter Three

ECONOMIC GROWTH AND DEVELOPMENT: SOME BASIC FACTS

SCOPE OF THE CHAPTER

To analyze the economics of developing countries, we need some basic facts about their growth and development. First, it is essential to understand the origins of modern economic growth and why, prior to this century, it was largely confined to the West. Second, we must examine the growth models of two leading non-Western countries, Japan and the Soviet Union. Third, we must look at the recent economic growth of developing countries, comparing their development in the years before and after World War II. Fourth, we sketch in the diverse economic performance among LDCs by comparing fast- and slow-growing countries, low- and middle-income countries, oil exporters and oil importers, different regions of the world, and socialist and nonsocialist countries.

According to the UN General Assembly resolutions on the new international order (Chapter 2), the major international problem is the widening income gap between rich and poor countries. Therefore a later section of this chapter draws on previous discussion to examine the meaning of this gap. Has it indeed widened, and is narrowing the gap an important goal? A final section looks briefly at population growth in the LDCs as it affects economic growth and development.

BEGINNINGS OF SUSTAINED ECONOMIC GROWTH

Historians hesitate to name a threshold period in history when economic growth took off. Although there were periods of economic growth during ancient and medieval times, rapid, sustained growth was rare. Living standards remained at a subsistence level for the majority of the world's population. The rapid, sustained increase in per capita GNP characteristic of **modern economic growth** began in the West (Western Europe, the United States, Canada, Australia, and New Zealand) one to two centuries ago. Industrialization and sustained economic growth had begun in Great Britain by the last half of the eighteenth century; in the United States and France in the first half of the nineteenth century; in Germany, the Netherlands, and Belgium by the middle of that century; and in Scandinavia, Canada, Japan (considered a non-Western country), Italy, and perhaps Russia, by the last half of the century.

THE WEST AND AFRO-ASIA: THE NINETEENTH CENTURY AND TODAY

GNP per capita for developed countries in Europe in the early 1980s was roughly fifteen to twenty times that of Afro-Asian less-developed countries. The gap was not so great 125 to 150 years ago, since people could not have survived on one-fifteenth the per capita income of European DCs in the nineteenth century. Updating a rough assessment by Nobel laureate Simon Kuznets indicates that at that time Western Europe, the United States, Canada, and Australia had an average real income higher than that of most African and Asian countries today. The DC economic growth has been much more rapid during the past century, and of course the DCs are adding to an already substantial economic base.[1]

CAPITALISM AND MODERN WESTERN ECONOMIC DEVELOPMENT

Why did sustained economic growth begin in the West? A major reason is the rise of **capitalism,** the economic system dominant there since the breakup of feudalism from the fifteenth to the eighteenth centuries. Fundamental to capitalism are the relations between private owners and workers. The means of production—land, mines, factories, and other forms of capital—are privately held; and legally free but capital–less workers sell their labor to employers. Under capitalism production decisions are made by private individuals operating for profit.

Capitalist institutions had antecedents in the ancient world, and pockets of capitalism flourished in the late medieval period. For example, a capitalist woolen industry existed in thirteenth-century Flanders and fourteenth-century Florence, but it died out because of revolutionary conflict between the workers and capitalists. Thus the continuous development of the capitalist system dates only from the sixteenth century.

Especially after the eleventh century, the growing long-distance trade between capitalist centers contributed to the collapse of the medieval economy. As European trade activity expanded during the next few centuries, certain institutions facilitated the growth of modern capitalism. Among them were private property,

[1] This is based on an updating of Simon Kuznets, *Economic Growth of Nations—Total Output and Production Structure* (Cambridge Mass.: Harvard University Press, 1971), pp. 23–28.

deposit banking, formal contracts, craft guilds, merchant associations, joint stock companies (the precursor of the corporation), insurance, international financial markets, naval protection of trade vessels, and government support in opening markets and granting monopoly privileges for inventions.

At the same time, burgeoning industrialization and urbanization further weakened the feudal economy, an agricultural system based on serfs bound to their lord's land. Ultimately these changes in trade, industry, and agriculture transformed the medieval economy into a new society fueled by capitalistic endeavors.

Prior to the twentieth century, only capitalist economies were successful in large capital accumulation and in generating and applying a vast scientific and technical knowledge to production. Why was capitalism first successful in the West?

1. The breakdown of the authority of the medieval Roman Catholic Church, together with the Protestant Reformation of the sixteenth and seventeenth centuries, stimulated a new economic order. Although Protestantism, like Catholicism, was ascetic, manifesting itself in the systematic regulation of the whole conduct of the Christian, the new **Protestant ethic** translated its "inner-worldly" asceticism into a vigorous activity in a secular vocation, or *calling* (in contrast to the "other-worldly" asceticism of the Catholic monastery). The Protestant ethic fostered hard work, frugality, sobriety, and efficiency, virtues coinciding with the spirit essential for capitalist development.[2] Acceptance of the Protestant idea of a calling led to the systematic organization of free labor and gave a religious justification for unstinting work even at low wages in the service of God (and incidentally the employer).

2. Between the sixteenth and nineteenth centuries, Western Europe witnessed the rise of strong national states that created the conditions essential for rapid and cumulative growth under capitalism. The nation-state established a domestic market free of trade barriers, a uniform monetary system, contract and property law, police and militia protection against internal violence, defense against external attack, and basic transportation and communication facilities—all of which fostered capitalism. Initially absolute monarchs wrested power from feudal lords and town authorities and consolidated territory into large political and economic units—the nation-state. The nation-state was necessary for the larger markets and economies of scale of capitalist expansion. Eventually monarchy ceded power to the **bourgeoisie,** the capitalist and middle classes. Where an absolute monarch existed, the capitalist class, who enjoyed only a precarious existence under autocratic authority, ultimately stripped the monarch of power and installed representatives more favorable to their economic interests.

3. The declining influence of the church coincided with the Enlightenment, a period of great intellectual activity in seventeenth- and eighteenth-century Europe that led to the scientific discoveries of electricity, oxygen, calculus, and so on. These discoveries found practical application in agriculture, industry, trade, and transport and resulted in extended markets, increased efficiency of large-scale production, and enhanced profits associated with capital

---

[2] Max Weber, *The Protestant Ethic and the Spirit of Capitalism* (New York: Charles Scribner's Sons, 1930). The first German edition was in 1904–1905.

concentration. Furthermore the rationalism permeating the new science and technology meshed with the spirit of capitalist enterprise.

4. Protestantism's spiritual individualism (the "priesthood of all believers"), coupled with the philosophical rationalism and humanism of the Enlightenment, emphasized freedom from arbitrary authority. In the economic sphere, this liberalism advocated a self-regulating market unrestricted by political intervention or state monopoly. These views were tailormade for the bourgeoisie in its struggle to overthrow the old order.

5. Intellectual and economic changes led to political revolutions in England, Holland, and France in the seventeenth and eighteenth centuries that reduced the power of the church and landed aristocracy. The bourgeoisie took over much of this power. Economic modernization in Europe would probably not have been possible without these revolutions.[3]

6. Modern capitalism is distinguished from earlier economic systems by a prodigious rate of capital accumulation. During the early capitalism of the sixteenth and seventeenth centuries, the great flow of gold and silver from the Americas to Europe inflated prices and profits and speeded up this accumulation. Inflation redistributed income from landlords and wage laborers, whose real earnings declined, to merchants, manufacturers, and commercial farmers, who were more likely to invest in new and productive enterprises.[4]

Capitalism, as an engine for rapid economic growth, spread beyond Europe to the outposts of Western civilization—the United States, Canada, Australia, and New Zealand. Indeed during most of the twentieth century, capitalism has been more successful in the United States than in other Western economies.

However, modern industrial capitalism was established in the West at great human costs. Physical violence, brutality, and exploitation shaped its early course. In England and Belgium, wages dropped and poverty increased markedly during the accelerated industrial growth of the latter eighteenth and early nineteenth centuries. In both countries, it took a half-century before the absolute incomes of the poor reached pre–Industrial Revolution levels.[5] Perhaps Charles Dickens best

[3] Even though capitalism originated in the modern West, much of what contributed to its rise originated in other civilizations. For example, much of its scientific and technical content came from the Middle East and India, the philosophical from ancient Greece, and the legal and political from ancient Greece and Rome.

[4] Much of this section is from Dudley Dillard, *Economic Development of the North Atlantic Community: Historical Introduction to Modern Economics* (Englewood Cliffs, N.J.: Prentice-Hall, 1967), pp. 72–149; Dudley Dillard, "Capitalism," in Charles K. Wilber, ed., *The Political Economy of Development and Underdevelopment* (New York: Random House, 1979), pp. 69–76; and Douglass C. North and Robert Paul Thomas, "An Economic Theory of the Growth of the Western World," *Economic History Review* 23 (April 1970): 1–17.

Neo-Marxists and dependency theorists (discussed in Chapter 5) argue that Western capitalism, through informal imperialism and late nineteenth- and early twentieth-century colonialism, developed at the expense of Latin America, Asia, and Africa, capturing their **surplus** (output above wages, depreciation, and purchases from other firms) through policies controlling their raw materials, markets, international trade, and planning. Most Western mainstream economists would not add imperialism as a contributor to Western capitalist success.

[5] Irma Adelman and Cynthia Taft Morris, "Growth and Impoverishment in the Middle of the Nineteenth Century," *World Development* 6 (March 1978): 245–73.

portrays the starvation, destitution, overcrowding, and death among the mid–nineteenth century unemployed and working class. The lives fictionalized in *Nicholas Nickleby, A Christmas Carol,* and *Oliver Twist* were grim indeed. Dickens's novels are an accurate portrayal of not only the English working class but of other Western workers during this time. Although these human costs may not be inevitable, similar problems have not been avoided by newly industrializing countries in subsequent periods. But despite these costs, even the late Marxist Maurice Dobb conceded that capitalism has improved the level of living for a large proportion of the Western population since the early nineteenth century.[6]

ECONOMIC MODERNIZATION IN THE NON-WESTERN WORLD

Capitalism led to modern economic growth in only a few non-Western countries. Chapter 5 discusses the relative importance of barriers to capitalism extant in traditional societies, as well as the effects of colonialism and other forms of Western political domination on the slow development of non-Western economies. Irrespective of the cause, it is clear that most non-Western countries lacked the strong indigenous capitalists and the effective bureaucratic and political leadership essential for rapid economic modernization.

The Japanese Development Model[7]

One notable exception was Japan, one of the five non-Western countries that escaped Western colonialism. Despite unequal treaties with the West from 1858 to 1899, Japan had substantial autonomy in economic affairs compared to other Afro-Asian countries.

Japan's level of economic development was much lower than Western countries in the middle to latter nineteenth century. However since 1867, when Japan abolished feudal property relationships, its economic growth has been the most rapid in the world.

Japan's "guided capitalism" under the Meiji emperor, 1868 to 1912, relied on state initiative for laws encouraging freedom of enterprise and corporate organization; for organizing a banking system (with the central Bank of Japan); for sending students and government officials for training and education abroad; for hiring thousands of foreigners to adapt and improve technology under local government or business direction; for importing machines sold on lenient credit terms to private entrepreneurs; for large investments in **infrastructure**—telegraphs, postal service, water supply, coastal shipping, ports, harbors, bridges, lighthouses, river improvements, railways, electricity, gas, and technical research; and for helping domestic business find export opportunities, exhibit products and borrow abroad, establish trading companies, and set marketing standards.

In the late nineteenth century, government initiated about half the investment outside agriculture but sold most industrial properties, often at bargain prices, to

[6] Maurice Dobb, *Capitalist Enterprise and Social Progress* (London: Routledge, 1926).

[7] This section is based on E. Wayne Nafziger, "The Japanese Development Model: Its Implications for Developing Countries," *Bulletin of the Graduate School of International Relations, International University of Japan* no. 5 (July 1986): pp. 1–26.

private business people. Additionally government aided private industry through a low-wage labor policy, low taxes on business enterprise and high incomes, a favorable legal climate, destruction of economic barriers between fiefs, lucrative purchase contracts, tax rebates, loans, and subsidies. Japan acquired funds for industrial investment and assistance by squeezing agriculture, relying primarily on a land tax for government revenue. From the state-assisted entrepreneurs came the fininical cliques or combines (**zaibatsu**) that dominated industry and banking through World War II.

Nevertheless unlike the contemporary Indian government, the Meiji government retained small industry, compelling the zaibatsu to provide technical advice, scarce inputs, and credit and encouraging small firms to take cooperative action. Creating small industry from scratch is not so effective as the Japanese approach of maintaining and upgrading workshop, handicraft, and cottage industry from an earlier stage of development.

Meiji Japan did not stress large leaps to the most advanced state of industrial technology available, but step-by-step improvements in technology and capital as government departments, regions, firms, and work units learned by doing. In the 1870s, this meant technical and management assistance and credit facilities to improve and increase the scale of crafts and small industry from the feudal period, causing less social disruption, since small industry's environment was not alien.

The fact that today Japan probably has the highest mass standards for primary and secondary schools in the world, and shares underlying national values, is no accident. Japan's rulers laid the foundation in the late feudal period, when Japan's primary enrollment rate was higher than the British, and in 1872, when a national system of universal education stressing scientific and technological education was established.

Moreover from 1868 to World War II, the Japanese had a policy (first forced and later chosen) of multilateral, nondiscriminatory foreign trade outside their empire (1904–45). Unlike today's LDCs, Japan did not discriminate against exports. Increased tariff protection in the first quarter of the twentieth century reduced the price of foreign exchange, but government export promotion brought the exchange rate close to a market-clearing rate (see Chapter 17 on foreign exchange rates). From 1868 to 1897, the Japanese yen, on a silver standard that declined relative to gold, chronically depreciated vis-à-vis the U.S. dollar.

Today's international economic conditions are not so favorable to LDC export expansion. The most rapidly expanding LDC manufactured exports during the 1970s and early 1980s were textiles, clothing, footwear, and simple consumer goods requiring widely available labor-intensive technology. But competition from other aspiring newly industrial exporting countries is more severe than it was for Meiji Japan. Still LDCs could benefit from the Japanese approach of using international competition and market-clearing exchange rates to spur exports.

While a contemporary LDC can learn useful lessons from the Japanese model, these lessons are limited because of Meiji Japan's historically specific conditions and because aspects of the Japanese approach also contributed to pathologies in growth, such as zaibatsu concentration, income inequality, labor union repression, militarism, and imperialism. These pathologies were not reduced until military defeat in 1945 was followed by the democratic reforms of an occupational government, a series of events not to be recommended nor likely to accelerate economic development and democratize the political economy in LDCs as it did in Japan.

The Soviet Development Model

The 1917 Communist revolution in Russia provided an alternative road to economic modernization. The main features of Soviet socialism, beginning with the first five-year plan in 1928, were replacing consumer preferences with planners' preferences, the Communist party dictating these preferences to planners, state control of capital and land, collectivization of agriculture, the virtual elimination of private trade, plan fulfillment monitored by the state banks, state monopoly trading with the outside world, and (unlike the Japanese) a low ratio of foreign trade to GNP. In a few decades, the Soviet Union was quickly transformed into a major industrial power. Indeed the share of industry in net national product (NNP) increased from 28 percent to 45 percent, and its share of the labor force from 18 percent to 29 percent, from 1928 to 1940, while agriculture's share in NNP declined from 49 percent to 29 percent and the labor force share dropped from 71 percent to 51 percent over the same period—an output shift that took 60–70 years, and a labor force shift that took 30–50 years in the West and Japan. Moreover a 60-percent illiteracy rate, an average life expectancy of about 40 years, and widespread poverty before the revolution have given way to universal literacy, a life expectancy of 70 years, and economic security.

The Soviets diverted savings from agriculture to industry (especially metallurgy, engineering, and other heavy industry) through collectivizing farming (1928–38), not through a direct tax like the Japanese, enabling the state to capture a large share of the difference between state monopsony procurement at below-market prices (sometimes below cost) and a sales price closer to market price.[8]

The extent of economic development in Russia before 1917 is a matter of controversy. Walter W. Rostow dates its takeoff into sustained growth in the decades just before the revolution when industrial growth was rapid, though discontinuous. Even so, growth in agriculture and other sectors lagged behind industry's. And surely the autocracy and social rigidity existing under the tsars would not have been consistent with the investment in education and capital equipment needed for economic modernization. Furthermore regardless of what might have occurred under an alternative system, the important point here is the exceptionally rapid economic growth and improvement in material living standards that took place under centralized socialism during the decades after 1928.[9]

Mikhail Gorbachev's **perestroika** (economic restructuring) recognized that, in the 1990s and twenty-first century, the Soviets could no longer rely on major sources of past growth—substantial *increases* in **labor participation rates** (ratio of the labor force to population), rates of investment, and educational enrollment rates. Continued growth requires increased productivity per worker through agricultural decollectivization, more decentralized decision-making, a reduced bureaucracy, greater management and worker rewards for increased enterprise profitabil-

---

[8] Paul R. Gregory and Robert C. Stuart, *Soviet Economic Structure and Performance* (New York: Harper & Row, 1986), pp. 141–52; and Simon Kuznets, "A Comparative Appraisal," in Abram Bergson and Simon Kuznets, eds., *Economic Trends in the Soviet Union* (Cambridge: Harvard University Press, 1963), pp. 345–47.

[9] Paul R. Gregory and Robert C. Stuart, *Soviet Economic Structure and Performance* (New York: Harper and Row, 1986), pp. 141–52; and Walter W. Rostow, *The Stages of Economic Growth: A Non-Communist Manifesto* (Cambridge: Cambridge University Press, 1971), pp. 65–67.

ity, more incentives for technological innovations, and more price reform. Yet ironically growth decelerated during Gorbachev's 1985 to 1989 leadership, increasing pressures for revoking economic reforms.

As indicated in Chapter 2, current levels of economic development form a continuum. Yet only capitalist and centralized socialist countries have achieved the large capital accumulation needed for the highly industrialized and modernized economy characteristic of high-income countries (see Table 2-1). It is not clear, however, whether these approaches can provide the same dramatic success in contemporary developing countries.

While few LDC leaders question the success of the first 50 years of socialism in the USSR, Soviet leadership's admission that centralized socialism was responsible for economic weaknesses of low consumption levels and low productivity (especially in agriculture) has increased LDC leaders' doubts about the Soviet model. The contemporary decentralized socialist LDCs of Yugoslavia, Hungary, and China (similar to the Soviet Union's New Economic Policy, 1921–28) have grown rapidly, but they have been plagued with internal inconsistencies and bureaucratic resistance, especially after the mid-1980s (Chapters 19 and 20). And while China in the 1950s learned from the Soviet model and Taiwan and South Korea have borrowed selectively from the Japanese model, lessons from past models are limited because of Meiji Japan's and the Soviet Union's historically specific conditions that cannot be replicated in other countries.

GROWTH IN THE LAST CENTURY

For the last 125 years or so, average annual growth rates of real GNP per capita in Japan, Sweden, Germany, and Canada have been at least 2 percent, a rate that multiplies income sevenfold in a hundred years. Except for the tiny oil enclaves Kuwait and the United Arab Emirates, whose extraordinary growth was concentrated in the 1960s and early 1970s, Japan's growth of 3.5 percent per year since the mid–nineteenth century has been the most rapid in the world (Table 3-1), increasing at a rate of thirty one times per century. This long period of growth in the West and Japan is unparalleled in world history.[10] It is much more rapid than that of the

---

[10] What explains UK and the U.S. slow and Japan's and Germany's accelerated growth since World War II? Lester Thurow, *The Zero-Sum Solution: Building a World-Class American Economy* (New York: Simon and Schuster, 1985), attributes Japan's superior performance to that of the United States to higher savings rates, higher primary and secondary educational standards, more emphasis on technical and applied science education, a higher propensity to import technology, the scientific and technological background of top managers, their longer time horizons, and the "leaner" management bureaucracy.

Mancur Olson, *The Rise and Decline of Nations: Economic Growth, Stagflation, and Social Rigidities* (New Haven: Yale University Press, 1982), argues that the growth of special interests in developed countries with long periods of stability (without invasion or upheaval), such as Britain and the United States, reduces efficiency and growth. Thus the Allied powers' defeat and occupation of Japan and Germany in the late 1940s abolished special interests that slowed economic growth, while encouraging the establishment of highly encompassing interests.

Paul Kennedy, *The Rise and Fall of the Great Powers: Economic Change and Military Conflict from 1500 to 2000* (New York: Random House, 1987), contends that great powers emerge because of a strong economic base but decline (for example, Britain in the mid–twentieth century and the United States in the late twentieth century) from military overcommitment obstructing economic growth.

TABLE 3-1   Annual Rate of Growth of Real GNP per Capita (percent)

Country	ANNUAL GROWTH RATES, COLUMNS 1–5					Multi-plication of 1860 GNP per Capita in 1986
	(1) 1860 or 1870 to 1910	(2) 1910 to 1950	(3) 1950 to 1975	(4) 1975 to 1986	(5) (long period) 1860 or 1870 to 1986	
Japan	2.9	1.8	7.6	3.4	3.5	76
Sweden	2.4	2.6	2.6	2.4	2.5	23
Germany[a]	2.0	0.7	4.5	2.4	2.1	14
Canada	2.2	1.3	2.4	2.2	2.0	11
Denmark[b]	1.8	1.3	2.9	2.5	1.9	11
France[c]	1.5	0.9	3.8	2.3	1.9	11[d]
U.S.	2.5	1.1	2.0	2.0	1.9	11
Russia-USSR[c]	1.0	2.0	2.7	1.9	1.8	9[d]
Ireland	1.7	1.4	2.6	1.9	1.8	9
Italy	0.8	1.3	4.3	2.2	1.8	9
U.K.	1.2	1.2	2.2	1.8	1.4	6

[a]Since World War II, West Germany.

[b]Figures for period 1 and the long period begin in 1840.

[c]The periods are (1) 1870–1913 and (2) 1913–50.

[d]Multiplication for period 1860–1986 at same annual growth as that in column 5.

Sources: Simon Kuznets, "Levels and Variations of Rates of Growth," *Economic Development and Cultural Change* 5 (October 1956): 13; David Morawetz, *Twenty-five Years of Economic Development, 1950 to 1975* (Baltimore: Johns Hopkins University Press for the World Bank, 1977), p. 80; Gur Ofer, "Soviet Economic Growth: 1928–1985," *Journal of Economic Literature* 25 (December 1987): 1778. The 1975 to 1986 rates (except for the USSR) are estimates based on World Bank, *World Bank Atlas, 1987* (Washington, D.C., 1987), pp. 6–9.

developing countries, whose growth (with a few exceptions, such as Brazil, Argentina, Mexico, and Malaysia) for the same period was only a fraction of 1 percent per year.[11]

ECONOMIC GROWTH IN EUROPE AND JAPAN AFTER WORLD WAR II

Europe and Japan were devastated economically during the war. In the late 1940s and early 1950s, the reorganization of the international trade and financial system coupled with U.S. technical and economic assistance (such as the Marshall Plan) provided the basis for the rapid recovery of war-torn economies, including the economic miracle in West Germany and Japan. Many expected the same pump

[11] David Morawetz, *Twenty-five Years of Economic Development, 1950 to 1975* (Baltimore: Johns Hopkins University Press for the World Bank, 1977), p. 14.

priming with capital and technological expertise to create similar economic miracles in underdeveloped countries. But this did not occur. Countries with cultures vastly different from those of the West, with undeveloped industrial complexes, low literacy, and few technical skills, were simply not able to use the capital fully.

It became obvious that the remarkable growth in Germany and Japan occurred because technical knowledge and human capital were still intact, even though factories, railroads, bridges, harbors, and other physical capital lay in ruins. Starting growth in an underdeveloped economy was far different from rebuilding a war-torn economy.[12]

RECENT ECONOMIC GROWTH IN DEVELOPING COUNTRIES

Economic growth in developing countries was much more rapid after World War II than before. Data before this war are generally poor or lacking altogether. From the start of the twentieth century until independence in 1947, real growth in India, the LDC with the best estimates, was no more than 0.2 percent per year, compared to an annual 1.7-percent growth from 1950 to 1986. World Bank studies indicate real growth rates for developing countries as a whole from 1870 to 1950 to be less than 1 percent a year compared to about 3.1 percent per year from 1950 to 1986, a rate that doubles income per head in about 23 years.[13] This rate was faster than that of developed countries during any comparable period before 1950. If maintained, this rate would be almost as rapid as the long-term growth for Japan and more rapid than the median growth rate (1.9 percent per year; see Table 3-1) for the last 125 years or so for developed countries on which there are data. Yet this comparatively favorable record does not satisfy developing countries, many of which made systematic planning efforts to condense into a few decades development that took the West more than a century.

This growth has been more rapid than earlier predictions and targets would indicate; at least this is true of growth since the 1960s. Forecasts in the 1960s by three prominent economists, Paul Rosenstein–Rodan, Hollis Chenery, and Alan Strout, underestimated the growth of LDCs in the 1960s, 1970s, and 1980s. Furthermore growth in the GNP of developing countries during the UN's first development decade of the 1960s exceeded the target.[14]

---

[12] With this awareness, scholars began thinking seriously in the 1950s about the economic development of Asia, Africa, and Latin America as a field of inquiry separate from the economics of the West. By the last part of the decade, several courses on the economic development of underdeveloped countries were introduced into U.S. universities.

[13] David Morawetz, *Twenty-five Years of Economic Development, 1950 to 1975* (Baltimore: Johns Hopkins University Press for the World Bank, 1977), pp. 12-14; Alan Heston and Robert Summers, "Comparative Indian Economic Growth: 1870–1970," *American Economic Review* 70, no. 2 (May 1980): 96–101; World Bank, *World Development Report, 1988* (New York: Oxford University Press, 1988), p. 187; World Bank, *World Bank Atlas: 1988 Update* (Washington, D.C., 1988), pp. 6–9; and Jogindar S. Uppal, *Economic Development in South Asia* (New York: St. Martin's Press, 1977), pp. 15–17.

[14] David Morawetz, *Twenty-five Years of Economic Development, 1950 to 1975* (Baltimore: Johns Hopkins University Press for the World Bank, 1977), pp. 16–22; Paul Rosenstein–Rodan, "International Aid for Underdeveloped Countries," *Review of Economics and Statistics* 43, no. 2 (May 1961): 107–38; and Hollis Chenery and Alan Strout, "Foreign Assistance and Economic Development," *American Economic Review* 56, no. 4 (September 1966): 679–733.

Rapid and Slow Growers

Such rapid growth masks a wide diversity of performance among the 4.1 billion people in the developing world. About twenty-nine of the developing countries, with 46 percent of LDC population in 1986 (1.9 billion), grew at an average annual rate of 3.5 percent or better from 1965 to 1984. These countries, which include South Korea, Taiwan, China, and Hong Kong (East Asia); Indonesia, Malaysia, Singapore, and Thailand (Southeast Asia); Yemen, Tunisia, Syria, and Jordan (Middle East); Brazil and Ecuador (Latin America); Yugoslavia and Hungary (the two most decentralized European socialist countries); and Cameroon, more than doubled GNP per capita during that period.[15] On the other hand, fifty-five of the less-developed countries, with 41 percent of the LDC population (1.7 billion) grew by less than 2 percent per year for the same period. All sub-Saharan African countries with six million or more people (except Cameroon); India, Bangladesh, Nepal (South Asia); early developing (1850–1950) but recently stagnating Peru, Bolivia, and temperate countries, such as Chile, Argentina, and Uruguay, oil-rich Venezuela, the Duvaliers' Haiti, Costa Rica, Honduras, and war-affected El Salvador (Latin America); Ferdinand E. Marcos's Philippines; and Morocco are included in this group.[16] A partial list of moderate-growing countries (2.0- percent to 3.4-percent annual growth) consisted of Pakistan, Sri Lanka, Burma, Egypt, Turkey, Greece, Spain, Colombia, and Mexico.

The contrast is instructive between West African oil-exporting neighbors Cameroon (3.9-percent annual growth) and Nigeria (1.9 percent), the only country to fall from the fast-growing (1975–80) to slow-growing group (1980–86). Nigeria's annual real growth from 1965 to 1975 was 7.0 percent compared to the Cameroon's 3.0 percent, while Nigerian growth, from 1975 to 1986 was -2.5 percent yearly compared to the Cameroon's 4.7 percent.

Sayre P. Schatz describes the period of Nigerian planning right after the quadrupling of world oil prices in 1973 to 1974 as euphoric planning:

> Projects involving huge sums were added hastily, with little investigation or appraisal. Issues of project interrelation and coordination were ignored in the belief that rapid economic growth would ensure the utility of whatever was undertaken. Economic reasoning gave way before economic enthusiasm. Problems of executive capacity (the ability to carry out the Plan) were ignored.[17]

The use of state levers by Nigeria's insecure military or civilian political elites (turning over frequently from coups), civil servants, and intermediaries for foreign capital, not to support capitalist production but to further their own private interests (substantially purchasing goods from, and transferring money to, foreign countries), was labeled pirate capitalism by Schatz.[18]

---

[15] Hong Kong and Singapore recently graduated from the LDC category to the DC category (see Table 2-1).

[16] Lloyd G. Reynolds, *Economic Growth in the Third World, 1950–1980* (New Haven: Yale University Press, 1985), pp. 81–134, discusses early-developing Latin America.

[17] Sayre P. Schatz, *Nigerian Capitalism* (Berkeley: University of California Press, 1978), p. 47.

[18] Sayre P. Schatz, "Pirate Capitalism and the Inert Economy of Nigeria," *Journal of Modern African Studies* 22 (March 1984): 45–57.

Cameroon, which began oil production off its west coast in 1978, avoided much of the Nigerian syndrome. While Cameroon's petroleum output was only one-tenth of Nigeria's, its potential for economic distortion was as great, since most of its export earnings were also from oil and its population was about one-tenth of Nigeria's. But in the 1970s, Cameroon's **real domestic currency depreciation** (inflation-adjusted decline of the CFA franc relative to the U.S. dollar), compared to the naira's **real appreciation,** made Cameroon's agricultural exports price competitive while Nigeria's traditional exports fell precipitously—cocoa from 24.5 percent of total exports in 1968 to 4.1 percent in 1979, palm kernels from 18.0 percent to 0.1 percent, rubber from 3.0 percent to 0.1 percent, and groundnuts from 18.0 percent, groundnut oil and cake from 6.8 percent, and raw cotton from 1.6 percent, all to 0.0 percent. All these commodities' export values (in constant naira prices) also fell. In fact the aggregate index of the volume of output of Nigerian agricultural

TABLE 3-2   GNP per Capita and Its Annual Growth Rate, Developing Countries, 1965–84

		GNP PER CAPITA		
		1984–86 U.S. Dollars		Annual Growth Rate 1965–86
Country	Population 1986 (millions)	1965	1986	(percent)
Twelve most populous countries				
China	1054.0	110	300	5.1
India	781.4	200	290	1.8
Indonesia	166.4	190	490	4.6
Brazil	138.4	750	1810	4.3
Bangladesh	103.2	150	160	0.4
Nigeria	103.1	430	640	1.9
Pakistan	99.2	210	350	2.4
Mexico	80.2	1080	1860	2.6
Viet Nam	63.3		210	
Philippines	57.3	380	560	1.9
Thailand	52.6	360	810	4.0
Turkey	51.5	360	1110	2.7
Twelve fastest growing countries[a]				
Korea, Rep. of	41.5	610	2370	6.7
Taiwan	19.6	1082	3580	6.5
China	1054.0	110	300	5.1
Yemen Arab Rep.	8.2	210	550	4.7
Indonesia	166.4	190	490	4.6
Brazil	138.4	750	1810	4.3
Malaysia	16.1	330	1830	4.3
Thailand	52.6	360	810	4.0
Yugoslavia	23.3	1030	2300	3.9
Hungary	10.6	900	2020	3.9
Cameroon	10.5	410	910	3.9
Tunisia	7.3	520	1140	3.8

Twelve slowest-growing
countries[a]

Uganda	15.2	400	230	−2.6
Zaïre	31.7	260	160	−2.2
Niger	6.6	410	260	−2.2
Ghana	13.2	560	390	−1.7
Madagascar	10.6	330	230	−1.7
Zambia	6.9	430	300	−1.7
Senegal	6.8	480	420	−0.6
Bolivia	6.6	650	600	−0.4
Tanzania	23.0	270	250	−0.3
Sudan	22.6	330	320	−0.2
Chile	12.2	1380	1320	−0.2
Ethiopia	43.5	120	120	0.0

[a]Countries with a population of 6 million or more. If countries between 1–5.9 million had been included, Botswana, Lesotho, and Jordan, with annual rates of 8.8 percent, 5.6 percent, and 5.5 percent, respectively, would have been among the fastest; and Nicaragua, Jamaica, Liberia, Central African Republic, Somalia, El Salvador, and Mauritania, with rates of −2.2 percent, −1.4 percent, −1.4 percent, 0.6 percent, 0.3 percent, 0.3 percent, and 0.3 percent, respectively, among the slowest.

Source: World Bank, *World Development Report, 1988* (New York: Oxford University Press, 1988), pp. 222–23.

export commodities declined from 100 in 1968 to 50.1 in 1978. Nigeria's agricultural exports as a percentage of total LDC agricultural exports declined during the oil boom, falling 5.7 percent annually from 1965 to 1983[19] (see Chapter 8 for a discussion of Dutch disease). (Remember that depreciation of the Japanese yen spurred exports in the late nineteenth century.)

The Cameroon government planned better than the Nigerian government, accumulating substantial foreign exchange reserves abroad and avoiding some of the painful adjustments of the 1980s' oil price fall. Moreover Cameroon used much of its oil revenues for manufacturing and agriculture, including maintaining coffee and cocoa producer prices despite softening world prices.[20]

Low- and Middle-Income Countries

If we exclude China, the disparity between low- and middle-income developing countries has increased significantly since 1965. The low-income countries, which

[19] World Bank, *World Development Report, 1986* (New York: Oxford University Press, 1986), p. 72; E. Wayne Nafziger, *The Economics of Political Instability: The Nigerian–Biafran War* (Boulder, Colo.: Westview, 1983), pp. 152–53; and Paul Collier, "Oil and Inequality in Rural Nigeria," in Dharan Ghai and Samir Radwan, eds., *Agrarian Policies and Rural Poverty in Africa* (Geneva: International Labor Office, 1983), pp. 191–217.

[20] E. Wayne Nafziger, *Inequality in Africa: Political Elites, Proletariat, Peasants, and the Poor* (Cambridge: Cambridge University Press, 1988), pp. 152–59; and Nancy C. Benjamin and Shantayanan Devarajan, "Oil Revenues and the Cameroonian Economy," in Michael G. Schatzberg and I. William Zartman, eds. *The Political Economy of Cameroon* (New York: Praeger, 1986), pp. 161–88.

include South Asia, sub-Saharan Africa (except as noted), parts of Southeast Asia (Burma, Laos, Kampuchea, and Viet Nam), and Haiti, grew by only 1.6 percent yearly (0.5 percent per year without India) compared to a 2.6-percent annual growth rate for middle-income countries (mainly the Middle East, East Asia, Latin America, the rest of Southeast Asia, and Cameroon, Nigeria, the Ivory Coast, Angola, Zimbabwe, South Africa, and some small sub-Saharan countries (see Table 2-1).

Oil Exporters and Importers

The fourfold increase in oil prices over 4 months from 1973 to 1974 and subsequent increases in the 1970s greatly benefited oil-exporting countries but severely disrupted oil-importing LDCs. The 1980 **terms of trade** (price index of exports divided by price index of imports) of high-income oil exporters (Saudi Arabia, Kuwait, the United Arab Emirates, and Libya) and oil-exporting LDCs (Iran, Iraq, Oman, Venezuela, Nigeria, Algeria, Indonesia, Mexico, Egypt, Malaysia, Cameroon, and Ecuador) were 241 percent and 195 percent, respectively, of 1973 levels while those of oil-importing LDCs were only 85.2 percent of 1973. (Chapter 17 shows how to compute the terms of trade.)

The 1973 to 1974 oil price shock slowed economic growth and accelerated inflation more in developing oil-importing countries than in rich countries, such as the United States, in the first two to three years. Petroleum accounted for almost one-half of the total energy supply of developing countries in the 1970s. Producers used oil largely to meet basic energy requirements, with only a tiny fraction for powering private automobiles, air conditioning, and other consumer items. Furthermore the energy crisis also affected agricultural output: Higher prices for petrochemicals contributed to sharp price increases for fertilizers and pesticides.

Developing countries imported 4.6 million barrels of oil per day in 1973 and 6.2 million barrels per day in 1980, but they paid $7 billion for petroleum imports in 1973 and $67 billion in 1980, almost a tenfold increase. The price per barrel (c.i.f.) rose from $4.20 in 1973 to $29.80 in 1980 (a sevenfold increase), and the real (inflation-adjusted) price increased by about three and one-third times (see Figure 3-1).[21]

Despite the adverse immediate effect of the oil shock, the medium-run growth impact was less severe, since oil-importing LDCs grew by 3.1 percent annually from 1973 to 1980, the same as oil-exporting LDCs, and more than the DC or high-income oil exporters' yearly growth rates—both 2.1 percent.[22] The greater cost of the oil price hike was the future **debt service** (interest and principal payments due in a given year on long-term debt) from the growth of LDC long-term debt, since LDCs were spurred to borrow funds at **negative real interest rates** (nominal interest

---

[21] C.i.f. includes the cost of insurance and freight in the price per barrel.

[22] When a country's terms of trade shift greatly, growth in GNP in constant price does not accurately reflect changes in purchasing power. The volume of imports that can be bought with a given export volume rises if the terms of trade increase and falls if they decline. There is no generally accepted way of adjusting for shifts in the terms of trade. The main point, however, is that the growth of oil importers is overstated and the growth of oil exporters is understated for the 1970s and vice versa for the 1980s. World Bank, *World Development Report, 1980* (New York: Oxford University Press, 1980), pp. 158–65.

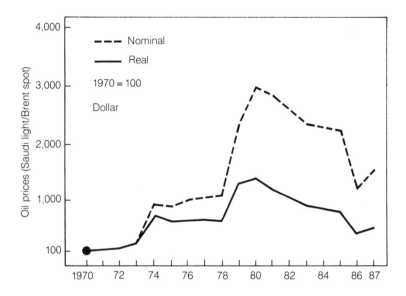

FIGURE 3-1   Changes in Petroleum Prices, 1970–87 (1970=100)   A major factor contributing to increased economic growth for oil-exporting LDCs and reduced economic growth for oil-importing LDCs in the 1970s was the more than threefold increase in real (inflation-adjusted) oil prices between 1973 and 1980. The subsequent fall in real oil prices helps explain the oil-importing LDCs' positive growth and the oil-exporting LDCs' negative growth during the 1980s.

Source: *Economist* (November 7, 1987), p. 113.

rates less than the inflation rate) from 1973 to 1975, but often had to **roll over the debt,** or borrow enough to cover debt service and imports, at positive world real rates of interest of 7–12 percent from 1982 to 1988. Oil-importing LDCs' long-term debt, which increased from $54.2 billion (1970) to $89.0 billion (1973) to $336.2 billion (1980) to $706.1 billion (1988), constrained 1980s' growth, sacrificed, along with other domestic goals of high employment and poverty reduction, for external goals.

From 1980 to 1987, while world real oil prices dropped more than 50 percent, oil-importing LDC growth was 2.1 percent yearly; oil-exporting LDCs, −1.6 percent; and high-income oil exporters, −6.3 percent. The 1987 terms of trade were 48.8 percent of 1980 (but 120.4 percent of 1965) for high-income oil exporters, 50.1 percent of 1980 (but 97.7 percent of 1965) for oil-exporting LDCs, and 83.3 percent of 1980 (and 93.2 percent of 1965) for oil-importing LDCs. Yet oil importers, with a 1986 population of 3223.1 million, had a GNP per capita of $560 compared to a 538.3 million population and $930 GNP per person for oil-exporting LDCs.[23]

[23] Calculated from World Bank, *World Development Report, 1988* (New York: Oxford University Press, 1988), pp. 187, 192, 222–23; and International Monetary Fund, *World Economic Outlook: Revised Projections* (Washington, D.C., October 1988), p. 127.

TABLE 3-3   GNP per Capita, Annual Growth Rate, and Relative Gap in GNP per Capita by Region, 1950–86

		GNP PER CAPITA				
	Popula-tion 1986 (mil-lions)	1984–86 U.S. Dollars		Annual Growth Rate 1950–86 (per-cent)	Relative Gap[a] (multiple)	
Region		1950	1986		1950	1986
South Asia	1018	154	282	1.7	31.0	47.4
China	1054	57	300	4.7	83.8	44.5
Africa[b]	504	232	426	1.7	20.6	31.4
Latin America	394	678	1,709	2.6	7.0	19.7
East Asia[c]	89	429	2,573	5.1	11.1	5.2
Middle East	142	1118	4,916	4.2	4.3	2.7
Developing countries	3861	201	624	3.2	23.8	21.4
Developed countries	699	4774	13,360	2.9	1.0	1.0

[a]GNP per capita of the developed countries as a multiple of GNP per capita of the region. Developed countries are the high-income countries in Table 2-1 (except Israel, Hong Kong, Singapore, and centrally planned).

[b]Includes Arab Africa and sub-Saharan Africa except South Africa.

[c]Does not include China.

Sources: David Morawetz, *Twenty-five Years of Economic Development, 1950 to 1975* (Baltimore: Johns Hopkins University Press, 1977), pp. 11, 27; and World Bank, *World Development Report, 1988* (New York: Oxford University Press), pp. 222–23.

Regions of the World

The growth rate of LDCs was faster than that of DCs from 1950 to 1986, and from 1950 to 1986, the most rapidly growing LDC region has been East Asia, which includes rapidly growing Taiwan, South Korea (both with 5.8-percent annual growth), and China (with 4.7-percent yearly growth) (see Table 3-3, which separates China from East Asia). The oil-rich Middle East, which has the highest GNP per capita ($4916), is the second fastest growing region. South Asia, with the lowest GNP per capita, and Africa, the slowest growing region (1965–86), are tied for the slowest growth over the 36-year period, with 1.7-percent annual growth, which takes 41 years to double average income.

Capitalist, Mixed, and Socialist Countries

Because of the difficulty Chapter 2 mentioned in adjusting socialist countries' measure of material product (excluding services) to national product, we lack up-to-date comparisons of mixed private–public and capitalist countries with socialist countries. If we use the most recent data (1980), the GNP per capita of capitalist and mixed countries is about twice that of socialist countries, whether comparisons are among developed or developing countries. But recall from Chapter 2 that the economic welfare of socialist countries is often understated; thus their average material well-being is more favorable than figures indicate.

However, from 1960 to 1980, growth in real GNP per capita for socialist countries was faster than for mixed and capitalist countries. Socialist LDCs grew at 3.9 percent compared to 2.4 percent per year for other LDCs, socialist DCs at 4.0 percent per year compared to 3.6 percent for other developed countries. When averaged these yearly growth rates are 3.9 percent socialist and 2.7 percent nonsocialist.

China's growth rate is faster than mixed and capitalist developing countries, and the Soviet Union's is faster than nonsocialist developed countries. But when these two socialist countries are not figured in, the rate differentials widen. Socialist LDCs' annual growth rate rises to 6.0 percent, socialist DCs' to 4.3 percent, and the average to 5.6 percent.[24]

Why have socialist economies grown faster than capitalist and mixed economies in recent years? In some cases, revolution replaced an order that inhibited economic modernization with leadership more committed to rapid economic transformation. Moreover the Soviet Union and Eastern Europe (except East Germany) industrialized late relative to the rest of Europe, as did China relative to other Asian countries. Thus some of this rapid growth may have involved catching up. Socialist countries, aware of their economic backwardness, relied on centralized state planning to transform their economies rapidly, especially in health, education, and industry. State-directed economic activity forced savings away from low-priority sectors, such as agriculture, to high-priority sectors, such as industry, particularly heavy industry and capital goods.

A Widening Gap?

In 1969, a commission on international development chaired by Lester Pearson (former Canadian prime minister) contended that "the widening gap between the developed and developing countries" is one of the central issues of our time.[25] Are rich countries getting richer and poor countries poorer? One measure, real per capita income, indicates that since World War II both developed and developing countries are better off. Is the gap widening? The answer is complex, since it depends on the definition of the gap, the time period used, how we define a rich country and a poor one, and whether or not we view a country at the beginning or the end of the time period.

Table 3-3 indicates that since 1950, the **relative economic gap** (GNP per capita of the developed countries as a multiple of the developing countries) has declined, especially in China, East Asia, and the Middle East, but the gap has increased in South Asia, Africa, and Latin America. However not a single developing country narrowed the **absolute** (arithmetical) **income gap** between 1950 and 1986. In fact U.S. annual growth in GNP per capita, 1.6 percent per year—about $280—is more than the *total* GNP per capita of very poor countries, such as Bangladesh or Ethiopia. Even the absolute gap between the United States and rapidly growing Taiwan

[24] Computed from World Bank, *World Development Report, 1982* (New York: Oxford University Press, 1982), pp. 110–11.

[25] Lester Pearson et al., *Partners in Development: Report of the Commission on International Development* (New York: Praeger, 1969), p. 1.

and South Korea more than doubled during the period, and the gap still continues to widen.

It is very difficult to narrow the absolute economic gap. To illustrate, suppose Gamma's GNP per capita of $5000 in 1990 increased by $500 in 1991, a growth rate of 10 percent, one-half the 20-percent rate for lower income Alpha and Beta in 1991 (see Figure 3-2, bar clusters a–b). Nevertheless the absolute gap between Gamma

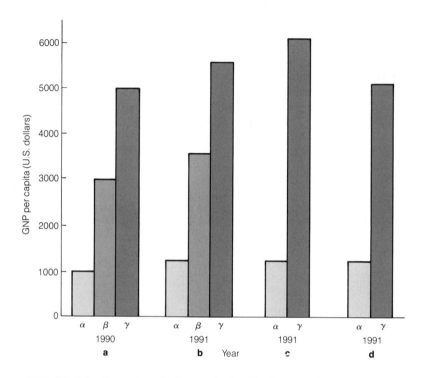

FIGURE 3-2   Examples of Changes in the Absolute and Relative Income Gaps

(a) Assume Alpha's 1990 GNP per capita is $1000, 20 percent of Gamma's $5000. Beta's 1990 GNP per capita of $3000 is 60 percent of Gamma's.

(b) Assume both Alpha's and Beta's 1991 GNP per capita growth (20 percent) is twice that of Gamma's (10 percent). Accordingly Beta narrows the absolute and relative gap vis-à-vis Gamma. However Alpha narrows the relative gap but widens the absolute gap vis-à-vis Gamma.

(c) If Alpha's 1991 GNP per capita increases by $200 (or 20 percent), Gamma's increase in 1991 GNP per capita must exceeed $1000 for both absolute and relative gaps to widen.

(d) A 1991 increase of $200 in GNP per capita for Alpha, and a 1991 increase of $100 in Gamma, will narrow both absolute and relative gaps.

and Alpha widened by $300, since Alpha's 20-percent growth rate on 1990 GNP per capita of $1000 yielded only $200 in 1991. On the other hand, Beta's 20-percent increase on GNP per capita of $3000 yielded $600 in 1983, narrowing the absolute gap vis-à-vis Gamma by $100 ($600 versus $500).

A lower-income country growing twice as fast as a higher-income country will not begin to reduce the *absolute* gap until its GNP per capita is one-half that of the richer country. Reducing the absolute gap is inevitably frustrating for most LDCs. If 1965 to 1986 growth rates remain the same, only Taiwan will narrow the gap by 2020, and only one other country will do so before the end of the twenty-first century (see Table 3-4).

TABLE 3-4   The Absolute Gap: When Might It Be Narrowed?

Country[a]	GNP per Capita 1986	Annual Growth Rate 1965–86 (percent)	Year When Gap[b] Is Reduced If 1965–84 Growth Continues
Spain	4860	2.9	2246
Greece	3680	3.3	2152
Taiwan	3580	6.5	2020
Algeria	2590	3.5	2155
Yugoslavia	2300	3.9	2124
Portugal	2250	3.2	2248
Hungary	2020	3.9	2125
Mexico	1860	2.6	4008
Malaysia	1830	4.3	2100
Brazil	1810	4.3	2101
Syria, Arab Rep.	1570	3.7	2170
Colombia	1230	2.8	2802
Ecuador	1160	3.5	2238
Tunisia	1140	3.8	2182
Turkey	1100	2.7	3267
Paraguay	1000	3.6	2229
Cameroon	910	3.9	2184
Botswana	840	8.8	2033
Thailand	810	4.0	2179
Egypt	760	3.1	2478
Yemen Arab Rep.	550	4.7	2137
Indonesia	490	4.6	2149
Sri Lanka	400	2.9	2887
China	300	5.1	2138

[a]All countries in Table 2-1 with a population of at least 6 million and GNP per capita of $6000 or less whose growth rate of per capita income exceeds 2.5 percent, that of high-income countries (except Israel, Hong Kong, Singapore, and centrally planned) during 1965–86.

[b]The gap is GNP per capita of developed countries ($13,360 in 1986) less GNP per capita of the individual country.

Source: Figures used in GNP per Capita and Annual Growth Rate columns are from data in Table 2-1; third column figures are the author's computations.

On the other hand, narrowing the *relative* gap makes little sense as a development objective. The 1986 GNP per capita of the United States, $17,680, was 110 times that of Bangladesh, $160. However if the GNP per capita of Bangladesh increases by $10 and that of the United States by $170, the *relative* gap narrows to 105, a goal hardly worth striving toward.

Studies indicate that ruling elites in developing countries emphasize such international comparisons more than their citizens. Poor people are concerned not so much with closing the gap but with the internal distribution of income and their own place within it.[26]

Population Growth

Since 1950 population in developing countries has grown at a rate of more than 2 percent per year, a rate faster than that in either developed or developing countries at any other time in history. Improvements in food production, nutrition, transport, communication, personal hygiene, health, medical care, the use of insecticides, immunization programs, and drainage and reclamation of land occurred rapidly after World War II. As a result, mortality rates declined. Average life expectancy in developing countries increased from 32 years in the 1930s to 42 years in the 1950s, 49 years in the 1960s, 54 years in the 1970s, and 61 years in the 1980s. Couples usually reduce family size only after changes in values, aspirations, social structure, and child-rearing costs associated with a later period of economic, technical, and educational development. Correspondingly, birth rates did not decline in developing countries as a whole until the 1970s, and the burden of nonworking dependents, 0–14 years old, until the 1980s. High birth rates require resources to be diverted to schools, food, health care, and social services for these dependents (see Chapter 9).

SUMMARY

1. In the last century or so, sustained economic growth occurred primarily in the capitalist countries of the West and Japan. During this period, the economic growth rate of a number of these countries was over 1.5 percent per year. Thus the gap between these countries and the developing countries of Afro-Asia has increased greatly.

2. The rise of capitalism in the West can be traced to the decline of feudalism, the breakdown of church authority, strong nation–states supporting free trade, a liberal ideology tailor made for the bourgeoisie, a price revolution that speeded capital accumulation, advances in science and technology, and a spirit of rationalism from the fifteenth to eighteenth centuries.

3. During the late nineteenth century, the Japanese government helped individuals and organizations acquire foreign technology, established a banking system, assisted private business people (including selling factories to them), aided technical improvement in small industry, implemented universal education, and kept foreign exchange rates close to market-clearing rates. However, the lessons contemporary LDCs can learn from early modern Japan are limited because of her historically specific conditions.

[26] See David Morawetz, *Twenty-five Years of Economic Development, 1950 to 1975* (Baltimore: Johns Hopkins University Press for the World Bank, 1977), pp. 26–30.

4. The 1917 Communist revolution in Russia provided an alternative to capitalism as a road to economic modernization. The state took control of economic planning and capital accumulation. In only a few decades, Soviet centralized socialism transformed Russia. Low literacy and life expectancy and widespread peasant poverty yielded to virtually universal literacy, a high life expectancy, and economic security. Yet many of the sources for this rapid growth have been exhausted, suggesting economic restructuring (perestroika) may be essential for continuing progress.

5. The economic growth of developing countries since World War II has been much more rapid than before the war. This postwar growth rate was faster than that of the developed countries in any comparable period before 1950.

6. However, this rapid growth masks a wide diversity of performance. From 1965 to 1984, almost half the LDC population lived in countries growing at an annual rate of 3.5 percent or better, but about two-fifths of this population grew by not more than 2 percent yearly. Middle-income countries grew more rapidly than low-income countries. Oil-importing countries grew as rapidly as oil-exporting countries during the 1970s and faster than oil exporters during the 1980s. Since 1950, East Asia (including China) and the Middle East have grown the most rapidly, while South Asia and Africa have been the slowest growing. The socialist countries, which have diverted savings to high-priority sectors, such as heavy industry and capital goods, have grown more rapidly than capitalist and mixed countries from 1960 to 1980.

7. Since World War II, developing countries have grown faster than the developed countries. However the *absolute* income gap has widened between developed and developing countries.

8. There is no historical precedent for the LDC population growth in excess of 2 percent per year since 1950. Improved health, production, and technology reduced death rates without significantly affecting birth rates.

   Despite the rapid overall economic growth in LDCs since World War II, its benefits have been unevenly distributed. Chapter 6 focuses on poverty and income inequality in LDCs and policies to reduce these.

TERMS TO REVIEW

- **modern economic growth**
- **capitalism**
- **bourgeoisie**
- **surplus**
- **Protestant ethic**
- **Japanese development model**
- **zaibatsu**
- **infrastructure**

- **Soviet development model**
- **perestroika**
- **labor participation rate**
- **real domestic currency depreciation**
- **real domestic currency appreciation**

- **terms of trade**
- **debt service**
- **debt roll over**
- **negative real interest rates**
- **relative economic gap**
- **absolute economic gap**

QUESTIONS TO DISCUSS

1. What are the characteristics of modern economic growth? Why was modern economic growth largely confined to the West (Western Europe, the United States, and Canada) before the twentieth century?

2. How important were noneconomic factors in contributing to modern capitalist development in the West?

3. How does the *relative* gap between the West and Afro-Asian LDCs today compare to the gap a century and a quarter or half ago? How do we explain this difference?

4. Which countries outside the West have had the most development success in the last century? Are these non-Western development models useful for today's LDCs?

5. Compare the economic growth of today's LDCs before and after World War II.

6. How good is the economic development record of developing countries since the 1950s and 1960s? Which LDC groups have the best records?

7. What are the differences in the post-1950s LDC development performances between (1) fast- and slow-growing countries, (2) low- and middle-income countries, (3) oil exporters and importers, (4) different regions of the world, and (5) socialist and nonsocialist countries? How do you explain these differences?

8. Which concept of the economic gap between LDCs and DCs is more useful? Has this gap widened, narrowed, or remained the same since 1950?

GUIDE TO READINGS

Simon Kuznets's *Economic Growth of Nations* (note 1) and *Modern Economic Growth: Rate, Structure, and Spread* (New Haven: Yale University Press, 1966) analyze the origin of modern economic growth. Initially modern growth meant capitalist growth as Dillard indicates in a book and article (note 4). For criticisms of Weber's thesis (note 2) on the Protestant ethic and capitalist development, see Chapter 13; R. H. Tawney, *Religion and the Rise of Capitalism* (New York: Harcourt, Brace, and Co., 1926); Kurt Samuelsson, *Religion and Economic Action: A Critique of Max Weber* (New York: Harper & Row, 1957); and H. M. Robertson, *Aspects of the Rise of Economic Individualism: A Criticism of Max Weber and His School* (New York: Kelley and Millman, 1959).

The annual *World Development Report* by the World Bank is the best of several sources on recent economic growth of LDCs and DCs (see the bibliographical note in Chapter 2). Morawetz's book (note 11) has an excellent analysis of major trends in the economic growth of LDCs since World War II. The books by Kuznets noted above, although somewhat dated, are the best sources on long-run economic growth. Paul Bairoch's careful statistical work in *The Economic Development of the Third World since 1900,* trans. Cynthia Postan (Berkeley and Los Angeles: University of California Press, 1975); "Europe's Gross National Product: 1800–1975," *Journal of European Economic History* 5 (Fall 1976): 273–340; and "International Industrialization Levels from 1750 to 1980," *Journal of European*

Economic History, 11 (Fall 1982): 269–333; is worth perusing, although I think Bairoch, unlike Kuznets, underestimates nineteenth-century differences between GNP per capita in the DCs and the third world. Gregory's and Stuart's book (note 8) on long-term Soviet growth is excellent.

Kazushi Ohkawa and Gustav Ranis, eds., *Japan and the Developing Countries* (Oxford: Basil Blackwell, 1985); Saburo Okita, *The Developing Economies and Japan: Lessons in Growth* (Tokyo: University of Tokyo Press, 1980); and Nafziger (note 7), with useful references, examine implications of the Japanese development experience for LDCs. G. C. Allen, *The Japanese Economy* (New York: Simon & Schuster, 1982); and Hiroshi Kitamura, *Choices for the Japanese Economy* (London: Royal Institute of International Affairs, 1976), discuss contemporary Japanese economic development.

Nigeria's real decline in GNP per capita during the 1980s (to $370 in 1987) was noted by World Bank, *World Development Report, 1989* (New York: Oxford University Press, 1989), pp. 164–65, which classified Nigeria as a low-income country. On Nigeria's planning, see P.N.C. Okigbo, *National Development Planning in Nigeria, 1900–92* (Portsmouth, N.H.: Heinemann, 1989).

Chapter Four

PROFILE OF DEVELOPING COUNTRIES

SCOPE OF THE CHAPTER

This chapter surveys the characteristics of developing countries. It looks at income distribution, political framework, family system, relative size of agriculture, technical and capital levels, saving rates, dualism, international trade dependence, export patterns, population growth, labor force growth, literacy, and skill levels. Subsequent chapters will expand on the economic pattern of development.

VARYING INCOME INEQUALITY

As the level of economic development rises, income inequality frequently follows an **inverted U-shaped curve,** first increasing (from low- to middle-income countries), and then decreasing (from middle- to high-income countries). Even so, the proportion of the population in poverty drops as per capita income increases (see Chapter 6).

POLITICAL FRAMEWORK

Varying Political Systems

Only about twenty eight of the LDCs are political democracies; that is, their people elect public officials. I say about twenty eight because what differentiates democracy from nondemocracy is not always clear. Since democracies include populous

India, they comprise more than one-third of the total population of LDCs and more than one-half of nonsocialist LDCs.

A Small Political Elite

Unlike Western democracies, political control in LDCs tends to be held by a relatively small **political elite.** This group includes not only individuals who directly or indirectly play a considerable part in government—political leaders, traditional princes and chiefs, high-ranking military officers, senior civil servants and administrators, and executives in public corporations—but also large landowners, major business people, and leading professionals. Even an authoritarian leader cannot rule without some consensus among this influential elite unless he or she uses police and military repression, perhaps with the support of a strong foreign power.

Low Political Institutionalization

For the political elite, economic modernization often poses a dilemma. Although achieving modernity breeds stability, the process of modernization breeds instability. Certainly modernization enhances the ability of a governing group to maintain order, resolve disputes, select leaders, and promote political community. But urbanization, industrialization, educational expansion, and so on, eventually involve previously inactive ethnic, religious, regional, or economic groups in politics. According to Samuel Huntington, the explosion of mass participation in politics relative to institutional capacity to absorb new participants leads to political instability.[1] (Of course civil conflict is not confined to newly modernizing countries. Currently ethnic, religious, and regional conflicts exist in Canada, Britain, and Belgium.)

Experience of Western Domination

Except for Japan, in the past two hundred years—and especially in the first half of the twentieth century—most of Africa and Asia were Western-dominated colonies. Even such countries as Afghanistan and Thailand, which were never Western colonies, experienced Western penetration and hegemony. And although most of Latin America became independent in the nineteenth century, it has been subject to British and U.S. economic and political suzerainty since then. Thus during the century or two of rapid economic growth in the Western countries, most LDCs have not had the political independence essential for economic modernization.

AN EXTENDED FAMILY

The **extended family,** including two or more nuclear families of father, mother, and children, is a common institution in developing countries. Although some scholars regard the extended family as an obstacle to economic development, I disagree. To be sure, if one family member earns a higher income and saves, others may demand the savings be shared, which hinders development, since

[1] Samuel P. Huntington, *Political Order in Changing Societies* (New Haven: Yale University Press, 1968).

funds are diverted from capital formation. However, if family members attend secondary school or university, acquire training, seek urban employment, or start a new business, the larger family unit may support them financially and so contribute to economic development.

PEASANT AGRICULTURAL SOCIETIES

Most low-income countries are predominantly peasant agricultural societies. **Peasants** are rural cultivators. They do not run a business enterprise as do farmers in the United States, but rather a household whose main concern is survival. Although patterns of land ownership, tenure, and concentration vary considerably, most of the land in these societies is worked by landless laborers, sharecroppers, renters, or smallholders rather than large commercial farmers. In Afro-Asia the average farm is usually less than 12 acres in size (see Chapter 6).

A HIGH PROPORTION OF THE LABOR FORCE IN AGRICULTURE

In low-income countries, 65–75 percent of the labor force is in agriculture, forestry, hunting, and fishing; 10–20 percent in industry (manufacturing, mining, construction, and public utilities); and 10–20 percent in services (see Table 4-1). In contrast high-income countries tend to have less than 10 percent of the labor force in agriculture; 30–40 percent in industry; and 50–65 percent in services. (A generation or two ago, the share of the labor force in agriculture in low-income countries may have been 90 percent, about the same as that of the United States in 1776.)

In low-income countries, the average agricultural family produces a surplus large enough only to supply a small nonagricultural population. In these countries, two-thirds of the labor force produce food, one-twenty-fifth do so in the United States. Obviously agricultural productivity in low-income countries is much lower than in the United States and other developed countries.

A HIGH PROPORTION OF OUTPUT IN AGRICULTURE

Figure 4-1 indicates that as countries develop, the output and labor force share in agriculture declines, and that in industry and services increases. The low-income countries of Asia and Africa are now in the early part of the labor force change, while the middle-income states of Latin America, East Asia, and the Middle East are in the later part. In high-income countries, the rising output and labor force share of services leads to stability and then an eventual decline in the share of industry.

Typically the shift in labor force shares from agriculture to industry lags behind the shift in production shares. One reason is the unprecedented growth of the labor force since the 1950s; it has far exceeded industry's capacity to absorb labor (see Chapter 10). In addition partly because of advanced technology and greater capital intensity, industry's labor productivity is higher than agriculture's. Thus the output percentage in agriculture for low-income countries, 25–35 percent, is lower than the labor force percentage and higher in industry, 30–40 percent. (See Table 4-1, where

TABLE 4-1   Industrial Structure in Developing and Developed Countries

	Percent of Labor Force in		Percent of Gross Domestic Product (GDP) in	
	Agriculture (1980)	Industry (1980)	Agriculture (1986)	Industry (1986)
Categories of countries				
Low-income	72	13	32	35
Middle-income	43	23	15	36
High-income oil exporters	35	21	2	58
Centrally planned economies	22	39	15	63
High income	7	35	3	35
Countries				
Bangladesh	75	6	47	14
India	70	13	32	29
Pakistan	55	16	24	28
China	74	14	31	46
Tanzania	86	5	59	10
Kenya	81	7	30	20
Nigeria	68	12	41	29
Indonesia	57	13	26	32
Egypt	46	20	20	29
Syria	32	32	22	21
Peru	40	18	11	38
Colombia	34	24	20	25
Brazil	31	27	11	39
Mexico	37	29	9	39
Argentina	13	34	13	44
South Korea	36	27	12	42
U.S.	4	31	2	31
Canada	5	29	3	36
U.K.	3	38	2	43

Source: World Bank, *World Development Report, 1988* (New York: Oxford University Press, 1988), pp. 226–27, 282–83.

output is **gross domestic product, GDP,** income earned within a country's boundaries instead of gross national product, income accruing to a country's residents.) Figure 4-1 indicates that although industry and agriculture account for equal shares of output at an income level of just under $700 per capita, parity in labor force shares is not reached until income is more than twice that level. In high-income countries, less than 10 percent of production is in agriculture, 30–40 percent in industry, and more than half in services.

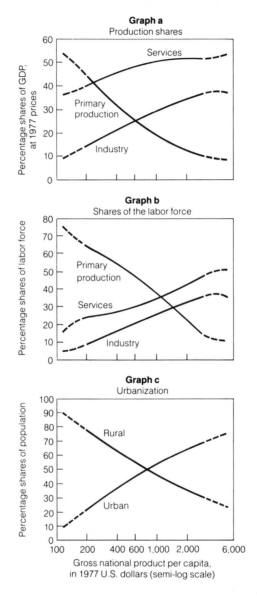

FIGURE 4-1 Economic Development and Structural Change As GNP per capita increases, the output and labor force share in agriculture decreases, while that in industry and services increases.

Source: World Bank, *World Development Report, 1979* (Washington, D.C., 1979), p. 44.

Although the relative size of the nonagricultural sector is positively related to per capita income, this relationship does not mean industrialization creates prosperity; instead industrialization may be a consequence of shifts in the composition of aggregate demand caused by higher per capita incomes. At the lowest levels of per capita income, almost one-half of total demand is for food, and relatively large shares are for shelter and clothing. However as average income increases, the percentage spent on food and other necessities falls (Table 4-2, line 3b), and the percentage spent on manufactured consumer goods and consumer services rises.

The correlation of increased shares of industry and services in output and employment with economic growth is closely related to shifts in economic activity from rural to urban areas (Graph c, Figure 3-1). Modern, nonagricultural activities benefit greatly from economies of location. As these activities increase their shares in output and employment, they spur the growth of urban centers.[2]

INADEQUATE TECHNOLOGY AND CAPITAL

Output per worker in LDCs is low compared to developed countries because capital per worker is low. Lack of equipment, machinery, and other such capital and low levels of technology, at least throughout most of the economy, hinder production. Although output per unit of capital in LDCs compares favorably to that of rich countries, it is spread over many more workers.

Production methods in most sectors are traditional. Many agricultural techniques, especially in low-income countries, date from biblical times. Wooden plows are used. Seed is sown by hand. Oxen thresh the grain by walking over it. Water is carried in jugs on the head, and the wind is used to separate wheat from straw.

Generally most manufacturing employment, although not output, is in **cottage industry.** These may be one-person enterprises, or at most, units with less than ten workers, many of whom are apprentices or family workers. Production is labor-intensive. Simple tools are used, and there is no mechanical power.

LOW SAVING RATES

Gross domestic saving as a percentage of GDP (1986) is 7 percent for low-income countries (excluding China and India) compared to 24 percent for middle-income countries and 21 percent for high-income countries. Capital inflows from abroad (in the form of equity investment, loans, and grants) increase the gross investment rate to 15 percent for low-income countries; capital outflows reduce middle-income countries' rate to 23 percent.[3]

A country's **capital stock** is the sum total of previous gross investments minus capital consumptions (or depreciations). During the 1960s and 1970s, saving rates for low-income countries were 10–15 percent of gross domestic product. Although

[2] World Bank, *World Development Report, 1979* (Washington, D.C., 1979), pp. 44–45.

[3] World Bank, *World Development Report, 1988* (New York: Oxford University Press, 1988), pp. 230–31.

TABLE 4-2 Normal Variation in Economic Structure with Level of Development

	PREDICTED VALUES AT DIFFERENT INCOME LEVELS (STATED IN 1964 PRICES)									
Process	Mean[a] Under $100	$100	$200	$300	$400	$500	$800	$1000	Mean[b] Over $1000	Change
1. Tax revenue	0.106	0.129	0.153	0.173	0.189	0.203	0.236	0.254	0.282	0.176
2. Education expenditure	0.026	0.033	0.033	0.034	0.035	0.037	0.041	0.043	0.039	0.013
3. Structure of domestic demand										
a. Government consumption	0.119	0.137	0.134	0.135	0.136	0.138	0.144	0.148	0.141	0.022
b. Food consumption	0.414	0.392	0.315	0.275	0.248	0.229	0.191	0.175	0.167	−0.247
4. Structure of trade										
a. Exports	0.172	0.195	0.218	0.230	0.238	0.244	0.255	0.260	0.249	0.077
b. Primary exports	0.130	0.137	0.136	0.131	0.125	0.120	0.105	0.096	0.058	−0.072
c. Manufactured exports	0.011	0.019	0.034	0.046	0.056	0.065	0.086	0.097	0.131	0.120
d. Service exports	0.028	0.031	0.042	0.048	0.051	0.053	0.056	0.057	0.059	0.031
e. Imports	0.205	0.218	0.234	0.243	0.249	0.254	0.263	0.267	0.250	0.045

[a]Approximately $70. Mean value of countries with per capita GNP under $100 vary slightly according to composition of the sample.

[a]Approximately $1500. Mean values of countries with per capita GNP over $1000 vary slightly according to composition of the sample.

Source: Hollis B. Chenery and Moises Syrquin, *Patterns of Development, 1950–1970* (New York: Oxford University Press, 1975), pp. 20–21.

figures on depreciation are rough, it is perhaps 6–9 percent of GDP. Accordingly net saving rates for these countries probably averaged 6–9 percent per year. With capital inflows, their net investment rates were probably not much more than 10–12 percent a year, an amount that approximated the 1980s' *net* rates. Thus overall levels of capital stock in low-income countries remain low.

A DUAL ECONOMY

Even though in the aggregate low-income countries have inadequate technology and capital, this is not true in all sectors. Virtually all low-income countries and many middle-income countries are **dual economies.** These economies have a traditional, peasant, agricultural sector, producing primarily for family or village subsistence. This sector has little or no reproducible capital, uses technologies handed down for generations, and has low marginal productivity of labor (that is, output produced from an extra hour of labor is less than the subsistence wage).

In the midst of this labor-intensive, subsistence, peasant agriculture (together with semisubsistence agriculture, petty trade, and cottage industry) sits a capital-intensive enclave consisting of modern manufacturing and processing operations, mineral extraction, and plantation agriculture. This modern sector produces for the market, uses reproducible capital and new technology, and hires labor commercially (where marginal productivity is at least as much as the wage). According to the Lewis model (Chapter 10), the dual economy grows only when the modern sector increases its output share relative to the traditional sector.[4]

In the 1950s and 1960s, this modern sector tended to be foreign owned and managed. Today as a result of limiting or banning foreign ownership shares, restrictions on conversion into foreign currency, and outright expropriation, it is increasingly owned domestically, often by government or quasi-governmental enterprises, and sometimes jointly with foreign capital. Despite local majority ownership, operation of the modern sector still depends on importing inputs, purchasing or leasing foreign patents and technology, and hiring foreign managers and technicians.

VARYING DEPENDENCE ON INTERNATIONAL TRADE

Contrary to a general impression, international trade as a percentage of GNP is slightly higher for rich countries than poor countries (see Table 4-2). This variation of the ratio of international trade to GNP is not caused by income but population size. Thus the United States and India have low ratios and the Netherlands and Jamaica high ratios.

Even so many developing countries are highly dependent on international trade and subject to volatile export earnings. Small countries especially depend a great deal on a few commodities or countries for export sales. For example, from 1973 to 1985, **export commodity concentration ratios,** the four leading commodities as a percentage of the *total* merchandise exports, were high for low-income sub-Saharan Africa, Central America, and a few other LDCs. Percentages included

---

[4] W. Arthur Lewis, "Economic Development with Unlimited Supplies of Labour," *Manchester School* 22 (May 1954): 139–91.

TABLE 4-3   Patterns of Trade among Economies by Types, 1981–87 (percentage of total exports)

	Exports to		
Exports from	Developed Countries	Developing Countries	Socialist Countries
Developed countries	72	26	2
Developing countries	63	31	5
Socialist countries[a]	32	17	51

[a]Developed socialist countries, 1984.

Sources: International Monetary Fund, *IMF Survey* 17, no. 15 (July 25, 1988): 251; and World Bank, *World Development Report, 1986* (New York: Oxford University Press, 1986), pp. 202–3.

Zambia 96 (with copper 90 percent); Somalia 94 (with livestock 90 percent); Ethiopia 87 (coffee, oilseeds, and hides and skin); Syria 86 (oil and cotton); Liberia 85 (iron ore, rubber, and wood); Malawi 84 (tobacco, tea, peanuts, and oilseeds); Ghana 82 (cocoa, wood, and aluminium); Panama 74; Paraguay 73; the Ivory Coast 73; Egypt 68; Nicaragua 67; Bolivia 66; Honduras 66; Sudan 65; Chile 64; El Salvador 63; Costa Rica 62; Colombia 62; Kenya 63; Bangladesh 59; Mexico 59; Sri Lanka 59; Tanzania 55; Guatemala 54; Ecuador 53; the Philippines 50; Pakistan 47; and Peru 46. But more diversified and industrially oriented South Korea had a percentage of 4, Brazil 23, Argentina 23, India 24, Malaysia 34, and Thailand 35. In 1985, six primary products accounted for more than 70 percent of sub-Saharan Africa's export earnings.[5] Oil-exporting countries, such as Saudi Arabia, Iraq, Libya, Nigeria, and Indonesia, are in a similar position; their major export is petroleum, of course.

Furthermore although 72 percent of the exports of developed countries is to other DCs and only 26 percent with LDCs; 63 percent of LDC trade is with DCs and only 31 percent with other LDCs (Table 4-3). (The residual is trade with socialist countries.) Some trade between rich and poor states—very important to developing countries—is not nearly so essential to developed countries. For example, one-third of Ghana's exports is cocoa to Britain, corresponding to only a fraction of 1 percent of its imports. And one-third of 1 percent of an English firm's sales comprise all the machinery bought by Ghana's largest shoe manufacturer.

Yet trade with other LDCs as a share of total LDC trade increased from 20 percent in 1970 to 23 percent in 1975 to 25 percent in 1980 to 32 percent in 1986, while LDC trade with other LDCs as a percentage of world exports increased from 3.5 percent in 1970 to 6.9 percent in 1986.[6]

[5] Mohammed El Samhouri, "Flexible Exchange Rates and Export Instability: The Impact of the Post-1973 International Monetary System on the Developing Countries," (Ph.D. diss., Kansas State University, 1989), calculated from United Nations, *Yearbook of International Trade Statistics* (New York: 1973–85); and E. Wayne Nafziger, *Inequality in Africa: Political Elites, Proletariat, Peasants, and the Poor* (Cambridge: Cambridge University Press, 1988), p. 55.

[6] John Sewell, Stuart K. Tucker, and contributors, *Growth, Exports, and Jobs in a Changing World Economy: Agenda, 1988,* Overseas Development Council U.S.–Third-World Policy Perspectives No. 9 (New Brunswick, N.J.: Transaction Books, 1988), p. 214.

A HIGH PROPORTION OF PRIMARY PRODUCT EXPORTS

Among LDCs **primary products** (food, raw materials, minerals, and organic oils and fats) comprise 47 percent of exports and 27 percent of imports. In developed countries, primary products are 20 percent of exports and 30 percent of imports. Developing countries supply 45 percent of the world's exports of primary products but only 17 percent of manufactured exports. Price instability is common for primary commodities, whose demand and supply tend to be inelastic (that is, the relative change in quantity is less than the relative change in price). The average deviation of world market prices of all fourteen major agricultural products from the price trend exceeded 14 percent from 1964 to 1984, while the deviation of manufactured products averaged less than 10 percent.

Yet the trend is changing. Primary product exports declined from 78 percent of total exports in 1965 to 47 percent in 1986, and the share of manufactures rose from 22 to 53 percent in the same period. And several middle-income countries have emerged as significant manufacturing exporters since 1960, especially in light manufactures, such as textiles and clothing. Four NICs—Taiwan, Hong Kong, South Korea, Singapore—comprise 44 percent of 1986 LDC manufactured exports. Adding middle-income Brazil, Yugoslavia, Poland, Portugal, Mexico, Turkey, and Thailand (which with the four are 12 percent of LDC population) accounts for 69 percent of the LDC exports of manufactures; also including highly populated, low-income China and India, which rank fourth and ninth, respectively, among LDC manufacturing exporters, brings the total to 79 percent. Exports of the thirteen countries just mentioned grew 7.9 percent yearly from 1965 to 1986; all LDC exports increased 3.6 percent annually, but low-income countries (other than China and India) only grew 0.5 percent per year.[7]

RAPID POPULATION GROWTH

About 3.9 billion people, or three-fourths of the world's 5.2 billion people in 1990, live in developing countries. Developing countries have a population density of 509 per cultivated square kilometer (53 per square kilometer) compared to 184 per cultivated square kilometer (22 per square kilometer) in the developed world. These figures contribute to a common myth that third-world people jostle each other for space. However, India, with 489 inhabitants per cultivated square kilometer, while more densely populated than Canada (56), the United States (132), and the Soviet Union (125), is less densely populated than Britain (800) and West Germany (813). Moreover China (1095) and Bangladesh (1164) are not so dense as the Netherlands (1622) and Japan (2657).[8]

The problem in LDCs is not population density but low productivity (low levels of technology and capital per worker) combined with rapid population growth. Between 1945 and 1988, death rates in developing countries were cut in half by better public health, preventive medicine, and nutrition. Additionally, improved transport and communication made food shortages less likely. While the

---

[7] World Bank, *World Development Report, 1988* (New York: Oxford University Press, 1988), pp. 242–47; and World Bank, *World Development Report, 1986* (New York: Oxford University Press, 1986), pp. 86–87.

[8] Computed from *Geographical Digest* (London: George Philip, 1986), pp. 30–31.

population growth rate in industrialized countries was 0.5 percent in 1990, LDC birth rates remained at high levels, resulting in an explosive annual growth of 2.1 percent (a rate doubling population in 33 years, estimated by dividing the percentage growth rate, 2.1, into 70). High fertility means a high percentage of the population in dependent ages, 0–14, and the diversion of resources to food, shelter, and education for a large nonworking population (see Chapter 9).

This rapid population is contributing to a LDC labor force growth estimated at 2.1 percent per year between 1985 and 2000—a much faster labor force growth than that of industrialized Europe in the nineteenth century (which grew at less than 1 percent a year). Industrial employment's demand growth lags behind this labor force growth, so that unemployment continues to rise in developing countries, especially in urban areas (Chapter 10).

LOW LITERACY AND SCHOOL ENROLLMENT RATES

When compared to developed countries, literacy and written communication are low in developing countries. Low-income countries have an adult literacy rate of 55 percent; middle-income countries, 73 percent; high-income oil exporters, 39 percent; and high-income countries, 99 percent. Among world regions, South Asia has a literacy rate of 42 percent; sub-Saharan Africa, 43 percent; China, 69 percent; the Middle East, 69 percent; Southeast Asia, 78 percent; Latin America, 85 percent; and East Asia, 90 percent (Table 2-1).

Recently a number of low-income countries made primary education free or compulsory, so that LDC primary enrollment rates (taken as a percentage of children aged 6–11) doubled from 1960 to 1980 (except in East Asia and Latin America, where 1960 rates were more than 60 percent). Enrollment was 81 percent in low-income countries, 87 percent in middle-income countries, 63 percent in sub-Saharan Africa, 79 percent in South Asia, 87 percent in developing Europe and the Middle East, 96 percent in East Asia (including China), and virtually 100 percent in Latin America and DCs. Secondary enrollment rates (children aged 12–17) were 23 percent in low-income countries, 31 percent in middle-income countries, 13 percent in sub-Saharan Africa, 30 percent in South Asia, 42 percent in East Asia, 43 percent in developing Europe and the Middle East, 44 percent in Latin America, 88 percent in DCs, and 92 percent for high-income socialist countries.[9]

It is difficult to determine if education is a cause or effect of economic development. A well-educated citizenry contributes to higher income and productivity, which in turn lead to a greater investment in primary education and adult literacy programs. In any case, literacy and enrollment rates are *not* so highly correlated to GNP per head as might be expected. First, there is little correlation at upper-income levels. Most countries have attained nearly 100 percent literacy by the time average yearly income reaches $4000 and virtually universal primary education before $4000. Second, such places as Kerala (in southwestern India), Sri Lanka, and Tanzania, which have tried to meet basic educational and other needs for even the poorest portion of the population, have higher literacy rates (79 percent, 87 percent, and 85 percent, respectively) than would be expected from a per capita

[9] Jee-Peng Tan, "Private Enrollment and Expenditure on Education: Some Macro Trends," *International Review of Education* 31 (May 1985): 103–17.

GNP of $400 a year of less. Third, literacy rates in countries like Saudi Arabia, the United Arab Emirates, Iran, Iraq, and Oman were relatively unaffected by the sudden oil-created affluence of the 1970s.[10]

Most LDCs continue to place a premium on education and employment opportunities for men. Enrollment and literacy rates for women in low-income countries tend to be two-thirds to three-fourths the rates for men.[11]

AN UNSKILLED LABOR FORCE

Production patterns and low literacy rates in LDCs correspond to a relatively unskilled labor force. In 1960, 12 percent of the labor force in low-income countries (under $700 per capita GNP) were in white-collar jobs (professional, technical administrative, executive, managerial, clerical, and sales) compared to 21 percent in middle-income countries ($700 to $1500 per capita GNP), and 31 percent in high-income countries (over $1500 per capita GNP). In developing countries, a large share of the labor force is unskilled and the population lower class (mostly peasants and manual workers); in developed countries, the reverse is true.

As economic development occurs, the structure of the work force changes. Capital and skilled labor are substituted for unskilled labor. Thus from 1960 to 1980, LDC white-collar worker shares increased by more than one-third. Moreover in the United States, the number of white-collar workers rose from 17 percent in 1900 to 45 percent in 1960, while the share of manual laborers declined sharply from 71 percent to 45 percent.[12]

Another characteristic of low-income countries is a small middle class of business people, professionals, and civil servants. As economic development takes place and the social structure becomes more fluid, the size of this middle class increases.

SUMMARY

1. Income inequality tends to increase from low- to middle-income countries and decrease from middle- to high-income countries (an inverted U-shaped curve). Poverty, on the other hand, drops as income rises.

2. The explosion of mass participation in politics relative to institutional capacity to absorb new participants may result in increased political instability.

3. Almost all LDCs experienced Western colonialism or political domination in the past 200 years.

4. Most low-income countries are predominantly peasant agricultural societies. Sixty-five to 75 percent of the labor force in these countries is in agriculture,

[10] Norman Hicks and Paul Streeten, "Indicators of Development: The Search for a Basic Needs Yardstick," *World Development* 7 (June 1979): 572–73.

[11] World Bank, *World Development Report, 1988* (New York: Oxford University Press, 1988), pp. 286–87; and World Bank, *World Tables, 1980* (Baltimore: Johns Hopkins University Press, 1980).

[12] Lyn Squire, *Employment Policy in Developing Countries: A Survey of Issues and Evidence* (New York: Oxford University Press, 1981), pp. 49–53; and Simon Kuznets, *Modern Economic Growth: Rate, Structure, and Spread* (New Haven: Yale University Press, 1966), pp. 191–92.

compared to less than 15 percent in high-income countries. Only 10–20 percent of the labor force in low-income countries is in industry compared to 35–45 percent in high-income countries. Because labor's productivity is higher in industry than in agriculture, the share of output in industry for low-income countries is higher, and the share of output in agriculture lower, than labor force shares.

5. Most low-income countries are dual economies. They have a capital-intensive enclave consisting of modern manufacturing and mining operations and plantation agriculture, and a traditional labor-intensive sector. Despite this modern sector, saving rates, capital per worker, and levels of technology are generally low in these countries.

6. The overwhelming majority of DC exports are manufacturing goods, and a disproportionate share of LDC exports are primary products. However, the share of manufactures in LDC exports has been growing steadily, especially among middle-income countries.

7. The population density of LDCs is two to three times that of DCs. Moreover population growth in LDCs is 2.1 percent per year compared to 0.5 in DCs. This rapid growth has contributed to a rapid growth in the labor force and increasing urban unemployment in LDCs.

8. Adult literacy rates are 55 percent in low-income countries and 73 percent in middle-income countries. These rates are expected to rise, particularly in low income countries, because of the expansion in primary enrollment rates.

9. As economic development takes place, the share of white-collar workers in the labor force increases and that of blue-collar workers declines.

TERMS TO REVIEW

- inverted U-shaped curve
- political elite
- extended family
- peasants

- gross domestic product
- cottage industry
- capital stock
- dual economy

- primary products
- export commodity concentration ratio

QUESTIONS TO DISCUSS

1. What are some common characteristics of LDCs? Which of these characteristics are causes and which accompaniments of underdevelopment?

2. How might today's LDCs differ from those of the 1950s?

3. How might a list of common characteristics of low-income countries vary from that of LDCs as a whole?

4. What is a dual economy? Are all LDCs characterized by economic dualism?

5. Will the skill composition of the labor force change as rapidly in LDCs as it did in the past in DCs?

GUIDE TO READINGS

Statistical sources that present data on the characteristics of LDCs include the World Bank's *World Tables* (note 11) and the annual *World Development Report* and *World Economic Survey* (guide to readings, Chapter 2). Even though parts of Chenery and Syrquin (note to Table 4-2) and Kuznets (note 1, Chapter 3) are out of date, they contain useful data on growth patterns.

The best-known model of the dual economy is that of W. Arthur Lewis (note 4), discussed in Chapter 10.

Huntington's book (note 1), although somewhat dated, is a standard work on the politics of LDCs. Critics of Huntington's approach are Donal Cruise O'Brien, "Modernization, Order, and the Erosion of a Democratic Ideal: American Political Science, 1960–1970," *Journal of Development Studies* 8 (July 1972): 353–80; and Terry Nardin, "Violence and the State: A Critique of Empirical Political Theory," Sage Professional Papers in Comparative Politics Series Number 01-020 (Beverly Hills, Calif.: Sage Publications, 1971).

Chapter Five

THEORIES OF ECONOMIC DEVELOPMENT

To many people, a **theory** is a contention that is impractical or has no factual support. Someone who says that free migration to the United States may be all right in theory, but not in practice implies that despite the merit of the idea, it would be impractical. Likewise the statement that the idea of lower wealth taxes in India stimulating economic growth is just a theory indicates an unverified hypothesis.

For the economist, however, a theory is a systematic explanation of interrelationships among economic variables, and its purpose is to explain causal relationships among these variables. Usually a theory is used not only to understand the world better, but also to provide a basis for policy. In any event, theorists cannot consider all the factors influencing economic growth in a single theory. They must determine which variables are crucial and which are irrelevant. However, reality is so complicated that a simple model may omit critical variables in the real world.[1] And although complex mathematical models can handle a large number of variables, they have not been very successful in explaining economic development, especially in the third world.

SCOPE OF THE CHAPTER

This chapter discusses a few of the major theories of economic development, reserving for subsequent chapters less comprehensive theories dealing with specific economic questions. Today scholars pay less attention to grand theories of develop-

[1] Charles P. Kindleberger and Bruce Herrick, *Economic Development* (New York: McGraw-Hill, 1977), p. 40.

76

ment than they did in the 1950s and 1960s. It is now apparent that the economic development of more than one hundred countries on six continents encompassing decades is too complex to explain with one vast theory.

The first two models of economic development discussed—that of the English classical economists, and of their foremost critic, Karl Marx—were developed more than a century ago, at the time of early capitalist development in Western Europe and the United States. Despite this focus on DC growth, the theories have some application today in LDCs.

Other theories presented in this chapter, largely formulated since World War II, concentrate on the experience of developing countries. Walter Rostow's model, written as an alternative to Marx's theory of modern history, sets forth five stages of economic growth for LDCs, based on the experience of the industrialized countries. The vicious circle theory, which focuses on the reasons for low saving rates in poor countries, was widely accepted in the early 1950s. The theoretical debate on balanced versus unbalanced growth has clarified important issues concerning the "big push" and economies of scale. Paul Baran's coalitions model draws on Marx's historical dynamics and Lenin's theory of imperialism to analyze economic backwardness in Asia, Africa, and Latin America. Finally dependency theory, which borrows from Baran's approach, argues that underdevelopment in third-world countries results from their participation in the international capitalist system.

THE CLASSICAL THEORY OF ECONOMIC STAGNATION

Model

The **classical theory,** based on the work of nineteenth-century English economist David Ricardo, *Principles of Political Economy and Taxation* (1817), was pessimistic about the possibility of sustained economic growth. For Ricardo, who assumed little continuing technical progress, growth was limited by land scarcity.

The classical economists—Adam Smith, Thomas R. Malthus, Ricardo, and John Stuart Mill—were influenced by Newtonian physics. Just as Newton posited that activities in the universe were not random but subject to some grand design, these men believed that the same natural order determined prices, rent, and economic affairs.

In the late eighteenth century, Smith argued that in a competitive economy, each individual, by acting in his or her own interest, promoted the public interest. A producer who charges more than others will not find buyers, a worker who asks more than the going wage will not find work, and an employer who pays less than competitors will not find anyone to work. It was as if an **invisible hand** were behind the self-interest of capitalists, merchants, landlords, and workers, directing their actions toward maximum economic growth.[2]

The classical model also took into account (1) the use of paper money, (2) the development of institutions to supply it in appropriate quantities, (3) capital accumulation based on output in excess of wages, (4) free foreign trade, and (5) division of labor (limited primarily by the size of the market). A major tenet of Ricardo was the **law of diminishing returns,** referring to successively lower extra outputs from

---

[2] Adam Smith, *An Inquiry into the Nature and Causes of the Wealth of Nations*, Cannan edition (New York: The Modern Library, 1937). First published 1776.

adding an equal extra input to fixed land. For him diminishing returns from population growth and a constant amount of land threatened economic growth. Since Ricardo believed technological change or improved production techniques could only temporarily check diminishing returns, increasing capital was seen as the only way of offsetting this long-run threat.

His reasoning took the following path. In the long run, the natural wage is at subsistence—the cost of perpetuating the labor force (or population, which increases at the same rate). The wage may deviate but eventually returns to a natural rate at subsistence. On the one hand, if the wage rises, food production exceeds what is essential for maintaining the population. Extra food means fewer deaths, and the population increases. More people need food and the average wage falls. Population growth continues to reduce wages until they reach the subsistence level once again. On the other hand, a wage below subsistence increases deaths and eventually contributes to a labor shortage, which raises the wage. Population decline increases wages once again to the subsistence level. In both instances, the tendency is for the wage to return to the natural subsistence rate.

With this **iron law of wages,** total wages increase in proportion to the labor force. Output increases with population, but other things being equal, output per worker declines with diminishing returns on fixed land. Thus the surplus value (output minus wages) per person declines with increased population. At the same time, land rents per acre increase with population growth, since land becomes more scarce relative to other factors.

The only way of offsetting diminishing returns is by accumulating increased capital per person. However, capitalists require minimum profits and interest payments to maintain or increase capital stock. Yet since profits and interest per person declines and rents increase with population growth, there is a diminishing **surplus** (profits, interest, and rent) available for the capitalists' accumulation. Ricardo feared that this declining surplus reduces the inducement to accumulate capital. Labor force expansion leads to a decline in capital per worker or a decrease in worker productivity and income per capita. Thus the Ricardian model indicates eventual economic stagnation or decline.

Critique

Paradoxically the stagnation theory of Ricardo was formulated amid numerous scientific discoveries and technical changes that multiplied output. Clearly he underestimated the impact of technological advance in offsetting diminishing returns. Before he wrote, the steam engine (1769), the spinning jenny (1770), the Arkwright water frame (1771), the puddling process for making wrought iron (1784), the power loom (1785), the cotton gin (1793), interchangeable parts (1798), improved soil tillage and improved breeds of livestock (around 1800), the steamboat (1807), the water mill for powering factories (1813), and the three-piece iron plow (1814) were all developed. Since Ricardo's time, rapid technological progress contributed to unprecedented economic growth.[3] Furthermore the iron law of wages did not

---

[3] Some contemporary economists, culminating with James E. Meade, *A Neoclassical Theory of Economic Growth* (New York: Oxford University Press, 1963), have added a variable reflecting technical progress while retaining most of the classical premises.

foresee the extent to which population growth could be limited, at least in the West, through voluntary birth control.

Moreover it did not occur to Ricardo that private ownership of land and capital is not an economic necessity. Land and capital would still be used even if rents and interest were not paid, as in state ownership of these means of production. Ironically Ricardian stagnation might result in a Marxian scenario, where wages and investment would be maintained only if property were confiscated by society and payments to private capitalists and landlords stopped.[4]

MARX'S HISTORICAL MATERIALISM

Karl Marx's views were shaped by radical changes in Western Europe: the French Revolution; the rise of industrial, capitalist production; political and labor revolts; and a growing secular rationalism. Marx (1818–83) opposed the prevailing philosophy and political economy, especially the views of utopian socialists and classical economists, in favor of a world view called **historical materialism.**

Theory

Marx wanted to replace the unhistorical approach of the classicists with a historical dialectic. Marxists consider classical and later orthodox economic analysis as a still photograph, which describes reality at a certain time. In contrast, the dialectical approach, analogous to a moving picture, looks at a social phenomenon by examining where it was and is going and its process of change. History moves from one stage to another, say, from feudalism to capitalism to socialism, on the basis of changes in ruling and oppressed classes and their relationship to each other. Conflict between the forces of production (the state of science and technology, the organization of production, and the development of human skills) and the existing relations of production (the appropriation and distribution of output as well as a society's way of thinking, its ideology, and world view) provide the dynamic movement in the materialist interpretation of history. The interaction between forces and relations of production shapes politics, law, morality, religion, culture, and ideas.

Accordingly feudalism is undercut by (1) the migration of serfs to the town, (2) factory competition with handicraft and manoral production, (3) expanded transport, trade, discovery, and new international markets on behalf of the new business class, and (4) the accompanying rise of nation-states. The new class, the proletariat or working class, created by this next stage, capitalism, is the seed for the destruction of capitalism and the transformation into the next stage, socialism. Capitalism faces repeated crises because the market, dependent largely on worker consumption, expands more slowly than productive capacity. Moreover this unutilized capacity creates, in Marx's phrase, a **reserve army of the unemployed,** a cheap labor source that expands and contracts with the boom and bust of business cycles. Furthermore with the growth of monopoly, many small business people, artisans, and farmers become propertyless workers who no longer have control over their workplaces. Eventually the proletariat revolts, takes control of capital, and estab-

---

[4] Stephen Enke has a detailed discussion of the classical model in *Economics for Development* (Englewood Cliffs, N.J.: Prentice-Hall, 1963), pp.70–90.

lishes socialism. In time socialism is succeeded by communism, and the state withers away.

Marx's ideas were popularized by his collaborator, Friedrich Engels, especially from 1883 to 1895, when he finished Marx's uncompleted manuscripts, interpreted Marxism, and provided its intellectual and organizational leadership.

Critique

Marx's main analysis was of capitalism, but his discussions of socialism and communism were not well developed. Even his analysis of capitalism, and the transition to socialism, had a number of flaws. He had theorized worker revolt in the industrialized West, but the revolution occurred first in Russia, one of the least developed capitalistic countries in Europe.

Marxists suggest several reasons why Western workers have yet to overthrow capitalism. Having realized the dangers of a rebellious working class at home, the capitalists have developed a tactic of divide and rule that depends on exploitation of workers outside the West. Furthermore the news media, educational institutions, and churches create a false consciousness supporting ruling-class ideologies. And the capitalist state has powerful legal, police, military, and administrative machinery to quell potential resistance.

Marx also overlooked the possibility that the interests of workers and capitalists might not conflict. Thus workers in the West may have supported capitalism because they gained more in the long run by receiving a relatively constant share of a rapidly growing output than by trying to acquire a larger share of what might have been a more slowly growing output under an alternative system.

Regardless of how we view Marxism, it remains a rallying point for discontented people. The irony is that nationalist groups that overthrow their rulers in the name of Marxism are frequently threatened by class antagonisms from those they rule. Almost no other socialist government is willing to go as far as the late Chairman Mao Zedong of China, who recognized the existence of classes under socialism, and called for a continuing revolution to oppose the encrusted, socialist, upper classes. Other theorists have revised or added to Marxism, including Paul Baran and the dependency theorists. We consider these views in succeeding sections of this chapter.

ROSTOW'S STAGES OF ECONOMIC GROWTH

People existed for centuries with little change in their economic life. When major changes occurred, as in the last five hundred years or so, they often took place abruptly. In *The Stages of Economic Growth* (1961), Walter W. Rostow, an eminent economic historian, sets forth a new historical synthesis about the beginnings of modern economic growth on six continents.

Five Stages

Rostow's economic stages are (1) the traditional society, (2) the preconditions for takeoff, (3) the takeoff, (4) the drive to maturity, and (5) the age of high mass consumption.

Rostow has little to say about the concept of traditional society except to indicate that it is based on attitudes and technology prominent before the turn of the eighteenth century. The work of Isaac Newton ushered in change. He formulated the law of gravity and the elements of differential calculus. After Newton, people widely believed "that the external world was subject to a few knowable laws, and was systematically capable of productive manipulation."[5]

Preconditions Stage

Rostow's **precondition stage** for sustained industrialization includes radical changes in three nonindustrial sectors: (1) increased transport investment to enlarge the market and production specialization; (2) a revolution in agriculture, so that a growing urban population can be fed; and (3) an expansion of imports, including capital, financed perhaps by exporting some natural resources. These changes, including increased capital formation, require a political elite interested in economic development. This interest may be instigated by a nationalist reaction against foreign domination or the desire to have a higher standard of living.

Takeoff

Rostow's central historical stage is the **takeoff,** a decisive expansion occurring over 20 to 30 years, which radically transforms a country's economy and society. During this stage, barriers to steady growth are finally overcome, while forces making for widespread economic progress dominate the society, so that growth becomes the normal condition. The takeoff period is a dramatic moment in history, corresponding to the beginning of the industrial revolution in late eighteenth-century Britain; pre–Civil War railroad and manufacturing development in the United States; the period after the 1848 revolution in Germany; the years just after the 1868 Meiji restoration in Japan; the rapid growth of the railroad, coal, iron, and heavy-engineering industries in the quarter-century before the 1917 Russian Revolution; and a period starting within a decade of India's independence (1947) and the Communist victory in China (1949).

Rostow indicates that three conditions must be satisfied for takeoff.

1. Net investment as a percentage of net national product (NNP) increases sharply—from 5 percent or less to over 10 percent. If an investment of 3.5 percent of NNP leads to a growth of 1 percent per year, then 10.5 percent of NNP is needed for a 3-percent growth (or a 2-percent per capita increase if population grows at 1 percent).

2. At least one substantial manufacturing sector grows rapidly. The growth of a leading manufacturing sector spreads to its input suppliers expanding to meet its increased demand and to its buyers benefiting from its larger output. In the last three decades of the 1700s, for example, the cotton textile industry in Britain expanded rapidly because of the use of the spinning jenny, water frame, and mule in textiles and the increased demand for cotton clothing. The development of textile manufactures, and their exports, had wide direct and

[5] Walter W. Rostow, *The Stages of Economic Growth: A Non-Communist Manifesto* (Cambridge: Cambridge University Press, 1961), p. 4.

indirect effects on the demand for coal, iron, machinery, and transport. In the United States, France, Germany, Canada, and Russia, the growth of the railroad, by widening markets, was a powerful stimulus in the coal, iron, and engineering industries, which in turn fueled the takeoff.

3. A political, social, and institutional framework quickly emerges to exploit expansion in the modern sectors. This condition implies mobilizing capital through retained earnings from rapidly expanding sectors; an improved system to tax high-income groups, especially in agriculture; developing banks and capital markets; and in most instances, foreign investment. Furthermore where state initiative is lacking, the culture must support a new class of entrepreneurs prepared to take the risk of innovating.

Drive to Maturity

After takeoff there follows the drive to maturity, a period of growth that is regular, expected, and self-sustained. This stage is characterized by a labor force that is predominantly urban, increasingly skilled, less individualistic, and more bureaucratic and looks increasingly to the state to provide economic security.

Age of High Mass Consumption

The symbols of this last stage, reached in the United States in the 1920s and in Western Europe in the 1950s, are the automobile, suburbanization, and innumerable durable consumer goods and gadgets. In Rostow's view, other societies may choose a welfare state or international military and political power.

Critique

Rostow's theory was the vogue among many U.S. government officials in the 1960s, especially in the international aid agencies, since it promised hope for sustained growth in LDCs after substantial initial infusions of foreign assistance. But among scholars, Rostow's work met with, at best, mixed reviews. Rostow is accused of overambition. Ian Drummond complains that "probably no theory has been so widely circulated from so slight a base of organized fact and careful analysis."[6]

Another economic historian, A. K. Cairncross, argues that one can believe in an abrupt takeoff, or industrial revolution, only if one's knowledge of history is flimsy and out of date. Cairncross argues that many of Rostow's conditions are defined so vaguely that they stretch to cover any case and he seems only too willing to admit exceptions when takeoff occurs at a time other than his theory suggests.[7]

Indeed, Rostow's stages, imprecisely defined, are difficult to test scientifically. For a theory to be meaningful, it must be possible to prove it wrong. If the stages are to explain how economic development is caused, the relationships cannot

[6] Ian Drummond, review of *The Stages of Economic Growth,* in *Canadian Journal of Economics and Political Science* 13 (February 1961): 112–13.

[7] A. K. Cairncross, "Essays in Bibliography and Criticism, XLV: The Stages of Economic Growth," *Economic History Review* 14 (April 1961): 454.

be circular. The stages must be defined in terms other than economic development, the variable the theory is trying to explain. For example, the concepts of *traditional society* and *high mass consumption society* define rather than explain reasons for the level of economic development. Furthermore past economies—primitive, ancient, medieval, and those of the presently developed countries of a century or two ago— are all grouped with presently underdeveloped countries in a single category, the traditional society.

The designation of traditional societies as pre-Newtonian neglects the dualism of many present-day LDCs. Much of the large manufacturing, plantation, and mining sectors of India, Indonesia, Nigeria, and Pakistan use modern methods and techniques and cannot be considered traditional in Rostow's sense.

Much of Rostow's thesis about conditions for takeoff is contradicted by empirical data. Increases in investment rates and growth do not occur in the 20–30 year span Rostow designates for takeoff. Growth in investment rates and net national product in Great Britain, Germany, Sweden, and Japan indicate a slow and relatively steady acceleration rather than an abrupt takeoff.

Frequently the characteristics of one of Rostow's stages are not unique to it. Why would the agricultural revolution, capital imports, and social overhead investment of the preconditions stage not be consistent with the abrupt increase in investment rates during the takeoff stage? Why could the development of leading sectors or the emergence of an institutional framework exploiting growth not take place in the preconditions stage as well as the takeoff stage? Why would the abrupt increase in growth and investment rates during takeoff not continue through the drive to maturity?

Unlike Marx's dialectical materialism, Rostow's approach does not show how the characteristics and processes of one stage move a society to the next stage. How do we explain the relatively effortless self-sustained growth after takeoff? Presumably some obstacles to growth have been removed. What are they, and how does his theory explain their removal?

Rostow's premise that economic modernization implies a change from an underdeveloped economy to one similar to those in North America and Western Europe today poses another problem. Rostow compares LDCs at independence to the formation of nation–states in the West. He assumes that the development of underdeveloped countries will parallel earlier stages of today's advanced countries, but he neglects the relationship of contemporary underdeveloped countries with developed countries as well as each LDC's highly individual history.

Rostow is ethnocentric when he chooses high mass consumption society, characterized by automobiles, suburbanization, and consumer gadgets, as the culminating stage of economic growth. For him today's modernized societies, the archetype of which is the United States, are an image of the future of traditional societies. Surely the study of comparative history should alert us to the danger of using the experience of the United States (or any other country) as a model for countries with very different cultural and political backgrounds to emulate.

VICIOUS CIRCLE THEORY

The **vicious circle** theory indicates that poverty perpetuates itself in mutually reinforcing vicious circles on both the supply and demand sides.

Supply Side

Because incomes are low, consumption cannot be diverted to saving for capital formation. Lack of capital results in low productivity per person, which perpetuates low levels of income. Thus the circle is complete. A country *is* poor because it *was previously* too poor to save and invest.

Demand Side

Furthermore because incomes are low, market size (for consumer goods, such as shoes, electric bulbs, and textiles) is too small to encourage potential investors. Lack of investment means low productivity and continued low income. A country *is* poor because it *was previously* too poor to provide the market to spur investment.

Insufficient Saving: A Critique

The vicious circle theory seems plausible to those Westerners who imagine that the *entire* population of the third world is poor and hungry. They are surprised that anyone in the LDCs saves. But you can probably identify some flaws in these views. Westerners may be judging the saving potential in LDCs on the basis of Western standards of living. Of course most of us find it difficult to imagine saving on the $7000 annual salary received by a middle manager in India. But remember the relative position that $7000 represents in India. There is reason for believing that low-income countries can save substantially more than they do. The highest income groups in low-income LDCs live far above subsistence levels. A study by World Bank economist Shail Jain indicates that their richest 5 percent receives about 15–35 percent of the income, an amount per head eight to twenty times that of the poorest 10 percent of the people.[8] Since evidence indicates that consumption levels are determined less by absolute levels of income than by relative income (income in comparison to neighbors and members of the community), the higher income classes in LDCs could save considerably if they were sufficiently motivated. One reason they may not do so is because of the **demonstration effect** of consumption levels in the West and of elites in the LDCs. That is, people may spend beyond their income in order to keep up with the Joneses, the Sridhars, or the Abdullahis.

You should also keep in mind that personal saving is usually a small proportion of total saving in a LDC. Corporate saving, government saving, public enterprise profits, social security contributions, life insurance premiums, and provident and pension fund reserves may be other sources for saving (see Chapter 14).

If we look at saving from this broader viewpoint, there are additional arguments to suggest that poor countries have a substantial capacity to save. Throughout history few societies have been too poor to wage war. Yet any war requires a share of the country's resources that would be sufficient for a significant rate of capital formation. The Overseas Development Council indicates that more than 3 percent of the GNP of nineteen low-income countries goes for military expenditures.[9] Per-

---

[8] Shail Jain, *Size Distribution of Income* (Washington, D.C.: World Bank, 1975).

[9] Roger D. Hansen and contributors to the Overseas Development Council, *U.S. Foreign Policy and the Third World: Agenda, 1982* (New York: Praeger, 1982), pp. 218–19. The *IDS Bulletin*, 16 (October 1985), has an entire issue devoted to disarmament and development.

haps if countries mobilized for economic development as they did for war, they could increase saving.

Furthermore some poor societies have been able to build magnificent monuments. As A. K. Cairncross argues, "Anyone who looks at the pyramids, cathedrals, and pagodas that civilizations have bequeathed, can hardly regard the construction of railways, dams, and power stations as imposing an unprecedented burden on a poor community."[10]

Small Markets: A Critique

Everett E. Hagen contends that the market is ample for using modern production methods effectively for products commonly consumed by low-income people— sugar, milled rice, milled flour, soap, sandals, textiles, clothing, cigarettes, matches, and candies. He argues that even a fairly small improvement in productivity for any of these commodities would capture a sizable market.[11]

Moreover large establishments require not only large markets but, more importantly, complex machinery and processes, which demand entrepreneurial, managerial, and technical skills and experience that are frequently scarce in developing countries. Hla Myint argues that cost advantages from early entry, or "economies of experience," are more important for large-scale production than economies of scale from increased market size.[12]

BALANCED VERSUS UNBALANCED GROWTH

A major development debate from the 1940s through the 1960s concerned **balanced growth** versus **unbalanced growth.** Some of the debate was semantic, since the meaning of *balance* can vary from the absurd requirement that all sectors grow at the same rate to the more sensible plea that some attention be given to all major sectors—industry, agriculture, and services. However, absurdities aside, the discussion raised some important issues. What are the relative merits of strategies of gradualism versus a big push? Is capital or entrepreneurship the major limitation to growth?

Balanced Growth

The synchronized application of capital to a wide range of different industries is called balanced growth by its advocates. Ragnar Nurkse considers this strategy the only way of escaping from the vicious circle of poverty. He does not consider the expansion of exports promising, since the **price elasticity of demand** (minus percentage change in quantity demanded divided by percentage change in price) for the

---

[10] A. K. Cairncross, "Capital Formation in the Take-off," in Walter W. Rostow, ed., *The Economics of Take-off into Sustained Growth* (London: Macmillan, 1963).

[11] Everett E. Hagen, *On the Theory of Social Change: How Economic Growth Begins* (Homewood, Ill.: Dorsey Press, 1962), pp. 42-43.

[12] Hla Myint, "An Interpretation of Economic Backwardness," *Oxford Economic Papers, New Series* 6 (June 1954): 132–63.

LDCs' predominantly primary exports is less than one, thus reducing export earnings with increased volume, other things being equal.[13]

Big Push Thesis

Those advocating this synchronized application of capital to all major sectors support the **big push thesis,** arguing that a strategy of gradualism is doomed to failure. A substantial effort is essential to overcome the inertia inherent in a stagnant economy. The situation is analogous to a car being stuck in the snow: It will not move with a gradually increasing weight; it needs a big push.

For Paul N. Rosenstein-Rodan, the factors that contribute to economic growth, like demand and investment in infrastructure, do not increase smoothly but are subject to sizable jumps or **indivisibilities.**[14] These indivisibilities result from flaws created in the investment market by **external economies,** that is, cost advantages rendered free by one producer to another. These benefits spill over to society as a whole, or to some member of it, rather than to the investor concerned. As an example, the increased production, decreased average costs, and labor training and experience that result from additional investment in the steel industry will benefit other industries as well. Greater output stimulates the demand for iron, coal, and transport. Lower costs may make vehicles and aluminum cheaper. In addition other industries may benefit later by hiring laborers who acquired industrial skills in the steel mills. Thus the social profitability of this investment exceeds its private profitability.

Indivisibility in Infrastructure.   For Rosenstein–Rodan a major indivisibility is in infrastructure, such as power, transport, and communications. This basic social capital reduces costs to other industries. To illustrate, the railroad from Kanpur to the Calcutta docks increases the competitiveness of India's wool textiles domestically and abroad. However, the investment for the 950–kilometer, Kanpur-Calcutta rail line is virtually indivisible in that a line a fraction as long is of little value. Building the Aswan Dam or the Monterrey-Mexico City telegraph line is subject to similar discontinuities.

Indivisibility in Demand.   This indivisibility arises from the interdependence of investment decisions; that is, a prospective investor is uncertain whether the output from his or her investment project will find a market. Rosenstein-Rodan uses the example of an economy closed to international trade to illustrate this indivisibility. He assumes that there are numerous subsistence agricultural laborers whose work adds nothing to total output (that is, the marginal productivity of their labor equals zero). If one hundred of these farm workers were hired in a shoe factory, their wages would increase income.

If the newly employed workers spend all of their additional income on shoes they produce the shoe factory will find a market and would succeed. In fact, however,

[13] Ragnar Nurkse, *Problems of Capital Formation in Underdeveloped Countries* (New York: Oxford University Press, 1953).

[14] Paul N. Rosenstein–Rodan, "Problems of Industrialization of Eastern and Southeastern Europe," *Economic Journal* 53 (June–September 1943): 202–11.

they will not spend all of their additional income on shoes. There is no "easy" solution of creating an additional market in this way. The risk of not finding a market reduces the incentive to invest, and the shoe factory investment project will probably be abandoned.[15]

However instead let us put 10,000 workers in one hundred factories (and farms) that among them will produce the bulk of consumer goods on which the newly employed workers will spend their wages. What was not true of the shoe factory is true for the complementary system of one hundred enterprises. The new producers are each others' customers and create additional markets through increased incomes. Complementary demand reduces the risk of not finding a market. Reducing interdependent risks increases the incentive to invest.

Critique of Balanced Growth

Advocates of balanced growth emphasize a varied package of industrial investment at the expense of investment in agriculture, especially exports. But Chapter 18 shows that a country cannot grow rapidly if it fails to specialize where production is most efficient. Recent experience indicates that LDCs cannot neglect agricultural investment if they are to feed their population, supply industrial inputs, and earn foreign currency. Chapter 15 points out that the recent demand for primary product exports increased so that their value grew as fast as GNP.

Furthermore infrastructure is not so indivisible as Rosenstein-Rodan implies. Roads, rivers, canals, or air traffic can substitute for railroads. Roads may be dirt, graveled, blacktopped, or paved and of various widths. Power plants can differ greatly in size, and telegram and telephone systems can be small, large, or intermediate. Large infrastructure facilities, though perhaps economical at high levels of economic development, are not essential for LDC growth.[16]

Some critics argue that the resources required for carrying out a policy of balanced growth are so vast that a country that could invest the required capital would not, in fact, be underdeveloped. In fact farm workers with zero marginal labor productivity are not available (Chapter 10). In any case, where will a LDC obtain the capital, skilled labor, and materials needed for such wide industrial expansion? We cannot forget that although new industries may be complementary on the demand side, they are competitors for limited resources on the supply side.

Advocates of balanced growth assume LDCs start from scratch. In reality every developing country starts from a position that reflects previous investment decisions. Thus at any time, there are highly desirable investment programs not balanced in themselves but well integrated with existing capital imbalances.[17]

---

[15] Paul N. Rosenstein–Rodan, "Notes on the Theory of the Big Push," in Howard S. Ellis, ed., *Economic Development for Latin America* (London: Macmillan, 1951), p. 62.

[16] Everett E. Hagen, *The Economics of Development* (Homewood, Ill.: Irwin, 1980), pp. 89–90.

[17] Hans Singer, "The Concept of Balanced Growth and Economic Development Theory and Facts," University of Texas Conference on Economic Development, April 1958, as cited in Benjamin Higgins, *Economic Development: Problems, Principles, and Policies* (New York: Norton, 1968), pp. 333–35; and Marcus Fleming, "External Economies and the Doctrine of Balanced Growth," *Economic Journal* 65 (June 1955): 241–56.

But perhaps the major discreditor of the balanced growth strategy was the widespread evidence in the 1960s and 1970s that LDCs were growing rapidly—without any attempt at the massive investments in the wide range of industries that advocates of the strategy considered essential.

Hirschman's Strategy of Unbalance

Albert O. Hirschman develops the idea of unbalanced investment to complement existing imbalances.[18] He contends that deliberately unbalancing the economy, in line with a predesigned strategy, is the best path for economic growth. He argues that the big push thesis may make interesting reading for economists, but it is gloomy news for the LDCs: They do not have the skills needed to launch such a massive effort. The major shortage in LDCs is not the supply of savings, but the ability to invest by entrepreneurs, the risktakers and decision makers. This ability is dependent on the amount and nature of existing investments. Hirschman believes poor countries need a development strategy that spurs investment decisions.

He suggests that since resources and abilities are limited, a big push is sensible only in strategically selected industries within the economy. Growth then spreads from one sector to another (similar to Rostow's concept of leading and following sectors).

However, investment should not be left solely to individual entrepreneurs in the market, since the profitability of different investment projects may depend on the order in which they are undertaken. For example, assume investment in a truck factory yields a return of 10 percent per year; in a steel factory, 8 percent, with the interest rate 9 percent. If left to the market, a private investor will invest in the truck factory. Later on as a result of this initial investment, returns on a steel investment increase to 10 percent, so then the investor invests in steel.

Assume, however, that establishing a steel factory would increase the returns in the truck factory in the next period from 10 to 16 percent. Society would be better off investing in the steel factory first, and the truck enterprise second, rather than making independent decisions based on the market. Planners need to consider the interdependence of one investment project with another so that they maximize overall *social* profitability. They need to make the investment that spurs the greatest amount of new investment decisions. Investments should occur in industries that have the greatest linkages, including **backward linkages** to enterprises that sell inputs to the industry, and **forward linkages** to units that buy output from the industry. The steel industry, having backward linkages to coal and iron production, and forward linkages to the construction and truck industries, has good investment potential, according to Hirschman.

Even a government that limits its major role to providing infrastructure can time its investment projects to spur private investments. Government investment in transport and power will increase productivity and thus encourage investment in other activities.

Initially planners trying to maximize linkages will not want to hamper imports too much, since doing so will deprive the country of forward linkages to domestic industries using imports. In fact officials may encourage imports until they reach a

[18] Albert O. Hirschman, *The Strategy of Economic Development* (New Haven: Yale University Press, 1958).

threshold in order to create these forward linkages. Once these linkages have been developed, protective tariffs will provide a strong inducement for domestic entrepreneurs to replace imports with domestically produced goods.

Critique of Unbalanced Growth

Hirschman fails to stress the importance of agricultural investments. According to him, agriculture does not stimulate linkage formation so directly as other industries. However despite its relatively weak linkages to other sectors, agricultural growth makes vital contributions to the nonagricultural sector through increased food supplies, added foreign exchange, labor supply, capital transfer, and larger markets.[19]

What constitutes the proper investment balance among sectors requires careful analysis. In some instances, imbalances may be essential for compensating for existing imbalances. On the other hand, Hirschman's unbalanced growth should have some kind of balance as an ultimate aim. Generally the concepts of *balance* and *imbalance* are of limited value. To be helpful, their meanings need to be defined carefully in specific decision-making contexts.

BARAN'S NEO-MARXIST THESIS

Africa, Asia, and Latin America were not of major interest to Marx. He regarded production in these regions as feudal and backward compared to the more progressive modes of capitalism. Thus he saw the introduction of European capitalism in these regions as beneficial. But in the twentieth century, Marxian analysis came to encompass an international class struggle, including the conflict between rich and poor countries. Vladimir Il'ich Lenin, who not only furnished intellectual and organizational leadership for the revolutionary takeover of power by the Communist party in Russia in October 1917 but was also chairman of the party from then until his death in 1924, provided much of this new Marxian revision. He argued that it was essential to recognize the difference between the monopoly capitalism of his period and the competitive capitalism of Marx's day. According to Lenin, a logical outgrowth of the monopoly stage of industrial and financial capitalism is the imperialist domination of poor countries by rich countries.

Thesis

The late U.S. Marxist, Paul A. Baran, incorporated Lenin's concepts of imperialism and international class conflict into his theory of economic growth and stagnation. For Baran capitalist revolution, homegrown variety, in LDCs was unlikely because of Western economic and political domination, especially in the colonial period. Capitalism arose not through the growth of small competitive firms at home, but through the transfer from abroad of advanced monopolistic business. Baran felt that as capitalism took hold, the bourgeoisie (business and middle classes) in LDCs, lacking the strength to spearhead thorough institutional change for major capital accumulation, would have to seek allies among other classes.

---

[19] Bruce F. Johnston and John W. Mellor, "The Role of Agriculture in Economic Development," *American Economic Review* 51 (September 1961): 571–81.

Thus in certain instances, the bourgeoisie would ally itself with the more moderate leaders of the workers and peasants to form a progressive coalition with a New Deal orientation (such as the Congress party governments under Prime Minister Jawaharlal Nehru, 1947–64, in India). At the outset, such a popular movement would be essentially democratic, antifeudal, and anti-imperialist and in support of domestic capitalism. However, the indigenous capitalist middle classes would ultimately be either unwilling or unable to provide the leadership for a sustained economic development that would also greatly reduce poverty and liberate the masses. In time the bourgeoisie, frightened by the threat of labor radicalism and populist upheaval and the possible expropriation of their property, would be forced into an alliance with the landed interests and the foreign bourgeoisie in their midst, whose governments could provide economic and military assistance to stave off impending disaster.

The differences within this counterrevolutionary coalition would not interfere with the overriding common interest in preventing socialism. Even so the coalition would be unable to raise the rate of capital accumulation significantly. A progressive income tax system to eliminate nonessential consumption; channeling savings from the landed aristocracy into productive investment; and undertaking substantial public investment in sectors where private capital does not venture, where monopolistic controls block expansion, or where infrastructure is required would be beyond the coalition's ability or desire. Thus this conservative alliance thrusts the popular forces even further along the road of radicalism and revolt, leading to further polarization. Finally Baran theorizes that the only way out of the impasse may be worker and peasant revolution, expropriating land and capital, and establishing a new regime based on the "ethos of collective effort," and "the creed of the predominance of the interests of society over the interests of a selected few."[20]

Critique

Although Baran's approach explains the difficulties that some reformed capitalist LDCs face in spurring economic development, the theory fails to examine a number of economic and political conflicts of interest. Although there are certainly many local agents, managers, merchants, industrialists, bureaucrats, and politicians who benefit considerably from foreign-controlled capital and technology, there are also some local capitalists whose interests compete with foreign business. These capitalists and their allies frequently lead movements for independence. (For example, the Ivory Coast cocoa farmers who opposed the formation of French cocoa plantations were major supporters of the nationalist Democratic party in the 1950s.) After independence these nationalist elements may become even stronger as colonial economic ties are gradually weakened. Economic policy under a coalition of domestic capitalists, politicians, and bureaucrats may erode the power of foreign capital. The allies and competitors of foreign business people are often locked in economic and political conflict.

Baran also ignores the probability that power is more frequently transferred

[20] Paul A. Baran, *The Political Economy of Growth* (New York: Monthly Review Press, 1957). His views are more succinctly presented in "On the Political Economy of Backwardness," *Manchester School* 20 (January 1952): 66–84, reprinted in A. N. Agarwala and S. P. Singh, *The Economics of Underdevelopment* (London: Oxford University Press, 1958), pp. 75–92.

from one elite to another when revolution occurs, rather than from the advantaged classes to the politically dispossessed masses: Very few of the Soviet and Chinese revolutionary leaders were workers or poor peasants.

For Baran the society closest to "a new social ethos [that] will become the spirit and guide of a new age"[21] is the Soviet Union after 1917. He argues that despite the political violence used by Stalin in the 1930s, and the loss of several million lives during this period, the collectivization of agriculture in the Soviet Union was the only possible approach to economic growth, given an irrational and illiterate peasantry. However, he ignores the substantial growth in both agriculture and industry from 1921 to 1928 under the Soviet New Economic Policy of market socialism. This policy consisted of widespread reliance on market prices, limited private ownership (especially in agriculture), and state ownership of most of the largest industrial enterprises. After Stalin began collectivization, agricultural production declined, the peasant's standard of living dropped significantly, and even the savings agriculture contributed to the industrial sector probably did not increase. There were widespread violence, famine, forced labor, and purges during collectivization. Although the performance of Soviet agriculture since then has improved, the relatively slow growth in agricultural productivity has frustrated Soviet leadership in its attempt to increase average consumption levels to those expected in a high-income economy.

Baran does not ask whether a more gradual, less-centralized approach to agricultural production would have resulted in more rapid development. But perhaps such a question cannot be resolved. Some historians argue that raising living levels, increasing life expectancy, and improving literacy during economic growth have inevitable human costs. The economic transition may be marked by squalor, poverty, unhealthy environment, high infant mortality rate, and a high premature death rate among the working poor, as occurred during Europe's Industrial Revolution, or by the disruption, famine, and death among peasants in the USSR in the 1930s. But in any case, the human costs cannot be avoided.

Several Marxian economists have argued that the Russian Revolution of 1917 did not erase divergent class interests. One French economist argues that the USSR abandoned the socialist road, creating a new ruling class—made up of the Communist party, the *Praesidium,* and the bureaucracy—whose economic interests are antagonistic to those of Soviet workers.[22]

DEPENDENCY THEORY

Celso Furtado, a Brazilian economist with the UN Economic Committee for Latin America, was an early contributor to the Spanish and Portuguese literature in **dependency theory** in the 1950s and 1960s. According to him, since the eighteenth century, global changes in demand resulted in a new international division of labor in which the peripheral countries of Asia, Africa, and Latin America specialized in primary products in an enclave controlled by foreigners while importing consumer goods that were the fruits of technical products in the central countries of the West.

---

[21] Paul A. Baran, "On the Political Economy of Backwardness," *Manchester School* 20 (January 1952): 84.

[22] Charles Bettelheim, *Class Struggles in the USSR,* I (New York: Monthly Review Press, 1978).

The increased productivity and new consumption patterns in peripheral countries benefited a small ruling class and its allies (less than a tenth of the population), who cooperated with the DCs to achieve modernization (economic development among a modernizing minority). The result is "peripheral capitalism, a capitalism unable to generate innovations and dependent for transformation upon decisions from the outside."[23]

A major dependency theorist, Andre Gunder Frank, is a U.S. expatriate recently affiliated with England's University of East Anglia. Frank, writing in the mid-1960s, criticized the view of many development scholars that contemporary underdeveloped countries resemble the earlier stages of now-developed countries. Many of these scholars viewed modernization in LDCs as simply the adoption of economic and political systems developed in Western Europe and North America.

For Frank the presently developed countries were never *under*developed, though they may have been *un*developed. His basic thesis is that underdevelopment does *not* mean traditional (that is, nonmodern) economic, political, and social institutions but LDC subjection to the colonial rule and imperial domination of foreign powers. In essence Frank sees underdevelopment as the effect of the penetration of modern capitalism into the archaic economic structures of the third world. He sees the deindustrialization of India under British colonialism, the disruption of African society by the slave trade and subsequent colonialism, and the total destruction of Incan and Aztec civilizations by the Spanish conquistadores as examples of the *creation* of underdevelopment.[24]

More plainly stated, the economic development of the rich countries contributes to the underdevelopment of the poor. Development in an LDC is not self-generating nor autonomous but ancillary. The LDCs are economic satellites of the highly developed regions of Northern America and Western Europe in the international capitalist system. The Afro-Asian and Latin American countries most *weakly* integrated into this system tend to be the most highly developed. Japanese economic development after the 1860s is the classic case illustrating Frank's theory. Japan's industrial growth remains unmatched: Japan was never a capitalist satellite.

Brazil best illustrates the connection between the satellite relationship and underdevelopment. Since the nineteenth century, the growth of major cities, São Paulo and Rio de Janeiro, has been satellite development—largely dependent on outside capitalist powers, especially Britain and the United States. As a result, regions in interior Brazil have become satellites of these two cities and through them, of these Western capitalist countries.

Frank suggests that satellite countries experience their *greatest* economic development when they are *least* dependent on the world capitalist system. Thus Argentina, Brazil, Mexico, and Chile grew most rapidly during World War I, the

---

[23] Celso Furtado, *Economic Development of Latin America: A Survey from Colonial Times to the Cuban Revolution* (Cambridge: Cambridge University Press, 1970), and *The Economic Growth of Brazil: A Survey from Colonial to Modern Times,* trans. by Ricardo W. de Aguiar and Eric Charles Drysdale (Berkeley and Los Angeles: University of California Press, 1968). The quote is from a short synopsis in Celso Furtado, "The Concept of External Dependence in the Study of Underdevelopment," in Charles K. Wilber, ed., *The Political Economy of Development and Underdevelopment* (New York: Random House, 1973), pp. 118–23.

[24] Andre Gunder Frank, *Latin America: Underdevelopment or Revolution?* (New York: Monthly Review Press, 1969), a collection of essays, most of which were first published in the mid-1960s.

Great Depression, and World War II, when trade and financial ties with major capitalist countries were weakest. Significantly the most underdeveloped regions today are those that have had the closest ties to Western capitalism in the past. They were the greatest exporters of primary products to, and the biggest sources of capital for, developed countries and were abandoned by them when for one reason or another business fell off. Frank points to India's Bengal; the one-time sugar-exporting West Indies and Northeastern Brazil; the defunct mining districts of Minas Gerais in Brazil, highland Peru, and Bolivia; and the former silver regions of Mexico as examples. He contends that even the *latifundium,* the large plantation or hacienda that has contributed so much to underdevelopment in Latin America, originated as a commercial, capitalist enterprise, not a feudal institution, which contradicts the generally held thesis that a region is underdeveloped because it is isolated and precapitalist.

It is an error, Frank feels, to argue that the development of the underdeveloped countries will be stimulated by indiscriminately transferring capital, institutions, and values from developed countries. He suggests that, in fact, the following economic activities have contributed to underdevelopment, not development:

1. Replacing indigenous enterprises with technologically more advanced, global, subsidiary companies.
2. Forming an unskilled labor force to work in factories and mines and on plantations.
3. Recruiting highly educated youths for junior posts in the colonial administrative service.
4. Workers migrating from villages to foreign-dominated urban complexes.
5. Opening the economy to trade with, and investment from, developed countries.

According to Frank, a third-world country can develop only by withdrawing from the world capitalist system. Perforce such a withdrawal means a large reduction in trade, aid, investment, and technology from the developed capitalist countries.

Critique

Many economic historians would agree with Frank that colonies paid dearly for economic dependency under foreign rule. They grant that development was not self-directed. Production was directed toward external rather than domestic needs, economic policies inhibited local industrial activity and led to uneven ethnic and regional economic progress; an elite oriented to foreign interests arose. However these costs were offset, at least in part, by the development of schools, roads, railroads, and administrative service under the colonial powers.

Moreover it is unfair to compare the experience of these countries under colonialism to what *might* have happened without foreign domination. The internal economic and political weaknesses of Afro-Asian and Latin American countries during the last part of the nineteenth and early part of the twentieth centuries probably made it inevitable that most of them would be economically dependent on some foreign power. The acute underdevelopment of Afghanistan, Thailand, and Ethiopia, which were not colonized, though they were influenced by the West, suggests that colonialism by itself may not have had so negative an impact as Frank indicates. Furthermore cutting economic ties with developed capitalist countries, as Frank recommends, is more likely to inhibit than expedite LDC development. To be sure, the People's Republic of China (through 1976) and the Soviet Union (since the 1930s) were not much hurt by a policy of economic self-sufficiency because they had large resource bases. However Frank's recommendation is often costly for small countries. Ghana's President Kwame Nkrumah lost a 1957 wager to President Felix Houphouet-Bogney of the neighboring Ivory Coast, similar in resource endowment to Ghana, that history would judge Ghana, which cut economic ties with capitalist countries, more successful economically than the Ivory Coast, dependent on the French for the majority of industrial investment (through the early 1970s) and for international trade. The Ivory Coast outperformed Ghana in annual growth: from 1950 to 1960, 1.5 percent to −0.3 percent; from 1960 to 1970, 4.2 percent to −0.3 percent; and from 1970 to 1980, 1.4 percent to −3.2 percent.[25] Moreover Cuba also stagnated during a period of drastically reduced economic ties to foreign capital. On the other hand, Taiwan and South Korea both experienced real growth of over 6 percent per year and decreased income inequality during the 1960s, 1970s, and 1980s (except for Korea's growing inequality after 1980) while highly dependent on trade, assistance, and investment from the United States and other capitalist countries.

Some changes to cut dependence have not had the anticipated effect. Dependence has taken new forms in the last quarter of the twentieth century. Beginning in the mid 1970s, Nigeria took several steps that, on the face of it, should have reduced its dependence on the West. The Lagos government cut substantially the share of its trade with the colonial power, Britain. Lagos acquired majority equity holdings in local petroleum extracting, refining, and distribution and promulgated an indigenization decree shifting the majority of ownership in manufacturing from foreign to indigenous hands. But these measures did not greatly reduce dependence on the West. Nigeria's trade was still virtually all with capitalist DCs (with the United States replacing Britain as the chief trading partner). In contrast to more diversified exports in the 1960s, petroleum comprised more than 80 percent of export value for the 1970s. Moreover only 15–20 percent of the petroleum industry's total expenditure on goods and services was spent on locally produced items, which do not include most basic requirements, such as drilling rigs, platforms, heavy structures, underwater engineering systems, and other advanced technologies. Further multinational corporate (MNC) ownership was replaced by MNC–state joint enterprises, which enriched private middlemen and women and enlarged the patronage base for state officials but did little to develop Nigerian administrative and technological skills for subsequent industrialization. Kenya, Tanzania, Zaïre, Malawi, and Bangladesh made even less progress than Nigeria in using indigenization requirements to reduce external dependence.[26]

There are however several instances where countries might have developed more rapidly with less dependence on foreign economic initiative. Pakistan, Bangladesh, Honduras, Guatemala, Zaïre, and the Philippines were probably hurt by excessive economic dependence on the United States and other Western countries.

[25] E. Wayne Nafziger, *Inequality in Africa: Political Elites, Proletariat, Peasants, and the Poor* (Cambridge: Cambridge University Press, 1988), pp. 54, 72–74.

[26] Ibid., pp. 53–54.

But the solution to these problems is not withdrawal from the world capitalist system but rather, a more selective policy in dealings with capitalist countries. Trade, economic aid, capital movements, and technological borrowing from developed countries should be such that investment is directed into priority industries. Discouraging foreign monopoly power, encouraging domestic enterprise, preventing heavy debt burdens, avoiding substantial technological dependence on outsiders, and protecting infant domestic industries should all be part of this selective policy. (Chapters 16–18 discuss further foreign trade and investment strategies.)

What characteristics of dependent economies are not found in independent ones? Frank defines dependence in a circular manner. The LDCs are underdeveloped because they are dependent. But the features Frank concentrates on in defining dependence are those characteristic of underdevelopment. Thus the theory does not offer an independent and verifiable explanation of the processes causing underdevelopment.

Are there degrees of economic dependence? Dependency theory fails to distinguish between regional powers in the third world, such as Brazil and OPEC countries, Venezuela, Libya, Saudi Arabia, and Nigeria, and more dependent countries, such as Senegal, Niger, Uganda, Nepal, and Lesotho.

Finally most developed countries are also dependent on foreign economic ties. In fact Canada and Belgium may be more dependent on foreign investment than India or Pakistan, but Frank does not consider them dependent countries. Rather than divide the world into dependent and independent countries, it seems more sensible to think in terms of a continuum of dependence from the weakest LDC to the most powerful capitalist country.

SUMMARY

1. English classical economist David Ricardo feared eventual stagnation from slow capital accumulation, and diminishing returns from population growth on fixed natural resources. However, he failed to see the possibility of sustained, rapid, economic growth because his theory understated scientific discoveries and technological progress.

2. Marx saw history dialectically—as progressing from feudalism to capitalism to socialism on the basis of class conflict. The oppressed classes overthrow the classes controlling the prevailing means of production. Nevertheless the socialist revolution did not take place in the most advanced capitalist countries, nor did workers overthrow capitalism when they became a majority of the labor force, as Marx expected.

3. Rostow's economic model has five stages; its central historical stage is the takeoff, a decisive period of increased investment, rapid growth in leading sectors, and institutional change during which the major blocks to steady growth are finally overcome. Rostow's theory has several weaknesses: insufficient empirical evidence concerning conditions needed for takeoff; imprecise definitions; no theoretical ground for a society's movement from one stage to another; and the mistaken assumption that economic development in LDCs will parallel the early stages of DC development.

4. The vicious circle theory contends that a country is poor because its income is too low to encourage potential investors and generate adequate saving. How-

ever high income inequality, funds spent on prestige projects and the military, and numerous products requiring few economies of scale suggest that the savings potential of LDCs is much greater than this theory envisions.

5. Balanced growth advocates argue that a big push is needed to begin economic development because of indivisibilities in demand and infrastructure. Critics indicate that most LDCs do not have the resources essential for launching such a big push.

6. Hirschman supports a deliberate unbalancing of the economy to facilitate economic decision making and investment. However he fails to stress the importance of agricultural investment.

7. For Baran, the coalition of the bourgeoisie and landed classes, helped by foreign capitalist governments, is incapable of undertaking the capital formation and political reform required for rapid economic growth and alleviation of mass poverty. Although Baran's vision of a ruling progressive coalition is intriguing, he underestimates the conflicts of interest and class antagonism that are likely to occur under its rule.

8. Furtado's dependency theory contends that increased productivity and new consumption patterns resulting from capitalism in the peripheral countries of Asia, Africa, and Latin America benefit a small ruling class and its allies.

9. Frank's dependency approach maintains that countries become underdeveloped through integration into, not isolation from, the international capitalist system. However, despite some evidence supporting Frank, he does not adequately demonstrate that withdrawing from the capitalist system results in faster economic development.

TERMS TO REVIEW

- theory
- classical theory
- invisible hand
- law of diminishing returns
- iron law of wages
- historical materialism
- reserve army of the unemployed

- preconditions stage
- takeoff
- vicious circle
- demonstration effect
- balanced growth
- unbalanced growth

- price elasticity of demand
- big push thesis
- indivisibilities
- external economies
- infrastructure
- backward linkages
- forward linkages
- dependency theory

QUESTIONS TO DISCUSS

1. Is Ricardian classical economic theory applicable to LDCs?

2. How valid is the assumption that the development of LDCs will parallel the earlier stages of today's DCs?

3. Choose one developed country (or one LDC that Rostow says has already experienced takeoff). How well does Rostow's stage theory explain that country's economic growth?

4. Which historical theory—Marx's or Rostow's—is more useful in explaining Western economic development? Contemporary LDC development?

5. Are some of today's LDCs closer to Marx's feudal stage than his capitalist stage? What might a Marxist recommend for a LDC in the feudal stage? Would a Leninist or Baranist prescription for a feudal LDC be any different from Marx's?

6. How might Marxian economic analysis (like Mao's or Bettelheim's) threaten political elites in socialist countries?

7. How valid is Baran's theory in explaining contemporary underdevelopment in Asia, Africa, and Latin America? Are revolution and a Soviet-type government essential for removing this underdevelopment?

8. How valid is Baran's theory in explaining the weaknesses of New-Deal-type regimes in LDCs?

9. How does Andre Gunder Frank differ from Karl Marx in judging Western capitalism's influence in Asia, Africa, and Latin America?

10. For which country has dependence on Western capitalist economies been most costly? For which country has dependence on Western capitalist economies been most beneficial? On the basis of arguments about these two countries, how persuasive is Frank's dependency theory?

11. What are some potential LDC vicious circles? How plausible are these as barriers to development?

12. How important are supply and demand indivisibilities in influencing LDC investment strategies?

13. Choose a country or world region. Which economic development theory best explains development in that country or region?

GUIDE TO READINGS

Higgins (note 17) has a detailed discussion and evaluation of the models of classical economists, Marx, Rostow, and balanced and unbalanced growth theorists. Irma Adelman's book devoted to *Theories of Economic Growth and Development* (Stanford: Stanford University Press, 1961) analyzes the classical and Marxian models, as well as several other major theories. Enke (note 4) has a concise outline and critique of the classical approach.

Rostow's stage theory was criticized by economists and historians at the 1963 International Economic Association meetings in Konstanz, West Germany. The papers have been compiled in a book edited by Rostow (note 10).

Nurkse's book (note 13) presents his views of the vicious circle and balanced growth theories. Nurkse's summary article, Rosenstein–Rodan's article on indivisibilities (note 14), Fleming's criticism of balanced growth (note 17), Myint's article (note 12), Rostow's presentation of his stage theory in condensed form, and Baran's article on economic backwardness are included in Agarwala and Singh (note 20).

The major statements of the dependency theory are three sources by Furtado (note 23), Frank (note 24), and Andre Gunder Frank, *Capitalism and Underdevelopment in Latin America: Historical Studies of Chile and Brazil* (New York: Monthly Review Press, 1969). A useful critique and bibliography of dependence theory are in Sanjaya Lall, "Is 'Dependence' a Useful Concept in Analysing Underdevelopment," *World Development* 3 (November–December 1975): 799–810.

James Weaver and Kenneth Jameson discuss competing approaches for explaining economic development, including orthodox and Marxist theories, in *Economic Development: Competing Paradigms* (Washington, D.C.: University Press of America, 1981).

Some may prefer to include W. Arthur Lewis's theory of industrial expansion (Chapter 10) and Joseph A. Schumpeter's theory of growth and business cycles (Chapter 13) with the theories of this chapter.

Chapter Six

POVERTY AND INCOME INEQUALITY

SCOPE OF THE CHAPTER

World Bank President Barber B. Conable, in his 1988 annual address to the board of governors, focused

> on the central goal of the Bank: the reduction of poverty. Poverty on today's scale prevents a billion people from having even minimally acceptable standards of living. To allow every fifth human being on our planet to suffer such an existence is a moral outrage. It is more: it is bad economics, a terrible waste of precious development resources. Poverty destroys lives, human dignity, and economic potential.[1]

Economic growth can reduce but probably cannot solve poverty without some attention to income and property distribution, for poverty rose in a number of countries in the 1960s, 1970s, and 1980s even when growth targets were met or surpassed. As indicated in Chapter 2, GNP growth can be a misleading indicator of development, since GNP is heavily weighted by the income shares of the rich.

Estimates of income distribution in most developing countries are, at best, approximations of the underlying distribution we wish to measure. Despite efforts since the early 1970s to investigate income inequality, these data are even weaker than national income statistics. The International Labor Organization suggests that

---

[1] Barber B. Conable, address to the World Bank Board of Governors, West Berlin, September 27, 1988 (Washington, D.C.: World Bank, 1988), p. 4.

using many of these data to make policy is like trying to run through the forest in the dark without a flashlight.[2] Frequently the sample procedure for looking at inequalities is not adequate. Furthermore, income is not only understated for subsistence farmers (see Chapter 2) but also for the rich, who often understate income for tax purposes.

Nevertheless a few careful studies help us generalize about differences in poverty and income inequality and suggest policies to reduce them. We begin by examining the amount and characteristics of absolute poverty in the world. We go on to consider the extent of global income inequality and to look at differences in poverty and inequality among the following types of countries: (1) those in early and late stages of economic development; (2) low-, middle-, and high-income countries; (3) slow and fast growers; (4) socialist and nonsocialist countries; (5) those from different world regions; and (6) oil importers and oil exporters. We identify subgroups within a country's population that are most hurt by poverty and present several case studies of policies developing countries have used to increase the income shares of their poorest people. Finally we suggest policies for reducing poverty and improving income distribution and discuss the relationship between inequality and political instability.

GLOBAL ABSOLUTE POVERTY

Income inequality and absolute poverty are different concepts. **Absolute poverty** is below the income that secures the bare essentials of food, clothing, and shelter. Determining this level is a matter of judgment, so that it is difficult to make comparisons between countries. Moreover what is considered poverty varies according to the living standards of the time and region. For example, some Americans now classified as poor are materially better off than many Americans of the 1950s or Africans today who are not considered poor.

Still despite measurement problems, some scholars designate an international line, below which people are assumed to be in poverty. Three World Bank economists—Montek S. Ahluwalia, Nicholas G. Carter, and Hollis B. Chenery— propose a poverty line based on a standard set in India, the country with the most extensive literature on the subject. They define the **poverty line** as the income needed to attain a daily supply of 2250 calories per person, a figure of $200 per capita in 1975 (adjusted upward by use of the Kravis factor to reflect purchasing power measured in U.S. dollars; see Chapter 2). The 2250 calories would be met by the following diet: 5 grams of leafy vegetables, 110 grams of other vegetables (potatoes, root vegetables, gourds, and so on), 90 grams of milk, 35 grams of oil, 35 grams of sugar, 10 grams of flesh foods (fish and meats), 45 grams of pulses (peas or other legumes), and 395 grams of cereals (rice, corn, millet, or wheat). To illustrate, the 395 grams of cereals might consist of about 2 cups of hot prepared rice, equivalent in weight to 54 percent of the total diet.[3]

---

[2] International Labor Organization, Jobs and Skills Program for Africa, *First Things First: Meeting the Basic Needs of the People of Nigeria* (Addis Ababa, 1981), p. 29.

[3] The figure for flesh foods is an average for a population that includes high Hindu castes who do not eat meat for religious reasons. For these castes, pulses combined with additional cereals make up the amino acids provided by meat. R. Rajalakshmi, *Preschool Child Malnutrition* (Baroda, India: University

Data on income distribution for 1975 indicate that 46 percent of the Indian population was below the poverty line (or potentially undernourished). Given information on income distribution, poverty in other countries is determined by finding the percentage of the population with an income of less than 200 adjusted U.S. dollars. Updating data based on about half of the population of LDCs indicate that 37 percent, or 1.5 billion people, in the developing world, and 28 percent of total world population, were poor in 1990.[4]

The estimated 1.5 billion people living in absolute poverty suffer the following deprivations:

1. Four-fifths of their income is spent on food; the diet is monotonous, limited to cereals, yams, or cassavas, a few vegetables, and in some regions, a little fish or meat.

2. All are undernourished (by our earlier definition of poverty line) and hundreds of millions are severely malnourished. Energy and motivation are reduced; performance in school and at work is undermined; resistance to illness is low; and the physical and mental development of children is often impaired.

3. Two of every ten children born die within the first year; another dies before the age of 5; and only five reach the age of 40.

4. Fewer than 25 percent of the children are vaccinated against measles, diphtheria, whooping cough, and polio, which have been virtually eliminated in rich countries. These diseases are widespread and frequently fatal in developing countries. A case of measles is one hundred times more likely to kill a child in a low-income country than in the United States.

5. Average life expectancy is about 40 years, compared to 76 years in developed countries.

6. Only about one-third of the adults are literate.

7. Only about four out of every ten children complete more than 3 years of primary school.[5]

---

of Baroda Press, 1975), pp. 106–9, refers to a usual adult Indian diet. I am grateful for the help of nutritionist Meredith Smith in preparing this material.

For constructing a least-cost diet, see Patrick J. Gormely, "Are High-Protein Foods Economically Efficient?" *Food Policy* 3 (November 1978): 280–88.

[4] Montek S. Ahluwalia, Nicholas B. Carter, and Hollis B. Chenery, "Growth and Poverty in Developing Countries," *Journal of Development Economics* 6 (September 1979): 299–341.

There are several problems with defining a poverty line in terms of income needed to ensure a given supply of calories: (1) There is a considerable variation in caloric intake at a given level of expenditure; (2) specifying a single caloric norm is questionable; (3) variations in caloric requirements for the same individual occur; and (4) other nutrients, such as protein, vitamins, and minerals, are not considered. Nevertheless Nevin S. Scrimshaw and Lance Taylor in "Food," *Scientific American* 243 (September 1980): 81 indicate that as income rises, the consumption of other nutrients rises along with caloric consumption.

For criticisms of Ahluwalia's approach and a proposal for an improved method of measuring poverty, see V. V. Bhanoji Rao, "Measurement of Deprivation and Poverty Based on the Proportion Spent on Food: An Explanatory Exercise," *World Development* 9 (April 1981): 337–53.

[5] Robert S. McNamara, presidential address to the World Bank, Washington, D.C., September 30, 1980, pp. 20–21; and World Bank, *World Development Report, 1980* (New York: Oxford University Press, 1980), p. 33, with adjustment for more recent data.

GLOBAL DISTRIBUTION OF INCOME

Indices of income inequality measure relative poverty rather than absolute poverty. At present most measures of income distribution are for countries, or regions within a country, but there is a growing perception of the international economy as an interdependent system. Those people who demand a new international economic order assume that the welfare of a jute farm laborer in Bangladesh, a foundry worker in Brazil, a textile manufacturer in Kenya, and a cabinet minister in India are linked to decisions made by bankers, industrialists, and economic policymakers in the United States, Western Europe, and Japan. Developing countries compare their living standards to those of developed nations. Accordingly there is some validity to the concept of a world distribution of income.

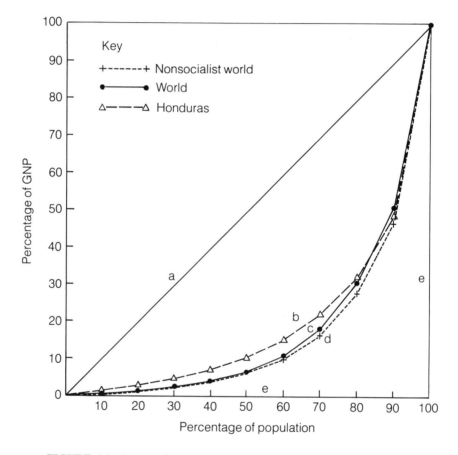

FIGURE 6-1   Lorenz Curves for Honduras and the World   The Lorenz curve indicates a higher income inequality for the world than for Honduras, the country with the world's highest household income inequality.

Source: Margaret E. Grosh and E. Wayne Nafziger, "The Computation of World Income Distribution," *Economic Development and Cultural Change* 34 (January 1986): 355.

TABLE 6-1   Household Income Distribution for Honduras and the World, 1970

(1) Population Decile	(2) Nonsocialist World (percent)	(3) World (percent)	(4) Honduras (percent)
1	0.4	0.5	1.4
2	0.8	0.8	1.6
3	1.2	1.2	1.8
4	1.6	1.7	2.5
5	2.4	2.5	3.4
6	3.7	4.1	4.8
7	6.4	7.3	6.7
8	11.1	12.3	10.1
9	18.8	20.3	16.8
10	53.6	49.3	50.9
Total	100.0	100.0	100.0
Gini coefficient	0.67	0.65	0.63

Source: Margaret E. Grosch and E. Wayne Nafziger, "The Computation of World Income Distribution," *Economic Development and Cultural Change* 34 (January 1986): 347–59. Adjustments for purchasing power are based on Irving B. Kravis, Alan W. Heston, and Robert Summers, "Real GDP *per Capita* for More than One Hundred Countries," *Economic Journal* 88 (June 1978): 215–42.

Inequalities of income distribution are often shown on a **Lorenz curve** (see Figure 6-1). If the global income distribution were perfectly equal, it would be represented by the 45° line (a). If one person, represented at the extreme right, received all the income, the Lorenz curve would follow half the perimeter of the box, the x-axis, and the right line parallel to the y-axis (e). In practice Lorenz curves are located between the 45° line and the line of complete inequality. Table 6-1, column 3, shows the world distribution of household income, arranged in ascending order from population decile 1 (the 10 percent with the lowest per capita GNP) to decile 10 (the 10 percent with the highest income.) These data are plotted on curve c in Figure 6-1.

Income inequality for the world exceeds that for any single country. The top 20 percent of the world's income-earning households receive 70 percent of the global income, and the bottom 40 percent receive only 4 percent. In Honduras, which according to a World Bank study has the highest household income inequality in the world, the top 20 percent of the households receive 68 percent of the income, and the bottom 40 percent, 7 percent. Honduras's curve b is generally to the left of the world's curve c in Figure 6-1.

When x and y are Lorenz curve coordinates and Δx and Δy are corresponding increments passing through these coordinates, then the **Gini index of inequality**

$$G = \frac{2}{10,000} \sum_0^{100} (x - y) \, \Delta x \qquad (6\text{-}1)$$

Summations are taken as many times as there are Δx increments between the limits.[6] The Gini index is the area between curve a and the Lorenz curve as a propor-

---

[6] Richard L. Merritt and Stein Rokkan, *Comparing Nations: The Use of Quantitative Data in Cross-National Research* (New Haven: Yale University Press, 1966), p. 364.

tion of the entire area below curve a. It ranges from a value of zero, representing equality, to 1, representing maximum inequality. The Gini for the world, 0.65, exceeds that for Honduras, 0.63. Thus, global income distribution is probably more unequal than that within any single country because it adds the effect of cross-national disparities in GNP per capita to that of internal inequalities.[7]

EARLY AND LATE STAGES OF DEVELOPMENT

Many development economists believe that inequality in LDCs follows an inverted U-shaped curve, first increasing and then decreasing with economic growth. Initially, growth results in lower income shares for the poor and higher income shares for the rich.[8] Irma Adelman's and Cynthia Taft Morris's explanation for the inverted U presupposes that LDCs are characterized by a dual economy (Chapter 4) in which the modern sector's income and productivity are significantly higher than the traditional sector's. They indicate that when economic growth and migration from the traditional to the modern sector begin in a subsistence agrarian economy (production mostly for the use of the cultivator and his family) through the expansion of a narrow modern sector (primarily manufacturing, mining, and processing), income inequality typically increases. Income inequalities have especially worsened where foreign exploitation of natural resources triggered growth. Data indicate that the income shares of the poorest 60 percent and middle 20 percent decline significantly in such a context while the share of the top 5 percent increases strikingly—particularly in low-income countries with a sharply dualistic economy dominated by traditional or foreign elites.

Once countries move beyond this early stage, further development generates no particular increase nor decrease in shares for the top 5 percent. At the very highest income level of a developing country, broad-based social and economic advances usually operate to its relative disadvantage, at least if the government *enlarges* its role in the economic sphere. However, the share of the top 5 percent increases if more natural resources become available for exploitation.

Middle-income groups are the primary beneficiaries of economic development beyond the early, dualistic stage. The first more widely based social and economic advances typically favor the middle sector.

As indicated earlier, the relative position of the poorest 60 percent typically worsens when growth begins. The modern sector competes with the traditional sector for markets and resources, and the result is a decline in the income shares of the poor. Such a decline occurred when peasants became landless workers during the European land consolidation of the sixteenth through the nineteenth centuries

---

[7] See also Henri Theil, "World Income Inequality and Its Components," *Economic Letters* 2 (1979): 99–102.

Global income distribution is less equal when the socialist countries are excluded because these countries have low income inequality; and they are generally not among those countries with the highest and lowest GNP per capita. However because data for socialist countries are not strictly comparable to those for nonsocialist countries, income distribution excluding the socialist countries is more reliable than that including them. Nevertheless income inequality for the world exceeds that for Honduras whether or not socialist countries are included.

[8] This proposition was first advanced by Simon Kuznets, "Economic Growth and Income Inequality," *American Economic Review* 45 (March 1955): 1–28.

and when high-yielding varieties of grains were first used on commercial farms in India and Pakistan. Even when economic growth becomes more broadly based, the poorest segments of the population increase their income shares only when the government expands its role, widening opportunities for education and training for lower-income groups.[9]

Do country data over time provide evidence that inequality follows an inverted U-shaped curve as economic development takes place? Time series data for individual countries are scarce and unreliable, and many LDCs have not yet arrived at a late enough stage of development to test the declining portion of the upside-down U curve. However, the time series data available suggest the plausibility of the inverted U-shaped curve. First records available for Britain, Germany, Belgium, and the United States indicate that income concentration increased from preindustrialization to early industrialization and decreased from early to late industrialization. Second the most reliable data for today's LDCs suggest that since World War II, inequality rose in low-income and lower-middle-income Bangladesh, India, the Ivory Coast, El Salvador, and the Philippines and fell in upper-middle-income Costa Rica, Taiwan, and Singapore, supporting the upside-down U, but declined in low-income Pakistan and Sri Lanka and increased in upper-middle-income Argentina and Brazil, exceptions to the inverted U.[10]

LOW-, MIDDLE-, AND HIGH-INCOME COUNTRIES

Income Inequality in Low-, Middle-, and High-Income Countries

Evidence for the inverse U is stronger when we classify a group of countries *in a given time period* by per capita income levels. The relationship between inequality (as measured by the Gini index) and gross domestic product per capita is an inverted U skewed to the right (Figure 6-2). Figure 6-2, based on Ahluwalia's study of income inequality in sixty six countries during the 1960s and early 1970s, exemplifies the upside-down U relationship. Ahluwalia focused on the extent to which the income shares of household groups differed from their population share. Income inequality is considered high if the income share of the poorest 40 percent is less than 12 percent of GNP; moderate if it is between 12 and 17 percent; and low if 17 percent and above.

The International Labor Office's 1984 survey of numerous LDC income distribution studies found grave weaknesses in individual country data frequently used for cross-national comparisons. The survey found only twenty two LDCs with

---

[9] Irma Adelman and Cynthia Taft Morris, *Economic Growth and Social Equity in Developing Countries* (Stanford: Stanford University Press, 1973), pp. 178–83; and Irma Adelman and Cynthia Taft Morris, "Growth and Impoverishment in the Middle of the Nineteenth Century," *World Development* 6 (March 1978): 245–73.

[10] Simon Kuznets, "Quantitative Aspects of the Economic Growth of Nations: VIII, Distribution of Income by Size," *Economic Development and Cultural Change* 11, no. 2, part 2 (January 1963): 58–67; Jacques Lecaillon, Felix Paukert, Christian Morrisson, and Dimitri Germidis, *Income Distribution and Economic Development: An Analytical Survey* (Geneva: International Labor Office, 1984), pp. 42–43; Cynthia Taft Morris and Irma Adelman, *Comparative Patterns of Economic Development, 1850–1914* (Baltimore: Johns Hopkins University Press, 1988); and Gary S. Fields, *Poverty, Inequality, and Development* (Cambridge: Cambridge University Press, 1980), pp. 78–98.

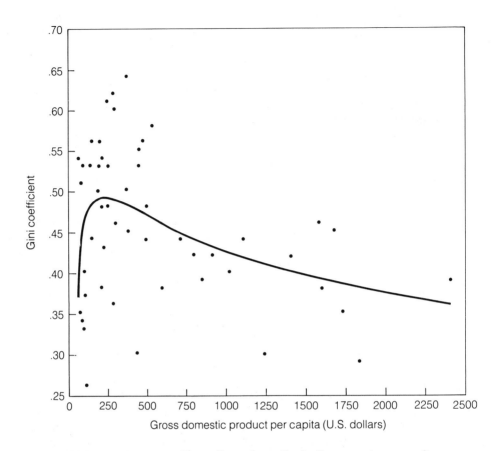

FIGURE 6-2   Income Inequality and per Capita Income   As per capita income increases, income inequality (the Gini index) first increases and then decreases. The trend line for the predicted Gini is an inverted U skewed to the right.

Source: Computed from Montek S. Ahluwalia, "Income Inequality," in Hollis Chenery, Montek S. Alhuwalia, C. L. G. Bell, John H. Duloy, and Richard Jolly, eds., *Redistribution with Growth* (London: Oxford University Press, 1974), p. 9.
Gini = 1.067 − 20.221(1/GDP per capita) − 0.089 ln (GDP per capita)
    (0.168)   (5.833)   (0.024)
My thanks to Paul Koch and Margaret Grosh, who are not responsible for errors.

reliable and comparable measures of household income concentration.[11] Table 6-2, which includes these twenty two and seventeen from subsequent World Bank compilations, indicates 25 percent of low-income countries, 52 percent of middle-income countries, and 0 percent of high-income countries have high income inequality. On the other hand, 25 percent of low-income countries, 4 percent of middle-income

[11] Jacques Lecaillon, Felix Paukert, Christian Morrisson, and Dimitri Germidis *Income Distribution and Economic Development: An Analytical Survey* (Geneva: International Labor Office, 1984).

countries, and 82 percent of high-income countries have low inequality. Accordingly income inequality increases as we move from low- to middle-income countries and declines from middle- to high-income countries, reconfirming the inverted U hypothesis. Thus cross-sectional and time series data support the hypothesis that inequality follows an inverted U-shaped curve as per capita income increases. Even so there is much more variation in relative inequality *within* country income groups than *between* them. (We discuss factors other than income below.) Income level is an imprecise predictor of a country's income inequality.[12]

Income Inequality in Developed and Developing Countries

Generally developed (high-income) countries have low income inequality, while almost half the developing countries have high inequality and almost half moderate inequality. The income shares of the poor are higher and their variance lower in DCs than in LDCs. While Table 6-2's conclusion that the poorest 40 percent of households in high-income countries receive 18 percent compared to 13 percent for low-income countries is not distorted, the indication that poor in middle-income countries receive 12 percent understates their inequality. First, in LDCs, individual and household income concentrations are approximately the same, whereas in DCs concentration for individuals is less than for households, since household size increases rapidly from lower- to upper-income classes. Second, in DCs, inequalities measured over a lifetime are markedly lower than those measured over a year, while in LDCs inequalities do not vary with the period chosen. Third, LDC life expectancies are highly correlated with average incomes, frequently contributing to interethnic, metropolitan-rural, and skilled-unskilled working life disparities of 10 to 15 years; in DCs the most underprivileged rarely die before retirement age. Fourth, progressive income taxes (with higher tax *rates* for higher incomes) and social welfare programs make income more equal in developed countries than Table 6-2 indicates. Fifth, however LDC (especially in a low-income country) urban-rural income discrepancies are overstated, since rural in-kind incomes are undervalued and rural living costs are usually 10–20 percent lower than urban costs. Sixth, retained corporate profits, which accrue disproportionately to upper-income classes, and are a significant fraction of GNP in DCs and many middle-income countries but usually omitted in income distribution estimates, contribute to overstating inequality in low-income countries. Thus overall the first four distortions are probably balanced by the fifth and sixth distortions, so that the comparison in Table 6-2 of DCs' and low-income countries' income distributions is unchanged. However, middle-income countries are affected so little by distortions 5 and 6 that these are outweighed by the first four distortions, which increase the disparity in income concentrations between DCs and middle-income countries in Table 6-2.[13] These distortions make the inverted U even more pronounced than data suggest.

[12] Gary S. Fields, *Poverty, Inequality, and Development* (Cambridge: Cambridge University Press, 1980), p. 67.

[13] Jacques Lecaillon, Felix Paukert, Christian Morrisson, and Dimitri Germidis, *Income Distribution and Economic Development: An Analytical Survey* (Geneva: International Labor Office, 1984), pp. 34–52; and Simon Kuznets, "Demographic Aspects of the Size Distribution of Income: An Exploratory Essay," *Economic Development and Cultural Change* 25 (October 1976): 1–44.

TABLE 6-2 Differences in Income Inequality between High-, Middle-, and Low-Income Countries

HIGH INEQUALITY—SHARE OF LOWEST 40 PERCENT LESS THAN 12 PERCENT

Country	Lowest 40%	Middle 40%	Top 20%
Kenya (1969)	8.9	30.7	60.4
Zambia (1976)	10.8	28.1	61.1
Ivory Coast (1985–86)	8.6	30.0	61.4
Mauritius (1980–81)	11.5	28.0	60.5
Zimbabwe (1968)	7.8	24.2	68.0
Honduras (1967–68)	7.3	25.2	67.5
Ecuador (1970)	7.6	22.9	69.5
Turkey (1973)	11.5	32.0	56.5
Malaysia (1973)	11.2	32.7	56.1
Colombia (1974)	10.5	31.0	58.5
Brazil (1972)	7.0	26.4	66.6
Peru (1972)	7.0	32.0	61.0
Mexico (1977)	9.9	32.4	57.7

MODERATE INEQUALITY—SHARE OF LOWEST 40 PERCENT BETWEEN 12 PERCENT AND 17 PERCENT

Country	Lowest 40%	Middle 40%	Top 20%
Senegal (1971)	13.3	25.8	60.9
Tanzania (1968)	13.5	25.5	61.0
India (1975–76)	13.5	25.5	61.0
Sri Lanka (1980–81)	15.9	34.4	49.7
Indonesia (1976)	14.4	36.2	49.4
Philippines (1985)	14.1	33.4	52.5
Egypt, Arab Rep. (1974)	16.5	35.5	48.0
Portugal (1973–74)	15.2	35.7	49.1
Costa Rica (1971)	14.5	30.4	55.1
Korea, Rep. of (1976)	16.9	37.8	45.3
Thailand (1975–76)	15.2	35.0	49.8
El Salvador (1976–77)	15.5	37.2	47.3
Uruguay (1967)	12.8	38.0	49.2
Chile (1968)	13.0	30.2	56.8
Argentina (1970)	14.1	35.6	50.3

LOW INEQUALITY—SHARE OF LOWEST 40 PERCENT, 17 PERCENT AND ABOVE

Country	Lowest 40%	Middle 40%	Top 20%
Bangladesh (1981–82)	17.3	37.4	45.3
Benin (1959)	18.0	32.5	49.5

Low Income (less than U.S. $450)

Middle Income (U.S. $450–$6000)

Country (Year)			
Panama (1973)	7.2	31.0	61.8
Iran (1971)	10.0	27.3	62.7
Venezuela (1970)	10.3	35.7	54.0
Spain (1980–81)	19.4	40.5	40.1
Ireland (1973)	20.3	40.3	39.4

High Income (more than U.S. $6000)

Country (Year)			
Hong Kong (1980)	16.2	36.8	47.0
New Zealand (1981–82)	15.9	39.4	44.7
Australia (1975–76)	15.4	37.5	47.1
Israel (1979–80)	18.0	42.1	39.9
Italy (1977)	17.5	38.6	43.9
Japan (1979)	21.9	40.6	37.5
U.K. (1979)	18.5	41.8	39.7
Canada (1981)	17.1	42.9	40.0
U.S. (1980)	17.2	42.9	39.9
Finland (1981)	18.4	43.9	37.7
France (1975)	17.0	40.8	42.2
Netherlands (1981)	22.4	41.4	36.2
Germany, Fed. Rep. (1978)	20.4	40.1	39.5
Denmark (1981)	17.4	44.0	38.6
Sweden (1981)	20.5	37.8	41.7
Norway (1982)	18.9	42.9	38.2
Switzerland (1978)	20.1	41.9	38.0

Sources: Jacques Lecaillon, Felix Paukert, Christian Morrisson, and Dimitri Germidis, *Income Distribution and Economic Development: An Analytical Survey* (Geneva: International Labor Office, 1984), pp. 26–27; World Bank, *World Development Report, 1987* (New York: Oxford University Press, 1987), pp. 252–53; and World Bank, *World Development Report, 1988* (New York: Oxford University Press, 1988), pp. 272–73.

Absolute Poverty in Developing Countries

Information on relative income inequality in developing countries does not indicate much about the extent of absolute poverty. Much of the current interest in income distribution reflects a concern that nutrition, shelter, health, education, sanitation, and so forth, meet certain minimum standards.

Previously in this chapter, we defined the concept of an international poverty line based on the income (200 adjusted U.S. dollars per capita in 1975) for supplying 2250 calories per person per day in India. According to this standard, 51 percent of the population of low-income countries, 31 percent of the lower-middle-income countries, 13 percent of the upper-middle-income countries, and 38 percent of all LDCs are in poverty (see Table 6-3). Although these estimates do not allow for variations in caloric requirements by age or sex (nor do they reflect expenditure patterns on other basic requirements), they are the best data available.

Most of the poor are from countries with low levels of per capita income. Only a relative few are from nations with a highly unequal income distribution. India, Indonesia, Bangladesh, and Pakistan, with 52 percent of the total population considered in Table 6-3, account for about 68 percent of the poor. These countries all have low to moderate income inequality. However, absolute poverty is present even in upper-middle-income countries. High income inequality may make poverty an equally serious problem for a country with several times the per capita income of another. About 14 percent of the people of Sri Lanka and Mexico are considered poor, although Mexico's GNP per head is four times that of Sri Lanka (Table 6-3).

Changes in Absolute Poverty in Developing Countries

Table 6-4, which divides countries into income categories in the same way as Table 6-3, indicates that the income shares of the poorest 40 percent in low- and lower-middle-income countries decreased from 1960 to 1975. Projections for 2000, based on a World Bank analysis of trends in income distribution policies, population, international trade, and capital flows, indicate a further deterioration in the income shares of the poorest group.

Using the definition of poverty line given earlier, the number of poor in *low-income countries* increased from 1960 to 1975 despite growing per capita income. This increase occurred because of population growth and declining income shares of the lowest 40 percent. However as a proportion of total population, the number of poor decreased during this same period from 62 percent to 51 percent. Furthermore projected higher growth rates for several low-income countries, notably India and Bangladesh, are expected to reduce the number of poor between 1975 and 2000 despite an anticipated decline in income shares for the bottom 40 percent of the population. The poverty rate during this period is expected to drop even more sharply—from 51 percent to 22 percent.

Lower-middle-income countries had an absolute and relative drop in the number of poor between 1960 and 1975, a reduction that is expected to continue from 1975 to 2000. Their growth, more rapid than in low-income countries, more than compensated for the slightly declining income share of the poorest 40 percent of the population. Although their poor had the *smallest* income shares, upper-middle-income countries were the only developing countries with an *increased* income share for this group from 1960 to 1975, a share expected to increase through the year 2000. The absolute and relative number of poor in these countries will have declined between 1960 and 2000, so that only 4 percent will be considered poor in 2000.

The income shares of the lowest 40 percent in the developing world as a whole have decreased (and are expected to continue to drop) more sharply than the lowest group's shares in any of the three groups of countries—the low-, lower-middle- or upper-middle-income countries. The increased income inequality *between* developing countries is a more important factor than the greater inequality *within* these countries in explaining the sharp decline in the income share of the poor in LDCs as a whole.[14]

SLOW AND FAST GROWERS

As already indicated, countries at earlier and lower levels of development are more likely to experience increases in income inequality. However, higher rates of economic growth, which are only weakly correlated with levels of economic development, are not associated with either greater equality or inequality. Both fast growers, such as Brazil, and slow growers, such as Zambia, have high income inequalities. And slow-growing Bangladesh and fast-growing Taiwan both have low income inequalities.

The following two examples illustrate the roles of economic growth and increased income equality in increasing the income of the bottom 60 percent of the population. In the 1960s and early 1970s, the growth rates for Peru and Sri Lanka were both about 2 percent per year, but because of increased income shares for the poor, the per capita income of the poorest 60 percent grew almost 5 percent yearly in Sri Lanka compared to only 2 percent in Peru. However in other cases, a high growth rate offsets a decline in the share of the bottom 60 percent to produce substantial increases in the income of the poor (see Table 5-6). Mexico, with an economic growth rate of over 5 percent per year from 1963 to 1968, experienced a decrease in the relative income share of the poorest 60 percent, but their absolute incomes grew by about 3 percent per year over the same period.

SOCIALIST AND NONSOCIALIST COUNTRIES

The socialist countries have a high degree of income equality. All five socialist countries in Ahluwalia's study, Yugoslavia, Bulgaria, Poland, Hungary, and Czechoslovakia, have low income inequality. The average income share of the poorest 40 percent in the five countries is 24 percent compared to 18 percent for developed countries and 12.5 percent for developing countries. This high income equality is to be expected, since people in socialist economies do not own land and capital.

[14] Montek S. Ahluwalia, Nicholas G. Carter, and Hollis B. Chenery, "Growth and Poverty in Developing Countries," *Journal of Development Economics* 6 (September 1979): 299–341.

TABLE 6-3 Per Capita Income, Population, and Poverty, 1975, and Poverty, 2000 (projected)

| Country[a] | 1975 GNP per Capita[b] | | Population 1975 (millions) | Percentage of Population in Poverty in 1975 | | Projected Percentage of Population in Poverty in 2000 (using official exchange rates) |
	At Official Exchange Rates	Using Adjustment for Purchasing Power		Using Adjustment for Purchasing Power	Using Official Exchange Rates	
Low income (under $350 adjusted GNP per capita)						
(1) Bangladesh	72	200	80.7	64	60	37
(2) Ethiopia	81	213	27.3	68	62	48
(3) Burma	88	237	30.9	65	56	56
(4) Indonesia	90	280	130.0	59	62	15
(5) Uganda	115	280	11.5	55	45	52
(6) Zaire	105	281	20.6	53	49	32
(7) Sudan	112	281	18.1	54	47	22
(8) Tanzania	118	297	14.8	51	46	30
(9) Pakistan	121	299	73.0	43	34	18
(10) India	102	300	599.4	46	46	17
Subtotal	99	284	1006.3	51	49	22
Lower-middle income ($350–$750 adjusted GNP per capita)						
(11) Kenya	168	413	13.4	55	48	35
(12) Nigeria	176	433	75.3	35	27	19
(13) Philippines	182	469	42.5	33	29	8
(14) Sri Lanka	185	471	14.1	14	10	9
(15) Senegal	227	550	4.3	35	29	26
(16) Egypt	238	561	37.2	20	14	9
(17) Thailand	237	584	41.6	32	23	5

	Col1	Col2	Col3	Col4	Col5	Col6
(18) Ghana	255	628	9.8	25	19	30
(19) Morocco	266	643	17.3	26	16	6
(20) Ivory Coast	325	695	5.9	25	14	8
Subtotal	209	511	261.4	31	24	14
Upper-middle income (greater than $750 adjusted GNP per capita)						
(21) Korea	325	797	34.1	8	6	2
(22) Chile	386	798	10.6	11	9	6
(23) Zambia	363	798	4.9	10	7	9
(24) Colombia	352	851	24.8	19	14	5
(25) Turkey	379	914	39.7	14	11	6
(26) Tunisia	425	992	5.7	10	9	0
(27) Malaysia	471	1006	12.2	12	8	5
(28) Taiwan	499	1075	16.1	5	4	0
(29) Guatemala	497	1128	5.5	10	9	9
(30) Brazil	509	1136	106.8	15	8	3
(31) Peru	503	1183	15.3	18	15	7
(32) Iran	572	1257	33.9	13	8	3
(33) Mexico	758	1429	59.6	14	10	5
(34) Yugoslavia	828	1701	21.3	5	4	0
(35) Argentina	1097	2094	24.9	5	3	3
(36) Venezuela	1288	2286	12.2	9	5	4
Subtotal	577	1220	427.6	13	8	4
Total	237	555	1695.3	38	35	16

Sources: Montek S. Ahluwalia, Nicholas G. Carter, and Hollis B. Chenery, "Growth and Poverty in Developing Countries," *Journal of Developmental Economics* 6 (September 1979): 302–3, 312–13. Purchasing power adjustment factors are from Irving B. Kravis, Alan W. Heston, and Robert Summers, "Real GDP *Per Capita* for More Than One Hundred Countries," *Economic Journal* 88 (June 1968): 215–42.

[a] Countries are ranked in ascending order by 1975 GNP per capita adjusted by a Kravis factor for purchasing power (see Chapter 2 and source below).

[b] In 1970 U.S. dollars.

TABLE 6-4 Growth and Poverty in Developing Countries

		1960 Estimates	1975[a]		Projections for 2000[b]	
(I)	Per capita income (PCI) ($ 1970 prices) (adjusted for purchasing power)					
	All LDCs	367	555	(2.8)	1462	(4.0)
	Low income	233	284	(1.3)	536	(2.6)
	Lower-middle income	337	511	(2.8)	1189	(3.4)
	Upper-middle income	714	1220	(3.6)	3724	(4.6)
(II)	PCI lowest 40 percent ($ 1970 prices) (adjusted for purchasing power)					
	All LDCs	109	136	(1.5)	236	(2.2)
	Low income	102	118	(1.0)	186	(1.8)
	Lower-middle income	104	153	(2.6)	288	(2.6)
	Upper-middle income	174	301	(3.7)	1114	(5.4)
(III)	Income shares lowest 40 percent (percentages)					
	All LDCs	11.9	9.8		6.4	
	Low income	17.5	16.7		13.9	
	Lower-middle income	12.4	12.0		9.7	
	Upper-middle income	9.7	9.9		12.0	
(IV)	Number of poor (millions)					
	All LDCs	597	644		475	
	Low income	438	510		375	
	Lower-middle income	86	81		70	
	Upper-middle income	72	54		30	
(V)	Percentages of population in poverty					
	All LDCs	50.9	38.0		16.3	
	Low income	61.7	50.7		22.4	
	Lower-middle income	49.2	31.0		14.2	
	Upper-middle income	24.9	12.6		4.0	

[a]Figures in parentheses are annual growth rates between 1960 and 1975.

[b]Figures in parentheses are annual growth rates between 1975 and 2000.

Source: Montek S. Ahluwalia, Nicholas G. Carter, and Hollis B. Chenery, "Growth and Poverty in Developing Countries," *Journal of Development Economics*, 6 (September 1979): 318.

Furthermore socialist countries have expanded mass education and reduced population growth, both of which contribute to greater income equality. Nonsocialist countries at the same income levels have not generally progressed so fast on these fronts. Income inequality in socialist countries is due mainly to wage discrepancies between sectors and skill classes. Perhaps the average income share of the bottom 40 percent in socialist countries may be taken as an upper limit to which policymakers in LDCs can aspire.[15]

[15]Montek S. Ahluwalia, "Income Inequality," in Hollis Chenery, Montek S. Ahluwalia, C. L. G. Bell, John H. Duloy, and Richard Jolly, eds., *Redistribution with Growth* (London: Oxford University Press, 1974), p. 7; and Montek S. Ahluwalia, "Inequality, Poverty, and Development," *Journal of Development Economics* 3 (December 1976): 327–28.

TABLE 6-5   Third-World Regions by Poverty Rates and Poor's Relative Income Shares

(1) Region of the World	(2) Population in Poverty, 1975 (in percent)	(3) Income Share of Lowest 20 Percent, 1970 (in percent)	(4) Income Share of Highest 5 Percent, 1970 (in percent)	Column 3/ Column 4 (in percent)
China	27	9	24	38
South Asia	47	7	24	29
Middle East	18	5	22	23
Southeast Asia[a]	59	6	28	21
East Asia[a]	7	6	28	21
Sub-Saharan Africa	51	4	26	15
Latin America	14	3	29	10
Developing countries	37	5	25	20
Developed countries	0[b]	10	23	43

[a]Southeast Asia's and East Asia's income shares of the poor relative to the rich included together.

[b]Comparable poverty data lacking.

Sources: World Bank, *World Tables, 1980* (Baltimore: Johns Hopkins University Press, 1980), pp. 460–61; E. Wayne Nafziger, *Inequality in Africa: Political Elites, Proletariat, Peasants, and the Poor* (Cambridge: Cambridge University Press, 1988), p. 22; and Table 6-3.

REGIONS OF THE WORLD

As Table 6-5 indicates, South Asia was the region of the developing world with the lowest income inequality in 1970. The lowest 20 percent received 7 percent of the income shares, while the highest 5 percent received only 24 percent. The Middle East and East Asia had medium income inequality; sub-Saharan Africa had high inequality, due largely to industrial productivity four to nine times agricultural productivity as compared to only two to three times in Asia and Latin America.[16] Still Latin America, with a high concentration of land ownership, had the highest income inequality, with the bottom 20 percent of its population receiving 3 percent and the top 5 percent, 29 percent of income.

South Asia's income inequality improved the most between 1960 and 1970, followed by East Asia's and the Middle East's. Sub-Saharan Africa's income inequality increased most, and Latin America's also rose during that period.

Despite its low income inequality, South Asia (together with Southeast Asia and sub-Saharan Africa) had one of the highest poverty rates in the world, due primarily to the low GNP per capita of its three most populous countries, India,

[16]Jacques Lecaillon, Felix Paukert, Christian Morrisson, and Dimitri Germidis, *Income Distribution and Economic Development: An Analytical Survey* (Geneva: International Labor Organization, 1984), pp. 54–58.

Bangladesh, and Pakistan (see Table 6-3). Southeast Asia and sub-Saharan Africa had even higher poverty rates than South Asia according to column 1, Table 6-5, but a small margin of error for the largest county of each regional grouping—Indonesia, Nigeria, and India—could change the ranking. East Asia, with the second highest LDC income per head, had the lowest poverty rate. Latin America had the second lowest rate, lower than the Middle East, with a higher GNP per capita and lower income inequality but highly dependent on food imports.

OIL IMPORTERS AND EXPORTERS

The rapid economic growth of major oil exporters during the early 1970s was accompanied by growing income inequalities that exceeded those in oil-importing LDCs. While inequality dropped during the slow growth of oil exporters in the late 1970s and 1980s, their poor performance on basic needs (Table 2-1) suggests that income inequality was high—probably still higher than that of oil importers. The poverty rate of high-income oil exporters was lower than oil-importing LDCs, who had the same rate as oil-exporting LDCs listed in Table 6-3 (Indonesia, Nigeria, Malaysia, Mexico, Venezuela, and Egypt). Overall oil exporters' poverty rates declined in the 1970s and 1980s, although probably not so rapidly as among oil importers.

Nigeria fits the income distribution pattern of oil-exporting countries. Personal income inequality in the modern sector increased from 1960 (Gini = 0.5) to 1975 (0.7), declining in 1979 (0.6) with sluggish oil growth. But relative wage and salary differences narrowed in both public and private sectors from 1965 to the later 1970s, even though these differentials were still larger than in most LDCs. The ratio of Nigeria's nonagricultural to agricultural labor productivity, 2.5 to 1 in 1966, increased to 2.7 to 1 in 1970 and 7.2 to 1 in 1975. The sharp rise from 1970 to 1975, was due largely to phenomenal oil output, price, and tax revenue expansion rather than technical change or skill development. Without oil the 1975 ratio would have been 3.0 to 1. The terms of trade also shifted toward industry. Moreover emigration drained rural areas of the most able-bodied young people, attracted by the 1975 oil-fueled doubling of government's minimum wage. In fact emigration selectivity resulted in a decline in inflation-adjusted agricultural productivity from 1970 to 1975. Rural income was so low that average urban income exceeded the average of the top 25 percent of rural incomes.[17]

IDENTIFYING POVERTY GROUPS

1. Half of the world's poor live in South Asia, mainly in India, Bangladesh, and Pakistan. One-sixth live in sub-Saharan Africa. Another sixth are in East and Southeast Asia, primarily in Indonesia. The remainder are mostly divided between Latin America and the Middle East.

[17] Peter Matlon, "The Structure of Production and Rural Incomes in Northern Nigeria: Results of Three Village Case Studies," and V. P. Diejomaoh and E. C. Anusionwu, "Education and Income Distribution in Nigeria," in Henry Bienen and V. P. Diejomaoh, eds., *The Political Economy of Income Distribution in Nigeria* (New York: Holmes & Meier, 1981), pp. 323–40.

2. Some minority groups are overrepresented among the poor; these include the Indians in Latin America and the outcastes in India.

3. Four-fifths of the poor live in rural areas, most of the rest in urban slums—but almost all in crowded conditions. The rural poor are the landless workers, sharecroppers, tenants, and small land owners. The urban poor include the unemployed, irregularly employed, menial workers, some small shopkeepers, artisans, and traders.

4. Compared to the lowest income classes in DCs, a much smaller percentage of the poor in the LDCs are wage laborers, or unemployed and searching for work (see below, on policies). Most of the poor work long hours as farmers, vendors, artisans, or hired workers. A few self-employed may own a small piece of land, some animals, or some tools, but many of the poor own no land and have virtually no assets.

5. Most of the poor are illiterate: They have not completed more than a year or two of school. As a result, their knowledge and understanding of the world are severely circumscribed.

6. Women are poorer than men, especially in one-quarter of the world's households where women alone head households. The female labor force is small, employed in the lowest paid jobs, and characterized by a far greater unemployment rate than the male labor force. In households with an adult male, females are often given more menial work and males are favored in the distribution of food and other consumer goods (see Chapter 10).

7. Forty percent of the poor are children under 10, living mainly in large families.

8. Even when living with an extended family, the elderly are poorer than other groups.

9. Many of the poor are beyond the gaze of the casual visitor to a village—away from roads, away from markets, or living on the outskirts of the village. Indeed Alan G. Hill contends that the wretched Sahel Africans presented dramatically on Western television screens represented the normal misery for poor populations in remote rural areas, discovered only when "the destitute collect on roadsides, in refugee camps or on the outskirts of towns and cities."[18]

WOMEN, POVERTY, AND MALE DOMINANCE

In most precolonial Afro-Asian societies, patriarchal authority severely limited the power of women, who were protected if they were deferential to the patriarchs. Yet some societies gave women clearly defined economic roles, allowing wealth accumulation and limited economic authority.

Most Afro-Asian women lost their limited power under colonialism. Men received land titles, extension assistance, technical training, and education. When

---

[18] World Bank, *World Development, 1980* (New York: Oxford University Press, 1980), pp. 33–35; Irene Tinker, Michèle Bo Bramsen, and Myra Buvinić, *Women and World Development* (New York: Praeger, 1976); Alan G. Hill, *Demographic Responses to Food Shortages in the Sahel,* ESD 801/13 (Rome: Food and Agriculture Organization, 1978), p. 1; and Peter Hendry, "Food and Population: Beyond Five Billion," *Population Bulletin* 43 (April 1988): 8.

men had to leave farms to seek employment, as in South Africa, women remained burdened with responsibility for the family's food. A few women, especially West African market traders, became wealthy, but the majority worked long hours to survive. In the 1930s through 1950s, colonial authorities colluded with patriarchal indigenous leaders to increase control over women. In some instances, where they had an independent economic base, women used traditional female organizations and methods, not confrontation to male authority, to oppose both European and local authorities. Women played a prominent role in many of the early nationalist struggles, especially when colonialists threatened their economic interests.

After independence low female literacy (two-thirds that for men), limited economic opportunity, and domestic burdens relegated women to the lowest economic rungs, even in countries claiming to be socialist, such as Ethiopia, which allocated land to male family heads during land reform in the 1970s. Government agricultural policy favored male heads of households and development plans often ignored women. Nevertheless economic or political crises sometimes benefit women, as men seek new alliances between sexes in rebuilding weak economies and polities.

The International Labor Organization estimates that women comprised 433 million, or 32 percent, of the LDC labor force of 1354 million and 676 million, or 35 percent, of the global labor force of 1955 million in 1985. Females receive an average income half that of males in LDCs, partly from **crowding,** the tendency to discriminate against women (and minorities) in well-paying jobs, forcing them to increase the supply of labor for menial or low-paying jobs. Though women are frequently the backbone of the rural economy, in a modernizing economy, they enjoy few advantages. While men seek wage employment in cities, women play the dominant role in small-scale farming, often on smaller plots and with lower returns than male-headed households. Women's workloads are heavy as a result of child-bearing (five children in the average rural LDC family), carrying water, collecting wood, increased weeding from new crop varieties, and other farm tasks due to growing rural population pressures. Additionally when technological innovations increase the productivity of cash crops, men frequently divert hectarage from women's food crops. Moreover women as a rule receive lower returns to training and education (university rates of return are negative for Kenyan women) because of discrimination, withdrawal from the labor force, and having to live in the same place as their husbands. Finally in Accra, Ghana female workers shoulder most of the responsibility for cooking, cleaning, laundry, and other housework, while two-thirds of the male workers do not do any housework.[19]

[19] Jane L. Parpart, "Women and the State in Africa," in Donald Rothchild and Naomi Chazan, eds., *The Precarious Balance* (Boulder, Colo.: Westview, 1986), pp. 278–92; United Nations, Department of International Economic and Social Affairs, *World Survey on the Role of Women in Development* (New York, 1986), pp. 12, 70; Jacques Lecaillon, Felix Paukert, Christian Morrisson, and Dimitri Germidis, *Income Distribution and Economic Development: An Analytical Survey* (Geneva: International Labor Office, 1984), pp. 80–81. William J. House and Tony Killick, "Social Justice and Development Policy in Kenya's Rural Economy," in Dharam Ghai and Samir Radwan, eds., *Agrarian Policies and Rural Poverty in Africa* (Geneva: International Labor Office, 1983), pp. 31–69; Arne Bigsten, *Education and Income Determination in Kenya* (Aldershot, England: Gower, 1984), pp. 134–47; Eugenia Date-Bah, "Sex Inequality in an African Urban Labour Market: The Case of Accra-Tema," Geneva, International Labor Organization, World Employment Program 2-21/Working Paper 122, pp. 59–65; and E. Wayne Nafziger, *Inequality in Africa: Political Elites, Proletariat, Peasants, and the Poor* (Cambridge: Cambridge University Press, 1988), pp. 45–46, 124–26.

CASE STUDIES OF COUNTRIES

Table 6-6 classifies countries into three groups on the basis of income shares of the bottom 60 percent of the population in the latest year for which figures are available and the share of increased income going to this 60 percent. The most recent income share for the poorest 60 percent ranges from 38 percent in Taiwan to 18 percent in Peru. The increased share of the poorest group in growth varied from Sri Lanka, which exceeded 50 percent, to Brazil, with only 15 percent.

The development strategy of Taiwan and Korea, which was successful, included land reforms, an emphasis on education, and a focus on labor-intensive expansion in industry, especially in manufactured exports. Yugoslavia's pre-1977 success can be attributed to the social ownership of the means of production and a strategy of large income transfers to poorer areas.[20]

China and Cuba

Although there are less detailed data available, China, since the Communist victory in 1949, and Cuba, since the 1959 revolution, have made much progress in increasing the income shares of their poorest people. Superficial and idealized accounts by numerous scholars and journalists in the early 1970s acclaimed China as the most egalitarian society in the world. Its income inequality fell between 1949 and 1957, but probably not after 1957. China's income inequality, low to moderate, is less than that of India and the Philippines. However largely because of substantial regional and urban/rural differences, its income inequality is greater than that of Taiwan, South Korea, and Sri Lanka.[21]

Nevertheless Mao Zedong's policy of building on the weakest link set an income floor below which no Chinese would sink. During the 1950s, redistribution policies greatly reduced the wretched poverty that had been the accepted lot of millions of peasants and menial workers for centuries.

From 1956 to 1957, GNP per capita in Cuba was $500, a high level among developing countries. Nevertheless unemployment was at 16 percent of the labor force; poverty was widespread; and a large fraction of the population, especially in rural areas, was illiterate and undernourished. Income was highly concentrated; and access to medical care and education was severely limited. Nine percent of the landowners held 73 percent of the land.

Although real GNP per capita probably declined in the two decades after the revolution, dire poverty and unemployment were virtually eliminated, since income was redistributed through several steps:

1. Tenants became owners of houses and small farm holdings.
2. The government expropriated property owned by foreigners and emigrants and nationalized, with partial compensation, property held by natives.
3. Expenditures for health, education, and other public services were mostly for the benefit of the poor.

[20] Montek S. Ahluwalia, Nicholas G. Carter, and Hollis B. Chenery, "Growth and Poverty in Developing Countries," *Journal of Development Economics* 6 (September 1979): 320–23.

[21] Nick Eberstadt, "China: How Much Success?" *New York Review of Books* 26, no. 7 (May 3, 1979): 39–46.

TABLE 6-6 Changes in Income Distribution in Selected Countries (in 1970 U.S. dollars adjusted for purchasing power)

Country	Period of Observation	Per Capita Income Initial Year	Increments in per Capita Income			Share of Bottom 60 Percent			Growth Rate in per Capita Income	
			Total	Top 40 Percent	Bottom 60 Percent	Initial	Final	Incremental	Total	Bottom 60 Percent
(I) Good performance										
Taiwan	1964–74	562	508	758	341	0.369	0.385	0.395	6.6	7.1
Yugoslavia	1963–73	1,003	518	822	316	0.357	0.360	0.365	4.2	4.3
Sri Lanka	1963–73	388	84	58	101	0.274	0.354	0.513	2.0	4.6
Korea	1965–76	362	540	938	275	0.349	0.323	0.311	8.7	7.9
(II) Intermediate performance										
India	1954–64	226	58	113	21	0.310	0.292	0.258	2.3	1.6
Philippines	1961–71	336	83	155	35	0.247	0.248	0.250	2.2	2.3
Turkey	1963–73	566	243	417	128	0.208	0.240	0.279	3.6	5.1
Columbia	1964–74	648	232	422	106	0.190	0.212	0.240	3.1	4.3
(III) Poor performance										
Brazil	1960–70	615	214	490	31	0.248	0.206	0.155	3.1	1.2
Mexico	1963–75	974	446	944	114	0.217	0.197	0.180	3.2	2.4
Peru	1961–71	834	212	435	63	0.179	0.179	0.179	2.3	2.3

Source: Montek S. Ahluwalia, Nicholas G. Carter, and Hollis B. Chenery, "Growth and Poverty in Developing Countries," *Journal of Development Economics* 6 (September 1979): 322.

4. Employment was guaranteed for able-bodied workers.

5. Minimum wages were increased, pensions were made universal, and salaries and perquisites for management were reduced.

6. Low prices for food, bus transport, and many other basic goods and services were maintained, and charges for education and medical care, and the loan obligations of small farm owners were eliminated.

Nevertheless progress was slow in providing food, housing, and consumer goods in the late 1960s, 1970s, and 1980s.[22]

Sri Lanka

From independence in 1948 to 1977, Sri Lanka, which spent about half of its recurrent governmental expenditures for food subsidy, health, and educational programs, has made much progress in meeting its population's basic needs. In the late 1960s and early to middle 1970s, about 20 percent of these expenditures (10 percent of GNP) was for food subsidies, including a free ration of 0.5–1.0 kilograms of rice per week for each person (the remainder sold at a subsidized price). Unlike its large, diverse neighbor, India, Sri Lanka's food programs effectively fed the poor and those in rural areas. The direct ration provided about 20 percent of the calories and 15 percent of the incomes of the poorest 20 percent of the population. In contrast to programs that redistribute cash or assets, there were fewer political obstacles to food redistribution.

One percent of Sri Lanka's population, compared to 25 percent in Bangladesh, subsisted on less than 1700 calories per day in 1970. The food subsidy program reduced mortality and malnutrition greatly. The mortality rate was much lower in Sri Lanka than in Bangladesh, although when cuts in the ration and subsidy were made during periods of high food prices in Sri Lanka, mortality rates increased significantly.[23]

Yet Sri Lanka's basic needs policies were achieved at the expense of resources needed for employment and investment. High enrollment rates and weak curricula contributed to a secondary-school-graduate unemployment rate of over 25 percent and to an overall unemployment rate of 20 percent in 1977. Additionally low food prices hurt agricultural growth, and high business taxes and pervasive government controls discouraged investment. The post-1977 Junius Jayewardene government cut food subsidies and other social spending as part of a strategy for improving farm incentives and attracting foreign investment.

Other Nonsocialist Countries

In many developing countries, including India, Brazil, Mexico (see Table 6-6), Argentina, Panama, and Malaysia, the income share of the poorest people apparently declined over time. In India the constitution and five-year plans stressed removing economic injustices, abolishing poverty, and improving income distribu-

---

[22] Dudley Seers, "Cuba," in Hollis Chenery, Montek S. Ahluwalia, C. L. G. Bell, John H. Duloy, and Richard Jolly, eds., *Redistribution with Growth* (London: Oxford University Press, 1974), pp. 262–68.

[23] Paul Iseman, "Basic Needs: The Case of Sri Lanka," *World Development* 8 (March 1980): 237–58; and World Bank, *World Development Report, 1980* (New York: Oxford University Press, 1980), p. 62.

tion. Beginning in the 1950s, numerous programs were undertaken to achieve these goals, including land reform, village cooperatives, community development, credit and services for the rural poor, educational and food subsidies, minimum wages, rural employment programs, and direct provision for upgrading health, sanitation, nutrition, drinking water, housing, education, transport, communication, and electricity for the poor. But overall progress was limited: Income shares for the poor dropped from the 1950s through the mid-1970s, and remained constant from the late 1970s to the late 1980s, while according to government studies, no appreciable dent was made on absolute poverty.

In India's democracy, the poor pressured political leaders to adopt programs aimed at improving the lot of weaker sections of the population. However, the landed and business classes dominated the government service and legislatures, and it was not in their interest to administer effectively programs that helped the underprivileged at their expense. Thus by 1970, only 0.3 percent of the total land cultivated had been distributed under land legislation. Furthermore, laws were frequently enacted with loopholes and exemptions that allowed land transfers to relatives, keeping land concentrated in the hands of a few families. Also large moneylenders, farmers, and traders controlled village cooperatives and used most of the social services and capital provided by community development programs.[24]

POLICIES TO REDUCE POVERTY AND INCOME INEQUALITY

As we discussed in an earlier section, the inverted U-shaped curve descriptive of income inequality rises in early stages of development and drops later on. Moreover income inequality worsens as income increases from low to middle levels and then improves as income advances from middle to high levels.

This pattern however may be a consequence of deliberate economic policies. Greater inequality is probably a result of past policies that incorrectly assumed benefits would eventually trickle down to the poor. Furthermore many mixed and capitalist LDCs emphasized the growth of the urban-oriented, highly technological, highly mechanized production of Western-style consumer goods. They neglected production patterns based on indigenous tastes, processes, and factor endowments.

Income inequality decreased in some countries that pursued other strategies in early stages of development—the socialist countries, as well as South Korea, Taiwan, and Sri Lanka. This section outlines some of the policies that may succeed in reducing poverty and income inequality.

Policies in Socialist LDCs

Income inequality is greatest between people whose principal income is from capital, land, and entrepreneurship and those whose primary income is from wages.

[24] Pranab K. Barhan, "India", in Hollis Chenery, Montek S. Ahluwalia, C. L. G. Bell, John H. Duloy, and Richard Jolly, eds., *Redistribution with Growth* (London: Oxford University Press, 1974), pp. 255–62; and David Morawetz, *Twenty-five Years of Economic Development, 1950 to 1975* (Baltimore: Johns Hopkins Press, 1977), pp. 39–41. For studies indicating a decline in the income and asset shares of the poor, see India, Ministry of Agriculture and Irrigation, *Report of the National Commission on Agriculture, 1976* (New Delhi, 1976); and R. P. Pathak, K. R. Ganapathy, and Y. U. K. Sarma, "Shifts in Patterns of Asset-Holdings of Rural Households, 1961–62 to 1971–72," *Economic and Political Weekly* 12 (March 19, 1977): 507–17.

Therefore socialist economists argue that, though capital and land are productive, their owners need not be paid, since private ownership is no more productive than social ownership. Under socialism profits, rents, and interest can be distributed to the whole society. Hence income is more evenly distributed in socialist countries than in mixed and capitalist countries.

Policies in Mixed and Capitalist LDCs

Still for reasons of efficiency, innovation, or resistance to radical change, a country may not wish to pursue socialist strategies. Opposition to radical change in the economic or political system may preclude reducing income inequality in highly concentrated, rigid social systems, such as those in Latin America. Even so, as empirical evidence indicates, *evolutionary* policy changes will improve income distribution in most mixed and capitalist LDCs.[25]

As might be expected, the initial distribution of assets and income is crucial in determining income inequality. People who already own property, hold an influential position, and have a good education are in the best position to profit as growth proceeds. Thus a society with high income inequality is likely to remain unequal or become more so, whereas one with small disparities may be able to avoid large increases in inequality. It simply may not be possible to grow first and redistribute later, because early social and economic position may have already fixed the distribution pattern. To reduce poverty and improve income equality, land reform (discussed in Chapter 7), mass education, and other such goals may have to be set immediately rather than taken up after growth is well under way.[26]

Capital and Credit. In LDCs generally, the poor live primarily from their labor and the rich on returns from property ownership. Not only do the poor have little capital, their poverty also limits their ability to respond to good investment opportunities, such as new seed varieties, fertilizer, tools or their children's education.

Government efforts to supplant traditional money lenders in providing credit for the poor have had only limited success. Even public agencies require collateral. People with few assets can rarely meet such a standard. Furthermore the substantial staff time needed to process and supervise loans and perhaps arrange technical assistance, as well as the higher risk of bad debts, make it difficult for these credit programs to be self-supporting. Moreover the limited amount of subsidized credit has frequently not wound up in the hands of the poor, but of more influential groups.

Public investment in roads, schools, irrigation projects, and other infrastruc-

---

[25] Montek S. Ahluwalia, Nicholas G. Carter, and Hollis B. Chenery, "Growth and Poverty in Developing Countries," *Journal of Development Economics* 6 (September 1979), 299–341; Irma Adelman and Sherman Robinson, *Income Distribution Policy in Developing Countries: A Case Study of Korea* (Stanford: Stanford University Press, 1978); and Charles R. Frank, Jr., and Richard C. Webb, eds., *Income Distribution and Growth in the Less-Developed Countries* (Washington, D.C.: Brookings Institution, 1977).

[26] David Morawetz, *Twenty-five Years of Economic Development, 1950 to 1975* (Baltimore: Johns Hopkins University Press, 1977), p. 41; and E. Wayne Nafziger, "Class, Caste, and Community of South Indian Industrialists: An Examination of the Horatio Alger Model," *Journal of Development Studies* 11 (January 1975): 131–48.

ture, if made in underprivileged areas, can provide direct benefits for the poor, increase their productivity, or provide jobs for them.[27]

Education and Training.   **Human capital** as well as physical capital can yield a stream of income over time. Nobel laureate Theodore W. Schultz argues that a society can invest in its citizens through expenditures on education, training, research, and health that enhance their productive capacity.[28] Universal, free, primary education is a major way of redistributing human capital to the relative benefit of the poor. High primary enrollment rates are associated with relatively high income shares for the bottom 40 percent of the population (see Chapter 10).[29]

Employment Programs.   Unemployment in LDCs is a major concern. It leads to economic inefficiency and political discontent as well as having obvious implications for income distribution. Open unemployment, in which a person without a job actively seeks employment, is largely an urban phenomenon in LDCs. The unemployed are mainly in their teens and early twenties and usually primary or secondary school graduates. It is rare for unemployed youth to seek an urban job without family support.

Some policies to reduce unemployment include faster industrial expansion, more labor-intensive production in manufacturing, a reduction in factor price distortion, greater economic development and social services in rural areas, a more relevant educational system, greater consistency between educational policy and economic planning, and more reliance on the market in setting wage rates.

Health and Nutrition.   Sickness and insufficient food limit the employment opportunities and earning power of the poor. Food subsidies or free rations increase the income of the poor, lead to better health and nutrition, permit people to work more days in a year, and enhance their effectiveness at work. However because of the expense of food programs, they are not likely to be continued unless food production per capita is maintained or raised. Poverty is a terribly circular affliction.

Population Programs.   Chapter 9 maintains that the living levels of the poor are improved by smaller family size, since each adult has fewer dependents.

Research and Technology.   The benefits of research and new technology in reducing poverty are most apparent in agriculture. The introduction of high-yielding varieties of wheat and rice—the **Green Revolution**—has increased food supplies for the poor and in some instances, small farmer incomes. But much more

[27] World Bank, *World Development Report, 1980* (New York: Oxford University Press, 1980), pp. 41–42.

[28] Theodore W. Schultz, *Transforming Traditional Agriculture* (New Haven: Yale University Press, 1964).

[29] Montek S. Ahluwalia, "Income Inequality," in Hollis Chenery, Montek S. Ahluwalia, C. L. G. Bell, John H. Duloy, and Richard Jolly, eds., *Redistribution with Growth* (London: Oxford University Press, 1974), p. 17; and George Psacharopoulos and Maureen Woodhall, *Education for Development: An Analysis of Investment Choice* (New York: Oxford University Press, 1985), pp. 258–64.

research is needed to improve the productivity of food crops on which many low-income farmers depend and to increase jobs and cheap consumer goods output in industry.

Migration.   As development proceeds, more jobs are created in the industrial, urban sector, so people move to the cities. Despite some problems, the living standards of migrants employed in the cities, though low, tend to be above those of the rural poor. Generally city workers send money home, so that farm land has to support fewer people, both of which benefit the rural poor.

Taxes.   Chapter 15 discusses tax schemes, such as the progressive income tax, to reduce income inequality.

Transfers and Subsidies.   In developed countries, antipoverty programs include income transfers to the old, the very young, the ill, the handicapped, the unemployed, and those whose earning power is below a living wage. But except for some middle-income countries, such as Brazil and Turkey, most developing countries cannot support such programs. For example, in Bangladesh, where almost two-thirds of the population is poor and undernourished (see Table 6-3), welfare payments to bring the population above the poverty line would undermine work incentives and be prohibitively expensive.

An alternative approach is subsidizing or rationing cheap foodstuffs. Subsidizing foods that higher income groups do not eat benefits the poor. For example, sorghum, introduced into ration shops in Bangladesh in 1978, was bought by nearly 70 percent of low-income households but by only 2 percent of high-income households.[30]

Emphasis on Target Group.   Another strategy for improving the lot of the poor is to target certain programs for the poorest groups. India has an affirmative action program favoring the placement of outcastes and other economically "backward castes" when openings in educational institutions and government positions occur. A number of countries, including India, use industrial incentives and subsidies to help economically backward regions and train business people from underprivileged groups. Some countries have tried to improve female literacy and educational rates. Others have stressed health and nutritional programs for expectant and nursing mothers and children. Improvements in social security, provident funds and pensions benefit the elderly. Upgrading housing in urban areas can increase real income among the poor. Finally some LDCs in a reversal of the policies of the 1950s and 1960s, have stressed development in the rural areas where most poor live.

Integrated War on Poverty.   A study by Irma Adelman and Sherman Robinson indicates that, taken singly, most of these policies cannot end rising income inequality occurring with development. Only a total mobilization of government policies toward programs to help the poor directly—a war on poverty—succeeds in reducing income inequality and increasing absolute incomes. And successful nonsocialist

---

[30] World Bank, *World Development Report, 1980* (New York: Oxford University Press, 1980), pp. 42–45, 51, 62.

countries, such as Taiwan, South Korea, Israel, and Singapore, all redistributed before growth. For Adelman and Robinson, the redistributed asset changes with the level of economic development. At first when the economy is primarily agricultural, land is redistributed. With further development, the primary asset is physical capital. At a later stage, the redistribution of human capital through education and training for the poor is emphasized.[31]

Growth-oriented Policies.   Accelerating economic growth is perhaps the most satisfactory *political* approach to reducing poverty. A number of upper-middle-income countries, such as Malaysia and Thailand, have decreased poverty a great deal through rapid economic growth; and historically workers gain more from a larger GNP pie than from a larger share of a pie that remains the same size. When the income pie is not enlarged, any gains the underprivileged classes make are at the expense of the more privileged classes: Such a redistribution from the higher to lower income classes is difficult to achieve politically. However when the GNP pie grows, the piece of pie can be larger for both privileged and underprivileged groups. Chapters 14–20 focus on ways of accelerating growth. As the next section indicates, the questions of poverty, inequality, and government policy are intertwined with those of political order.

INEQUALITY AND POLITICAL INSTABILITY

Only rarely has peasant discontent led to revolutionary insurrection. China's civil war (1927–49) is a modern example. Yet given the substantial income inequalities within many developing states, the noteworthy point may not be the few economically deprived that rebel against political authority, but the vast majority who do not. Karl Marx expected that as workers united and became more powerful and comprised a majority of the population, they would revolt and appropriate capital and land. Yet wage earners did not revolt when they were in a majority in the West, and there is no indication that this will occur among workers in the developing world. The state has the military and police power to neutralize or suppress rebellion. Furthermore the economically disadvantaged are rarely united, since their interests vary; and in any event, the political elite can usually reward potentially restive groups who cooperate with it and thus remains in control. The poor remain unorganized; the state remains intact.

Despite the popularly *perceived* economic discrepancy between what ought to be and what is, a tension termed **relative deprivation,** actual political violence rarely occurs. The likelihood of powerfully felt relative deprivation, common experiences and beliefs that sanction violence, the ideological support of other groups, protection from retribution, and cues for violence all determine whether or not the deprived will rebel.[32] Furthermore the political leadership does not simply rule by force and fraud but represents the interests and purposes of important and influential groups in society. Usually the power elite sees to it that the ideological positions of the media, schools, and religious communities do not contradict its interest.

---

[31] Irma Adelman and Sherman Robinson, *Income Distribution Policy in Developing Countries: A Case Study of Korea* (Stanford: Stanford University Press, 1978).

[32] Ted Robert Gurr, *Why Men Rebel* (Princeton: Princeton University Press, 1970).

Prevailing political and religious ideologies legitimate inequalities associated with class, occupation, and caste.

Despite all of these tendencies to maintain political stability, representatives of the developing world increasingly stress the inequalities, injustices, and tensions of the *global* economy and polity when explaining poverty and underdevelopment in their own countries. Their views of income distribution and class antagonisms go beyond differences within countries to include greater discrepancies between countries. Rich countries are seen as controlling the international economy, and most of the U.S. and Canadian readers of this book are viewed as members of an international upper class and beneficiaries of an unjust international order.

Thus people who perceive a highly interrelated global system dominated by rich countries are not surprised when political enmities and disorder in Latin America, West Africa, and the Middle East threaten the material comforts and political tranquility of middle-class Americans. This perception is a far cry from that of most Americans, for whom riots, terrorism, holding hostages, and armed attacks directed against rich countries are often capricious, arbitrary, and inexplicable. Herman E. Daly argues that the wide gap in economic well-being between the rich and poor, the increasing material aspirations of poor countries, and the rich's tenacious defense of their living standards are a threat to all of our human activities, a threat to "spaceship earth" itself (see Chapter 8).[33]

SUMMARY

1. The best current definition of the international poverty line is the income needed for a daily supply of 2250 calories per person in India. Based on this figure, in 1990 about 1.5 billion of the 4.0 billion population in LDCs were poor.

2. People in absolute poverty are undernourished and have low resistance to disease. A high infant mortality rate, a life expectancy of about 40 years, and illiteracy characterize this group.

3. Only 4 percent of the real income in the world goes to the poorest 40 percent of the world's population, while the richest 20 percent receives 70 percent of it. Income inequality worldwide exceeds that for any single country.

4. Early economic development in LDCs often results in increasing poverty for the lowest income groups. Inequality follows an inverted U-shaped pattern, first increasing and then decreasing with growth in per capita income.

5. Although middle-income countries tend to have higher income inequality than low-income countries, inequality increases in low-income states with economic development.

6. Developed countries have lower income inequality than developing countries.

7. Although absolute poverty is present in upper-middle-income countries with high inequalities, such as Mexico and Brazil, most absolute poverty is in Indonesia, India, Bangladesh, Pakistan, and parts of sub-Saharan Africa, which have low per capita income and low to moderate inequality.

[33] Herman E. Daly, *Steady-state Economics: The Economics of Biophysical Equilibrium and Moral Growth* (San Francisco: W. H. Freeman, 1977).

8. The rate of economic growth is not associated with the degree of income inequality.

9. Socialist countries have the lowest income inequality mainly because individuals do not receive income from property ownership.

10. Among developing regions, South Asia has the greatest poverty, even though its income inequality is lowest. Latin America has the highest inequality but the lowest poverty percentage of LDC regions.

11. Oil-exporting LDCs have lower poverty rates and higher income inequality than oil-importing LDCs.

12. Minority groups, rural residents, women, children, the elderly, and the illiterate are highly represented among the world's poor.

13. Women comprise 32 percent of the LDC labor force and receive an average income half that of men, partly because of discrimination.

14. Cuba's emphasis on land redistribution and low-priced social services for the poor; Taiwan's and South Korea's stress on land reform, education, and labor-intensive manufacturing; and Sri Lanka's programs for universal primary education and free rice distribution have succeeded in increasing income shares of the poorest segments of their populations. On the other hand, many of India's programs to aid the poor were circumvented by administrators, landlords, and business people whose economic interests were threatened by such efforts.

15. Policies used to reduce poverty and income inequality include socialization of the means of production, credit for the poor, universal primary education, employment programs, rural development schemes, progressive income taxes, food subsidies, health programs, family planning, food research, inducements to migration, income transfers, and affirmative action programs. However an integrated war on poverty requiring a total mobilization of government policies toward programs to help the poor is probably necessary if poverty and inequality are to be substantially reduced.

16. Despite the vast poverty and inequality in LDCs, the economically disadvantaged rarely rebel against the state.

TERMS TO REVIEW

- absolute poverty
- poverty line
- Lorenz curve

- Gini index of inequality
- human capital
- Green Revolution

- crowding
- relative deprivation

QUESTIONS TO DISCUSS

1. What is an international poverty line? What are some of its advantages and disadvantages?

2. What is meant by absolute poverty? What are some characteristics of absolute poverty?

3. Assess the reliability and validity of LDC statistics on poverty and income inequality.

4. Which of the following have been more successful in reducing absolute poverty and income inequality in recent decades: Developed or developing countries? Low- or middle-income countries? Countries in early or late stages of development? Slow or fast growers? Socialist or nonsocialist countries? Oil importers or exporters?

5. Does the rising segment of the inverted U-shaped curve imply that the poor suffer from economic growth?

6. Why are cross-national income distribution data for different per capita income levels *at a given time* inadequate for generalizing about income distribution changes with economic development over time?

7. Which policies do you think are most effective in reducing poverty and income inequality in mixed and capitalist LDCs?

8. Discuss why LDC women have higher poverty rates than men. What LDC policies would reduce female poverty rates?

9. What is the tradeoff between LDC policies seeking to reduce income inequality and those trying to stimulate growth? Should the tradeoff vary between different LDCs?

10. What conditions do you think are necessary for economic inequalities to contribute to political upheaval?

GUIDE TO READINGS

Data on LDC poverty and income distribution are included in Lecaillon, Paukert, Morrisson, and Germidis (note 10), Ahluwalia, Carter, and Chenery (note 4), Ahluwalia (first citation, note 15), and the appendix to the annual *World Development Report*. The International Labor Organization has published studies on income distribution and basic needs in a number of LDCs (similar to note 2). Fields (note 10) has a good survey of the literature; however, it does not include the studies just noted and may be difficult for some undergraduate students. Major studies with data from earlier periods are Morris and Adelman (note 10); Chenery et al (note 15); and William Loehr and John P. Powelson, eds., *Economic Development, Poverty, and Income Distribution* (Boulder, Colo.: Westview, 1977).

Major studies of policies for improving income distribution include Chenery et al. (note 15), Adelman and Robinson, and Frank and Webb (note 25). Graham Pyatt and Erik Thorbecke discuss planning to reduce poverty in *Planning Techniques for a Better Future* (Geneva: International Labor Office, 1976).

Eberstadt (note 21) and World Bank, *China: Socialist Economic Development* I (Washington, 1983) have an excellent discussion of poverty and income inequality in China. Contrary to the prevailing view, Whyte (Chapter 7, note 42) concludes that China's income inequality declined from the Maoist period (1949–76) to the post-1979 period of decentralized agricultural reform (see "Collective Farms or Communes," Chapter 7).

R. M. Sundrum, *Growth and Income Distribution in India* (Newbury Park, Calif.: Sage, 1987), analyzes poverty and income distribution in India. Nafziger (note 19) focuses on explanations for income inequality in sub-Saharan Africa.

World Development 16 (January 1988), has a special issue devoted to South Korea, and *World Development* 15 (January 1987), an issue on Cuba. Tinker, Bramsen, and Buvinić (note 18), Parpart, and the UN (note 19) look at the role of women in economic development.

Gerry Rodgers, ed., *Urban Poverty and the Labour Market: Access to Jobs and Incomes in Asian ad Latin American Cities* (Geneva: International Labor Office, 1989), discusses how the labor market influences urban poverty.

Chapter Seven

RURAL POVERTY AND AGRICULTURAL TRANSFORMATION

About 70 percent of the population and 80 percent of the poor in LDCs live in rural areas. Thus any strategy to reduce poverty and accelerate economic growth should focus on rural development.

SCOPE OF THE CHAPTER

This chapter examines rural poverty and indicates policies to ameliorate it. Our approach is ninefold;

1. We look at the nature of poverty in rural areas in LDCs (though the information available is limited).
2. We identify major rural groups comprising the poor.
3. We discuss the differences between rural and agricultural development.
4. We show that present-day, rural-urban differences in LDCs are greater than in the West in the nineteenth century.
5. We compare agricultural productivity in DCs and LDCs and in China and India.
6. We examine the transition from subsistence to specialized farming to clarify what farming is like in LDCs.
7. We compare the growth of food production per capita in LDCs and DCs.

8. We discuss factors contributing to low income in rural areas.

9. Finally and perhaps most importantly, we examine policies that might increase income and reduce poverty in rural areas.

TRENDS IN RURAL POVERTY IN DEVELOPING COUNTRIES

Despite real economic growth (both overall and in agriculture) in several major South and Southeast Asian countries during the 1960s and 1970s, the proportion of the rural population in poverty in these regions increased (see Figure 7-1), and the average real wages of agricultural laborers declined. Even in the Indian state of Punjab, where the green revolution raised average income dramatically from the 1960s to the 1970s, the percentage of the rural population living in poverty rose (Figure 7-1).[1] For other LDCs, the evidence is less clear except in sub-Saharan Africa, which experienced negative growth in agriculture and increasing rural poverty rates from the late 1960s through the mid to late 1980s.[2] Data suggest that although the number of rural poor may have increased slightly, the percentage of the rural population in poverty in the third world as a whole decreased during the 1960s and 1970s. In the 1980s, both LDC rural poverty and its percentage probably declined.

MAJOR RURAL GROUPS IN POVERTY

The widespread assumption among development economists in the 1950s and 1960s that agrarian societies are characterized by roughly uniform poverty is a myth.[3] Rural society is highly differentiated, comprising a complex structure of rich landowners, peasants, sharecroppers, tenants, and laborers, in addition to artisans, traders, and plantation workers. In most LDCs, it is the agricultural laborers, the landless, and the near-landless who comprise the poor. As an example, if we use the poverty line definition formulated in Chapter 6 (the income needed for a 2250-calorie diet per day per person in India), 48 million, or 56 percent, of the 85 million people in Uttar Pradesh state, India, in 1969 were poor. Seventy-five percent of the total state population is in agriculture, but 85 percent of the poor (41 million people) were farm workers or farmers with no more than one–half to one hectare of land. About 12 million, or 93 percent, of the 13 million agricultural laborers in the state were living below the poverty line.[4]

---

[1] Data on poverty for the 1960s and 1970s are comparable in a given region, but not between regions. Thus comparisons in Figure 7-1 between Tamil Nadu during the 1960s and 1970s are more reliable than those between Tamil Nadu and Malaysia during a given period.

International Labor Office (ILO), *Profiles of Rural Poverty* (Geneva, 1979); World Bank, *World Development Report, 1988* (New York: Oxford University Press, 1988), p. 285; and Keith Griffin and Azizur Rahman Khan, "Poverty in the Third World: Ugly Facts and Fancy Models," *World Development* 1 (March 1978): 295–304.

[2] E. Wayne Nafziger, *Inequality in Africa: Political Elites, Proletariat, Peasants, and the Poor* (Cambridge: Cambridge University Press, 1988), pp. 16–34, 140–56.

[3] See Henry J. Bruton, *Principles of Development Economics* (Englewood Cliffs, N.J.: Prentice-Hall, 1965), p. 100.

[4] International Labor Office, *Profiles of Rural Poverty* (Geneva, 1979), pp. 9–12.

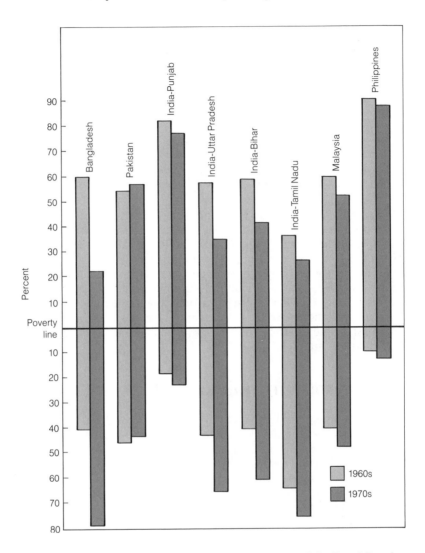

FIGURE 7-1 The Advance of Poverty: Percentage of the Rural Population in South and Southeast Asia Living above and below the Poverty Line The percentage of the rural population in poverty was higher in the 1970s than it was in the 1960s for seven of the eight South and Southeast Asian cases studied.

Source: International Labor Office, *Profiles of Rural Poverty* (Geneva, 1979), p. 8.

RURAL AND AGRICULTURAL DEVELOPMENT

Rural development is not the same as agricultural development. The agrarian community requires a full range of services such as schools, shops, banks, machinery dealerships, and so on. Often rural areas use surplus agricultural labor, either seasonally or full-time, in industry. Thus in Maoist China from 1958 to 1976, rural development was based on the people's commune, which provided economies of scale for social services and mobilized underemployed labor for manufacturing, constructing machine tools, building roads and dams, and digging irrigation channels. Furthermore many LDC farmers are employed part-time, and other family members full-time, in off-farm enterprises. Finally some farmers actually live in urban areas. Thus rural development includes more than agricultural income growth.

RURAL-URBAN INCOME DIFFERENTIALS IN NINETEENTH-CENTURY EUROPE AND PRESENT-DAY LDCS

Contemporary rural-urban differentials in LDCs are much greater than they were in Europe in the nineteenth century. Output per person outside agriculture, as a multiple of the figure in agriculture, is eight in Africa and four in Asia and Latin America. It was two in Europe in the nineteenth century (see Table 7-1). However, discrepancies between urban and rural areas in income per person are not so high as nonagricultural-agricultural differences indicate because (1) urban agriculturalists have a lower average income than others in urban areas; (2) rural nonagriculturalists have a higher average income than others in rural areas; and (3) rural worker participation rates (which include proportionally more women and children) are high.

AGRICULTURAL PRODUCTIVITY IN DCS AND LDCS

How does agricultural productivity differ between LDCs and DCs? Agricultural output per worker in developing countries is one–eighteenth of that in developed countries and one–eightieth of that in North America (Table 7-2). Obviously world agriculture is highly diverse. On the one hand is the highly efficient agriculture of the affluent countries where high levels of capital accumulation, technical knowledge, and worker productivity permit a small farm population to feed entire nations. In contrast is the low-productive agriculture in most developing countries that barely sustains the population, including a minority off the farm, at a subsistence level.

SMALL-SCALE LDC AGRICULTURE

The evolution of agricultural production commonly occurs in three stages: (1) **peasant farming,** where the major concern is survival; (2) **mixed farming;** and (3) **commercial farming.**[5] If you have seen only the highly specialized, mechanized farms of the United States and Canada, it may be hard for you to visualize the subsistence agriculture that is the livelihood of most farmers in LDCs. On the traditional peasant farm, output and consumption are almost identical, and the staple crop (usually wheat, barley, sorghum, rice, or corn) is the chief source of

[5] This discussion draws on Raanan Weitz, *From Peasant to Farmer: A Revolutionary Strategy for Development* (New York: Columbia University Press, 1971), pp. 6–28.

TABLE 7-1 Output per Person Outside Agriculture As a Multiple of Output per Person in Agriculture: Contemporary LDCs Compared to Europe and Japan in the Nineteenth Century

LDCs (1970)		Europe and Japan (nineteenth century)		
Zaïre	40.8			
Zambia	34.9			
Saudi Arabia	23.5			
Tanzania	10.9			
Ivory Coast	9.5			
Kenya	8.9			
Lebanon	8.0			
Mexico	7.2			
Thailand	6.7			
South Vietnam	6.6			
Sierra Leone	6.0			
Turkey	6.0			
Philippines	5.4			
Ethiopia	4.6			
Chile	4.4			
Iraq	4.0			
Venezuela	4.0			
Brazil	3.9			
Malaysia	3.8			
South Africa	3.8			
Syria	3.7			
Burma	3.6			
Morocco	3.5			
South Korea	3.5			
		Norway	1865	3.4
Pakistan	3.2			
India	3.1			
Jordan	3.1			
Taiwan	3.0			
Iran	2.8			
		Japan	1880	2.7
		Sweden	1863	2.7
Costa Rica	2.6			
Indonesia	2.4			
Colombia	2.2			
Sri Lanka	2.2			
Nigeria	2.0			
		Germany	1857	1.7
		Netherlands	1860	1.7
Benin	1.6	Italy	1898	1.6
		Denmark	1872	1.1
		France	1830	1.1
		Great Britain	1801	1.1

Source: Michael Lipton, *Why Poor People Stay Poor: A Study of Urban Bias in World Development* (London: Maurice Temple Smith, 1977), pp. 435–37.

TABLE 7-2 Agricultural Output per Agricultural Worker—World and Regions, 1964–66 to 1986–88 (1979–81 world = 100)

Region	AGRICULTURAL OUTPUT PER AGRICULTURAL WORKER					
	1964–66	1969–71	1974–76	1979–81	1984–86	1986–88
Developed capitalist	553	733	917	1231	1532	1611
North America	2268	2873	3115	3617	4332	4429
Western Europe	435	593	742	968	1233	1318
Oceania	2666	3110	3149	3288	3782	3982
Other	120	160	216	319	389	423
Developed socialist (Eastern Europe and USSR)	220	306	371	419	541	600
All developed countries	372	502	613	765	964	1032
Developing nonsocialist	52	57	60	65	70	71
Africa	39	41	41	39	40	41
Far East	34	38	41	45	50	50
Latin America	186	205	226	261	280	286
Near East	78	88	102	114	128	286
Other	58	62	65	73	76	78
Developing socialist (Asia)	25	27	29	32	38	39
All developing countries	40	43	46	50	55	56
World	82	90	95	100	107	107

Source: J. Ay, "Agricultural Output per Agricultural Worker," Rome: Food and Agriculture Organization of the United Nations, June 1989. I am grateful to J. Ay for compiling this table for this book.

food. Land and labor are the key production factors, and capital is small. Labor, however, is underutilized except for peak seasons, such as planting and harvest. Cultivators—small owners, tenants, or sharecroppers—farm only as much land as their families can work without hired labor.

For many this way of life is changing. An increasing number of peasants, pressured by a growing rural population per cultivated acre, attracted by productivity gains from new capital and technology, and stirred by mass communications to higher consumer expectations, are producing crops for the market. Yet change does not take place so rapidly as the Western observer expects. Peasant resistance to change, which appears irrational to the Westerner, may in fact be prudent. The prime objective of the peasant is not to maximize income but his or her family's chance of survival.

Attempts to improve the situation of subsistence farmers by an indiscriminate introduction of cash crops often result in a greater risk to the survival of the peasant's family without any major increase in its average consumption. In parts of South Asia and Latin America, peasants who grow cash crops earn so little that at least three-quarters of their income is spent on food. In fact commercial farming is often a more precarious operation than subsistence farming: Prices fluctuate, necessary materials are scarce, and the weather remains unpredictable.

For many mixed farming rather than highly specialized commercial farming is the first step away from subsistence agriculture. Production branches off into other enterprises besides the staple crop, such as fruits, vegetables, and animal husbandry. This change begins with improved productivity through technological advances, capital formation, or using resources underemployed in subsistence farming, and it varies depending on the particular conditions of the farm. For example, if the staple crop is grown only part of the year, new crops may be introduced in the slack season to use idle land and family labor, or more crops may be grown as a result of mixed cropping, irrigation, or using new seed varieties. Reducing labor requirements in the peak seasons by introducing simple labor-saving techniques can lead to new enterprises, such as cattle or poultry farming. Improved seeds, fertilizer, and irrigation may yield more food and free some land for cash crops. Thus the farmer will have a marketable surplus for cash income. By spreading the work load more evenly throughout the year, diversified farming uses more of the available labor. Mixed farming can also provide more security to the operator. If one crop is destroyed by pests, disease, or natural calamity or sells at a low price, others may do better.

The specialized farm, the most advanced agricultural phase in a market economy, usually emphasizes cultivating one crop. Such a farm is capital intensive, uses advanced technology, and takes advantage of economies of scale and expanding national and international markets. The farmer no longer grows crops for the family but for the market.

Concentrating on one major crop appears quite risky. It seems to return the farm to the unbalanced work schedule and dependence on a single crop of the subsistence phase. However, the specialized farm uses labor-saving devices that decrease the work load at peak periods, so that the slack season can be used for other activities, such as plowing, fertilizing, maintaining equipment, and catching up with the latest literature. Furthermore some of the risks of one-crop farming can be overcome by insurance policies, pesticides, market research, and irrigation. Also the income from specialized farming is so much higher than from other forms of farm production that it outweighs occasional losses from bad weather or price fluctuations.

Even when agricultural output per person grows, the transition from peasant to specialized farmer usually increases the number of landless laborers. Indeed the change of many farm cultivators to hired workers during growing commercialization may be partly responsible for the increased rural poverty noted in South and Southeast Asia in the 1960s and 1970s.

GROWTH OF AVERAGE FOOD PRODUCTION IN DCS AND LDCS

Both agricultural and food outputs per worker in LDCs are fractions of the same measures in DCs. How does the *growth* of food production per capita in LDCs compare to that in DCs? Figure 7-2 indicates that food output per person in developed countries grew at an annual rate of 0.9 percent from 1952 to 1984, and in developing countries, at a rate of 0.6 percent per year (DCs, 0.7 percent and LDCs, 0.4 percent yearly, 1960–84). Even India, whose food system is considered by two agriculturalists to be too inefficient and antiquated to be saved through assistance,[6]

---

[6] William Paddock and Paul Paddock, *Famine—1975! America's Decision: Who Will Survive?* (Boston: Little, Brown, 1967), pp. 217–22.

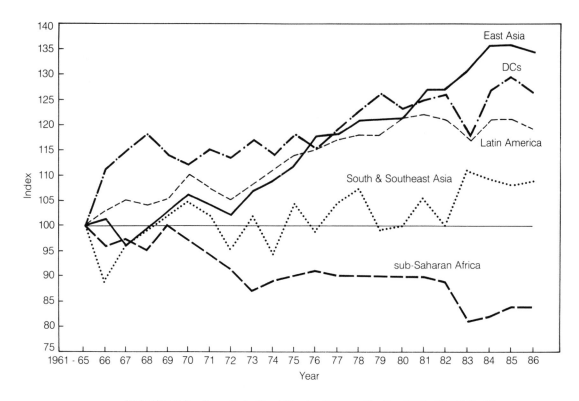

FIGURE 7-2   Growth in Food Production per Capita, 1961–86 (1961–65 = 100)   Per capita food production grew by 33 percent in developed countries from 1952 to 1984, and by 21 percent in developing countries during the same period (28 percent in Latin America; 32 percent in East Asia, excluding Japan and China; 22 percent in South and Southeast Asia; and −13 percent in sub-Saharan Africa). From 1960 to 1984, growth was 19 percent in the DCs and 12 percent in the LDCs (22 percent in Latin America; 15 percent in East Asia, excluding Japan and China; 28 percent in South and Southeast Asia; and −14 percent in sub-Saharan Africa). Although the graph shows year-to-year fluctuations, the figure for per capita food output for a given year *t* is an average of the figures for year *t* − 2 through *t* + 2.

Sources: U.S. Department of Agriculture, International Economic Division, *World Indices of Agricultural and Food Production, 1950–85* (Washington, D.C., 1986); U.S. Department of Agriculture, Economic Research Service, *World Indices of Agricultural and Food Production, 1976–85* (Washington, D.C., 1986); U.S. Department of Agriculture, Economic Research Service, *World Indices of Agricultural and Food Production, 1977–86* (Washington, D.C., 1988).

increased food production per person by 1.2 percent per year from 1952 to 1984. (Of course since the vagaries of weather make farm production volatile, alarmists can always distort figures to show reduction in per capita food grain production by beginning with a bumper crop, as in 1970 to 1971 in India, and ending with a poor harvest, as in 1972 to 1973 or 1979 to 1980. To avoid distortions due to weather fluctuations, I use a 5-year moving average in which food output in the year 1984, for instance, is computed as an average of the outputs of 1982 through 1986.)

Food output per capita increased from 1952 to 1984, in all LDC regions except sub-Saharan Africa, where it declined 0.4 percent annually (0.6 annually, 1960–84). Africa's daily calorie consumption per capita—2115 in the early 1960s and 2197 in the mid 1970s—was 20 percent below the Economic Commission for Africa's (ECA's) critical minimum. According to the World Bank, only the Ivory Coast, the Congo, Liberia, Senegal, and Madagascar had a daily consumption in 1983 that was not less than the minimum required. Ironically the World Bank's Berg report emphasizes Africa's marked contrast to India (and Pakistan), where expanded irrigated land used new high-yielding varieties of seeds in the Green Revolution.[7]

Africa's deteriorating food position began before the droughts in the Sahel, the Sudan, and Ethiopia in 1968 to 1974 and in 1984 to 1985. While the roots of Africa's food crisis began during colonialism, the continuing crisis is due to African governments' neglect of agriculture. Colonial policy contributed to today's agricultural underdevelopment. (1) Africans were systematically excluded from participating in colonial development schemes and producing export crops and improved cattle. British agricultural policy in Eastern Africa benefited European settlers and ignored and discriminated against African farmers, prohibiting Kenyans from growing coffee. (2) Colonial governments compelled farmers to grow selected crops and work to maintain roads. (3) Colonialism often changed traditional land tenure systems from communal or clan to individual control. This created greater inequalities from new classes of affluent farmers and ranchers, and less secure tenants, sharecroppers, and landless workers. (4) Colonialists failed to train African agricultural scientists and managers. (5) Research and development concentrated on export crops, plantations, and land settlement schemes, neglecting food production and small farmers and herders. (6) Europeans gained most from colonial land grants and agricultural export surpluses.[8] As indicated later in this chapter, the contemporary neglect of Africa's agriculture results partly from the political advantage to state leaders to intervene in the market to improve prices and incomes that urban classes receive relative to farmers.

World food production per capita, which grew between the 1950s and the 1980s, is expected to continue growing in the 1990s—even in LDCs, albeit at a slower rate than in the DCs. Meanwhile food demand per capita will continue to rise, though not so rapidly as increases in GNP per capita.

[7] Economic Commission for Africa, *ECA and Africa's Development, 1983–2008: A Preliminary Perspective Study* (Addis Ababa, 1983), p. 9; World Bank, *World Development Report, 1986,* (New York: Oxford University Press, 1986), pp. 88–94; and World Bank, *Accelerated Development in sub-Saharan Africa: An Agenda for Action* (Washington, D.C., 1981), p. 47. The last report is sometimes named for its coordinator, Elliot Berg.

[8] Carl K. Eicher and Doyle C. Baker, *Research on Agricultural Development in sub-Saharan Africa: A Critical Survey,* East Lansing: Michigan State University International Development Paper no. 1, 1982, pp. 20–23; and Dharan Ghai and Samir Radwan, eds., *Agrarian Policies and Rural Poverty in Africa* (Geneva: International Labor Office, 1983), pp. 16–21.

TABLE 7-3   Food Consumption and Food Deficits in Developing Countries, 1980 and 2000 (million metric tons and percentages)

Region	1980			2000[a]		
	Food Consumption (m.m.t.)	Food Deficit (Food Consumption Minus Production) (m.m.t.)	Food Deficit/ Food Consumption (percent)	Food Consumption (m.m.t.)	Food Deficit (Food Consumption Minus Production) (m.m.t.)	Food Deficit/ Food Consumption (percent)
East and Southeast Asia	110.8	0.6	0	180	(31)	(7.2)
China	313.9	15.0	4.8	494	(7)	(1.4)
South Asia	188.0	3.3	1.8	310	(13)	(10.0)
Middle East	86.9	18.9	21.7	183	64	35.0
Sub-Saharan Africa	78.3	5.9	6.8	160	47	29.4
Latin America	115.9	8.2	7.1	214	9	4.2
Total	893.8	51.9	5.7	1541	69	4.5

[a]Consumption projections assume a trend based on 1966–80 average annual growth rate of real GNP per capita.

Note: () indicates surplus.

Source: Leonardo A. Paulino, *Food in the Third World: Past Trends and Projections to 2000,* Research Report 52, International Food Policy Research Institute, Washington, D.C., June 1986.

The LDC **food deficit** (amount of food imported) as a percentage of food consumption in LDCs is expected to decline by 2000. Indeed East, Southeast, and South Asia should turn their 1980 deficit into a surplus, and Latin America's relative deficit will fall. Yet the LDCs' *absolute* deficit, especially in sub-Saharan Africa and the Middle East, continues to increase (Table 7-3). The major developing countries with food deficits in the 1990s and first decade of the twenty-first century are indicated in Chapter 9, which examines the population-food balance in more detail. Of course if a country can afford to import food, food deficits need not mean undernourishment. Food importers, such as Britain, West Germany, and Japan, generate enough industrial surplus (and Kuwait, enough oil surplus) to maintain a high level of nutrition.

An American Association for the Advancement of Science symposium argues that annual food production is enough to feed everyone on earth adequately if distribution were more equal. However while *intra* regional distribution would be adequate for Asia and Latin America, sub-Saharan Africa's caloric intake, if equally distributed, would still be below minimal nutritional standards.[9] Chapter 9's discussion of the food-population balance and the following section on Sino-Indian com-

[9] Philip H. Abelson, ed., *Food: Politics, Economics, Nutrition, and Research* (Washington, D.C.: American Association for the Advancement of Science, 1975); and U.S. Department of Agriculture, Economics, Statistics, and Cooperative Service, International Economic Division, *Food Problems and Prospects in sub-Saharan Africa: The Decade of the 1980's* (Washington, D.C.: U.S. Agency for International Development, 1980).

parisons suggest that local food shortages are due not so much to inadequate world production as to deficiences in food distribution and entitlement. Although world-wide food output per capita should grow in the 1990s and the first decade of the 2000s, unequal food distribution means that some people in LDCs will be undernourished.

Food output figures omit fish, an important part of the diet throughout the world and especially in LDCs. The world's population ate 54 million tons of fish in 1983 (half in LDCs) compared to 105 million tons of red meat and 25 million tons of fowl. Since most people harvest fish without practicing husbandry, fish, if available, has cost advantages over other kinds of food.[10]

FOOD IN INDIA AND CHINA

China is omitted from data on LDCs in Figure 7-2. During the Chinese Cultural Revolution from 1966 to 1976, some Western economists accepted the official claim that the country had no malnutrition. French economist Al Imfeld maintained that "in contrast to India, China has eliminated hunger."[11] The best evidence indicates that food production per capita in China fell more than 12 percent between the 1930s and the late 1970s. Although growth in food production per capita of the world's most populated country, China from 1952 to 1984, was slightly faster than that of the second most populated country, neighboring India, breaking down the analysis into the pre–1977 to 1979 period, when China had primarily cooperative and collective farming, and the period after the 1979 agricultural reforms, is more revealing. India's annual growth in food output per person, from 1954 to 1977, was 0.4 percent compared to China's 0.3 percent.[12] (The 5-year moving average avoids much influence from the abnormal growth just following China's post-1949 war rehabilitation and India's recovery fom disruption due to the 1947 Indian-Pakistani partition or following China's reforms and India's post-1978 liberalization.)

Yet because China's food grain output per person in the early 1950s was roughly 25–30 percent higher than India's, China's average *level* of food output per person remained higher than India's through the 1980s. Furthermore since income inequalities are less in China than India, the percentage of the population that is malnourished is lower than in India. Nevertheless China's Communist Party Central Committee admitted that in 1977, about one hundred million people, or more than one-tenth of China's population, did not have enough to eat,[13] thus contradicting Imfeld's contention.

[10] "World Fishing Flounders," *Economist* (June 23, 1984): pp. 70–71.

[11] Al Imfeld, *China as a Model of Development,* trans. Matthew J. O'Connell (New York: Orbis, 1976), p. 157.

[12] E. Wayne Nafziger, "India versus China: Economic Development Performance," *Dalhousie Review* 65 (Fall 1985): 366–92, with updated information from U.S. Department of Agriculture, International Economic Division, *World Indices of Agricultural and Food Production, 1950–85* (Washington, D.C., 1986); and U.S. Department of Agriculture, Economic Research Service, *World Indices of Agricultural and Food Production, 1977–86* (Washington, D.C., 1988).

[13] Christopher Howe, *China's Economy: A Basic Guide* (New York: Basic Books, 1978), pp. xxiii, 180–84; Dwight H. Perkins, *China's Agricultural Development: 1368–1968* (Chicago: Aldine, 1969); Nick Eberstadt, "Has China Failed?" *New York Review of Books,* 26 (April 5, 1979): 33–46; and A. Doak Barnett, *China's Economy in Global Perspective* (Washington, D.C.: Brookings Institute, 1981), p. 305.

Stanford economist John G. Gurley argues that "the Chinese have what is in effect an insurance policy against pestilence, famine, and other disasters."[14] But though China normally has a lower malnutrition rate and distributes food more equally than does India, China is more subject to famine than is India.

Amartya K. Sen emphasizes that having enough to eat does not depend on merely egalitarian income distribution or low poverty rates but on society's system of entitlement. **Entitlement** refers to the set of alternative commodity bundles that a person can command in a society using the totality of rights and opportunities that he or she possesses. An entitlement helps people acquire capabilities (like being well nourished). In a market economy, the entitlement limit is based on ownership of factors of production and exchange possibilities (through trade or a shift in production possibilities). For most people, entitlement depends on the ability to find a job, the wage rate, and the prices of commodities bought. In a welfare or socialist economy, entitlement also depends on what families can obtain from the state through the established system of command. A hungry, destitute person will be *entitled* to something to eat, not by society's low Gini concentration and a high food output per capita, but by a relief system offering free food. Thus in 1974, thousands of people died in Bangladesh despite its low inequality, because floods reduced rural employment along with output, and inflation cut rural laborers' purchasing power.

Sen argues that food is purchased with political pressure as well as income. Accordingly one-third of the Indian population goes to bed hungry every night and leads a life ravaged by regular deprivation. India's social system takes nonacute endemic hunger in stride; there are no headlines nor riots. But while India's politicians do not provide entitlements for chronic or endemic malnutrition, they do so for potential severe famine through food imports, redistribution, and relief. In Maoist China, the situation was almost the opposite. Its political commitment ensured lower regular malnutrition through more equal access to means of livelihood and state-provided entitlement to basic needs of food, clothing, and shelter. In a normal year, China's poor were much better fed than India's. Yet if there were a political and economic crisis that confused the regime so that it pursued disastrous policies with confident dogmatism, then it could not be forced to change its policies by crusading newspapers or effective political opposition pressure, as in India.

Famines result from a failure of the entitlement system. Sen, using Beijing University figures, calculates an extra mortality of 14–16 million people from famine in China from 1959 to 1961, greater in absolute or relative terms than the 3 million extra mortality in India's largest twentieth-century famine, the Great Bengal Famine of 1943. So although China was more successful than India before 1977 to 1979 in eliminating regular malnutrition, China has had more famines than India.[15]

---

[14] John G. Gurley, *China's Economy and the Maoist Strategy* (New York: Monthly Review Press, 1976), p. 134. The book is based on essays written during the Cultural Revolution.

[15] Amartya K. Sen, "Development: Which Way Now?" *Economic Journal* 93 (December 1983): 757–60; and Amartya K. Sen, *On Economic Inequality* (Oxford: Clarendon Press, 1983). For further discussion of Sen's entitlement theory of famine, see Peter Bowbrick, "The Causes of Famine: A Refutation of Professor Sen's Theory," *Food Policy* 11 (May 1986), 105–24; Amartya K. Sen, "The Causes of Famine: A Reply," *Food Policy* 11 (May 1986), 125–32; Peter Bowbrick, "Rejoinder: An Untenable Hypothesis on the Causes of Famine," *Food Policy* 12 (February 1987), 5–9; Amartya K. Sen, "Reply: Famine and Mr. Bowbrick," *Food Policy* 12 (February 1987), 10–14; Stephen Devereux,

China's per capita food production dropped sharply during the 1959 to 1961 famine (1960's figure was 25 percent below 1952's), resulting in widespread malnutrition. The cause of this decline was not only bad weather, floods, and drought, but also poor quality work during the emphasis on collective labor-intensive projects during the Great Leap Forward (GLF) from 1958 to 1960. Reservoir construction work destroyed soil, rivers, and existing irrigation systems. Reservoir and water conservation work raised underground water levels, led to alkalized, salinized, and water-logged soil, halted stream and river flows, left irrigation channels unfinished, and failed to provide for drainage. Moreover GLF water projects removed land from cultivation. Yet the GLF political pressure for agricultural success made local officials unwilling to report food shortages.[16]

In reforms beginning in 1979, China decontrolled (and increased) prices for farm commodities, virtually eliminated their compulsory deliveries to the state, reduced multitiered pricing, relaxed interregional farm trade restrictions, encouraged rural markets, allowed direct sales of farm goods to urban consumers, and decollectivized agriculture, instituting individual household management of farm plots under long-term contracts with collectives and allowing farmers to choose cropping patterns and nonfarm activities. From 1977 to 1984, even India's 3.0– percent annual growth in food output per capita under a modest post-1978 liberalization was outstripped by China's 4.6-percent growth, which was not so rapid as gains in oilseed, livestock, and cotton output. Indeed China reversed its pre-1979 dependence on imported grains, exporting corn, other coarse grains, and soybeans (as well as raw cotton), which competed with exports from the U.S. Midwest and South, especially to Japan. These remarkable gains were achieved without increased farm inputs except for chemical fertilizer.[17] Although China's price decontrol of food inputs and outputs was only partial, its success reinforces the World Bank's emphasis in the Berg report (discussed later in the chapter) of "getting prices right."

FACTORS CONTRIBUTING TO LOW INCOME AND POVERTY IN RURAL AREAS

Average income in rural areas is substantially less than in urban areas in LDCs. Rural inequality is greater than urban inequality in Latin America but less in the rest of the developing world.[18] Not surprisingly in LDCs as a whole, there are

"Entitlements, Availability, and Famine: A Revisionist View of Wollo, 1972–74," *Food Policy* 13 (August 1988), 270–82; and Erhun Kula, "The Inadequacy of The Entitlement Approach to Explain and Remedy Famines," *Journal of Development Studies* 25 (October 1988), 112–16.

[16] Jan S. Prybyla, *The Political Economy of Communist China* (Scranton, Pa.: International Textbook, 1970), pp. 264–69; A. Doak Barnett, *China's Economy in Global Perspective* (Washington, D.C.: Brookings Institute 1981), pp. 271, 302; and Nicholas R. Lardy, *Agriculture in China's Modern Economic Development* (Cambridge: Cambridge University Press, 1983), pp. 152–53.

[17] World Bank, *World Development Report, 1986* (New York: Oxford University Press, 1986), pp. 104–6. Chinese-Indian comparisons come from E. Wayne Nafziger, "India versus China," *Dalhousie Review* 65: 366–92, with later data from U.S. Department of Agriculture, *World Indices of Agricultural and Food Production, 1950–85* (Washington, D.C., 1986); and U.S. Department of Agriculture, *World Indices of Agricultural and Food Production, 1977–86* (Washington, D.C., 1988).

[18] Shail Jain, *Size Distribution of Income: A Compilation of Data* (Washington, D.C.: World Bank, 1975).

higher poverty rates in rural areas than in cities. This section discusses why this is so.

Lack of Resources and Technology

Agricultural income and productivity in LDCs are low because of minimal capital per worker and inadequate technology. Small farm *owners* receive limited credit and tenants, sharecroppers, and landless laborers receive almost none. There is little research and development to improve technology appropriate for small farmers, partly because they lack effective demand and political power.

Concentration of Capital, Land, and Technology

Agricultural technology and capital are concentrated among large farmers. The development of commercial agriculture, as in the case of the high-yielding seed varieties of the Green Revolution, compelled some cultivators to work for a wage, and made many other farmers even more marginal than they had been. Although still less than urban inequality, rural income inequality has increased since 1970.[19]

Incomes of farm households are highly correlated with the amount of nonfarm income (urban wages, remittances, and so forth), especially in Kenya and Nigeria. Indeed household nonfarm income is the key to determining farm productivity and household incomes in Kenya. Farm families receiving urban wages bought land, hired farm labor, financed innovations, purchased farm inputs, and increased farm income. Most farm families without a regularly employed person earn no more than enough to satisfy the necessities of life. A study of northern Nigerian villages found that off-farm income accounts for nearly 40 percent of the total income of the top quintile (fifth), but only 22–27 percent of income of the four bottom quintiles, while a western central Nigerian survey indicated rural family income and capital per acre correlated significantly with the percentage of income from nonfarm sources.[20]

Land holdings are severely concentrated in many LDCs (see Chapter 6). This is especially true in Latin America, where the average farm size is over 80 hectares (twenty times larger than in Afro-Asia), and size dispersion is substantial (Gini coefficient = 0.84) (see Table 7-4).[21] In Brazil a small fraction of landholders (16 percent) commands 87 percent of agricultural land. Land inequality is greater than data indicate because many small holders sharecrop or lease their holdings, and many rural have no land at all.[22] Since the colonial period more than 100 years ago, most of Latin America has been characterized by **latifundios,** large land-grant

---

[19] Ibid.; and International Labor Office, *Profiles of Rural Poverty* (Geneva, 1979).

[20] E. Wayne Nafziger, *Inequality in Africa: Political Elites, Proletariat, Peasants, and the Poor* (Cambridge: Cambridge University Press, 1988), p. 85; Paul Collier and Deepak Lal, *Labour and Poverty in Kenya, 1900–1980* (Oxford: Clarendon Press, 1986), pp. 249–50; and Peter Matlon, "The Structure of Production and Rural Incomes in Northern Nigeria," in Henry Bienen and V. P. Diejomaoh, *The Political Economy of Income Distribution in Nigeria* (New York: Holmes & Meier, 1981), pp. 323–72.

[21] Lyn Squire, *Employment Policy in Developing Countries: A Survey of Issues and Evidence* (New York: Oxford University Press, 1981), p. 156.

[22] Robert Repetto, "Population, Resources, Environment: An Uncertain Future," *Population Bulletin* 42 (July 1987): 13–14.

TABLE 7-4 Distribution of Agricultural Landholders and Area by Size of Holdings, Selected Countries: 1980

	Under 5 Hectares		Size of Holdings 5–50 Hectares		Over 50 Hectares	
	Percent of Land-holders	Percent of Area	Percent of Land-holders	Percent of Area	Percent of Land-holders	Percent of Area
Uruguay	12	0	46	4	42	96
Brazil	37	1	45	12	16	87
Panama	66	4	27	30	7	66
Guatemala	78	11	19	25	3	64
Turkey	62	20	37	68	1	11
Thailand	72	39	28	61	0	0
Niger	58	33	42	67	0	0
Pakistan	86	51	14	37	0	9
Philippines	86	51	14	37	0	12
India	91	51	9	46	0	3
Nepal	97	71	3	29	0	0

Source: Robert Repetto, "Population, Resources, Environment: An Uncertain Future," *Population Bulletin* 42 (July 1987): 14.

estates owned by the few, and **minifundios,** small poor holdings that rarely provide adequate employment for a family (see Table 7-5). To obtain a subsistence income, holders of *minifundios* generally work as seasonal labor on the *latifundios.* And of course, these large estates, characterized by extensive cultivation, high capital intensity, and much unused land, have a higher output per agricultural worker.

Low Educational and Skill Levels

Average incomes in urban areas are higher than in rural areas, where skill levels and demands are lower. Years of schooling, a major indicator of skill and productivity (see Chapter 11), are fewer in rural than in urban areas. For example, in India the city-born child has twice the chance of receiving a primary or secondary education as the one born in a rural community and eight times the chance of receiving a university education. More and better quality schools are available to city children than to rural children. In addition much rural schooling is irrelevant to its community's economic needs. Some economists even question how much rural areas benefit from a child's education, since the most able and educated young people usually emigrate to the cities.[23]

Rural-Urban Migration

Attracted by the prospect of better-paying jobs in urban areas, rural emigrants tend to have education, skill, and income that are higher than average in the rural areas. Poorer villagers are often at a disadvantage in migrating: (1) They simply cannot

[23] Michael Lipton, *Why Poor People Stay Poor: A Study of Urban Bias in World Development* (London: Maurice Temple Smith, 1977), pp. 259–60; 446.

TABLE 7-5 *Minifundios,* Medium-sized Farms, and *Latifundios* in the Agrarian Structure of Selected Latin American Countries, 1966

	MINIFUNDIOS[a]		MEDIUM-SIZED AND FAMILY FARMS[b]		*LATIFUNDIOS*[c]	
	Percent of Farms	Percent of Occupied Land	Percent of Farms	Percent of Occupied Land	Percent of Farms	Percent of Occupied Land
Argentina	43.2	3.4	56.8	59.7	0.8	36.9
Brazil	22.5	0.5	72.8	40.0	4.7	59.5
Colombia	64.0	4.9	34.7	45.6	1.3	49.5
Chile	36.9	0.2	56.2	18.5	6.9	81.3
Ecuador	89.9	16.6	9.7	38.3	0.4	45.1
Guatemala	88.4	14.3	11.5	44.9	0.1	40.8
Peru	88.0	7.4	10.9	10.2	1.1	82.4

[a]Employ less than two people.

[b]Family farms employ two to four people and medium-sized farms four to twelve workers.

[c]Employ more than twelve people.

Source: Celso Furtado, *Economic Development in Latin America* (New York: Cambridge University Press, 1970), pp. 54–55.

afford to migrate—acquiring job information, emigrating, and searching for work are expensive propositions, especially if they are financed at the high interest rates charged by the village money lender. And of course emigrés must subsist as they wait for their first paychecks. (2) Their families find it more difficult to release them from work. (3) They are not so well educated as most other villagers. Many urban employers use education to screen job applicants, even for unskilled work (see Chapter 11). Even when the poorer villagers surmount these obstacles and move to the city, they frequently do not stay. Poverty forces them back to the village. The jobless, ill, pregnant, and elderly eventually return to relatives in the rural areas, eroding average incomes already reduced by the large economic burden from high rural birth rates.[24]

Policies of Urban Bias

British economist Michael Lipton argues that the most significant class conflicts and income discrepancies are not between labor and capital, as Karl Marx contended, but between rural and urban classes. Despite development plans that proclaim agriculture as the highest priority sector, and political rhetoric that stresses the needs of the poor rural masses, government allocates most of its resources to cities, a policy of **urban bias.** Planners and politicians in LDCs are more likely to respond to the concerns of the more powerful, organized, and articulate urban dwellers. Thus farm land is diverted from growing millet and beans for hungry villagers to produce meat and milk for urban middle and upper classes or to grow cocoa, coffee, tea, sugar, cotton, and jute for export. Scarce capital is spent on highways and steel

[24]Ibid., pp. 66, 147–49, 231–35.

mills instead of on water pumps, tube wells, and other equipment essential for growing food. High-cost administrative and management talent is used to design office buildings and sports stadiums rather than village wells and agricultural extension services.

Urban bias may take these forms:

1. Policies that raise industrial prices relative to the prices of farm goods. Government may set price ceilings on food and guarantee minimum prices for industrial goods. High taxes and low prices force agriculture to transfer income and capital to industry and social infrastructure. The most frequently cited model for such policies is the Soviet Union of the 1930s, which used low prices, sales taxes, and government monopsony purchases to divert the surplus from agriculture into heavy-industry output and investment growth unmatched by any Western country.

2. Concentration of investment in industry. Although over half of the LDC population is in agriculture, only about 20 percent of investment is in agriculture.

3. Tax incentives and subsidies to pioneering firms in industry, but not in agriculture.

4. Setting below-market prices for foreign currency, which reduces domestic currency receipts from agricultural exports. This policy lowers the price of capital goods and other foreign inputs, which benefits large industrial establishments with privileged access to import licenses. In Pakistan such a foreign exchange policy coupled with industrial price guarantees resulted in the transfer of about 70 percent of agricultural savings and over 24 percent of its gross product to the nonagricultural sector in 1964 and 1965.

5. Tariff and quota protection for industry, contributing to higher fertilizer, seed, equipment, materials, and consumer prices for farmers.

6. Spending more for education, training, housing, plumbing, nutrition, medical care, and transport in urban areas than in rural areas (see Chapter 10).[25] Thus life expectancy, an indicator of the quality of the health care system, varies widely among regions. Buenos Aires had a 1985 life expectancy of 75 years; the rest of Argentina, 69; the poor rural areas, 63; and Argentina as a whole, 70. Algiers's life expectancy is 68; the rest of Algeria, 61; the poor rural areas, 58; and Algeria generally, 61.

Seasonal Poverty and Hunger

Ironically *moderate* undernourishment is higher in rural than urban areas, since it is most likely to result from inadequate income than food shortages. However, Food and Agriculture Organization (FAO) studies of several LDCs indicate that, because of greater access to subsistence food production, the percentage of the population suffering *severe* malnourishment in rural areas is lower than in urban areas.[26]

[25] Ibid.; and Keith Griffin and Azizur Rahman Khan, eds., *Growth and Inequality in Pakistan* (London: Macmillan, 1972).

[26] Food and Agriculture Organization of the United Nations, *The Fourth FAO World Food Survey* (Rome, 1977), pp. 29–46.

Yet there is substantial hunger in rural areas. A "hungry season" before the beginning of a new harvest is widespread in many LDCs, especially in West Africa. Poor rural households are caught in a poverty trap in which selling labor and obtaining credit at high interest rates to ensure survival through the hungry season result in less income and high interest payments in future years. The poverty trap is circular. Initially farmers sacrifice self-sufficiency to produce cash crops. Accordingly they no longer grow early maturing crops that would fill the hunger gap between harvests. Poor farm families are also more vulnerable than previously as a result of individualized consumption replacing community or clan sharing. Furthermore poor farm families cannot afford to purchase food just before harvests, when cash resources are lowest and prices are highest. At this juncture, many poor farmers neglect their own farms and sell their labor to richer farmers. They accept a lower income from their own farm to guarantee short-term survival. Reduced calorie and protein consumption during a period of more work leads to weight loss and greater chances of contracting diseases. The situation may become worse each year.[27]

POLICIES TO INCREASE RURAL INCOME AND REDUCE POVERTY

This section focuses on increasing average rural incomes and reducing the percentage of the rural population in poverty by improving income distribution.

Agrarian Reform and Land Redistribution

In many LDCs, land holdings are severely concentrated: A small fraction of landholders own the bulk of the land. However most holdings are less than 2 hectares apiece. The UN Food and Agricultural Organization (FAO) indicates that in Latin America, the region with highest concentration, 1.3 percent of the landowners hold 71.6 percent of the land under cultivation.

Redistributing land to the poor reduces income inequality. Yet poverty stems not only from unequal land distribution but also from low farmer productivity. Frequently the land tenure system provides the cultivator little incentive for innovation, long-term investment, harder work, increased fertilization, and improved seeds. And in many instances, landowners raise rents and crop shares when production goes up. The cultivator gains little from higher production.

Giving the poor more land has been tried in a number of countries, with mixed results. Land reform has frequently failed because of the political opposition of landlords (as in India), the transfer of holdings to relatives, or because the new landowners do not have access to credit, water, fertilizer, extension assistance, and other services. However in the early 1950s in Taiwan and South Korea, where land redistribution was coupled with credit and extension services for small farmers, incomes rose substantially.

[27] Derek Byerlee, Carl Eicher, and David Norman, "Farm Systems in Developing Countries" (unpublished manuscript, 1982); and Mark Newman, Ismael Ouedraogo, and David Norman, "Farm-level Studies in the Semiarid Tropics of West Africa," Proceedings of the Workshop on Socioeconomic Constraints to Development of Semiarid Tropical Agriculture, International Crop Research Institute for Semiarid Tropics (ICRISAT), Hyderabad, India, February 19–23, 1979, pp. 241–63.

By the 1960s, economists believed that redistributing land to small farmers led to lower crop yields. However recent research indicates that land redistribution to the poor *usually* increases LDC agricultural output, at least after a period of adjustment, for two reasons: (1) A small farmer who receives security of ownership is more likely to undertake improvements; and (2) small farms often use more labor per acre—labor that otherwise might not have been used. When small-sized farms have lower productivity per hectare, it is more often because farmers are illiterate and thus tend to adopt technological innovations more slowly or because they have virtually no access to credit. Furthermore land fragmentation eventually inhibits productivity.

Alternatives to distributing individual land parcels center on creating cooperatives or revising land tenure rules. But even these methods have dangers. Quite often cooperatives are dominated by money lenders and landed interests, or they have management and incentive problems. Revised land tenure rules that give the tenant farmer greater security, and thus more incentive to invest, are hard to enforce. Numerous landless workers are willing to replace existing tenants and forego the revised rules, and landlords try to make up for lost rent in other tenant transactions. They raise interest on money lent to tenants or lower wages. Despite the difficulties, land and tenure reforms are still used to reduce poverty in many LDCs.[28]

Capital

Agriculturalists have often assumed that the success of mechanization in raising production in the United States and Canada can be duplicated in LDCs. However as Chapter 10 contends, technology developed for DCs frequently is not suitable for LDCs, where labor tends to be low cost and capital is expensive. In these countries, planning has to be such that production increases from new machinery justify its high cost.

Here are a few sensible policy guidelines. When farms are small, improve farm implements rather than use tractors and combines. If costly machinery is used, it should be rented to all farmers to spread the cost over enough units to be economical. New machinery is more likely to pay for itself if it is used during planting and harvesting to reduce labor shortages rather than during slack farm seasons, when labor is at a surplus. Moreover machinery prices should probably not be subsidized. Eastern Nigerian farm settlement schemes in the 1960s, for instance, used tractors and earthmovers when they were subsidized, but returned to labor-intensive means of clearing and cultivation when machinery was priced more realistically.[29]

[28] World Bank, *World Development Report, 1980* (New York: Oxford University Press, 1980), p. 41; Montek S. Ahluwalia, "Income Inequality," in Hollis Chenery, Montek S. Ahluwalia, C. L. G. Bell, John H. Duloy, and Richard Jolly, eds., *Redistribution with Growth* (London: Oxford University Press, 1974), p. 24; R. Albert Berry and William R. Cline, *Agrarian Structure and Productivity in Developing Countries,* a study prepared for ILO (Baltimore: Johns Hopkins University Press, 1979); and Clarence Zuvekas, Jr., *Economic Development: An Introduction* (New York: St. Martin's, 1979), p. 220.

[29] Uma Lele, *The Design of Rural Development: Lessons from Africa* (Baltimore: Johns Hopkins University Press, 1975), p. 35; and Clarence Zuvekas, Jr., *Economic Development: An Introduction* (New York: St. Martin's, 1979), p. 217.

As indicated in Chapter 5, direct social investment (roads, schools, and so on) in poor rural areas will increase income and jobs.

Credit

The major source of credit for many small farmers is the village money lender-large landlord, who may charge interest rates of 5 to 10 percent per month. Still, some small farmers prefer this credit to bank or government credit, since repayment schedules are more flexible. Frequently money lender and debtor are bound by a semipermanent patron-client relationship, in which the creditor provides virtually unconditional access to money in emergencies and for marriage celebrations for daughters in the family. (Remember the discussion of Balayya in Chapter 1.)

Commercial farmers cannot make a profit if they pay usurious interest rates. Yet these farmers have a unique need for credit that may require a separate loan agency. Expenses for the time between sowing and harvest frequently have to be financed, and since small farmers have little fixed capital, they must offer their land as collateral. Yet government loans boards rarely accept such collateral, since it is difficult politically to foreclose land if the farmer fails to repay. Farming is also subject to risks, such as weather, that cannot be controlled.

Government-administered credit may be necessary to pay for technological innovation, such as high-yielding varieties of grain, as well as the extension help, storage facilities, irrigation, and fertilizer required to take advantage of a new technique. Despite great need, government-administered credit programs are rarely self-supporting and have a limited success.[30]

Research and Technology

The section in Chapter 9 on the food-population balance emphasizes the importance of research and technology, especially as generated by an international network of agricultural research centers, in improving agricultural technology. Here we want to stress that the technology used should depend on available resources. For example, Japan, with a ratio of farm workers per cultivated hectare almost 50 times as high as that of United States, has emphasized biological and chemical technology (such as new seeds and fertilizer) rather than mechanical technology. For the majority of LDCs with high worker-land ratios, the Japanese approach is more sensible than that of the United States.[31]

The introduction of new technology in rural areas is often quite risky. Understandably farmers are reluctant to accept change unless their risks are adequately covered. From long experience, peasants have reason to be skeptical of the findings of experimental research farms. In a number of instances in LDCs, peasant income has fallen, sometimes threatening household survival, when innovation occurred. Too often the new methods were not adapted to local farming conditions: They were inadequately tested in a different soil, climate, and environment and had adverse side effects that destroyed any benefit they may have had. When family

---

[30] Guy Hunter, ed., *Agricultural Development and the Rural Poor: Declaration of Policy and Guidelines for Action* (London: Overseas Development Institute, 1978), p. 83.

[31] Yujiro Hayami and Vernon W. Ruttan, *Agricultural Development: An International Perspective* (Baltimore: Johns Hopkins University Press, 1971), pp. 111–28.

survival is at stake, it is more important to avoid any probability of crop failure than to maximize long-run output.

Clearly introducing new technology requires active initial monitoring, so that probable social and economic effects are foreseen: While on-farm tests are required, small farmers are free to experiment with only a fraction of their land holdings, using the remainder to produce food by the old techniques in case the experiment should fail.

Perhaps China best illustrates the importance of adequate agricultural research policies. It has had a very slow growth in food output per person. Since the 1950s, Chinese agricultural institutes were isolated from international institutes and did little basic agricultural research. During the height of the Cultural Revolution from 1966 to 1970, some leading agricultural scientists were sent to rural areas to learn from the peasants and workers. At about the same time, the matriculation of agricultural students was disrupted because the educational system was shut down. Deng Xiaoping, China's foremost political leader during the late 1970s and 1980s, argued that lagging research and low-quality education, especially in agriculture, constitute the "greatest crisis" in contemporary China.[32] China's dilemma underscores the importance of fundamental agricultural research, either undertaken in local research institutes or borrowed and adapted from abroad.

Chapter 10 also takes up these issues. It too stresses the importance of technology that matches resources and social conditions. The LDC agricultural institutes must develop and adapt technology suitable for small farmers and laborers and disseminate this technical information.[33]

Extension Services

Extension personnel must take the results of agricultural research to the farmers. The agent's role is crucial and varied. Agents must contact and speak with farmers; pass on simple technical information; be able to demonstrate it personally; identify difficulties; know sources of technical advice and training; identify farmers who are good credit risks; arrange for fertilizer, seeds, and other inputs from government depots; and clearly report farm problems and characteristics to researchers and planners.

Unfortunately agricultural extension programs in LDCs are not very successful. Extension agents are often few and far between, ill paid, ill trained, and ill equipped to provide technical help. In many instances, they are beholden to the large, influential farmers and neglect the small farmers, who have far less education and political power. They especially neglect women, even though women manage a sizable proportion of farm activities, particularly food crops, in traditional agriculture.

Extension services based on the U.S. model are not effective. Edward B. Rice has found that in Latin America and other LDCs, the independent extension service based on the U.S. model introduces few innovations and contributes little to rapid growth. He suggests that extension personnel might be more effective if integrated with development organizations, such as loan banks, irrigation authori-

[32] Christopher Howe, *China's Economy: A Basic Guide,* (New York: Basic Books, 1978), pp. 26–27, 81.

[33] Guy Hunter, ed., *Agricultural Development and the Rural Poor: Declaration of Policy and Guidelines for Action* (London: Overseas Development Institute, 1978), pp. 78–82.

ties, seed and fertilizer distribution centers, agrarian reform agencies, or cooperative organizations.[34]

Access to Water and Other Inputs

Irrigation increases agricultural productivity. It enlarges the land area under cultivation, permits the growth of several crops per year, and regulates the flow of water.
Water may be essential with fertilization and improved seed use. But water access
and availability are often problematical for small farmers. For example, in Pakistan's century-old irrigation system in the Indus River basin, large, influential
farmers get first chance at available water, wasting it, since cost is unrelated to used
amount. Even were water access not a problem, the small farmer seldom has the
savings, credit, or incentive to invest in wells and other water projects. When
government funds are inadequate, water courses deteriorate. Obviously water
rights management and user fees must be planned to avoid inequity and inefficiency. Competent technical management must foresee salinity or sedimentation
problems. But even when these matters are competently handled, irrigation is not a
panacea for LDC agriculture. Many irrigation systems in LDCs have failed to
increase agricultural output to pay for their high construction and operating costs.
These enduring monuments to failure underline the need for detailed
preinvestment feasibility studies of irrigation projects, including careful estimates
of capital, personnel, inputs, and maintenance costs over time and how to increase
output (see Chapters 12 and 18).

Aside from water access, farmers require other inputs such as seeds and
fertilizer. These are generally supplied through government ministries or agencies.
In this case, government must guarantee input quality, accessibility, and quantity.[35]
The Nigerian bureaucracy failed to plan for its Operation Feed the Nation in 1979:
One-half million tons of imported fertilizer were delivered two months too late for
the planting season.

Transport

The LDC crops otherwise competitive with those in other countries often cannot
enter world markets because of high transport costs. Investment in roads, railroads,
port dredging, canals, and other transport can lower the cost of producing farm
goods and delivering them to markets. The U.S. Midwest became a center of
specialized production of corn, wheat, beef, and pork in the mid–nineteenth century only after several decades of road, railroad, steamboat, and canal expansion.
Bolivia illustrates the transport problem for LDCs. Agricultural commodities in
Bolivia's lush subtropical and tropical eastern lowlands are at a competitive disad-

[34] Ibid., p. 55; Edward B. Rice, *Extension in the Andes: An Evaluation of Official U.S. Assistance
to Agricultural Extension Services in Central and South America* (Cambridge, Mass.: MIT Press, 1974);
World Bank, *World Development Report, 1978* (New York: Oxford University Press, 1978), p. 43; and
Uma Lele, *Design of Rural Development. Lessons from Africa* (Baltimore: Johns Hopkins University
Press, 1979) pp. 62–63.

[35] World Bank, *World Development Report, 1978* (New York: Oxford University Press, 1978, pp.
40–42; Clarence Zuvekas, Jr. *Economic Development: An Introduction* (New York: St. Martin's, 1979),
p. 216; and Douglas Ensminger and Paul Bomani, *Conquest of World Hunger and Poverty* (Ames: Iowa
State University Press, 1980), p. 63.

vantage because of high transport costs: Crops must get over the Andes mountains to the west or travel the great distance to the eastern coasts of Brazil and Argentina. Farmers near La Paz pay about twice, and those in remote rural areas of Bolivia several times, the price of fertilizer paid in the United States or Mexico. Thus agricultural export potential in Bolivia is severely limited.[36]

Marketing and Storage

Poor marketing channels and insufficient storage facilities often hamper grain sales outside the region of production and limit production gains from the improved seeds of the Green Revolution.[37] For example, the lack of storage and drying facilities in the Philippines in the 1960s prevented many farmers from growing two rice crops a year. And in northern India, the increase in wheat production in 1968 had to be stored in schools or in the open air. As much as one-third of this crop was destroyed by rats and rain.

Government must plan for the impact of new seeds and improved agricultural techniques on marketing and storage. Government can provide the infrastructure, such as roads and grain bins; set uniform grades and standards that sharpen the incentive to improve product quality; and by supplying national price information, help farmers decide which crops to plant, when to sell, and what storage facilities to build.

Many LDCs have established official marketing boards to buy crops from farmers to sell on the world market. However these boards have a tendency to demand a monopsony position to ensure financial success and frequently accumulate funds to transfer from agriculture to industry. Nevertheless the boards can stabilize crop prices and provide production and market research, promotion, extension assistance, and other services.

Many government marketing institutions in LDCs have been established to replace open markets considered inefficient, antisocial, and subject to exploitation by middlemen and women. However a government should examine whether its use of scarce capital and skilled personnel to establish such an enterprise to replace the private intermediary is socially beneficial. Ironically such marketing institutions are more likely to eliminate the small, competitive grain trader than the agent or distributor for the large, influential agribusiness. Furthermore the private middleman or woman operating in a competitive market is likely to have a smaller markup than the state enterprise, which frequently has a monopoly. Moreover empirical evidence indicates that the farm market is relatively efficient in transmitting price information, providing incentives, allocating production among commodities, and rationing goods among consumers.

Price and Exchange Rate Policies.

Irma Adelman's and Sherman Robinson's simulations of the effect of government policy interventions warn against confining rural development projects to those that

[36] Clarence Zuvekas, Jr., *Economic Development: An Introduction* (New York: St. Martin's, 1979), p. 135, 230.

[37] This section draws from Yujiro Hayami and Vernon W. Ruttan, *Agricultural Development*, pp. 216, 267; Guy Hunter, ed., *Agricultural Development and The Rural Poor: Declaration of Policy and Guidelines for Action* (London: Overseas Development Institute, 1978), pp. 89–91; and Oma Lele, *The Design of Rural Development: Lessons from Africa* (Baltimore: Johns Hopkins University Press, 1975), pp. 100–101.

only increase agricultural productivity—making more machinery and credit available; improving irrigation, fertilizer, and seeds; adding new technology; enhancing extension services; and so on. Increased agricultural production and an inelastic demand are likely to reduce the agricultural terms of trade as well as rural real income and to increase urban-rural inequalities in the short run.[38] Thus to reduce rural poverty, production-oriented programs must be combined with price and exchange rate policies, improved rural services, land reform, farmer cooperation, and more rural industry.

Empirical studies indicate a high *long-run* **elasticity of supply** (that is, a high percentage change in quantity supplied in response to a 1-percentage change in price) in LDC agriculture. Long run means the farmer can vary the hectares devoted to a given crop.

In response to consumer pressure, LDC governments frequently establish maximum producer, wholesale, or retail prices for food. But the long-run effects of such policies, given high supply elasticity, may raise prices by discouraging domestic production and increasing reliance on imports. This effect occurred in Argentina in the late 1940s. Subsequent government measures to increase relative farm prices in the early 1950s did not stimulate output as expected because farmers felt the more favorable prices would not be permanent. Subsidizing food is the only way of reducing consumer food prices without harming production incentives (even in socialist countries).

The benefits of research, technology, extension and credit programs, and so on, can be lost with ill-conceived pricing policies. Technological development is more efficient when farm input and output prices are competitive. Researchers and extension agents are more likely to innovate when farm prices clear the market than when they are controlled. Lastly farmers tend to press research institutions for technological innovations with a high payoff—for example, those that save resources with an inelastic supply.[39]

The World Bank's Berg report criticizes African states for keeping farm prices far below market prices, dampening farm producer incentives, using marketing boards to transfer peasant savings to large industry, and setting exchange rates that discourage exports and encourage **import substitutes** (domestic production replacing imports). World Bank economist Kevin M. Cleaver shows that the **real exchange-rate change** (domestic inflation divided by foreign inflation times the percentage change in the foreign exchange price of domestic currency), from 1970 to 1981, is negatively related to agricultural (and overall) growth rates. Kenya and Lesotho, whose farm exports remained competitive as the real value of their domestic currency depreciated, grew faster than Ghana and Tanzania, whose real domestic currency value appreciated (increased).[40] These state interventions into the price system hurt farmers, increasing industry and agricultural income differentials.

Agricultural resource allocation is highly affected by the foreign exchange

---

[38] Irma Adelman and Sherman Robinson, *Income Distribution Policy in Developing Countries: A Case Study of Korea* (Stanford: Stanford University Press, 1978), pp. 128–46.

[39] Yujiro Hayami and Vernon W. Ruttan, *Agricultural Development: An International Perspective* (Baltimore: Johns Hopkins University Press, 1971), pp. 56–59; and Clarence Zuvekas, Jr., *Economic Development: An Introduction* (New York: St. Martin's, 1979), pp. 233–34.

[40] World Bank, *Accelerated Development in sub-Saharan Africa: An Agenda for Action* (Washington, D.C., 1981); and Kevin M. Cleaver, "The Impact of Price of Exchange Rate Policies on Agriculture in sub-Saharan Africa," World Bank Staff Working Paper no. 728, Washington, D.C., 1985.

rate. As discussed in Chapters 10 and 18, a domestic price for foreign currency lower than equilibrium price reduces farm export receipts and wastes capital goods imports by those people acquiring foreign currency.

Improving Rural Services

Urban areas have far more schools, medical services, piped water, and so on, than rural areas. If rural, middle, and lower classes opposed the urban bias of the national political leadership, they might be able to increase their share of social investment. It is especially important to narrow the educational gap existing between the rural and urban child. As argued in Chapter 11, increasing the share of public educational expenditures in rural areas redistributes income to the poor. And if rural schools begin to place a greater emphasis on curricula that prepare children for rural employment, the rural areas will retain *and* attract more skilled people.

Cooperative and Collective Farms

When population density is high and holdings small and fragmented, farmers are more likely to engage in cooperative or collective use of land, equipment, and facilities. The major advantages in this case are economies of scale in the shared use and cost of tractors, irrigation pumps, and other specialized capital equipment; and improved division of labor and administration.

Cooperatives.   The **cooperative,** involving the least radical break from the individual or family farm, may include the common use of facilities, pooling land, the combined purchase of inputs, or the shared marketing of crops. The cooperative ownership or hire of a tractor, irrigation channel, peanut sheller, or grain harvester divides high overhead costs. Sharing land use but retaining individual ownership is a big first step in improving rural resource efficiency. However cooperatives are rarely successful in nonsocialist countries: Political commitment to these programs is weak.[41]

Collective Farms or Communes.   Here the state or community owns the land and capital. Pre-1985 Soviet Union and Maoist China are the chief exemplars of collectivism. Soviet leader Joseph Stalin introduced the **collective farm (kolkhoz)** in 1929. Between 1921 and 1928, a new class of **kulaks** (prosperous small landholders) and private traders whom the party could not control had arisen. Collectivization

---

[41] Clarence Zuvekas, Jr., *Economic Development: An Introduction* (New York: St. Martin's, 1979), p. 34; and Guy Hunter, ed., *Agricultural Development and the Rural Poor: Declaration of Policy and Guidelines for Action* (London: Overseas Development Institute, 1978), p. 60. The remainder of this section uses Jan S. Prybyla, *The Chinese Economy: Problems and Policies* (Columbia: University of South Carolina Press, 1978), pp. 43–46, 60–64; Paul R. Gregory and Robert C. Stuart, *Soviet Economic Structure and Performance* (New York: Harper and Row, 1986); E. L. Wheelwright and Bruce Mc-Farland, *The Chinese Road to Socialism: Economics of the Cultural Revolution* (New York: Monthly Review Press, 1970), pp. 43–65; Alec Nove, *An Economic History of the U.S.S.R.* (Middlesex, U.K.: Penguin, 1972); Christopher Howe, *China's Economy, a Basic Guide* (New York: Basic Books, 1978) pp. xxiii–xxv; and Carmelo Mesa-Lago, *Cuba in the 1970s: Pragmatism and Institutionalization* (Albuquerque: University of New Mexico Press, 1978), pp. 97–101.

was Stalin's way of regaining control. The Chinese stressed the slogan, "Learn from the Soviet Union," but their people's commune (or collective farm) was shaped over several years (1949–59). The Chinese commune, with an average of 15,000 members, consisted of several production brigades divided into decentralized production teams of one hundred to four hundred people, the basic unit of production and distribution.

What are some of the advantages of collective farms?

1. Using official price policies to increase saving. (However the net result of these policies is income transfer from rural to urban areas. Recall that the Soviet Union used low prices to squeeze agriculture for the benefit of heavy industry.)
2. Exploiting internal economies of scale in production and social services. The Soviet *kolkhoz,* usually more than 400 hectares, uses tractors, combines, an accountant, an engineer, and sometimes an agronomist. The Chinese commune may be large enough for a tractor station, high school, hospital, credit cooperative, radio station, reservoir, dam, hydroelectric power station, processing plant, sawmill, and a variety of rural industries.
3. Off-season employment of underutilized farm workers in rural industry (as on the Chinese communes). The rural underemployed stay home, reducing the blight, population density, and pressure on food prices in urban areas that result when they migrate.
4. State control of the grain market. This control was especially important in the Soviet Union, where the Communist leadership *believed* (perhaps erroneously) that peasant marketing declined during the steep drop in farm prices relative to industrial prices from 1922 to 1924.

Many economists, especially from Western countries, question whether the benefits of collective agriculture surpass the costs. During the Soviet collectivization of 1929 to 1933, the forcible collection of grain, the confiscation of farm property, the arrest and deportation of real and alleged kulaks, the destruction of tools and livestock, the class warfare between peasants and kulaks, the administrative disorder, the disruption of sowing and harvest, and the accompanying famine led to the deaths of about five million people. Gross agricultural output per person declined from 1928 to 1937. Although Soviet agricultural performance has since improved, even the leadership has expressed disappointment in the average level of food production, still below that of Italy. In China although industrial output per capita grew by 8.3 percent per year between 1952 and 1975, food output per person increased only 0.2 percent per year. Moreover small private plots in the Soviet Union and Maoist China have produced a disproportionate share of vegetables, livestock, and peasant's money income, albeit with more labor per acre than on the collective. Furthermore in both socialist Poland and Yugoslavia, farmers have resisted collectivization. In these countries, the private sector accounts for more than four-fifths of the agricultural area and output. To be sure, the Soviet people are adequately nourished, and Maoist China met the nutritional needs of its poorest 40 percent better than most other low-income countries. Nevertheless the low productivity of Eastern European and Soviet agriculture compared to capitalist DCs, and of socialist Asia (primarily China) relative to nonsocialist LDCs (Table 7-2), together with the slow pre-1979 growth in Chinese food output per person, hardly suggests collective agriculture as a model for developing countries.

Collectivism's advantages are probably not so great as their proponents claim. Low farm prices and the transfer of agricultural savings to industry can hamper agricultural growth. The same economies of large-scale production can be achieved instead through cooperatives, renting machinery, and technical and managerial assistance provided by extension agents. Local or provincial government or private enterprise can provide many of the social services mentioned. Even in a mixed or capitalist economy, off-farm employment opportunities can be made available to farmers during the slack season. Although the state leadership may wish to control the grain market for political reasons, there is no evidence that this increases agricultural efficiency and growth.

There are other problems with the collective farms. The link between individual initiative and effort, on the one hand, and income, on the other, is not so powerful as on the individually or family-owned farm. Also the collectivist system for paying labor is complicated, time consuming, and cumbersome: The output of the production unit is usually distributed by work points based on the type of task and work performance. Disputes concerning its accuracy and equity are common. Additionally there are marked differences in average income between collective farms. Effort and efficiency cannot usually overcome poor location and soil. Moreover collective farm investment tends to be made for political reasons rather than prospective rates of return. Furthermore collective farms are rewarded on the basis of output rather than efficiency (which considers cost) and demand for what is produced.

Ironically despite Deng Xiaoping's repudiation of Mao's slogans of egalitarianism and increasing moral (not material) incentives, Martin King Whyte thinks Deng's decollectivization and price decontrol probably reduced China's income inequality. While Mao attacked privilege among encrusted bureaucrats and intellectuals, his opposition to financial incentives reduced income, especially among peasants. Mao's urban bias policies widened the urban-rural gap from the mid-1950s to the mid-1970s. While post-1979 agricultural reforms encouraged enterprising peasants "to get rich" and widen interrural income differentials, the rapid growth of agricultural income vis-à-vis industrial income reduced the difference between town and countryside, perhaps even reducing overall income inequality. Additionally relaxing restrictions on urban emigration permitted rural families from depressed areas to reduce populations and benefit from nonfarm remittances.[42] As implied before, market-oriented reforms may cut inequalities fostered by the state's town-biased allocation system.

State Farms. Partly because of the cumbersome way of paying wages on the collective farm, the Soviet Union has gradually increased the percentage of land in **state farms** from the early 1950s to the mid-1980s. By the late 1970s, over one-half of the country's total cultivated land was used for state farms. Their workers, as well as an increasing number of collective farm workers, are being paid a fixed wage, which protects peasant income against the effects of weather fluctuations and

---

[42] Martin King Whyte, "Social Trends in China: The Triumph of Inequality?" in A. Doak Barnett and Ralph N. Clough, eds., *Modernizing China: Post-Mao Reform and Development* (Boulder, Colo.: Westview, 1986), pp. 103–23.

soil deficiencies. Since 1959, Cuba, which has followed the Soviet model more closely than China, has taken several steps toward state ownership of land. By 1975, about 80 percent of the arable land was in state farms.

Rural Industry

As discussed in Chapter 10, demand for agricultural labor grows slowly (and in later stages may even decrease). Technical advances and capital accumulation displace some farm labor. The LDC demand for food grows slowly, since its income elasticity (percentage change in per capita food purchases relative to percentage change in per capita income) is only about one-half. On the other hand, population growth in rural areas is usually more rapid than in LDCs as a whole, so the labor supply usually grows rapidly. Off-farm employment must expand to take care of these extra workers.

Public works projects and small- and medium-scale manufacturing, agribusiness, and processing increase relative incomes and reduce unemployment and underemployment in rural areas. Since 1958, China has had a policy of "walking on two legs," with large urban manufacturing augmented by a "second leg," small- and medium-sized industry on the rural communes. India has limited industrial expansion and new enterprises in metropolitan areas, while firms locating in industrially "backward" nonmetropolitan areas are given favored access to materials and facilities.

Industries and retail enterprises complementary to agriculture—firms producing and selling basic consumer items, blacksmithing, repair, and maintenance shops—are certainly worth developing. However many industrial operations cannot be competitive without the materials, power, markets, financial institutions, communication network, and skilled labor usually concentrated in major urban centers. For example, except in a few metropolitan areas in Nigeria, the electricity supply is too unreliable for many enterprises, including those using plastic injector molding machines, iron-smelting furnaces, or refrigerators. In the 1980s, Deng Xiaoping admitted that the emphasis by rural communes during the Chinese Cultural Revolution on making their own lathes and tractors was very uneconomical, even given the high transport and distribution costs.

Political Constraints

Improved rural social services, greater price incentives, effective farm cooperatives, and public spending on research, credit, rural industry, extension services, irrigation, and transport are frequently not technical, but political, problems. The political survival of state leaders in fragile LDCs requires marshaling the support of urban elites (civil servants, private and state corporate employees, business people, professionals, and skilled workers) through economic policies that sacrifice income distribution and agricultural growth. Moreover LDCs may lack the political and administrative capability, especially in rural areas, to undertake programs to reduce poverty. Established interests—large farmers, money lenders, and the urban classes—may oppose the policy changes and spending essential to improving the economic welfare of the small farmer, tenant, and landless workers.

Additionally state intervention in the market is an instrument of political control and assistance. Government, quasi-government corporations, and private business pressure political elites for inexpensive food policies to keep down wages, and governments sometimes use troops to quell food-related riots (as in Brazil, Egypt, and Tunisia in the mid-1980s). Unrest by urban workers over erosion of their purchasing power has threatened numerous LDC governments. Real wage declines under Nigeria's Abubakar Tafewa Balewa government in 1964 and the Yakubu Gowon government in 1974 to 1975, as well as Ghana's Kofi Busia government in 1971, contributed to political unrest and violence that precipitated military coups. Politicians may also help emerging industry reduce raw material or processing costs. Market intervention provides political control for elites to use in retaining power, building support, and implementing policies.

In 1954 in Ghana, Kwame Nkrumah's Convention People's Party (CPP) passed a bill freezing cocoa producer prices for four years, anticipating use of the increased revenues for industry. But the CPP government undercut the newly formed opposition party in the cocoa-growing regions by selectively providing subsidized inputs—loans, seeds, fertilizer, and implements—for prospective dissidents. Additionally state farm programs in each constituency in the 1960s made available public resources to organize support for the Nkrumah government.

Market-clearing farm prices and exchange rates, whose benefits are distributed indiscriminately, erode urban political support and secure little support from the countryside. In comparison, project-based policies allow benefits to be selectively apportioned for maximum political advantage. Government makes it in the interest of numerous individuals to cooperate with programs that harm the interest of producers as a whole.[43]

Rural dwellers, who are often politically weak and fear government reprisals, rarely organize to oppose antirural policies. While poor farmers have little tactical power, rich ones have too much to lose from protest. Moreover they have less costly options—selling in black markets, shifting resources to other commodities, or migrating to urban areas. Yet eventually rural classes harmed by state market intervention may have to mobilize to oppose the urban and large-farm bias of many contemporary LDC political leaders.

SUMMARY

1. Rural inequality is probably less than urban inequality in LDCs as a whole. Nevertheless rural populations have a higher percentage in poverty than urban populations, because of much lower average incomes in rural areas. Most rural poverty is concentrated among agricultural laborers, the landless, and the near landless.

2. Output per person outside agriculture as a multiple of that in agriculture, which is eight in Africa and four in Asia and Latin America, was only about two in Europe in the nineteenth century.

---

[43] Robert H. Bates, *Markets and States in Tropical Africa: The Political Basis of Agricultural Policies* (Berkeley and Los Angeles: University of California Press, 1981); Douglas Rimmer, *The Economies of West Africa* (London: Weidenfeld and Nicolson, 1984); E. Wayne Nafziger, *Inequality in Africa: Political Elites, Proletariat, Peasants, and the Poor* (Cambridge: Cambridge University Press, 1988), pp. 140–56, 173–75; and Peter Hendry, "Food and Population: Beyond Five Billion," *Population Bulletin* 43 (April 1988): 11.

3. Because of high levels of capital accumulation, technical knowledge, and worker productivity, agricultural output per worker in developed countries is more than ten times as high as in developing countries.

4. Subsistence farming dominated LDC agriculture in the past. The major goal of the peasant farmer has not been to maximize income, but the family's probability of survival. Nevertheless many peasants, attracted by the potential for improving productivity and living standards, have begun to produce more crops for the market.

5. Food production per capita in the developed countries grew at a rate of 0.9 percent per year from 1952 to 1984, compared to 0.6 percent annually in developing countries. Growth rates for both India and China are positive, though generally slower than for LDCs before the late 1970s, and more rapid than other LDCs after liberalization in the late 1970s. Food output per person in LDCs is expected to increase, and their food deficit should decline during the 1990s.

6. Colonial and postcolonial policies biased against agriculture helped contribute to sub-Saharan Africa's decline in food output per capita from the early 1950s to the mid-1980s.

7. Inadequate capital (including that for health and social services), lack of technology, low educational and skill levels, the brain drain to urban areas, food price policies, below-market foreign exchange rates, and governmental urban bias contribute to low incomes in rural areas. Land concentration, the bias of technology toward large farmers, and large seasonal variations in income also affect rural poverty rates.

8. Policies that would increase rural income and reduce rural poverty are manifold. Land reform and redistribution; developing labor-intensive capital equipment; establishing rural credit agencies, agricultural research centers that conduct on-farm tests, institutes to develop and adapt technology for small farmers, an extension service integrated with development agencies, an irrigation authority that conducts careful feasibility studies of proposed projects, and government ministries that provide suitable and timely inputs to farmers are estimable goals. So, too, farm commodity and foreign exchange prices close to market-clearing rates; greater expenditure on social and educational services in rural areas; redistributing land to the rural poor; establishing agro industries, basic consumer goods industries, and other small industries in rural areas; and investment in marketing, transport, and storage facilities for agricultural commodities would improve the lot of the rural poor.

9. Well-planned, cooperative ventures can help small farmers improve productivity by allowing them to take advantage of economies of large-scale production. Collective farms have the same advantage and also use farm workers in rural industry during the slack season. However, collectivism has not generally increased productivity because of some inherent disincentives.

10. Production-oriented rural development projects such as small-farmer credit, agricultural innovations and new technology, and improved extension services are likely to reduce agricultural terms of trade and thus reduce rural incomes in the short run. To increase incomes of the rural poor, production-oriented

programs need to be combined with policies to improve relative agricultural prices and rural income distribution.

The following subjects related to food and agriculture are covered in subsequent chapters: natural resources, land, and climate (Chapter 8); the food-population balance (Chapter 9); disguised unemployment in agriculture and rural-urban migration (Chapter 10); and the substantial dependence of many low-income countries on primary product exports (Chapter 18).

TERMS TO REVIEW

- **peasant farming**
- **mixed farming**
- **commercial farm-ing**
- **food deficit**
- **import substitutes**

- **real exchange-rate change**
- **entitlement**
- *latifundios*
- *minifundios*
- **urban bias**

- **elasticity of supply**
- **cooperative**
- *kolkhoz*
- **collective farm**
- **kulak**
- **state farm**

QUESTIONS TO DISCUSS

1. Give arguments in favor of LDCs concentrating their antipoverty programs in rural areas.

2. Why is agricultural productivity in DCs so much higher than in LDCs?

3. How would the theory of a peasant economy differ from that of a commercial farm economy?

4. Are agriculturalists Paddock and Paddock (note 6) correct in pointing out "the failure of agriculture to produce food in pace with the expanding population?"

5. Explain and compare India's progress since the early 1950s in increasing average food output and reducing hunger to China's progress.

6. Explain sub-Saharan Africa's negative growth in food output per person between the early 1950s and the mid-1980s.

7. What factors contribute to the high incidence of rural poverty in LDCs?

8. Give examples of policies of urban bias (or rural bias) in your own country or another one you know well. Has such a policy bias hampered development?

9. What policies are most effective in increasing rural income and reducing rural poverty? What strategies are needed to prevent rural development policies from increasing rural poverty through reduced agricultural terms of trade?

10. Is Soviet and Chinese collectivism (similar to that before 1975) practicable in LDCs? Compare and explain China's agricultural progress in the Maoist period (1949–76) to that of the period after the 1979 agricultural reforms.

GUIDE TO READINGS

Data on food output and imports in DCs and LDCs are in publications by the U.S. Department of Agriculture (similar to those cited in the note to Figure 7-2), the International Food Policy Research Institute (see note to Table 7-3), and the Food and Agriculture Organization of the United Nations. On Africa's food problem, see Ghai and Radwan, Eicher and Baker (note 8), Nafziger (note 2), and various volumes by the World Bank (for example, the last item in note 7). Material on food and agriculture in socialist countries is contained in Howe; Eberstadt (note 13); Lardy (note 16); Sylvan Wittwer, Yu Youtai, Sun Han, and Wang Lianzheng, *Feeding a Billion: Frontiers of Chinese Agriculture* (East Lansing: Michigan State University Press, 1987); Carl Riskin, *China's Political Economy: The Quest for Development since 1949* (Oxford: Oxford University Press, 1987); and Gregory and Stuart (note 41).

Some of the major works on rural poverty in LDCs are Lipton (note 23), and the World Bank's annual *World Development Report,* and a series of volumes by the ILO (see Chapter 6, guide to readings). Weitz (note 5) has a thorough treatment of the evolution from peasant to specialized farmers. Excellent discussions of agricultural policies are in Lela (note 29); Hunter (note 30); Hayami and Ruttan (note 31); Lipton (note 23); and Bruce F. Johnston and Peter Kilby, *Agriculture and Structural Transformation: Economic Strategies in Late Developing Countries* (New York: Oxford University Press, 1975).

Ajit Kuman Ghose, ed., *Agrarian Reform in Contemporary Developing Countries,* prepared for the ILO (London: Croom Helm, 1983), pp. 3–28; M. R. El Ghonemy, K. H. Parsons, R. P. Sinha, N. Uphoff, and P. Wignaraja, *Studies on Agrarian Reform and Rural Povery* (Rome: Food and Agriculture Organization of the United Nations, 1984), pp. 19–57; and Berry and Cline (note 28) discuss agrarian reform.

Chapter Eight

NATURAL RESOURCES, LAND, AND CLIMATE

This chapter analyzes the relationships between natural resources and economic development. Prior to the main body of the chapter, however, we want to introduce Chapters 8–13. For now the discussion shifts from a general view of economic development, including theories (Chapters 1–7), to the factors that contribute to economic growth (Chapters 8–13).

THE PRODUCTION FUNCTION

Since aggregate growth refers to increases in total production, we can visualize growth factors if we examine the factors contributing to production. We do this in a **production function** stating the relationship between capacity output and the volume of various inputs.

$$Y = F(L,K,N,E,T) \tag{8-1}$$

means that output (or national product) (Y) during a given time period depends on the input flows of labor (L), capital (K), natural resources (N), and entrepreneurship; (E) and prevailing technology (T).

The formula implies that each input, such as labor (L), is homogeneous. We could assume that L represents a number of labor units in which a skilled person is more than one unit. More realistically, though, L stands for a list of skills, together with the number of individuals possessing each skill, available during the unit of time.

Capital goods—plant, equipment, machinery, buildings, and inventories—are produced goods used as inputs in further production. To avoid circularity, where the value of capital is determined by its output potential, the *stock* of capital consists of a heterogeneous complex of specific capital goods. Variable K, however, refers to the *flow* of capital services available for production during the period.

Analogous to the other inputs in our equation, N is a heterogeneous complex of natural resources. Although the stock of natural resources may be gradually depleting, only the flow is relevant for the production function. When new discoveries or techniques allow increased exploitation of natural resources, the flow of N increases per time period.

Entrepreneurship is the production resource coordinating labor, capital, natural resources, and technology. Variable E lends itself even less to quantification than the other production factors.

Technology (T), or technical knowledge, connotes the practical arts, ranging from hunting, fishing, and agriculture through manufacturing, communication, and medicine. T can be a direct production input, as in Equation 8-1, or a variable affecting the relationship between inputs L, K, N, and E and output Y. From the latter perspective, technologies are skills, knowledge, procedures, and activities for transforming inputs into outputs, and an increased T reduces inputs per output.[1]

The scale of production is a variable that might have been included in Equation 8-1. With a given technology, increasing the inputs—labor, capital, natural resources, and entrepreneurship—by some multiple may not result in the same multiplication in output because of economies or diseconomies of scale.

Since our focus is on income or production per worker (or per person), we could restate Equation 8-1 with the independent variable Y/L or Y/P (with P, population). In this case, the production function would become more complex.

This chapter concentrates on the role of land and natural resources in economic development. The next three chapters focus on the relationships among population, labor skills, employment, and development. These chapters clarify how population growth affects economic development, how fertility affects labor force participation and development, how population growth affects labor force growth and unemployment, and what factors affect labor skills—a major component of population quality. Chapters 12 and 13 discuss the remaining independent variables (besides natural resources and labor) in Equation 8-1—capital, technology, and entrepreneurship.

SCOPE OF THE CHAPTER

This chapter analyzes land, climate, and natural resources as economic resources in LDCs.

1. We examine the importance of natural resources for economic development.
2. We look at differences between land, natural resources, and capital.
3. We discuss the growth of arid and semiarid lands.
4. We examine economic development in tropical climates.

[1] Martin Fransman, *Technology and Economic Development* (Boulder, Colo.: Westview, 1986), p. 23.

5. We assess the effect of changing real oil prices on consumption in the 1970s, 1980s and 1990s.

6. We analyze the adverse impact that Dutch disease in a booming export sector can have on other sectors of the economy.

7. We consider the extent to which growth is limited by a scarcity of natural resources.

8. We examine the ethical dilemmas of rich nations in a world of limited resources and income inequalities.

IMPORTANCE OF NATURAL RESOURCES

How important to economic development are land and natural resources? Simon Kuznets wrote in 1955 that economic growth "is unlikely to be inhibited by an absolute lack of natural resources."[2] Other economists have argued that natural resources are fixed factors and therefore unrelated to growth.[3] Japan, Switzerland, and Israel have grown rapidly despite a paucity of natural resources. Yet national product and its growth do not depend on the *stock* of natural resources but their *flow* per unit of time. In fact if technology is fixed, the flow of natural resources places an absolute limitation on physical production in such industries as steel and aluminum.[4]

Kuwait and the United Arab Emirates have some of the world's highest per capita incomes, while those in Saudi Arabia and Libya are higher than the LDCs'. Still incomes and revenues in these oil exporting states varied widely from 1970 to 1988, following boom and bust cycles similar to those in Texas, Louisiana, Oklahoma, and Alberta.

THE CONCEPTS OF LAND, NATURAL RESOURCES, AND CAPITAL

Land and **natural resources** are considered nonproducible, since unlike capital, they cannot be replenished through production. In practice, however, the line between these resources and capital is blurred. Thus we say land is nonproducible, but in some major port cities, such as Singapore, Bombay, and Boston, where land was scarce, landfills extended overall area. Although only about 11 percent of the earth's land area is cultivated, new arable land is continually created through drainage, irrigation, and the use of fertilizer, new seeds, and new machinery. New techniques and cheap transport have made economical the exploitation of resources that were previously unused.

Land and natural resources, although often lumped together, have highly distinguishable properties. Land is immobile and potentially renewable. Natural

[2] Simon S. Kuznets, "Toward a Theory of Economic Growth," in Robert Lekachman, ed., *National Policy for Economic Welfare at Home and Abroad* (Garden City, N.Y.: Doubleday, 1955), p. 36.

[3] James E. Meade, *A Neoclassical Theory of Economic Growth* (Oxford: Oxford University Press, 1961). p. 10.

[4] However advances in technology, such as transistors and silicon chips, reduce the natural resources required per unit of output.

resources, on the other hand, are mobile, but most are nonrenewable—they cannot be replenished at a rate fast enough to be meaningful in terms of the human life span. Nonrenewable energy sources include petroleum, coal, lignite, peat, natural gas liquids, terrestrial heat flows, oil shale, tar sands, uranium, and thorium. Renewable energy sources consist of photochemical energy stored in plants and animals (for example, food, wood, animal excrement, and vegetable fuel), and sun, water (including tidal energy), wind, and animal power.[5]

ARID AND SEMIARID LANDS

A desert is a region supporting little vegetation because of insufficient rainfall (less than 25 centimeters of rain annually) and dry soil. About 23 percent of the earth's land area is desert, or **arid land,** and an additional 20 percent is semiarid. In 1980, about 14 percent of the world population (630 million people) lived in arid or semiarid lands. According to UN estimates, about 80 million people live on almost useless lands—lands damaged by erosion, dune formation, vegetational change, and salt encrustation. Perhaps 50 million of these 80 million people, because of their dependence on agriculture, face the gradual loss of their livelihoods as fields and pastures turn into wastelands.

In the last half-century, particularly since the late 1960s, the Sahara Desert has expanded southward into the areas of the African Sahel (parts of Mauritania, Senegal, Mali, Burkina Faso, Niger and Chad). Such encroachment in Africa, as well as in the Middle East, Australia, and the Americas, results more from irresponsible land use patterns—deforestation, overgrazing, overcultivating, and shortsighted farming practices—than from climatic fluctuations.[6]

TROPICAL CLIMATES

Geographically the **tropics** lie in a band 2500 kilometers wide on each side of the equator, but climatically they are wider. There are three types of tropical climates, all hot but widely varied in rainfall. The wet equatorial climate, a band 1100 kilometers wide centered on the equator, is characterized by constant rainfall (190 to 300 centimeters a year) and humidity. A monsoon strip, alternately wet and dry, lies 1100 kilometers on either side of the wet equatorial tropics. Still farther north and south are the arid tropics, about 1600 kilometers wide, where rain-fed agriculture is practically impossible.

In 1945, the geographer Ellsworth Huntington, contended that different climates, through their direct effects on human energies and achievement, determined different levels of civilization. He argued that the highest level of achievement is affected by the degree to which the weather is moderate and variable.[7] Following strong reaction against his theories, few recent scholars have tried to explain or even declare a relationship between climate and human achievement. At

[5] Earl Cook, *Man, Energy, Society* (San Francisco: W. H. Freeman, 1976), pp. 17, 51.

[6] Erik Eckholm and Lester R. Brown, *Spreading Deserts—The Hand of Man* (Washington, D.C.: Worldwatch Institute, 1977).

[7] Ellsworth Huntington, *Mainsprings of Civilization* (New York: Wiley, 1945).

present they do not know if hot tropical weather has a direct adverse impact on our work efficiency, creativity, and initiative.

However Andrew W. Kamarck enumerates other less questionable notions about why economic underdevelopment occurs in the tropics.[8] There is no winter in the tropics. Weeds, insect pests, and parasitic diseases that are enemies to crops, animals, and people are not exterminated. This disadvantage outweighs any benefit that might accrue from luxuriant plant growth. Intestinal parasites occur in nearly all domestic animals in the tropics. They retard the development of young animals, reduce yields of milk and meat, impair the working capacity of draft animals, and kill many infected animals. For example, trypanosomiasis, a disease carried by the tsetse fly, inhibits farm and transport development because it attacks cattle and transport animals in much of tropical Africa. Gigantic swarms of locusts can fly over 1200 miles nonstop and attack crops anywhere from West Africa to India.

In the tropics, soil is damaged by the sun, which can burn away organic matter and kill microorganisms, and by torrential rains, which can crush soil structure and leach out minerals. And when the lush tropical vegetation is removed, soil deteriorates unless recent alluvial or volcanic overflow replenishes it. Thus reddish and yellowish brown laterite soils predominate in large parts of the humid tropics.

Disease is also a factor in economic underdevelopment in the tropics. This region offers far more hospitable conditions for human disease than the temperate zones. The incidence of parasitic infections in temperate zones is much lower than in the tropics, since winter kills most parasites. At least three-fourths of the adult population of the tropics is infected with some form of parasite. In fact infectious, parasitic, and respiratory diseases account for about 44 percent of the deaths in LDCs but only 11 percent in DCs. For example, about 200 million people suffer from bilharzia, a disease carried by a parasitic worm, that may produce severe, irreversible liver damage, an enlarged spleen, and a bloated abdomen, while the rest of the body becomes emaciated. River blindness, a fly-borne infection, affects approximately 20 million people, mostly in large river valleys in tropical Africa, and causes partial or total blindness. Because constant warm temperature plays a part in this parasite's life cycle, the fly cannot successfully carry this infection into temperate areas. Amoebic and bacillary dysentery spread more rapidly in tropical areas than in temperate zones. The idea that only visitors "not used to the water" suffer from dysentery is fiction.[9] Overall these parasitic diseases substantially impair the health, well-being, and productivity of people living in the tropics.

Poor soil and plant, animal, and human diseases endemic in the tropics explain some of their underdevelopment. An exception is the industrialized highlands of southern Brazil. Although they are located in the tropics, their altitudes foster a cool climate similar to the eastern Appalachians in the United States.

No doubt problems of plague (like desert locusts, which spread from Ethiopia-Sudan in 1985 through much of the Sahara, Northern Africa, and Saudi Arabia by 1988), disease, and soil can be ameliorated by international cooperative research and centralized services in tropical agriculture and medicine. Clearly capital transfer or adaptation of existing research and technology from developed tem-

---

[8] Most of this section relies on Andrew M. Kamarck, *The Tropics and Economic Development: A Provocative Inquiry into the Poverty of Nations* (Baltimore: Johns Hopkins University Press, 1976).

[9] Everett E. Hagen, *Economics of Development* (Homewood, Ill.: Irwin, 1975), p. 191.

perate countries is limited as a spur to tropical economic growth until these other problems are dealt with.

ENERGY

The fourfold price increase in crude petroleum over four months in 1973 and 1974 sent many LDC economies reeling. The LDC imports of fuels and lubricants (largely petroleum) as a percentage of total merchandise imports more than doubled from 8.0 percent in 1970 to 17.5 percent in 1977. The **balance of trade** (merchandise exports minus merchandise imports) for oil-importing LDCs dropped from −$18.0 billion in 1973 to −$42.2 billion in 1974 to −72.1 billion in 1980, while it rose in oil-exporting countries from $18.9 billion in 1973 to $87.1 billion in 1974 to $170.8 billion in 1980. For India oil import payments as a percentage of export receipts more than doubled from 18.6 percent in 1973 to 38.4 percent in 1974. Yet oil-importing LDCs recovered some from the 1973 to 1974 shock, growing as fast as oil-exporting LDCs from 1973 to 1980. Nonoil LDCs' balance of trade recovered during the slump in oil prices in the 1980s, falling to −$35.7 billion in 1983 and −$6.1 billion in 1986, before turning positive in 1987 to 1988, while oil-exporting countries' positive trade balance dropped. While oil-importing LDCs maintained their growth from the 1970s to 1980s, oil-exporting countries' growth, the major determinant of which is the oil export price, declined to a negative rate[10] (see Chapter 3 and Table 8-1).

The Organization of Petroleum Exporting Countries (OPEC) is a **cartel** whose members agree to limit output and fix prices. Though founded in 1960, OPEC achieved its major success through concerted action to increase oil prices in 1973 and 1974. During the 1970s, OPEC countries took over ownership of the oil concessions within their territories, and international oil companies became a combination of contractor and sales agent for these countries.

However by the early 1980s, conservation, the development of alternative energy sources, and a recession among much of the **Organization of Economic Cooperation and Development (OECD**—the United States, Canada, Western Europe, Japan, Australia, and New Zealand) dampened the growth of demand. Meanwhile OPEC was finding it more difficult to enforce prices and quotas, since members, such as Iran, Iraq, and Nigeria, that faced a costly war or mounting debt problems, exceeded their quotas or offered discounts below posted prices, and major nonmember producers, such as Mexico and China, increased their production shares. Saudi Arabia (population 12 million), with 19 percent of the world's estimated reserves (Table 8-2) and the lowest cost production, has a dominant role in OPEC pricing. When members violate OPEC agreements, the Saudis can increase production and lower prices, as from 1986 to 1988, threatening to drive high-cost producers out of the market. Trying to predict the responses of the Saudis and OPEC's weaker members indicates the difficulty of predicting how successful price collusion and future price trends will be.

Energy use depends on both income and price effects (with conservation measures being part of the price impact). The price elasticity of demand for energy

---

[10]Alireza Rahimibrougerdi, "An Empirical Investigation of the Effects of Major Exogenous Shocks on the Growth of Non-Oil- and Oil-Exporting Developing Countries from 1965 to 1985" (Ph.D. diss., Kansas State University, 1988), pp. 147–68.

TABLE 8-1 Balance of Trade by Country Group, 1970–89 (billions of U.S. dollars)[a]

Country Group	1970	1971	1972	1973	1974	1975	1976	1977	1978	1979
Developed countries	-6.7	-5.7	-7.4	-13.5	-54.7	-19.4	-45.5	-51.2	-29.2	-85.2
Oil-exporting and high-income oil-exporting countries	7.7	10.8	11.1	18.9	87.1	58.5	70.5	62.1	106.5	170.0
Oil-importing countries	-14.2	-19.5	-16.4	-18.0	-42.2	-55.6	-41.5	-42.0	-61.5	-91.6

Country Group	1980	1981	1982	1983	1984	1985	1986	1987	1988	1989
Developed counties	-67.0	-19.7	-14.9	-16.6	-43.9	-38.3	-0.5	-18.7	-4.2	-6.6
Oil-exporting and high-income oil-exporting countries	170.8	124.9	64.4	44.2	54.7	55.7	11.5	37.8	25.8	30.4
Oil-importing countries	-72.1	-77.0	-57.0	-35.7	-17.2	-20.5	-6.1	1.2	5.9	-3.2

[a]Socialist countries are not included.

Sources: International Monetary Fund, *International Financial Statistics Yearbook, 1981* (Washington, D.C., 1981), pp. 67–73; and International Monetary Fund, *World Economic Outlook* (Washington, D.C., October 1988), pp. 93, 106.

TABLE 8-2 The World's Twenty Leading Crude Oil Countries (by 1986 production and 1988 estimated proven crude oil reserves, millions of barrels)

Country	1986 Production	1988 Reserves
USSR	4,290	59,000
U.S.	3,169	25,270
Saudi Arabia[a]	1,795	166,980
China	954	18,400
United Kingdom	915	5,200
Mexico	887	48,610
Iran[a]	710	92,850
Iraq[a]	626	100,000
Venezuela[a]	575	56,300
Canada	537	6,825
Nigeria[a]	533	15,980
Kuwait[a]	491	91,920
United Arab Emirates[a]	486	92,205
Indonesia[a]	461	8,400
Libya[a]	415	21,000
Norway	307	15,980
Egypt	297	4,300
Algeria[a]	245	8,500
India	228	4,250
Brazil	210	
Oman		4,012
	17,640	845,982
Other	2,689	41,366
Total world	20,329	887,348

[a]OPEC members (also includes Ecuador and Gabon).

The second leading producer, the United States, is a net oil importer, and the majority of both Soviet and Chinese productions is consumed domestically. Also note that Brazil ranks twentieth in 1986 production and Oman twentieth in 1988 reserves.

Source: American Petroleum Institute, *Basic Petroleum Data Book,* VIII, *Petroleum Industry Statistics* (Washington, D.C., 1988), section II, table 4d, and section IV, table 2d.

increases with response time. Thus in the first several months of the abrupt 1973 to 1974 oil price increase, the elasticity of demand for energy was close to zero (*growth* in amount demanded decreased little). Over the next 7-year period, price elasticities were about 0.4 percent in DCs and 0.3 percent in LDCs (*growth* in quantity demanded dropped substantially). The full effect of changing energy prices takes place 15–25 years later, when demand elasticities (in reponse to 1973–74 prices) may well be twice as high as for the 7-year period.[11]

[11] Robert Stobaugh, "After the Peak: The Threat of Imported Oil," in *Energy Future: Report of the Energy Project at the Harvard Business School,* ed. Robert Stobaugh and Daniel Yergin (New York: Random House, 1979), pp. 31–33; and World Bank, *World Development Report, 1981* (New York: Oxford University Press, 1981), pp. 36–37.

DUTCH DISEASE

Michael Roemer analyzes **Dutch disease,** named when the booming North Seas' gas export revenues in the 1970s appreciated the guilder, making Dutch industrial exports more costly in foreign currencies and increasing foreign competition and unemployment. Analogously the United States suffered from a similar disease from 1980 to 1984, experiencing a farm export crisis and deindustrialization from the decline of traditional U.S. export industries (automobiles, capital goods, high technology, railroad and farm equipment, paint, leather products, cotton fabrics, carpeting, electrical equipment and parts, and basic chemicals) during substantial capital inflows strengthening the dollar. Yet LDCs are less likely to catch Dutch disease from capital inflows than from a major world price increase, a cost-reducing technological change, or a major discovery of a primary resource. The pathology might better be called the Indonesian, Nigerian, Mexican, Venezuelan (from petroleum), Thai (rice, rubber, tin), Malaysian (rubber, tin), Brazilian (coffee, sugar), Colombian (coffee), Ivory Coast (coffee, cocoa, wood), Bangladesh (foreign aid inflows), Egyptian (tourism, remittances, foreign aid inflows), Jordanian (remittances), Zambian, Zaïrian (copper), Ghanaian (cocoa), or Kenyan (tourism, coffee) disease, a 1970s' and 1980s' economic distortion resulting from dependence on one to three booming exports.

Roemer's three-sector model shows that growth in the booming export sector reduces the price of foreign exchange, retarding other sectors' growth by reducing incentives to export other commodities and replace domestic goods for imports and raising factor and input prices for nonbooming sectors. Moreover labor moves from the lagging export and import substitution sectors to the booming and nontradable sectors. Other ill effects of the export boom may be relaxed fiscal discipline, increased capital-intensive projects, and wage dualism. Government can minimize the negative effects of Dutch disease by investing in the lagging traded goods sector before the natural resource is exhausted, so that the rest of the economy can capture the potential benefits of the export boom.[12]

The oil boom of the 1970s proved a blessing for many oil-exporting countries but a curse for others. In 1976, Nigeria's head of state, General Olusegun Obasanjo, responding to political unrest and an overheated economy, pointed out that petroleum revenue was not a cure-all. "Though this country has great potential she is not yet a rich nation. . . . Our resources from oil are not enough to satisfy the yearnings, aspirations and genuine needs of our people, development and social services."[13]

Oil revenues increased average material welfare, widened employment opportunities, and increased policy options. But they also altered incentives, raised expectations, distorted and destabilized nonoil output, frequently in agriculture.

[12] Michael Roemer, "Dutch Disease in Developing Countries: Swallowing Bitter Medicine," in Mats Lundahl, *The Primary Sector in Economic Development* (New York: St. Martin's, 1985), pp. 234–52. See also Ronald Findlay, "Primary Exports, Manufacturing, and Development," in Mats Lundahl, *The Primary Sector in Economic Development* (New York: St. Martin's, 1985), pp. 218–33; and W. Max Corden and J. Peter Neary, "Booming Sector and Deindustrialisation in a Small Open Economy," *Economic Journal* 92 (December 1982): 825–48.

[13] Alan Rake, "And Now the Struggle for Real Development," *African Development* 10 (December 1976): 1263; E. Wayne Nafziger, *The Economics of Political Instability* (Boulder, Colo.: Westview, 1983), p. 187.

Middle-income Indonesia and Nigeria, which had more than 40 percent of pre-1973 GNP originating in agriculture, provide a revealing contrast. While Indonesia's agricultural output increased 3.7 percent annually from 1973 to 1983, output in Nigeria declined 1.9 percent and exports, 7.9 percent yearly over the same period. Agricultural imports as a share of total imports rose from 3 percent in the late 1960s to 7 percent in the early 1980s in Nigeria, while in Indonesia, the share remained unchanged at about 1 percent.

Several differences in agricultural pricing and investment explain Indonesia's more favorable agricultural development. The real value of the Nigerian naira appreciated substantially from 1970 to 1972 and from 1982 to 1983, depreciating relative to the dollar only under pressure in 1986, while Indonesia's rupiah real value increased much more slowly, and depreciated via-à-vis the dollar, from 1978 to 1983. Additionally Indonesia invested a substantial amount of government funds in agriculture, especially rice, while less than 10 percent of the Nigerian plan's capital expenditures were in agriculture. The attempt by Nigeria, beginning in the mid-1980s, to increase incentives and investment in agriculture had little initial impact.[14] The country will require sustained policy changes to reverse the effects of years of neglect.

The Dutch disease from the oil boom in the 1970s may seem a mild case of influenza for Nigeria, Mexico, Venezuela, and Iran compared to **reverse Dutch disease** from the oil bust of the 1980s. For a top Nigerian economic official in 1988, striking it rich on oil in the 1970s was "like a man who wins a lottery and builds a castle. He can't maintain it, and then has to borrow to move out."[15] Dependence on one or two exports makes these countries especially vulnerable to external price shocks.

LIMITS TO GROWTH

The nineteenth-century English, classical economists feared eventual economic stagnation or decline from diminishing returns to natural resources. The concept of diminishing returns was the foundation for Malthus's *Essay on the Principles of Population* (1798, 1803) which argued that population growth tended to outstrip increases in food supply. Economists have long disputed whether diminishing returns and Malthusian population dynamics place limits on economic growth.

In the early 1970s, the influential Club of Rome, a private international association organized by Italian industrialist Aurelio Peccei, commissioned a team of scholars at MIT to examine the implication of growth trends for our survival. The study, *The Limits to Growth,* based on computer simulations, uses growth trends from 1900 to 1970 as a base for projecting the effects of industrial expansion and population growth on environmental pollution and the consumption of food and nonrenewable resources. The study suggests that as natural resources diminish,

[14] World Bank, *World Development Report, 1986* (New York: Oxford University Press, 1986), p. 72.

[15] Flora Lewis, "Oil Crisis of '73 Wreaking Economic Havoc," *Kansas City Times* (November 22, 1988), p. 7. See David Evans, "Reverse Dutch Disease and Mineral-Exporting Developing Economies," *IDS Bulletin* 17 (October 1986): 10–13, on reverse Dutch diseases from depressed primary product prices.

costs rise, leaving less capital for future investment. Eventually new capital formation falls below depreciation, so that the industrial base, as well as the agricultural and services economies, collapse. Shortly after population drops precipitously because of food and resource shortages. The study concludes that if present growth continues, the planetary limits to growth will be reached sometime in the twenty-first century, at which time the global economic system will break down.

The message of the book is that since the earth is finite, any indefinite economic expansion must eventually reach its limits. Without environmental controls, economic growth and the attendant exponential increase in carbon dioxide emissions from burning fossil fuel, thermal pollution, radioactive nuclear wastes, and soluble industrial, agricultural, and municipal wastes severely threaten our limited air and water resources. Biologist Garrett Hardin explains the environmental pollution economists attribute to external diseconomies (Chapters 7 and 12) as a **"tragedy of the commons."** Just as the herder's cattle eventually overgraze a pasture open to all, so do businesses and individuals overpollute air and water free for all to use.[16]

Yet many of the assumptions the MIT scholars make are seriously flawed. For example, their estimates indicate that they apparently believe that *proven* petroleum reserves represent *all* the petroleum reserves of the world. However, proven reserves are not satisfactory for making long-term projections, since they are only the known reserves that can be recovered profitably at prevailing cost and price levels. Proven reserves are no more than an assessment of the working inventory of minerals that industry is confident is available. Profit-motivated, commercial exploration tries to find only sufficient new reserves to meet the industry's requirements over its forward planning period (typically 8 to 12 years), plus any new reserves that promise to be more profitable than previous discoveries.

Thus it is not surprising that proven reserves are rather meager in comparison to the reserves that can ultimately be recovered. Thus we have the spectacle in 1864 of W. Stanley Jevons, one of the great economists of the nineteenth century, predicting that England's industry would soon grind to a halt with the exhaustion of England's coal. A modern example of this disparity between proven and ultimately recoverable reserves is that in 1970, the proven reserves of lead, zinc, and copper were much larger than those in 1949, even though the amount of these metals mined between 1949 and 1970 was greater than proven reserves in 1949.

A further criticism of the MIT team is that their model analyzes the world's population, capital stock, natural resources, technology, and output without discussing differences by world region. It also treats food output as a single entity, ignoring differences between cereals, fruits, vegetables, and animal products.

Another flaw in the MIT study is the assumption of exponential growth in industrial and agricultural needs, but the arbitrary placement of nonexponential limits on the technical progress that might accommodate these needs.

A complex computer model only aids understanding if its assumptions are valid. Critics argue that *Limits* is not a "rediscovery of the laws of nature," as the authors' press agents claim, but a "rediscovery of the oldest maxim of computer science: Garbage In, Garbage Out."[17]

---

[16] Garrett Hardin, "The Tragedy of the Commons," *Science* 162 (December 13, 1968): 1244–45.

[17] Donella H. Meadows, Dennis L. Meadows, Jørgen Randers, and William W. Behrens, III, *The Limits to Growth* (New York: Universe Books, 1972); Colin Robinson, "The Depletion of Energy Resources," in *The Economics of Natural Resource Depletion*, ed. D. W. Pearce (New York: Wiley,

Herman E. Daly more clearly indicates the assumptions, calculations, and causal relationships behind limits to economic growth and unlike *Limits,* goes on to calculate their effect on increased international conflict.[18] According to him, a U.S.-style, high mass consumption, growth-oriented economy is impossible for a world of 5.2 billion people. The stock of mineral deposits in the earth's crust and the ecosystem's capacity to absorb enormous or exotic waste materials and heat drastically limit the number of person-years that can be lived at U.S. consumption levels. Daly believes that how we apportion these person-years of mass consumption among nations, social classes, and generations will be the dominant political and economic issue of the future. The struggle for these limited high-consumption units will shape the nature of political conflict, both within and between nation-states.

Daly's argument that the entire world's population cannot enjoy U.S. consumption levels—the **impossibility theorem**—can be illustrated in the following way. Today it requires about one-third of the world's flow of nonrenewable resources and 26 percent of **gross planetary product** (the gross production value of the world's goods and services) to support the 5 percent of the world's population living in the United States. On the other hand, the 79 percent of the world's population living in LDCs use only about one-seventh of the nonrenewable resources and produce only 17 percent of the gross planetary product.[19] Present resource flows would allow the extension of the U.S. living standard to a maximum of 15 percent of the world's population with nothing left over for the other 85 percent.

For some the solution to this dilemma is to increase world resource flows sixfold, the amount needed to raise world resource use per capita to that in the United States. However to increase resource flows this much, the rest of the world would have to attain the capitalization and technical extracting and processing capacity of the United States. Such an increase in capital would require a tremendous increase in resource flows during the accumulation period. Harrison Brown estimates that it would take more than 60 years of production at 1970 rates to supply the rest of the world with the average industrial metals per capita embodied in the artifacts of the ten richest countries. Furthermore due to the law of diminishing returns, a sixfold increase in net, usable resources, energy, and materials implies a much greater than sixfold increase in gross resources and environmental impact. Enormous increases in energy and capital devoted to mining, refining, transporta-

---

1975), pp. 28–31; A. J. Surrey and William Page, "Some Issues in the Current Debate about Energy and Natural Resources," in *The Economics of Natural Resource Depletion,* ed. D. W. Pearce (New York: Wiley, 1975), pp. 56–64; Julian L. Simon, *The Ultimate Resource* (Princeton: Princeton University Press, 1981); Colin Clark, *Population and Depopulation,* The 11th Monash Economics Lecture, Monash University, Clayton, Victoria, Australia, October 3, 1977; and the last quote is from Peter Passell, Marc Roberts, and Leonard Ross, Review of *Limits to Growth, New York Times Book Review* (April 2, 1972).

[18] Herman E. Daly, *Steady-State Economics: The Economics of Biophysical Equilibrium and Moral Growth* (San Francisco: W. H. Freeman, 1977).

[19] Chapter 2 indicates that cross-cultural comparisons of income understate the gross national product per capita of the poor countries. Even when figures are adjusted for these distortions, the share of the poorest countries increases only from 17 percent to 20 percent. U.S. Department of State, *The Planetary Product "Back to Normalcy" in 1976–77,* Special Report No. 44, Washington, D.C., Bureau of Public Affairs, 1978, adjusted to 1989.

tion, and pollution control are essential for mining poorer grade and less-accessible minerals and disposing safely of large quantities of wastes.[20]

Brown's estimates are based on rough input-output relationships with no allowance for new discoveries and technological improvements. Nevertheless the required increases in resource flows suggest the difficulty, if not impossibility, of the world attaining a U.S.-style consumption level by the 2020s.

Entropy and the Economic Process

The application of the physical law of **entropy** to production shows, from a scientific perspective, the finite limits of the earth's resources. What goes into the economic process represents valuable natural resources; what is thrown out is generally waste. That is, matter-energy enters the economic process in a state of low entropy and comes out in a state of high entropy. To explain, entropy is a measure of the *unavailable* energy in a thermodynamic system. Energy can be free energy, over which we have almost complete command, or bound energy, which we cannot possibly use. The chemical energy in a piece of coal is free energy because we can transform it into heat or mechanical work. But when the coal's initial free energy is dissipated in the form of heat, smoke, and ashes that we cannot use, it has been degraded into bound energy—energy dissipated in disorder, or a state of high entropy. The second law of thermodynamics states that the entropy of a closed system continuously increases, or that the order of such a system steadily turns into disorder. The entropy cost of any biological or economic enterprise is always greater than the product. Every object of economic value—a fruit picked from a tree or a piece of clothing—has a low entropy. Our continuous tapping of natural resources increases entropy. Pollution and waste indicate the entropic nature of the economic process. Even recycling requires an additional amount of low entropy in excess of the renewed resource's entropy.[21]

We have access to two sources of free energy, the stock of mineral deposits and the flow of solar radiation intercepted by the earth. However we have little control over this flow. The higher the level of economic development, the greater the depletion of mineral deposits and hence the shorter the expected life of the human species. For theorist Nicholas Georgescu–Roegen, every time we produce a Cadillac, we destroy low entropy that could otherwise be used for producing a plow or a spade. Thus we produce Cadillacs at the expense of future human life. Economic abundance, a blessing now, is against the interest of the human species as a whole. We become dependent on, and addicted to, industrial luxuries, so that, according to Georgescu–Roegen, the human species will have a short but exciting life.

Georgescu–Roegen's perspective is one not of decades but of millenia, since his preoccupation is with our survival as a species. But even if we have little concern beyond the lifetime of our great-grandchildren, we ignore pessimists such as Daly and Georgescu-Roegen at our peril.

---

[20] Harrison Brown, "Human Materials Production as a Process in the Biosphere," *Scientific American* 223, no. 3 (September 1970): 195–208.

[21] Nicholas Georgescu–Roegen, *The Entropy Law and the Economic Process* (Cambridge, Mass.: Harvard University Press, 1971).

LIVING ON A LIFEBOAT

What impact do limited resources have on the ethics of whether or not rich countries should aid poor countries? Hardin, who uses the metaphor of living on a lifeboat, argues that food, technical, financial, and other assistance should be *denied* to desperately poor countries as a way of ensuring the survival of the rest of the human species. Hardin sees the developed nations as a lifeboat with a load of rich people. In comparison,

> The poor of the world are in other, much more crowded lifeboats. Continuously . . . the poor fall out of their lifeboats and swim for a while in the water outside, hoping to be admitted to a rich lifeboat, or in some other way to benefit from the "goodies" on board.[22]

Hardin sees only three options for the passengers on the rich lifeboat, filled to perhaps 80 percent of its capacity:

1. Take all the needy aboard so that the boat is swamped and everyone drowns—complete justice, complete catastrophe.
2. Take on enough people to fill the remaining carrying capacity. However this option sacrifices the safety factor represented by the extra capacity. Furthermore how do we choose whom to save and whom to exclude?
3. Admit no more to the boat, preserve the small safety factor, and assure the survival of the passengers. This action may be unjust, but those who feel guilty are free to change places with those in the water. Those people willing to climb aboard would have no such qualms, so the lifeboat would purge itself of guilt as the conscience-stricken surrender their places.

This ethical analysis aside, Hardin supports the **lifeboat ethic** of the rich on practical grounds: The poor (that is, the LDCs) are doubling in numbers every 33 years, the rich (DCs), every 115 years. During these 115 years, the 3 to 1 ratio of those outside to those inside the rich life boat will increase to 16 to 1.[23]

[22] Garrett Hardin, "Living on a Lifeboat," *Bio Science* 24 (October 1974): 561–68.

[23] The doubling time and ratios are based on 1988 population growth figures. A view similar to Hardin's, but with less support among scholars, is that of agriculturists William Paddock and Paul Paddock, *Famine—1975! America's Decisions: Who Will Survive* (Boston: Little, Brown, 1967). The Paddock brothers propose that the United States allocate aid on the basis of **triage,** a medical concept used by the Allies in World War I to classify casualties. When the wounded crowd medical facilities to the point that all cannot be cared for by a limited staff, some decision must be made as to who will be treated. All incoming casualties are placed in one of three classes: (1) those who will survive regardless of treatment, (2) those who will survive only with prompt treatment, and (3) those who will die regardless of treatment. The limited medical aid is concentrated on the second group alone. Analogously the Paddocks recommend that the United States provide food assistance to only countries that can become self-sufficient in food, but not countries in category (3), such as India, which they believe to be incapable of attaining sufficiency. Giving aid to the third group would not prevent, but only postpone its inevitable famine.

However food production per capita in India (and the LDCs as a whole) increased from the 1950s through the 1980s (see Chapter 7). In addition evidence presented in Chapter 9 indicates that the Paddocks' view of inevitable widespread famine in LDCs is incorrect.

Hardin's premises about population growth are faulty. He expresses concern that some of the "goodies" transferred from the rich lifeboat to the poor boats may merely "convert extra food into extra babies."[24] However food production has grown faster than population in developing countries in every decade since World War II. Moreover although population *has* increased in LDCs since World War II, it has been because of falling mortality rates, not greater fertility (which instead has been dropping slowly). Furthermore evidence indicates that economic assistance to LDCs generally facilitates development, thus reducing the fertility rate rather than increasing it. (For elaboration, see Chapters 7 and 9.)

In addition Hardin's lifeboat metaphor is flawed. In contrast to Hardin's lifeboats that barely interact, nations in the real world interact enormously through trade, investment, military and political power, and so on. His metaphor is not realistic enough to be satisfactory. Hardin must admit that the rich lifeboats are dependent on the poor lifeboats for many of the materials and products of their affluence. Furthermore the rich lifeboats command a disproportional share of the world's resources. Indeed one seat on the lifeboat (that is, access to a given amount of nonrenewable resources) can support ten times the population from a LDC as from the DC. Daly and Georgescu–Roegen would argue that it is the Americans and Canadians, not the Indians and Africans, who most endanger the stability of the lifeboat. The average American, for instance, consumes 156 times as much energy per capita as the average citizen of Bangladesh (see the last column, Table 2-1). Also Hardin fails to acknowledge that the carrying capacity of the planet, unlike that of the lifeboat, is not fixed but can increase with technical change. Indeed technical assistance can enhance output in the poor countries without hurting the rich countries. Finally Hardin's rich lifeboat can raise the ladder and sail away. In the real world, we may not be able to abandon the poor. See Chapter 16 for more discussion on economic aid to LDCs.

SUMMARY

1. Production depends on the flow of natural resources, capital, labor, entrepreneurship, and technology per unit of time.

2. Land and natural resources are distinguishable. Land is immobile and potentially renewable. Natural resources are mobile, but most are nonrenewable.

3. About 14 percent of the world population lives on arid or semiarid land. Increases in arid lands in the last several decades are traceable to overcultivation, deforestation, and so forth.

4. Economic underdevelopment in the tropics is partly a matter of geography. There is no winter to exterminate weeds and insect pests. Parasitic diseases are endemic and weaken the health and productivity of people. The heat and torrential rains damage the soils, removing needed organic matter, microorganisms, and minerals.

5. The Club of Rome's study, *The Limits to Growth,* concluded that the global economic system will collapse during the twenty-first century. However a major shortcoming of the study is the assumption of exponential growth in indus-

---

[24] Garrett Hardin, "Living on a Lifeboat," *BioScience* 24 (October 1974): 564.

trial and agricultural needs and the arbitrary placement of nonexponential limits on the technical progress that might accommodate these needs.

6. Daly's impossibility theorem argues that there are not enough resources in the world to support the whole world at U.S.-style consumption levels.

7. Our continuous use of natural resources increases entropy, a measure of the unavailable energy in a thermodynamic system. Georgescu–Roegen argues that luxury production decreases the expected life span of the human species.

8. Oil crises in the 1970s worsened the balance of trade deficit, debt burden, and inflation rate and slowed the growth rate of oil-importing LDCs, but the oil glut in the 1980s reduced these problems for some oil importers.

9. Dutch disease is the adverse competitive effect that local currency appreciation due to a booming export sector has on other exports and import substitutes. Among two highly populated oil-exporting LDCs, this disease was less severe in Indonesia than in Nigeria in the late 1970s and early 1980s, since Indonesia appreciated more slowly and used oil revenues to expand agricultural investment.

10. Lifeboat ethics, used as an argument for denying economic assistance to LDCs, is based on a number of flawed premises. Rich nations command a disproportional share of the world's resources, depend economically on poor nations, and have access to technical knowledge that can increase LDC productivity without decreasing their own.

The following subjects related to natural resources are covered in subsequent chapters: the food-population balance (Chapter 9), the increased international debt burden of oil-importing LDCs (Chapter 17), the international trade of natural resources, and cartels for primary producers (Chapter 18)

TERMS TO REVIEW

- **production function**
- **capital goods**
- **entrepreneurship**
- **technology**
- **land**
- **natural resources**
- **arid land**
- **tropics**
- **balance of trade**

- **cartel**
- **Organization of Economic Co-operation and Development (OECD)**
- **Dutch disease**
- **reverse Dutch disease**

- **tragedy of the commons**
- **proven reserves**
- **Daly's impossibility theorem**
- **gross planetary product**
- **entropy**
- **lifeboat ethic**
- **triage**

QUESTIONS TO DISCUSS

1. What inputs determine the level of national product in a given year? Are these inputs stocks or flows?

2. How does geography affect economic development in the tropics? What measures are needed to overcome these adverse effects?

3. Indicate in broad outline the movements of *real* world crude petroleum prices in the last quarter of a century. What impact have these prices had on oil-importing LDCs?

4. Assume you are asked as an economic practitioner to analyze a patient with Dutch disease. Analyze the causes of the disease, describe the patient's symptoms, and prescribe an antidote to improve the patient's health. Also do the same for reverse Dutch disease.

5. How severely will a shortage of natural resources limit economic growth in the next half-century, especially in LDCs?

6. Evaluate the following statement by Paddock and Paddock (*Famine— 1975!,* p. 229) on the global food crisis.

> Triage would seem to be the most clean-cut method of meeting the crisis. Waste not the food on the "can't-be-saved" [like India, Egypt, and Haiti]. . . . Send it to those nations [like Pakistan and Tunisia] which, having it, can buttress their own resources, their own efforts, and win the fight through to survival.

GUIDE TO READINGS

Robert Repetto, "Population, Resources, Environment: An Uncertain Future," *Population Bulletin* 42 (July 1987): 1–43, provides data on the relationship between the world's resources and population. The annual *State of the World,* by Lester R. Brown and associates at the Worldwatch Institute, (New York: Norton), assesses resources, environment, and sustainable economies.

A.P. Thirlwall, *Growth and Development with Special Reference to Developing Countries* (New York: Wiley, 1977), pp. 48–80; and Henry J. Bruton, *Principles of Development Economics* (Englewood Cliffs, N.J.: Prentice-Hall, 1965), pp. 11–21, provide a more detailed analysis of the aggregate production function.

Does scarcity of natural resources place substantial limitations on future economic growth? Although the best-known analyses of the yes answer to this question are the Club of Rome studies by Meadows et al. (note 17) and Mihajlo Mesarovic and Eduard Pestel, *Mankind at the Turning Point* (New York: Signet, 1974), the arguments by Daly (note 18) and Georgescu–Roegen (note 21) are more compelling. On the negative side of this question is Simon (note 17). Short articles by growth optimist J. E. Stiglitz and pessimist Daly, plus a critique by Georgescu–Roegen, are in V. Kerry Smith, *Scarcity and Growth Reconsidered* (Baltimore: Johns Hopkins University Press, 1979), pp. 36–105. Clear expositions for the two sides, written for the lay reader, are Georgescu–Roegen, "The Entropy Law and the Economic Process," in H. E. Daly, ed., *Essays toward a Steady-State Economy* (Cuernavaca, Mexico: Centro Intercultural de Documentacion, 1971); and Simon, "The Scarcity of Raw Materials," *Atlantic Monthly* (June 1981): 33–41. The next chapter provides sources for the debate between Malthusians and optimists, such as Simon, concerning whether population and resources limit food output growth.

A wide-ranging study of the energy future is the Harvard Business School report edited by Stobaugh and Yergin (note 11). *World Development Report, 1981,* pp. 35–48, examines the effect of high energy prices on LDCs.

For Hardin (note 22) and the Paddocks (note 23), limited resources demonstrate the need for the West to reduce economic assistance to low-income countries. On the other hand, the annual Overseas Development Council study of the United States and world development uses the premise of limitations to argue for greater aid to LDCs.

Roemer, Findlay, and Corden and Neary (note 12) examine Dutch disease in LDCs. The *IDS Bulletin* 17 (October 1986) has three articles dealing with Dutch disease: Evans (note 15); Ahmad Jazayeri, "Prices and Output in Two Oil-Based Economies: The Dutch Disease in Iran and Nigeria," pp. 14–21; and Alan Gelb, "From Boom to Bust—Oil Exporting Countries over the Cycle, 1970–84," pp. 22–29.

Kamarck (note 8) has written the definitive study on economic development in the tropics. Eckholm and Brown (note 6) discuss how LDC policies have led to growth of arid lands.

Christopher Flavin, *Slowing Global Warming: A Worldwide Strategy* (Washington, D. C.: Worldwatch Institute, 1989), warns that global average temperatures increased 0.6 degrees Celsius in the last century and are expected to rise 2.5–5.5 degrees Celsius by the late twenty-first century. He estimates that carbon dioxide (from coal, oil, natural gas, and deforestation) added 57 percent of this "greenhouse effect," chlorofluorocarbons (from foams, aerosols, refrigerants, and solvents) 25 percent, methane (from wetlands, rice, fossil fuels, and livestock) 12 percent, and nitrous oxide (from fossil fuels, fertilizers, and deforestation) 6 percent. Global warming will increase drought, heat waves, and tropical storms, raise sea level, and shift vegetation zones so as to disrupt grain and other crop production.

One-fourth of the world's population, primarily in the rich world, accounts for 70 percent of its fossil fuel based carbon emissions. The United States' carbon emissions from fossil fuels per capita (1987) is 5.03, Canada's is 4.24, and the world's is 1.08. Besides North America, the Soviet Union, China, Brazil, and Japan are the largest producers of greenhouse gas, a major external diseconomy.

Chapter Nine

POPULATION AND DEVELOPMENT

Between 1980 and 1990, the world's population grew at 1.7 percent per year, from 4.4 billion to 5.2 billion. During the same period, LDC population grew at 2.1 percent per year, from 3.2 billion to 3.9 billion. This chapter explains this phenomenal growth rate and looks at its implications.

SCOPE OF THE CHAPTER

After a brief historical sketch, we consider population growth in DCs and LDCs and by world regions. Next we explain the rapid growth in LDCs by looking at trends in death and birth rates during a period of demographic (population) transition. With this background, we assess the effect of population growth on economic development and review the work of classical economist Thomas Robert Malthus, who argues that population growth outstrips economic growth. In this connection, we discuss the present and future balance between food and population. Population growth also affects urbanization, labor force growth, and the number of dependents workers must support; we look at all of these elements, too. In the last section, we consider the relative merits of birth control programs and socioeconomic development in reducing population growth.

WORLD POPULATION THROUGHOUT HISTORY

Throughout most of our existence, population grew at a rate of only 0.002 percent (or 20 per million people) per year. This growth was subject to substantial fluctuations from wars, plagues, famines, and natural catastrophes. However since about 8000 BC, population growth rates have accelerated. Worldwide population reached one billion in the early nineteenth century, millions of years after our appearance on earth. The second billion was added about a century later, in 1930. The third billion came along in only 30 years, in 1960; the fourth took only 15 years, in 1975; the fifth, 11 years, in 1986; and the sixth billion is expected 11 years later, in 1997 (see

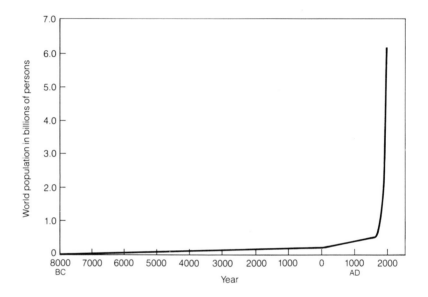

FIGURE 9-1 World Population Growth through History The graph shows how explosive population growth has been in the last 200 years. World population grew at an annual rate of about 0.002 percent between the appearance of humanity and 8000 BC, 0.05 percent between 8000 BC and 1650, 0.43 percent between 1650 and 1900, 0.91 percent between 1900 and 1950, 1.93 percent between 1950 and 1980, and is expected to grow 1.62 percent per year between 1980 and 2000.

Sources: Based on Paul R. Ehrlich, Anne H. Ehrlich, and John P. Holdren, *Ecoscience: Population, Resources, Environment* (San Francisco: W. H. Freeman, 1977), p. 183; Warren S. Thompson and David T. Lewis, *Population Problems* (New York: McGraw-Hill, 1965), p. 384; Alexander Morris Carr-Saunders, *World Population: Past Growth and Present Trends* (Oxford: Clarendon Press, 1936), pp. 15–45; U.S. Bureau of the Census, *World Population: 1977—Recent Demographic Estimates for the Countries and Regions of the World* (Washington, D.C., 1978), p. 15; U.S. Bureau of the Census, *Illustrative Projections of World Populations in the Twenty-first Century* (Washington, D.C., 1979), p. 17; and World Bank, *World Development Report, 1987* (New York: Oxford University Press, 1987), pp. 254–55.

Figure 9-1). Nearly 80 percent of the world's population in 1997 will live in what are now LDCs.

POPULATION GROWTH IN DEVELOPED AND DEVELOPING COUNTRIES

Figure 9-2 indicates the great variation in birth rates, death rates, and population growth among nations. Countries can be roughly divided into three groups: (1) the DCs, consisting of countries in Europe, North America, Australia, New Zealand, and Japan, with population growth rates below 1 percent per year; (2) Argentina, Chile, Uruguay, Cuba, China, Taiwan, South Korea, Sri Lanka, and Thailand, with annual rates between 1 and 2 percent (and Yugoslavia and Romania with less than 1 percent), whose demographic behavior is closer to DCs than to LDCs; and (3) the bulk of the LDCs—most of Africa, Asia, and Latin America, with population growth rates in excess of 2 percent per year. (Note that the birth rates and population growth rates of affluent oil countries, such as Kuwait, the United Arab Emirates, Saudi Arabia, Libya, and Venezuela, are similar to those of other third-world countries.)

A major distinction between the three groups is the birth rate. (Following the conventional use, **crude birth and death rates** denote a number per 1000, *not* percent.) The DCs' crude birth rate (except for the Soviet Union's) are no more than 16 per thousand. Most developing countries have birth rates above 26 per 1000. Countries in category 2 generally fall between these two figures.

WORLD POPULATION BY REGION

The world's population is unevenly distributed geographically. Figure 9-3 shows regional distribution in 1950 and 1987, and projected distribution in 2020. The most rapidly growing regions are in the developing world: Asia, Africa, and Latin America. Their share of the global population increased from 70.0 percent in 1950 to 78.7 percent in 1987, and is expected to reach 84.8 percent in 2020. Today LDCs grow at a rate of 2.1 percent per year, a rate that doubles population in 33 years. Such growth is unprecedented in world history.

Africa is expected to have the most rapid growth in the three decades before 2020, 2.7 percent annually. Its present rate, 2.8 percent yearly, is the result of a traditionally high crude birth rate, 44 per 1000 (with only 3–4 percent of married couples using contraceptives), and a crude death rate, 18 per thousand. The death rate plummeted in the last four decades because of improvements in health, nutrition, medicine, and sanitation. While growth in Latin America until 2020 is projected at 1.6 percent annually, its present yearly rate, 2.2 percent per year, is based on 30 births and 8 deaths per 1000. Although Asia's annual growth, 1.8 percent (birth rate of 28 and death rate of 10), will decline to 1.4 percent in the 30 years before 2020 it is by far the most heavily populated region, with almost 60 percent of the world's people (excluding Asiatic Soviet Union).[1]

[1] Population Reference Bureau, *1987 World Population Data Sheet* (Washington, D.C., 1987); and Nancy Birdsall and Frederick T. Sai, "Family-Planning Services in sub-Saharan Africa," *Finance and Development* 25 (March 1988): 29.

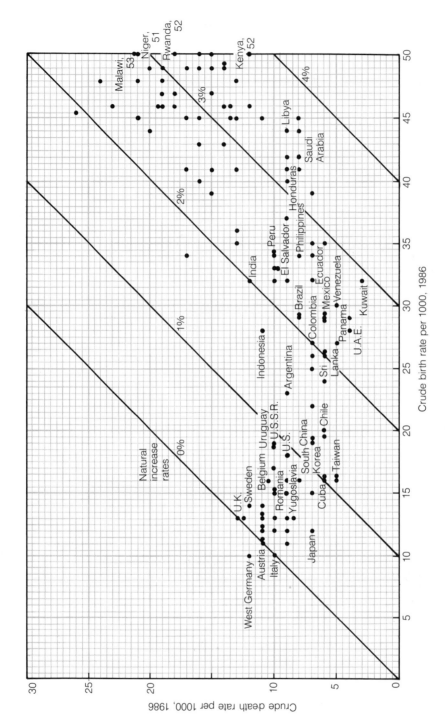

FIGURE 9-2 Population Growth in Developed and Developing Countries A population growth rate of 1–2 percent per year divides the DCs from the LDCs.

Source: World Bank, *World Development Report, 1988* (New York: Oxford University Press, 1988), pp. 276–77. Author's estimate for Taiwan.

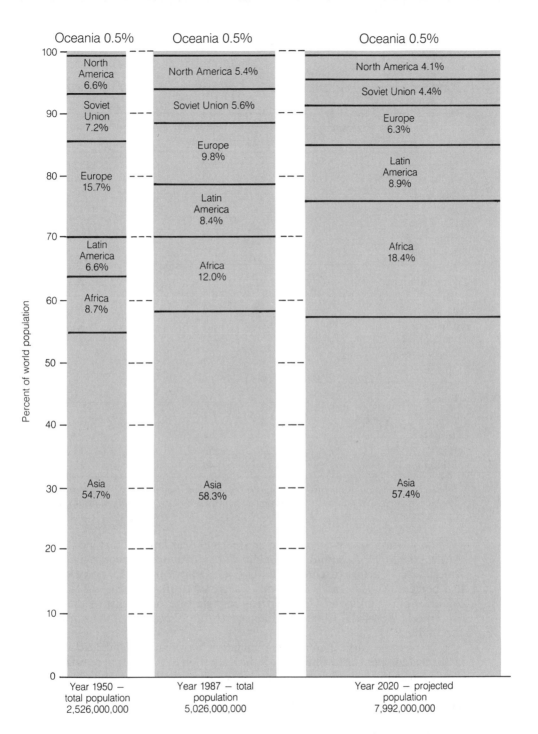

FIGURE 9-3 World Population by Region: 1950, 1987, and 2020 (projected) Asia's, Africa's, and Latin America's share of the world population is increasing over time.

Sources: Based on United Nations, Department of Economic and Social Affairs, *Demographic Yearbook, 1976* (New York, 1977), p. 115; Paul R. Ehrlich, Anne H. Ehrlich, and John P. Holdren, *Ecoscience: Population, Resources, Environment* (San Francisco: W. H. Freeman, 1977), pp. 200–201; and Population Reference Bureau, *World Population Data Sheet, 1988* (Washington, D.C., 1988).

TABLE 9-1   Population of the Twenty-one Largest Countries in the World: 1987 and 2020 (projected)

	Total Population, 1987 (millions)	Projected Population, 2020 (millions)
China	1062	1394
India	800	1310
USSR	284	355
U.S.	244	297
Indonesia	175	284
Brazil	142	234
Japan	122	123
Nigeria	109	274
Bangladesh	107	202
Pakistan	105	242
Mexico	82	138
Vietnam	62	121
Philippines	62	115
West Germany	61	50
U.K.	57	57
Italy	57	54
France	56	58
Egypt	52	103
Turkey	51	92
Iran	50	131
Ethiopia	46	111

Source: Population Reference Bureau, *1987 World Population Data Sheet* (Washington, D.C., 1987); and Thomas W. Merrick, "World Population in Transition," *Population Bulletin* 41 (April 1986): 6.

Population size is a factor in shifting political and military power from the North Atlantic to Asia and the Pacific. The percentage of people living in North America and Europe (excluding the USSR) declined from 23.0 percent in 1900 to 15.2 percent in 1987, and is expected to decrease to 10.4 percent in 2020. Six Asian countries plus the Soviet Union (partly in Asia) are on the list of the ten largest countries in the world. China and India constitute 37 percent of the world's population (Table 9-1).

Most of the large increases in population between 1987 and 2020 are expected in the developing world. China's or India's addition to population during this period should exceed U.S. total population in 2020. Nigeria, Pakistan, Indonesia, Bangladesh, Brazil, Iran, Ethiopia, Vietnam, Kenya, and Mexico will each grow more during the period from 1987 to 2020 than the United States, the world's fourth largest country.

THE DEMOGRAPHIC TRANSITION

In the ancient and medieval periods, famine, disease, and war were potent checks to population growth throughout the world. During the Black Death (1348–50), for example, Europe lost one-fourth to one-third of its population.

After 1650, the population of Western countries increased more rapidly and steadily. The rate increased first in England (especially from 1760 to about 1840), then in other parts of Western Europe, and later in several areas Europeans had settled—the United States, Canada, Australia, and New Zealand. However between 1930 and the present, population growth rates declined in these Western countries in about the same order in which they had increased.[2] On the other hand, except for China and Japan, non-Western countries did not experience initial rapid population growth until after 1930.

The **demographic transition** is a period of rapid population growth between a preindustrial, stable population characterized by high birth and death rates and a later, modern, stable population marked by low fertility and mortality. The rapid natural increase takes place in the early transitional stage when fertility is high and mortality is declining. Figure 9-4 illustrates the four-stage demographic transition theory.

Stage 1: High Fertility and Mortality

We were in this stage throughout most of our history. Although annual population growth was only 5 per 10,000 between AD 1 and AD 1650, growth in eighteenth- and nineteenth-century Western Europe was about 5 per 1000, and birth and death rates were high and fairly similar. High mortality in North America is not so historically remote, as the following quote illustrates:

> Abraham Lincoln's mother died when she was thirty-five and he was nine. Prior to her death she had three children: Abraham's brother died in infancy and his sister died in her early twenties. Abraham's first love, Anne Rutledge, died at age nineteen. Of the four sons born to Abraham and Mary Todd Lincoln, only one survived to maturity. Clearly, a life with so many bereavements was very different from most of our lives today.[3]

High mortality rates were inevitable in the absence of modern sanitation, medicine, industry, agriculture, trade, transportation, and communication. Premodern socioeconomic groups, such as village communities, tribes, lineages, and principalities, were small and largely self-sufficient. Even so, food shortages brought on by floods, droughts, insect plagues, and warfare, although confined to a small locality, were very serious. Roads and vehicles for transporting surplus food from other areas were rarely adequate to the need during these times.

For such populations to survive, fertility must at least match mortality. Thus it is not surprising that prevailing ideology, values, religion, and social structure in the ancient, medieval, and early modern world supported high birth rates. Large families were considered a blessing from God. A woman gained acceptance in her husband's family, as well as her community, by bearing children. However, values and institutions supporting high fertility changed slowly as mortality rates declined. We bear the burden of these outmoded views today, long after they have lost their original function.

Preindustrial Western continental Europe had lower birth and death rates than have twentieth-century developing countries in a comparable stage of develop-

---

[2] Warren S. Thompson and David T. Lewis, *Population Problems* (New York: McGraw-Hill, 1965), pp. 396–418.

[3] David M. Heer, *Society and Population* (Englewood Cliffs, N.J.: Prentice-Hall, 1975), p. 56.

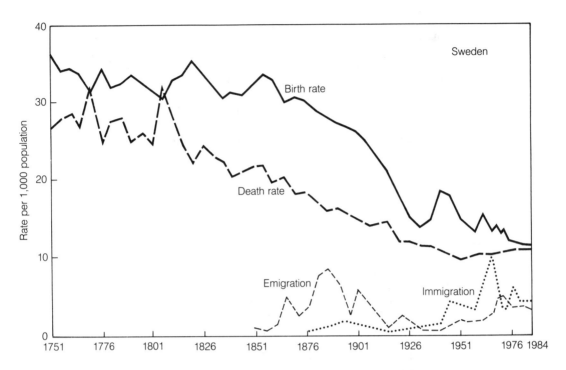

FIGURE 9-4   **The Demographic Transition in Representative Developed and Developing Countries**   The following shows the transition from a preindustrial, stable population (stage 1) to a late expanding population (stage 3) for both developed (Sweden) and developing (Mexico) countries, and to a later, modern stable population for the DC.

    Stage 1—early stable (Sweden before 1810, Mexico before 1920). Birth and death rates are high. Death rates vary widely due to famines, epidemics, and disease. The average life expectancy is 30–35 years.

    Stage 2—early expanding (Sweden, c1810–65; Mexico, 1920–70). Birth rates remain high. Death rates fall rapidly as a result of advances in health, medicine, nutrition, sanitation, transportation, communication,

ment (shown in Figure 9-4). Early and near-universal marriage are practiced in these developing countries in contrast to the nineteenth-century European pattern of late marriage or sometimes no marriage at all.[4] This difference accounts, in part, for the LDCs' higher birth rates.

Stage 2: Declining Mortality

This stage began in nineteenth-century Europe as modernization gradually reduced mortality rates. Food production increased as agricultural techniques improved. The introductions of corn and the potato, either of which could sustain a large

[4] Michael S. Teitelbaum, "Relevance of Demographic Transition Theory for Developing Countries," *Science* 188 (May 2, 1975): 420–25.

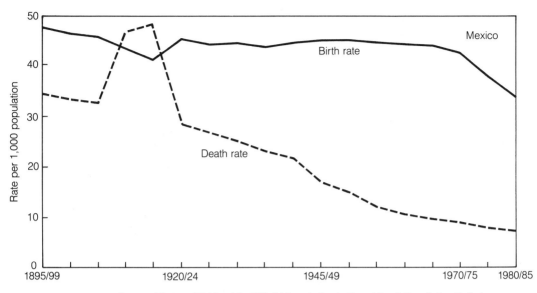

Source: Thomas W. Merrick, "World Population in Transition," *Population Bulletin* 41 (April 1986): 9.

FIGURE 9-4   (continued)

commerce, and production. Since techniques that reduce deaths can be dispersed more quickly to recently modernizing countries, the decline in the death rate is steeper in developing countries than in developed countries. Stage 2 is the period of most rapid population explosion. Stage 2 may take 50–100 years in the developed country and 15–50 years in the developing country.

Stage 3—late expanding (Sweden, c1865–1980; Mexico, 1970–?). Death rates continue to decline. By the end of the period, average life expectancy is at least 70 years. Birth rates fall rapidly, reflecting not only more effective contraceptives and more vigorous family planning programs, but also the increased cost of children, enhanced mobility, higher aspirations, and changing values and social structure associated with urbanization, education, and economic development. Population growth is positive but decelerating. Except for such countries as China, Sri Lanka, South Korea, Taiwan, Chile, and Argentina, which have birth rates of less than 25 per 1000 population, most developing countries (including Mexico) are at the beginning of stage 3. Developed countries are further along in stage 3, but only a few (noted below) have furnished stage III. Developed countries that have completed this stage have taken at least 50 years to do so.

Stage 4—late stable (Sweden, c1980–, Mexico ?) Both death and birth rates are low and nearly equal. Birth rates however may fluctuate. Eventually the population is stationary. Only a few countries in Europe (West and East Germany, Austria, Sweden, Denmark, Belgium, and Britain) are close to equality in birth and death rates.

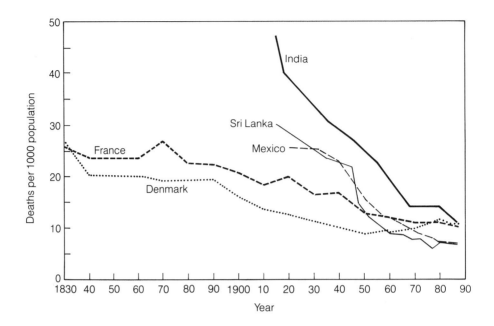

FIGURE 9-5   Changes in Death Rates (selected countries)   Mortality rates declined in LDCs faster than in DCs.

Sources: Warren S. Thompson and David T. Lewis, *Population Problems* (New York: McGraw-Hill, 1965); United Nations, *Demographic Yearbook, 1976* (New York, 1976); World Bank, *World Development Report, 1979* (Washington, D.C., 1979); World Bank, *World Development Report, 1982* (New York: Oxford University Press, 1982); and World Bank, *World Development Report, 1988* (New York: Oxford University Press, 1988).

family on a small plot of land, were especially important at this time. Improvements in trade, transportation, and communication meant people were less vulnerable to food shortages. Death from infectious diseases, such as tuberculosis and smallpox, declined as nutrition and medical science improved, and after the introduction and adoption of soap, cheap kitchen utensils, and cotton clothing led to better personal hygiene. Drainage and land reclamation reduced the incidence of malaria and respiratory diseases.[5]

Mortality rates decreased about a century earlier in developed countries than developing countries. However today's LDCs have lowered their mortality rates much more rapidly once they began. Figure 9-5 indicates a gradual, long-term reduction in Western death rates, with Denmark's declining from 27 to 11 and France's from 26 to 12, over a period of 130 years (1830–1960). Sri Lanka's and India's mortality rates, however, decreased sharply from 1915 to 1986—Sri Lanka's from 30 to 6, and India's from 47 to 12 (infants 500 to 89), per 1000 population.

[5] Paul R. Ehrlich, Anne H. Ehrlich, and John P. Holdren, *Ecoscience: Population, Resources, Environment* (San Francisco: W. H. Freeman, 1977), pp. 186–92.

These rapid declines are based on techniques that the developed countries acquired over decades—improved agriculture, transport, commerce, medicine, sanitation, and so forth.

Why have some LDC death rates dropped to 5–9 per 1000, below those of many industrialized countries? With a stable population, these mortality rates would be consistent with a life expectancy of more than 100 years! These low death rates are possible because birth rates higher than replacement levels create an age structure more youthful than exists in a stable population (one only replacing itself). (Figure 9-9 shows that DCs, with a more stable population, have an older population than the LDCs.) If the death rates for specific age groups were applied to a stable population, death rates in LDCs would be, in fact, in excess of 10 per 1000.

In the late 1930s, average life expectancy in developing countries was 32 years compared to 56 in developed countries. Life expectancy in LDCs increased to 61 between 1985 and 1990, compared to 76 in the developed countries (Table 9-2). Since World War II, mortality rates have dropped sharply in developing countries because of declines in infant mortality and better medical treatment for major infectious diseases—malaria, cholera, yellow fever, typhoid fever, smallpox, tuberculosis and other respiratory ailments. Despite such improvements, Figure 9-6 shows that people still live longer in rich countries. (Life expectancy in several oil-exporting nations has been unaffected by their recent, sudden wealth.) The positive relationship between life expectancy and income per capita persists until income reaches a certain level, perhaps corresponding to some critical level of health practice and economic productivity. Beyond this level, there appears to be little, if any, positive relationship between average income and life expectancy. Accordingly, although developed, and a few developing, countries have a life expectancy figure of over 70 years, the only countries with a life expectancy between 35 and 70 years are developing countries.

TABLE 9-2   Life Expectancy at Birth, by Region, 1935–39, 1950–55, 1965–70, 1975–80, and 1985–90

Region	Years				
	1935–39	1950–55	1965–70	1975–80	1985–90
South Asia	30	41	46	49	56
East Asia	30	45	55	61	71
Africa	30	36	43	47	54
Latin America	40	52	60	64	68
China	n.a.[a]	48	60	64	70
Developing countries	32	42	49	54	61
Developed countries	56	65	70	73	76

[a]Not available.

Sources: David Morawetz, *Twenty-Five Years of Economic Development* (Baltimore: Johns Hopkins University Press, 1977), p. 48; World Bank, *World Tables, 1980* (Baltimore: Johns Hopkins University Press, 1980), pp. 442–47; and John W. Sewell, Stuart K. Tucker, and contributors for the Overseas Development Council, *Growth, Exports, and Jobs in a Changing Economy: Agenda, 1988* (New Brunswick, N.J.: Transaction Books, 1988), pp. 246–57.

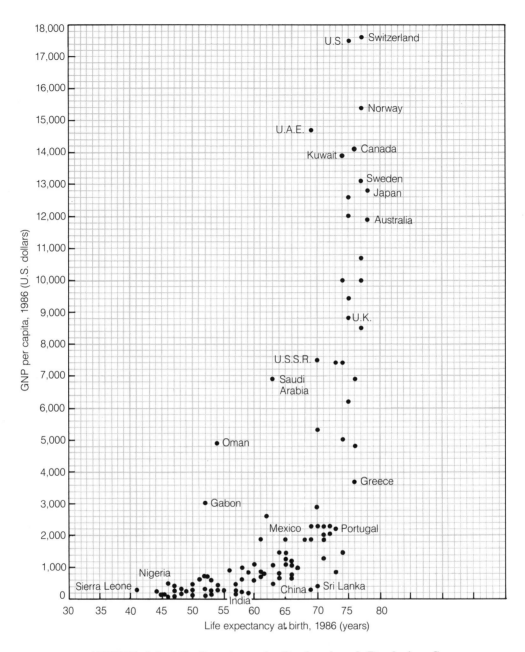

FIGURE 9-6 Life Expectancy in Developed and Developing Countries Among LDCs life expectancy increases with average income. Beyond a certain income level, perhaps corresponding to some critical levels of health practices and economic productivity, there is little relationship between average income and life expectancy.

Source: World Bank, *World Development Report, 1988* (New York: Oxford University Press, 1988), pp. 222–23.

It may be several decades before lowered mortality rates are matched by a decline in fertility rates. One element in this decades-long process—values and institutions supporting high fertility rates—are quite resistant to change. It is much easier in the contemporary world to lower a mortality rate than to change a value system that promotes fertility. The technology needed to increase life expectancy is widely available to all developing countries. They have access to the accumulated improvements in health, medicine, agriculture, and industry of the nineteenth century and the much more radical innovations of this century—immunization, pesticides, high-yielding grain varieties, and so on. To illustrate our thesis, the Allied powers (in the 1940s) and the World Health Organization (in the 1950s) sprayed a new insecticide, DDT, over large areas of Sri Lanka to destroy malaria-carrying mosquitos. The cost was less than two dollars per head. Malaria was largely eradicated, contributing in part to a steep decline in Sri Lanka's death rate from 21.7 per 1000 in 1945 to 14.6 in 1948 to 9.1 in 1959 (see Figure 9-5). Since most people desire health and long life, new life extension methods are easily and quickly adopted.[6]

Stage 3: Declining Fertility

Stage 3, declining fertility, of the demographic transition did not begin in Europe for several decades, and in some instances, a century, after the beginning of declining mortality in stage 2. However, in developing countries, stage 3 has followed much more rapidly stage 2. Nevertheless stage 2 was more explosive, since the initial birth rate was higher and the drop in death rate steeper.

What are the most important determinants of fertility decline? There are two competing answers. Organized **family-planning programs,** which provide propaganda and contraceptives to reduce the number of births, is one answer. The other is motivating birth control through the more complicated processes of education, urbanization, modernization, and economic development. This view is expressed in the slogan of the 1974 World Population Conference held in Bucharest, "Development is the best contraceptive."

Those who support family planning programs point to the substantial decline in the world's **total fertility rate (TFR)**—the number of children born to the average woman during her reproductive years—from the 1960s to the 1980s, even in the poorest developing countries. To the surprise of many demographers, the TFR of eighty two of one hundred thirteen developing countries, and all thirty five developed countries, decreased, so that the world's TFR dropped from 4.6 births per woman in 1968 to 4.1 in 1975 and to 3.6 in 1987. In the early 1960s, a number of developing countries began major family planning programs. At least one study suggests that declines in crude birth rates in developing countries were strongly associated with substantial, organized, family planning efforts.[7]

However, other evidence indicates that fertility also decreases with economic development, modernization, urbanization, and industrialization. For example, Figure 9-7 indicates that among developing countries (those with a 1986 GNP per

[6] Michael S. Teitelbaum, "Relevance of Demographic Transition Theory for Developing Countries," *Science* 188 (May 2, 1975): 420–25.

[7] Amy Ong Tsui and Donald J. Bogue, "Declining World Fertility: Trends, Causes and Implications," *Population Bulletin* 33, no. 4 (October 1978): 1–55; World Bank, *World Development Report, 1988* (New York: Oxford University Press, 1988), pp. 276–77; and Peter Hendry, "Food and Population: Beyond Five Billion," *Population Bulletin* 43 (April 1988): 14.

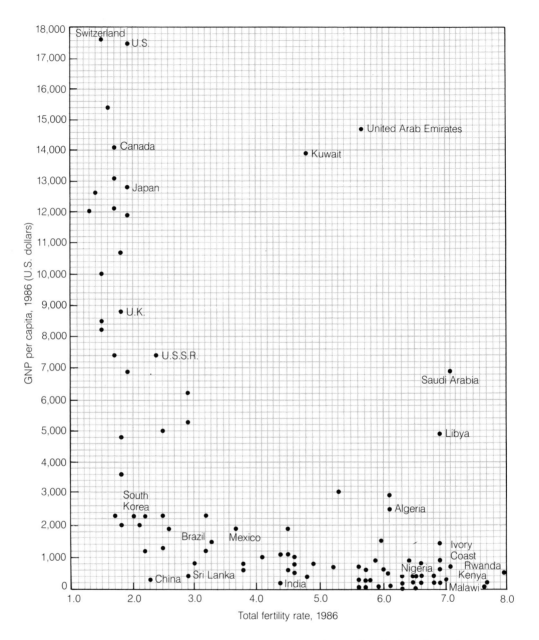

FIGURE 9-7   Fertility Rates in Developed and Developing Countries
Fertility rates decline as average income rises.

Source: World Bank, *World Development Report, 1988* (New York: Oxford University Press, 1988), pp. 222–23, 276–77.

capita of less than $6000), average income and fertility are negatively related; that is, low income is associated with high fertility rates. The relative importance of family planning programs versus economic development for population control is discussed in a later section on strategies for reducing fertility.

The Demographic Transition in the 1990s

In the early 1990s, most countries were still in stage 3 of the demographic transition. Virtually all countries had experienced some decline in mortality. The highest death rates in the world, primarily in sub-Saharan Africa, were in the lower 20s, substantially below mortality in stage 1. We cannot always identify precisely what stage a country is in. However, even the most demographically backward countries were in the latter part of stage 2, if not in the earlier part of stage 3, by the 1990s. On the other hand, only West Germany, East Germany, Austria, Sweden, Denmark, Belgium, and Britain were in stage 4—low, stable population growth—with virtually equal fertility and mortality rates.

Beyond Stage 4: A Stationary Population

World Bank projections indicate that most developing countries will not reach an exact replacement rate before 2020 to 2040. At this rate, the average woman of child-bearing age bears only one daughter—her replacement in the population. However **population momentum** or growth continues after **replacement-level fertility** has been reached because previous fertility rates have produced an age structure with a relatively high percentage of women in or below reproductive age. Thus most developing countries will not have a **stationary population** (where growth is zero) until 2075 to 2175, about 5 to 14 decades after attaining exact replacement level.

Let us examine this process more fully. Take as an example China, a country with a population of 1117 million and a total fertility rate of 5–6 in the early 1970s that dropped precipitously to 2.3 in 1986. If it reached replacement-level fertility in 2000, its population would then be 1279 million. Even if it maintains this fertility level, population will grow to 1508 million by 2050, and 1570 million by 2105, the year a stationary population level is reached. The LDCs can expect substantial future population growth even if measures are undertaken immediately to reduce fertility rates.[8]

IS POPULATION GROWTH AN OBSTACLE TO ECONOMIC DEVELOPMENT?

Does population growth hamper economic development as Malthus contends, or does population spur innovation and development as Julian L. Simon argues? This section examines some possible costs of high fertility rates and rapid population

[8] Thomas W. Merrick, "World Population in Transition," *Population Bulletin* 41 (April 1986): 6; World Bank, *World Development Report, 1980* (New York: Oxford University Press, 1980), pp. 142–43, 162–63; World Bank, *World Development Report, 1988* (New York: Oxford University Press, 1988), pp. 274–75; and Thomas Frejka, "The Prospects for a Stationary Population," *Scientific American* 228, no. 3 (March 1973): 15–23.

growth, including (1) diminishing returns to natural resources, with an adverse impact on average food consumption; (2) increased urbanization and congestion; (3) a higher labor force growth rate and higher unemployment; and (4) a working population that must support a larger number of dependents.

Population and Food

The Malthusian View.   The best-known work on the food and population balance is Malthus's *Essay on the Principle of Population* (1798, 1803). The essay, written in reaction to the utopian views of his father's friends, was one reason economics came to be referred to as the dismal science. Malthus's theory was that population, which increased geometrically—1, 2, 4, 8, 16, 32, and so on—outstripped food supply, which grew arithmetically: 1, 2, 3, 4, 5, 6. For Malthus, a clergyman as well as an economist, the only check to population growth would be wars, epidemics, infanticide, abortion, and sexual perversion, unless people practiced moral restraint, that is, later marriages and abstention. Even then he believed living standards would remain at a subsistence level in the long run.[9]

However, Malthus failed to envision the capital accumulation and technical progress that would overcome diminishing returns on land. Rough estimates are that between 1650 and 1990, the world's food production multiplied thirteen to fifteen times, while population increased only eight times. The world's cultivated land probably doubled or tripled during this period, largely from increases in cultivation in the United States, Canada, Australia, and New Zealand. Output per hectare probably increased at least fourfold during these 330 years through irrigation, multiple cropping, improved seeds, increased use of commercial fertilizer, better farm implements, and other agricultural innovations. Malthus also underestimated the extent to which education, economic modernization, industrialization, urbanization, and improved contraception would reduce fertility rates.

The Present and Future Population-Food Balance.   Some scientists believe the Malthusian population and food relationship is applicable to the contemporary world. For them the rapid population growth of LDCs since World War II confirms Malthus's thesis. Presently these neo-Malthusians appear to be wrong. Food production has continued to grow more rapidly than population, even in LDCs, in every decade since World War II (see Chapter 7). However, the question remains—Will this increase in average food production continue into the 1990s and the first decade of the twenty-first century when world population growth is expected to increase 1.7 percent per year?

Major studies of world food supply indicate that with present resources and the expected technological improvements, food increases should stay ahead of population growth in the 1990s. It is expected that the substantial agricultural capabilities of North America, Australia, New Zealand, Western Europe, and Japan will increase during this period.

Simon's View.   Some economists' optimism about technological change makes them not only believe that output will continue to grow more rapidly than population but also that population growth stimulates *per capita* output growth.

[9] Thomas Robert Malthus, *Essay on the Principle of Population* (Homewood, Ill.: Irwin, 1963).

Simon argues that the level of technology is enhanced by population. More people increase the stock of knowledge through additional learning gains compounded by the quickening effect of greater competition and total demand spurring "necessity as the mother for invention." Division of labor and economies of large-scale production increase as markets expand. In short as population size rises, both the supply of, and demand for, inventions increase thereby increasing productivity and economic growth. Because population growth spurs economic growth, Simon's model requires no government interference and is consistent with a **laissez-faire** population policy.

While Simon criticizes the Club of Rome's *Limits to Growth* (Chapter 8) for underestimating technical change, he goes to the other extreme by assuming that population growth causes technological progress. Indeed Simon's assumption that technological progress arises without cost contradicts the second law of thermodynamics, which states that the world is a closed system with ever-increasing entropy (see Chapter 8). Moreover Simon's model, like that of the Club of Rome, yields the intended results because they are built into the assumptions. Simon's premise is that "the level of technology that is combined with labour and capital in the production function must be influenced by population directly or indirectly."[10]

Food Research and Technology.   Despite increased world food production per person from the 1950s through the 1980s (and expected to continue through the 1990s), there *are* reasons to be concerned about the Malthusian balance in LDCs. About 80 percent of the world's expenditures on agricultural research, technology, and capital are made in developed countries. Vernon Ruttan's study indicates that these expenditures bear directly on the greater agricultural labor productivity in DCs. This greater productivity has little to do with superior resource endowment.[11] To be sure, some agricultural innovations used in DCs can be adapted to LDCs. However, these innovations must be adapted carefully in the developing countries. Usually LDCs need their own agricultural research, since many of their ecological zones are quite different from those of North America and Europe. The discovery of improved seed varieties and the improvement of agricultural methods in third-world countries are mainly the work of an **international network of agricultural research centers.** The principal food commodities and climate zones of the developing world have been brought into this network. Such donors as the World Bank, the UN Development Program, the Ford Foundation, the Rockefeller Foundation, the U.S. Agency for International Development, and agencies of other governments have financed the network. Its goals are to continue and extend the work generally known as the Green Revolution—the development of high-yielding varieties of wheat and rice. Prototypes of these centers are International Center for the Improvement of Maize and Wheat (CIMMYT), the Mexican institute, founded in

---

[10] Julian L. Simon, *Theory of Population and Economic Growth* (Oxford: Basil Blackwell, 1986) (quote on p. 3); Julian L. Simon, "The Case for More People," *American Demographics* 1 (November/December 1979): 26–30; H. W. Arndt, Review of Simon's *Theory of Population and Economic Growth, Population and Development Review* 13 (March 1987): 156–58; and John Ermisch, Review of Simon's *Theory of Population and Economic Growth, Population Studies* 41 (March 1987): 175–77.

[11] Vernon Ruttan, "Induced Technical and Institutional Change and the Future of Agriculture," in the Fifteenth International Conference of Agricultural Economists, *Papers and Reports* (Sao Paulo, Brazil, 1972).

1943, where a team led by Nobel Peace Prize winner Norman Borlaug developed dwarf wheats; and International Rice Research Institute (IRRI) in the Philippines, founded in 1960, which stresses research on rice and the use of multiple cropping systems.

The network has difficulties in helping national research centers adapt its research to local conditions and encourage its adoption by farmers. Furthermore many crop scientists in developing countries leave local research centers because of low salaries, politics on the job, government roadblocks to research, small budgets, and other grievances.[12]

Network critics charge that research projects emphasize high-yielding grain varieties that benefit the large commercial farmers. To elaborate, scientists tended to develop these varieties as part of a package, which included capital inputs, such as irrigation, fertilizers, tractors, mechanical pumps, threshers, reapers, combines, pesticides, and so on. For example, in India and Pakistan, new wheat varieties were adapted to cropland under controlled irrigation—land owned primarily by relatively affluent Punjabi farmers. Some of the negative effects of the package were increased land concentration, displacement of farm labor, and rising rural unemployment and emigration. Yet the net impact of new high-yielding grain varieties is probably positive. They did mitigate food shortages in South Asia during the 1970s and 1980s.

Food Distribution. There is more than enough food produced each year to feed everyone on earth adequately, yet millions are hungry. Food distribution is the difficulty. The Japanese, who are well nourished, consume about the same amount of calories and protein per person as the world average. James D. Gavan and John A. Dixon estimate that in the 1970s calorie and protein availability in India would have exceeded minimal requirements if distribution had not been so unequal.[13] Furthermore although Brazil, a country with high income inequalities, has over six times the GNP per capita of China, it has a large amount of malnutrition; and China, with lower income inequalities, has little. In general malnutrition is strongly correlated with poverty, which in turn is correlated with inequality in income distribution. Except for sub-Saharan Africa, food shortages are not due to inadequate production but to deficiencies in food distribution.

Even though global food supplies for the 1990s appear adequate, unequal food distribution means that some countries and localities are likely to face food deficits. Despite increased agricultural productivity in developing countries, their absolute food deficits are expected to increase, especially in Bangladesh, Nigeria, and most other sub-Saharan African countries. Domestic food deficits by themselves need not mean undernourishment if a country can afford to import food. However with higher prices for farm inputs and increased capital goods imports for

---

[12] Nicholas Wade, "International Agricultural Research," in Philip H. Abelson, ed., *Food: Politics, Economics, Nutrition, and Research* (Washington, D.C.: American Association for the Advancement of Science, 1975), pp. 91–95; and World Bank, *World Development Report, 1982* (New York: Oxford University Press, 1982), pp. 57–77.

[13] James D. Gavan and John A. Dixon, "India: A Perspective on the Food Situation," in Philip H. Abelson, ed., *Food: Politics, Economics, Nutrition, and Research* (Washington, D. C., American Association for the Advancement of Science, 1975), pp. 49–57.

industrialization, many developing countries may not have the foreign currency to import enough food to relieve the deficit.[14]

Energy Limitations.   Higher energy prices could seriously weaken our assumptions about the global food balance. The substantial gains made in food productivity since the 1940s have been partly dependent on cheap, abundant energy supplies. Would food production continue to grow in the 1990s and the first decade of the twenty-first century at previous rates if energy constraints were substantial? Obviously the energy-intensive U.S. food system cannot be exported intact to developing countries. Two scientists estimate that to feed the entire world with a food system like that of the United States would require 80 percent of today's entire world energy expenditures.[15]

A Recapitulation.   In the recent past, the world avoided the Malthusian specter but did not support Simon's view that population growth spurred output growth. Indeed there is reason to be wary about the population-food balance for future years in LDCs. The uncertainty concerning future growth in agricultural productivity, especially in sub-Saharan Africa, probably means that we should continue our efforts at population control.

Urbanization and Congestion

LDCs are congested and overpopulated in certain areas and especially so in major cities. Although 30 percent of the population of Africa is urban, it remains the least urbanized of the six continents. Yet some scholars argue that urban growth in Africa hampers economic development, employment growth, and the alleviation of poverty. In the early 1980s, highways to the central business district in Lagos, Nigeria, were so choked with traffic that it took 4 to 5 hours for a taxi to drive 24 kilometers from the international airport in rush-hour traffic. Although the premium on space in the inner city made it almost impossible for the working poor to afford housing there, the cost of transport made it difficult to live even on the outskirts of Lagos. Ironically the demand for transport (and congestion) in Lagos fell from 1981 to 1988 as a result of an economic depression triggered by reduced real oil export prices!

Urban areas in LDCs are not only experiencing a rapid natural increase in population but are also serving as a magnet for underemployed and poorly paid workers from the rural areas. A World Bank study estimates that urban populations in LDCs will triple between 1975 and 2000 (see Chapter 11.)[16] Overurbanization means it is necessary to limit population growth not just in cities but in an entire nation.

[14] Consultative Group on International Agricultural Research, *Report of the Review Committee* (Washington, D.C., 1977).

[15] John S. Steinhart and Carol E. Steinhart, "Energy Use in the U.S. Food System," in Philip H. Abelson, ed., *Food: Politics, Economics, Nutrition, and Research* (Washington, D. C., American Association for the Advancement of Science, 1975), pp. 33–42.

[16] Michael A. Cohen, "Cities in Developing Countries: 1975–2000," *Finance and Development* 13 (March 1976): 13.

Rapid Labor Force Growth and Increasing Unemployment

The LDC labor force growth rate is 2.1 percent per year, the same rate as population growth. The vast pool cannot be readily absorbed by industry, resulting in increased unemployment and underemployment. Chapter 10 indicates some of the political and social problems, as well as economic waste, ensuing from such underemployment. These problems underscore the urgent need to reduce population growth.

The Dependency Burden

Although the LDC labor force is growing rapidly, the number of children dependent on each worker is high. High fertility rates create this dependency burden. The **dependency ratio** is an index of this load. It is the ratio of persons 0–14, and 65 years

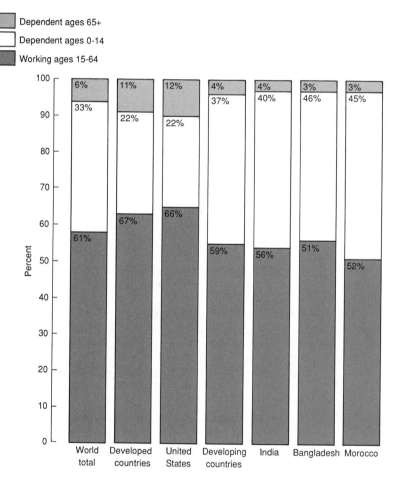

FIGURE 9-8   Dependency Loads   Dependency loads are higher for LDCs than DCs.

Source: Based on Population Reference Bureau, *World Population Data Sheet, 1988* (Washington, D.C., 1988).

and older to persons of working ages, 15–64 years. Figure 9-8 compares the dependency ratio in developing and developed countries. For example, 66 percent of the population in the United States is 15–64 years old, compared to 52 percent in Morocco. Despite the higher elderly percentage in the United States, dependency in Morocco is more burdensome, since 45 percent of its population is aged 0–14 compared to only 22 percent in the United States. Morocco, with a high birth rate (33 per 1000 in 1985), has almost as many people in the dependent ages as in the working ages. The United States, with a lower birth rate (16 per 1000), has only about half as many persons in the dependent ages as in the working ages. Another way of viewing age structure is a **population age pyramid** showing the percentage distribution of a population by age and sex (Figure 9-9).

Some LDCs narrowed the base of the pyramid in the 1970s and 1980s. For example, in 1960, when the birth rate in Costa Rica was 47 per 1000, it had a population structure with a wider base and a narrower peak than the pyramid on the left in Figure 9-9. However, after the country launched a vigorous family-

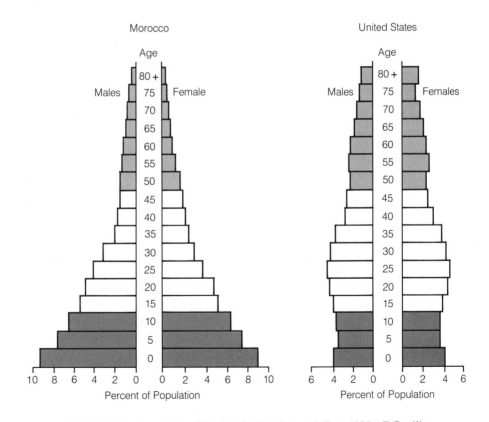

FIGURE 9-9   Population Distribution by Age and Sex, 1985 DCs, like the United States, with a low birth rate, have an older population than the LDCs, like Morocco, with a high birth rate.

Source: Carl Haub, "Understanding Population Projections," *Population Bulletin* 42 (December 1987): 21.

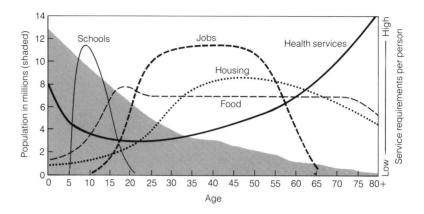

FIGURE 9-10   Population Age Profile and Service Requirements: Bangladesh, 1975   Bangladesh's high birth rate necessitates high spending levels on food, health care, and education for children. (Total population, 74 million)

Source; Madgda McHale and John McHale, "World of Children," *Population Bulletin* 33, no. 6 (January 1979): 14.

planning program in 1968, the birth rate dropped to 29 per 1000 from 1978 to 1987, so that the two bottom bars, corresponding to ages 0–9, narrowed substantially.

Of course the ratio of the labor force to population is not only a function of dependency ratios. Because of cross-national differences in the participation of women, old people, youths, and children in the labor force, countries with similar dependency ratios may have different ratios of labor force to population.

Dependency loads vary within developing countries according to income. The living standards of the poor are hurt by high fertility and large families. Each adult's earnings support more dependents than is the case in richer families. Thus in peninsular Malaysia, 71 percent of the richest 10 percent (by household) are 15–64 years old compared to only 45 percent for the poorest 10 percent.[17]

Figure 9-10, which plots the relationships between age and service requirements, shows the higher educational and health costs of caring for those 15 years or under. Thus the high dependency ratio in Bangladesh means that a substantial proportion of its resources must be diverted to provide schools, food, health care, and social services for the young. Households in Bangladesh have a large number of consumers per earning member, which means a high ratio of consumption to income. Very little income is left over for savings or capital information.

Overall neither Malthusian pessimism or Simon's optimism is warranted. The two centuries since Malthus wrote demonstrate that technological innovation, capital accumulation, and birth control more than compensate for diminishing returns to fixed land. On the other hand, Simon's model fails to consider how population

[17] World Bank, *World Development Report, 1980* (New York: Oxford University Press, 1980), pp. 42–43.

growth increases the costs of agricultural resources, congestion, environmental degradation, labor force underemployment, and the burden of dependency.[18]

STRATEGIES FOR REDUCING FERTILITY

Increasing urban congestion, rapid labor force growth, a high dependency burden, and uncertainty about food output growth indicate the importance of limiting population growth in LDCs. The only possible approach here is a reduction in fertility. Let us examine two strategies: (1) birth control programs and (2) socioeconomic development.

Birth Control Programs

From time immemorial, societies have had available a number of contraceptive methods. Intercourse without penetration and coitus interruptus have been known and practiced in one form or another in nearly all societies. Abortion; high celibacy rates; no marriage at all; late marriage; sanctions against the remarriage of widows; and taboos against coitus outside marriage, while nursing an infant, or on certain religious holidays have all been used to reduce fertility. Ireland, with land and food shortages throughout much of the eighteenth, nineteenth and early twentieth centuries, had less and later marriage than other parts of Europe. In the early twentieth century, the average Irish bridegroom was over 30. Marriage had to be postponed until the son could obtain land and independence from his father.

Moreover a large number of premodern cultures have practiced infanticide (a control on family size, though not births). In some preindustrial cultures a newborn child is not considered a member of society, so that destruction of the child is viewed psychologically in much the same light as we view abortion.

Furthermore chemical and mechanical contraceptives were known and applied in many primitive and peasant societies. Women in nineteenth-century Martinique and Guiana used rather effectively a douche containing lemon juice mixed with a decoction of the husks of the mahogany nut. However some of these contraceptives—the vaginal insertion of an okralike seed pod, rags of finely chopped grass, or dung—were clumsy, sexually unsatisfactory, or unhealthy. By and large, the technology of preindustrial societies was not equal to providing a chemical or mechanical contraceptive that was cheap, satisfactory, effective, and readily available.[19]

But since most of these societies had high mortality rates, population growth rates were low anyway. However, maintaining a stable population today requires lowered fertility rates and more adequate contraceptives. Because of the cost of

---

[18] Regressions of the effect of population growth on economic growth from 1965 to 1984, in David E. Bloom and Richard B. Freeman, "The Effects of Rapid Population Growth on Labor Supply and Employment in Developing Countries," *Population and Development* 12 (September 1986): 403–5, provide no support for either the optimists' or pessimists' points of view.

However in the relatively unsettled areas of Asiatic Soviet Union, inland Brazil, Australia, and Canada, population growth may be subject, other things being equal, to increasing returns and growing per capita income, resulting from increased division of labor.

[19] Kingsley Davis and Judith Blake, "Social Structure and Fertility: An Analytical Framework," *Economic Development and Cultural Change* 4 (April 1956): 211–35.

modern contraceptives and their social benefits, many LDC governments subsidize birth control devices, so that users receive them free or for a nominal cost.

Modern Contraceptives.   In the 1980s, the abortion-inducing drug (only available in a few countries), the oral contraceptive (the Pill), the intrauterine device (IUD), abortion, and sterilization were all used as methods of birth control. Condoms, diaphragms, spermicides, coitus interruptus, and the rhythm method are cheap but less effective than the first grouping.

Male sterilization via vasectomy, which involves a 10-minute out-patient operation with local anesthesia, is relatively inexpensive. It is usually irreversible, safe, and has no effect on subsequent sexual performance. Vasectomies were widely used in India before a reversal of policy in 1977. Female sterilization, a more expensive and more serious operation, is rarely performed in LDCs.

The IUD is an effective contraceptive and except for male sterilization, the cheapest (though it has to be inserted by medical personnel). However, because of high rates of expulsion or removal, use of the IUD requires follow-up. A study in the early 1970s in Lucknow, India, indicates that less than one-half of the women using IUDs retained them for as long as a year and only about one-fourth for as long as two years.[20]

The oral contraceptive, nearly 100 percent effective if taken on schedule, is more expensive than the IUD. The Pill must be taken daily except for an interval of several days per month, a difficult system for people in both DCs and LDCs.

Abortion is expensive and where illegal, performed under conditions hazardous to the woman's life and health. However, it is a widely used method of birth control, as indicated by estimates of four abortions for every ten live births in the world in 1971.[21] In Chile and Hungary, nominally Roman Catholic countries, abortions are more numerous than live births. In the early 1990s, over two-thirds of the world's population live in countries where abortions are legal.

Family-Planning Programs.   By the mid-1980s, 85 countries in the third world, comprising 95 percent of its population, had embarked on official family-planning programs to reduce population growth. India established a program in 1951, Pakistan in 1960, South Korea in 1961, China and North Vietnam in 1962, and a wave of others occurred thereafter.[22] In 1979, there may have been as many as 40 million new users of birth control devices and methods provided by family-planning programs worldwide, including sterilizations, IUDs, the Pill, abortion, condoms, or others.

The five Asian countries—China, Taiwan, South Korea, Sri Lanka, and Thailand—whose fertility rates are almost as low as those in developed countries (see Figure 9-7), all launched family-planning programs in the 1960s that substantially reduced fertility rates during the subsequent decade. In 1962, China advocated "birth planning" to protect the health of mothers and children. During the Cultural Revolution from 1966 to 1976, many neighborhood groups collectively set

---

[20] Joginder S. Uppal, *Economic Development in South Asia* (New York: St. Martin's, 1977), p. 48.

[21] Timothy King, coordinator, *Population Policies and Economic Development* (Baltimore: Johns Hopkins University Press, 1974).

[22] World Bank, *World Development Report, 1984* (New York: Oxford University Press, 1984), p. 127.

targets for births and awarded the privilege of having babies to "deserving couples." Even in rural areas, where contraceptives dispensed by health care centers included "paper bills," sheets of water-soluble paper impregnated with oral contraceptives, over one-half of the couples practiced contraception. China's birth control programs reduced the crude birth rate from 36 per 1000 in 1960 to 19 in 1986 (a greater success than India's). In 1973, contraceptive users as a percentage of women of reproductive age exceeded 50 percent in Taiwan and reached 30 percent in South Korea. This progress in family planning contributed to a decrease in crude birth rate from the lower 40s to the teens per 1000 in both countries between 1960 and 1988. Sri Lanka's relatively strong family-planning program resulted in a decline in the birth rate from 36 to 24 per 1000 between 1960 and 1988, while Thailand's program was instrumental in a reduction from 46 to 29 during the same period.[23]

Cost-Effectiveness of Family-Planning Programs   How cost-effective are family-planning programs? Is the cost less than the benefit to society? Suppose the present value of benefits from preventing a birth is $100, a figure equal to the saved hospital, medical, food, educational, and other costs minus the expected earnings of the person whose birth was prevented.[24] Assume the cost of providing contraceptives to prevent one birth amounts to $50. If a subsidy of $40 induces a family not to have another child, program costs would still be only $90 per prevented birth, $10 less than the $100 the birth would cost a society.

Simulation models developed by Stephen Enke indicate high returns to investment in birth control programs.[25] As a result of slowed population growth, labor force growth also slows—decreasing the ratio of labor to capital and natural resources and increasing labor's marginal productivity. In addition slowing population growth reduces the ratio of nonworking dependents to the economically productive population (a ratio discussed earlier in this chapter). Nevertheless Enke's models overstate the returns to family-planning programs. Frequently they attribute to these programs prevented births that would not have occurred anyway because traditional methods of birth control would have succeeded. The models also understate the increased cost per user as the programs reach out to families resistant to birth control and overstate the net benefits of a prevented birth to society. Underestimating overhead costs in the population centers and understating the present value of future earnings are also problems.[26]

[23] Paul R. Ehrlich, Anne H. Ehrlich, and John P. Holdren, *Ecoscience: Population, Resources, Environment* (San Francisco: W. H. Freeman, 1977); World Bank, *World Development Report, 1979* (Washington, D.C., 1979), pp. 56–58; and Population Reference Bureau, *1988 World Population Data Sheet* (Washington, D.C., 1988).

[24] To obtain present value, evaluate the present worth of each part of the stream of future receipts and expenditures. Thus if the interest rate is 15 percent, the present value of earnings of $5000 18 years into the future is, $5000/(1 + .15)^{18}, or $404.03. The present value of $1000 spent on food, housing, health care, schooling, and other items 8 years into the future is $1000/(1 + .15),^{8} or $326.90. Once the present worth of future receipts and expenditures for every year is known, simply add together all these separate, discounted values. See Chapter 12.

[25] Stephen Enke, "The Economics of Government Payments to Limit Population," *Economic Development and Cultural Change,* 8 no. 4 (July 1960): 239–48; and Stephen Enke, "The Economic Aspects of Slowing Population Growth," *Economic Journal* 76 (March 1966): 44–56.

[26] Clarence Zuvekas, Jr., *Economic Development: An Introduction* (New York: St. Martin's, 1979), pp. 92–93.

Motivation to Limit Family Size   A successful family-planning program requires more than making a supply of contraceptives available; it also requires a demand for birth control. A number of programs in developing countries, especially in highly populated South Asia, have had only a limited impact on reducing fertility, partly because of a lack of motivation to limit family size. India's program encountered active resistance during the early 1960s. Opposition, which led occasionally to riots, had numerous causes. The programs were directed by Western instead of local medical services. Frequently religious and ethnic minorities viewed the program as discriminatory, and peasants believed that it was contrary to their economic interests. However India's program was reorganized in 1965 with strong governmental support. Incentive payments were increased. For example, transistor radios were given to the users as well as persons who "motivated" the use of the birth control devices. A "cafeteria" approach to contraceptive methods and devices was used. Funding increased, so that by 1975 there were 50,000 family-planning centers and subcenters throughout the country. Nevertheless despite the effort, the birth rate fell from 44 to only 33 per 1000 between 1960 and 1988, a drop not much in excess of countries investing little in family-planning programs. Furthermore the public outcry following a sterilization campaign in 1976 and 1977 set back the entire family-planning program by more than a decade.

The varying success of organized family-planning efforts in developing countries indicates that making contraceptives available is not enough to reduce fertility rates. Couples will not use contraceptives unless they are motivated to limit births. The next section discusses ways in which socioeconomic change affects birth control decisions.

Socioeconomic Development

Children in a Peasant Society.   In most low-income countries, especially in South and Southeast Asia, farming is predominantly peasant agriculture. Peasants cultivate bits of land they usually do not own. Agricultural methods are traditional, technology stagnant, and little capital is available. Compared to their counterparts in urban society, children in a peasant society are more likely to be perceived as an economic asset. Boys as young as 8 to 10 years tend or herd animals, weed, pick, and sell produce. Girls fetch water, prepare meals, tend to younger children, and sometimes farm. Children place fewer economic demands on a peasant family. Food is raised domestically; housing is constructed by the family from local materials; and the cost of education, entertainment, and travel is negligible. Although the family may receive a dowry when a daughter marries out of the village, major financial security is usually provided by sons, who add to the family's farm output or earn money from trade or another occupation. Having a larger family permits more income and asset transfer to balance temporary deficits or surpluses. When social insurance is inadequate, the larger the family, the smaller the risk of a poverty-ridden old age.

The literate, urban white-collar worker in South and Southeast Asia is more likely to limit family size than is an illiterate peasant in the same region. Consider, for example, the family in a two-room apartment in Delhi, India, with husband and wife employed and their children expected to get an education. The cost of children is more for this family than for one in a less densely populated village in rural

TABLE 9-3 Average Number of Children Born per Couple, by Selected Characteristics, in India, 1961–65 (by income, education, residence, and occupation)

Characteristics	Average Number of Children
Household income and expenditure (1960–61)	
Up to Rs 10 per month	3.40
Rs 11–20 per month	3.02
Rs 21–30 per month	2.95
Rs 30 and over per month	2.70
Educational level attained by women (1961)	
Illiterate	3.5
Primary school	3.4
Secondary school	3.1
College	3.0
Postgraduate	2.5
Residence (1963–64)	
Urban	3.19
Rural	3.76
Occupation of head of household	
Agriculture	4.4
Industry	4.2
Professional—law, medicine, teaching	3.7
Average for all occupations	4.3

Source: Joginder S. Uppal, *Economic Development in South Asia* (New York: St. Martin's, 1977), p. 41.

southeastern India. Childrearing, particularly when children are too young to attend school, interferes with work for women outside the home. In addition, children are more likely to interfere with the urban worker's aspirations for a better job or geographic mobility.

Indian village values support high fertility. In much of rural India, the status of the new bride in her husband's village is tied to having children, especially sons. A son not only provides added security for old age, but also performs essential religious rites on the death of a parent.

As child mortality rates fall, fewer births are needed to achieve any given desired family size. Parents may need only two to three children to be virtually certain of a surviving son, in contrast to the six to eight essential when death rates are high.

In general modernization affects the birth rate. For example, as Table 9-3 indicates, fertility in India declines with increased income, education, urban living, and improved occupational status.

Income Distribution.   A number of studies in the 1970s indicate that fertility is lower when income distribution is more even. Income redistribution to lower classes increases the percentage of the population above the poverty level. Increased economic security and higher income for the poor mean having children is not the only way of securing one's old age. Higher absolute incomes and redistribution policies (discussed in Chapters 6 and 7) increase lower-class literacy, mobility, and urbanization, factors reducing birth rates. Thus in Taiwan, high enrollment rates in schools, which reduce child labor, are associated with lowered fertility.[27] Furthermore, with allowances for time lags, low birth rates increase income equality by decreasing unemployment and increasing per capita expenditure on training and education.

Taiwan and the Philippines illustrate this relationship between income distribution and fertility. In the early 1970s, per capita income in Taiwan was approximately the same as in the Philippines. However, there was a considerable discrepancy between the income distribution in the two countries. The top 10 percent of the population in the Philippines was significantly richer than the same group in Taiwan, but the bottom 20 percent was more than twice as well off in Taiwan. This fact explains why Taiwan's fertility rate is lower than the Philippines'.[28] More people had reached a socioeconomic level in Taiwan that promoted birth control. And income inequality is lower in low-fertility Yugoslavia, Romania, Argentina, Chile, Uruguay, Cuba, China, Taiwan, South Korea, and Sri Lanka than in high-fertility Venezuela, Mexico, Brazil, Colombia, Peru, Ecuador, Panama, El Salvador, and Honduras (Figure 9-2).

Religion.   When factors measuring modernization are held constant, religion explains few cross-national fertility differences. Thus fertility rates in predominantly Roman Catholic Latin America, Italy, France, Spain, Portugal, and Poland given their level of development, are about what demographers would expect. Yet religious (prolife) politics (along with a belief that population was neutral in development) influenced the U.S. government, previously the major donor to LDC population programs, to refuse to support programs promoting or condoning abortion or (what was perceived as) coercive population control from 1984 to 1988, thus substantially reducing LDC family-planning funding.[29]

A Summary of Variables.   Interestingly enough, a study by Anne D. Williams indicates income is not important in reducing a fertility rates when other factors are held constant.[30] How then do we explain the negative relationship between per capita income and fertility in Figure 9-7? Variables *positively* associated with income, such as education and literacy, occupational status, women in the labor force, urbanization, and income equality, are all *negatively* correlated with fertility. On the other hand, child mortality rates and children in the labor force—*negatively* related to income—are *positively* associated with the birth rate.

[27] Julian L. Simon, "Income, Wealth, and Their Distribution as Policy Tools in Fertility Control," in Ronald G. Ridker, ed., *Population and Development: The Search for Selective Interventions* (Baltimore: Johns Hopkins University Press, 1976), pp. 36–76.

[28] William Rich, "Smaller Families through Jobs and Justice," *International Development Review,* 14, no. 4 (1972/73): 10–15.

[29] Peter Hendry, "Food and Population: Beyond Five Billion," *Population Bulletin* 43 (April 1988): 32.

[30] Anne D. Williams, "Determinants of Fertility in Developing Countries," in M. C. Keeley, ed., *Population, Public Policy, and Economic Development* (New York: Praeger, 1976), pp. 117–57.

Development or Family Planning?

What policies then can a developing country pursue to lower fertility rates? Programs promoting social and economic development by improving health, nutrition, education, and urban development will lower fertility rates. In addition improving income distribution—including more educational and job opportunities for women, the underprivileged classes, and lower-income groups—will also contribute to a reduced birth rate. In a sense, lower fertility is a by-product of strategies widely considered socially desirable in themselves.

Which is more important in contributing to reduced fertility, family planning or socioeconomic development? We cannot choose one as more important, since birth reduction depends on both. Birth control devices offered by family-planning agencies will not be accepted if the social and economic circumstances of the population are such that reduced fertility does not seem an advantage. On the other hand, people wanting smaller families must have access to birth control devices and information. Developing countries serious about reducing fertility need both family-planning programs and policies promoting socioeconomic development and increased income equality.

The reader should keep in mind that development and population are interacting variables. Each affects the other.

SUMMARY

1. Population growth in the second half of the twentieth century, especially among LDCs, is unprecedented in human experience. The developing world has a current population growth rate in excess of 2 percent per year. More than one-half of the world's population lives in Asia.

2. The demographic transition is a period of rapid population growth occurring between a preindustrial, stable population characterized by high fertility and mortality rates and nearly equal birth and death rates in a late modern period. The fast growth takes place in the early transitional stage, when fertility rates remain high but mortality rates decline.

3. Contemporary LDC population growth has been more explosive than that of the DCs during their early transitional period because of a sharper drop in mortality rates in LDCs. Today's developing countries were able to take advantage of advances in food production, new pesticides, improvements in transport and communication, improved nutrition, better personal hygiene, medical innovations, and immunization in a short time—many of which were not available to DCs during their early demographic transition.

4. Fertility decreases with economic development, urbanization, industrialization, mobility, literacy, female labor force participation, reduced income inequality, and greater family-planning efforts. However these efforts are not likely to be successful unless socioeconomic development and improved income distribution make birth control seem advantageous. Development and family-planning programs have both contributed to the decrease in LDC fertility rates since the 1960s.

5. The young age structure in LDCs means that their populations will continue to grow even after the average woman of childbearing age bears only enough daughters to replace herself.

6. Malthus's predictions that population would outgrow food supply were wrong in the past because he did not foresee that technological change, capital accumulation, and voluntary birth control would maintain a safe food and population balance. Present agricultural production is sufficient to feed everyone on earth adequately. However, deficiencies in food distribution between and within nations, inadequate agricultural research, and limited energy make future food availability in LDCs rather uncertain, especially in sub-Saharan Africa.

7. Simon, who contends that population growth stimulates technology, division of labor, and economic growth, argues against a LDC government population policy. However, Simon's assumptions contradict the second law of thermodynamics, which states that the world is a closed system with ever-increasing entropy.

8. Increased urbanization and congestion, rapid labor force growth, growing unemployment, and high dependency burdens are some major costs of high fertility rates and rapid population growth. That 35–40 percent of LDC population is 0–14 years old compared to only 20–25 percent in the DCs means that resources have to be diverted from capital formation to take care of the young in the LDCs.

TERMS TO REVIEW

- crude birth rate
- crude death rate
- family-planning programs
- total fertility rate
- demographic transition

- replacement-level fertility
- population momentum
- stationary population
- international net-

- work of agricultural research centers
- dependency ratio
- population age pyramid
- laissez-faire

QUESTIONS TO DISCUSS

1. What factors have contributed to a rising LDC population growth rate since 1950? Why has the LDC population growth rate not slowed down much in recent years?

2. Explain the demographic transition theory. At what stages in the theory are LDCs? Why are they in different stages?

3. Compare and contrast the historical population growth patterns of DCs and today's LDCs. Why are the patterns different?

4. What, if any, is the statistical relationship between birth rate and GNP per

capita? Between birth rate and income distribution? What are the reasons for these relationships?

5. Why would population continue to grow for several decades after it reaches a replacement-level fertility?

6. What are some of the costs of a high fertility rate and rapid population growth?

7. How well does Malthusian population theory explain Western population growth? Contemporary LDC population growth?

8. What do you expect to happen to food production per capita (especially in LDCs) in the late twentieth century?

9. Discuss and evaluate views of economic optimists like Simon who argue that LDC governments do not need a policy to limit population growth.

10. Which policies are more important for reducing fertility: family-planning programs or socioeconomic development?

GUIDE TO READINGS

United Nations Department of Economic and Social Affairs, *The Population Debate: Dimensions and Perspectives—Papers of the World Population Conference, 1974,* 2 vols. (New York, 1975), provides perspectives on the population controversy from scholars in the capitalist, socialist, and developing world. Robert Repetto, "Population, Resources, Environment: An Uncertain Future," *Population Bulletin* 42 (July 1987): 1–43; and Ehrlich, Ehrlich, and Holdren (note 5) discuss population, resources, and the environment. Merrick (note 8); Haub (note to Figure 9-9); Robert H. Cassen, "Population and Development: A Survey," *World Development* 4 (October–November 1976): 785–830; and Allen C. Kelley, "Economic Consequences of Population Change in the Third World," *Journal of Economic Literature* 26 (December 1988): 1685–1728, are good surveys of the literature. Teitelbaum (note 4) expounds and criticizes the theory of demographic transition. The literature on factors affecting fertility in LDCs is reviewed by Williams (note 30) and Simon (note 27). Despite their overemphasis on family planning, Tsui and Bogue (note 7) present a useful discussion of the relative impact of family-planning programs and socioeconomic development on reducing fertility in developing countries. But Kingsley Davis's critique of Tsui and Bogue more accurately assesses the relative impact in "Declining Birth Rates and Growing Populations," *Population Research and Policy Review* 3 (1984): 61–75.

Hendry (note 7) surveys the literature on the relationship between food and population, while a special compendium from *Science* edited by Abelson (notes 12, 13, and 15) contains a multidisciplinary perspective on the world food problem. Leonardo A. Paulino, *Food in the Third World: Past Trends and Projections to 2000,* Research Report 52 (Washington, D.C.: International Food Policy Research Institute, 1986) (see note to Table 7-3) examines LDC food output trends.

Bloom and Freeman (note 18) summarize the effect of rapid population growth on LDC labor force growth.

The United Nations, *Demographic Yearbook* (note to Figure 9-3); United States Bureau of the Census, *World Population* (note to Figure 9-1); Population Reference Bureau, *World Population Data Sheet;* and *World Development Report* publish current world population statistics periodically.

John S. Aird, "Population Studies and Population Policy in China," *Population and Development Review* 8 (June 1982): 267–97, is an excellent demographic study of China's population.

Chapter Ten

EMPLOYMENT, MIGRATION, AND URBANIZATION

Questions concerning population and the labor force are intertwined. The dependency burden of the working population depends on fertility rates, and labor force growth is a function of natural population increase and migration. Labor skills are a major component of population quality. This chapter examines employment, unemployment, underemployment, and labor migration, while the next chapter considers the quality of labor resources.

You cannot understand LDC unemployment unless you realize how it is different from that in the West. The openly unemployed in LDCs are usually 15–24 years old, educated, and residents of urban areas. The unemployed in LDCs, usually supported by an extended family in a job search, are less likely to be from the poorest one-fifth of the population than in DCs.

Still, the employment problem is of major concern to developing countries. Obviously providing adequately paid, productive jobs for the very poor is a major way of reducing poverty and inequality in LDCs. High unemployment rates represent a vast underutilization of human resources; the unemployed, who are most often young, urban, educated males, are a potential source of social unrest and political discontent.[1]

In the West, economic development was accompanied by a large internal and international migration from rural areas, where technical progress freed labor, to urban areas, where rapid, industrial expansion increased labor demand. Many

[1] E. Wayne Nafziger, *The Economics of Political Instability: The Nigerian-Biafran War* (Boulder, Colo.: Westview, 1983).

economists expected that rapid industrialization would resolve the employment problem in LDCs. Unfortunately for reasons to be discussed below, this strategy of rapid industrial growth did not have the same results in LDCs as in the West.

SCOPE OF THE CHAPTER

The first two sections of this chapter discuss the types of underutilized labor and the extent of LDC unemployment and underemployment. The next section examines whether LDC industrial expansion can absorb labor force growth. Following that, we look at disguised unemployment in agriculture. We examine the Lewis and Harris–Todaro models of rural-urban migration and consider why Western explanations for unemployment may not apply to LDCs. The subsequent section explains LDC unemployment by looking at LDC technology, factor-price distortions, and educated labor markets. The final section considers policies to reduce unemployment.

DIMENSIONS OF UNEMPLOYMENT AND UNDEREMPLOYMENT

The openly **unemployed** are those without a job who are actively seeking one. An article in the *International Labor Review* estimates that LDC unemployment rose from 36 million in 1960 to 66 million in 1980, an increase of 83 percent. The Economic Commission for Africa estimates 1975 urban unemployment rates of 10.8 percent in Africa, 6.9 percent in Asia, and 6.5 percent in Latin America. The LDC unemployment as a percentage of the labor force increased from 7.4 percent in 1970 to 7.8 percent in 1980 to 8.2 percent in 1990.[2]

Who are the unemployed in LDCs? Mainly city residents—unemployment in urban areas is twice that of rural areas. Most unemployed are first-time entrants to the labor force: The unemployment rate for youths, 15 to 24, is twice that of people over 24. The unemployed are often women—although there are fewer unemployed females than males, the rate for women is higher. Finally the unemployed are fairly well educated. Unemployment correlates with education until after secondary levels, when it begins to fall.[3] These patterns are explained later in the chapter.

To the unemployed, we must add the **underemployed,** those who work less than they would like to work. Probably over 25 percent of the total LDC labor force was unemployed or underemployed in 1990. Combined unemployment and underemployment rates in LDCs are regularly as high as they were in the West during the worst years of the Great Depression.

UNDERUTILIZED LABOR

Besides the openly unemployed and underemployed, Edgar O. Edwards identifies three other forms of labor underutilization:

[2] Yves Sablo, "Employment and Unemployment, 1960–90," *International Labour Review* 112 (December 1975): 408–17; and Economic Commission for Africa, *ECA and Africa's Development, 1983–2000: A Preliminary Perspective Study* (Addis Ababa, 1983), pp. 7–59.

[3] Lyn Squire, *Employment Policy in Developing Countries: A Survey of Issues and Evidence* (New York: Oxford University Press, 1981), pp. 66–69.

1. The visibly active but underutilized—those who would not be classified as either unemployed or underemployed, but who have in fact found alternative means of "marking time," including,

    (a) Disguised unemployment. Many people seem occupied on farms or employed in government on a full-time basis even though the services they render may actually require much less than full time. Social pressures on private industry also may result in disguised unemployment. The concept is discussed in more detail below.

    (b) Hidden unemployment. Those who are engaged in nonemployment activities, especially education and household chores, as a "second choice," primarily because job opportunities are not (i) available at the levels of education already attained; or (ii) open to women, due to discrimination. Thus educational institutions and households become "employers of last resort." Moreover many students may be among the less able. They cannot compete successfully for jobs, so they go to school.

    (c) The prematurely retired. This phenomenon is especially apparent in the civil service. In many LDCs, retirement age is falling as longevity increases, primarily as a means of creating job opportunities for younger workers.

2. The impaired—those who may work full time but whose work is seriously impaired through malnutrition or inadequate medical care.

3. The unproductive—those who work long hours but lack the skill or capital needed to acquire even the essentials of life.[4]

The remainder of the chapter focuses on the openly unemployed, the underemployed, and the disguised unemployed.

LABOR FORCE GROWTH, URBANIZATION, AND INDUSTRIAL EXPANSION

Growing LDC unemployment is caused by the labor force growing faster than job opportunities. By 2000 the LDC labor force will have increased more than 2.5 times—from 500 million in 1950 to 1325 million (Figure 10-1). Today's developing countries must contend with a much more rapid labor force growth than the industrialized countries had at a similar stage in their growth. The labor force in Western Europe, North America, and Japan grew at 0.8 percent a year in the nineteenth century compared to 2.1 percent per year in the developing countries in 1986. (Labor force growth lags behind population growth. China's 1980 to 1985 labor force growth of 2.5 percent yearly is a reflection of population growth in the early to mid-1960s, while the 1985 to 2000 annual labor force growth of 1.4 percent is linked to a declining 1970 to 1985 population growth. The echo of East Asia's reduced labor force growth at the turn of the twenty-first century is the falling 1.4-percent yearly population growth that occurred from 1980 to 1985.) It took almost 90 years

[4] Edgar O. Edwards, ed., *Employment in Developing Nations* (New York: Columbia University Press, 1974), pp. 10–11.

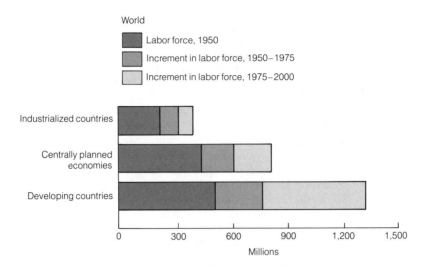

FIGURE 10-1   Labor Force Estimates and Projections, 1950–2000

Source: World Bank, *World Development Report, 1979* (Washington, D.C., 1979) p. 48.

for the labor force to double in industrialized countries; it now takes about 33 years in the developing countries.

Economic growth is usually accompanied by a decline in the proportion of labor force in agriculture and an increase in the share of labor in the more productive industrial and services sector. Yet in 1980, 72 percent of the labor force in low-income countries was in agriculture and only 13 percent in industry, while in middle-income countries, 43 percent was in agriculture and 23 percent in industry (see Table 4-1).

Annual industrial employment expanded at 0.4 to 0.7 percent of the total labor force in developing countries in 1980—higher than the 0.3 percent figure for industrialized Europe at the turn of the twentieth century.

Because of fast labor force growth, industry in today's developing countries absorbs only 20–35 percent of the increased labor force, compared to about 50 percent in Europe in 1900. Let us illustrate. Assume the labor force is growing at 2.7 percent per year, the rate for sub-Saharan Africa from 1985 to 2000 (see Table 10-1). Assume agricultural employment remains constant, so that growth is in industry and services. The nonagricultural sector in sub-Saharan Africa in the 1980s employs 25 percent of the labor force. This sector would have to increase its total employment 10.8 percent per year to absorb a labor force growth of 2.7 percent (that is $0.25 \times 0.108 = 0.027$). Table 10.2 indicates that although two sub-Saharan countries increased manufacturing output by 11 percent or more per year, this growth substantially exceeds manufacturing employment growth in all sub-Saharan countries. Indeed only two LDCs, South Korea and Taiwan, increased manufacturing employment by more than 11 percent. Both countries have had a rapid rate of industrial growth and an emphasis on labor-intensive manufactures, especially in exports. Since *nonagricultural* employment rarely grows faster than

TABLE 10-1 Growth of the Labor Force, 1950–2000

	AVERAGE ANNUAL PERCENTAGE GROWTH RATE				
	1950–60	1960–70	1970–80	1980–85	1985–2000
East Asia and Pacific[a]	2.1	2.4	2.5	2.1	1.8
Low-Income Asia[b]	1.4	1.7	1.9	2.0	2.0
Latin America and Caribbean	2.2	2.4	2.6	2.6	2.5
Middle East and North Africa[c]	1.6	1.9	2.5	3.3	3.3
Sub-Saharan Africa[d]	1.7	2.2	2.1	2.4	2.7
Southern Europe	1.1	0.8	1.2	1.7	1.3
Developing countries	1.6	1.8	2.1	2.4	2.1
Developed countries	n.a.[e]	1.2	1.2	1.0	0.5

[a]Excludes Japan.

[b]Includes Afghanistan, Bangladesh, Bhutan, Burma, India, Indonesia, Kampuchea, Laos, Maldives, Nepal, Pakistan, Sri Lanka, and Vietnam.

[c]Excludes high-income oil exporters.

[d]Excludes the Republic of South Africa.

[e]Not available.

Sources: World Bank, *World Development Report, 1979* (Washington, D.C., 1979), p. 47; Lyn Squire, *Employment Policy in Developing Countries: A Survey of Issues and Evidence* (New York: Oxford University Press, 1981), pp. 44–45; and World Bank, *World Development Report, 1988* (New York: Oxford University Press, 1988), pp. 282–83.

manufacturing employment achieving the needed employment growth in most LDCs is difficult.[5]

Sluggish employment growth in the industrial and services sectors has contributed to high rates of urban unemployment, underemployment, and low rural productivity. The rest of this chapter explores the relationship between rural development and productivity, and labor migration from rural to urban areas and the consequent rising urban unemployment.

DISGUISED UNEMPLOYMENT

Many economists believe **disguised unemployment,** that is, **zero marginal productivity of labor,** is endemic among LDC agricultural labor: Withdrawing a labor unit from agriculture does not decrease output. *Disguised unemployment* was a term first used during the Great Depression to describe workers in DCs who took inferior jobs as a result of being laid off. Between the 1930s and early 1950s, LDCs had little visible industrial unemployment, so economists surmised that the LDC counterpart of mass unemployment in the West was disguised unemployment: People

[5] Peter Gregory, "An Assessment of Changes in Employment Conditions in Less-Developed Countries," *Economic Development and Cultural Change* 28 (July 1980): 673–700; and World Bank, *World Development Report, 1979* (Washington, D.C.: 1979), p. 46.

TABLE 10-2   Industrialization and Employment Growth in Developing Countries

Region/Countries	Annual Manufacturing Output Growth[a] (in percentage) 1963–69	Annual Manufacturing Employment Growth (in percentage) 1963–69
Africa		
Algeria	−0.5	−27.0
Egypt	11.2	0.7
Ethiopia	12.8	6.4
Ghana	10.6	6.3
Kenya	6.4	4.3
Nigeria	14.1	5.7
Uganda	6.6	4.8
Asia		
Korea, Rep. of	18.4	13.0
India	5.9	3.3
Israel	12.1	3.0
Pakistan	12.3	2.6
Philippines	6.1	4.8
Taiwan	16.8	13.3
Thailand	10.7	−12.0
Latin America		
Brazil	6.5	1.1
Chile	4.8	4.2
Colombia	5.9	2.8
Costa Rica	8.9	2.8
Dominican Rep.	1.7	−3.3
Ecuador	11.4	6.0
Panama	12.9	7.4

[a]More precisely annual growth rate in the contribution of manufacturing to GNP.

Source: David Morawetz, "Employment Implications of Industrialization in Developing Countries," *Economic Journal* 84 (September 1974): 492–95.

continued to work on the farm despite depressed conditions. At that time, foreign experts viewed LDC agricultural production as inefficient. Compared to workers in advanced economies, agricultural workers in LDCs seemed to be producing little and appeared to be idle much of the time. Some agricultural economists assumed that peasant agriculture could be organized to employ all farm workers 10 hours a day, 6 days a week, all year long. But disguised unemployment had many mistaken premises. Many observers misunderstood the seasonality of LDC agricultural work and the difference in economic behavior between subsistence and commercial farmers (see Chapter 7).[6]

The theoretical basis for zero marginal productivity of labor was the concept

[6] Charles H. C. Kao, Kurt A. Anschel, and Carl K. Eicher, "Disguised Unemployment in Agriculture: A Survey," in Carl K. Eicher and Lawrence Witt, eds., *Agriculture in Economic Development* (New York: McGraw-Hill, 1964), pp. 129–44.

of **limited technical substitutability of factors.** Economic theory frequently assumes that you can produce a good with an infinite number of combinations of capital and labor, adjusting continuously by substituting a little more of one factor for a little less of another. However, in practice, there may be only a few productive processes available to a LDC, these being perhaps highly mechanized processes developed in the capital-abundant West. The extreme case is where production requires an unalterable ratio of capital to labor, so that the capital available to the economy cannot fully employ those in the labor force.[7] In peasant agriculture, labor less than fully employed is supposedly reflected in disguised unemployment.

However, the assumption of rigid factor proportions in LDC agriculture is not correct. Jacob Viner notes,

> I find it impossible to conceive of a farm of any kind on which, other factors of production being held constant . . . it would not be possible, by known methods, to obtain some addition to the crop by using additional labor in more careful selection and planting of the seed, more intensive weeding, cultivating, thinning, and mulching, more painstaking harvesting, gleaning and cleaning of the crop.[8]

Whether or not disguised unemployment exists depends on how an economist defines the term *marginal unit.* Zero marginal productivity in agriculture is much less plausible if it refers to a *marginal hour of work* rather than a *marginal worker.* It is not difficult to imagine a village or clan applying simple and unchanging techniques and capital equipment to a plot of land whose size has remained the same for years. Since financial incentives do not work and frequent negotiations would be costly, tasks are assigned by custom. People of the same age and sex work about the same amount of time and get the same wage. Everyone is fed to a subsistence level as long as enough food is available. If population and the labor force increase, for example, by one-fifth, each worker's hours decrease by one-fifth. Output does not change. However even if an extra worker's output is zero, an extra hour's output may be considerable. Where hours worked is the relevant measure, labor has a positive marginal productivity.

Even though capital-labor ratios are alterable in agriculture, they might not be so in industry, especially in such sectors as steel or chemicals. The last resort for labor not employed in profit-maximizing industry is with the clan, or extended family, in agriculture. Agriculture's absorption of this labor means marginal productivity and wage that will be lower than in industry. Yet the possibilities of substantial labor-intensive agricultural jobs, as Viner indicates, means that the marginal product of agricultural labor would be positive.

Do field investigations support this supposition? Several studies between 1930 and the early 1950s purported to show that LDC output in agriculture remained constant or increased with reduced labor. But these studies lacked evidence that capital formation and the level of technology remained constant.[9] Obviously labor's

[7] R.S. Eckhaus, "The Factor-Proportions Problem in Underdeveloped Areas," *American Economic Review* 45 (September 1955): 539–65.

[8] Jacob Viner, "Some Reflections on the Concept of Disguised Unemployment," *Indian Journal of Economics* 38 (July 1957): 19.

[9] Charles H. C. Kao, Kurt A. Anschel, and Carl K. Eicher, "Disguised Unemployment in Agriculture: A Survey," in Carl K. Eicher and Lawrence Witt, eds., *Agriculture in Economic Development* (New York: McGraw–Hill, 1964), pp.129–44.

marginal productivity can be positive—even if output expands with less labor—if capital and technology increase.

RURAL-URBAN MIGRATION

While overall the LDC labor force grows at an annual rate of about 2 percent, the urban labor force and population are growing annually by 4 percent! If this growth rate continues through 2000, UN projections are that the urban share of total LDC population will increase from 28 percent in 1975 to 42 percent in 2000. During this same period, the number of cities in LDCs with populations over 1 million is expected to increase from 90 to 300. Projections from Table 10-3 indicate that nineteen LDC urban areas will have populations of at least 10 million by 2000.

Low returns to agriculture and the prospect of higher wages in industry spur

TABLE 10-3   Populations of Selected Urban Areas, 1950, 1975, and 2000 (in millions)

Urban Area	1950	1975	2000
Developing countries			
Mexico City, Mexico	2.9	10.9	31.0
Sao Paulo, Brazil	2.5	9.9	25.8
Shanghai, China	5.8	11.5	22.7
Beijing, China	2.2	8.9	19.9
Rio de Janeiro, Brazil	2.9	8.3	19.0
Bombay, India	2.9	7.1	17.1
Calcutta, India	4.5	8.1	16.7
Jakarta, Indonesia	1.6	5.6	16.6
Seoul, Korea	1.0	7.3	14.2
Cairo, Egypt	2.4	6.9	13.9
Manila, Philippines	1.5	4.4	12.3
Buenos Aires, Argentina	4.5	9.3	12.1
Karachi, Pakistan	1.0	4.5	11.8
Bogota, Colombia	0.7	3.4	11.7
Lagos, Nigeria	0.3	2.1	9.4
Kinshasa, Zaïre	0.2	2.0	7.8
Developed countries			
Tokyo, Japan	6.7	17.5	24.2
New York, U.S.	12.3	17.0	22.8
Paris, France	5.4	9.2	11.3
London, U.K.	10.2	10.7	9.8

Other urban areas with more than 10 million in 2000 (in millions): Los Angeles, U.S. 14.2; Madras, India 12.9; Tehran, Iran 11.3; Baghdad, Iraq 11.1; Bangkok, Thailand 11.9; Delhi, India 11.7; Istanbul, Turkey 11.2; Osaka, Japan 11.1.

Sources: Michael A. Cohen, "Cities in Developing Countries: 1975–2000," *Finance and Development* 13 (March 1976): 12–15, based on UN projections; and World Bank, *World Development Report, 1984* (New York: Oxford University Press, 1984), p. 68.

migration from rural to urban areas. A substantial proportion of the growth in the urban labor force is because of such migration, especially in predominantly agricultural countries that are newly industrializing. Thus migration to the cities is a larger contributor than natural population growth to urban labor growth in sub-Saharan Africa, the least industrialized LDC region, than it is in more industrialized Latin America, where natural increase is the major source of urban growth.[10]

The Lewis Model

The simplest explanation for rural-urban migration is that people migrate to urban areas when wages there exceed rural wages. Sir W. Arthur Lewis elaborates on this theory in his explanation of labor transfer from agriculture to industry in a newly industrializing country. In contrast to those economists writing since the early 1970s, who have been concerned about overurbanization, Lewis, writing in 1954, is concerned about possible labor shortages in the expanding industrial sector.

Lewis believes in zero (or negligible) marginal productivity of labor in subsistence agriculture, a sector virtually without capital and technological progress. Yet he contends that the wage (w) in agriculture is positive at subsistence (s): w_s (see Figure 10-2). For this to be true, it is essential only that the *average* product of labor be at a subsistence level, since agricultural workers divide the produce equally among themselves until food availability is above subsistence. Lewis feels equilibrium wages in agriculture stay at w_s through the classical mechanism of the iron law of wages, in which higher wages are brought down by population growth, and lower wages raised as output spread over a smaller population is reduced by an increased mortality rate.

For the more capital-intensive urban industrial sector to attract labor from the rural area, it is essential to pay w_s plus a 30-percent inducement, or w_k (the capitalist wage). This higher wage compensates for the higher cost of living as well as the psychological cost of moving to a more regimented environment. At w_k the urban employer can attract an unlimited supply of unskilled rural labor. The employer will hire this labor up to the point Q_{L1}, where the value of its extra product (or the left marginal revenue product curve MRP_{L1}) equals the wage w_k. The total wages of the workers are equal to OQ_{L1}, the quantity of labor, multiplied by w_k, the wage (that is, rectangle OQ_{L1} BA). The capitalist earns the surplus (ABC in Figure 10-2), the amount between the wage and that part of the marginal product curve above the wage.

Lewis assumes that the capitalist saves all the surplus (profits, interest, and rent) and the worker saves nothing. Further he suggests that all the surplus is reinvested, increasing the amount of capital per worker and thus the marginal product of labor to MRP_{L2}, so that more labor Q_{L2} can be hired at wage rate w_k. This process enlarges the surplus, adds to capital formation, raises labor's marginal productivity, increases the labor hired, enlarges the surplus, and so on, through the cycle until all surplus labor is absorbed into the industrial sector. Beyond this point

---

[10]The merging or expansion of villages can create a statistical illusion of townward migration. For example, two villages of 2000 each can, through natural increase, expand their built-up areas until they meet to form a single village of 5000, the usual threshold for reclassification as an urban area. Bombay and Delhi, India, and Kuala Lampur, Malaysia, contain villagelike enclaves. Michael Lipton, *Why Poor People Stay Poor: A Study of Urban Bias in World Development* (London: Temple Smith, 1977), pp. 225–26.

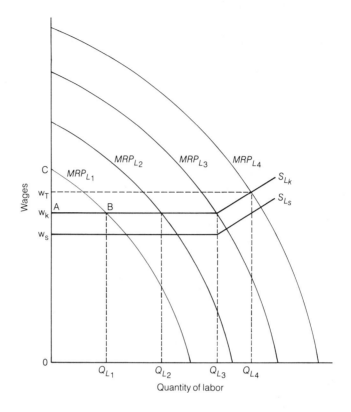

FIGURE 10-2   Industrial Expansion in the Lewis Model.   An unlimited supply of labor facilitates capital accumulation and economic growth.

Source: Based on W. Arthur Lewis, "Economic Development with Unlimited Supplies of Labor," *Manchester School* 22 (May 1954): 146.

Q_{L3}, the labor supply curve (S_{Lk}) is upward sloping and additional laborers can be attracted only with a higher wage. As productivity increases beyond MRP_{L3} to MRP_{L4}, the MRP_L (or demand for labor) curve intersects the labor supply curve at a wage w_T and at a quantity of labor Q_{L4} in excess of surplus rural labor.[11]

In the Lewis model, capital is created by using surplus labor (with little social cost). Capital goods are created without giving up the production of consumer goods. However, to finance surplus labor, additional credit may sometimes be needed.

The significance of Lewis's model is that growth takes place as a result of structural change. An economy consisting primarily of a subsistence agricultural sector (which does not save) is transformed into one predominantly in the modern capitalist sector (which does save). As the relative size of the capitalist sector grows, the ratio of profits and other surplus to national income grows.

[11] W. Arthur Lewis, "Economic Development with Unlimited Supplies of Labor," *Manchester School* 22 (May 1954): 139–91.

Critics question the theoretical underpinning of the Lewis model, the assumption of an unlimited labor supply. They believe the capitalist wage rate may have to be raised before all surplus rural labor is absorbed. As workers with zero marginal productivity migrate from the subsistence agricultural sector, it will then divide *constant* output among *fewer persons* resulting in a *higher wage.* Industrial wages, then, must increase to motivate rural workers to migrate. Or Lewis's critics argue that the larger industrial labor force contributes to greater food demand, but the capacity to produce food is unchanged. Thus food prices rise. Accordingly the industrial sector must increase wages to pay for the increased price of food. Lewis overestimates the extent that the availability of cheap rural migrant labor can stimulate industrial growth.

The Harris–Todaro Model

The Lewis model does not consider why rural migration continues despite high urban unemployment. John R. Harris and Michael P. Todaro, whose model views a worker's decision to migrate on the basis of wages *and* probability of unemployment, try to close this gap in the Lewis model. They assume that migrants respond to urban-rural differences in expected rather than actual earnings. Suppose the average unskilled rural worker has a choice between being a farm laborer (or working his or her own land) for an annual income of Rs. 1000 or migrating to the city where he or she can receive an annual wage of Rs. 2000. Most economists, who assume full employment, would deduce that the worker would seek the higher paying urban job. However, in developing countries with high unemployment rates, this supposition might be unrealistic. Assume that the probability of the worker getting the urban job during a 1-year period is 20 percent. The worker would not migrate, since the **expected income** is Rs. 2000 × .20, or Rs. 400, much less than Rs. 1000 (1000 × a probability of 1) on the farm. But if the probability of success is 60 percent, expected urban earnings would be Rs. 2000 × .60, or Rs. 1200. In this case, it would be rational for the farm worker to seek the urban job. And since most migrants are young (under 25), it would be more realistic to assume an even longer time span in the decision to migrate. The migrant may consider lifetime earnings. Thus if the present value of expected lifetime earnings in the urban job is greater than on the farm, it would be rational to migrate.

According to Harris and Todaro, creating urban jobs by expanding industrial output is insufficient for solving the urban unemployment problem. Instead they recommend that government reduce urban wages, eliminate other factor price distortions, promote rural employment, and generate labor-intensive technologies, policies discussed below.[12]

Criticisms of the Harris–Todaro Model

Even without amenities, an ILO study indicates that the ratio of average urban to rural income is more than 2 in Asia and Latin America and 4–5 in Africa (after adjustments for living costs). Assuming a ratio of 2, urban unemployment must be

[12] John R. Harris and Michael P. Todaro, "Migration, Unemployment, and Development: A Two-sector Analysis," *American Economic Review* 60, no. 1 (March 1970): 126–42; and Michael P. Todaro, "Income Expectations, Rural-Urban Migration and Employment in Africa," *International Labor Review* 104 (November 1971): 387–413.

50 percent to equate urban and rural expected income. But LDC urban unemployment rarely exceeds 10–20 percent, indicating migration does not close the urban and rural expected wage gap. We can explain the gap by adding to the Harris–Todaro urban **formal** and rural sectors the urban **informal sector,** where petty traders, tea shop proprietors, hawkers, street venders, artisans, shoe shiners, street entertainers, garbage collectors, repair persons, artisans, cottage industrialists, and other self-employed generate employment and income for themselves in activities with little capital, skill, and entry barriers. These small enterprisers have low start-up costs and profit margins, negotiate agreements outside the formal legal system, and hire workers at less than the legal minimum wage. A substantial share of the LDC urban labor force is relegated to the informal sector: 34 percent of Mexico City's; 45 percent of Bogota, Colombia's; 43 percent of Calcutta, India's; and 50 percent of Lagos, Nigeria's.

The informal-sector's labor supply is affected primarily by wages and population growth in the rural sector. The substantial absorption of rural emigrants in the informal sector explains why migration stops long before rural expected incomes attain urban formal sector ones. Many migrants are neither unemployed nor receiving the prevailing formal sector wage but are working in informal jobs, which facilitate their entry into the urban economy.[13]

The Effect of Other Amenities

The decision to migrate is not based merely on differences in earnings. Workers considering migration will look at many other factors; they will compare housing, shops, transport, schools, hospitals, and other amenities in the two places. This decision encompasses much more than the difficulty of keeping youths on the farm once they have seen the bright lights of Paris, Lagos, New Delhi, or São Paulo. In fact it is rare in developing countries for a rural youth to seek a city job without family support. Typically job applicants are sent to the city by their families to diversify family income. While in the city, they may stay with relatives during the job search. The Western stereotype of young urban immigrants as rebels against the family is not common in developing countries, where young people rarely have cars or money essential for independence and they depend heavily on the family for employment, a good marriage, and economic security.

The concentration of social services in LDC urban areas has led to overurbanization, especially in Africa. A visitor who ventures beyond an African capital city is likely to be shocked by the economic and social disparity existing between the city and the hinterlands. For example, in 1968, the eight-story, five hundred-bed Centre Hospitalier Universitaire, one of the largest and most modern hospitals in Africa, was built in the affluent section of Abidjan. But the project's funds, given by the French government, were originally intended for twelve regional

---

[13] Jacques Lecaillon, Felix Paukert, Christian Morrisson, and Dimitri Germidis, *Income Distribution and Economic Development: An Analytical Survey* (Geneva: International Labor Office, 1984), pp. 54–57; N. Vijay Jagannathan, *Informal Markets in Developing Countries* (New York: Oxford University Press, 1987), pp. 57–58; S. V. Sethuraman, *The Urban Informal Sector in Developing Countries* (Geneva: International Labor Office, 1981), p. 17; William E. Cole and Richard D. Sanders, "Internal Migration and Urban Employment in the Third World," *American Economic Review* 75 (June 1985): 481–94; and Malcolm Gillis, Dwight H. Perkins, Michael Roemer, and Donald R. Snodgrass, *Economics of Development* (New York: Norton, 1987), pp. 190–91.

hospitals in the Ivory Coast. Housing, transport, sewerage, fuel, and staple foods are often government subsidized in urban areas, where their cost is far more than in rural areas.[14]

WESTERN APPROACHES TO UNEMPLOYMENT

The classical view of employment, prevalent in the West for about 100 years before the Great Depression, was that in the long run, an economy would be in equilibrium at full employment. Flexible wage rates responding to demand and supply ensured that anyone who wanted to work would be employed at the equilibrium wage rate. In the idealized world of classical economics, there would never be involuntary unemployment!

John Maynard Keynes's general theory of income and employment was a response to failure of the classical model in the West in the 1930s. In the Keynesian model, a country's employment increases with GNP. Unemployment occurs because aggregate (total) demand by consumers, businesses, and government for goods and services is not enough for GNP to reach full employment. The Keynesian prescription for unemployment is to increase aggregate demand through more private consumption and investment (by reduced tax rates or lower interest rates) or through more government spending. As long as there is unemployment and unutilized capital capacity in the economy, GNP will respond automatically to increased demand through higher employment.[15]

However, Keynesian theory has little applicability in the LDCs. First, businesses in LDCs cannot respond quickly to increased demand for output. The major limitations to output and employment expansion are usually on the supply side, in the form of shortages of entrepreneurs, managers, administrators, technicians, capital, foreign exchange, raw materials, transportation, communication, and smoothly functioning product and capital markets. In fact where there are severe limitations in supply response (where output or supply is price inelastic), increased spending may merely result in higher inflation rates.

Second, open unemployment may not be reduced even if spending increases labor demand. As indicated previously, open unemployment occurs primarily in urban areas. However, labor *supply* in urban areas responds rapidly to new employment opportunities. The creation of additional urban jobs through expanded demand means even more entrants into the urban labor force, mainly as migrants from rural areas.

Third, LDCs cannot rely so much as DCs do on changes in fiscal policy (direct taxes and government spending) to affect aggregate demand and employment. Direct taxes (personal income, corporate income, and property taxes) and government expenditures make up a much smaller proportion of GNP in LDCs than in DCs (see Chapter 15).

Fourth, as the discussion concerning Table 10-2 suggested, employment growth is likely to be slower than output growth. In fact in some instances, increas-

---

[14] Josef Gugler and William G. Flanagan, *Urbanization and Social Change in West Africa* (London: Cambridge University Press, 1978).

[15] Michael P. Todaro, *Economic Development in the Third World* (London: Longman, 1977). pp. 174–79, has a thorough discussion of the classical and Keynesian theories of employment.

ing employment may decrease output. In the 1950s, when Prime Minister Jawaharlal Nehru asked economists on the Indian Planning Commission to expand employment, they asked him how much GNP he was willing to give up. The idea of a tradeoff between output and employment, which astounded the Indian prime minister, is consistent with a planning strategy in which capital and high-level technology are substituted for labor in the modern sector. For example, milling rice by a sheller machine rather than pounding by hand increases output at the expense of employment. However, this tradeoff between employment and output may not be inevitable, as we indicate in the discussion of employment policies.

CAUSES OF UNEMPLOYMENT IN DEVELOPING COUNTRIES

This section focuses on the reasons for urban unemployment in LDCs. As indicated earlier, the LDC urban labor force is growing at about 4 percent per year due to population increases and rural-urban migration. The first two parts of this section indicate why this labor supply cannot be absorbed. Then we look at supply and demand factors that contribute to high unemployment rates among the educated in LDCs.

The Unsuitability of Technology

As indicated in Chapter 4, most LDCs are dual economies having a modern manufacturing, mining, agricultural, transportation, and communication sector. But organizational methods and ideas, management systems, machines, processes, and so on, are imported from the DCs to run this modern sector. This technology was designed primarily for the DCs, which have high wages and relatively abundant capital. But as we have pointed out before, technology developed for DCs may not be suitable for LDCs, where wages are low and capital is scarce. On the basis of capital resources available, Frances Stewart estimates that the appropriate capital stock per person in the United States might be eight times that of Brazil, twenty times that of Sri Lanka, and over forty five times that of Nigeria and India.[16]

Often LDCs do not adopt more appropriate technology because of the rigid factor requirements of the production processes in many industries. There simply may be no substitute for producing a good with a modern, highly capital-intensive technique. China learned this the hard way during its Great Leap Forward in 1958 to 1960, which actually resulted in a great leap backward in industrial output. At that time, China emphasized labor-intensive projects that included digging canals, repairing dams, leveling mountains, and building backyard furnaces. Take the case of iron and steel. In 1958, iron and steel utensils and fixtures were taken from Chinese households for use in hundreds of thousands of backyard, steel-and-iron-smelting blast furnaces. To one observer, these furnaces shone like innumerable glowworms in the night. However by 1959, China's backyard furnaces were producing only one-fourth of the planned annual output of 20 million tons of pig iron. Some of this metal was too brittle even to use for simple farm tools. By 1960, the

---

[16] Frances Stewart, "Technology and Employment in LDCs," in Edgar O. Edwards, ed., *Employment in Developing Nations* (New York: Columbia University Press, 1974), pp. 86–88.

backyard furnaces were abandoned in order to concentrate on large, conventional smelting, blast, and open-hearth furnaces.[17]

When capital-labor ratios in industry are inflexible, the small amount of capital available in LDCs may not make it possible to employ all the labor force.

Factor Price Distortions

However even when there is a wide choice of various capital-labor combinations, LDCs may not choose labor-intensive methods because of **factor price distortions** that make wages higher and interest rates and foreign exchange costs lower than market-clearing rates.

High Wages in the Modern Sector.   Marx's collaborator, Friedrich Engels, who wrote in the late nineteenth century, referred to Britain's regularly employed industrial proletariat, with its wages and privileges in excess of other European workers, as a **labor aristocracy.** Today some scholars apply Engels's concept to LDCs, pointing out that urban workers tend to be economically far better off than the rural population.

It is true that the prevailing wage for unskilled labor in the modern sector in LDCs is frequently higher than the market wage because of minimum wage legislation, labor union pressure, and the wage policies of foreign corporations operating in these countries. Often trade unions try to influence wages in the modern sector through political lobbying rather than collective bargaining. Frequently unions became political during a colonial period, when the struggle for employment, higher wages, and improved benefits was tied to a nationalist movement. After independence was gained, the political power of the unions often led to the widespread establishment of official wage tribunals, which frequently base a minimum living wage on the standards of more industrialized countries rather than on market forces in their own country. When foreign firms pay higher wages than domestic firms, the motive may be to gain political favor, avoid political attack, and prevent labor strife, as well as to ensure getting workers of high quality.

In many LDCs, the income of workers paid the legal minimum wage is several times the country's per capita GNP. Even when we adjust for the average number of dependents supported by these workers, the per capita incomes of their households are still usually in excess of the average for the country as a whole. This disparity exists because the minimum wage (when enforced) usually applies to only a small fraction of the labor force, workers in government and in firms with, say, fifteen to twenty or more employees. The wage structure for these workers in the **formal sector** is usually higher than those with comparable jobs in the **informal sector.** Wage-employment studies indicate that wages higher than equilibrium reduce employment in the formal sector.

Low Capital Costs.   Capital costs in LDCs may be artificially low. Programs encouraging investment, such as subsidized interest rates, liberal depreciation allowances, and tax rebates are common. But at least as important are policies that keep the **price of foreign exchange,** that is, the price of foreign currency in terms of domestic currency, lower than equilibrium.

---

[17] Jan S. Prybyla, *The Political Economy of Communist China* (Scranton, Pa.: International Textbook, 1970), pp. 256, 276–77, 299.

The LDC central bank restrictions on imports and currency conversion, although ostensibly made to conserve foreign exchange, may actually create foreign currency shortages by keeping the foreign exchange price too low. For example, such restrictions may allow India to keep the foreign exchange rate at Rs. 13 = $1 rather than a market-clearing rate of Rs. 26 = $1. This low price of foreign currency means that an imported machine tagged at $1000 costs Rs. 13,000, instead of Rs. 26,000 (at equilibrium exchange rates). The low foreign exchange price gives importers of capital goods (as well as other goods) an artificial inducement to buy. However since most countries assign a high priority to importing capital goods, these importers have a better chance of acquiring licenses for foreign exchange from the central bank than do other importers (see Chapter 18).

The low foreign exchange price and the official preference for imported capital goods combine to make the actual price of capital cheaper than its equilibrium price. And when this occurs with wages higher than market rates, LDCs end up using more capital-intensive techniques and employing fewer people than would happen at equilibrium factor prices. Distortions in these prices and fairly inflexible factor requirements for some production processes result in higher unemployment. The end effect is increased income inequalities between property owners and workers and between highly paid workers and the unemployed.

Unemployment among the Educated

The overall secondary school enrollment rate in LDCs is about 23 percent. Regrettably scattered studies suggest that LDCs, especially those with secondary enrollment rates over 20 percent, have unemployment rates of well over 10 percent among persons with some secondary schooling. Sri Lanka (where the overwhelming majority of youths receive some secondary education), India, and Malaysia have unemployment rates in this educational group in excess of 20 percent. The unemployment rate for people with some primary education may be close to 10 percent; for those with some postprimary education even lower; and those with no schooling lower yet.[18] Even so, there is no evidence of a rising unemployment trend among the educated in LDCs, although there is an indication of higher unemployment in particular countries that have instituted universal primary education or rapidly expanded secondary enrollment during the past decade.

Unemployment among the educated appears to be associated with how the labor market adjusts to an influx of school graduates (and dropouts). While political pressures force many LDC public education systems to expand, there are rarely enough jobs for these people once they graduate. Job aspirations among the educated simply cannot be met. During the initial years of educational expansion and replacement of foreigners by locals just after independence from colonial rule, graduates were readily absorbed in high-level positions in the civil services, armed forces, government corporations, schools, and private business. However in subsequent years, there have been far fewer vacancies at these levels.

High unemployment among the educated is in part due to the fact that the wage structure may adjust slowly, especially if the public sector is the major employer of educated workers. Frequently in government service, wages are based on the cost of

---

[18] Lyn Squire, *Employment Policy in Developing Countries: A Survey of Issues and Evidence* (New York: Oxford University Press, 1981), p. 70.

acquiring the training essential to meet the legal requirements for the job rather than on labor supply and productivity. The signals from this perverse wage-setting mechanism do not provide consistency between educational output and employment opportunities. Furthermore graduates may be encouraged to wait for well-paid jobs rather than immediately accept a job that pays much less. If the wage difference is high enough and the probability of obtaining a higher paid job is sufficiently large, a period of job seeking will yield a higher expected, lifetime income.

These explanations are consistent with the unemployment patterns indicated earlier. Illiterate people cannot wait for a better paid job. They remain on the farm or take the first job offer. At the other extreme, highly trained people are scarce enough in most LDCs that university graduates get well-paid jobs immediately. But those in between, primary and secondary school graduates (or dropouts), are neither assured of high-paying jobs nor completely out of the running for them. Thus there may be a substantial pay off in a full time search for a job. The educated unemployed tend to be young, with few dependents, and supported by their families. Most eventually find work, usually within two years, although some have to lower their job expectations. Mark Blaug, P. R. G. Layard, and Maureen Woodhall found that while 65 percent of secondary school graduates in India were unemployed in the first year after completing their education, only 36 percent were in the second year, 20 percent in the third, 11 percent in the fourth, 6 percent in the fifth, and 2 percent in the sixth. Except for possible political discontent, the costs associated with this unemployment are not so serious as they might appear.[19]

POLICIES FOR REDUCING UNEMPLOYMENT

Population Policies

As we have already said, rising LDC unemployment is caused by slowly growing job opportunities and a rapidly growing labor force. Family planning programs and programs to improve health, nutrition, education, urban development, income distribution, and opportunities for women can reduce fertility and population growth, thus decreasing labor force size 15 to 20 years hence (Chapter 9). Such fertility reduction should be pursued.

Policies to Discourage Rural-Urban Migration

Unemployment can be reduced by decreasing rural-urban migration. The key to such a decrease is greater rural economic development. As indicated in Chapter 7, this development can be facilitated by eliminating the urban bias in development projects; removing price ceilings on food and other agricultural goods; setting the foreign exchange price close to a market-clearing rate; increasing capital-saving, technological change in agriculture; locating new industries in rural areas; and providing more schools, housing, food, sewerage, hospitals, health services, roads, entertainment, and other amenities.

[19] World Bank, *World Development Report, 1980* (New York: Oxford University Press, 1980), p. 51; and Mark Blaug, P. R. G. Layard, and Maureen Woodhall, *The Causes of Graduate Unemployment in India* (London: Allen Lane, Penguin Books, 1969), p. 90.

However, such expenditures to reduce urban migration may reach diminishing returns quickly. Unemployment among even a fraction of urban migrants may be preferable to widespread low worker productivity in rural areas. In some instances, the problem of urban migration may be a political not an economic one.

Appropriate Technology

In general **appropriate technologies** in LDCs use more unskilled labor than in DCs. The use of more appropriate technology can be stimulated by (1) intraindustry substitution, (2) interproduct substitution, (3) greater income equality, (4) providing fewer refined products and services, (5) government purchase of labor-intensive goods, (6) making sounder choices among existing technologies, (7) factor substitution in peripheral or ancillary activities, (8) using less-modern equipment, (9) the local generation of technologies and, (10) the local adaptation of technologies. In addition policies reducing factor price distortion, as discussed in a subsequent section, encourage the use of more appropriate technology. Let us examine the items in this list more carefully.

1. Encouraging the production of more labor-intensive goods within each industry is possible (for example, manufacturing cotton shirts rather than nylon and sandals instead of fancy leather shoes).
2. A single need may be fulfilled by several goods whose production varies in labor intensity. Housing needs may be more or less fulfilled by the sidewalks of Calcutta, caves, mud huts, multistory apartments, single-family houses, or palaces. In Calcutta bamboo-reinforced mud huts with tin roofs are more labor-intensive (and affordable) than Western-style, single-family dwellings.
3. Macroeconomic studies indicate that goods consumed by the poor are somewhat more labor-intensive than those consumed by the rich. Government policies, including progressive taxes, the subsidized distribution of public goods and essential comodities, and high tariffs or excise taxes on luxury items, may improve income equality. Such policies are likely to increase the demand for labor-intensive goods, such as cotton shirts, sandals, mud huts, and ungraded rice, and reduce the demand for more capital-intensive, luxury goods, particularly imports.[20]
4. One can remove luxury components from existing goods and services. Poor-quality soap produced with labor-intensive techniques can perhaps substitute for Western detergents. Traditional medicine as practiced by barefoot doctors in China may be used instead of the high-income medicine from the West.
5. Government can influence employment by directing official purchases toward labor-intensive goods.
6. Planners or entrepreneurs may choose a more labor-intensive existing technology. However, David Morawetz's survey concludes that the substitution of labor for capital is drastically limited depending on the good specified for production. Labor-intensive methods in textiles, brick making, road building,

[20] David Morawetz, "Employment Implications of Industrialization in Developing Countries," *Economic Journal* 84, (September 1974): 505–6, 512–14; and Edgar O. Edwards, *Employment in Developing Nations* (New York: Columbia University Press, 1974), p. 29.

and iron and steel output may be greatly limited if high-quality products are to be produced.[21]

7. Peripheral and ancillary activities, such as materials receiving, handling, packaging, and storage probably offer more factor substitution than materials processing. It is usually possible to use people instead of fork lifts and conveyer belts. However, product quality may sometimes dictate the use of mechanized materials handling.

8. Using less modern equipment from DCs (for example, animal-drawn hay rakes or precomputer office equipment) offers some possibilities for more labor-intensive approaches. However, older equipment in good condition is usually not readily available from the industrialized countries.

9. The LDCs can generate technology locally. During the Cultural Revolution from 1966 to 1976, Chinese managers, engineers, and workers were compelled to be inventive, since they were cut off from the outside world. Although Chinese factory workers learned to make their own tools and machines, it was later admitted that this approach was more costly than using available technology.

   The LDCs open to outside techniques can generate some technology through industry research or research organizations designed specifically to producing technology appropriate to their needs and resources. However, many government institutes have failed in developing appropriate technology. Industrial research is usually best done in the context of the producing unit by entrepreneurs, managers, engineers, technicians, and marketing specialists familiar with the industry and the work force. But even this work on labor-intensive technology will not be carried out if factor and product prices are distorted (see below).

   Perhaps the most successful example of generating appropriate technology is the high-yielding wheat varieties used in the Green Revolution in Mexico, India, and Pakistan. Appropriate technology institutes have also been effective in developing natural resources and infrastructure where there is little incentive for private research.

10. Foreign technology may be scaled down to fit LDC skills and resources. Such adaptations in South and Southeast Asia include a 5-horsepower tiller, a low-lift water pump, a McCormick-style thresher, and a jeep-type vehicle.[22]

    Sometimes adaptation may, however, require costly use of scarce engineers, managers, and other skilled persons. It may be cheaper to transfer the technology outright rather than to spend the resources to modify it.

    Nor may appropriate technologies always save capital, since it is not the only scarce factor in LDCs. Skilled entrepreneurs, managers, government administrators, and labor may be scarce as well. Thus capital-intensive, machine-paced, or process-oriented operations, which save on scarce management, may be appropriate in some cases. For example, modern factory methods for making shoes and wooden furniture use more capital per worker than cottage methods but save on skilled labor, since each operative needs a nar-

[21] David Morawetz, "Employment Implications of Industrialization in Developing Countries," *Economic Journal* 84 (September 1974), 515–23.

[22] Amir U. Khan, "Appropriate Technologies: Do We Transfer, Adapt, or Develop?" in Edgar O. Edwards, ed., *Employment in Developing Nations* (New York: Columbia University Press, 1974), pp. 223–33.

rower range of skills than the shoemaker or carpenter who makes the whole product. Thus if skilled labor is a limitation, using the more modern, capital-intensive methods may be suitable.[23]

To conclude this section, there is some scope for more appropriate technology to increase the use of labor. Nevertheless, cheaper alternative technologies to those used in DCs are not as widely available as many economists have thought.

Policies to Reduce Factor Price Distortion

The LDCs can increase employment by decreasing distortions in the prices of labor and capital. These distortions can be reduced through the following policies: (1) curtailing wages in the organized sector, (2) encouraging small-scale industry, (3) decreasing subsidies to capital investors, (4) revising worker legislation—reviewing termination practices and severance payment requirements, (5) reducing social security programs and payroll taxation, (6) increasing capital utilization and, (7) setting market-clearing exchange rates.

1. Reducing wages increases employment opportunities when the price elasticity of labor demand (minus the percentage change in the quantity of labor demanded divided by the percentage change in the wage for a unit of labor) is greater than one (or elastic). However, wage cuts are not effective when labor demand is inelastic. Labor demand is more inelastic (1) when product demand is inelastic, (2) the smaller the fraction labor is of total cost, (3) the less other factors can be substituted for labor, (4) when factor supplies other than labor are inelastic, and (5) the more inflexible the product's administered price.[24] Moreover although there may be some labor aristocrats around, they do not comprise the bulk of LDC wage earners. Furthermore care should be taken not to weaken the ability of trade unions to protect worker rights and income shares against powerful employers.

2. Encouraging the informal sector, especially small-scale industry, usually has a favorable employment effect. Firms with less than fifty workers employ over half the industrial labor force in LDCs, including 71 percent in Colombia, 70 percent in Nigeria, and 40 percent in Malaysia (43 percent in Japan and 34 percent in Switzerland!).

   Small firms have a more favorable employment effect than large firms, because they require less capital and more labor per unit of output and because their factor prices are much closer to market prices. Wage legislation often does not apply to, or is not enforced in, small firms; their wages are lower than in large ones. Additionally the small firm's less-subsidized capital costs are close to market rates.

   Government can encourage small-scale industry through such policies as industrial extension service, technical help, and preferred, official buying. However subsidized credit and imports for small firms merely encourage the use of more capital-intensive techniques.[25]

[23] David Morawetz, "Employment Implications of Industrialization in Developing Countries," *Economic Journal* 84 (September 1974), 517.

[24] Paul A. Samuelson, *Economics* (New York: McGraw-Hill, 1980), p. 525.

[25] David Morawetz, "Employment Implications of Industrialization in Developing Countries," *Economic Journal* 84 (September 1974), 524–26.

3. As just implied, a country can decrease capital-intensive techniques and unemployment by not subsidizing capital and credit.

4. A number of economists contend that worker legislation in many LDCs holds back industrial employment growth as much as high wages. Such legislation makes it difficult to fire an employee and requires large severance pay when termination occurs. These economists reason that employers may not hire extra workers when they see opportunities for sales expansion if they know that they will not be able to release them if the expansion is only temporary. So far evidence fails to demonstrate that the effect of these worker policies is positive.

5. A reduction in social security payments and payroll taxes will increase the demand for, and supply of, labor at a given wage and thus increase employment. However, the cost of these policies would be a reduction in overall savings and an increase in poverty among the aged, physically impaired, and in families losing a bread winner.

6. A simple way of increasing employment is to utilize capital stock more intensively by working two or three shifts rather than one. Since LDCs appear to have low capital utilization rates compared to DCs, employment could be substantially increased in there were enough skilled managers and foremen for extra shifts.

7. The LDCs can reduce foreign trade and currency restrictions to raise the price of foreign exchange to a market-clearing rate. This rate discourages using foreign-made capital goods by raising their domestic currency price. This increase in the price of capital will stimulate the greater use of labor-intensive techniques. Furthermore a foreign exchange rate close to equilibrium is probably a more effective policy for promoting exports and import replacements than subsidies, tariffs, quotas, and licenses, all of which distort the efficient allocation of resources.

Educational Policy

The challenge here is to reform the educational system to achieve a balance between LDC educational output and labor needs. Several strategies are suggested.

1. Where politically feasible, educational budgets in many LDCs should grow more slowly and be more oriented toward primary education and scientific and technical learning. The problem of unemployed secondary school graduates and dropouts is usually greatest where secondary education has expanded rapidly in recent years. In addition many secondary school graduates are trained in the humanities and social sciences but lack the scientific, technical, and vocational skills for work in a modern economy. Even though rapidly expanding primary education may increase unemployment, such a negative effect is somewhat offset by the higher literacy rate achieved and increased income equality. (See also Chapter 11, which indicates that the rate of return to primary education in LDCs is generally higher than to secondary education.)

2. Subsidies for secondary and higher education should be reduced, since they encourage a surplus of educated people, some of whom become unemployed. In addition as indicated in Chapter 11, they redistribute income to the rich.

However in order to improve income distribution, subsidies might be made for scholarships for the poor.

3. Increase the flexibility of pay scales. Occupational choice should change with shifts in supply and demand. When there is a surplus of engineers or lawyers (as in India in the early 1970s), salaries should fall, so that both graduates and prospective students will shift to another field.

4. Inequalities and discrimination in both education and employment should be minimized. To reduce the burden on the educational system and improve its performance, LDCs should pursue policies that encourage greater reliance on job-related learning experiences for advancement; they should use successful work experience as a criterion for educational advancement and reduce discrimination in hiring and promotion. In some instances where the highly educated are severely underutilized, it is because ethnic, regional, and sex discrimination keeps the most qualified workers from finding appropriate jobs.

5. Job rationing by educational certification must be modified. Frequently overstated job specifications make overeducation necessary for employment. Requiring a secondary education to sweep the factory floor or a university degree to manage a livestock ranch is counterproductive. Employers should be encouraged to set realistic job qualifications, even though the task of job rationing may be made somewhat more difficult.[26]

The policies on migration, education, technology, and factor price distortions discussed in the last four sections may not always be politically feasible. Governments sometimes lose the political support they need to function when they revise labor codes, curtail wages, eliminate capital subsidies, adjust foreign exchange rates, reduce secondary and higher education subsidies, or make government pay scales more flexible.

Growth-oriented Policies

Clearly South Korea and Taiwan achieved rapid employment growth partly through policies like those we have discussed and partly through rapid economic growth. Other things being equal, faster rates of growth in production contribute to faster employment growth. But other things are not always equal, as suggested by our discussion on rural-urban migration, appropriate technology, factor prices, and the educated labor market.

SUMMARY

1. The openly unemployed, those without a job who are actively looking for one, are usually urban, 15–24 years old, and among the well educated.

2. The underemployed, the visibly active but underutilized, the impaired, and the unproductive are all underutilized in LDC labor forces. Combined unem-

---

[26] Edgar O. Edwards and Michael P. Todaro, "Education, Society, and Development: Some Main Themes and Suggested Strategies for International Assistance," *World Development* 2 (January 1974): 29–30; and Lyn Squire, *Employment Policy in Developing Countries: A Survey of Issues and Evidence* (New York: Oxford University Press, 1981), pp. 194–205.

ployment and underemployment rates in LDCs were probably over one-fourth of the total labor force in 1990.

3. The labor force grows faster than job opportunities, so unemployment grows. About 30 percent of the labor force in low-income countries is employed outside agriculture. The labor force in these countries is growing at more than 2 percent per year. If employment in agriculture remains constant, the industrial sector must increase employment by roughly 7 percent or more per year to absorb this extra labor. Industrial employment rarely grows this fast in these countries.

4. Although many economists believe that there is widespread disguised unemployment, or zero marginal productivity, in LDC agriculture, the available evidence does not support the contention.

5. Rural-urban migration contributes almost as much to the rapid growth of the urban labor force in LDCs as population growth. Lewis argues that an unlimited supply of underutilized farm labor migrates to urban areas for wages only slightly in excess of rural, subsistence wages. Harris and Todaro indicate, however, that farm workers considering a move to an urban area consider urban-rural differences in unemployment as well as wages.

6. Keynesian unemployment from deficient aggregate demand is not important in LDCs because of the slow response in output to demand increases, ineffective fiscal policy, rural-urban migrants in the labor market, and possible trade-offs between employment and output from inappropriate technology.

7. Technology designed for the industrialized countries, which have a relative abundance of capital and scarcity of labor, is often not suitable for LDCs, with their abundant labor and scarce capital. This inappropriate technology increases unemployment. However in some instances, such as in the iron and steel industries, the capital-labor ratios may be invariable. The LDCs must use the same technology as DCs in such a case.

8. Capital may be priced higher and labor priced lower than equilibrium prices in LDCs because of government wage and social legislation, trade union pressures, and a low price for foreign exchange.

9. The LDC unemployment is higher among the educated than the uneducated because the educated may have unrealistic earnings expectations or job preferences and because wages paid to educated workers are often inflexible.

10. Policies to reduce unemployment include programs to reduce fertility; encourage rural development and amenities; substitute labor-intensive production techniques for capital-intensive approaches; substitute products that use labor more intensively; redistribute income to the poor; increase official purchases from small-scale, labor-intensive firms; generate new technology locally; adapt existing technology; curtail wages in the organized sector; decrease subsidies to capital; increase capital utilization; set equilibrium foreign exchange rates; resist pressures for a too rapid expansion of upper-level education and refuse to subsidize this level of education; increase the share of spending for primary schooling; stress scientific and technical education; improve wage flexibility at the higher levels; and reduce job rationing by educational certification.

TERMS TO REVIEW

- unemployment
- underemployment
- disguised unem-
  ployment
- zero marginal pro-
  ductivity of la-
  bor
- limited technical
- substitutability
  of factors
- expected income
- Keynesian theory
  of income and
  employment
- factor price distor-
  tions
- labor aristocracy
- formal sector
- informal sector
- price of foreign ex-
  change
- appropriate tech-
  nology

QUESTIONS TO DISCUSS

1. What supply and demand factors for industrial labor explain rising LDC unemployment rates?

2. How widespread is disguised unemployment in LDCs?

3. Explain urban-rural migration in LDCs.

4. What factors contribute to high urban unemployment in LDCs? Why are macroeconomic theories based on Western experience inadequate in explaining this high unemployment?

5. What policies can LDC governments undertake to reduce the unemployment rate?

6. Explain why rural-urban migration persists in light of substantial urban unemployment (for example, 15 percent or more). How would the Harris–Todaro model explain this situation? Evaluate the Harris–Todaro model.

7. What is the urban informal sector? How does the informal sector labor market affect (or how is it affected by) labor markets in the urban formal and rural sectors?

8. What causes unemployment among the educated in LDCs? What educational policies will reduce this unemployment?

9. How are wages determined in the subsistence and capitalist sectors in the Lewis model?

10. What is Lewis's explanation for rural-urban migration? For the expansion of the industrial capitalist sector? Why do critics think that the Lewis model overstates rural-urban migration and industrial expansion?

GUIDE TO READINGS

World Development Report, 1979, pp. 46–58, and Morawetz (note 20) analyze the inability of modern industry to provide adequate employment opportunities for the rapidly growing LDC labor force. Policies to reduce unemployment are discussed in these two sources in addition to Squire (note 3) and the edited volume by Edwards (note 4), especially Stewart (note 16). Unemployment among the educated is treated by Edwards and Todaro (note 26) and the *World Development Report, 1980,* pp. 46–51.

Kao, Anschel, and Eicher (note 9) have a comprehensive review of the theoretical and empirical literature on disguised unemployment in agriculture. Lewis (note 16), and Harris and Todaro (note 12) discuss the determinants of migration from rural and urban areas. See also Oded Stark, "Rural-to-Urban Migration in LDCs: A Relative Deprivation Approach," *Economic Development and Cultural Change* 32 (January 1984): 475–86; and Oded Stark and David Levhari, "On Migration and Risk in LDCs," *Economic Development and Cultural Change* 31 (October 1982): 191–96.

Lisa Peattie, "An Idea in Good Currency and How It Grew: The Informal Sector," *World Development* 15 (July 1987): 851–60, discusses different concepts of the informal sector and why they are so fuzzy. For a critique, see Nasreen Khundker, "The Fuzziness of the Informal Sector: Can We Afford to Throw Out the Baby with the Bath Water? (A Comment)," *World Development* 16 (October 1988): 1263–65.

Chapter Eleven

HUMAN RESOURCE DEVELOPMENT

SCOPE OF THE CHAPTER

Nobel laureate Simon S. Kuznets argues that the major stock of an economically advanced country is not its physical capital but "the body of knowledge amassed from tested findings and discoveries of empirical science, and the capacity and training of its population to use this knowledge effectively."[1] The contrast in economic growth between Japan and Germany, on the one hand, and third-world countries, on the other after World War II illustrates the importance of labor quality. Although much of the physical capital in Germany and Japan was in ruins or depleted, their economies grew rapidly after the war, since the skill, experience, education, training, health, discipline, and motivation of the existing labor force remained intact.

Why is labor productivity higher in DCs such as Japan and Germany than in LDCs? In this chapter, we are not interested in productivity differences attributed to capital and land. Rather we focus on the effect of variables, such as (1) formal education and training; (2) socialization, childrearing, motivation, and attitudes; and (3) the health and physical condition of the labor force.

[1] Simon S. Kuznets, "Toward a Theory of Economic Growth," in Robert Lekachman, ed., *National Policy for Economic Welfare at Home and Abroad* (Garden City, N.Y.: Doubleday, 1955), p. 39.

EDUCATION AND TRAINING

Investment in Human Capital

Remember the discussion of human capital in Chapter 6. Theodore W. Schultz argues that

> Capital goods are always treated as produced means of production. But in general the concept of capital goods is restricted to material factors, thus excluding the skills and other capabilities of man that are augmented by investment in human capital. The acquired abilities of a people that are useful in their economic endeavor are obviously produced means of production and in this respect forms of capital, the supply of which can be augmented.[2]

Economic Returns to Education

Education helps individuals fulfill and apply their abilities and talents. It increases productivity, improves health and nutrition, and reduces family size. Schooling presents specific knowledge, develops general reasoning skills, causes values to change, increases receptivity to new ideas, and changes attitudes toward work and society. But our major interest is its effect in reducing poverty and increasing income.

World Bank economists George Psacharopoulos and Maureen Woodhall indicate that the average return to education (and human capital) is higher than that to physical capital in LDCs but lower in DCs. Among human investments, primary education may be the most effective for overcoming absolute poverty and reducing income inequality. In the 1960s, planners in developing countries favored secondary and higher education that met the high-level labor requirements of the modern sector rather than establishing literacy and general education as goals for the labor force as a whole. Studies made in the 1970s and early 1980s on the economic rates of return to educational investment indicate the highest returns are from primary education. They show that between 1957 and 1978 returns to primary education were 24 percent per year, secondary education 15 percent, and higher education 12 percent (Table 11-1). The higher rates of returns to primary education are consistent with diminishing returns to increased dollars per pupil. Public expenditure per student is more for higher and secondary education than for primary education. Sub-Saharan Africa spends one hundred times as much per pupil for higher education as for primary education! (See Table 11-2.) Africa's higher education costs result partly from an inability to achieve economies of scale. Thus in the 1970s, in Ghana educating 20,000 students costs $3500 per student, while in India, 2,700,000 (with a network of local affiliated colleges to major universities in each state) costs only $250 per student.[3] On the other hand, returns to primary education reach a point of diminishing returns, declining as literacy rates increase (Table 11-1).

---

[2] Theodore W. Schultz, *Transforming Traditional Agriculture* (New Haven: Yale University Press, 1964).

[3] George Psacharopoulos and Maureen Woodhall, *Education for Development: An Analysis of Investment Choices* (New York: Oxford University Press, 1985), pp. 21–22, 196–97, analyze returns to education relative to physical capital, and Ghanaian, Indian, and other LDC university costs.

TABLE 11-1   Rates of Return to Education

Country Group	Primary Education (percent)	Secondary Education (percent)	Higher Education (percent)	Number of Countries
All developing countries	24.2	15.4	12.3	30
Low income/adult literacy rate under 50 percent[a]	27.3	17.2	12.1	11
Middle income/adult literacy rate over 50 percent	22.2	14.3	12.4	19
Industrialized countries	n.a.[b]	10.0	9.1	14

[a]In this sample of thirty developing countries, those countries with low incomes also had literacy rates below 50 percent (at the time the studies were done). All the middle-income countries had literacy rates above 50 percent.

[b]Not available.

Note: In all cases, the figures are "social" rates of return: The costs include foregone earnings (what the students could have earned had they not been in school) as well as both public and private outlays; the benefits are measured by income before tax. (The "private" returns to individuals exclude public costs and taxes, and are usually larger.) The studies refer to various years between 1957 and 1978, mainly in the latter half of the period.

Source: World Bank, *World Development Report, 1980* (New York: Oxford University Press, 1980), p. 49.

How do educational differentials in lifetime earnings vary internationally (assuming a 10-percent annual interest rate on future earnings)? In the late 1960s, the ratio of higher educational to primary education earnings in Africa (8–10) was much higher than Latin American (4–5), Asian (3–6), and North American (3) ratios. Indeed in Africa, where university and even secondary graduates have been

TABLE 11-2   Public Expenditures on Elementary and Higher Education per Student, 1976

Region	Higher (Postsecondary) Education	Elementary Education	Ratio of Higher to Elementary Education
Sub-Saharan Africa	3819	38	100.5
South Asia	117	13	9.0
East Asia	471	54	8.7
Middle East and North Africa	3106	181	17.2
Latin America and Caribbean	733	91	8.1
Industrialized countries	2278	1157	2.0
USSR and Eastern Europe	957	539	1.8

Note: Figures shown are averages (weighted by enrollment) of costs (in 1976 dollars) in the countries in each region for which data were available.

Source: World Bank, *World Development Report, 1980* (New York: Oxford University Press, 1980), p. 46.

scarce, the premium to graduates of both levels of education (highly subsidized) is high, while the premium is low for both levels in North America.[4]

Noneconomic Benefits of Education

As we have hinted at earlier, schooling is far more than the acquisition of skills for the production of goods and services. Education has both consumer-good and investment-good components. The ability to appreciate literature or to understand the place of one's society in the world and in history—although they may not help a worker produce steel or grow millet more effectively—are skills that enrich life, and they are important for their own sakes. People may be willing to pay for schooling of this kind even when its economic rate of return is zero or negative.

Some returns to education cannot be captured by increased individual earnings. Literacy and primary education benefit society as a whole. In this situation where the social returns to education exceed private returns, there is a strong argument for a public subsidy.

Education as Screening

It may be inadequate to measure social rates of return to education through the wage, which does not reflect added productivity in imperfectly competitive labor markets. In LDCs access to high-paying jobs is often limited through educational qualifications. Education may certify an individual's productive qualities to an employer without enhancing them. In some developing countries, especially in the public sector, the salaries of university and secondary graduates may be artificially inflated and bear little relation to relative productivity. Educational requirements serve primarily to ration access to these inflated salaries. Earnings differences associated with different educational levels would thus overstate the effect of education on productivity.

On the other hand, using educational qualifications to screen job applicants is not entirely wasteful and certainly preferable to other methods of selection, such as class, caste, or family connections. Moreover the wages of skilled labor relative to unskilled labor have steadily declined as the supply of educated labor has grown. Even the public sector is sensitive to supply changes: Relative salaries of teachers and civil servants are not so high in Asia, where educated workers are more abundant, as in Africa, where they are more scarce.

The World Bank, which surveys seventeen studies in LDCs that measure increases in annual output based on 4 years of primary education versus no primary education, tries to eliminate the screening effect by measuring productivity directly rather than wages.[5] All these studies were done in small-scale agriculture where

---

[4] Keith Hinchliffe, "Education, Individual Earnings, and Earnings Distribution," *Journal of Development Studies* 11 (January 1975): 152–56.

[5] The next three sections rely on World Bank, *World Development Report, 1980* (New York: Oxford University Press, 1980), pp. 46–53; Henry J. Bruton, *Principles of Development Economics* (Englewood Cliffs, N.J.: Prentice-Hall, 1965), pp. 205–21; M. Boissière, J. B. Knight, and R. H. Sabot, "Earnings, Schooling, Ability, and Cognitive Skills," *American Economic Review* 75 (December 1985): 1016–30; and E. Wayne Nafziger, *Inequality in Africa: Political Elites, Proletariat, Peasants, and the Poor* (Cambridge: Cambridge University Press, 1988), pp. 133–34.

educational credentials are of little importance. The studies found that, other things being equal, the returns to investment in primary education were as high as those to investment in machines, equipment, and buildings. These studies conjectured that primary education helps people to work for long-term goals, to keep records, to estimate the returns of past activities and the risks of future ones, and to obtain and evaluate information about changing technology. All in all, these studies of farmer productivity demonstrate investment in education pays off in some sectors even where educational qualifications are not used as screening devices.

M. Boissière's, J. B. Knight's, and R. H. Sabot's study in Kenya and Tanzania, which separates skills learned in school from its screening effect, shows that earning ability increases substantially with greater literacy and numeracy (as measured by tests given by researchers), both in manual and nonmanual jobs. These skills enable mechanics, machinists, and forklift drivers, as well as accountants, clerks, and secretaries, to do a better job. But cognitive skills, especially literacy and numeracy, are not certified by schooling but discovered on the job by the employer, who is willing to pay for them by giving a wage premium over time. Earnings do not, however, increase much with increased reasoning ability (measured by Raven's Progressive Matrices' pictorial pattern matching, for which literacy and numeracy provide no advantage) or increased years of school.

In both countries, learning school lessons, not just attending school and receiving certification, substantially affects performance and earnings in work. However, earning differences between primary and secondary graduates could reflect screening or alternatively unmeasured noncognitive skills acquired in secondary education. Research in countries at other levels of economic development is essential before we can generalize about the effects of screening and cognitive achievement.

Education and Equality

Expanding primary education favorably affects equality of opportunity. As primary schooling expands, children in rural areas, the poorest urban children, and girls will all have more chance of going to school. In general public expenditures on primary education redistribute income toward the poor, who have larger families and almost no access to private schooling. Public spending on secondary and higher education, on the other hand, redistributes income to the rich, since poor children have little opportunity to benefit from it (Table 11-3).

The links between parental education, income, and ability to provide education of quality mean educational inequalities are likely to be transmitted from one generation to another. Public primary school, while disproportionately subsidizing the poor, still costs the poor to attend. Moreover access to secondary and higher education is highly correlated with parental income and education. In Kenya those from a high socioeconomic background are more likely to attend high-cost primary schools, with more public subsidy; better teachers, equipment, and laboratories; and higher school–leaving examination scores; which admit them to the best secondary schools and the university. The national secondary schools, which receive more government aid and thus charge lower fees, take only 5 percent of primary school graduates. Additionally the explicit private cost for secondary school graduates to attend the university (highly subsidized) is low, and the private benefit is high. Yet this cost (much opportunity cost) of secondary and higher education is still often a barrier to the poor. Moreover those with affluent and educated parents can

TABLE 11-3 Public Education Spending per Household (in dollars)

Income Group[a]	Malaysia, 1974[b]		Colombia, 1974[c]	
	Primary	Postsecondary	Primary	University
Poorest 20 percent	135	4	48	1
Richest 20 percent	45	53	9	46

[a]Households ranked by income per person.

[b]Federal costs per household.

[c]Subsidies per household.

Source: World Bank, *World Development Report, 1980* (New York: Oxford University Press, 1980), p. 50.

not only finance education more easily, but are more likely to have the personal qualities, good connections, and better knowledge of opportunities to receive higher salaries and nonmanual jobs. Climbing the educational ladder in Kenya (and many other LDCs) depends on income as well as achievement.

Even if girls never enter the labor force, educating them may be one of the best investments a country can make in future economic welfare. Studies indicate clearly that educating girls substantially improves household nutrition and reduces fertility and child mortality. Yet in most parts of the developing world, especially South Asia, the Middle East, and Africa, the educational bias in favor of male enrollment is pronounced (Figure 11-1). Parents view education for their daughters as less useful than for their sons. Frequently they fear that education will harm a daughter's marriage prospects or domestic life. A girl's education may result in fewer economic benefits, especially if she faces job discrimination, marries early and stops working, or moves to her husband's village. However, educating her does increase the opportunity for paid employment, and families waste no time in educating their daughters when cultural change improves a woman's opportunities in the labor market.

Secondary and Higher Education

A renewed emphasis on primary education is quite important in LDCs, but secondary and higher education should not be abandoned. Despite the high numbers of educated unemployed in some developing countries, especially among humanities and social sciences (but not economics!) graduates,[6] there are some severe shortages of skilled people. Although these shortages vary from country to country, quite often they are shortages in vocational, technical, and scientific areas.

One possible approach to reduce the unit cost of training skilled people is to use more career in-service or on-the-job training. The following discussion suggests other ways.

In most countries, government subsidizes students beyond the primary level.

[6] George Psacharopoulos, "Returns to Education: A Further International Update and Implications," *Journal of Human Resources* 20 (Fall 1985): 590–91, 603–4, indicates that the average returns to human capital investment for fourteen DCs and LDCs are higher for economics than six other fields, which suggests that unemployment rates for economic graduates are also low.

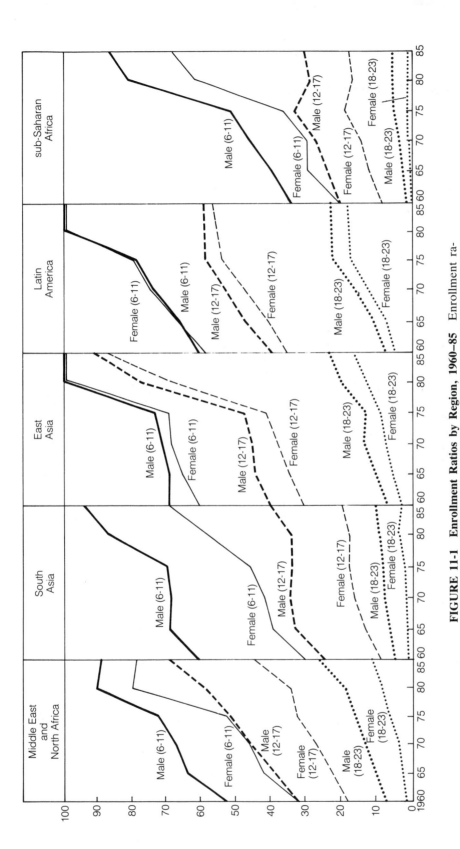

FIGURE 11-1 Enrollment Ratios by Region, 1960–85 Enrollment ratios are generally higher in East Asia and Latin America and lower in sub-Saharan Africa than other LDC regions. These ratios are higher among males than females, especially in South Asia, the Middle East, and Africa.

Sources: World Bank, *World Development Report, 1980* (New York: Oxford University Press, 1980), p. 47; World Bank, *World Development Report, 1983* (New York: Oxford University Press, 1983), pp. 266–67; and World Bank, *World Development Report, 1988* (New York: Oxford University Press, 1988), pp. 280–81.

Yet the families of these students are generally much better off than the national average (Table 11-3). For example, in Tunisia, the proportion of children from higher income groups is nine times larger in universities than in primary schools. These students should probably be charged tuition and other fees to cover the costs of their higher education, since its individual rewards are large. Charging these richer students allows government to spend more on poorer children, who can be granted scholarships. These policies may be difficult to implement. Parents of postprimary children are usually politically influential and will probably resist paying greater educational costs.

Correspondence courses can dramatically reduce the cost of some postprimary schooling, including teacher training. Such courses may not be feasible for lab subjects and the like; however where they are possible, they can usually be provided at a fraction of the cost of traditional schools and allow would-be students to earn income while continuing their education. Studies indicate that Brazil, Kenya, and the Dominican Republic have all conducted correspondence courses that have effectively taught people in remote areas.

In many instances, LDCs can reduce the number of university specializations, relying instead on foreign universities for specialized training in fields where few students and expensive equipment lead to excessive costs per person. However care must be taken to prevent either a substantial brain drain from LDCs to DCs (more on this later) or a concentration of foreign-educated children among the rich and influential.

Planning for Specialized Education and Training

The following three skill categories require little or no specific training. The people having these skills move readily from one type of occupation to another.

1. The most obvious category comprises skills simple enough to be learned by short observation of someone performing the task. Swinging an ax, pulling weeds by hand, or carrying messages are such easily acquired skills that educational planners can ignore them.
2. Some skills require rather limited training (perhaps a year or less) that can best be provided on the job. These include learning to operate simple machines, drive trucks, and perform some construction jobs.
3. Another skill category requires little or no specialized training but considerable general training—at least secondary and possible university education. Many administrative and organizational jobs, especially in the civil service, require a good general educational background, as well as sound judgment and initiative. Developing these skills means more formal academic training than is required in the two previous categories.

We have already discussed how public expenditures are best allocated between primary, secondary, and postsecondary education to ensure these skill levels, but we add that *highly* specialized training and education are usually not essential in these skill categories.

It is very important how a LDC develops the more specialized skills it will need in its labor force. There is a wide range of skills especially relevant to LDCs that require specific training and among which there is very little substitution. Most professionals—medical doctors, engineers, accountants, teachers, lawyers, social workers, and geologists—are included in this category. Generally a person with these skills has gone through 12–20 years of training, several of which have involved specialized training. The skill has been created at great cost, and the worker's productivity depends very much on the general pattern of the country's economic development.

Educational and personnel planning are most pressing where little substitution among skills is possible. For example, if a country has large oil deposits and its educational system produces only lawyers, sociologists, and poets but no geologists and petroleum engineers, establishing an oil industry will be difficult unless the country can import the needed technicians.

The fixed input-output planning method uses past information to derive a relationship between specialized human inputs and outputs. This approach first estimates the future level and composition of output. The assumed input-output relationship then enables the planner to estimate the demand for persons to fill the expected jobs. Given the length of training required for highly skilled jobs, the production of highly trained persons to fill them is nearly fixed in the short run. However, plans might be made for, say, 5 years, 10 years, and 20 years hence, with educational programs to meet the needs of specialized personnel. These programs would include training teachers by the time needed.

Yet the fixed input-output approach does not recognize some possibilities for substitution. First, if the supply of teachers is inadequate or too costly, planners might hire foreign teachers or send students abroad. Second, one category of high-level skills may substitute for another—nurses or paramedics for a medical doctor, technicians for an engineer, and elementary teachers trained in postprimary teachers' colleges for university graduates in education. Third, it is not necessarily true that the array of skills produced should adapt to the desired output composition. Perhaps the relationship can be reversed, especially in an economy open to international trade and specialization. For example, if a country has an abundance of potters and brass workers and a scarcity of chemical engineers, it may be less costly, especially in the short run, to export pottery and brass goods and import chemicals. Other alternatives would be to hire foreign chemical engineers or provide economic incentives to encourage foreign enterprises to produce chemicals domestically.[7]

Achieving Consistency in Planning for Educated Personnel

What can be done to reduce the shortages and surpluses of particular types of high-level personnel in LDCs? Various government departments (or ministries) must coordinate their activities. For example, the Department of Education's planning may conflict with that of the Department of Economic Planning. Educational policy may be to turn out historians, psychologists, and artists, while the development plan calls for engineers, accountants, and agronomists.

Chapter 10 mentioned some of the distortions that occur in the market for educated labor. The educated may have unrealistic earning expectations and job preferences, and wage rates may adjust slowly to changes in the supply and demand

---

[7] This and the next two sections rely heavily on Henry J. Bruton, *Principles of Development Economics* (Englewood Cliffs, N. J.: Prentice Hall, 1965), pp. 205–21.

for skills. Chapter 10 suggested certain policies to handle this market distortion. These included slower growth in educational budgets, orientation toward scientific and technical learning, a reduction in subsidies for secondary and higher education to high- and middle-income students, a modification of job rationing by educational certification, and more flexible wages.

In most LDCs, the supply and demand for high-level personnel could be equalized if wages were adjusted to productivity. For example, in Kenya a primary school teacher is paid one-third as much as a secondary school teacher, and in Cyprus, the primary teacher earns 48 percent of a clerical officer's salary, while one in New Zealand makes 414 percent.[8] Another example is that existing wages in LDC agriculture departments frequently encourage the rare extension worker skilled in analyzing plant or animal diseases or in designing farm machinery to seek an urban desk job. A shift in wage structure will not only spur job shifts among the presently employed, but will also encourage changes in spending for education and training. But even if wages are more closely related to productivity, the long gestation period required for the production of some skills may cause difficulty. Yet the market might still work effectively if government keeps people informed about future trends in the supply and demand for skilled labor.

Vocational and Technical Skills

It is often inefficient to rely heavily on schools to develop vocational skills. Technical skills change rapidly, and vocational and technical schools often find it difficult to keep up. Frequently these institutions should simply provide generalized training as a basis for subsequent on-the-job training or short courses. On-the-job training balances supply and demand. Firms train people for only those slots already in existence or virtually certain to come into existence. Training processes operating independently of specific job demands are less effective, and the instructors in such situations may have no idea of the needs of the firms where students will ultimately be placed.

Where on-the-job training is not possible, short-term training institutions for people already at work are often superior to vocational or technical schools. A firm's production may be substantially disrupted if an entrepreneur in a small firm or a key management person in a large firm leaves for long-term training. Thus it is best perhaps to offer a short course oriented toward those skills that are lacking. The key person's productivity will improve, and production will not be appreciably impaired.

Another approach may be to use extension agents to teach specific knowledge and skills to an owner, manager, or technician in a firm or farm. The extension agent can visit the enterprise, provide one-on-one instruction at the extension center, or have the client consult with a technical or management expert. I have observed leatherworking, woodworking, and shoemaking experts in Nigeria's industrial extension centers helping small-scale entrepreneurs, who had capital and management experience, master the mechanical skills and establish the production line essential for their firms to expand.

Should vocational training or extension programs be subsidized? We know

---

[8] Peter Heller and Alan Tait, "Government Employment and Pay: Some International Comparisons," *Finance and Development* 20 (September 1983): 44–47.

that even in the case of small farmers or industrialists, the recipient of such assistance is usually economically better off than average. Subsidies are questionable. However, there may be some economic rationale for subsidies to programs that provide direct entrepreneurial and technical assistance to small productive units. Thus a small firm may not be able to pay a highly specialized person; however if this person's scarce managerial and technical skills are used in thirty or forty firms a year, the economic cost per firm is likely to be low. Furthermore, given the external economies and the difficulty of billing each firm for the service, there may be merit in not charging for it at all.

Reducing the Brain Drain

The market for persons with scientific, professional, and technical training is an international one. In 1962, U.S. immigration laws were liberalized to admit persons having certain skills. The result is that almost half a million individuals with professional, scientific, and engineering training migrated to the United States between 1962 and 1980. Altogether other Western countries may have attracted just as many skilled immigrants. The overwhelming majority of these people came from LDCs, especially Asian countries, such as South Korea, India, the Philippines, and Taiwan.

According to the marginal product approach, the developing country does not lose from the emigration of high-level personnel, or **brain drain.** In a competitive economy, a worker earns an income equivalent to his or her marginal product. Since the emigrant removes both contribution to national product and the income that gives a claim to this share, the income of those remaining behind is not reduced. In fact the welfare of the people born in the country increases, since the emigrant increases his income.[9]

Another argument is that emigration is an "overflow" of high-level persons who would otherwise be underutilized and discontented in their home countries.[10] For example, it is argued that someone like European-based Pakistani Nobel physicist Abdus Salam would not have had at home the research facilities and intellectual stimulation from colleagues needed for his specialized work in chromodynamics.

However there are several reasons to question these two analyses. Criticisms 1–3, following, are of the marginal product model, and 4 deals with the overflow approach.

1. The marginal product model assumes that individuals pay the full cost of their education. Yet in most LDCs the government subsidizes schooling. When educated persons emigrate, the country loses human capital, a cost borne by its taxpayers in the past.
2. Many LDC labor markets are not competitive but nearly **monopsonistic** (one buyer), with only one major employer, the government. In this situation, marginal product is in excess of the wage. Accordingly the country loses more output than income from emigration.

[9] Herbert B. Grubel and Anthony D. Scott, "The International Flow of Human Capital." *American Economic Review* 56 (May 1966): 268–74.

[10] George B. Baldwin, "Brain Drain or Overflow," *Foreign Affairs* 48 (January 1970): 358–72.

3. High-level technical, professional, and managerial skills increase the productivity of other production factors, such as capital and unskilled labor. Thus emigration of high-level personnel reduces the productivity of other factors.
4. The overflow theory probably applies to only a fraction of the skilled people who emigrate. Furthermore government could reduce overflow by encouraging students and trainees to take programs relevant to the home country.

All in all, there is reason for LDC concern about the brain drain. They might undertake several policies.

1. Scholarships and training grants can be awarded only within the country, except where needed programs are not available. Students studying abroad should receive scholarships funds only for programs of study relevant to the home country.
2. Many students sent abroad could go to another LDC offering the needed specialization.
3. Even when the student is sent to a developed country for graduate study, joint degree programs between universities in DCs and LDCs, in which research is done locally under the supervision of a scholar living in the LDC, would improve the chance of that student's remaining at home.
4. The government can provide temporary salaries to its foreign-educated graduates in their job searches, guarantee employment in the home country, or financially assist recruiters seeking nationals abroad.
5. Eliminating discriminatory policies and barriers to free inquiry might encourage highly educated nationals abroad to return.

Some policies to reduce the brain drain may have negative effects. For example, the insights and creativity garnered from overseas study and travel may have to be sacrificed.

SOCIALIZATION AND MOTIVATION

Socialization is the process whereby personality, attitudes, motivation, and behavior are acquired through child rearing and social interaction. In this process, the group imparts its expectations to the individual concerning food habits, religion, sexual attitudes, world view, and work attitudes. Do cross-national differences in labor productivity and work commitment result from different socialization processes?

Commitment to Work

During the colonial period, many Western government officials, managers, and economists argued that Afro-Asians were not motivated by economic incentives and lacked a commitment to work. Many of these Westerners opposed raising native wages on the grounds that the labor supply curve was backward bending at an early stage. The prevailing view was that Afro-Asians would work less if wages were increased because they had few wants and valued their leisure. If there were some validity to the **backward-bending labor supply curve** during the early part of this century, it was because of Western colonial policy. Traditionally many peasants sold no agricultural products; instead they farmed for consumption by the family, clan, or village. However when the colonial government required money taxes, the peasant had either to produce what the European traders would buy or work at least part-time for the colonial government or a foreign firm. Not surprisingly many worked for money only long enough to pay the enforced tax. Accordingly if wages per hour were raised, they worked fewer hours and disappeared to their villages sooner.

The supply curve for labor for most individuals, whether in LDCs or DCs, is backward bending at some point. Most people take part of their higher income in leisure. However despite the backward bending *individual* curve, the *aggregate* supply curve of labor is upward sloping (that is, more hours of work are forthcoming at higher wages).

Attitudes toward Manual Work

Gunnar Myrdal, the Swedish economist who won the Nobel prize partly for his detailed inquiry into Asian poverty, argues that a major barrier to high labor productivity is a class system in which the elite are contemptuous of manual work.[11] The implication is that upper- and middle-class Westerners, who are more likely to carry their own briefcases, mow their lawns, and repair their automobiles, have different attitudes.

Yet affluent Europeans and North Americans may do more manual work than affluent Asians simply because cheap labor is not readily available to them. In general unskilled labor is more abundant in LDCs than in DCs. However Northern Europeans have hired Turkish, Yugoslav, and Italian "guest workers" to do menial jobs, and farmers in the southwestern United States employ large numbers of Hispanics to do "stoop" work. Furthermore as the minimum wage for cooks, nannies, gardeners, and other servants increases in LDCs, as in Nigeria during the oil boom of the 1970s, elites in LDCs increasingly resort to manual work themselves. Thus attitudes toward manual work may differ between DCs and LDCs, but these appear to be primarily related to the supply of cheap labor.

Creativity and Self-reliance

Psychologists argue that differences in skills and motivations are created by the child's environment. Cultures vary widely in approaches to child rearing and training. We cannot reject out of hand the possibility that cross–national differences in labor productivity may be affected by attitudes and capabilities derived from different socialization processes.

Some childhood development scholars suggest that the environment in traditional societies, such as exist in most LDCs, produces an authoritarian personality. Children brought up in these societies view the world as consisting of arbitrary forces rather than one that can be rationally manipulated. They are less likely to be independent, self-reliant, creative, imaginative, and reliable than children from

---

[11] Gunnar Myrdal, *Asian Drama: An Inquiry into the Poverty of Nations,* vol. 2 (Middlesex, Eng.: Penguin Book, 1968), pp. 1020–1285.

societies that encourage reasoning and initiative. These theories are discussed in more detail when we look at entrepreneurship and innovation (see Chapter 13).

HEALTH AND PHYSICAL CONDITION

Poor nutrition and bad health contribute not only to physical suffering and mental anguish, but also to low labor productivity. A mother malnourished during pregnancy, and inadequate food during infancy and early childhood may lead to disease as well as deficiencies in a child's physical and mental development. Future productivity is thereby impaired. Furthermore malnutrition and disease among adults saps their energy, initiative, creativity, and learning ability and reduces their work capacity.

Malnourishment is mostly a problem among the poor. Millions of people in LDCs suffer from malnutrition, not because they do not know what to eat or because the right kind of food is not available, but because they cannot afford it. One billion people, one–fourth of the developing world, are trapped in a vicious circle of poverty, malnutrition, and low productivity.

World Bank nutrition economists Shlomo Reutlinger and Marcelo Selowsky, as well as most other experts, are not certain whether the *proportion* of people in LDCs suffering from malnutrition has been increasing, decreasing, or constant since 1960. It is clear, however, that with improved transport and communication and greater awareness of the need for emergency food aid, fewer people starve to death as a result of severe food crises and famines today than in 1960. Yet countries with any lengthy disruption in planting, harvesting, and food distribution—as often happens with internal political conflict, such as in Cambodia in the late 1970s and early 1980s—remain vulnerable to starvation.

Life expectancy is probably the best single indicator of national health levels. As indicated in Chapter 9, life expectancy in LDCs increased steadily between the 1930s and 1970s. These increases were more the result of general improvements in living conditions than in medical care. Nevertheless medical progress has been considerable, especially in controlling communicable diseases. By 1975, plague and smallpox were virtually eliminated, and malaria and cholera kill fewer people today than they did in 1950.

Obviously good health and nutrition are intertwined with a country's economic and social development. Although people are healthier and nutrition has probably not declined in LDCs since the 1960s, progress has been slow—with the result that labor productivity has grown slowly. And overall the physical and mental well-being among the poorest segments of LDC population has improved but modestly. In Abidjan, Ivory Coast, the probability of dying between 1–4 years of age is fifteen times greater in slum areas than in affluent areas where housing and health standards are comparable to DCs.[12]

[12] David Morawetz, *Twenty-five Years of Economic Development, 1950 to 1975* (Baltimore: Johns Hopkins University Press, 1977), pp. 44–50; Shlomo Reutlinger, "Malnutrition: A Poverty or a Food Problem," *World Development* 5 (1977): 715–24; Shlomo Reutlinger and Marcelo Selowsky, *Malnutrition and Poverty: Magnitude and Policy Options* (Baltimore: Johns Hopkins University Press, 1976), pp. 8–9; Johanna T. Dwyer and Jean Mayer, "Beyond Economics and Nutrition: The Complex Basis of Food Policy," in Philip H. Abelson, ed., *Food: Politics, Economics, Nutrition, and Research*, (Washington, D.C.: American Association for the Advancement of Science, 1975), pp. 74–78; Halfdan Mahler, "People," *Scientific American* 243 (September 1980); 66–77; and Peter Hendry, "Food and Population: Beyond Five Billion," *Population Bulletin* 43 (April 1988): 8.

SUMMARY

1. Despite destruction of physical capital during World War II, the economies of Germany and Japan grew rapidly in the postwar period because their labor forces—with high degrees of skill, experience, education, health, and discipline—remained intact.

2. Investment in human capital includes expenditures on education, training, research, and health, enhancing a people's future productivity.

3. Returns to investment in primary education in LDCs, especially those with low literacy rates, are high, especially when compared to returns for secondary and higher education and to those in material investment.

4. While employers sometimes use secondary and university education as a screening device, they discover and pay wage premiums for literacy and numeracy, even in manual work.

5. Public expenditure per student for higher education in LDCs is about ten times as high as for primary education.

6. In LDCs the expansion of primary education redistributes benefits from the rich to the poor, while the growth of secondary and higher education redistributes income from the poor to the rich. In light of this pattern, LDCs may want to charge their richer citizens for the full cost of secondary and higher education.

7. In most LDCs, boys are sent to school far more often than girls. Yet a number of studies indicate that educating girls has a high pay off in improving nutrition, reducing fertility and child mortality, and increasing labor force productivity.

8. One planning method for producing specialized skills is to use input-output relationships to determine future demand for various types of high-level personnel. However, assuming a fixed input-output relationship does not recognize the possibility of substituting one skill for another or adapting output to skills array.

9. If wages are adjusted more closely to productivity, LDC educational planning is easier.

10. On-the-job training tends to balance demand for, and supply of, training. In addition extension agents and training at short-term vocational or technical institutions can help people improve their skills without appreciably disrupting production.

11. Some economists argue that LDCs do not lose from the brain drain, since the worker earns an income equal to his or her marginal product. However we can question this analysis, since marginal product may exceed the wage, high-level skills increase the productivity of other production factors, and government highly subsidizes education in developing countries.

12. There is no evidence of a backward bending supply curve for labor unique to LDCs. Furthermore the aggregate supply curve of labor in LDCs is clearly upward sloping.

13. Although affluent Asians may be more likely to consider manual work degrading than affluent Westerners, these attitudes appear to be primarily related to the more abundant supply of cheap labor in Asia.

14. Poor nutrition and health reduce labor productivity. However health has improved, and nutrition has probably not deteriorated in LDCs since the 1960s.

Terms to Review

- education as screening
- brain drain
- monopsonistic
- socialization
- backward-bending
- labor supply curve

Questions to Discuss

1. Would you expect the returns to a dollar of investment in education to vary from those in industrial plant, machinery, and equipment? Would noneconomic educational benefits affect the decision under perfect competition to equalize the expected marginal rate of return per dollar in each investment?

2. Why are returns to LDC primary educational investment higher than those in secondary and higher education? How do you expect their relative returns to change as economic development takes place?

3. To what extent is education a screening device for jobs rather than a way of increasing productivity in LDCs? How might the importance of screening and enhancing productivity vary by educational and skill level, sector, or world region in the developing world?

4. How does LDC government investment in educational expansion affect income distribution?

5. What are some of the ways, other than enrollment reduction, that an LDC can increase its rate of returns to investment in secondary and higher education?

6. What advice would you give to the top official in the Department of Education in a LDC who is designing a long-run program of education, training, and extension in his country? (You may either focus on LDCs in general, a particular LDC world region, or a particular LDC.)

7. How might government wage policies contribute to unemployment and underutilization of labor among the educated?

8. How can LDCs reduce the brain drain?

9. How do you explain cross-national differences in labor productivity?

Guide to Readings

Theodore W. Schultz, *The Economic Value of Education* (New York: Columbia University Press, 1963); Schultz, "Investment in Human Capital," *American Economic Review* 51 (March 1961)1–17; and Gary S. Becker, *Human Capital* (New York: Columbia University

Press, 1975), are some of the major works on investment in human capital. Psacharopoulos and Woodhall (note 3); Psacharopoulos (note 6); Boissière, Knight, and Sabot; and the *World Development Report, 1980* (note 5) analyze returns to education. *World Development Report, 1980,* pp. 32–64, has an excellent discussion of current issues in human resource development, especially in education, training, health, and nutrition. This report, Bruton (note 5), works by Edwards, and Edwards and Todaro cited in the readings for Chapter 10 consider the question of educational planning.

Morawetz, Reutlinger, Mahler, Reutlinger and Selowsky (note 12), Alan Berg, *Malnutrition: What Can Be Done? Lessons from World Bank Experience* (Baltimore: Johns Hopkins University Press, 1987), and Nevin S. Scrimshaw and Lance Taylor, "Food," *Scientific American* 243 (September 1980): 78–88, analyze nutrition, health, and economic development. Burton A. Weisbrod and Thomas W. Helminiak, "Parasitic Diseases and Agricultural Labor Productivity," *Economic Development and Cultural Change* 25 (April 1977): 505–22, measure the impact of parasitic diseases on labor productivity. The effect of tropical climate on human efficiency is examined in Chapter 8.

World Development 3 (October 1975) and the *Journal of Development Economics* 2 (September 1975) are entirely devoted to a discussion of the brain drain. *IDS Bulletin* 20 (January 1989) focuses on adjusting LDC education to the economic crisis.

Kusum Nair; "Asian Drama—A Critique," *Economic Development and Cultural Change* 17 (July 1969): 453–56, presents a skillful argument against Myrdal's discussion (note 13) of Asian attitudes toward manual work.

The effect of childhood environment on the creativity and self-reliance of the labor force is discussed by David C. McClelland, *The Achieving Society* (Princeton: D. Van Nostrand, 1961), and Everett E. Hagen, *On the Theory of Social Change: How Economic Growth Begins* (Homewood, Ill.: Dorsey Press, 1962). See also Chapter 13.

Chapter Twelve

CAPITAL FORMATION, INVESTMENT CHOICE, AND TECHNICAL PROGRESS

The rapid economic growth of the West, Japan, and Russia since the mid–nineteenth century has not been equaled by any other country. Since then the United States, Canada, Japan, Russia, and most Western European countries experienced real growth rates in gross national product per capita in excess of 1 percent per year, a rate that means a rise to at least four times initial value by 1990 (Chapter 3). The most important sources of this growth were capital formation and increased knowledge and technology. But now such continuous rapid growth may be more difficult. Given limited mineral resources, improved technology and increased capital accumulation will be essential for expanding (and perhaps just maintaining) real planetary product per capita in the future. Technical advances, such as better mining techniques (especially for using ocean resources), may mitigate our limited mineral supplies; and microminiaturization with integrated circuits (for substantial reductions in metals required), and the development of renewable power sources based on the sun, either directly through solar cells, or indirectly through water power, wind power, and photosynthesis, will help us use our resources more wisely.

Each of the next three chapters on capital formation and technology has a different perspective. This chapter discusses the contribution of capital formation and technical progress to economic growth, investment allocation among economic sectors, and the choice of techniques, or input combinations, to be used. Chapter 13 considers the role of the entrepreneur in undertaking innovation, technical change, and capital formation. Finally Chapter 14 looks at the sources of capital formation.

SCOPE OF THE CHAPTER

The first section summarizes studies that review how capital formation and technical progress contribute to economic growth and indicates why the contribution of the two differs in DCs and LDCs. The second part tries to identify the composition of what is sometimes called **technical progress**—the residual factor in growth, the increased worker productivity arising from factors other than increases in capital per worker-hour. Third, we consider technical change as a prolonged process of learning by doing. The fourth section asks whether growth can be attributed only to increases in measured inputs. Fifth, we define research, development, and invention, and their relationship to technical change.

The sixth section looks at the investment criterion, maximum labor absorption, and some of its inadequacies. Next we discuss social benefit-cost analysis, the planner's most comprehensive gauge for investment choice. We raise questions about the appropriate discount rate and how to treat risk and uncertainty. Subsequently we indicate how private profitability must be adjusted for externalities, income distribution, indivisibilities, monopoly, savings effects, and factor price distortions to obtain social profitability. The next section analyzes and assesses shadow prices, a way of adjusting prices more closely to social costs and benefits. Our final topic is the Soviet emphasis on unbalanced investment in the capital goods sector.

CAPITAL FORMATION AND TECHNICAL PROGRESS AS SOURCES OF GROWTH

In the 1950s, UN economists considered capital shortage the major limitation to LDC economic growth. By capital they meant tools, machinery, plant, equipment, inventory stocks, and so on, but not human capital.

On the basis of nineteenth- and twentieth-century Western growth, however, British economic historian Sir Alex Cairncross, writing in 1955, questioned whether capital's role was central to economic growth. To be sure, he agreed with UN economists that capital and income grow at about the same rate. But he felt that capital increases do not explain economic growth, that, in fact, the reverse was true: The amount of capital responds to increases in its demand, which depends on economic growth.[1]

Since 1955, econometricians have tried to resolve this controversy with studies measuring how factor growth affects output growth. The studies' primary concern has been to determine the relative importance of the two major sources of economic growth—capital formation and technical progress.

Initial attempts at statistical measurement in the West and Japan in the late 1950s and 1960s indicated that capital per worker-hour explained 5–33 percent of growth in output per worker-hour. Scholars usually attributed the residual, 67–95 percent, to technical progress.[2] A development economist used this evidence to

---

[1] Alex Cairncross, "The Place of Capital in Economic Progress," in Léon H. Dupriez, ed., *Economic Progress: Papers and Proceedings of a Round Table Held by the International Economic Association* (Louvain, France: Institut de Recherches Economiques et Sociales, 1955), pp. 235–48.

[2] Moses Abramovitz, "Resources and Output Trends in the United States since 1870," *American Economic Review* 44 (May 1956): 5–23; Robert Solow, "Technical Change and the Aggregate Produc-

argue that capital formation has been stressed too much and technical progress too little.[3]

Studies of non-Western economies published after 1960 contradict findings based on Western data. These studies indicate that the contribution of capital per worker to growth is 50–90 percent, while that of the residual is only 10–50 percent.[4] (Table 12-1 details the sources of growth in Western and non-Western countries.)

The aggregate models used in studies of the sources of economic growth in developed and developing countries are rough tools. Yet these studies point in the same general direction. First the major source of growth per worker in developing countries is capital per worker; increased productivity of each unit of capital per worker is of less significance. Second the major source of growth per worker in developed countries is increased productivity, with increases in capital per worker being relatively unimportant. Accordingly capital accumulation appears to be more important and technical progress less important as a source of growth in developing countries than in developed countries. (The appendix to this chapter derives the annual growth rates of output, labor, capital, and the residual from a production function similar to Equation 8-1; shows how to compute the residual; and discusses why capital's contribution to growth in LDCs exceeds that in DCs.)

In 1965, Nobel prize winner John R. Hicks argued that econometric studies of growth sources in Western countries understate capital formation's contribution to growth. Since many significant advances in knowledge are embodied in new capital, its separation from technical progress may lead to underestimating its contribution. Furthermore accumulation of new capital is frequently offset by a decrease in value in old capital, partly from obsolescence. Thus, Hicks contended, it is very wrong to give the impression to a LDC, having relatively small amounts of old capital, that capital accumulation is a matter of minor importance.[5] Econometric studies of

---

tion Function," *Review of Economics and Statistics* 39 (August 1957): 312–20; Warren T. Hogan, "Technical Progress and Production Functions," *Review of Economics and Statistics* 40 (November 1958): 407–11; Herbert S. Levine, "A Small Problem in the Analysis of Growth," *Review of Economics and Statistics* 42 (May 1960): 225–28; Benton F. Massell, "Capital Formation and Technological Change in United States Manufacturing," *Review of Economics and Statistics* 42 (May 1960): 182–88; Benton F. Massell, "Another Small Problem in the Analysis of Growth," *Review of Economics and Statistics* 44 (August 1962): 330–35; Olavi Niitamo, "The Development of Productivity in Finnish Industry, 1925–52," *Productivity Measurement Review* 33 (November 1958): 30–41; O. Aukrust and J. Bjerke, "Real Capital and Economic Growth in Norway, 1900–1956," in International Association for Research in Income and Wealth, *The Measurement of National Wealth*, Income and Wealth, series VIII (London: Bowes & Bowes, 1959); W. B. Reddaway and A. D. Smith, "Progress in British Manufacturing Industries in the Period, 1948–1954," *Economic Journal* 70 (March 1960): 6–37; and Henry J. Bruton, "Productivity Growth in Latin America," *American Economic Review* 57 (December 1967): 1099–1116.

[3] Everett E. Hagen, *The Economics of Development* (Homewood, Ill.: Irwin, 1980), pp. 201–3.

[4] A. L. Gaathon, *Capital Stock, Employment, and Output in Israel, 1950–59* (Jerusalem: Bank of Israel Research Department, 1961); M. Bruno, *Interdependence, Resource Use, and Structural Change in Israel* (Jerusalem: Bank of Israel Research Department, 1962); Henry J. Bruton, "Productivity Growth in Latin America," *American Economic Review* 57 (December 1967), 1099–1116; Angus Maddison, *Economic Progress and Policy in Developing Countries* (London: Allen and Unwin, 1970); and Sherman Robinson, "Sources of Growth in Less Developed Countries: A Cross Section Study," *Quarterly Journal of Economics* 85 (August 1971): 391–408.

[5] John R. Hicks, *Capital and Growth* (New York: Oxford University Press, 1965).

TABLE 12-1 Share of Growth in Output per Worker from Increased Capital per Worker

(1) Author, Year of Study	(2) Country	(3) Measure of Output per Worker or Person	(4) Period	(5) Proportion of Growth in Output per Worker Attributed to Increases in Capital per Worker
Abramovitz (1956)	U.S.	Net National Product (NNP) per capita	1869–78 to 1944–53	0.05–0.20
Solow (1957), with correction by Hogan (1958) and Levine (1960)	U.S.	Gross private nonagricultural output per manhour	1909–59	0.10–0.19
Massell (1960, 1962)	U.S.	Manufacturing output per manhour	1919–57	0.10–0.33
Niitamo (1958)	Finland	Output per man-year	1925–52	<0.50
Aukrust and Bjerke (1959)	Norway	NNP per capita	1900–56	0.38
Reddaway and Smith (1960)	U.K.	Net manufacturing output per worker	1948–54	0.33
Gaathon (1961)	Israel	GNP per capita	1950–59	0.60
Bruno (1962)	Israel	GNP per capita	1958–60	0.50–0.60
Bruton (1967)	U.S., Northwestern Europe, Japan, Israel	Output per manhour	1940–64	0.42
Bruton (1967)	Argentina, Brazil, Chile, Colombia, Mexico	Output per manhour	1940–64	0.74
Maddison (1970)	22 developing countries	Output per manhour	1950–65	0.90
Robinson (1971)	39 developing countries	Output per manhour	1958–66	0.88

Sources: Notes 2 and 4 of this chapter.

LDCs done since 1965 seem to confirm Hicks's point. The rates of capital growth in developing countries (as well as Israel, which received substantial inflows of funds in the 1950s) were rapid enough to offset some of the understatement of capital in the production function. Developing countries concerned about rapid economic growth ignore capital accumulation at their peril. Chapters 14 and 15 concentrate on policies to increase capital formation in LDCs.

COMPONENTS OF THE RESIDUAL

Studies of Western growth find that the residual is a major contributor to economic growth. However, to label this residual technical knowledge without explaining it is to neglect a major cause of economic growth. Critics object to elevating a statistical residual to the engine of growth, thus converting ignorance into knowledge.[6]

In any case, what does this residual include? Edward F. Denison has studied the contribution that twenty three separate sources made to growth rates in 9 Western countries for the period from 1950 to 1962.[7] His estimates, particularly of labor quality, are based on reasonable and clearly stated judgments rather than on econometric exercises. Thus he *assumes* that three-fifths of the earnings differentials between workers of the same age, geographical area, and family economic background are the result of education. Moreover individuals in the labor force having the same years of school and hours in school per year obtained at the same age are considered to have an equivalent education, no matter when or where they received their education. Furthermore 70 percent of the decrease in average hours worked is assumed to be offset by productivity increases. The reader aware of Denison's assumptions and approximations can benefit from his work; he is careful in handling empirical data, stating assumptions, and in investigating how results may be sensitive to variations in assumptions.

In all countries, growth in national income per worker is attributed more to increases in output per unit of input (the residual factor) than to increases in inputs, labor, capital, and land. Denison indicates that sources for increased output per worker for the United States or Northwestern Europe include advances in knowledge, economies of scale, improved allocation of resources, reduction in the age of capital, and decreases in the time lag in applying knowledge. Other empirical studies have included organizational improvements, increased education and training, and learning by experience.

LEARNING BY DOING

Technical change can be viewed as a prolonged learning process based on experience and problem solving. Each successive piece of capital equipment is more productive, since learning advances are embodied in new machines. Learning not only takes place in research, educational, and training institutions, but also through

[6] Thomas Balogh and Paul P. Streeten, "The Coefficient of Ignorance," *Bulletin of the Oxford Institute of Statistics* 25 (May 1963): 99–107.

[7] Edward F. Denison, *Why Growth Rates Differ: Postwar Experience in Nine Western Countries* (Washington, D.C.: Brookings Institution, 1967).

using new capital goods. Japan, which copied Western techniques for producing toys, cameras, and electronics after World War II, has become a leader in these industries through this kind of hands-on learning.

A **learning curve** measures how much labor productivity (or output per labor input) increases with cumulative experience. Thus a Swedish ironworks increased its output per worker-hour 2 percent per year despite no new investment and no new production methods for 15 years. Likewise U.S. Air Force engineers assume a constant relative decline in labor required for an airplane body as the number of airframes previously produced increases. A constant relative decline in labor requirements as output expands means labor costs approach zero as cumulative production tends to infinity—a nonsensical idea if output runs were long, but since in practice they tend to be less than 20 years, economists can safely use this form of the learning curve. Furthermore British scholars of technical progress, Charles Kennedy and A. P. Thirlwall, argue that since product types are constantly changing, we can assume there is no aggregate limit to the learning process.[8]

Because of external economies, that is, cost reductions spilling over to other producers (Chapter 7), firms whose workers learn by using capital equipment cannot hold on to some of the benefits of this learning. The **social profitability** (profits adjusted for divergences between social and private benefits and costs) of investment exceeds profitability to the firm. Thus investment rate under competitive conditions may be lower than the one optimal for society or the one prevailing with central planning. A capitalist government may wish to subsidize investment to the point that its commercial profitability equals its social profitability.

GROWTH AS A PROCESS OF INCREASE IN INPUTS

Some economists contend that virtually all economic growth can be explained by increases in inputs. In Chapters 6 and 11, we discussed the importance of the human capital input in increasing labor quality and economic growth. Theodore W. Schultz, in his presidential address to the American Economic Association in 1961, suggests that most of the residual can be attributed to investment in this input rather than to technical progress. He argues that

> Studies of economic growth based on increases in man-hours worked and on increases in capital restricted to structures, equipment, and inventories, presumably with quality held constant, do not take account of the important changes that occur over time in the quality of labor and of material capital goods. The advance in knowledge and useful new factors based on such knowledge are all too frequently put aside as if they were not produced means of production but instead simply happened to occur over time. This view is as a rule implicit in the notion of technological change.[9]

[8] Kenneth Arrow, "The Economic Implications of Learning by Doing," *Review of Economic Studies* 29 (June 1962): 154–94; and Charles Kennedy and A. P. Thirlwall, "Technical Progress: A Survey," *Economic Journal* 82 (March 1972): 38–39.

[9] Theodore W. Schultz, "Investment in Human Capital," *American Economic Review* 51 (March 1961): 1–17; and Theodore W. Schultz, *Transforming Traditional Agriculture* (New Haven: Yale University Press, 1964).

Economists contending that output is explained by increases in inputs attribute technical change to research, education, or other factor inputs. Knowledge as an intermediate or final investment good may be viewed as a direct production input. Dale W. Jorgenson and Zvi Griliches purport to show that if quantities of output and input are measured accurately, the observed growth in total factor productivity in the United States is negligible, accounting for only 3.3 percent of economic growth. However, in reply to Denison's careful analysis, Jorgenson and Griliches admit they erred in adjusting for changes in utilization of capital and land. Adjusting for the error leaves Denison's findings intact.[10] Thus the evidence still suggests that a large percentage of the productivity increase per person in the United States is unexplained by input increases. However, for developing countries, a much smaller growth share is unexplained by increased inputs.

From one perspective, capital includes anything that yields a stream of income over time. Investment is net addition to material, human, and intellectual capital. Improvements in people's health, discipline, skill, and education; transfers of labor to more productive activities; and the discovery and application of knowledge constitute human and intellectual capital. Economic development, then, may be viewed as a generalized process of capital accumulation.[11] This approach is valuable, since it emphasizes the relative return from alternative resource investments. However, we do not have precise enough measures of this concept of capital to analyze its contribution to growth.

THE COST OF TECHNICAL KNOWLEDGE

Choices among technologies, which continually change, are poorly defined. Technical knowledge, which is unevenly distributed internationally and *intra*nationally, is acquired only at a cost and is almost always incomplete, so that any person's knowledge is smaller than the total in existence. Less-developed areas can almost never acquire technical knowledge in its entirely, since blueprints, instructions, and technical assistance fail to include technology's implicit steps. Learning and acquiring technology does not result automatically from buying, producing, selling, and using but requires an active search to evaluate current routines for possible changes. Search involves people gathering intelligence by purchasing licenses, doing joint research, experimenting with different processes and designs, improving engineering, and so forth. The LDC firms and governments obtain technical knowledge through transfer from abroad as well as internal innovation, adaptation, and modification. Paradoxically LDCs can only buy information from abroad before its value is completely assessed, since this implies possessing the information.

---

[10] Dale W. Jorgenson and Zvi Griliches, "The Explanation of Productivity Change," *Review of Economic Studies* 34 (July 1967): 249–83; Edward F. Denison, "Some Major Issues in Productivity Analysis: An Examination of Estimates by Jorgenson and Griliches," *Survey of Current Business* 52 (May 1972): 37–64; and Dale W. Jorgenson and Zvi Griliches, "Issues in Growth Accounting: A Reply to Edward F. Denison," *Survey of Current Business* 52 (May 1972): 65–94.

[11] Harry G. Johnson, "Development as a Generalized Process of Capital Accumulation," in Gerald M. Meier, *Leading Issues in Economic Development* (New York: Oxford University Press, 1976), pp. 542–47.

The **price of knowledge,** determined in the wide range between the cost to the seller (often a monopolist) of producing knowledge and the cost to the buyer of doing without, depends on the respective resources, knowledge, alternatives, and bargaining strengths of both parties. Selling knowledge, like other public goods, does not reduce its availability to the seller but does decrease the seller's monopoly rents.[12]

RESEARCH, INVENTION, DEVELOPMENT, AND INNOVATION

Technical progress results from a combination of research, invention, development, and innovation. **Basic research** consists of systematic investigation aimed at fuller knowledge of the subject studied. **Applied research** is concerned with the potential applications of scientific knowledge, frequently to commercial products or processes. **Development** refers to technical activities that apply research or scientific knowledge to products or processes.[13] Some research and development results in **invention,** devising new methods or products. At times invention may require development. The commercial application of invention is innovation, discussed in Chapter 13.

According to one study, investment in agricultural research in the United States from 1940 to 1950, yielded a return of at least 35 percent per year, while that in hybrid corn research from 1910 to 1955 yielded at least 700 percent yearly.[14] In his 1968 presidential address to the American Economic Association, Kenneth E. Boulding speculated that the rate of return on the small investment in economic research was several hundred percent per year over the period from 1945 to 1965.[15]

Despite these spectacular results, *organized* research and development (abbreviated as R and D) as a whole has had only a modest impact on the rate of economic growth, since much of it generates no new knowledge. Denison estimates that only 7.5 percent of U.S. per capita growth from 1929 to 1957 can be attributed to organized R and D.[16] Today over half of these expenses are for defense and space programs, which have had only incidental benefits to civilian production. Furthermore many economists are skeptical that creativity flourishes in the institutionalized R and D setting. Much technical progress results from on-the-job problem

[12] R. R. Nelson, "Innovation and Economic Development: Theoretical Retrospect and Prospect," IDB/CEPAL Studies on Technology and Development in Latin America, Buenos Aires, 1978, p. 18; and Martin Fransman, *Technology and Economic Development* (Boulder, Colo.: Westview, 1986).

[13] Charles Kennedy and A. P. Thirlwall, "Technical Progress: A Survey," *Economic Journal* 82 (March 1972): 11–72.

[14] Zvi Griliches, "Research Costs and Social Returns: Hybrid Corn and Related Innovations," *Journal of Political Economy* 66 (October 1958): 419–31.

[15] Kenneth E. Boulding, *Economics as a Science* (New York: McGraw-Hill, 1970), p. 151, emphasizes the great depressions prevented by economic research. The rate of return on economic research has probably decreased, however, since Boulding wrote. In the late 1970s, an economic adviser to the Carter administration, Alfred Kahn, admitted that economists do not know how to reduce inflation substantially without increasing unemployment. A number of difficult economic problems exist in developing countries. However, in contrast to U.S. economic issues, few of these problems have been researched, suggesting that returns to economic research in the third world would be high.

[16] Edward F. Denison, *The Sources of Economic Growth in the United States and the Alternatives before Us* (New York: Committee for Economic Development, 1962).

solving and performance improvement rather than from work done in R and D departments. Moreover a very large portion of privately financed R and D is irrelevant to measured growth. And in developing countries, where R and D is usually a smaller percentage of GNP, its contribution to growth is likely to be less. However, these countries may be able to purchase or borrow technology from abroad (see Chapter 16).

Yet studies like Denison's assume R and D spending is a flow cost used to produce output in a given year rather than an asset that accumulates through time. Thus these studies, which assume current spending alone measures innovation, leave out accumulated knowledge.[17]

A firm's size, monopoly power, and product diversification will determine how much R and D it does. If it is large, monopolistic, and diverse, the enterprise is more likely to capture the benefits from R and D.[18]

However, in competitive product markets like grain, the individual producer can appropriate only a small fraction of the benefits accruing from research. For example, Griliches indicates that consumers received almost all of the social returns of government-sponsored research on hybrid seed corn in the United States.[19] Corn farmers, or even the hybrid seed corn industry, would probably not have undertaken the research, since private rates of return were far below social rates. When such a divergence in these rates exists, the case for government investment in research is strong.

In the 1950s and 1960s, U.S. and British technological leaders, with the highest ratio of R & D spending to GNP, had some of the lowest rates of productivity growth. There are important advantages for countries that are **technology followers,** like early post–World War II Japan, and South Korea in the late 1970s and early 1980s. While followership requires an early emergence of indigenous technological capacity, it may not require deep levels of knowledge.

Since World War II, rapidly growing Japan and West Germany have been large net importers of technology, while slow-growing Britain and the United States are not, suggesting that part of the latters' industrial problems is too little awareness of others' inventions and development.[20]

INVESTMENT CRITERIA

Investable resources can be used in a number of ways: to build steel mills or fertilizer plants, to construct schools, to expand applied research, to train agricultural extension agents, and so on. And since there are not enough resources to go around, we must choose among investments. The rest of this chapter indicates how we can make these choices in an economically rational way.

[17] M. I. Kamien and N. L. Schwartz, *Market Structure and Innovation* (Cambridge: Cambridge University Press, 1982), p. 51.

[18] Charles Kennedy and A. P. Thirlwall, "Technical Progress: A Survey," *Economic Journal* 82 (March 1972): 61–62.

[19] Zvi Griliches, "Research Costs and Social Returns: Hybrid Corn and Related Innovations," *Journal of Political Economy* 66 (October 1958): 419–37.

[20] Lawrence G. Franko, *The Threat of Japanese Multinationals—How the West Can Respond* (Chichester, U.K.: Wiley, 1983), p. 24.

Maximum Labor Absorption

In LDCs labor—often underemployed and having low alternative costs—is usually considered the abundant factor, and capital, the scarce factor. Thus we might expect LDCs to specialize in labor-intensive goods (that is, those with high labor-capital ratios). Specifically this means that LDCs should replace the capital-intensive industrial techniques common in DCs with more labor-intensive approaches.

As indicated in Chapter 10, appropriate technology for LDCs should fit their factor proportions. According to E. F. Schumacher, the advocate of small is beautiful (Chapter 2), an **intermediate technology** is needed—techniques somewhere between Western capital-intensive processes and the LDCs' traditional instruments.[21] In practice however, many LDCs use capital-intensive methods. Sometimes entrepreneurs, bound in inertia, may not question existing capital-intensive designs. But these techniques have other attractions in LDCs as well.

1. Business people often want to use the most advanced design without knowing that it may not be the most profitable. James Pickett, D. J. C. Forsyth, and N. S. McBain, on the basis of field research in Africa, attribute this attitude to an **engineering mentality.**

> Engineers . . . are professionally driven by . . . "the half-artistic joy in technically perfecting the productive apparatus." . . . The engineer's interest is in technical efficiency—in extracting the maximum amount of sucrose from a given input of sugar cane; and from this standpoint machines are often more reliable than men. . . . A decision is taken, for example, to establish a plant of some given productive capacity in a developing country. Engineers trained according to developed country curricula are asked to design the plant. They produce blueprints for a limited number of alternatives, each of which is a variant on current "best-practice" technique. The alternatives are submitted to economic . . . scrutiny, the most attractive chosen, and another capital-intensive, technologically inappropriate plant is established.[22]

2. For many commodities, there may be no substitute for a highly capital-intensive production process. Recall Chapter 10, where we discussed an unalterable ratio of capital to labor. With fixed factor proportions, a given amount of capital may not fully employ the labor force. Yet there may be no other technologies available using higher ratios of labor to capital to produce the specified commodities.

3. Capital-intensive methods embodying technical advances may be cheaper per

[21] E. F. Schumacher, "Industrialization through 'Intermediate Technology,' " in Ronald Robinson, ed., *Industrialization in Developing Countries,* Cambridge University Overseas Studies Committee Conference on Role of Industrialization in Development, Cambridge, U.K., 1965, pp. 91–96.

[22] James Pickett, D. J. C. Forsyth, and N. S. McBain, "The Choice of Technology," *World Development* 2 (March 1974): 47–54.

The economist rejects the technically most efficient process where less costly inputs or improved revenue prospects increase social profitability. Economic efficiency implies that the use of a resource should be expanded when the extra social revenue associated with it exceeds the extra social cost, and contracted when the reverse occurs, even if this implies substituting crude labor-intensive machines for the "best-practice" sucrose-extracting machines.

output unit than either traditional labor-intensive approaches or newly designed intermediate technologies. Business people may find that modifying existing technologies is more expensive than using them without alteration. For as Chapter 13 indicates, adapting existing Western technology to LDC conditions often requires substantial (and sometimes costly) creativity.

4. Automatic machinery may reduce the need for skilled workers, managers, or administrators, all of whom are scarce in developing countries. Conserving on expensive personnel may be as important as conserving capital in LDCs (see Chapter 10).

5. Factor-price distortions may make capital, especially from abroad, cheaper than its equilibrium price. The reasons for these distortions, as indicated in Chapter 10, include minimum wage legislation, pressure from organized labor, subsidies to capital, and artificially low foreign exchange prices.

Thus maximizing a project's labor intensity is not a sound investment criterion. Nevertheless LDC planners need to examine carefully technologies in which labor can be substituted for capital.

Social Benefit-Cost Analysis

Suppose society has a given amount of resources to invest to raise output. The objective is to allocate these limited resources to achieve the largest possible increase in the economy's capacity to produce goods and services. A standard approach, **social benefit-cost analysis,** more comprehensive than the just-discussed labor absorption criterion, states that you maximize the net social income (social benefits minus social costs) associated with a dollar of investment.

The **net present value** (V) of the stream of benefits and costs is calculated as

$$V = B_0 - C_0 + \frac{B_1 - C_1}{(1 + r)} + \frac{B_2 - C_2}{(1 + r)^2} + \ldots \frac{B_T - C_T}{(1 + r)^T} = \sum_{t=0}^{T} \frac{B_t - C_t}{(1 + r)^t} \qquad (12\text{-}1)$$

where B is social benefits, C is social costs, r is the social discount rate (the interest rate set by planners), t is time, and T is the life of the investment project.

Interest on capital reflects a discount of future income relative to present income, because more capital invested now means society produces a higher income in the future. Thus even where there is no risk or inflation, a dollar's worth of future income is never worth so much as today's dollar. Future values are always discounted, and the more distant the payoff, the greater the discount.

Suppose an irrigation project results in a net stream of $200 per year for 20 years, but nothing thereafter. The total net income stream is $200 \times 20 = \$4000$ over the investment life. Assume however that the discount rate is 15 percent. This discounts the $200 annual net return to $173.91 in the first year, $99.43 in the fifth year, $49.44 in the tenth year, $24.58 in the fifteenth year, and $12.22 in the twentieth year. The discounted value of the total income stream over the 20-year period is not $4000, but only $1,251.87.

Now to return to decisions about investment, you should rank investment projects by their V (Table 12-2 shows how to rank two hypothetical investment projects by V). Choose projects with the highest ratio of V to K (the amount of capital to be allocated), then the next highest V/K, and so on, until the funds to be

TABLE 12-2 Present Value of Hypothetical 20-Year Net Income Streams from Two Alternative Investment Projects in Year 0 Discounted at 15 Percent per Year

Year	TEXTILE FACTORY ($1 MILLION INITIAL K) Net Income $(B_t - C_t)$	Net Income (discounted to year 0)	Year	SUGAR REFINERY ($1 MILLION INITIAL K) Net Income $(B_t - C_t)$	Net Income (discounted to year 0)
1	125,000	108,696	1	175,000	152,174
2	125,000	94,518	2	175,000	132,325
3	125,000	82,190	3	175,000	115,065
4	125,000	71,469	4	175,000	100,057
5	125,000	62,147	5	175,000	87,006
6	125,000	54,041	6	175,000	75,657
7	200,000	75,187	7	175,000	65,789
8	200,000	65,380	8	175,000	57,208
9	200,000	56,852	9	175,000	49,746
10	200,000	49,437	10	175,000	43,257
11	200,000	42,989	11	175,000	37,615
12	200,000	37,381	12	175,000	32,709
13	200,000	32,506	13	175,000	28,442
14	200,000	28,266	14	175,000	24,733
15	200,000	24,579	15	175,000	21,506
16	200,000	21,373	16	175,000	18,701
17	200,000	18,585	17	175,000	16,262
18	200,000	16,161	18	175,000	14,141
19	200,000	14,053	19	175,000	12,296
20	200,000	12,220	20	175,000	10,693
	3,550,000	$V = 968,030$		3,500,000	$V = 1,095,382$

$$\frac{V}{K} = \frac{968,030}{1,000,000} = 0.97 \qquad \frac{V}{K} = \frac{1,095,382}{1,000,000} = 1.10$$

Even though the summation of *undiscounted* net incomes is higher for the textile factory than the sugar refinery, planners should invest in the refinery, since its present value is higher. The example illustrates the importance of higher net incomes in the first few years before the discount factor is very high.

invested are exhausted.[23] Thus a government agency choosing among investment projects, say, high-yielding varieties of seeds, oil wells, textile factories, sugar refineries, flour mills, primary education, and training industrial managers, should be guided by the following rule: *Maximize the contribution to national product arising from a given amount of investment.*

[23] After the projects are ranked, you may be able to increase the present value of all projects by shifting resources from projects with low V/K to those with high V/K. Assume project A has a V/K of 1.8 and project B of 1.0. Switching a marginal dollar from project B to project A means that V/K for that dollar investment is increased from 1.0 to 1.8. Switches can continue until V/K is maximized; V/K is equalized for the last dollar invested in each project. However, in practice, where the project size is lumpy or discontinuous, as in the case of a dam or steel mill, these switches may not be possible.

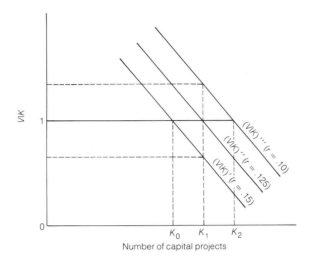

FIGURE 12-1 V/K, Discount Rates, and Capital Projects   Planners should choose a discount rate (for example, $r = 0.125$ below) so that the number of capital projects is consistent with V/K of 1 $(V/K)''$.

What Discount Rate to Use?   The present value of the net income stream is critically dependent on the **discount** (or interest) **rate** used. To illustrate, the present value of an investment of $1000, with a net income stream of $130 per year over the next 20 years, can change from more than $1000 to less than $1000, if the discount rate is raised from 10 percent to 15 percent.

The influential manual written by Oxford professors Ian M. D. Little and James Mirrlees for the OECD (an organization of developed capitalist countries) indicates that the discount rate should be set high enough to equate new capital formation (investment) with the supply of domestic savings and capital imports available (say K_1 in Figure 12-1). At a given discount rate (r), V/K diminishes (the V/K curve is downward sloping) as capital projects increase. The V/K schedule rises (shifts to the right) as discount rates decrease and falls (shifts to the left) as discount rates increase.

Given the supply of savings and capital imports, planners should choose a discount rate so that the number of investment projects is consistent with a V/K equal to one; that is, present value of the net income stream is equal to the value of the capital invested (Equation 12-2). A too-low discount rate $(r = 10$ percent in Figure 12-1) results in excessive demand for investment, $K_1 K_2$ and often a large international balance of payments deficit. For V/K to equal 1 (in Figure 12-1) at the point corresponding to the number of capital projects available, K_1, the discount rate must be 12.5 percent. A too-high discount rate $(r = 15$ percent) results in too little investment, K_0, so that the discount rate must be lowered to 12.5 percent to spur decisionmakers to use the savings and capital imports available.

Little and Mirrlees think most LDCs should use a real, or inflation-adjusted, interest rate of 10 percent. To illustrate, suppose $100 today and $200 next year are equivalent in buying power. A real interest rate of 10 percent would require a nominal interest rate of 120 percent per year so that $220 would be repaid next year for a loan of $100 today.

In practice they suggest the trial use of three rates—high, medium, and low—to sort out projects that are obviously good and obviously bad. The marginal ones can be put off until the planners see how large the investment program will be and whether any better projects come along to displace the marginal ones.[24]

Risk and Uncertainty. It is difficult to rank investment projects whose net income streams are risky or uncertain. **Risk** is a situation where the probabilities of future net returns occurring are known. To calculate V (Equation 12-1), decisionmakers can specify the whole set of alternative net income streams, computing the expected present value of the alternative outcomes, each weighted by its probability. This approach is especially appropriate for risk-indifferent government planners who have numerous projects, a long time in which to work, and considerable borrowing capacity in the event of unexpected shortfalls, especially since governments (or even giant corporations) can pool risk. Indeed the larger the population, the lower the projects' risk per individual citizen. To be sure, private individuals bear some risks, for example, students enrolled in courses in mechanics, farmers using high-yielding varieties of rice, and slum dwellers resettled in public housing. Moreover individual risks from public investments vary depending on the distribution of income, preferences, and tax rates.[25] Decisionmakers can however adjust expected present value for risk-taking or aversion. For example, the risk averter can place less value on probability distributions with a wide dispersion around the mean.

Many LDC investment choices are characterized by **uncertainty,** where the probabilities of net returns occurring are unknown. Yet this does not mean that planners must forgo project appraisal. While the outcome of a particular investment may be uncertain, the risk of the entire investment program is negligible. Although the characteristics of success are uncertain, the ingredients for outright failure (political unacceptability, management incompetence, and so on) may not be. Meticulous feasibility studies of the project will help planners evaluate their abilities to respond to difficulties (often unforeseen). Although planners may not be able to rank some projects by V/K, they may still be able to make careful nonquantitative comparisons between projects.[26]

[24] Ian M. D. Little and James A. Mirrlees, *Social Cost Benefit Analysis,* vol. 2 of *Manual of Industrial Project Analysis in Developing Countries* (Paris: Organization for Economic Cooperation and Development, 1968); George B. Baldwin, "A Layman's Guide to Little/Mirrlees," *Finance and Development* 9 (March 1972): 20; and Armen A. Alchian and William R. Allen, *University Economics: Elements of Inquiry* (Belmont, Calif.: Wadsworth, 1972), pp. 467–68.

[25] Kenneth J. Arrow and Robert C. Lind, "Uncertainty and the Evaluation of Public Investment Decisions," *American Economic Review* 60 (June 1970): 364–78.

[26] Pan A. Yotopoulos and Jeffrey B. Nugent, *Economics of Development: Empirical Investigations* (New York: Harper & Row, 1976), pp. 376–77; and Frank Knight, *Risk, Uncertainty, and Profit* (Boston: Houghton Mifflin, 1921).

DIFFERENCES BETWEEN SOCIAL AND PRIVATE
BENEFIT-COST CALCULATIONS

Under restrictive assumptions, the invisible hand of the market, dependent on thousands of individual decisions, will guide producers toward maximum social welfare. In an economy that consists of perfectly competitive firms that: (1) produce only final goods, (2) render no external costs or benefits to other production units, (3) produce under conditions of constant (marginal opportunity) costs, and (4) pay market-clearing prices for production factors, a private firm that maximizes its rate of return will also maximize the increase in national product.

However, the social and private profitability of any investment are frequently different. When Equation 12-1 is used for the private firm rather than national-planning authorities, B becomes benefits and C costs incurred by the firm from the project, and r becomes the prevailing rate of interest that the firm pays on the capital market. Private investors want to maximize the commercial profitability of the investment. On the other hand, the national planner is likely to consider not only the internal rate of return to a given investment project, but also its effect on the profitability of other production units and on consumers. The following discussion examines the divergence between private and social marginal productivity.

External Economies

As indicated in Chapter 5, external economies are cost advantages rendered free by one firm to another producer or a consumer. So though the irrigation authority may not recover its investment in dams, reservoirs, canals, pumps, and tubewells directly, increased farm yields because of improved water supplies may make the social profitability of their investment quite high. Likewise revenues generated by vaccinating people for measles, rubella, polio, and cholera may not cover costs but may substantially increase net social benefits by improving the health and productivity of the population. On the other hand, the costs of external diseconomies, such as environmental pollution arising from iron smelting, chemical, and fertilizer plants, must be added to direct costs to arrive at any investment's net social impact.

The Dakha, Bangladesh, municipal authorities should consider externalities when they decide whether to build an underground railway of a given design. Officials can estimate the initial capital outlays spread over 8 years (compounding to get the value of K in year 0) and against which must be set the stream of future net social benefits (gross benefits less operating costs) spread over 40 years but discounted to year 0.

Net social benefits will exceed net financial benefits if only because a lower fare would produce greater social benefits while reducing net receipts. The largest net benefit occurs when the fare is equal to the marginal operating cost, which varies throughout the day. But it is less cumbersome to hold the fare constant at average operating cost (or above average at peak hours, with a concessionary rate for other times).

Part of the annual gross benefit of the railway is the total receipts expected in each of the 40 years (say, 50 cents per ride times the number of riders). External benefits include the difference between 50 cents and the most people are prepared to pay for alternative road transport (auto, taxi, bus, bicycle, and rickshaw—a human-powered carriage) and the time, comfort, and safety benefits to riders (or to road users from less congestion).

If the capitalized value were $200 million in year 0 and the discount rate is correct, Dakha should build the underground if the sum of discounted future net benefits exceeds $200 million.

How do we calculate benefit cost if the railway adds equipment and other capital costs during the life of the underground? E. J. Mishan favors putting capital costs and operating costs together and entering all payments and external diseconomies as costs and all gross receipts and external economies as benefits. Thus we invest if annual net benefits $(B - C)$, which replace V in Equation 12-1, are at least zero.[27]

Planners be forewarned. Politicians have discovered the concept of *external economies,* using vague references to them to support unviable steel plants, dams, or port projects in their local districts. But even though planning agencies are generally responsible to the political leadership, careful feasibility studies, including evidence of the existence and the extent of externalities, can make a planning agency's recommendations difficult to override.

Distributional Weights

The social value of an investment may depend on who receives its benefits and bears its costs. In Equation 12-1 consumer goods produced for the rich count as much as for the poor. A government may express its goals of improving income distribution by weighing an investment's net benefits to the poor more heavily than to the rich.[28]

Indivisibilities

The returns to many indivisible investment projects, such as bridges, dams, rail lines, and electrical plants, depend on economies of scale in the use of technology, capital, or labor (see Chapter 5). Electricity can be generated, for example, in small-scale coal or oil-based steam plants or in large-scale hydroelectric or nuclear power plants.

The benefit-cost calculation still applies in the presence of indivisibilities. However, they make the role of engineers and others who formulate the project more important. Thus before evaluating a project on the basis of a given technology and scale, the project evaluator should be certain to ask engineers and others if all feasible technologies and scales have been considered.[29]

Monopoly

A **monopoly** is a single seller of a product without close substitutes; an **oligopoly** has few sellers, with interdependent pricing decisions among the larger firms in the industry. Unlike pure competition, where the individual firm faces a horizontal

---

[27] E. J. Mishan, *Cost-Benefit Analysis: An Informal Introduction* (London: Allen and Unwin, 1982); Edward M. Gramlich, *A Guide to Benefit–Cost Analysis* (Englewood Cliffs, N.J.: Prentice Hall, 1990).

[28] United Nations, Industrial Development Organization, *Guidelines for Project Evaluation* (New York, 1972), pp. 75–80, 135–48.

[29] Pan A. Yotopoulos and Jeffrey B. Nugent, *Economics of Development: Empirical Investigations* (New York: Harper & Row, 1976), p. 374.

(perfectly elastic) demand curve, the pure monopolist faces a downward-sloping demand curve. Prices are higher and outputs lower in monopolistic resource and product markets than they are under pure competition.

Monopolistic restraints are frequent in LDCs, especially in the early stages of manufacturing. In many instances, industrial concentration is a by-product of official government policy, especially of fiscal incentives and controls. Also large firms know how to deal with the bureaucracy. Rare is the LDC government with the political ability and willpower to pursue antimonopoly policies. But if such a course *is* followed, trusts can be broken up; subsidies or preferential licensing of monopolistic pioneer companies eliminated; foreign ownership shares reduced; foreign companies made to divest themselves of ancillary production or marketing channels; or nationalization of monopolies undertaken.

However, nationalized enterprises may still behave as a private monopolist in pricing and output policies. In other instances, a monopoly may be natural, as when internal economies of scale bring about a continuously falling average cost curve that makes having more than one firm in an industry inefficient. Examples of these **natural public monopolies** may be telephone, electricity, water, or postal service. In these cases, fixed production and distribution costs are so large that large-scale operations are necessary for low unit costs and prices. Where competition is inappropriate, LDC governments can place monopolies under public ownership or regulation, so that consumers benefit from scale economies. Government can further reduce resource misallocation from public monopolies if they are required to use competitive pricing policies—where marginal cost is equal to price.

Planners must realize that monopolistic behavior at a later stage in the production process can affect benefits at an earlier stage. Suppose an irrigation project leads to growing more sugar beets, so more sugar is refined. If the sugar refiner has a monopoly, the sugar beet farmers' demand for irrigation water will not be a sufficient indication of such a project's merits. If refiners were producing sugar competitively, they would use more beets, in turn increasing the demand for water. Obviously the more monopolistic an industry, the more scope there will be for improving allocation through antimonopoly policies and marginal cost pricing. Even though economists can recommend such improvements, their only recourse in calculating benefit cost is to accept present and future prices and correct them for measurable externalities.[30]

Saving and Reinvestment

The usual benefit-cost analysis does not consider the effect of an investment's income streams on subsequent saving and output. Let us compare the irrigation project discussed above to a rural luxury housing project. Assume both projects have the same annual net income streams over a 20-year investment life. Let us focus only on the $200 annual net return ($99.43 discounted to the present) in the fifth year. Suppose that the commercial farmers whose incomes increased by $200 from the irrigation project invest $100 in farm machinery and buildings, which in turn increases net farm earnings for the next 20 years. Assume though that all of the

---

[30] A. R. Prest and R. Turvey, "Cost-Benefit Analysis: A Survey," *Economic Journal* 75 (December 1965): 683–735; E. J. Mishan, *Cost-Benefit Analysis: An Informal Introduction* (London: Allen & Unwin, 1982), pp. 111–53, and Karl E. Case and Ray C. Fair, *Principles of Economics* (Englewood Cliffs, N.J.: Prentice Hall, 1989), pp. 323–26.

income from the luxury housing project is spent on consumer goods. Should the additional income (discounted back to the present) attributed to the commercial farmers' investment not also be included in the net income streams of the initial irrigation project? On the other hand, that none of the net earnings from luxury housing is reinvested would make that project less desirable.

Though it is not usually done, benefit-cost analysis can consider the effect of a project's net returns on subsequent saving and output.[31] In some instances, the savings effect will conflict with the distributional effect, since higher income recipients usually save and reinvest more. Furthermore since the income streams are even further in the future, their discounted value may be small, especially with high interest rates. Although accurate prediction is not possible, we can consider how much people are likely to save from income resulting from a particular investment project.

Factor Price Distortions

Chapter 10 indicates that wages in LDCs are frequently higher, and interest rates and foreign exchange costs lower, than market-clearing rates. Because of these distortions, the private investor may use more capital goods and foreign inputs and less labor than is socially profitable.

SHADOW PRICES

Prices do not measure social benefits and costs of an investment project if external economies and diseconomies, indivisibilities, monopolies, and price distortions are present. Prices observed in the market adjusted to take account of these differences between social cost-benefit and private cost-benefit calculations are **shadow prices.**

Planners use shadow (or accounting) prices to rectify distortions in the price of labor, capital, and foreign exchange. The following examples illustrate how this adjustment is usually made. The shadow wage for unskilled industrial labor, based on its alternative price in agriculture, may be only Rs. 0.50 per hour when the prevailing wage is Rs. 1.00 per hour. Even though business people borrow money at subsidized rates from government loan boards at only a 12-percent interest rate, the shadow interest rate, based on the cost of capital on the world market, may be 18 percent. The shadow (equilibrium) foreign exchange rate may be Rs. 26=$1, while the actual rate, repressed by import and exchange restrictions, may be Rs. 13=$1. Thus the foreign-made computer purchased by a domestic firm for only Rs. 26,000 ($2000) has a shadow price of Rs. 52,000. Correspondingly the accounting price of raw jute exported for $1000 a ton is Rs. 26,000 compared to the Rs. 13,000 received by the seller at the official exchange rate.

Little and Mirrlees determine the shadow prices of both inputs and outputs by their world prices, since these "represent the actual terms on which the country can trade." However, they argue that, since traded goods are valued in world prices,

---

[31] Walter Galenson and Harvey Leibenstein, "Investment Criteria, Productivity, and Economic Development," *Quarterly Journal of Economics* 69 (August 1955): 343–70; and Otto Eckstein, "Investment Criteria for Economic Development and the Theory of Intertemporal Welfare Economics," *Quarterly Journal of Economics* 71 (February 1957): 56–85.

nontraded goods must be similarly valued, in order to "ensure that we are valuing everything in terms of a common yardstick."[32]

Very few economists favoring the use of shadow prices question Little's and Mirrlees's valuations of goods that are or could be traded. But to value nontraded items in world prices involves a lot of trouble for doubtful advantage. Usually input-output data and purchasing power equivalents do not exist, so we cannot accurately value local goods in terms of world prices. In most countries, it is probably simpler and sufficiently accurate to (1) use world prices for inputs and outputs that are traded; (2) convert these values into domestic currency at an exchange rate (using a market rate if the official rate is badly out of line); and (3) value at domestic factor costs (shadow or market prices as appropriate) for nontraded inputs. In most investment projects, any distortions in the values of nontraded inputs are not likely to be important.[33]

Shadow pricing can open up Pandora's box. To illustrate, the shadow price of capital may depend on a distorted wage whose shadow rate requires calculation, and so on for other factors. Scarce planning personnel may have more important tasks than computing shadow prices from a complex system of interindustry equations, especially when data are lacking and shadow rates continually change. In addition a government that, say, hires labor on the basis of a shadow wage lower than the wage paid increases its payroll costs and budget deficit.[34]

Many developed capitalist countries have prices near enough to equilibrium that shadow prices are not needed for government planning. It would seem much easier for LDC governments to change foreign exchange rates, interest rates, wages, and other prices to equilibrium prices, which would make planning less cumbersome and time consuming and improve the efficiency of resource allocation.

Chapter 10 discussed how to decrease factor price distortions by (1) cutting wages and fringe benefits, (2) reducing interest rate subsidies, and (3) increasing the price of foreign exchange to an equilibrium rate. Yet price distortions are difficult to remove. Low elasticities of demand for urban labor may limit how much wage reductions expand employment (see Chapter 10). Increased foreign exchange prices (say, from Rs. 13=$1 to Rs. 26=$1) will not improve the balance of trade (exports minus imports of goods) if sums of the export and import demand elasticities are too low. An inelastic demand for an LDC's exports results in only a modest increase in rupee export receipts, which may not compensate for the increase in rupee import payments from inelastic import demand (that is, a relatively small quantity decline in response to the relatively large rupee price increase from the increased foreign exchange price). In LDCs import demand elasticity is often low as a result of high tariffs, extensive quantitative and other trade restrictions, and exchange controls.

Moreover equilibrium prices may conflict with other policy goals. The LDC

[32] Ian M. D. Little and James A. Mirrlees, *Social Cost Benefit Analysis,* vol. 2 of *Manual of Industrial Project Analysis in Developing Countries* (Paris: Organization for Economic Cooperation and Development, 1968), p. 92.

[33] George B. Baldwin, "A Layman's Guide to Little/Mirrlees," *Finance and Development* 9 (March 1972): 16–21.

[34] Wolfgang F. Stolper, *Planning without Facts: Lessons in Resource Allocation from Nigeria's Development* (Cambridge, Mass.: Harvard University Press, 1966), pp. 82–90.

governments may not want to weaken labor unions' ability to protect the rights and shares of workers against powerful employers. Subsidized capital may be part of a government plan to promote local enterprise. Young, growing debtor nations borrowing capital to increase future productivity (for example, the United States and Canada in the late nineteenth century) may not be able to attain a foreign exchange rate that eliminates an overall balance of payments deficit.

Furthermore existing distortions may be supported by economic interests too powerful for government to overcome. These interests may include organized labor, local enterprises receiving subsidies, industries competing with imports, firms favored with licensed foreign inputs, industrial and import licensing agencies, and central banks.

The LDC governments may be faced with a choice between the Scylla of cumbersome shadow price calculations and the Charybdis of factor price modification. Although the case for adjusting LDC prices nearer to their equilibrium rate is strong, the technical and political obstacles to doing so are often formidable.

SOVIET PRIORITY ON INVESTMENT IN THE CAPITAL GOODS INDUSTRY

The Model

One of the most creative periods for debate on investment choice was from 1924 to 1928, a time of acute capital shortage in the Soviet Union. During this period, Joseph Stalin, who was consolidating his power as successor to Lenin as the leader of the Communist party, was not so rigid in his approach to economic policy as he was after 1929. The Soviet industrialization dispute during this period anticipated many current controversies on development strategies, including those of balanced versus unbalanced growth (see Chapter 5).

The driving force in G. A. Fel'dman's unbalanced growth model, developed for the Soviet planning commission in 1928, was rapid increase in investment in machines to make machines. Long-run economic growth was a function of the fraction of investment in the capital goods industry (λ_1).

The **Fel'dman model** implies not merely sacrificing current consumption for current investment, but also cutting the fraction of investment in the consumer goods industry (λ_2) to attain a high λ_1. A high λ_1 sacrifices the short-run growth of consumer goods capacity to yield high long-run growth rates for capital goods capacity and consumption. A low λ_1 (or high λ_2) yields a relatively high short-term rate and relatively low long-term growth rate in consumption.

Soviet investment and growth patterns bear a close resemblance to the Fel'dman model. Between 1928 and 1937, heavy manufacturing's share of the net product of total manufacturing increased from 31 percent to 63 percent, whereas light manufacturing's share fell from 68 percent to 36 percent. During this same period, gross capital investment grew at an annual rate of 14 percent, and the ratio of gross investment to GNP doubled from 13 percent to 26 percent. However, household consumption scarcely increased (0.8 percent per year during the period), while the share of consumption in GNP (in 1937 prices) declined from 80 percent to 53 percent. Over the period from 1928 to the present, the Soviet Union's unbalanced approach to investment not only contributed to its greatest economic successes—

rapid economic growth and industrialization—but also to its chief failure—an average consumption level lower than almost all of Western Europe.

Indian Adaptation of the Soviet Model

For India's second five-year plan (1955/56–1960/61), Jawaharlal Nehru, India's first prime minister, and Professor P. C. Mahalanobis, a statistician who headed the Indian planning commission, tried to combine the Fel'dman–Stalin investment strategy with democratic socialism to reduce capital shortages. The Mahalanobis planning model, like that of Fel'dman, stressed expanding the investment share in steel and capital goods. Eventually even agriculture was supposed to benefit from this emphasis, since the production of inputs, such as fertilizer and farm machinery, was to increase.

The actual investment pattern differed from the plan. Setting a fraction of investment in the capital goods industry as a target had little practical effect on investment decisions. To begin with, planning in India does not represent a binding commitment by a public department to spend funds. Moreover it was extremely difficult to identify capital and consumer goods sectors in the industrial statistics at any reasonable level of disaggregation (or subdivision). The division between capital and consumer goods completely ignored intermediate goods, which comprise the bulk of manufacturing output in most economies. Furthermore most industries produce at least two types of goods. For example, the automotive industry produces automobiles (consumer goods), trucks (capital goods), and replacement parts (intermediate goods). In practice the Mahalanobis model left investment choice in a number of enterprises and industries virtually unaffected.

Additionally new investments in heavy industry occurred more slowly than had been planned because of technical and managerial problems, and the increased output from each unit of investment was lower than expected. Yet heavy industry still had high rates of surplus capacity because of a lack of demand. Not only had planners miscalculated the demand for consumer and capital goods as a result of unreliable figures on population growth, income distribution, and demand elasticities, more fundamentally, they had failed to consider that there were not enough investors ready to buy the capital goods produced. In contrast in the Soviet Union, where planning is comprehensive and industry is state-owned, the government provided the market for capital goods from other industries producing capital goods and armaments.

During India's second five-year plan, real GNP grew by only 3.7 percent per year compared to the 5.5-percent annual target, and the 2.5-percent annual growth rate in the early 1960s was even further below the 5.4-percent third-plan target. Slow growth in agricultural and capital goods sectors, as well as balance of payments crises from rapidly growing food and capital imports, convinced the Indian government to abandon the Mahalanobis approach by the late 1960s.[35]

Past experience with unbalanced investment in the capital goods industry suggests several lessons: (1) A larger investment share in this industry is likely to

[35] Lance Taylor, *Macro Models for Developing Countries* (New York: McGraw-Hill, 1979), pp. 119–27; Paul R. Gregory and Robert C. Stuart, *Soviet Economic Structure and Performance* (New York: Harper & Row, 1981), pp. 63–92, 327–96; Angus Maddison, *Class Structure and Economic Growth: India and Pakistan since the Moghuls* (New York: Norton, 1971), pp. 111–15; and India, Planning Commission, *Fourth Five-Year Plan, 1969–74* (Delhi, 1969).

increase economic growth if there is sufficient demand for capital goods; (2) the squeeze on current consumption implied by the unbalanced investment pattern may be at least as long as a generation; and (3) planners in capitalist and mixed economies may have too limited a control over total investment to implement a Fel'dman investment strategy. (The question of what these planners can do to influence investment rates is discussed in Chapters 14 and 19.)

SUMMARY

1. Capital formation and technical progress are major factors responsible for the rapid economic growth of the West and Japan in the last 125–150 years.

2. Economic growth cannot be explained merely by increases in inputs.

3. Econometric studies of *developed* countries indicate that the increase in the productivity of each worker per unit of capital is a more important source of growth than the addition in capital per worker. Major explanations for this increase in productivity are advances in knowledge, greater education and training, learning by experience, organizational improvement, economies of scale, and resource shifts.

4. However, research on the sources of growth in *developing* countries provides evidence that the contribution of capital per worker is more important to economic growth than that of worker productivity per unit of capital. Reasons for the greater contribution of capital to growth in LDCs are higher marginal productivity of capital and higher growth rates of capital.

5. Technical progress results from a combination of research, development, invention, and innovation.

6. Technical knowledge acquired from abroad is costly and usually incomplete.

7. LDC planners must examine existing technologies for possible substitution of labor for capital. Nevertheless the maximization of labor absorption is inadequate as an investment criterion. Labor-intensive techniques may sometimes not be used because of fixed capital-labor ratios in the industry, the high cost of adapting and modifying existing technologies, scarce administrative and managerial resources needed to implement labor-intensive techniques, and distortions that increase the price of labor relative to that of capital.

8. Social benefit-cost analysis chooses investment projects that maximize the discounted net social benefits per unit of capital invested.

9. The discount rate should be set high enough to equate investment with savings and capital imports.

10. The investment planner who wants to avert risk can place less value on probability distributions with a wide relative dispersion around the average.

11. Market prices must be adjusted for externalities, distribution, indivisibilities, monopolies, and factor price distortions to obtain shadow prices. These prices aid the planner in adjusting returns away from commercial profitability to social profitability.

12. Computing shadow prices is usually a cumbersome and time-consuming task. Setting factor and foreign exchange prices closer to equilibrium rates may be more effective in improving resource allocation.

13. After 1928, the Soviet unbalanced investment strategy emphasized investment in the capital goods sector at the expense of the consumer goods sector. The strategy probably increased Soviet economic growth, but it might not be applicable to mixed and capitalist economies, where planners have limited control over total investment.

TERMS TO REVIEW

- technical progress
- learning curve
- social profitability
- price of knowledge
- basic research
- applied research
- development
- invention
- technological fol-lowership

- maximum labor ab-sorption
- intermediate tech-nology
- engineering mental-ity
- social benefit-cost analysis
- present value (*V*) of the net in-come stream

- discount rate
- risk
- uncertainty
- monopoly
- oligopoly
- natural public mo-nopolies
- shadow prices
- Fel'dman model

QUESTIONS TO DISCUSS

1. What is the relative importance of capital formation and technical progress as sources of economic growth? In the West? In LDCs?

2. Why is capital accumulation more important as a source of growth in LDCs than in DCs? Why is technical progress less important?

3. What contributes to growth in output per worker-hour besides increases in capital per worker-hour?

4. How do economists conceptualize technical knowledge? What effect does cost have in technology search?

5. What implications does learning by doing have for LDC domestic and international technological policies?

6. How is the price of knowledge determined?

7. What are some of the advantages and disadvantages of technology followership?

8. What criterion would you recommend that a planner use in allocating investable resources among different projects and sectors in a less developed economy?

9. What is the maximum labor absorption investment criterion? What are its flaws?

10. What are the attractions of capital-intensive techniques in capital scarce LDCs?

11. What is social benefit-cost analysis? Explain how it is used to rank alternative investment projects.

12. How would Sichuan (China) provincial authorities decide whether to build a bridge across the Yangtze River in a major city, Chóngqing?

13. What are the differences between social and private benefit-cost calculations?

14. How do planners choose what discount rate to apply to investment projects?

15. What are shadow prices? Give some examples. What is a planning alternative to the use of shadow prices? Evaluate this alternative.

16. What was the Fel'dman–Stalin investment strategy? How applicable is it in capitalist and mixed private-public LDCs?

GUIDE TO READINGS

Fransman (note 12) and Giovanni Dosi, Christopher Freeman, Richard Nelson, Gerald Silverberg, and Luc Soete, eds., *Technical Change and Economic Theory* (London: Pinter, 1988), are important analyses of technical progress, while Kennedy's and Thirlwall's survey (note 8) of technological change is excellent though dated. A. P. Thirlwall, *Growth and Development with Special Reference to Developing Countries* (New York: Wiley, 1977), pp. 48–80, has an excellent survey of the literature on sources of growth in developing countries.

The major manuals providing guidelines for investment choice and benefit-cost analysis are Mishan (note 27), Little and Mirrlees (note 24), and UN, *Guidelines* (note 28). Baldwin's essay (note 24) provides a brief, simple explanation of benefit-cost analysis, while Morawetz (see note 20, Chapter 10), includes employment considerations in his analysis. Arrow and Lind (note 25) analyze the effect of uncertainty on public investments. Chapter 14 indicates some serious limitations in using the incremental capital-output ratio (ICOR) as an investment criterion. Gramlich (note 27) has the most current benefit–cost textbook.

Henry J. Bruton, *Principles of Development Economics* (Englewood Cliffs, N.J.: Prentice-Hall, 1965), pp. 281–316; Yotopoulos and Nugent, pp. 369–92 (note 26); and Thirlwall, *Growth and Development,* pp. 169–211, in ascending level of difficulty, provide surveys of technological choice, investment criterion, and resource allocation.

Taylor (note 35) has a clear exposition of the Fel'dman–Mahalanobis model.

E. F. Schumacher, "Industrialization through 'Intermediate Technology' " (note 21), *Small Is Beautiful* (note 26, Chapter 2), and *Good Work* (New York: Harper & Row, 1979), make a strong case for using intermediate technology, especially in LDCs.

For lessons in technology transfer from the Japanese experience, see Ichirou Inukai, "Experience in Transfer of Technology from the West: Lessons from False Starts," in H. Nagamine, ed., *Nation-Building and Regional Development: The Japanese Experience* (Nagoya, Japan: UN Center for Regional Development, 1981), pp. 77–98.

APPENDIX TO CHAPTER 12

DERIVING THE EQUATION FOR GROWTHS OF FACTOR INPUTS AND OUTPUT

For econometricians measuring sources of output growth, the primary question is the relative importance of the growths of capital formation and technical progress. To understand how to pose this question, we must return to the production function (Equation 8-1). Aggregate output *(Y)*, you recall, is written as a function of factor inputs and technology, that is,

$$Y = F(T, L, K, N, E) \tag{12-3}$$

where T is prevailing technology, L is labor, K capital, N natural resources, and E entrepreneurship. Let us reduce the variables to three, by regarding natural resources as a form of capital and entrepreneurship as a type of labor, so that

$$Y = G(T, L, K) \tag{12-4}$$

The Cobb–Douglas production function is used most commonly to distinguish between the sources of growth. In the 1920s, mathematician Charles Cobb and economist Paul Douglas (later U.S. Senator from Illinois) wrote this function as

$$Y = TL^{\alpha}K^{\beta} \tag{12-5}$$

The parameter α is $(\Delta Y/Y)/(\Delta L/L)$, the elasticity (responsiveness) of output with respect to labor (holding capital constant). (The symbol Δ means increment in, so that, for example, $\Delta Y/Y$ is the rate of growth of output and $\Delta L/L$ the rate of growth of labor.) The parameter β is $(\Delta Y/Y)/(\Delta K/K)$, the elasticity of output with respect to capital (holding labor constant).[36] If we assume $\alpha + \beta = 1$, which represents constant returns to scale (that is, as you increase capital and labor inputs proportionately, output increases proportionately), then α also equals labor's share and β capital's share of total income. Additional assumptions are perfect competition, with production factors paid their marginal product, and neutral technological change.

The natural logarithms of Equation 12-5 give

$$\ln Y = \ln T + \alpha \ln L + \beta \ln K \tag{12-6}$$

Differentiating with respect to time gives us

$$\frac{dY}{dt} \times \frac{1}{Y} = \left(\frac{dT}{dt} \times \frac{1}{T} \right) + \alpha \left(\frac{dL}{dt} \times \frac{1}{L} \right) + \beta \left(\frac{dK}{dt} \times \frac{1}{K} \right) \tag{12-7}$$

Equation 12-7 is in continuous time. The discrete approximation, taking annual rates of changes of the variables, is

---

[36] Charles Cobb and Paul Douglas, "A Theory of Production," *American Economic Review* (supplement) 18, no. 1 (March 1928): 139–65; and A. P. Thirlwall, *Growth and Development with Special Reference to Developing Countries* (New York: Wiley, 1977), pp. 52–54.

$$\frac{dY}{Y} = \frac{dT}{T} + \alpha \frac{dL}{L} + \beta \frac{dK}{K} \tag{12-8}$$

These are the annual rates of change of the variables, which are expressed as

$$r_Y = r_T + \alpha r_L + \beta r_K \tag{12-9}$$

where r_Y is the annual rate of growth of output, r_L the annual rate of growth of labor, and r_K the annual rate of growth of capital. r_T is a residual, the portion of output growth not attributable to increases in production factors, or growth in output per unit of total inputs. In econometric studies, this residual (rightly or wrongly) is attributed to technical progress (or technological advance).

COMPUTING THE RESIDUAL

Empirical studies solve for r_T after calculating r_Y, r_L, r_K, α, and β. Let us illustrate. Suppose economic growth (r_Y) is 5 percent, r_L 2 percent, r_K 12 percent, and the factor shares $\alpha = 0.75$ and $\beta = 0.25$. Substituting in Equation 12-9, we have

$$5.0 = r_T + 0.75(2) + 0.25(12) \tag{12-10}$$

Labor's contribution to measured growth is $0.75(2) = 1.5$ percentage points; the contribution of capital is $0.25(12) = 3$; and r_T is left as residual with a contribution of 0.5 percentage points.

EXPRESSING INCREASED PRODUCTIVITY PER WORKER ATTRIBUTED TO INCREASED CAPITAL PER WORKER AND THE RESIDUAL

Statistical measures of the sources of growth examined the percentage of growth in output per worker-hour that could be attributed to an increase in capital per worker $[\beta(r_K - r_L)/(r_Y - r_L)]$ (Table 12-1); and the residual, the increase in output per worker-hour that could *not* be accounted for by increases in capital per worker, $[r_T/(r_Y - r_L)]$, was usually attributed to technical progress.

We can derive these two terms by subtracting αr_L from both sides of Equation 12-9 to get

$$r_Y - \alpha r_L = r_T + \beta r_K \tag{12-11}$$

Since $-\alpha = \beta - 1$

$$r_Y + \beta r_L - r_L = r_T + \beta r_K \tag{12-12}$$

Subtracting βr_L from both sides results in

$$r_Y - r_L = r_T + \beta(r_K - r_L) \tag{12-13}$$

Dividing both sides by $r_Y - \alpha r_L$ gives us

$$\frac{\beta(r^K - r_L)}{r_Y - r_L} + \frac{r_T}{r_Y - r_L} = 1 \tag{12-14}$$

In words, increases in output per worker attributed to increases in capital per worker plus increases in output per worker that cannot be attributed to increases in output per worker are equal to one.

WHY CAPITAL'S CONTRIBUTION TO GROWTH IN LDCS EXCEEDS THAT IN DCS

The parameter β is $(\Delta Y/Y)/(\Delta K/K)$ or $(\Delta Y/\Delta K)(K/Y)$. Capital's contribution to growth is βr_K or $\beta(\Delta K/K)$ or product of three factors, $(\Delta Y/\Delta K)(K/Y)(\Delta K/K)$. Let us compare the values of each one of these factors in DCs and LDCs.

The average capital output ratio (K/Y) is the stock of capital divided by the annual flow of output. This ratio does not systematically differ between DCs and LDCs. To be sure, the less capital-intensive production and more immediate yields from capital (due to a shorter period of life for capital goods) are factors making the LDC capital output ratio less (that is, less capital essential to produce one unit of output). But these factors are offset by others making LDC capital output ratios greater than DC ratios—the lower rates of capital utilization and lower technological levels in LDCs.

However, the marginal productivity of capital $(\Delta Y/\Delta K)$ in less-developed countries exceeds that in developed countries because capital is combined with more labor in the former.

Furthermore developing countries, with low levels of initial capital, have had a high rate of growth of capital $(\Delta K/K)$, especially during the 1950s and 1960s, the period included in most of the quantitative studies.

Thus since $(\Delta Y/\Delta K)$ and $(\Delta K/K)$ are higher, and (K/Y) no lower in developing countries, capital's contribution to output growth, equal to $(\Delta Y/\Delta K)(K/Y)(\Delta K/K)$, is more in developing than developed countries. Roughly speaking since the rate of growth of output per person is about the same in LDCs and DCs (Chapter 4), and capital's contribution to growth is relatively greater in LDCs than in DCs, the residual, attributed to technical change, is smaller in LDCs than DCs.

Chapter Thirteen

ENTREPRENEURSHIP, ORGANIZATION, AND INNOVATION

Perhaps one day a saga may be written about the modern captain of industry. Perhaps, in the civilization which succeeds our own, a legend of the entrepreneur will be thumbed by antiquarians, and told as a winter tale by the firelight, as today our sages assemble fragments of priestly mythologies from the Nile, and as we tell to children of Jason's noble quest of the Golden Fleece. But what form such a legend may take it is not at all easy to foresee. Whether the businessman be the Jason or the Aetes in the story depends on other secrets which those unloved sisters keep hid where they store their scissors and their thread. We have, indeed, the crude unwrought materials for such a legend to hand in plenty, but they are suitable, strange to say, for legends of two sharply different kinds. The Golden Fleece is there, right enough, as the background of the story. But the captain of industry may be cast in either of two roles: as the noble, daring, high-souled adventurer, sailing in the teeth of storm and danger to wrest from barbarism a prize to enrich his countrymen; or else as a barbarous tyrant, guarding his treasure with cunning and laying snares to entrap Jason, who comes with the breath of a new civilization to challenge his power and possession.[1]

The entrepreneur, with a dream and will to found a private kingdom, to conquer adversity, to achieve success for its own sake, and to experience the joy of creation, is a heroic figure in economic development, according to Joseph A. Schumpeter—

[1] Maurice Dobb, *Capitalist Enterprise and Social Progress* (London: George Routledge and Sons, 1926), p. 3.

sometime finance minister in an Austrian Socialist government and professor of economics in Bonn, Tokyo, and at Harvard.[2] In a similar vein. Harvard psychologist David C. McClelland perceives the efforts of the entrepreneur, in controlling production in both capitalist and socialist economies, as largely responsible for rapid economic growth. For McClelland, the entrepreneur, driven by an inner urge to improve, is motivated by profits as a measure of achievement rather than as a source of enrichment.[3]

Economic historians emphasize that such Schumpeterian captains of industry as John D. Rockefeller (oil), Andrew Carnegie (steel), Cornelius Vanderbilt (railroads), James B. Duke (tobacco and power), and Jay Gould and J. P. Morgan (finance) led the 50-year economic expansion before World War I that made the United States the world's leading industrial nation. Rockefeller combined managerial genius, capacity for detail, decisiveness, frugality, and foresight with a ruthless supression of competition, the use of espionage and violence to gain competitive advantages, and a general neglect of the public interest to become the symbol of the virtues and vices of these "robber barons."[4]

But surely an economy does not require Rockefellers, Vanderbilts, and Goulds for rapid development. The functions of entrepreneurship, organization, and innovation are not limited to the large private sector but can be exercised by the Argentine flour miller, the Malaysian cobbler, the Chinese planner and factory manager, or the Yugoslav workers' council or regional (republic) ministry. Except in an anarchist utopia, the need for entrepreneurship is free of ideology.

Despite exceptions, such as Jamshedjee Tata, responsible for India's first steel mill in 1911, the political, cultural, and technological milieu was not right for vigorous, industrial, entrepreneurial activity in present LDCs, especially prior to 1950.

SCOPE OF THE CHAPTER

The **entrepreneur** can be viewed in at least four ways: (1) as the coordinator of other production resources—land, labor, and capital; (2) as the decisionmaker under uncertainty; (3) as the innovator; and (4) as the gap filler and input completer. The last two concepts, which are the most relevant for economic development, are discussed in the first two sections of this chapter.

We next look at entrepreneurial functions in LDCs. After this we consider the family as an entrepreneurial unit. The multiple entrepreneurial function is then discussed. The next two sections examine McClelland's and Hagen's analyses of the effect of social and psychological factors on entrepreneurship. Subsequent sections consider the entrepreneur's socioeconomic profile—occupational background, religious and ethnic origin, social origin and mobility, education, and sex. The last section discusses technological mobilization and innovation in socialist economies.

[2] Joseph A. Schumpeter, *The Theory of Economic Development* (Cambridge, Mass.: Harvard University Press, 1961). (First German ed., 1911.)

[3] David C. McClelland, *The Achieving Society* (Princeton, N.J.: D. Van Nostrand, 1961).

[4] Gerald D. Nash, ed., *Issues in American Economic History: Selected Readings* (Boston: Heath, 1964), pp. 347–48.

ENTREPRENEUR AS INNOVATOR

The rapid economic growth of the Western world during the past century is largely a story of how novel and improved ways of satisfying wants were discovered and adopted. But this story is not just one of inventions or devising new methods or products. History is replete with inventions that were not needed or that, more frequently, failed to obtain a sponsor or market. For example, the Stanley Steamer, invented early in the twentieth century, probably failed not because it was inferior to the automobile with the internal combustion engine but because the inventors, the Stanley brothers, did not try to mass produce it. No, to explain economic growth, we must emphasize innovation rather than invention. Economists have paid little systematic attention to the process of **innovation**—the embodiment in commercial practice of some new idea or invention—and to the innovator.

Schumpeter's Theory

Schumpeter is the exceptional economist who links innovation to the entrepreneur, maintaining that the source of private profits is successful innovation and that innovation brings about economic growth.[5] He feels that the entrepreneur carries out new economic combinations by: (1) introducing new products, (2) introducing new production functions that decrease inputs needed to produce a given output, (3) opening new markets, (4) exploiting new sources of materials, and (5) reorganizing an industry.

The Schumpeterian model begins with a **stationary state,** an unchanging economic process that merely reproduces itself at constant rates without innovators or entrepreneurs. This model assumes perfect competition, full employment, and no savings nor technical change; and it clarifies the tremendous impact of entrepreneurs on the economic process. In the stationary state, no entrepreneurial function is required, since the ordinary, routine work, the repetition of orders and operations, can be done by workers themselves. However, into this stationary process, a profit-motivated entrepreneur begins to innovate, say, by introducing a new production function that raises the marginal productivity of various production resources. Eventually such innovation means the construction of new plants and the creation of new firms, which imply new leadership.

The stationary economy may have high earnings for management, monopoly gains, windfalls, or speculative gains, but has no entrepreneurial profits. Profits are the premium for innovation, and they arise from no other source. Innovation however sets up only a temporary monopoly gain, which is soon wiped out by imitation. For profits to continue, it is necessary to keep a step ahead of one's rivals—the innovations must continue. Profits result from the activity of the entrepreneur, even though he or she may not always receive them.

New bank credit finances the innovation, which, once successfully set up, is more easily imitated by competitors. Innovations are not isolated events evenly distributed in time, place, and sector; they arise in clusters, as a result of lowered risk. Eventually the waves of entrepreneurial activity not only force out old firms

---

[5] Joseph A. Schumpeter, *The Theory of Economic Development* (Cambridge, Mass.: Harvard University Press, 1961); and Joseph A. Schumpeter, *Business Cycles,* 2 vols. (New York: McGraw-Hill, 1939).

but exhaust the limited possibilities of gain from the innovation. As borrowing diminishes and loans are repaid, the entrepreneurial activity slackens and finally ceases. Innovation, saving, credit creation, and imitation explain economic growth, while their ebb and flow determine the business cycle.

The Schumpeterian Entrepreneur in Developing Countries

According to Schumpeter, his theory is valid only in capitalist economies prior to the rise of giant corporations. Thus it may be even less appropriate for mixed and capitalist LDCs, since many industries in these countries, especially in manufacturing, are dominated by a few large firms. It seems unrealistic to preclude the possibility that innovation may mean expansion of already-existing firms. In fact, in the real world, characterized by imperfect competition, an established organization would frequently have an advantage in developing new techniques, markets, products, and organizations.

Furthermore Schumpeter's concept of the entrepreneur is somewhat limited in developing countries. The majority of LDC Schumpeterian entrepreneurs are traders whose innovations are opening new markets. In light of technical transfers from advanced economies, the development of entirely new combinations should not unduly limit what is and is not considered entrepreneurial activity.

People with technical, executive, and organizational skills may be too scarce in less-developed countries to use in developing new combinations in the Schumpeterian sense. And in any case, fewer high-level people are needed to adapt combinations from economically advanced countries.

Stages in Innovation

Technical advance involves (1) the development of pure science, (2) invention, (3) innovation, (4) financing the innovation, and (5) the innovation's acceptance. Science and technical innovation interact; basic scientific advances not only create opportunities for innovation, but economic incentives and technical progress can affect the agenda for, and identify the payoffs from, scientific research. Links from production to technology and science are often absent in LDCs. Yet low-income countries can frequently skip stages 1 and 2 and sometimes even stage 3, so that scarce, high-level personnel can be devoted to adapting those discoveries already made.[6]

ENTREPRENEUR AS GAP-FILLER

The innovator differs from the manager of a firm, who runs the business along established lines. Entrepreneurs are the engineers of change, not its products. They are difficult to identify in practice, since no one acts exclusively as an entrepreneur. Though they frequently will be found among heads or founders of firms, or among the major owners or stockholders, they need not necessarily hold executive office in the firm, furnish capital, or bear risks.

[6] W. Robert Maclaurin, "The Sequence from Invention to Innovation and Its Relation to Economic Growth," *Quarterly Journal of Economics* 67 (February 1953): 97–111; and Martin Fransman, *Technology and Economic Development* (Boulder, Colo.: Westview, 1986), pp. 47–48.

Entrepreneurship indicates activities essential to creating or carrying on an enterprise where not all markets are well established or clearly defined, or where the production function is not fully specified nor completely known. An entrepreneur (an individual or groups of individuals) has the rare capability of making up for market deficiencies or filling gaps. There is no one-to-one correspondence between sets of inputs and outputs. Many firms operate with a considerable degree of slack.[7] Thus the entrepreneur, especially in LDCs, may need to seek and evaluate economic opportunities; marshall financial resources; manage the firm; and acquire new economic information and translate it into new markets, techniques, and products, since it may not be possible to hire someone to do these tasks. To illustrate, if an upper skiving machine is essential for making men's fine leather shoes; if no one in the country produces this machine; and if imports are barred, then only entrepreneurs who know how to construct the machine can enter the fine leather footwear industry.

The entrepreneur must also be an "input completer." For any given economic activity, a minimum quantity of inputs must be marshaled. If less than the minimum is available, the entrepreneur steps in to make up for the lack of marketable inputs by developing more productive techniques; accumulating new knowledge; creating or adopting new goods, new markets, new materials, and new organizational forms; and creating new skills—all important elements in economic growth. As indicated in Chapter 12, growth cannot be explained merely by increases in standard inputs, such as labor and capital. Entrepreneurial gap filling and input completing help explain why labor and capital do not account for all outputs. No fixed relationship between inputs and outputs exists, partly because entrepreneurial contributions cannot be readily quantified, predicted, planned for, or controlled.

FUNCTIONS OF THE ENTREPRENEUR

As we hinted earlier, we feel Schumpeter's concept of the entrepreneur should be broadened to include those who adapt and modify already existing innovations.[8] Most business activity in a nonstationary state requires some innovation. Each firm is uniquely located and organized, and its economic setting changes over time. Absolute imitation is therefore impossible, and techniques developed outside the firm must be adapted to its circumstances. This necessity is especially apparent when a LDC firm borrows technology from an advanced economy with different, relative factor prices—for example, a higher labor price relative to capital. These adaptations require, if you will, innovation if defined in a less restrictive sense than Schumpeter used it.

In a changing economy, it is difficult to distinguish between the adaptations of day-to-day management and the entrepreneur's creative decisions. Thus the following list of thirteen entrepreneurial roles includes some management functions.

[7] Harvey Leibenstein, "Allocative Efficiency versus 'X-Efficiency'," *American Economic Review* 56 (June 1966): 392–415; and Harvey Leibenstein, "Entrepreneurship and Development," *American Economic Review* 58 (May 1968): 72–83.

[8] Although Schumpeter did not consider the imitator to be an entrepreneur, he did contrast the imitating entrepreneur with the innovating entrepreneur. Entrepreneurs who adapt innovations already in existence could be said to be involved in both imitation and innovation.

Exchange relationships
1. Seeing market opportunities (novel or imitative)
2. Gaining command over resources
3. Marketing the product and responding to competition
4. Purchasing inputs

Political administration
5. Dealing with the public bureaucracy (concessions, licenses, taxes, and so forth)
6. Managing human relations in the firm
7. Managing customer and supplier relations

Management control
8. Managing finances
9. Managing production (control by written records, supervision, coordinating input flows with customer orders, maintaining equipment)

Technological
10. Acquiring and overseeing plant assembly
11. Minimizing inputs with a given production process—industrial engineering
12. Upgrading processes and product quality
13. Introducing new production techniques and products

The economist who analyzes Western economies frequently limits the entrepreneurial function to activities 1 and 2: It is assumed that the remaining skills can be purchased in the marketplace. But the extent to which the entrepreneur can delegate these activities to competent subordinates depends on many variables: the scale of production; how well developed the market is for such highly skilled labor; the social factors governing how responsible hired personnel will be; and the entrepreneur's efficiency in using high-level managerial employees. Since many of the markets for skilled people in developing countries are not well developed, entrepreneurs frequently have to perform these tasks themselves. Studies of entrepreneurs in LDCs indicate that production, financial, and technological management are least satisfactory.[9]

FAMILY AS ENTREPRENEUR

The family enterprise, which is widespread in less-industrialized countries, is usually small and managed primarily by the father or eldest son. As the dominant form of economic organization in nineteenth-century France, the family firm was conceived of as a fief to maintain and enhance the position of the family, and not as a mechanism for wealth and power.[10] However, some of the leading industrial conglomerates in developing countries are family owned. For example, India's largest

[9] Peter Kilby, ed., *Entrepreneurship and Economic Development* (New York: Free Press, 1971), pp. 1–40.

[10] David S. Landes, "French Entrepreneurship and Industrial Growth in the Nineteenth Century," *Journal of Economic History* 9 (May 1949): 45–61.

private manufacturers are usually members of old trading families, who control several companies. Frequently family members specialize their roles according to industry, location, or management function.

Family entrepreneurship can mobilize large amounts of resources, make quick, unified decisions, put trustworthy people into management positions, and constrain irresponsibility. Thus among the Ibo people in Nigeria, families guarantee that debts are paid, and their solidarity provides strong sanctions against default, since individual failure reflects on family reputation. The extended family frequently funds apprentice training and initial capitalization, even though it may hinder the firm's expansion by diverting resources to current consumption.[11]

Family entrepreneurship may be conservative about taking risks, innovating, and delegating authority. Paternalistic attitudes in employer-employee relationships prevail, and family-owned firms are often reluctant to hire professional managers. This reluctance however may reflect the critical shortage of professionals and managers in LDCs—especially those who can occupy positions of authority without ownership—rather than the idiosyncracies of the family. In addition most family firms are too small to afford outside managers. And we must add that paternalism and authoritarianism are feudal legacies characteristic of many enterprises in developing countries, and not unique to family businesses.

MULTIPLE ENTREPRENEURIAL FUNCTION

Frequently today with the increased complexity of business firms, the entrepreneurial function may be divided among a business hierarchy. Such a hierarchical functioning might be more appropriately labeled **organization** rather than entrepreneurship. Organization connotes not only the constellation of functions, persons, and abilities used to manage the enterprise, but also how these elements are integrated into a common undertaking.[12] Organization may be either profit or social service oriented, giving the concept applicability in capitalistic economies and centrally planned ones.

ACHIEVEMENT MOTIVATION AND ENTREPRENEURSHIP

Psychological evidence indicates that in early childhood, a person unconsciously learns behavior that is safest and most rewarding and that such learning substantially influences adult behavior. For example, the individual who is encouraged to be curious, creative, and independent as a child is more likely to engage in innovative and entrepreneurial activity as an adult. Although a society may consciously attempt to nurture imagination, self-reliance, and achievement orientation in child rearing and schooling, scholars used to consider this process slow and uncertain at best and requiring at least a generation before it would affect entrepreneurship and economic growth.

[11] E. Wayne Nafziger, "The Effect of the Nigerian Extended Family on Entrepreneurial Activity," *Economic Development and Cultural Change* 18 (October 1969): 25–33.

[12] Frederick Harbison, "Entrepreneurial Organization as a Factor in Economic Development," *Quarterly Journal of Economics* 64 (August 1956): 364–79.

McClelland contends that a society with a generally high **need for achievement** or urge to improve produces more energetic entrepreneurs, who, in turn, bring about more rapid economic development. He argues that entrepreneurs can be trained to succeed. Scholars are quite skeptical of the validity of McClelland's findings. Nevertheless achievement motivation training (along with practical training in management, marketing, and finance and assistance in project conception and planning) is more and more a part of programs at entrepreneurship development centers.[13]

THEORY OF TECHNOLOGICAL CREATIVITY

Hagen's Theory

On the Theory of Social Change (1962), by economist Everett E Hagen, uses psychology, sociology, and anthropology to explain how a traditional agricultural society (with a hierarchical and authoritarian social structure where status is inherited) becomes one where continuing technical progress occurs. Since the industrial and cultural complex of low-income societies is unique, they cannot merely imitate Western techniques. Thus economic growth requires widespread adaptation, creativity, and problem solving, in addition to positive attitudes toward manual labor.

Hagen suggests that childhood environment and training in traditional societies produce an authoritarian personality with a low need for achievement, a high need for dependence and submission, and a fatalistic view of the world. If parents perceive children as fragile organisms without the capacity for understanding or managing the world, the offspring are treated oversolicitously and prevented from taking the initiative. The child, repressing anger, avoids anxiety by obeying the commands of powerful people.

Events that cause peasants, workers, and lower elites to feel they are no longer respected and valued may catalyze economic development. For Hagen this process occurs over many generations. Increasingly adults become angry and anxious; and sons retreat and reject their parents' unsatisfying values. After several generations, women, reacting to their husbands' ineffectiveness, respond with delight to their sons' achievements. Such maternal attitudes combined with paternal weakness provide an almost ideal environment for the formation of an anxious, driving type of creativity. If sons are blocked from other careers, they will become entrepreneurs and spearhead the drive for economic growth.[14]

A Critique

One problem with Hagen's theory is that loss of status respect is an event so broadly defined that it may occur once or twice a decade in most societies. Nor does the theory explain groups, such as seventeenth-century English Catholics, who lost

---

[13] David C. McClelland, *The Achieving Society* (Princeton, N.J.: D. Van Nostrand, 1961); and David C. McClelland and David G. Winter, *Motivating Economic Achievement* (New York: Free Press, 1971). See E. Wayne Nafziger, *Entrepreneurship, Equity, and Economic Development* (Greenwich, Conn.: JAI Press, 1986), pp. 61–70, for an elaboration of criticisms of the McClelland approach.

[14] Everett E. Hagen, *On the Theory of Social Change: How Economic Growth Begins* (Homewood, Ill.: Dorsey Press, 1962).

status but did not become entrepreneurs. Furthermore the interval between status loss and the emergence of creativity varies from 30 to 700 years, so that Hagen's hypothesis fits almost any case.

Although Hagen charges economists with ethnocentrism, he applies a Western-based personality theory to vastly different societies and historical periods. In addition his case studies provide no evidence of changes in parent-child relationships and child-training methods during the early historical periods of status loss. Moreover one economic historian convincingly argues that the position, training, and discipline of the child in modern Germany, Austria, and Sweden resemble those described in Hagen's traditional society.[15] Finally Hagen slights the effect on entrepreneurial activity of changes in economic opportunities, such as improved transport, wider-reaching markets, the availability of foreign capital and technology, and social structure. But despite its inadequacies, Hagen's work has made economists more aware of the importance of noneconomic variables in economic growth.

OCCUPATIONAL BACKGROUND

Many studies of industrial entrepreneurs in developing countries indicate trade was their former occupation.[16] A trading background gives the entrepreneur a familiarity with the market, some general management and commercial experience, sales outlets and contacts, and some capital. A number of traders enter manufacturing to ensure regular supplies or because they can increase profits. Frequently a major catalyst for this shift is government policy following independence from colonial control. At that time, governments often encourage import substitution in manufacturing through higher tariffs, tighter import quotas, and an industrial policy that encourages the use of domestic inputs. Even with government encouragement, traders going into manufacturing often have trouble setting up a production line and coordinating a large labor force.

Writers on entrepreneurship occasionally mention a "trader mentality" that leads to an irrational preference for the quick turnover rather than the long-run returns that manufacturing offers. Frequently however, the trader may lack industrial management and technical skills. In addition the business milieu, social overhead services, and government policies may not encourage industry. It is not irrational for entrepreneurs to prefer trade to manufacturing if they believe incomes

[15] Alexander Gerschenkron, Review of Hagen, *On the Theory of Social Change, Economica* 32 (February 1965): 90–94.

[16] The following studies were consulted: Yusif A. Sayigh, *Entrepreneurs of Lebanon: The Role of the Business Leader in a Developing Economy* (Cambridge, Mass.: Harvard University Press, 1962); Alec P. Alexander, "Industrial Entrepreneurship in Turkey: Origins and Growth," *Economic Development and Cultural Change* 8 (July 1960): 349–65; Alec P. Alexander, *Greek Industrialists: An Economic and Social Analysis* (Athens: Center of Planning and Economic Research, 1964); Peter Kilby, *African Enterprise: The Nigerian Bread Industry* (Stanford: Hoover Institution, 1965); John R. Harris, "Industrial Entrepreneurship in Nigeria" (Ph.D. diss., Northwestern University, 1967); James J. Berna, *Industrial Entrepreneurship in Madras State* (New York: Asia Publishing House, 1960); E. Wayne Nafziger, *Class, Caste, and Entrepreneurship: A Study of Indian Industrialists* (Honolulu: University Press of Hawaii, 1978); Gustav F. Papanek, "The Development of Entrepreneurship," *American Economic Review* 52 (May 1962): 46–58; and John J. Carroll, *The Filipino Manufacturing Entrepreneur, Agent and Product of Change* (Ithaca: Cornell University Press, 1965).

are higher in trade. For some traders, an industrial venture may await government programs in technical and management training, industrial extension, and financial assistance.

In most developing countries, numerous young people are apprenticed to learn such skills as baking, shoemaking, tinsmithing, blacksmithing, tanning, and dress-making from a parent, relative, or other artisan. Even though some have argued that artisans trained in this way have less drive and vision and direct relatively small firms, some of them have, nonetheless, become major manufacturers. This transformation is especially pronounced in early phases of industrialization, such as in England's Industrial Revolution and today's less-developed countries. The scale of the enterprise may gradually expand over several years or even generations. Even so, relatively few artisans can make the leap from the small firm owner to manufacturer. However, artisans and their students benefit from industrial innovation as well as from training and extension programs. Apprentice systems inevitably improve with the introduction of new techniques. Economists should not overlook these artisans, since they contribute to industrial growth.

In general most successful industrial entrepreneurs have borne or shared chief responsibility for the management of at least one enterprise prior to their present activity, whether this work was in another manufacturing unit or in handicrafts, trade, transport, or contracting. Few industrialists, however, were once farmers. Except for landowners, very few farmers have had the funds to invest in industry. And even landlords are poorly represented. They tend to place a high value on consumption and real estate expenditure and lack experience in managing and coordinating a production process with specialized work tasks and machinery and in overseeing secondary labor relations.

Few people in developing countries move from government employment to entrepreneurship. In studies in Lebanon, Turkey, Greece, Pakistan, and India, less than 10 percent of the entrepreneurs were once in the civil service. Frequently potentially capable entrepreneurs in government service have relatively high salaries, good working conditions, attractive fringe benefits, and tenure. Leaving such a job to enter entrepreneurial activity involves substantial risk.

Empirical studies indicate that an even smaller fraction of industrial entrepreneurs were previously blue-collar workers. Blue-collar workers are most likely to become entrepreneurs because of "push" factors, such as the lack of attractive job options or the threat of persistent unemployment, rather than "pull" factors, such as the prospect of rapidly expanding markets.

RELIGIOUS AND ETHNIC ORIGIN

Weber's Thesis: The Protestant Ethic

Capitalism is an economic system where private owners of capital and their agents, making decisions based on private profit, hire legally free, but capital–less, workers. Max Weber's *The Protestant Ethic and the Spirit of Capitalism* (1904–05) tried to explain why the continuous and rational development of the capitalist system originated in Western Europe in about the sixteenth century.[17] Weber noted that

---

[17] Max Weber, *The Protestant Ethic and the Spirit of Capitalism,* translated by Talcott Parsons in 1930 (New York: Charles Scribner's Sons, 1958).

European businessmen and skilled laborers were overwhelmingly Protestant and that capitalism was most advanced in Protestant countries, such as England and Holland. He held to the view, discussed in Chapter 4, that Protestant asceticism was expressed in a secular vocation. Although Puritans (or ascetic Protestants) opposed materialism as much as the Roman Catholic Church, they did not disapprove of accumulating wealth. They did however restrict extravagance and conspicuous consumption and frowned on laziness. These attitudes resulted in a high savings rate and continued hard work—both factors favorable to economic progress.

Calvinists (Reformed churches and Presbyterians), Pietists, Methodists, Baptists, Quakers, and Mennonites made up the major ascetic Protestant denominations. Sixteenth-century French reformer John Calvin taught that those elected by God were to be diligent, thrifty, honest, and prudent, virtues coinciding with the spirit essential for capitalist development.

Critique of Weber

The Protestant Reformation and the rise of capitalism, though correlated, need not indicate causation. A third factor—the disruption of the Catholic social system and loss of civil power—may have been partly responsible for both. Alternatively the Protestant ethic may have changed to accommodate the needs of the rising capitalist class. Another explanation is that the secularization, ethical relativism, and social realism of Protestantism may have been as important as its "this-worldly" asceticism in explaining its contribution to economic development.

Marginal Individuals as Entrepreneurs

Despite criticisms Weber's work has stimulated scholars to ask important questions about how entrepreneurial activity is affected by religious, ethnic, and linguistic communities. One question concerns marginal ethnic and social groups, that is, those whose values differ greatly from the majority of the population. To what extent do **marginal individuals,** because of their ambiguous position, tend to be innovative?

In a confirmation of Weber's study, Hagen finds that Nonconformists (Quakers, Methodists, Congregationalists, Baptists, Anabaptists, and Unitarians), with only 7 percent of the population, contributed 41 percent of the leading entrepreneurs during the English Industrial Revolution (1760–1830). Other marginal communities disproportionally represented in entrepreneurial activity include Jews in medieval Europe, Huguenots in seventeenth- and eighteenth-century France, Old Believers in nineteenth-century Russia, Indians in East Africa before the 1970s, Chinese in Southeast Asia, Lebanese in West Africa, Marwaris in Calcutta, and Gujaratis in Bombay. Refugees from the 1947 partition between India and Pakistan, and the exchange of minorities between Turkey and Greece in the 1920s, were overrepresented among industrialists in these four countries. Displaced Armenians, Jews, Europeans, Palestinians, and Arab expatriates, escaping persecution, political hostility, and economic depression, were responsible for the rise in entrepreneurial activity in the Middle East between 1930 and 1955. For migrants the challenge of a new environment may have a beneficial educational and psychological effect, and the geographical dispersion of friends and relatives may allow the rejection of local values, obligations, and sanctions that impede rational business practice.

In the contemporary world, most dominant communities value economic achievement. Thus leading business communities include the Protestants of Northern and Western European origin living in the United States, and Hindu high castes in India. In Lebanon in 1959, the politically dominant Maronites and other Christians comprised 80 percent of the innovative entrepreneurs, although only 50 percent of the population. The Yorubas and Ibos, the largest ethnic communities in the more industrialized region of southern Nigeria, are the leading entrepreneurs.

Unlike the preceding groups, aliens have usually not been innovative in industry requiring large fixed investment, which can easily be confiscated. Furthermore the technical change they introduce is usually not imitated by other groups. The English Nonconformists, Huguenots, Old Believers, Marwaris, Gujaratis, and the south Asian and Mediterranean refugees mentioned previously are not considered alien groups, since their roots have been in their country's culture. Even though there are instances where aliens have made important contributions to technical change, there is no evidence they are generally more innovative than natives.

Are marginal individuals especially innovative? Since no one has conducted a systematic worldwide test, we simply cannot say.

SOCIAL ORIGINS AND MOBILITY

The United States

The dominant American folk hero has been the person who goes from rags to riches through business operations. One of the most celebrated was the steel magnate Andrew Carnegie (1835–1919), an uneducated immigrant, the son of a workingman, forced to seek employment at a young age. Through cleverness and hard work, he rose from bobbin boy to messenger to assistant railroad superintendent to industrial leader. For him, "The millionaires who are in active control started as poor boys and were trained in the sternest but most efficient of all schools—poverty."[18] Even so, his story is atypical. The Horatio Alger stories of the nineteenth century are largely legend. The typical successful industrial leader in the late nineteenth and early twentieth centuries was usually American by birth, English in national origin, urban in early environment, educated through high school, and born and bred in an atmosphere in which business and a relatively high social status were intimately associated with his family life.[19]

Other Nonsocialist Countries

It should not be surprising that industrialists outside the United States have a similar sociological profile. Innovators during the English Industrial Revolution were primarily sons of men in comfortable circumstances.[20] Industrial entrepreneurs from

[18] Andrew Carnegie, *The Empire of Business* (New York: Doubleday, Page, and Co., 1902), p. 109.

[19] William Miller, ed., *Men in Business: Essays on the Historical Role of the Entrepreneur* (New York: Harper & Row, 1962).

[20] Everett E. Hagen, *On the Theory of Social Change: How Economic Growth Begins* (Homewood, Ill.: Dorsey Press, 1962).

Greece, Nigeria, Pakistan, India, and the Philippines had an occupational and family status substantially higher than the population as a whole. Industrial corporate managers, mostly from families having the funds to pay for a university education, generally have an even higher socioeconomic status than entrepreneurs.

The Soviet Union and China

In the Soviet Union in 1936, the latest date for reliable information on parental occupational origins, sons of white-collar employees, professionals, or business-owners had six times the representation in industrial, executive positions that the sons of manual workers and farmers had. This situation existed despite the 1917 revolution, which had ostensibly overturned the existing class structure.[21] Even in China, capitalists, supporting the 1949 revolution who had not been allied to foreign interests, continued (except for the Cultural Revolution, 1966–76) to receive interest on their investments and to be paid fairly high salaries for managing joint public-private enterprises. Members and children of the prerevolutionary Chinese bourgeoisie still hold a large number of positions in industry, administration, and education, despite attacks on their privileges from 1966 through 1976.[22]

Advantages of Privileged Backgrounds

The entrepreneur or manager frequently profits from having some **monopoly advantage.** This advantage (except for inherited talent) is usually the result of greater opportunities, such as (1) access to more economic information than competitors, (2) superior access to training and education, (3) a lower discount of future earnings, (4) larger firm size, and (5) lucrative agreements to restrict entry or output. All five are facilitated by wealth or position.[23]

Accordingly in India, high castes, upper classes, and large business families use such monopoly advantages to become industrial entrepreneurs in disproportionate numbers. In one Indian city, 52 percent of these entrepreneurs (in contrast to only 11 percent of blue-collar workers) were from high Hindu castes, which comprise only 26 percent of the total population. None of the entrepreneurs, but a disproportionate share of blue-collar workers, was from low-caste backgrounds (that is, Harijans and Protestant or Roman Catholic Christians). This lopsided distribution of business activity—shown in Table 13-1, which reflects differences in economic opportunities between the privileged and less-privileged portions of the population—is typical of many other countries as well.

Entrepreneurial activity is frequently a means of moving one or two notches up the economic ladder. Research indicates that the socioeconomic status of entrepreneurs is higher than their parents' status, which is substantially higher than that of the general population.

[21] David Granick, *The Red Executive: A Study of the Organization Man in Russian Industry* (New York: Anchor Books, 1961).

[22] Jan Deleyne, *The Chinese Economy* (New York: Harper & Row, 1971); and Thomas P. Lyons, *Economic Integration and Planning in Maoist China* (New York: Columbia University Press, 1987).

[23] Maurice Dobb, *Capitalist Enterprise and Social Progress* (London: George Routledge and Sons, 1926).

TABLE 13-1 Caste and Religious Community of Entrepreneurs and Workers in an Indian City

Caste/Religion	Percentage of Entrepreneurs	Percentage of Blue-Collar Workers	Percentage of Total Population
High Hindu			
Brahmin (priest)	20.4	2.2	21.4
Kshatriya (ruler, warrior)	9.3	8.9	2.3
Vaishya (trader)	22.2	0.0	2.2
Middle Hindu			
Sudra (artisan, peasant)	27.8	57.8	56.9
Low Hindu			
Harijan (outcaste)	0.0	15.5	11.2
Non-Hindu			
Muslim	13.0	6.7	1.3
Christian (high caste)	1.8	0.0	0.1
Christian (low caste)	0.0	8.9	4.5
Sikh, Parsi, other	5.5	0.0	0.1
Total	100.0	100.0	100.0

Source: E. Wayne Nafziger, *Class, Caste, and Entrepreneurship: A Study of Indian Industrialists* (Honolulu: University Press of Hawaii, 1978), p. 65.

EDUCATION

Most studies indicate a higher level of education among entrepreneurs than for the population as a whole, and a direct relationship between education and the entrepreneur's success. People with more education probably make sounder business decisions; in addition their verbal skills are better and make acquiring new ideas and methods, corresponding and conversing in business relationships, and understanding instruction manuals and other routine, written information easier. Finally the educated entrepreneur probably has a sound mathematical background, facilitating computation and recordkeeping.

However, the education of the entrepreneur may be negatively related to success in crafts requiring a lengthy apprenticeship such as weaving, blacksmithing, goldsmithing, shoemaking, and leathermaking. Time and money spent on formal education may represent relinquished opportunities in training more closely related to entrepreneurial activities.[24]

Education may limit entrepreneurship by giving people other occupational choices. Thus in the early 1960s, when Nigerians were replacing the remaining Britons in the civil service, Nigeria's few university graduates turned to these jobs with their high salary, security, prestige, and other perquisites rather than to entrepreneurial activity with its relatively low earnings and high risk. On the other hand, in areas where university graduates are in excess supply, such as south India, some choose entrepreneurship to avoid unemployment or blue-collar jobs.

[24] E. Wayne Nafziger, *African Capitalism: A Case Study in Nigerian Entrepreneurship* (Stanford: Hoover Institution, 1977).

GENDER

In the United States, there are relatively few women in business—not merely because of sex discrimination (though that plays a part) but because of the whole female socialization pattern in America. Some feminists charge that girls are brought up to aspire to be secretaries, nurses, dancers, and kindergarten teachers rather than to start a business.

In many developing countries, the percentage of female businesspersons is lower than in the United States. Despite certain exceptions, such as the concentrations of female traders in some large open-air market places in West Africa, only a small proportion of large-scale entrepreneurs in LDCs are women.

Most LDCs have cultural norms dictating how males and females should behave at work. Frequently a woman's physical mobility and social contact are restricted in LDCs. The anthropologist Johanna Lessinger states that in India women are not allowed to deal directly with strange men, since it is assumed that all unmonitored contact between unrelated men and women must be sexual.[25] Furthermore according to Lessinger, Indian women are viewed as naturally weaker, more emotional, less socially adept, less rational, and inferior to men. These views have been used not only to limit competition between women and men in business, but also, in some instances, to justify a woman's restriction to the household.

Moreover the culture may view the characteristics of the successful entrepreneur—shrewdness, quick judgment, gregariousness, and force of personality—as inconsistent with those of a good and proper woman. Even where a woman is determined to be an entrepreneur, she is daily reminded that she is going against the norm: Sexual harassment is likely if she steps beyond the bounds of accepted behavior. Although a woman can get around these restrictions by surrounding herself with relatives, neighbors, and other women who can vouch for her good behavior, this strategy is cumbersome for the entrepreneur, who must be mobile. In addition to these social restrictions, the LDC businesswoman may be refused credit by bankers and suppliers. In general despite some slight variations, these attitudes toward female entrepreneurial activity are prevalent in developing countries.

TECHNOLOGICAL MOBILIZATION IN SOCIALIST ECONOMIES

Motivating innovative activity in centrally planned economies is usually difficult. In 1959, Soviet Premier Nikita Khrushchev complained about an unsatisfactory rate of technological change.

> In our country some bureaucrats are so used to the old nag that they do not want to change over to a good race horse, for he might tear away on the turn and even spill them out of the sleigh! Therefore, such people will hold on to the old nag's tail with both hands and teeth.[26]

[25] Johanna Lessinger, "Women Traders in Madras City," unpublished paper, Barnard College, 1980.

[26] Joseph S. Berliner, "Bureaucratic Conservatism and Creativity in the Soviet Economy," in Frederick W. Riggs, ed., *Frontiers of Development Administration* (Durham, N.C.: Duke University Press, 1971), pp. 585–86, citing *Pravda*, 2 July 1959.

Soviet managers resist innovation, since effort and resources diverted to it might threaten plan fulfillment. While kinks in the new technology are being ironed out, managers may lose part of their take-home pay, which is often tied to plan targets, or they may be demoted. When evaluating managers for bonuses and promotions, party officials give little weight to their innovative abilities. Also the tightly planned system has little latitude for servicing and spare parts for new equipment or for acquiring new resources and suppliers. Furthermore the prices of new products usually count for less in computing plan fulfillment than older, standard goods. Finally introducing new models requires extensive testing and negotiations with research institutes as well as approval from official agencies before production is authorized.[27] The bureaucratic maze hampers innovation. However, a goal of economic reorganization, **perestroika,** begun by Soviet leader Mikhail Gorbachev in 1985, is to spur innovation among Soviet managers.

From 1966 to 1970, the early years of the Cultural Revolution, China's leaders took control of industrial innovation and management from the professional managerial elite. Management changed from one person to a "three-in-one" revolutionary committee, consisting of government officials, technicians, and workers. Campaigns urged workers to invent or improve machines, tools, and processes—a policy that began after Soviet technicians took their blueprints and withdrew from unfinished factories in 1960.

According to the Chinese press in the late 1960s, numerous technical activists among the workers, previously unrecognized, introduced new techniques, persevered when criticized by bureaucrats and peers, and received support from the Communist party. Through its help, they acquired more sophisticated technical advice and frequently received further training and education leading to promotion.[28] Since the 1978 industrial reforms, professional managers and technicians reasserted their authority and quelled the innovation of technical activists.

China's **individual economy** has grown rapidly as the number of privately self-employed in cities and towns (primarily in services, commerce, handicrafts, and catering) grew from 150,000 in 1978 to roughly 5–10 million in 1988, increasing industrial output and soaking up underemployed labor. While privately owned and operated proprietorships could employ only five outside the family, vertically or horizontally integrated cooperatives and corporations had higher employment limits that varied by locality. In 1984, Wan Runnan persuaded six Academy of Sciences engineering colleagues to join him in borrowing $5400 and renting a small office to found the Beijing Stone Group Company, which grossed $85.5 million sales in electronic equipment, earned $6.7 million after taxes, employed eight hundred, and had fifteen subsidiaries (including Japan and Hong Kong) by 1987. The Stone Group controlled ownership and provided technical knowledge for joint ventures with Japan's Mitsui in producing an English–Chinese electronic typewriter, word processors, and printers suitable for China, and software. Chinese law and social sanctions limit annual after-tax income of company President Wan to $8500, yet as

---

[27] Joseph S. Berliner, "Bureaucratic Conservatism and Creativity in the Soviet Economy," in Frederich W. Riggs, ed., *Frontiers of Development Administration* (Durham, N.C.: Duke University Press, 1971), pp. 569–97.

[28] Richard P. Suttmeir, *Research and Revolution: Science Policy and Societal Change in China* (Lexington, Mass.: Heath, 1974).

an entrepreneur, he has independence, prestige, and an income twenty five times his academy salary.[29]

SUMMARY

1. The political and cultural milieu in LDCs was generally not conducive to large-scale industrial entrepreneurship prior to 1950 or so. Although LDC governments should encourage their entrepreneurs, it is not essential that they be captains of industry as glorified by Schumpeter.

2. To Schumpeter the entrepreneur is an innovator, one who carries out new combinations. These innovations are the source of private profit and economic growth. However, LDCs need not unduly emphasize developing new combinations, since some technology can be borrowed or adapted from abroad.

3. The entrepreneur differs from the manager of a firm, who runs the business on established lines. The entrepreneur can fill gaps, complete inputs, and make up for market deficiencies.

4. Since they assume that most skills needed for an enterprise can be purchased in the market, Western economists frequently limit the entrepreneurial function to perceiving market opportunities and gaining command over resources. However, LDC entrepreneurs may have to provide some basic skills themselves, such as marketing, purchasing, dealing with government, human relations, supplier relations, customer relations, financial management, production management, and technological management, which are all skills in short supply in the market.

5. Although the family enterprise has the advantage of quick, unified decision making, its disadvantages include a conservative approach to taking risks, reluctance to hire professional managers, and paternalism in labor relationships.

6. McClelland contends that a society with a generally high need for achievement produces energetic entrepreneurs who bring about rapid economic growth. Some training institutions have used achievement motivation training as a part of programs at centers to develop entrepreneurship.

7. Hagen argues that societies where children are raised democratically, so that they are encouraged to take initiative and be self-reliant, are more likely to produce entrepreneurs. However, critics are skeptical about Hagen's claim that this creativity is linked to a prior period of lost status.

8. Industrial entrepreneurs in LDCs come from a wide variety of occupational backgrounds, including trade, sales, and crafts. Few manufacturing entrepreneurs, however, come from farming, government employment, or factory work.

---

[29] Harry Harding, *China's Second Revolution: Reform after Mao* (Washington, D.C.: Brookings Institution, 1987), pp. 124–28; Thomas B. Gould, "China's Private Entrepreneurs," *China Business Review* (November–December 1985): 46–50; Shi Zulin, "Individual Economy in China," paper presented to the U.S. People to People Economics Delegation, Beijing, May 14, 1987; and Adi Ignatius, "Fast-growing Chinese Electronics Firm Emulates IBM," *Wall Street Journal* (June 3, 1988): 10.

9. According to Weber, the spirit of the modern capitalist entrepreneur in Western Europe in the sixteenth century was found disproportionally among Puritans, whose religious asceticism manifested itself in worldly activity. Despite criticism of Weber's thesis, his work has stimulated scholars to ask questions about how differences between religious and ethnic groups affect entrepreneurial activity. One such question, concerning the representation of marginal ethnic and social groups in entrepreneurial activity, has not been satisfactorily answered.

10. Generally entrepreneurs come from a much higher socioeconomic background than the general population. In addition they tend to be upwardly mobile.

11. Although education can increase the entrepreneurial supply by making available skills needed for business, it can decrease this supply by increasing a person's job options.

12. Cultural norms in LDCs defining how women should behave at work limit female entrepreneurial activity. (Such problems occur in developed countries as well.)

13. Organization and innovation are important for growth in socialist as well as capitalist economies. It has been difficult for socialist countries, particularly the Soviet Union, to motivate managers and technicians to innovate.

14. Under China's post-1978 industrial reform, self-employed individuals can innovate, start a new enterprise, combine capital and personnel, and eventually, albeit with certain limits, expand the firm. The last part of the twentieth century and the first part of the twenty-first century will indicate whether individual entrepreneurial activity will expand or whether the Communist party, state, and bureaucracy will resist this capitalist encroachment.

TERMS TO REVIEW

- **entrepreneur**
- **innovation**
- **stationary state**
- **multiple entrepreneurial function**
- **organization**
- **need for achievement**
- **marginal individuals**
- **monopoly advantage**
- **perestroika**
- **China's individual economy**

QUESTIONS TO DISCUSS

1. What is Schumpeter's theory of economic development? What is the role of the entrepreneur in this theory? How applicable is Schumpeter's concept of the entrepreneur to developing countries?

2. Which steps in the process of developing technical advances are essential for LDCs? Which steps in the process can they skip in full or in part?

3. What is meant by the entrepreneur as gap-filler? Why is this entrepreneurial concept more relevant to LDCs than DCs?

4. What are the functions of the entrepreneur in LDCs? How might these functions differ from those of the entrepreneur in DCs?

5. What are the advantages and disadvantages of family enterprises in LDCs?

6. What are some of the noneconomic factors affecting entrepreneurship in LDCs?

7. What are the socioeconomic factors that affect the supply of industrial entrepreneurs in mixed and capitalist LDCs?

8. Are marginal individuals more innovative than nonmarginal individuals as entrepreneurs?

9. Is the concept of entrepreneurship applicable to socialist economies?

10. Can socialist economies encourage innovation and enterprise without sacrificing their collective and egalitarian goals?

GUIDE TO READINGS

The UN's *Journal of Development Planning* no. 18 (1988), edited by Harvey Leibenstein and Dennis Ray, devotes a whole issue to entrepreneurship and economic development, including Dennis Ray's "The Role of Entrepreneurship in Economic Development," pp. 3–18; William J. Baumol, "Is Entrepreneurship Always Productive?" pp. 85–94; Lois Stevenson, "Women and Economic Development: A Focus on Entrepreneurship," pp. 113–26; E. Wayne Nafziger, "Society and the Entrepreneur," pp. 127–52; Linsu Kim, "Entrepreneurship and Innovation in a Rapidly Developing Country," pp. 183–94; Peter Kilby, "Breaking the Entrepreneurial Bottleneck in Late-Developing Countries: Is There a Useful Role for Government?" pp. 221–50; and several other articles. Harris's survey of empirical studies of entrepreneurship (note 16), primarily in LDCs, is the most comprehensive available. Kilby's discussion of various perspectives on entrepreneurship (note 9) is not so exhaustive as the Harris survey but emphasizes the correlation of the theoretical literature from a large number of disciplines with existing empirical literature. In addition Schumpeter, McClelland, and Hagen summarize their views on entrepreneurship in short articles in the Kilby volume. Nafziger (note 16) sketches the concept of the entrepreneur in the history of economic theory and in contemporary economic analysis.

Merle Goldman, "Vengeance in China," *New York Review of Books* 36 (November 9, 1989): 5–9; and Adi Ignatius, "Computer Whiz Leads China's Opposition," *Wall Street Journal* (August 22, 1989): p. A1, discuss the 1987–89 alliance of Wan Runnan (see pp. 297–98) with dissident Chinese students and intellectuals, his going into exile in June 1989 as a leader of the Chinese Democratic Front opposing the Chinese government, and the government suppressing private enterprise.

Chapter Fourteen

MOBILIZING DOMESTIC RESOURCES

In this chapter we discuss the requirements and sources of capital formation. The following national accounts equation shows the relationship between saving, investment, and the international balance on goods and services (that is, exports minus imports of goods and services). National income is equal to

$$C + I + (X-M) = C + S \tag{14-1}$$

where C = consumption, I = domestic capital formation (or investment), X = exports of goods and services, M = imports of goods and services, and S = saving. If we subtract C from both sides of the equation,

$$I + (X-M) = S$$

Subtracting X from and adding M to both sides results in

$$I = S + (M-X) \tag{14-2}$$

If M exceeds X, the country has a deficit in its balance on goods and services. It may finance the deficit by borrowing, attracting investment, or receiving grants from abroad (surplus items). Essentially

$$M - X = F \tag{14-3}$$

where F is a **capital import,** or inflow of capital from abroad. Substituting this variable in Equation 14-2 gives us

$$I = S + F \tag{14-4}$$

Equation 14-4 states that a country can increase its new capital formation (or **investment**) through its own domestic saving (see below and Chapter 15) and by inflows of capital from abroad (Chapter 16). (When a politically or economically unstable LDC exports capital through capital flight, as discussed in Chapter 17, there is an outflow of domestic savings, and F is negative in Equation 14-4.)

SCOPE OF THE CHAPTER

A major goal of this chapter is to compare output devoted to consumer goods versus capital goods (those that increase the system's capacity). Both kinds of items are urgently needed in LDCs. Increased consumption is important because large parts of the population live close to subsistence. Greater capital formation raises the productivity of consumer goods output in the future. The heart of the issue is the conflict between resources for present consumption and future consumption (present saving).

The first section of this chapter examines a widely used method for calculating capital requirements, the *ICOR* approach. The remainder of the chapter discusses how an economy can increase its rate of capital formation.

CAPITAL REQUIREMENTS

W. Arthur Lewis's model (see Chapter 10) focuses on increasing capital formation as a percentage of national income. He contends that

> The central problem in the theory of economic development is to understand the process by which a community which was previously saving and investing 4 or 5 percent of its national income or less, converts itself into an economy where voluntary saving is running at about 12 to 15 percent of national income or more. This is the central problem because the central fact of economic development is rapid capital accumulation (including knowledge and skills with capital).[1]

We can illustrate the need for raising the investment rate if we examine the following equation:

$$G = i/ICOR \qquad (14\text{-}5)$$

where G is the rate of economic growth, i investment as a percentage of income, and **ICOR, the incremental capital output ratio,** the inverse of the ratio of increase in productive capacity to investment. If Y is income, K capital stock, and I investment, then $G = (\Delta Y/Y)$, $i = (I/Y)$, and the *ICOR* is $(\Delta K/\Delta Y)$, the same as $(I/\Delta Y)$, since $\Delta K \equiv I$ by definition.[2] Thus Equation 14-5 is an identity

$$\frac{\Delta Y}{Y} \equiv \frac{I/Y}{I/\Delta Y} \qquad (14\text{-}6)$$

[1] W. Arthur Lewis, "Economic Development with Unlimited Supplies of Labor," *Manchester School* 22 (May 1954): 139–91.

[2] Since *actual* savings (income not spent for consumption) equals *actual* investment (output not used for consumption), you can substitute *s*, savings as a percentage of income, for *i*. This adjustment gives you the fundamental Harrod equation (14-9), discussed in the appendix to this chapter.

Assume that the *desired rate of growth in GNP per capita* is 4 percent per year. As a rough approximation, we can add this desired figure to *population growth per year* (say, 2 percent) to get *G*, the *targeted rate of growth in total income per year* (6 percent).

The *ICOR*, used to calculate the investment rate required to achieve the economic growth target, is a simple and crude empirical ratio between added capital stock and the resulting increase in output per year. For reasons indicated below, *ICORs*, range widely, from about 2 to 7. At best a 2-percentage-*point* increase in investment rate in a year may increase growth by 1-percentage *point*. Here an *i* (**investment rate**) of 12 percent, divided by *ICOR* 2 results in the targeted growth rate of 6 percent (Equation 14-5). At worst it may require a 7-percentage *point* increase in investment rate to increase growth by 1 percentage *point*. However, a growth target of 6 percent with a *ICOR* of 7 requires an investment rate of 42 percent—rarely if ever, attained. (See Table 14-1 for investment rates by country groups.)

A major condition for the takeoff in Walter Rostow's theory of economic growth is a sharp increase in investment as a percentage of national income, say, from 5 percent or less to over 10 percent (see Chapter 5). Both Lewis and Rostow emphasize that abrupt increases in growth rates during the West's industrial revolution (late eighteenth through late nineteenth centuries) resulted from increased investment rates. But there is little historical evidence of an abrupt increment in

TABLE 14-1   Saving and Investment Rates by Country Group, 1960 and 1986[a]

	Gross Domestic Saving/ Gross Domestic Product, 1960	Gross Investment/ Gross Domestic Product, 1960	Gross Domestic Saving/ Gross Domestic Product, 1986	Gross Investment/ Gross Domestic Product, 1986
Low-income countries	0.17	0.19	0.25	0.29
China and India	0.19	0.21	0.30	0.32
Other low-income	0.09	0.11	0.07	0.15
Middle-income countries	0.19	0.20	0.24	0.23
High-income oil exporters[b]	0.22	0.21	0.30	0.29
High-income capitalist and mixed countries	0.22	0.21	0.21	0.21
Centrally planned economies[c]	0.27	0.25	0.25	0.24

[a]Figures are weighted averages for the country groups.

[b]Figures for 1960 and 1985.

[c]Figures for 1960 and 1982.

Sources: World Bank, *World Development Report, 1988* (New York: Oxford University Press, 1988), pp. 230–31; World Bank, *World Development Report, 1987* (New York: Oxford University Press, 1987), pp. 210–11; and World Bank, *World Development Report, 1982* (New York: Oxford University Press, 1982), pp. 118–19.

either growth rate or investment rate (as we indicated in our discussion of Rostow's theory in Chapter 5).

Nevertheless we can see the importance of investment rates of over 10 percent if we look at it from the following perspective, similar to Rostow's. Assume that the *ICOR* for an economy in its early stages of economic development is 3.5. If population grows by 2 percent per year, it is essential to invest 7 percent of national income regularly if income per capita is to be sustained. In Equation 14-5, $(i/ICOR) = (.07/3.5) = 0.02$, an aggregate growth rate that keeps income per capita constant. A mere 1-percent growth rate in income per capita, or a 3-percent overall growth rate, requires investing 10.5 percent of national income. Thus under typical assumptions concerning *ICORs* and population growth, investment as a proportion of national income should exceed 10 percent.

Although the weighted average of the domestic savings rate in low-income countries (other than China and India) is only 7 percent, when you add the rate of foreign capital inflow to income, 8 percent (see Equation 14-4), you get an investment rate of 15 percent (Table 14-1). Of the 105 countries for which there are data in the *World Development Report, 1988,* only five—Ethiopia, Mozambique, Guinea, Bolivia, and Uruguay— had investment rates of less than 10 percent. Even in 1960, the year that Rostow first published the *Stages,* only 8 of 105 countries had an investment rate of less than 10 percent.

However, Rostow assumed that *net* investment rates of over 10 percent, *not* gross investment rates, were relevant in determining growth rates. **Depreciation** (or capital consumption) must be subtracted from **gross investment** to give **net investment**. Data on depreciation, and thus net investment, are poor.

The net investment rate for LDCs is about 60 percent of gross investment rate (see Table 14-2), which suggests that a gross investment rate of about 16 percent roughly corresponds to a net investment rate of 10 percent. Most LDCs have attained this result—45 percent (15 out of 33) of the low-income countries in *World Development Report, 1988* have a gross investment rate of at least 16 percent, and 81 percent (42 out of 52) of the middle-income countries. Yet in 1960, only half of the LDCs had a gross investment rate of 16 percent or above. Fourteen percent (4 out of 27) of today's low-income countries had an investment rate of at least 16 percent in 1960, while 68 percent (36 out of 53) of today's middle-income countries attained this rate. Thus rough calculations suggest that several low-income countries have net investment rates below Rostow's threshold of 10 percent, although there are not nearly so many of them in the late 1980s and early 1990s as there were in the 1950s and early 1960s.

The *ICOR,* although used to express simple relationships in Equation 14-5, has serious limitations. A low *ICOR* (that is, little investment per unit of increased output) may not necessarily indicate highly productive capital. First the *ICOR* excludes the costs of inputs other than capital. An *ICOR* may be low because complementary factors—entrepreneurship, management, labor, and technical knowledge—are high per unit of capital, not because the capital projects chosen have high yields. Second as with the private benefit-cost analysis discussed in Chapter 12, *ICOR* ignores externalities and interdependencies among different projects. Third *ICORs* may be misleading because of variations in capital utilization. Thus two otherwise similar manufacturing plants may have different *ICORs* because of differences in the number of shifts worked per day, the utilization of capacity in a given shift, and so forth. Fourth the *ICOR* neglects the timing of costs and benefits and ignores those beyond the period measured (usually only 1 year).

Consider the firm in Table 14-3 choosing between investing $10,000 in a pickup truck or ten bullocks and wagons. For an enterprise, the Y in the *ICOR's* denominator is *not* net output but its **net value added** (net output minus purchases from other enterprises). The conventional *ICOR,* computed for 1 year, is $(I/\Delta Y)$, or $(10,000/4,000) = 2.50$ for the truck, and $(10,000/3,000) = 3.33$ for the bullocks with wagons. However, because of frequent monsoons, rough roads, and the high cost of spare parts, the truck's investment life is only 5 years and the bullocks' and wagons', 15 years. The longer life of the bullock project makes the discounted value of its net value added greater, $17,542.11, compared to $13,408.64 for the truck.

The *ICORs* can be computed for longer than 1 year but are still misleading because timing of inputs and outputs is ignored. Let us assume the investment life of the pickup truck is 10 years instead of 5 years, so that its net value added is $40,000. If computed over a 15-year period, the *ICOR* for the bullock project is lower, $10,000/45,000$ (or 0.22), compared to $10,000/40,000$ (or 0.25) for the truck. Yet because its returns are earlier, the truck's present net value added (discounted at a rate of 15 percent per year), $20,075.08, is greater than the bullocks' and wagons' $17,542.11.

Of course costs and benefits could be discounted to the present so that the *ICOR* were the reciprocal of the private marginal product criterion. Further we could adjust for externalities, distribution, indivisibilities, monopoly, saving and reinvestment, and factor price distortion so that the *ICOR* became the reciprocal of the social benefit-cost approach (see Chapter 12). However, this adjusted *ICOR* would add nothing to existing investment criteria.

The *ICOR* for a particular type of industrial project, or even at an aggregate level, is often unstable, varying with changes in technical levels, complementary factors, capital utilization, discount rates, and investment life. Even when used in equations, such as 14-5, to estimate capital requirements, the *ICOR* is a rough tool rather than a precise instrument for investment planning. The *ICOR* approach is simple, but using it is more likely to distort than clarify relationships in the development process.

How then does a country determine its desired investment rate? For some countries, the investment rate goal is set a bit higher than a past rate or close to the rate attained by another country in a comparable situation. One resolution of the issue is to devote as many resources as possible to capacity-increasing projects.

HOW TO INCREASE THE RATE OF CAPITAL FORMATION

How can a LDC government increase net capital formation as a percentage of national income? This section discusses several ways of achieving this goal. Although the first measure assumes no government role in capital formation decisions, remaining measures do involve some government action.

Free Market Inducement: The Classical Mechanism

The nineteenth-century English classical economists assumed a purely competitive economy. They believed that government interference in privately made saving and investment decisions would hurt economic efficiency and that indeed the capital formation rate corresponding to these decisions meant full employment and optimal economic growth.

TABLE 14-2 Rates and Sources of Capital Formation, ca. 1985

Country	(1) Gross Investment as a Percentage of Domestic Product	Proportion of Gross Capital Formation Financed by					
		(2) Foreign Saving	(3) Depreciation	(4) Domestic Net Saving (5 + 6 + 7)	(5) Corporate Saving	(6) Government Saving	(7) Household Saving
Developed countries							
Australia	0.24	0.06	0.43	0.51	0.23	0.13	0.15
Austria	0.24		0.46	0.54	0.42	0.12	
Canada	0.20	0.01	0.38	0.61	0.23	0.08	0.30
Finland	0.24	0.01	0.50	0.49	0.28	0.04	0.17
France	0.19	0.01	0.50	0.49	0.32	0.05	0.12
Germany, Fed. Rep. of	0.20	−0.02	0.51	0.51	0.47	0.03	0.01
Italy	0.19	0.01	0.09	0.90	0.83	0.07	
Japan	0.28	−0.04	0.45	0.59	0.28	0.05	0.26
Netherlands	0.20	0.01	0.50	0.49	0.46	0.03	
Norway	0.22	0.02	0.37	0.61	0.24	0.09	0.28
Sweden	0.19	0.06	0.61	0.33	0.45	−0.10	−0.01

Developing Countries

Botswana	0.25	0.06	0.48	0.46	0.33	0.13	0.47
Cameroon	0.26		0.50		0.02	0.01	0.03
Congo	0.30	−0.06	0.34	0.72	0.30	0.39	
Greece	0.21	0.08	0.62	0.30	0.93	−0.63	0.15
Honduras	0.18	0.07	0.47	0.46	0.17	0.14	0.08
India	0.25	0.02	0.50	0.48	0.24	0.16	0.07
Korea, Rep. of	0.30	0.01	0.50	0.49	0.41	0.01	
Nicaragua	0.12		0.50	0.50	0.50		
Paraguay	0.20	0.03	0.62	0.35	0.11	0.01	0.23
Philippines	0.16	−0.06	0.67	0.39	−0.03	0.20	0.22
South Africa	0.20	−0.24	0.80	0.44	0.37	−0.05	0.12
Spain	0.19	−0.07	0.63	0.44	0.23	−0.07	0.28
Thailand	0.23	0.19	0.41	0.40	0.06	−0.03	0.37

Source: United Nations, *National Accounts Statistics: Main Aggregates and Detailed Tables, 1985* (New York, 1987).

TABLE 14-3   Comparison of the ICORs and the Present Discounted Values of Two Projects

	One Pickup Truck	Ten Bullocks and Ten Wagons
Initial investment	$10,000	$10,000
Annual net value added	$ 4,000	$ 3,000
Investment life	5 years	15 years
Total net value added over one investment life	$4,000 × 5 = $20,000	$3,000 × 15 = $45,000
Net value added discounted to the present (15 percent discount rate)	$13,408.64	$17,542.11

Household Saving.   These economists analyzed saving by households, a major source of net capital formation then and now (see Table 14-2). They argued that the interest rate equalizes household saving supply and business investment demand. A higher interest rate rewards thrift, resulting in an upward, supply-of-savings curve. A lower interest rate decreases the cost of business borrowing, so that investment demand is downward sloping. The intersection of demand and supply determines the interest rate and the amount of saving households make available to businesses.

Retained Earnings.   Classical economists also recognized a business's retained earnings as a major source of capital formation. Business saving, which consists of corporate saving as well as saving from unincorporated business (a small fraction of household saving), is the leading source of net capital formation (see Table 14-2).

Remember Lewis's model in which labor migrates when urban wages exceed rural wages (Chapter 10). He assumes that the capitalist saves all surplus (profits, interest, and rent), and the worker saves nothing. The model is based on the classical tradition, positing no technical change, a prevailing wage at subsistence, zero saving by wage earners, and economic development based on increasing capital per worker (Chapter 5). But the problem with Lewis's model is that wages are likely to increase well before surplus agricultural labor is hired by the capitalist sector (Chapter 10). When wages rise, there is a profit squeeze, and saving and growth in the capitalist sector are reduced.

Contemporary Attitudes toward the Classical Approach.   Few contemporary economists favor the classical approach, especially its view of the determination of capital formation rates. For Keynesian economists, the interest rate is determined by the demand for, and supply of, money. They reject the classical view that the interest rate equates the saving plans of households and the investment plans of businesses. Keynesians believe these plans are largely unrelated to the interest rate. They point out that saving plans usually do not coincide with investment plans, since savers and investors are different groups motivated by different considerations. Saving depends on income; investment is a function of its expected rate of return. Keynesian economists do not expect a market economy's actual saving to equal the amount needed for maximum economic growth.

Although classical economists advocated investments in infrastructure, such as roads and canals, they generally emphasized a free market with minimal government intervention—a view having little appeal to leaders and economists in developing countries. The LDCs are even less inclined than DCs to accept the saving decisions of households and businesses based on the market. Perhaps they are reluctant to do so because they see that governments taking an active role in increasing capital formation rates generate high saving rates. Most noteworthy here is the Soviet Union, where saving as a percentage of national income has exceeded 20 percent in peacetime since highly centralized planning began in the 1930s. And as Table 14-1 indicates, the saving rates of socialist countries exceeded those of developed, nonsocialist (primarily capitalist) countries in both the 1960s and the 1980s. In any event, the rest of our discussion of ways of increasing capital formation stresses government-initiated measures.

Capital Imports

The LDCs may prefer to increase capital formation without the pain of reducing current consumption, that is, with capital inflows from abroad or by exploiting idle resources. The success of importing capital, discussed in Chapter 16, depends on how much capacity increases in the future, so that a country can raise domestic saving to export capital.

Exploiting Idle Resources

Redundant Labor.   According to Ragnar Nurkse, a government should use labor with low or zero marginal productivity in agriculture to work on capital projects, such as roads, railways, houses, and factories. Workers on these projects continue to depend on their relatives on the farm for food. It is as if workers in capital goods production carry their own subsistence bundles with them. In essence new capital formation, or saving, is created at virtually no cost.[3]

The problem with Nurkse's theory is that we can expect those remaining on the farm *and* those beginning work on capital projects to increase consumption. To persuade idled agricultural laborers to work harder off the farm probably requires money wages. In fact just as in the Lewis model, these laborers will leave the farm only if they receive a wage exceeding the subsistence that all members of the rural community receive (see Chapter 10). Those remaining on the farm will inevitably increase their consumption as existing output (barely reduced by the withdrawal of labor) is spread over fewer people. Thus financial and social costs of the capital projects are actually greater, and the potential for saving less, than Nurkse anticipates.

Although in theory government could use taxes or low agricultural procurement prices to prevent those staying on the farms from consuming more, in practice government cannot capture the saving potential from unutilized labor except in economies like the Soviet Union. Even there, from 1929 to 1933, immediate gains from forced agricultural saving were more than offset when peasants disrupted production; they ate a major form of agricultural capital stock—animal herds. Chapter 7 discusses other disruptions to Soviet farm output.

---

[3] Ragnar Nurkse, *Problems of Capital Formation in Underdeveloped Countries* (New York: Oxford University Press, 1967), first published 1953.

Another problem with Nurkse's approach is that employing previously unutilized farm labor activates resources with high alternative costs. The workers on the capital project will need some capital (such as crude tools) to build the roads, railways, houses, and factories. In addition, entrepreneurs, supervisors, and planners will be needed to initiate, plan, and administer the project. Furthermore if workers move to the city, its housing, transport, schools, hospitals, and other services will have to be expanded.

Unused Capital Capacity.   Visitors to many capital poor LDCs are shocked by the evidence of widespread capital underutilization: earthmovers rusting away for lack of servicing or spare parts; empty housing projects; abandoned irrigation ditches; and factories producing at a fraction of capacity because of mechanical breakdowns, materials shortages, or insufficient markets. Surely, they ask, cannot output be increased through wiser capital utilization?

Yet existing capacity is not fully utilized for many reasons. LDCs use more capital than is socially most profitable because technology transferred from DCs is not suited to their needs and because of factor price distortions and low foreign exchange prices (see Chapters 10 and 12). Furthermore many developing countries can profitably absorb only so much additional capital. The small size of the construction industry, poor transport and communication facilities, irregular power, slow and undependable deliveries, unsatisfactory servicing of equipment, and inadequate housing for foreign personnel constitute major technical limitations to more effective use of existing and potential capital. LDCs also lack skilled people; competent civil servants, innovative entrepreneurs, experienced managers and technicians, and educated workers. However, in the long run, expanding educational and training facilities, transportation and communication, and other infrastructure should increase **absorptive capacity.**

Factories producing textiles, shoes, motor vehicles, beer, soft drinks, paper products, and so on, could reach full capacity by running 24 hours a day, running three shifts instead of one. Even so, more managers, supervisors, technicians, and other skilled persons in short supply in most LDCs would be needed.

In the short run, some of these skilled people can be hired from abroad. Still it is difficult and expensive to find foreigners who will work and respond well in the local culture and economy. Furthermore using foreign specialists may prevent local workers from getting experience, learning, and control of domestic production—a long-run benefit that would increase the future ability of the country to use capital effectively.

Labor with low marginal productivity in agriculture cannot be easily utilized cheaply; increasing capital utilization is difficult, and the success of capital imports depends on increasing future capacity. Thus increasing saving usually requires diverting resources from consumption, discussed in the remainder of this chapter.

Moral Suasion

Many poor countries have a substantial but unexploited capacity to save. Societies spending resources for guns, tanks, cathedrals, or palaces surely could divert funds into productive investment (Chapter 5). Moreover, households in low-income countries accumulate assets of one kind or another that represent saving—for a rainy day, marriage festivities, religious observances, and other purposes. Many a poor rural Indian woman wears a lifetime of savings in the form of a gold necklace.

Political leaders have often stirred up the populace to sacrifice for a war effort. Could not some of this enthusiasm support the program for economic development? The government could convince people that development is taking place, that saving is bearing fruit. Sound national economic management, coupled with a social security system, might make people less insecure about economic emergencies, so that they might invest more in productive activity.[4]

Persuasion is more likely to be effective, especially among lower- and middle-income groups, if real personal income is increasing. It is easier to convince people to save when income is going up than when it is constant, since saving would then mean a decrease in consumption.[5]

Improvement in the Tax System

Saving is unconsumed current production. Taxation is one form of saving (a part of S in the national accounts Equation 14-1). Improving the tax system increases saving.

An Emphasis on Direct Taxes.   In the West, a major source of government revenue is direct taxes—those levied on property, wealth, inheritance, and personal and corporate income. Many LDCs lack the administrative or political capacity to raise large amounts of revenue in this way. Nonetheless direct taxes, especially on affluent individuals and enterprises, increase government revenue substantially. Chapter 15 discusses some of the problems involved in collecting taxes.

Taxes on Luxuries.   Through luxury taxes, government can command some resources that would otherwise have been used for air conditioners, automobiles, and the like. An excise tax, levied on the production or sale of the individual luxury commodity, is the most common luxury tax. A tax on imports of luxuries should probably be avoided, since it would stimulate domestic investment in luxury goods.

A word of caution is necessary. Excessively widespread and steep taxes on nonessential goods may either encourage evasion and smuggling or adversely affect incentives—most people will not work harder if they cannot spend the extra income earned.

Sales (or Turnover) Taxes.   Since the early 1930s, the Soviet Union has used high sales taxes on, and government monopoly purchases of, farm goods to capture agricultural saving. Some LDC governments use agricultural marketing boards with monopsony buying power to set low purchase prices for farm goods in order to sell them later on the world market for a substantial profit. However, such action may hamper the growth of agricultural output. Furthermore the substantial price spread gives rise to smuggling. As an example, in 1975, Ethiopia was the largest exporter

---

[4] Some of the material from this and subsequent sections is from Henry J. Bruton, *Principles of Development Economics* (Englewood Cliffs, N.J.: Prentice-Hall, 1965), pp. 154–58.

[5] Economists, especially from DCs, should be careful about prescribing expenditure reductions for marriage feasts, religious observances, cathedrals, mosques, and so on, in order to increase productive investment for material goods.

of sesame seeds in the world, though it produced little of this crop domestically. Two-thirds of the sesame seeds were smuggled from the Sudan, where the Sudan Oil Seed marketing board paid prices significantly below world prices.[6]

A well-designed tax program can help government acquire resources for capital formation, and eliminate obstacles to private saving. However, such improvements in tax machinery are a long, slow process.

Developing Financial Intermediaries

Many people hold physical assets or money as a precaution against a rainy day. Traditionally many LDC savers hold assets in gold, jewels, or foreign bank accounts. These holdings will probably be shifted to stocks, bonds, or short-term saving deposits once people are convinced that a piece of paper represents a legitimate claim to an asset, which can be relatively liquid.

People are more likely to save if financial instruments and institutions exist. **Financial intermediaries** are institutions that serve as middlemen between savers and investors; examples are commercial banks, savings banks, community savings societies, development banks, stock and bond markets, mutual funds, social security, pension and provident funds, insurance funds, and government debt instruments.

These financial intermediaries need not merely be "demand-following"—responding merely to investor and saver demand—but may be "supply-leading," facilitating entrepreneurship and capital formation that would otherwise not occur.[7] As an example, in the last decades of the nineteenth century in Russia, the czar's minister of finance created state banks that actively sought to lend to local and foreign entrepreneurs in heavy industry. And development banks in LDCs, such as the Industrial Credit and Investment Corporation of India established in 1954, have financed both local and foreign private ventures, although these have usually been limited to large-scale enterprises.

Increasing Investment Opportunities

In many instances, an investment opportunity will generate saving that otherwise would not be made. Government subsidies, tariffs, loans, training facilities, technical and managerial help, and construction of infrastructure may increase saving because prospective entrepreneurs perceive higher investment returns. As an example, a small-town shoemaker whose capital consists of a hammer, pliers, knife, rasp, bench, and other simple tools may begin to save to buy skiving, sewing, tacking, lasting, and pulling-over machines once the government has provided electricity in the area or has set up an industrial extension center to help the shoemaker order machines, design production lines, repair and maintain machines, and manage a labor force.

[6] Based on Food and Agriculture Organization of the United Nations, *Trade Yearbook,* Rome, 1952–1980, and calculated by Abdalla Sidahmed, who brought this example to my attention.

[7] Hugh T. Patrick, "Financial Development and Economic Growth in Underdeveloped Countries," *Economic Development and Cultural Change* 14 (January 1966): 174–77.

Redistributing Income

The government can encourage particular sectors and economic groups by its tax, subsidy, and industrial policies. It can redistribute income to people with a high propensity to save or stimulate output in sectors with the most growth potential and in which saving and taxation are high.

Local Financing of Social Investment

Political integration and national loyalty are often weak in many young LDC nations. In such cases, government frequently lacks the political will and administrative ability essential for expanding tax revenue (see Chapter 15). However, local government can levy taxes that the central government cannot *if* the funds are used to finance schools, roads, or other social overhead projects that clearly benefit local residents. In fact some new urban services, such as roads, sewers, aqueducts, street lighting, and parks, can be financed by special assessments on those businesses, property owners, and individuals that benefit most from construction.[8]

Inflationary Financing

The banking system can provide credit and the treasury can print money to lend to those with high rates of saving and productive investment. Creating new money, although inflationary, increases the proportion of resources available to high savers, so that real capital formation rises. However, this approach is not sustainable, and it is fraught with perils, as Chapter 15 indicates.

Confiscation, Foreign Exchange Conversion Restrictions, and Indigenization Decrees

Expropriating private capital can increase capital formation if foreign companies have repatriated a large proportion of earnings abroad or if domestic investors have dissipated much of their income in luxury consumption or investment in luxury housing or foreign assets. Martin Bronfenbrenner argues that confiscating capital did not kill the "goose that laid the golden egg" in the Soviet Union and China.[9] In fact expropriation seems to have permitted these countries to industrialize faster than most other non-Westen economies.

Bronfenbrenner uses an arithmetic model of confiscation. He assumes a plausible quantitative relationship between national income, income shares, and saving in LDCs. He shows that productive investment rates can be significantly increased in societies whose income distributions include high property income (profits, rents, and interest), only a small proportion of which are plowed back into economic development. The model assumes that saving originates only in this sector, which

---

[8] William G. Rhoads and Richard M. Bird, "Financing Urbanization by Benefit Taxation," in Richard M. Bird and Oliver Oldman, eds., *Readings on Taxation in Developing Countries* (Baltimore: Johns Hopkins University Press, 1975), pp 453–63.

[9] Martin Bronfenbrenner, "The Appeal of Confiscation in Economic Development," *Economic Development and Cultural Change* 3 (April 1955): 201–18.

makes up 15 percent of national income. One-third of this property share (or 5 percent of national income) comprises net saving. Of this 5 percent, 2 percent is invested productively. After government confiscates all capital goods without compensation, all property income can be invested. Even if the share of property income declines by one-third, to 10 percent of national income, as a result of less efficient management by government, this 10 percent can be productively invested. Thus the previous rate of productive investment (2 percent) is multiplied by a factor of five.

Confiscation runs counter to Western moral premises and economic interest. Yet the temptation to confiscate may be great, especially when the value of existing private assets relative to potential, future private investment is high. However, LDCs are less likely to benefit from the confiscation of foreign capital when (1) its returns are high enough to satisfy both foreign investors and domestic political leaders; (2) the country is highly dependent on future funds and personnel from abroad; (3) when foreign companies provide knowledge and technology not otherwise available; or (4) the country is vulnerable to military, political, or economic retaliation by the foreign power losing from expropriation.

This list suggests that in practice the net benefits from confiscation are often negligible or even negative, especially for small countries. The loss of foreign trade, aid, and investment resulting from international economic sanctions is difficult to replace. To be sure, for example, Cuba established close economic ties with the Soviet Union and other socialist countries when it expropriated U.S. foreign capital after the 1959 revolution. Yet despite some gains (noted in Chapter 2), the overall, economic growth of postrevolutionary Cuba has been slow, partly because Cuba no longer exports sugar to the United States and other Western countries. Furthermore once expropriation has occurred, domestic economic mismanagement may ruin whatever benefits may have accrued. Wasteful government spending and public enterprise losses from inefficiency and corruption may severely limit the state's productive investment.

The LDC governments can be selective in confiscation policies. They can exempt companies from countries that, it is expected, may one day provide significant aid and investment or exempt all foreign companies. Moreover capital outflows from foreign companies can be reduced, short of confiscation, by restricting the conversion of profits, dividends, royalties, management fees and other earnings into foreign currency but at the cost of discouraging foreign investment and reducing allocative efficiency, which dampens exports and import substitutes (see Chapter 17).

Another LDC strategy, short of confiscation, is an **indigenization** decree requiring majority local ownership in certain sectors and reserving other sectors entirely for local enterprises. The primary objectives of indigenization are greater self-reliance and self-sustaining growth.

But even many LDC nationals believe indigenization's prospects are poor, since if complete, it means doing without international aid, capital, imported technology, and imported consumer goods. Zaïre nationalized its largest copper-producing firm, a Belgian concern, GECAMINES (Général de Carriers et des Mines du Zaïre), in 1967. While its dominant position and privileged access to inputs make it financially profitable, the firm uses more foreign exchange than it generates, is highly capital intensive, has large excess capacity, and is not well integrated with other Zaïrian sectors.

Zaïre's 1973 nationalization of palm oil changed it from a leading export to a net import by 1977. Government-appointed Zaïrian plantation managers, most of whom lacked interest and competence, systematically depleted the plantations' working capital to rescue their own financial position, hedging against future loss of power.[10]

The Nigerian Enterprises Promotion Decrees of 1972, 1977, and 1981, shifted the manufacturing sector from foreign majority ownership in the 1960s to indigenous majority ownership in the mid and late 1970s, even though some foreigners naturalized, converted equity into debt holdings, or used other loopholes to continue ownership or control. Chibuzo S. A. Ogbuagu argues that indigenization became an instrument for a few civil servants, military rulers, business people, and professionals to amass considerable wealth by manipulating state power. Several top politicians and military officers benefiting from fraud resigned to join business or were forced from government because of conflicts of interest. Ironically an indigenization policy designed partly to reduce foreign concentration created Nigerian monopolies and oligopolies, especially among those with the wealth and influence to obtain capital and government loans to purchase foreign shares.

Additionally Nigerian entrepreneurs still lacked the capital and management and technical skills to replace foreigners effectively in most industries reserved for them by law. As a result, some industries covered under previous indigenization acts were reclassified under the 1981 law to permit more foreign participation. Many Nigerians acquiring shares in indigenized companies were content with dividends paid to them by foreign managers. So most Nigerians increased shares of foreign firms without the enterprising zeal and managerial or technical know-how to take on the higher responsibility of running the economy.[11]

SUMMARY

1. A country can increase its new capital formation through domestic saving or by inflows of capital from abroad.

2. The *ICOR* (incremental capital-output ratio) is the ratio of investment to increments in national income. If an economy's *ICOR* is 3.5, a targeted rate of overall growth of 3 percent (2 percent for population growth and 1 percent for growth in output per capita) requires 10.5 percent of national income to be invested. Crude estimates indicate that two-thirds of present LDCs have net investment rates of at least 10 percent, compared to about one-half of LDCs in 1960.

3. The *ICOR* has serious limitations as an investment criterion and a guide for figuring capital requirements because it (1) excludes the cost of inputs other than capital, (2) ignores externalities, (3) does not consider variations in capital utilization, and (4) neglects the timing of costs and benefits.

---

[10] Claude Ake, "The Political Context of Indigenization," in Adebayo Adedeji, ed., *Indigenization of African Economies* (London: Hutchinson University Library for Africa, 1981), pp. 32–41; and Guy Gran, ed., *Zaïre: The Political Economy of Underdevelopment* (New York: Praeger, 1979).

[11] Chibuzo S.A. Ogbuagu, "The Nigerian Indigenization Policy: Nationalism or Pragmatism?" *African Affairs* 82 (April 1983): 241–66; and E. Wayne Nafziger, *Inequality in Africa: Political Elites, Proletariat, Peasants, and the Poor* (Cambridge: Cambridge University Press, 1988), pp. 88–90.

4. In both DCs and LDCs, the major source of domestic net saving is household saving, with corporate saving second, and government saving third.

5. The English classical economists believed that government interference in capital formation decisions made by private individuals in the market would hurt efficiency and growth.

6. Most contemporary leaders and economists in LDCs do not accept the saving decisions of households and businesses arising from the market. The following are some of the measures LDC governments can take to increase saving rates: (1) exploitation of unused capital capacity, (2) moral suasion, (3) increased collection of personal income, corporation, and property taxes, (4) taxes on luxuries, (5) sales taxes, (6) development of financial intermediaries, (7) increased investment opportunities, (8) redistribution of income to people or sectors with high saving or tax rates, (9) increased local financing of social investment, (10) inflationary financing for high savers, (11) restrictions on converting profits, dividends, royalties, management fees, and other earnings into foreign currency, (12) indigenizing local ownership, and (13) confiscation of private capital. Needless to say, governments must consider the costs associated with any one of these measures.

TERMS TO REVIEW

- **capital import**
- **investment**
- **investment rate**
- **gross investment**
- **net investment**
- **depreciation**
- **incremental**

- **capital-output ratio (ICOR)**
- **net value added**
- **absorptive capacity**
- **financial intermediaries**

- **indigenization**
- **Harrod–Domar growth model**
- **accelerator theory of investment**

QUESTIONS TO DISCUSS

1. Using national income equations, show two ways of explaining capital inflow from abroad.

2. Use the equation stating economic growth equals investment rate divided by the incremental capital-output ratio to explain why Walter Rostow's theory of economic growth emphasizes a sharp increase in investment rate from 5 percent to over 10 percent of national income. What are some criticisms of Rostow's emphasis on this increased investment rate?

3. What is the incremental capital-output ratio (*ICOR*)? What problems occur when using *ICOR*s to estimate capital requirements?

4. What measures can LDC governments take to increase net capital formation as a percentage of national income?

5. How useful is the Lewis model in explaining early growth in capital formation in developing countries?

6. How adequate is the market for making saving decisions in LDCs?

7. Is there much potential for using previously idle resources to increase LDC capital formation rates?

8. How can LDCs improve the tax system to increase saving?

9. Evaluate foreign exchange conversion restrictions, indigenization decrees, and confiscation of foreign-owned private capital as measures for increasing productive capital formation.

GUIDE TO READINGS

The World Bank (note, p. 65) has information on LDC saving and investment rates. Yotopoulos and Nugent, pp. 393–95 (note 26, p. 268), and V. R. Panchamukhi, *Capital Formation and Output in the Third World* (New Delhi, Radiant, 1986), critically review *ICORS* and growth.

Adelman and Enke (guide to Chapter 5) discuss the classical approach to saving decisions. The models of Lewis (note 1) and John C. H. Fei and Gustav Ranis, "A Theory of Economic Development," *American Economic Review* 51 (September 1961): 533–65, analyze the increase in saving in a dual economy. Bruton, pp. 121–73 (note 4) is a good source for ideas on how to raise rates of capital formation in LDCs.

APPENDIX TO CHAPTER 14

THE HARROD–DOMAR MODEL

Capital formation and the *ICOR* are fundamental variables in the **Harrod–Domar growth model.** Evsey D. Domar emphasizes that present investment, while contributing to aggregate demand today, also provides new productive capacity. If this capacity is not adequately used, it discourages future investment, thus increasing surplus capital and depressing the economy. But if investment increases at the correct rate, aggregate demand will be sufficient to use fully the newly added capacity. Domar indicates the rate at which investment would have to grow for this process to take place. Investment must grow at a constant percentage rate

$$\frac{\Delta I}{I} = \frac{1}{ICOR} \, (\alpha)$$

(14-7)

where α is the marginal propensity to save, the ratio of the increment in savings to the increment in income.

Roy F. Harrod is also concerned with keeping total spending and productive capacity in balance, but he focuses on the growth path of income, unlike Domar's concentration on the growth rate of investment. In the Harrod model, the equilibrium (or warranted) growth rate keeps planned savings equal to planned investment, that is,

$$sY_t = ICOR \ (Y_t - Y_{t-1}) \tag{14-8}$$

$$\frac{Y_t - Y_{t-1}}{Y_t} = \frac{s}{ICOR} \tag{14-9}$$

where s is (S_t/Y_t), the average propensity to save.

Harrod goes beyond Domar's explanation of what investment must be for sustainable growth to include a theory of what determines investment. He calls his notion the **accelerator theory of investment;** that is, investment today (I_t) is partly dependent on income today minus that of yesterday $(Y_t - Y_{t-1})$, reflected in the *ICOR* relationship.

Harrod also discusses what happens if the actual growth rate does not equal the warranted rate, that is, planned savings does not equal planned investment. He concludes that the warranted growth path is like a razor's edge, since a departure of the actual growth rate $[(Y_t - Y_{t-1})/Y_t]$ from the warranted path causes a further departure in the same direction, throwing the economy into a period of either explosive growth (producing inflation) or stagnation.

The model's instability follows from some peculiar assumptions about producer behavior. If producers guessed correctly yesterday about demand and their supply just equaled market demand, they will plan today to increase their output by the *same percentage* as they increased it yesterday. If they produced too much, they will reduce yesterday's growth rate of output and again produce too much today because demand will fall below expectations. If they produced too little yesterday, so there was excess demand, today's output growth will increase over yesterday's and there will again be excess demand. One possibility Harrod considers is that the warranted growth path may not be attainable because of limitations in the growth of capacity, that is, his "natural" growth rate.

There are several problems with the Harrod–Domar model. The first is Harrod's assumption about producer behavior, including the premise that producers do not modify behavior as they learn how the economy previously responded to divergences between warranted and actual growths. Harrod's behavioral assumptions may be even less relevant where the state has a major role in planning output expansion. The second problem is that Harrod's accelerator has no lag, implying that capital goods are produced simultaneously with the increased output requiring this production. A third problem, which is also characteristic of the Domar model, is the assumption of fixed capital-labor proportions, which omits the possibility of adjusting capital-labor ratios to avoid surplus capital, and output ceilings that might cause the warranted rate to be the actual rate. Models that allow for substitution between factors—often called neoclassical growth models (for example, the Cobb–Douglas approach in Chapter 12)—overcome this last problem of the Harrod–Domar model.[12]

[12] Roy F. Harrod, "An Essay in Dynamic Theory," *Economic Journal* 49 (March 1939): 14–33; Evsey D. Domar, "The Problem of Capital Accumulation," *American Economic Review* 37 (March 1947): 34–55; Gardner Ackley, *Macroeconomic Theory* (New York: Macmillan, 1961), pp. 513–26; and Edward Shapiro, *Macroeconomic Analysis* (New York: Harcourt, Brace, Jovanovich, 1978), 402–13. I am grateful for the help of Edgar S. Bagley.

Chapter Fifteen

MONETARY AND FISCAL POLICY, GROWTH, AND INFLATION

Monetary policy affects the supply of money (basically currency plus commercial bank demand deposits) and the rate of interest. **Fiscal policy** includes the rate of taxation and level of government spending.

The DC governments use monetary and fiscal policies to achieve goals for output and employment growth and price stability. Thus during a recession, with slow or negative growth, high unemployment, and surplus capital capacity, these governments reduce interest rates, expand bank credit, decrease tax rates, and increase government spending to expand aggregate spending and accelerate growth. On the other hand, DC governments are likely to respond to a high rate of inflation (general price increase) with increased interest rates, a contraction of bank credit, higher tax rates, decreased government expenditures, and perhaps even wage-price controls in order to reduce total spending.

The DCs do not often attain their macroeconomic goals because of ineffective monetary and fiscal tools, political pressures, or contradictory goals. Thus we have the quandary during **stagflation** or inflationary recession (a frequent economic malady in the West during the 1970s and 1980s) of whether to increase aggregate spending to eliminate the recession or decrease spending to reduce inflation.

SCOPE OF THE CHAPTER

The LDCs encounter even greater limitations than DCs in using monetary and fiscal policies to achieve macroeconomic goals. The first section of this chapter discusses some of the limitations of monetary policy in LDCs. Second we look at the low tax rates in LDCs. The third section examines tax policy goals, including limitations LDCs face in using various taxes. Political constraints on implementing tax policies are mentioned in the fourth section. A fifth part on government expenditures indicates the limits of using spending policies to stabilize income and prices. The final section, on the problem of inflation, analyzes accelerated worldwide inflation since 1970; the demand-pull, cost-push, ratchet, structural, expectational, and political explanations for inflation; the benefits and costs of inflation; and the relationship between inflation and growth.

LIMITATIONS OF MONETARY POLICY

In DCs central banks (like the Bank of England or the U.S. Federal Reserve) can increase the supply of money by buying government bonds, lowering the interest rate charged commercial banks, and reducing these banks' required ratio of reserves to demand deposits. The increased money supply and decreased interest rate should increase investment spending and raise output and employment during recession. And a decreased money supply should curtail investment, so that inflation is reduced.

The banking system, often limited in its ability to regulate the money supply to influence output and prices in DCs, is even more ineffective in LDCs. Usually the money market in developing countries is externally dependent, poorly organized, fragmented, and cartelized (more on this last point when we discuss financial repression later in the chapter).

1. Many of the major commercial banks in LDCs are branches of large private banks in DCs, such as Chase Manhattan or Barclay's Bank. Their orientation is external: They are concerned with profits in dollars, pound sterling, or other convertible currency, not rupees, nairas, pesos, and other currencies that cannot be exchanged on the world market.

2. Many LDCs are so dependent on international transactions that they must limit the banking system's local expansion of the money supply to some multiple of foreign currency held by the central bank. Thus the government cannot always control the money supply because of the variability of foreign exchange assets.

3. The LDC central banks do not have much influence on the amount of bank deposits. They generally make few loans to commercial banks. Furthermore since securities markets are usually not well developed in LDCs, the central bank usually buys and sells few bonds on the open market.

4. Commercial banks generally restrict their loans to large and medium enterprises in modern manufacturing, mining, power, transport, construction, and plantation agriculture. Small traders, artisans, and farmers obtain most of their funds from close relatives or borrow at exorbitant interest rates from local money lenders and landlords. Thus LDC banking systems have less influence than DCs on the interest rate, level of investment, and aggregate output.

5. Demand deposits (checking accounts) as a percentage of the total money supply are generally lower in LDCs than DCs. In the United States, they make up three-fourths of the total money supply, but in most developing countries, the figure is less than half. Checks are not widely accepted for

payment in LDCs. Generally commercial banks in LDCs control a smaller share of the money supply than in DCs.[1]

6. The links between interest rate, investment, and output assumed in DCs are questionable in LDCs. Investment is not very sensitive to the interest rate charged by commercial banks, partly because a lot of money is lent by money lenders, landlords, relatives, and others outside the banks. Furthermore because of supply limitations, increases in investment demand may result in inflation rather than expanded real output. The LDCs often face these limitations at far less than full employment because of poor management, monopolistic restraints, bureaucratic delay, and the lack of essential inputs (resulting from licensing restrictions on foreign exchange or domestic materials).

TAX RATIOS AND GNP PER CAPITA

We have seen the monetary policy limitations in LDCs. Fiscal policy—taxation and government spending—comprises another tool for controlling income, employment, and prices. Tax policy also has other purposes—raising funds for public spending being the most obvious one. The next four sections examine changes in tax revenues as an economy develops, factors to be considered in formulating tax policy, political obstacles to tax collections, and patterns of government spending in DCs and LDCs.

The concept of systematic state intervention to stimulate economic development has been a major part of the ideology of many developing countries. Yet perhaps surprisingly, taxes as a percentage of GNP in LDCs are generally less than in DCs. According to Table 15-1, tax revenue as a percentage of GNP is 17.8 percent for developing countries and 37.7 percent for developed countries.[2] If social security contributions are included, the differences in tax ratios widen. The LDC ratio is 20 percent, the DC ratio, 46 percent.

Among the sample of LDCs, the tax ratio is 12.9 percent for low-income countries and 23.1 percent for middle-income countries. Percentages range from a high of 36.5 percent for Israel, 32.6 percent for Yugoslavia, and 29.8 percent for Egypt to 2.6 percent for Uganda (where government ceased to operate in many areas during a civil war in the early 1980s) and 5.5 percent for Ghana (see Table 15-1). Data also indicate that the tax ratio for a given country increases with economic growth.[3]

---

[1] U Tun Wai, "Interest Rates in the Organized Money Markets of Underdeveloped Countries," *International Monetary Fund Staff Papers* 5 (August 1956): 249–78, and U Tun Wai, "Interest Rates Outside the Organized Money Markets of Underdeveloped Countries," *International Monetary Fund Staff Papers* 6 (November 1957): 80–125; excerpts of which are reprinted in Gerald M. Meier, *Leading Issues in Economic Development* (New York: Oxford University Press, 1976), pp. 299–305.

[2] Tax revenue does not include contributions to social security or those of government as employer. The tax ratios in the study, which adjusts "off-budget" items to improve the ratios' comparability, are at least rough indicators of the true rankings.

[3] Vito Tanzi, "Quantitative Characteristics of the Tax Systems of Developing Countries," in David Newbery and Nicholas Stern, eds., *The Theory of Taxation for Developing Countries* (New York: Oxford University Press, 1987), pp. 205–41; David B. Perry, "International Tax Comparisons," *Canadian Tax Journal* 28 (January-February 1980): 89–93; Alan A. Tait, Wilfred L. M. Grätz, and Barry J. Eichengreen, "International Comparisons of Taxation for Selected Developing Countries, 1972–76," *International Monetary Fund Staff Papers* 26 (March 1979): 123–56; and Raja J. Chelliah, Hessel J. Baas, and Margaret R. Kelly, "Tax Ratios and Tax Effort in Developing Countries, 1969–71," *International Monetary Fund Staff Papers* 22 (March 1975): 187–205. See Table 15-1.

TABLE 15-1   Tax Ratios and GNP per Capita

DEVELOPED COUNTRIES			DEVELOPING COUNTRIES		
	Taxes as a Percent of GNP[a]	GNP per Capita 1981 ($)		Taxes as a Percent of GNP[a]	GNP per Capita 1981 ($)
Sweden	53.1	14,870	Israel[b]	36.5	5,160
Norway	47.3	14,060	Yugoslavia[b]	32.6	2,790
Netherlands	46.7	11,790	Egypt	29.8	650
Belgium	44.4	11,920	Portugal	28.2	2,520
Denmark	43.2	13,120	Greece[b]	27.3	4,420
Austria	41.3	10,210	Congo	26.9	1,100
France	39.4	12,190	Botswana	25.9	1,010
Finland	38.9	10,680	Liberia	25.4	520
Germany, Fed. Rep.	38.0	13,450	Tunisia[b]	25.1	1,420
U.K.	35.2	9,110	Chile[b]	24.8	2,560
Italy	34.5	6,960	Togo	24.4	380
Ireland	33.7	5,230	Nicaragua	23.6	860
New Zealand	32.3	7,700	Brazil[b]	23.5	2,200
Canada	32.3	11,400	Zimbabwe	23.1	870
Switzerland	31.5	17,430	Zambia[b]	23.0	600
U.S.	30.4	12,820	Malaysia	22.8	1,840
Australia	29.7	11,080	Morocco	21.7	860
Japan	22.2	10,080	Panama[b]	21.5	1,910
			Kenya[b]	21.4	420
Average[c]	37.7		Indonesia[b]	20.8	530
			South Africa[b]	20.7	2,770
			Senegal	20.5	430
			Uruguay	20.4	2,820
			Ivory Coast	20.4	1,170
			Venezuela[b]	20.0	4,220
			Argentina	19.9	2,560
			Yemen Arab Rep.	19.8	460
			Sri Lanka[b]	19.6	300
			Cyprus	19.3	3,740
			Nigeria	18.9	870
			Papua New Guinea	18.6	840
			Singapore	18.4	5,240
			Zaïre	18.3	210
			Jordan	17.9	1,620

Tanzania	17.8	280
Costa Rica[b]	17.5	1,430
Peru	17.0	1,170
Somalia[b]	16.9	280
Cameroon	16.8	880
Mexico[b]	16.6	2,250
Turkey	16.6	1,540
Korea, Rep. of	16.3	1,700
Benin	16.3	320
India[b]	15.9	260
Malawi[b]	15.8	200
Madagascar[b]	15.1	330
Central African Rep.	15.0	320
Thailand	13.5	770
Pakistan	13.1	350
Burkina Faso	12.9	240
Colombia[b]	12.2	1,380
Ecuador[b]	12.2	1,180
Sierra Leone	11.8	320
Ethiopia[b]	11.5	140
Philippines[b]	11.2	790
El Salvador	11.2	650
Paraguay[b]	11.1	1,630
Haiti	10.5	300
Dominican Rep.[b]	10.3	1,260
Syrian Arab Rep.	10.0	1,570
Burma	9.8	190
Guatemala[b]	9.8	1,140
Sudan	9.7	380
Bangladesh	8.1	140
Honduras	6.3	600
Bolivia	6.3	600
Nepal	6.1	150
Ghana	5.5	400
Uganda	2.6	200
Average[c]	17.8	

[a]1978 for DCs, 1981–83 for LDCs (or some other earlier 3-year period not beginning before 1977).

[b]State and local tax revenues are included.

[c]Five other DCs and fifteen other LDCs are included in the original.

Sources: David B. Perry, "International Tax Comparisons," *Canadian Tax Journal* 28 (January–February 1980): 91; Vito Tanzi, "Quantitative Characteristics of the Tax Systems of Developing Countries," in David Newbery and Nicholas Stern, eds., *The Theory of Taxation for Developing Countries* (New York: Oxford University Press, 1987), pp. 205–41; International Monetary Fund, *Government Finance Statistics Yearbook* vol. 8 (Washington, D.C., 1984); and World Bank, *World Development Report, 1983* (New York: Oxford University Press, 1983), pp. 148–49.

The increase in tax ratio with GNP per capita is a reflection of both demand and supply factors—demand for **social goods** (collective goods like education, highways, sewerage, flood control, and national defense) and the capacity to levy and pay taxes.

Wagner's law, named for the nineteenth century German economist Adolph Wagner, states that as real GNP per capita rises, people demand relatively more social goods and relatively fewer private goods. A poor country spends a high percentage of its income on food, clothing, shelter, and other essential consumer goods. After these needs have been largely fulfilled, an increased proportion of additional spending is for social goods.[4]

GOALS OF TAX POLICY

The most important taxation goal in LDCs is to mobilize resources for public expenditure. According to the IMF, the amount of these resources is determined by GNP per capita, the share of the mining sector in GNP, the share of exports in GNP, and tax policy. Part of this section looks at how tax policies affect public spending. In addition we consider the impact of taxes on stability of income and prices. However, achieving these crucial taxation goals must be viewed in light of other goals, such as improved income distribution, efficient resource allocation, increased capital and enterprise, and administrative feasibility. The LDC governments must consider all of these goals when designing tax schemes to achieve rapid economic growth, to improve the lot of the poor, and to stabilize prices.

Mobilizing Resources for Public Expenditure

A major reason that tax ratios increase with GNP per capita is that richer countries rely more heavily on taxes with greater elasticity (that is, percentage change in taxation/percentage change in GNP). An **elastic tax,** whose coefficient exceeds one, rises more rapidly than GNP. **Direct taxes**—primarily property, wealth, inheritance, and income taxes (such as personal and corporate taxes)—are generally more elastic than **indirect taxes** such as import, export, turnover, sales, and excise taxes (except for sales or excise taxes on goods purchased mostly by high-income groups).

Direct taxes account for 31.8 percent of the revenue sources in LDCs. The two leading direct taxes, the corporate income and personal taxes, comprise only 19.0 percent and 10.3 percent, respectively, of total LDC revenue sources.

The major source of tax for LDCs is international trade, an indirect tax comprising 30.6 percent of the total—with import duties 25.0 percent and export duties 4.9 percent. Other important indirect taxes—excise, sales, and other taxes on production and internal transactions—account for 27.9 percent of the total (see Table 15-2).

The proportion of taxes raised from direct taxes is 22 percent in low-income countries, 42 percent in middle-income countries, and about 65 percent in high-income countries.[5] Accordingly the average ratio of direct taxes to GNP is 2.9

---

[4] Adolph Wagner, "Three Extracts on Public Finance," in Richard A. Musgrave and Alan Peacock, eds., *Classics in the Theory of Public Finance* (New York: Macmillan, 1958), pp. 1–16. Wagner wrote in the 1880s.

[5] This includes taxes raised from national, regional, state, and local governments.

TABLE 15-2 Revenue Sources in Developing Countries, 1981–83 (percent of total tax revenue)

Country	DIRECT TAXES				INDIRECT TAXES			OTHER TAXES	
	Personal Income Taxes (1)	Corporate and Other Income Taxes (2)	Wealth and Property Taxes (3)	(cols. 1 + 2 + 3)	Taxes on International Trade (4)	Taxes on Production and International Transactions (5)	Total Indirect Taxes (cols. 4 + 5)	Social Security Taxes	Other Taxes
Bangladesh	13.5	1.7	3.2	18.4	38.2	15.7	53.9	0	27.7
Ethiopia	10.3	14.6	2.1	27.0	42.0	28.5	70.5	0	2.5
Nepal	5.3	2.1	8.8	16.2	38.9	44.2	83.1	0	0.7
Malawi	14.6	22.1	3.3	40.0	24.3	35.4	59.7	0	0.3
Zaire	16.5	20.9	0	37.4	35.8	19.1	54.9	3.7	4.0
Uganda	6.0	5.6	0	11.6	55.8	32.5	88.3	0	0.1
Burkina Faso	11.7	7.4	1.3	20.4	46.3	18.9	65.2	10.8	3.6
India	7.2	8.1	1.3	16.6	17.7	62.8	80.5	0	2.9
Somalia	7.8	0.8	2.1	10.7	45.4	26.9	72.3	0	17.0
Tanzania	9.6	22.2	0.7	32.5	18.0	48.7	66.7	0.3	0.5
Haiti	6.1	14.2	1.7	22.0	36.8	27.7	64.5	1.2	12.3
Sri Lanka	3.4	10.5	0.5	14.4	36.9	27.7	64.6	0	21.0
Benin	3.2	14.0	0.2	17.4	57.3	14.0	71.3	9.7	1.6
Central African Rep.	8.5	9.3	0.5	18.3	43.8	22.9	66.7	11.2	3.8
Sierra Leone	11.7	15.3	0	27.0	46.5	24.4	70.9	0.5	1.6
Madagascar	9.2	7.8	0	17.0	23.9	40.0	63.9	12.6	6.5
Pakistan	5.8	3.7	0.3	9.8	40.4	22.3	62.7	0	27.5
Sudan	7.0	11.5	0.2	18.7	56.4	24.4	80.8	0	0.6
Togo	7.0	30.5	1.5	39.0	36.4	17.0	53.4	7.3	0.3
Ghana	13.8	13.0	0	26.8	37.1	36.0	73.1	0	0.1
Senegal	13.7	11.0	2.6	27.3	38.5	27.8	66.3	5.4	1.0
Yemen Arab Rep.	8.0	5.0	0.9	13.9	61.2	9.0	70.2	0	15.9
Liberia	27.7	9.2	1.0	37.9	32.0	27.7	60.5	0	1.6

TABLE 15-2 Continued

Country	DIRECT TAXES				INDIRECT TAXES			OTHER TAXES	
	Personal Income Taxes (1)	Corporate and Other Income Taxes (2)	Wealth and Property Taxes (3)	(cols. 1 + 2 + 3)	Taxes on International Trade (4)	Taxes on Production and International Transactions (5)	Total Indirect Taxes (cols. 4 + 5)	Social Security Taxes	Other Taxes
Indonesia	1.9	79.3	1.5	82.7	6.0	10.7	16.7	0	0.6
Bolivia	10.7	7.1	2.1	19.9	33.9	42.5	76.4	0	3.7
Honduras	9.8	18.3	0.9	29.0	43.1	26.8	69.9	0	1.1
Zambia	19.6	19.0	3.4	42.0	7.7	46.7	54.4	3.2	0.4
Egypt	7.6	20.4	1.9	29.9	27.6	17.6	45.2	17.2	7.7
El Salvador	9.8	12.7	7.3	29.8	28.9	2.8	31.7	0	38.5
Thailand	8.9	11.8	1.3	22.0	23.0	49.0	72.0	0	6.0
Philippines	10.9	12.0	4.2	27.1	24.8	46.4	71.2	0	1.7
Papua New Guinea	30.2	30.9	0	61.1	22.6	15.2	37.8	0	1.1
Morocco	9.9	11.4	2.5	23.8	24.7	39.1	63.8	6.4	6.0
Nicaragua	0	0	5.9	5.9	18.2	48.6	66.8	13.3	14.0
Nigeria	0.1	77.1	0	77.2	19.4	3.3	22.7	0	0.1
Zimbabwe	26.7	25.9	0.3	52.9	9.4	34.8	44.2	0	2.9
Cameroon	12.1	33.4	2.4	47.9	29.0	15.0	44.0	6.7	1.4
Botswana	0	46.0	0.3	46.0	52.1	1.6	53.7	0	0.3
Congo	11.0	10.1	0.1	21.2	17.0	10.0	27.0	7.7	44.1
Guatemala	2.7	9.9	1.0	13.6	23.4	32.2	55.6	12.3	18.5
Peru	2.4	20.5	6.3	29.2	30.1	45.5	75.6	4.4	-9.2
Ecuador	0	29.2	3.5	32.7	33.7	12.1	45.8	0	21.5
Ivory Coast	6.8	7.3	2.3	16.4	46.3	26.8	73.1	10.2	0.3
Dominican Rep.	8.4	16.2	1.0	25.6	34.5	32.5	67.0	5.0	2.4
Colombia	11.0	13.0	2.5	26.5	18.8	32.8	51.6	15.5	6.4
Tunisia	8.6	10.6	2.8	22.0	33.4	29.4	62.8	12.3	2.9
Costa Rica	15.4	0.1	2.4	17.9	20.4	32.1	52.5	28.3	1.3

Turkey	48.9	11.5	2.3	62.7	9.1	24.1	33.2	0	4.1
Paraguay	0.3	15.3	6.6	22.2	22.7	20.0	42.7	14.3	20.8
Korea, Rep. of	14.0	12.6	1.1	27.7	16.4	51.5	67.9	1.2	3.2
Malaysia	9.4	32.4	0.5	42.3	35.9	19.8	55.7	0.5	1.5
Brazil	0.6	12.4	1.8	14.8	3.6	48.3	51.9	32.3	1.0
Mexico	15.8	19.7	1.6	37.1	15.6	32.3	47.9	14.8	0.2
Portugal	7.7	12.4	1.3	21.4	5.5	36.4	41.9	31.3	5.4
Argentina	0.2	14.0	6.9	21.1	9.4	44.4	53.8	16.5	8.6
Chile	11.4	9.1	2.3	22.8	6.4	53.0	59.4	12.2	5.6
South Africa	20.3	37.4	6.5	64.2	4.5	28.5	33.0	1.4	1.4
Yugoslavia	3.5	4.6	0.4	8.5	10.1	27.2	37.3	54.2	0
Uruguay	0.9	7.0	4.8	12.7	12.3	46.0	58.3	27.5	1.5
Cyprus	15.1	9.1	3.3	27.5	24.5	23.9	48.4	22.8	1.3
Venezuela	4.1	70.3	1.5	75.9	9.8	6.8	16.6	5.6	1.9
Greece	13.1	4.9	3.5	21.5	5.1	36.9	42.0	30.4	6.1
Israel	33.3	13.0	3.2	49.5	4.4	28.4	32.8	16.3	1.4
Oman	0	91.9	0.3	92.2	5.2	1.6	6.8	1.0	0
Low-income countries[a]	8.7	11.7	2.0	22.4	39.2	32.3	71.5	3.2	2.9
Middle-income countries[a]	12.0	26.9	3.0	41.9	21.3	23.1	44.4	10.9	2.8
LDCs[a]	10.3	19.0	2.5	31.8	30.6	27.9	58.5	6.9	2.8

[a]Includes twenty-two other countries (six low income and sixteen middle income) listed in the original sources.

Sources: Vito Tanzi, "Quantitative Characteristics of the Tax Systems of Developing Countries," in David Newbery and Nicholas Stern, eds., *The Theory of Taxation for Developing Countries* (New York: Oxford University Press, 1987), pp. 205–41; International Monetary Fund, *Government Finance Statistics Yearbook* vol. 8 (Washington, D.C., 1984); and World Bank, *World Development Report, 1983* (New York: Oxford University Press, 1983), pp. 148–49.

percent in low-income countries, 9.4 percent in middle-income countries, and 24.5 percent in high-income countries.

Although personal income taxes rarely comprise more than 5 percent of GNP in LDCs, they often account for 10–20 percent of GNP in the DCs. In most DCs, the income tax structure is **progressive,** which means that people with higher incomes pay a higher percentage of income in taxes. For example, in 1988, a married couple with two children in the United States earning $12,500 would pay no tax; one earning $25,000 would pay $1826 (7.3 percent); one earning $50,000, $8553 (17.1 percent); one earning $100,000, $19,280 (19.9 percent); and one earning $200,000, $54,314 (27.2 percent). Many people feel the progressive tax is just—that those with higher incomes should bear a larger tax burden, since they have a much greater ability to pay. Moreover a progressive income tax has an elasticity greater than one, so that a rising GNP pushes taxpayers into higher tax brackets. Let us examine the personal income tax and others in light of overall tax policy goals before discussing some of the administrative and political reasons why LDCs rely so little on the individual income tax.

Stability of Income and Prices

As we said earlier, developed countries use fiscal and monetary policies to achieve macroeconomic goals of economic growth, employment, and price changes. When there is high unemployment, the government can increase spending and decrease taxes to increase aggregate demand and employment. In times of inflation, government can reduce spending and increase taxes to decrease aggregate demand and diminish price rises.

At times fiscal policy has a limited effect in stabilizing employment and prices in DCs, and not surprisingly, it is even less effective in LDCs. There are several reasons for this ineffectiveness.

First as indicated above, tax receipts as a share of GNP in LDCs are typically smaller than in DCs.

Second LDCs, relying more on indirect taxes, have less control than DCs over the amount of taxes they can raise. Personal and corporate income taxes can generally not be used to stabilize aggregate spending, since they comprise only 5.1 percent of GNP in LDCs. Furthermore LDC indirect taxes are subject to wide variation—especially taxes on international trade, which are frequently affected by sharp fluctuations in volume and price (see Chapter 4). In the 1970s, Zaïre raised about four-fifths of its revenue from export taxes. However, when the price of its leading export, copper, fell by 40 percent from 1974 to 1975, export receipts dropped 40 percent, too, resulting in a 36-percent decline in export tax revenue and a 19-percent decline in total government revenue.[6]

Third prices and unemployment are not so sensitive to fiscal policy in LDCs as in DCs. Chapter 10 details (and we reiterate here) why expansionary fiscal policies (increased government spending and decreased tax rates) may have only a limited effect in reducing unemployment in LDCs: (1) There are major supply limitations, such as shortages of skills, infrastructure, and efficient markets; (2) creating urban jobs through expanded demand may result in more people leaving rural areas; (3) employment may not rise with output because of factor price distortions or unsuit-

---

[6] World Bank, *World Tables, 1980* (Baltimore: Johns Hopkins University Press, 1980).

able technology; and (4) government may set unrealistically high wages for educated workers. On the other side of the coin, although contractionary fiscal policies may reduce Keynesian demand-pull inflation, they are not likely to reduce cost-push, ratchet, and structural inflation (discussed below).

Generally tax policy, as monetary policy, is a very limited tool for achieving income and price stability.

Improving Income Distribution

The progressive personal income tax takes a larger proportion of income from people in upper-income brackets and a smaller proportion from people in lower-income brackets. Thus income distribution after taxes is supposed to be less unequal than before taxes.

Excise taxes or high import tariffs on luxury items redistribute income from higher-income to lower-income groups. These taxes are especially attractive when the income would otherwise be spent on lavish living and luxury imports.

The broad-based **sales tax,** used widely by state and local governments in the United States, is usually **regressive,** in that people with lower incomes pay a larger percentage of income in taxes. This tax is usually levied as a fixed percentage of the price of retail sales. Since the poor save a smaller proportion of income than the rich, a LDC government wanting to use the tax system to reduce income inequality should not rely much on a general sales tax. However, the regressive feature of the sales tax can be modified by exempting basic consumer goods, such as food and medicine. But this modification is often opposed by treasury officials because it reduces revenues substantially.

Efficiency of Resource Allocation

One goal of a tax system is to encourage efficient use of resources or at least to minimize inefficiencies. Export taxes reduce the output of goods whose prices are determined on world markets. Such taxes shift resources from export to domestic production with a consequent loss of efficiency and foreign exchange earnings.[7]

Import duties raise the price of inputs and capital goods needed for agricultural and industrial exports and domestic goods. The price of locally produced goods requiring imported inputs increases, altering consumer choice.

An economy maximizes output and optimizes resource efficiency when price equals marginal cost. If government raises revenue from indirect taxes, price cannot equal marginal cost in all industries. However, indirect taxes can be levied at uniform rates on all final goods and exemptions and differential rates applied only to improve income distribution or encourage rapidly growing sectors. In this way, price will be proportional to marginal costs in all industries, and a minimum distortion of consumer choice will occur. Essentially a sales tax distorts efficiency least if it is broad based; that is, if it applies to the final sale of producer goods as well as to consumer goods and services.[8]

[7] John F. Due and Ann F. Friedlaender, *Government Finance: Economics of the Public Sector* (Homewood, Ill.: Irwin, 1981), p. 548.

[8] A uniform tax rate based on value added has a similar effect to the sales tax on resource allocation and tax incidence, but it is usually more difficult for LDC governments to administer effec-

Increasing Capital and Enterprise

The LDC governments can mobilize saving through direct taxes (on personal income, corporate profits, and property), taxes on luxury items, and sales taxes. These taxes result in a higher rate of capital formation if government has a higher investment rate than the people taxed. Moreover the state can use taxes and subsidies to redistribute output to sectors with high growth potential and to individuals with a high propensity to save (see Chapter 14).

The government can use tax policy to encourage domestic and foreign entrepreneurship. Tax revenues can be used for transport, power, and technical training to create external economies for private investment. Government development banks, development corporations, and loans boards can lend capital to private entrepreneurs. **Fiscal incentives** to attract business, especially from abroad, include tax holidays (for the first few years of operation), income averaging (where losses in one year can be offset against profits in another), accelerated depreciation, import duty relief, lower tax rates for reinvested business profits, and preferred purchases through government departments. The LDC governments may limit these incentives to enterprises and sectors that are high priority in their development plan.

Surveys suggest that fiscal incentives have, at best, only a slight effect on the amount of investment. Moreover subsidized investment may crowd out existing firms or firms that might have been willing to invest without subsidy. Using tax incentives successfully requires careful economic planning, skillfully structuring taxes, competent tax administration, quick decisions on applications, and no political favoritism.[9]

Is there a conflict between the redistributive effect of the progressive income tax and increased capital accumulation? As we indicated in Chapter 14, profits are a major source of new capital formation. Since for the successful business person, expansion takes precedence over the desire for higher consumption, taxes on profits affect consumption far more than saving. Nicholas Kaldor even argues that progressive taxation, by curbing luxury spending that distorts the investment pattern, may even stimulate capital accumulation. Before progressive taxation, too much capital is invested in industries catering to the rich. After taxation some investment shifts from luxury production to necessities.[10] Thus while there are conflicts between income redistribution and capital accumulation, they are probably less than is commonly believed in LDCs.

---

tively. Charles E. McLure, Jr., "The Proper Use of Indirect Taxation," in Richard M. Bird and Oliver Oldman, eds., *Readings on Taxation in Developing Countries* (Baltimore: Johns Hopkins University Press, 1975), pp. 339–49. See also John F. Due, "Value-Added Taxation in Developing Economies," in N. T. Wang, ed., *Taxation and Development* (New York: Praeger, 1976), pp. 164–86.

[9] S. M. S. Shah and J. F. J. Toye, "Fiscal Incentives for Firms in Some Developing Countries: Survey and Critique," in J. F. J. Toye, ed., *Taxation and Economic Development* (London: Frank Cass, 1978), pp. 269–96; and Walter W. Heller, "Fiscal Policies for Underdeveloped Countries," in Richard M. Bird and Oliver Oldman, eds., *Readings on Taxation in Developing Countries* (Baltimore: Johns Hopkins University Press, 1975), pp. 5–28.

[10] Nicholas Kaldor, "Will Underdeveloped Countries Learn to Tax?" in Richard M. Bird and Oliver Oldman, eds., *Readings on Taxation in Developing Countries* (Baltimore: Johns Hopkins University Press, 1975), p. 33.

Administrative Feasibility

Some developed countries use income taxes (especially the progressive personal tax) to mobilize large amounts of resources for public expenditures, improve income distribution, stabilize income and prices, and prevent inefficient allocation that comes from a heavy reliance on indirect taxes. However, few LDCs rely much on income taxes, because they have trouble administering them.

The following conditions must be met if income tax is to become a major revenue source for a country: (1) existence of a predominantly money economy, (2) a high standard of literacy among taxpayers, (3) widespread use of accounting records honestly and reliably maintained, (4) a large degree of voluntary taxpayer compliance, and (5) honest and efficient administration. Even DCs, to say nothing of LDCs, have trouble fulfilling these conditions.[11] Tanzania under President Julius K. Nyerere from 1974 to 1985, was probably the only African country that used its tax system to redistribute income to low-income classes.

Taxes on international trade are the major source of tax revenue in LDCs, especially for low-income countries with poor administrative capacity. Import duties can restrict luxury goods consumption, which reduces saving and drains foreign exchange.[12] However, government can exempt the import of capital goods and other inputs needed for the development process. Export taxes, on the other hand, can substitute for income taxes on (commercial) farmers, as, for example, in Ghana.

Exports and imports usually pass through a limited number of ports and border crossings. A relatively small administrative staff can measure volume and value and collect revenue. To be sure, traders may underinvoice goods or seek favors or concessions from customs officials. However, these problems are not so great as those encountered with an income, sales, or value-added tax.

The LDCs may be able to administer excise taxes if the number of producers is small. Rates are usually specific rather than percentage of value to simplify collection. The principal excises in LDCs, just as in DCs, are motor fuel (often for road finance), cigarettes, beer, and liquor. However, as the economy develops, introducing more excise taxes complicates administration and discriminates against consumers of taxed items.

The inadequacies of segmented excise taxes have led a number of developing countries to introduce sales taxes. In the poorest countries, using a retail tax is impossible. Enumerating, let alone collecting from, the numerous, very small, uneducated peddlers, traders, and shopkeepers is the major difficulty. Thus a number of African countries have levied a sales tax on manufacturers, where numbers are fewer and control is easier. But this tax discriminates between products, favors imports, and interferes with the allocation of functions by production stage. Other

---

[11] Richard Goode, "Personal Income Tax in Latin America," in Joint Tax Program, Organization of American States/Inter-American Development Bank/Economic Commission for Latin America, *Fiscal Policy for Economic Growth in Latin America* (Baltimore: Johns Hopkins University Press, 1962), pp. 157–71; and Vito Tanzi, "Personal Income Taxation in Latin America: Obstacles and Possibilities," *National Tax Journal* 19 (June 1966): 156–62.

[12] Note, however, some of the unintended side effects of a tax on luxury items (Chapter 14).

countries restrict the sales tax to large retail firms, which also introduces distortions and inequities.[13]

POLITICAL CONSTRAINTS TO TAX POLICY

Politics may be as obstructive as administration in using direct taxes in LDCs. Property owners and the upper classes often successfully oppose a progressive income tax or sizable property tax, introduce tax loopholes beneficial to them, or evade tax payments without penalty.

The United States has a reputation for less legal tax avoidance and illegal evasion than most of the third world. However, a Brookings Institution study indicates that even in the United States taxes as a percentage of income remain nearly constant for virtually all income levels because of tax loopholes and the effect of indirect taxes. Furthermore the U.S. Internal Revenue Service assumes that the average U.S. citizen is rather resistant to taxation. Tax evasion is low because of the high probability and serious consequences of being caught.[14]

Tax collection in an LDC depends not only on the appropriate tax legislation, but also, more importantly, on administrative capability and political will. A noted tax authority wrote in 1963 that

> In many underdeveloped countries the low revenue yield of taxation can only be attributed to the fact that the tax provisions are not properly enforced, either on account of the inability of the administration to cope with them, or on account of straightforward corruption. No system of tax laws, however carefully conceived, is proof against collusion between the tax administrators and the taxpayers; an efficient administration consisting of persons of high integrity is usually the most important requirement for obtaining maximum revenue, and exploiting fully the taxation potential of a country.[15]

EXPENDITURE POLICY

Many Afro-Asian leaders have been convinced that colonialism meant slow economic growth, largely as the result of laissez-faire capitalism (implying a minimum of government interference into the economy). These leaders focused populist and antiimperialist sentiments in these countries into an ideology of African or Asian socialism. This socialism, frequently misunderstood by outsiders, usually did not imply that government was to own a majority of land and capital. Nor did it mean that tax revenue was a large proportion of GNP. As we indicated earlier, Wagner's

[13] John F. Due and Ann F. Friedlaender, *Government Finance: Economics of the Public Sector* (Homewood, Ill.: Irwin, 1981), pp. 539–48.

[14] Joseph A. Pechman and Benjamin A. Okner, *Who Bears the Tax Burden?* (Washington, D.C.: Brookings Institution, 1974); and Vito Tanzi, "Personal Income Taxation in Latin America," in Richard M. Bird and Oliver Oldman, eds., *Readings On Taxation in Developing Countries: Obstacles and Possibilities* (Baltimore: Johns Hopkins University Press, 1975), pp. 234–36.

[15] Nicholas Kaldor, "Taxation for Economic Development," *Journal of Modern African Studies* 1 (May 1963): 23.

law of demand and administrative limits on tax collections restricted the social goods sector in most of these economies.

What socialism in the third world often does mean is systematic planning (see Chapter 19) by the state to assure a minimum economic welfare for all its citizens. Yet World Bank statistics indicate that LDC governments spend a relatively small percentage of GNP on health, welfare, social security, and housing (in low-income countries, the 1986 expenditures on these categories were 2 percent of GNP and 10 percent of the central government budget; in middle-income countries, 4 percent of GNP and 20 percent of the budget; and in high-income countries, 15 percent of GNP and 52 percent of the budget), and a relatively large share on education, electricity, gas, water, transport, communication, and training programs. Doubtless because in countries where a large part of the population is poor, welfare and social security payments to bring everyone above the poverty line would not only undermine work incentives but would also be prohibitively expensive (see Chapter 6). Moreover as we have said before, infrastructure and education are important investments creating external economies in early stages of development.[16]

Can government vary spending to regulate income, employment, and prices? Sound investment projects in education, power, transport, and communication are difficult to prepare and require a long lead time. Furthermore as indicated, macroeconomic variables are not so sensitive to demand management in LDCs as in DCs. Spending policy, just as monetary and tax policies, is a limited instrument for influencing economic growth and price stability.

INFLATION

Accelerated Inflation since 1970

Inflation is an increase in the general level of prices. During the 1950s and the 1960s, economists considered inflation as a phenomenon affecting individual countries in isolation. To be sure, inflation in Latin America was 22.5 percent per year from 1960 to 1970. But if we exclude the 41.1 percent annual inflation rate of the contiguous region of Brazil-Uruguay-Argentina-Chile, Latin America's annual rate for the decade was only 5.0 percent, comparable to that of Afro-Asia, that is, 6.1 percent (see Table 15-3). However, since 1970, LDC annual inflation has accelerated, increasing from 9 percent to 18 percent in the 1970s and 34 percent in the 1980s. Most of this increase came from rapid inflation in Latin America, 35 percent annually in the 1970s and 107 percent in the 1980s! The DC inflation rates, while increasing from 4 percent in the 1960s to 8 percent in the 1970s, fell to 5 percent in the 1980s.

Instability in the international economy since the early 1970s has exacerbated inflation. In 1971, the post-1945 Bretton Woods system of fixed exchange rates broke down. It was replaced by a floating exchange rate system, under which DCs experienced large swings in exchange rates. H. Johannes Witteveen, while president of the International Monetary Fund in 1975, argued that exchange fluctuations in an imperfectly competitive world exacerbated inflation by increasing prices in

---

[16] Richard A. Musgrave and Peggy B. Musgrave, *Public Finance in Theory and Practice* (New York: McGraw-Hill, 1980), p. 813.

TABLE 15-3   Inflation Rates in Developed and Developing Countries, 1960–89

	Average Annual Rate of Inflation[a] (percent)					
	1960–70		1970–79		1979–89	
Country groups						
Developed countries	4.3		8.1		5.0	
Developing countries[b]	8.9		18.1		34.3	
Latin America		22.5		34.8		106.8
Afro-Asia		6.1		10.2		9.8
High-income oil exporters	2.2		12.0		20.5	
Developing countries by region						
Latin America	22.5		34.8		106.8	
Brazil		46.1		28.0		157.1
Excluding Brazil		9.3		38.6		79.6
Africa	5.3		12.7		16.0	
Asia	6.4		9.5		8.1	
India		7.1		7.5		7.8
Excluding India		5.3		13.1		8.4
Middle East	2.5		11.6		13.6	

[a]GNP deflator.

[b]China not included.

Sources: World Bank, *World Development Report, 1981* (New York: Oxford University Press, 1981), pp. 134–35, 181; World Bank, *World Development Report, 1988* (New York: Oxford University Press, 1988), pp. 222–23; and International Monetary Fund, *World Economic Outlook* (Washington, D.C., October 1988), p. 67.

countries with a depreciating currency, but not decreasing prices in countries with an appreciating currency. Poor world harvests in 1972 to 1973 increased food prices, wage rates, and cost-push inflation substantially in 1972 to 1974. Higher oil prices also pushed up costs and prices, especially in industry and power, in 1973 to 1975. Worldwide inflation remained high between 1975 and 1978, a period when, according to a Brookings Institution study, the effect of oil prices was not important. Inflation in the DCs radiated out to the LDCs through trade links.[17] Yet from 1978 through the end of the 1980s (as in the 1960s), inflation rates varied too widely among LDCs (note the differences between Latin America and Afro-Asia in Table 15-3) to attribute to a common cause. We cannot blame Paraguay's rapid inflation in the early 1950s; Brazil's, Uruguay's, Chile's, and Bolivia's in the decade before 1974; or Brazil's, Argentina's Peru's, Bolivia's, and Israel's inflations in the 1980s at more than 100 percent yearly, on international instability. Let us examine several causes in the following sections.

[17]United Nations, Department of International Economic and Social Affairs, *World Economic Survey, 1980–1981* (New York, 1981), pp. 37–39; H. Johannes Witteveen, "Inflation and the International Monetary System," *American Economic Review* 65 (May 1975): 108–14; and William R. Cline and Associates, *World Inflation and the Developing Countries* (Washington, D.C.: Brookings Institution, 1981).

Demand-pull Inflation

The next six sections consider the (1) demand-pull, (2) cost-push, (3) ratchet, (4) structural, (5) expectational, and (6) political explanations for inflation, and what government can do to reduce them.

Demand-pull inflation results from consumer, business, and government demand for goods and services in excess of an economy's capacity to produce. The International Monetary Fund, when financing the international payments deficit for a rapidly inflating LDC, requires contractionary monetary and fiscal policies—reduced government spending, increased taxes, a decreased money supply, and a higher interest rate—to curb demand. Sometimes these demand restrictions do not moderate inflation. The LDC government may have to decrease substantially the employment rate and real growth to reduce the inflation rate. As a result, many LDC economists question the importance of demand-pull inflation and look for other causes of inflation.

Cost-push Inflation

The presence of cost-push and structural (supply-side) inflationary pressures may explain why a contraction in demand may cause unemployment and recession rather than reduce inflation. **Cost-push inflation** means prices increase even when demand drops or remains constant, because of higher costs in imperfectly competitive markets.

Labor unions may force up wages although there is excess labor supply—particularly by applying political pressure on government, the major employer and wage-setter in the modern sector. Higher food prices may also come into play, as during the poor worldwide harvests in 1972 to 1973. If food costs more, workers may press for higher wages.

Similarly large businesses may increase prices in response to increased wage and other costs, even though demand for their products does not increase. Because of labor's and business's market power, economists sometimes label cost-push inflation "administered price" or "seller's" inflation.

Economists may blame rising costs from demand pull on cost push. Increased aggregate demand for finished goods and services expands business's derived demand for raw materials and labor. When their short-run supply is inelastic, costs go up before finished-good prices rise. Despite appearances, here excess demand, not cost, is inflation's cause.[18]

Ratchet Inflation

A ratchet wrench only goes forward, not backward. Analogously prices may rise, but not go down. Assume aggregate demand remains constant but demand increases in the first sector and decreases in the second. With **ratchet inflation,** prices rise in the first sector, remain the same in the second, and increase overall.

The LDC governments could use antimonopoly measures and wage and price controls to moderate cost-push and ratchet inflationary pressures. Yet they may lack the political and administrative strength to attack monopolies and restrain

---

[18]Maxwell J. Fry, *Money, Interest, and Banking in Economic Development* (Baltimore: Johns Hopkins University Press, 1988), pp. 330–31.

wages. Several LDCs have instituted price controls but usually with mixed results. Price controls should be limited to highly imperfect markets, rather than competitive markets, where these controls cause shortages, long lines, and black markets. In addition some business firms circumvent price controls by reducing quality, service, or in some instances, quantity (for example, the number of nuts in a candy bar). Most LDC governments lack the administrative machinery and research capability to obtain the essential data, undertake the appropriate analysis, change price ceilings in response to movements in supply and demand in thousands of markets, and enforce controls.

Structural Inflation: The Case of Latin America

Some Latin American economists argue that structural rigidities, not demand-pull, cost-push, or ratchet inflation, cause rapid inflation in Latin America. Structural factors include the slow and unstable growth of foreign currency earnings (from exports) and the inelastic supply of agricultural goods. A price rise from these factors is termed **structural inflation.**

Sluggish growth in foreign exchange earnings relative to import demand occurs because a disproportional share of exports in Latin America are primary products (food, raw materials, minerals, and organic oils and fats) other than fuels (see Chapter 4). The slow growth in demand for these primary exports decreases the country's terms of trade, that is, the ratio of its export prices to its import prices. Government restricts imports to adjust to foreign exchange shortages. Import demand, which grows with national income, exceeds import supply, and inflation sets in. Even expanding the supply of **import substitutes** (domestic production replacing imports) increases prices and input costs above import prices. The slow growth of export income necessitates frequent exchange-rate devaluation, which increases import prices. In addition export sluggishness keeps export tax revenues down, reducing government saving and further increasing inflation.

Food output is especially unresponsive to price rises—a second structural rigidity in LDC economies. This supply inelasticity is largely due to defective land tenure patterns, such as concentrated land ownership, poor production incentives, and insecure tenancy.

All of these factors—deterioration in terms of trade, cost of import substitution, devaluation, and rise in agricultural prices—initiate cost-push inflation. Structuralists contend that contractionary monetary and fiscal policies, such as those advised by the International Monetary Fund, depress the economy and exacerbate political discontent without going to the heart of the problem, the need for fundamental structural change—land reform, expanding the industrial sector, antimonopoly measures, and improved income distribution.[19]

Critics of the structuralists argue that the pressure on food supplies is not peculiar to Latin America. In fact the United Nations and the U.S. Department of Agriculture indicate both total and per capita food production grew about as rap-

---

[19] Much of the analysis of structural inflation in this section borrows from Roberto de Oliveira Campos, "Economic Development and Inflation with Special Reference to Latin America," in Organization for Economic Cooperation and Development, *Development Plans and Programmes* (Paris: OECD Development Center, 1964), pp. 129–37, reprinted in Gerald M. Meier, *Leading Issues in Economic Development* (New York: Oxford University Press, 1984), pp. 268–73.

idly in Latin America in the 1970s and 1980s as in any other region of the developing world.[20]

In addition Latin American export growth has not been sluggish. From 1970 to 1989, the real value of exports from Latin America grew 1.6 percent annually, its terms of trade increased slightly, and the real purchasing power of export earnings increased 8.3 percent yearly.[21]

Moreover when export growth is sluggish, the cause is not structural but an overvalued domestic currency relative to foreign exchange. Assume the market-clearing exchange rate is 50 pesos per dollar and the actual exchange rate 25 pesos per dollar. The farmer selling $1000 worth of sugar cane on the world market receives only 25,000 pesos at the existing exchange rate rather than 50,000 pesos at an equilibrium rate. Devaluing the domestic currency to reflect the market exchange rate would spur farmers and other producers to export.

All in all, cost-push inflation generated by import substitution, decline in the terms of trade, and inelastic agricultural supplies are of limited use in explaining the chronic high rates of inflation found in many Latin American countries.

Expectational Inflation

Inflation gains momentum once workers, consumers, and business people expect it to continue. **Inflationary expectations** encourage workers to demand higher wage increases. Business managers expecting continued inflation grant workers' demands, pass cost increases on to consumers, buy materials and equipment now rather than later, and pay higher interest rates because they expect to raise their prices. Lenders demand higher interest rates because they expect their money to be worth less when the loan is repaid, after prices have risen. Consumers purchase durable goods in anticipation of higher future prices. Thus once started, inflation continues because people expect it to continue.[22]

A major justification for wage-price controls is to break the vicious circle of inflationary expectations among workers, consumers, and business people. But as noted earlier, few LDC wage-price controls are effective, and people may view any success controls have as an aberration rather than as a basis for changing long-run expectations.

Political Inflation

Some Chileans explain their chronic hyperinflation as "a 'struggle' or even 'civil war' between the country's major economic interest groups." Albert O. Hirschman contends that in Latin America, inflation, as civil war, can be caused by "a group

---

[20] Figure 7-2, and United Nations, Department of International Economic and Social Affairs, *World Economic Survey, 1980–1981* (New York, 1981), p. 28.

[21] Computed from International Monetary Fund, *World Economic Outlook* (Washington, D.C.: October 1988), pp. 59–137. See also William R. Cline and Associates, *World Inflation and the Developing Countries* (Washington, D.C.: Brookings Institution, 1981). See also the discussion of the long-run terms of trade in Chapter 17.

[22] William J. Baumol and Alan S. Blinder, *Economics—Principles and Policy* (New York: Harcourt Brace Jovanovich, 1982), pp. 328–91; Daniel R. Fusfeld, *Economics* (Lexington, Mass.: Heath, 1976), p. 332; and Robert L. Heilbroner and James K. Galbraith, *The Economic Problem* (Englewood Cliffs, N.J.: Prentice Hall, 1987), pp. 404-05, 480-81.

which wrongly believes that it can get away with 'grabbing' a larger share of the national product than it has so far received." When communication between economic groups is poor, one or more classes may overestimate its strength and make excessive money demands that can be worked out only through inflation. Such a process may reduce tension that may otherwise result in revolution or war. Many LDC ministers of labor have averted a political strike by granting inflationary wage increases.[23]

Social tensions and class antagonisms causing this **political inflation** are too deep seated to be cleared up by short-run government policies. In fact the political threat of the conflict may be so great that the government may have little choice but to tolerate persistent inflation.

Benefits of Inflation

Inflation need not be all bad. In fact would we not welcome inflation if it contributed to economic growth and higher material well-being? As a matter of fact, Robert A. Mundell's monetarist model indicates that rapid inflation may add 1 percentage point to annual, real economic growth by spurring extra capital formation.[24]

Some economists argue that inflation can promote economic development in the following ways.

1. The treasury prints money or the banking system expands credit so that a modernizing government can raise funds in excess of tax revenues. Even if real resources remain constant, inflationary financing allows government to control a larger resource share by bidding resources away from low-priority uses.
2. Government can use inflationary credit to redistribute income from wage earners who save little to capitalists with high rates of productive capital formation. Business people usually benefit from inflation, since product prices tend to rise faster than resource prices. For example, wages may not keep up with inflation, especially in its early stages when price increases are greater than anticipated. Furthermore inflation reduces the real interest rate and real debt burden for expanding business.
3. Inflationary pressure pushes an economy toward full employment and more fully utilizes labor and other resources. Rising wages and prices reallocate resources from traditional sectors to rapidly growing sectors.

Costs of Inflation

Yet inflation can be highly problematical.

1. Government redistribution from high consumers to high savers through inflationary financing may work during only the early inflationary stages. When

---

[23] Albert O. Hirschman, *Journeys toward Progress: Studies of Economic Policy-Making in Latin America* (New York: Twentieth Century Fund, 1963), pp. 192–223.

[24] Robert A. Mundell, "Growth, Stability, and Inflationary Finance," *Journal of Political Economy* 73 (April 1965): 97–109.

people expect continued inflation, they find ways of protecting themselves against it. Wage demands, automatic cost-of-living adjustments, for example, reflect inflationary expectations. Retirees and pensioners pressure government to increase benefits to keep up with inflation. Government may respond to other political interests to control increases in the prices of food, rents, urban transport, and so forth. Official price ceilings inevitably distort resource allocation, frequently resulting in shortages, black markets, and corruption.

2. Inflation imposes a tax on the holders of money. Government or business people benefiting from inflationary financing collect the real resources from the **inflation tax.** To restore the real value of their money, people must accumulate additional balances at a rate equal to inflation. People attempt to evade the tax by holding onto goods rather than money.

3. Inflation distorts business behavior, especially investment behavior, since any rational calculation of profits is undermined. Entrepreneurs do not risk investing in basic industries with a long payoff period but rather in capital gains assets (for example, luxury housing) as a protection against inflation. Business people waste much effort forecasting and speculating on the inflation rate, or in hedging against the uncertainties involved.[25]

4. Inflation, especially if it is discontinuous and uneven, weakens the creation of credit and capital markets. Uncertainties about future price increases may damage the development of savings banks, community savings societies, bond markets, social security, pension funds, insurance funds, and government debt instruments. For example, Brazil's annual growth rate in GNP per capita declined from 11 percent in 1968 to 1973 to 5 percent in 1973 to 1979, partly from the adverse impact of inflation on savings. Nominal interest rates remained almost constant while annual inflation accelerated from 13 percent in 1973 to 44 percent in 1977. Because of the resulting negative *real* interest rates, savings were reduced and diverted from productive investment.[26]

5. Monetary and fiscal instruments in LDCs are usually too weak to slow inflation without sacrificing real income, employment, and social welfare programs.

6. Income distribution is usually less uniform during inflationary times. Inflation redistributes income, at least in the early stages, from low-income workers and those on fixed income to high-income classes. This redistribution may not increase saving, since the rich may buy luxury items with their increased incomes. A study of seven LDCs (including Brazil, Uruguay, Argentina, and Chile) by the Organization for Economic Cooperation and Development concluded that "there is no evidence anywhere of inflation having increased the flow of saving."[27]

[25] Harry G. Johnson, "Is Inflation the Inevitable Price of Rapid Development or a Retarding Factor in Economic Growth?" *Malayan Economic Review* 11 (April 1965): 22–28, reprinted in Gerald M. Meier, *Leading Issues in Economic Development* (New York: Oxford University Press, 1976), pp. 311–15.

[26] World Bank, *World Development Report, 1981* (New York: Oxford University Press, 1981); and William R. Cline, "Brazil's Aggressive Response to External Shocks," in Cline and Associates, *World Inflation*, pp. 102–35.

[27] Ian Little, Tibor Scitovsky, and Maurice Scott, *Industry and Trade in Some Developing Countries: A Comparative Study* (London: Oxford University Press, 1970), p. 77.

7. Inflation increases the prices of domestic goods relative to foreign goods—decreasing the competitiveness of domestic goods internationally and usually reducing the **international balance of merchandise trade** (exports minus imports of goods). Inflation also discourages the inflow of foreign capital, since the real value of investment and of future repatriated earnings erodes. The large international deficits that often come with rapid inflation can increase debt burdens and limit essential imports.

With inflation in excess of 30 percent a year in the mid-to-late 1970s, Brazil depreciated the cruzeiro relative to the U.S. dollar at a steady, predictable rate to keep domestic prices competitive. However, devaluation stimulated inflation through the increased demand for Brazilian goods and cost-push pressures from higher import prices. Furthermore Brazilian inflation was too erratic for steady exchange-rate changes to prevent fluctuations in real export and import prices. Yet most LDCs are not even so capable as Brazil in managing monetary, fiscal, and exchange-rate policies to limit the evils of inflation.

Inflation and Growth: Empirical Evidence

As indicated above, Mundell's monetarist model suggests that inflation can increase real economic growth. However, the empirical evidence is mixed, depending on the time period, country group, and range of inflation examined. Opposing Mundell's work, Henry C. Wallich's study of forty three countries from 1956 to 1965, finds a negative relationship between inflation and real economic growth. A. P. Thirlwall's and C. A. Barton's review of fifty one countries from 1958 to 1965 finds no significant correlation between inflation and growth. But U Tun Wai's study of thirty one LDCs from 1946 to 1954, and Graeme S. Dorrance's research on forty nine DCs and LDCs from 1953 to 1961, indicate a positive relationship between the two variables.[28]

However, Thirlwall, Barton, Tun Wai, and Dorrance find that among LDCs, growth declines when annual inflation exceeds 10 percent. We might expect that Latin American inflation (and LDC inflation generally in the 1970s), which increased at an annual rate greater than 10 percent, would be either negatively related or unrelated to growth. Figures 15-1 and 15-2, presenting data for 1960 to 1979, indicate no relationship between inflation and growth in either Afro-Asia or Latin America. Although there is not enough evidence for a strong statement, it appears that inflation in LDCs in the 1960s and 1970s has *not* contributed to economic growth.[29]

[28] Henry C. Wallich, "Money and Growth: A Country Cross-Section Analysis," *Journal of Money, Credit, and Banking* 1 (May 1969): 281–302; A. P. Thirlwall and C. A. Barton, "Inflation and Growth: The International Evidence," *Banca Nazionale del Lavoro Quarterly Review* no. 99 (September 1971): 263–75; U Tun Wai, "The Relation between Inflation and Economic Development: A Statistical Inductive Study," *International Monetary Fund Staff Papers* 7 (October 1959): 302–17; and Graeme S. Dorrance, "Inflation and Growth: The Statistical Evidence," *International Monetary Fund Staff Papers*, 13 (March 1966): 82–102.

[29] Jeffrey R. Nugent and Constantine Glezakos, "Phillips Curves in Developing Countries," *Economic Development and Cultural Change* 30 (January 1982): 321–34.

Could the causal relationship lead from growth to inflation rather than the other way around? Thirlwall and Barton argue that "if growth is a supply phenomenon, higher growth should lower

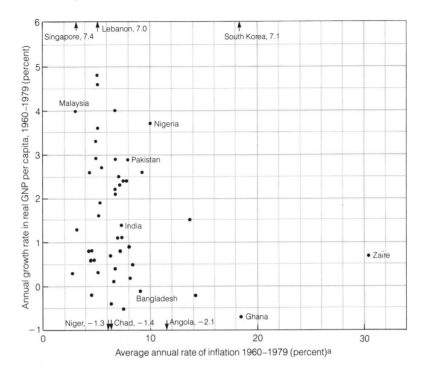

FIGURE 15-1   Growth and Inflation in Afro-Asia   Growth rates are not related to inflation rates in Afro-Asia.

*a*Measured by the implicit gross domestic price deflator.

Source: World Bank, *World Development Report, 1981* (New York: Oxford University Press, 1981), pp. 134–35.

FINANCIAL REPRESSION AND LIBERALIZATION

The LDC money markets tend to be highly oligopolistic even when dominated by domestic banks and lenders. Government **financial repression**—distortions of the interest rates, foreign exchange rates (Chapter 18), and other financial prices— reduce the relative size of the financial system and the real rate of growth. Frequently the motive for LDC financial restriction is to encourage financial institutions and instruments from which the government can expropriate **seigniorage** (or claim resources in return for controlling currency issue and credit expansion).

---

inflation not exacerbate it. Real growth by itself cannot be the cause of inflation unless it sets in motion forces which themselves generate rising prices and persist"—such as shortages in the produce and factor markets. Attempts to expand demand in excess of the growth rate of productive potential can cause inflation, but it is a non sequitur to argue from this that real growth causes inflation. A. P. Thirlwall and C. A. Barton, "Inflation and Growth: The International Evidence," *Banca Nazionale del Lavoro Quarterly Review* no. 99 (September 1971): 269–70.

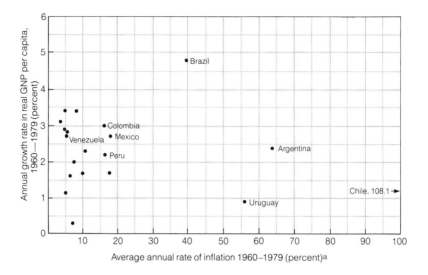

FIGURE 15-2   Growth and Inflation in Latin America   Growth rates are not related to inflation rates in Latin America.

*a*Measured by the implicit gross domestic price deflator.

Source: World Bank, *World Development Report, 1981* (New York: Oxford University Press, 1981), pp. 134–35.

Government favors and protects an oligopolistic banking system whose reserve requirements and obligatory holdings of government bonds enable the state to tap savings at zero or low interest rates. Authorities suppress private bond and equity markets through transactions taxes, special taxes on income from capital, and inconducive laws because of the difficulty of extracting seigniorage from private assets. The state imposes interest rate ceilings to stifle private sector competition in fund raising. Imposing these ceilings, foreign exchange controls, high reserve requirements, and restrictions on private capital markets increases the flow of domestic resources to the public sector without higher taxes, inflation, or interest rates. Banks engage in nonprice rationing of loans, facing pressure for loans to those with political connections but otherwise allocate credit according to transaction costs, all of which leave no opportunity for charging a premium for risky (and sometimes innovative) projects. Overall these policies also encourage capital-intensive projects (Chapter 10) and discourage capital investment. The LDC financially repressive regimes, uncompetitive markets, and banking bureaucracies not disciplined by market and profit tests may encourage adopting inefficient lending criteria. The high arrears, delinquency, and default of many LDC (especially official) banks and development lending institutions result from (1) failure to tie lending to productive investment, (2) neglect of marketing, (3) delayed loan disbursement and unrealistic repayment schedules, (4) misapplication of loans, (5) ineffective supervision, (6) apathy of bank management in recovering loans, and (7) irresponsible and undisciplined borrowers, including many who (for cultural reasons or misunderstanding government's role) fail to distinguish loans from grants. Additionally Argentina's,

Brazil's, Chile's, Uruguay's, Mexico's, Turkey's, Thailand's, and pre–World War II Japan's bank-lending policies have suffered from collusion between major corporations and banks.

Combatting financial repression, which is as much political as it is economic, can reduce inflation. Financial liberalization necessitates abolishing ceilings on interest rates (or at least raising them to competitive levels), introducing market incentives for bank managers, encouraging private stock and bond markets, and lowering reserve requirements. At higher (market-clearing) interest rates, banks make more credit available, increasing the economy's capacity and relieving inflationary pressures. Trade liberalization, which threatens (often) politically influential import-competing industrialists, increases product competition and reduces import prices (see Chapter 18), reducing input prices and cost-push inflation.[30]

ISLAMIC BANKING

While Islam, like early medieval Christianity, interprets its scriptures to ban interest, it encourages profit as a return to entrepreneurship together with financial capital. Moreover like Western banks, Islamic banks are financial intermediaries between savers and investors and administer the economy's payment system. Bank depositors are treated as if they were shareholders of the bank. Islamic banks receive returns through markup pricing (for example, buying a house, then reselling it at a higher price to the borrower and requiring the borrower to repay over 25 years) or profit-sharing, interest-free deposits (mutual-fund-type packages for sale to investor-depositors). These banks operate alongside traditional banks in such countries as Malaysia, but in Ayatollah Ruhollah Khomeini's Iran (1979–89) and Mohammad Zia ul-Haq's Pakistan (1985–88), the government eliminated interest-based transactions from the banking system. Interest-free banking can improve efficiency, since profit shares are free from interest rate controls. Indeed World Bank and International Monetary Fund economist Mohsin S. Khan argues that Islamic banking, with its equity participation, is more stable than Western banking, since shocks are absorbed by changes in the values of deposits held by the public. However, profit-sharing is problematic where businesses use double bookkeeping for tax evasion, making their profits difficult for banks to determine.[31]

---

[30] Maxwell J. Fry, *Money, Interest, and Banking in Economic Development* (Baltimore: Johns Hopkins University Press, 1988), pp. 7–18, 261–335; Ronald I. McKinnon, *Money and Capital in Economic Development* (Washington, D.C.: Brookings Institution, 1973); Edward S. Shaw, *Financial Deepening in Economic Development* (New York: Oxford University Press, 1973); Mario I. Blejer, "Liberalization and Stabilization Policies in the Southern-Cone Countries: An Introduction," *Journal of Interamerican Studies and World Affairs* 25 (November 1983): 441; Felipe Morris, "India's Financial System: An Overview of Its Principal Structural Features," Washington, World Bank Staff Working Paper no. 739, 1985, p. 21; David Gill, "Securities Market Structural Issues and Challenges," paper prepared for the annual meeting of the International Federation of Stock Exchanges, Toronto, September 12–14, 1983; and Yoon Je Cho, "The Effect of Financial Liberalization on the Efficiency of Credit Allocation: Some Evidence from Korea," *Journal of Development Economics* 29 (July 1988): 101-10.

[31] Maxwell J. Fry, *Money, Interest, and Banking in Economic Development* (Baltimore: Johns Hopkins University Press, 1988), p. 266; Zubair Iqbal and Abbas Mirakhor, "Islamic Banking," Washington, D.C., International Monetary Fund Occasional Paper 49, March 1987; and Mohsin S. Khan, "Islamic Interest-Free Banking," *International Monetary Fund Staff Papers* 33 (March 1986): 1–27.

SUMMARY

1. Central banks in LDCs generally have less effect on expenditure and output than in DCs because of an externally dependent banking system, a poorly developed securities market, the limited scope of bank loans, the low percentage of demand deposits divided by the total money supply, and the relative insensitivity of investment and employment to monetary policies.

2. Tax revenue as a percentage of GNP in LDCs is about 18 percent compared to 38 percent in DCs.

3. The increase in tax ratios with GNP per capita reflects both the growth in the demand for public services and the capacity to levy and pay taxes.

4. Direct taxes (such as taxes on property, wealth, inheritance, and income) account for about one-third of revenue sources in LDCs and about two-thirds in DCs. Major indirect taxes in most LDCs are those on international trade, production, and internal transactions, which, however, distort resource allocation. Direct taxes generally have a higher elasticity (that is, percentage change in taxation/percentage change in GNP) than indirect taxes.

5. Some DCs use the progressive income tax to mobilize large amounts of public resources, improve income distribution, stabilize income and prices, and prevent inefficient use of resources, often arising from a heavy reliance on indirect taxes. However, import, export, and excise taxes are the major sources of tax revenue in LDCs. Most LDCs lack the administrative capacity to emphasize an income tax.

6. Developing countries cannot use fiscal policy to stabilize income and prices so effectively as developed countries can. The LDC governments have less control over the amount of taxes raised and less scope for speeding up or delaying expenditures.

7. A relatively small percentage of government spending in LDCs is on health, social security, and welfare, and a relatively high percentage on education and infrastructure.

8. Instability in the international economy, including poor world harvests and oil price rises, increased the annual inflation rate in LDCs from less than 10 percent in the 1960s to over 10 percent in the 1970s and early 1980s.

9. Demand-pull is not an adequate explanation for inflation in LDCs. Inflation may be cost push (from the market power of businesses and unions), ratchet (from rigid prices downward), or structural (slow export growth and inelastic food supply), with added momentum, once started, from inflationary expectations. Policies to moderate inflation include market-clearing exchange rates, wage-price controls, antimonopoly measures, land reform, structural change from agriculture to industry, and improved income distribution. With the possible exception of exchange-rate policy, most LDCs lack the administrative and political strength to undertake these policies, especially in the immediate future.

10. Some economists argue that inflation can promote economic growth by redistributing income from low savers to high savers. However, inflation distorts resource allocation, weakens capital markets, imposes a tax on money holders, undermines rational business behavior, increases income inequality, hurts

the balance of trade and, beyond the early stages of inflation, probably does not redistribute income to high savers.

11. There is not enough evidence to support the hypothesis that inflation contributes to economic growth.

12. The LDC money markets are often highly oligopolistic and financially repressive, distorting interest rates, foreign exchange rates, and other financial prices. Government protects oligopolistic banks to be able to tap savings at low interest rates. If political elites have the will to undertake financial liberalization, they can reduce inflation and spur growth.

13. An Islamic economic system prohibits interest as a part of a political system that emphasizes equitable income and wealth distribution. Islam forbids only a fixed or predetermined return on financial transactions, not uncertain returns, such as profits, which are encouraged. In Islamic banks in Pakistan, Iran, and Malaysia, bank depositors are treated as if they were shareholders of the bank.

TERMS TO REVIEW

- **monetary policy**
- **fiscal policy**
- **stagflation**
- **Wagner's law**
- **elastic tax**
- **direct taxes**
- **indirect taxes**
- **progressive tax**
- **regressive tax**
- **sales tax**

- **fiscal incentives**
- **inflation**
- **demand-pull inflation**
- **cost-push inflation**
- **ratchet inflation**
- **structural inflation**
- **inflationary expectations**
- **political inflation**

- **inflation tax**
- **import substitutes**
- **international balance of merchandise trade**
- **financial repression**
- **seigniorage**
- **social goods**

QUESTIONS TO DISCUSS

1. What prevents LDC use of monetary and fiscal policies from attaining goals of output and employment growth, and price stability?

2. Why are taxes as a percentage of GNP generally lower for LDCs than for DCs?

3. What obstacles do LDCs encounter in reaching their tax policy goals?

4. Why are direct taxes as a percentage of GNP generally lower, and indirect taxes as a percentage of GNP, generally higher, for LDCs than DCs? Why is heavy reliance on indirect taxes as sources of revenue often disadvantageous to LDCs?

5. What tax measures can LDCs take to reduce income inequality? To increase capital and enterprise?

6. What, if any, is the tradeoff between tax policies that reduce income and wealth concentration and those that increase capital formation?

7. Why is health, social security, and welfare spending as a percentage of GNP less in LDCs than DCs? Why is health, social security, and welfare spending as a percentage of total government spending less in LDCs than DCs?

8. Why did the LDC inflation rate increase from the 1960s to the 1980s?

9. How do you expect inflation in the 1990s to compare to that of the 1980s?

10. What causes LDC inflation? Which causes are most important? How might LDCs reduce inflation?

11. Why was inflation so rapid in Latin America in the 1960s, 1970s, and 1980s?

12. In what way might inflation avert civil war or political violence?

13. What are the costs and benefits of inflation? Which are greater for LDCs, costs or benefits?

14. What is the empirical relationship between inflation and growth?

15. Explain the political and economic reasons for frequent LDC government financial repression and the effects it has on economic development. Indicate policies for LDC financial liberalization and ways in which they could affect inflation and real growth.

GUIDE TO READINGS

Tun Wai (note 1) discusses the limitations of monetary policy in LDCs. Due and Friedlaender (note 7) have an excellent chapter on public finance in LDCs. Fry (note 30); Newbery and Stern (note 3); Bird and Oldham (note 8); Stephen R. Lewis, Jr., *Taxation for Development: Principles and Applications* (New York: Oxford University Press, 1984); and Eprime Eshag, *Fiscal and Monetary Policies and Problems in Developing Countries* (Cambridge: Cambridge University Press, 1983), are excellent general works on LDC monetary and fiscal policies. Tanzi; Perry; Tait, Gratz, and Eichengreen; Chelliah, Baas, and Kelly (note 3); and the World Bank (note to Table 15-1) discuss tax rate figures in DCs and LDCs. Shah and Toye (note 9) analyze fiscal incentives to increase capital and enterprise in developing countries. World Bank, *World Development Report, 1989*, discusses LDC financial systems.

Recent information on inflation is available from the World Bank's annual *World Development Report;* the International Monetary Fund's annual *World Economic Outlook;* and the UN's annual *World Economic Survey* (note 17).

Campos (note 19) analyzes the controversy between monetarists and structuralists concerning Latin American inflation. *World Development* 15 (August 1987) devotes a special issue to inflation in Latin America. Eliana A. Cardoso analyzes "Hyperinflation in Latin America," in *Challenge* 32 (January/February 1989): 11–19.

Johnson (note 25) has a systematic discussion of arguments for and against inflation. A. P. Thirlwall, *Growth and Development with Special Reference to Developing Countries* (New York: Wiley, 1977), pp. 283–87, summarizes evidence on the relationship between inflation and economic growth.

Fry, McKinnon, Shaw, and Blejer (note 30) analyze financial repression and liberalization and their impacts on development.

Khan, and Iqbal and Mirakhor (note 31) have thorough discussions of Islamic banking.

Chapter Sixteen

BALANCE OF PAYMENTS, AID, AND FOREIGN INVESTMENT

DEMAND FOR A NEW INTERNATIONAL ECONOMIC ORDER

The demand by developing countries for a new international economic order was in response to dissatisfaction with their record during the UN's first development decade, from 1960 to 1970, when these countries and international agencies emphasized internal economic policies. Their call for a new order intensified in the mid-1970s, when their modest gains from previous years were threatened by world wide inflation, a fourfold increase in oil prices in 1973 to 1974, and the subsequent deterioration in LDC foreign exchange and debt position. Leaders of developing countries increasingly attributed LDC underdevelopment to a weak position in the international economic system.

The UN General Assembly's sixth and seventh special sessions (1974–75) adopted a declaration on principles and programs for a change in the international economic order. This order comprises all economic relations and institutions linking people from different nations, including the World Bank and the UN Development Program that lend capital to LDCs; the **International Monetary Fund (IMF),** which provides credit to ease short-term international payments imbalances; the **General Agreements on Tariffs and Trade,** which administers rules of conduct in international trade; bilateral and multilateral trade, aid, banking services, currency rates, capital movements, and technological transfers; capitalist and socialist aid consortiums; and international commodity stabilization agreements. Third-world countries want more policy influence in international institutions, more control over international economic relations, and a restructured world order that emphasizes their needs.

One of their aims is to be less dependent on rich countries. The UN declaration proclaims that every state has permanent sovereignty over its natural resources and economic activities. Furthermore each state is entitled to control its natural resources and their exploitation, "including the right to nationalization or transfer of ownership to its nationals." Although OPEC achieved full local ownership and a price-setting producer cartel that raised prices and revenues substantially in the mid to late 1970s, the cartel's effectiveness broke down due to several members' lack of discipline in the 1980s (violating the agreement, ignoring quotas, and undercutting prices) and the expansion of non-OPEC oil exploration and energy substitutes. No other raw material producers' group has been able to achieve even the temporary success that OPEC did in controlling its resources and setting prices.

In 1974, when the UN General Assembly declared principles for the new order, it also adopted a plan of action. Clearly the UN ratification implies only vague intentions, not the plan's implementation, which required discussions and painstaking negotiations in a number of international forums. But progress on specific measures during the 1970s and 1980s was limited due to LDC division and much DC opposition. At the end of Chapter 18, following our discussion of foreign aid and investment, the debt crisis, and international trade policy in Chapters 16–18, we will return to a more detailed discussion of what changes LDCs want in the international economic order and what progress they have made.

SCOPE OF THE CHAPTER

This chapter discusses international aid and investment. We look first at DC–LDC economic interdependence. The second section discusses capital inflows, and the third, their roles in reducing savings and foreign exchange gaps. The fourth section reviews the balance of payments. Finally the last section analyzes how to finance the deficit.

NORTH–SOUTH INTERDEPENDENCE

The countries of the North (DCs) and the South (third world) are economically interdependent. Even the United States, which has the lowest *ratio of international trade to GNP* among the capitalist and mixed DCs, depended more on the third world in the late 1980s than in the early 1970s, despite some reduction in dependency in the 1980s. The U.S. merchandise imports as a percentage of GNP, which increased from 6 percent in 1970 to 12 percent in 1980, fell to 9 percent in 1987. However, U.S. exports to third-world countries (LDCs and high-income oil exporters) as a percentage of the total increased from 31 percent in 1970 to 38 percent in 1975 to 41 percent in 1981 before dropping to 34 percent in 1986, as U.S. capital, automotive, electronic, and consumer goods became less competitive abroad with competition from Japan, Western Europe, and such NICs as Taiwan, South Korea, Hong Kong, and Singapore. The U.S. imports from the third world increased from 25 percent in 1970 to 42 percent in 1975 (soon after the 1973–74 great oil price hike) to 46 percent in 1981 before declining to 34 percent in 1986, as oil prices fell and the

United States became more competitive with dollar depreciation. Although the *share* of U.S. *trade with the third world* was slightly less than Japan's, it was more than the European Community, Canada, Australia, or New Zealand.

In 1986, 31 percent of U.S. petroleum consumption was imported, of which 90 percent was from the third world. In about the same year, imports from the third world as a percentage of total consumption were high for a number of vital minerals—100 percent for strontium, 83 percent of columbium, 88 percent for natural graphite, 86 percent for bauxite and alumina, 80 percent for maganese ore, 74 percent for tin, 62 percent for flourspar, 58 percent for barite, 57 percent for diamonds, and 51 percent for cobalt.[1]

In 1980, an independent commission, consisting of twenty diplomats from five continents chaired by former West German Chancellor Willy Brandt, stressed that interdependence created a mutual interest by both North and South in reforming the world economic order. However in the 1980s, LDC government remained dissatisfied with the lack of progress made by North–South conferences in reshaping old international economic institutions (or setting up new ones) to implement the Brandt Commission recommendations or the UN General Assembly's call for a new international economic order in the mid–1970s (see Chapter 18). Among northern governments, the United States, still the world's major trader, banker, investor, and aid-giver, despite a relative decline in international economic power from the late 1940s to the 1990s, was the most vocal in arguing that major changes in international economic institutions were not in the U.S. interest and perhaps of limited benefit even to LDCs. Keep this background in mind as we discuss external financing and technology in LDCs.

CAPITAL INFLOWS

The LDCs obtain a capital inflow from abroad when institutions and individuals in other countries give grants or make loans or (equity) investments to pay for a balance on goods and services deficit (or import surplus). Thus in 1987, Ghana received grants and transfers of $172 million and a new inflow of capital of $274 million to pay for a merchandise deficit of $54 million, a service deficit of $284 million, and a reduction in official liabilities by $108 million. [See Table 16-1 for the **international balance of payments statement,** an annual summary of a country's international economic and financial transactions. A double-entry bookkeeping system ensures that current (income) and capital accounts equal zero.]

This inflow of foreign funds enables a country to spend more than it produces, import more than it exports, and invest more than it saves (Equations 14-1–14-4), and thus fills the gaps that limit development. A study by three MIT economists indicates that without **capital goods imports** (electrical, mechanical, and transport

[1] Sources for this section are the U.S. Council for Economic Advisers, *The Economic Report of the President, 1982* (Washington, D.C.; U.S. Government Printing Office, 1982), p. 233; U.S. Department of State, "Trade Patterns of the West, 1977," Special Report no. 48 (Washington, D.C.: Bureau of Public Affairs, 1978); John W. Sewell, Stuart K. Tucker, and contributors, *Growth, Exports, and Jobs in a Changing World Economy* (New Brunswick, N.J.: Transaction Books, 1988), pp. 216–19; and Independent Commission on International Development Issues (Brandt report), *North-South: A Program for Survival* (Cambridge, Mass.: MIT Press, 1980).

TABLE 16-1   Ghana's International Balance of Payments, 1987 ($ million)

	Goods and Services Account	Current Account	Capital Account (+ increases in foreign liabilities)
	(− debits or payments)		
Merchandise exports	+787		
Merchandise imports	−841		
Service exports, minus service imports (net travel, transport, investment income, and other services)	−284		
Balance on goods and services		−338	
Net grants, remittances, and unilateral transfers		+172	
Balance on current account		−166	
Net capital inflows			+274
Net official reserve asset change			−108
		−166	+166

Source: International Monetary Fund, *IMF Survey* 16 (November 30, 1987): 365.

equipment, machinery, and instruments, not the same as capital imports in Chapter 14), LDCs run an export surplus. The World Bank estimates that foreign capital as a share of LDC total capital formation was 10–20 percent in the 1960s and 1970s, although this share declined to 8–12 percent in the 1980s.[2]

But when a country imports capital, domestic saving declines. Two economists who have noticed this relationship argue that using foreign capital makes a country less thrifty. They suggest that foreign capital distorts the composition of capital, frustrates indigenous entrepreneurship, and inhibits institutional reform.[3]

Their explanation is wrong. A careful look shows that an increase in capital inflow associated with a decrease in domestic saving occurs because of the way economists define these aggregates. From Equation 14-4,

$$S = I - F \qquad (16\text{-}1)$$

where S is saving, I is investment, and F is capital imports. Investment does not rise because the increase in capital formation from the capital inflow is counterbalanced by the negative foreign investment, or an increase in foreign claims on the country.

[2] F. Desmond McCarthy, Lance Taylor, and Cyrus Talati, "Trade Patterns in Developing Countries, 1964–82," *Journal of Development Economics* 27 (October 1987): 5–39; World Bank, *World Development Report, 1988* (New York: Oxford University Press, 1988), pp. 230–31; and World Bank, *World Development Report, 1984* (New York: Oxford University Press, 1984), pp. 226–27.

[3] K. B. Griffin and J. L. Enos, "Foreign Assistance: Objectives and Consequences," *Economic Development and Cultural Change* 18 (April 1970): 313–27.

TWO GAPS

Hollis B. Chenery and Alan M. Strout, in a model based on empirical evidence from fifty LDCs from 1957 to 1962, identify three development stages in which growth proceeds at the highest rate permitted by the most limiting factors. These factors are (1) the skill limit (see Chapter 14 on inability to absorb additional capital), (2) the savings gap (investment minus savings), and (3) the foreign exchange gap (imports minus exports).

In stage 1, foreign skills and technology reduce the skill limit. The authors however focus on stage 2, **investment-limited growth,** and stage 3, **trade-limited growth**—both stages where foreign aid and capital can reduce the gap that limits accelerated growth.

But why differentiate between the two gaps, since the *actual* savings gap is always equal to the *actual* foreign exchange gap? The answer is that gap analysis does not focus on *actual* shortages but rather on discrepancies in plans between savers and investors, and exporters and importers. Planned saving depends on income and income distribution, but planned investment is determined by the expected rates of return to capital. Export plans depend on international prices and foreign incomes, but import plans are determined by international prices, domestic income, and income distribution. Given the independence of decisions, it is not surprising that the excess of planned investment over saving might differ from the amount that planned imports exceed exports.

Chenery's and Strout's evidence indicates that at early development stages, growth is likely to be investment limited. If planned investment minus planned saving is greater than planned imports minus planned exports at a given GNP, then all the investment will not be realized. Actual investment equals actual saving plus foreign borrowing at a lower level of GNP than would have been realized if there had been a small savings gap. The required foreign assistance equals the larger of the two gaps, the savings gap. This import of capital will remove the limitation that investment places on growth.

If on the other hand the foreign exchange gap is larger than the savings gap, imports will fall, reducing the foreign capital and inputs available for the development effort. In this case, growth is trade limited. Capital imports equal to the foreign exchange gap will remove the limitation that trade places on growth.

In reality foreign borrowing reduces both the savings and foreign exchange gaps by equal amounts. A machine acquired by international transfer represents both an import for which no foreign exchange needs to be expended and an investment good that does not have to be offset by domestic saving.

The Chenery–Strout, three-stage approach only approximates reality in the many LDCs, where the three limitations often coexist or interact with one another. In fact limits may vary from one sector to another. One sector may be limited by a savings gap, another by a foreign exchange gap, and a third by a skill constraint.

Furthermore the **two-gap analysis,** which focuses on an aggregate approach, does not look at specific needs that foreign funds can meet. Moreover the emphasis on external development limitations diverts attention from internal economic factors that are often important constraints on growth. Nevertheless the Chenery–Strout three-stage and two-gap approaches, even though stereotypical, can be useful tools in analyzing foreign capital requirements in a number of different LDCs.[4]

STAGES IN THE BALANCE OF PAYMENTS

As we have said, foreign loans enable a country to spend more than it produces, invest more than it saves, and import more than it exports. But eventually the borrowing country must service the foreign debt. Debt service refers to the interest plus repayment of principal due in a given year. Sometimes a country can arrange debt relief, convert debt into equity, or postpone payment by rescheduling the debt or borrowing in excess of the debt due for the year (see Chapter 17). In rare instances, a country may repudiate its debts despite potential economic sanctions and credit restraints (see Chapter 14).

Paying back the loan requires a country to produce more than it spends, save more than it invests, and export more than it imports. Doing this need not be onerous, however. In fact it is typical for a newly industrializing country to encounter a growing debt. The United States, from the Revolutionary War until after the Civil War, was a **young and growing debtor nation,** borrowing from England and France to finance an import surplus for domestic investments, such as railroads and canals. However the United States proceeded to a subsequent stage, **mature debtor nation,** 1874 to 1914, when the economy's increased capacity facilitated the export surplus to service the foreign debt. Similarly contemporary industrializing countries effectively using capital inflows from abroad should usually be able to pay back loans with increased output and productivity.[5]

SOURCES OF FINANCING THE DEFICIT

Exports minus imports of goods and services equal the **international balance on goods and services.** Aid, remittances, loans, and investment from abroad finance a LDC's balance on goods and services deficit.

Both oil-importing developed and developing countries had a deficit in 1974, mainly as a result of the quadrupling of oil prices over four months in 1973 and 1974. However from 1975 through 1980, while the DCs had surpluses, the oil-

---

[4] Hollis B. Chenery and Alan M. Strout, "Foreign Assistance and Economic Development," *American Economic Review* 56 (September 1966): 679–733; Charles P. Kindleberger and Bruce Herrick, *Economic Development* (New York: McGraw-Hill, 1977), pp. 296–98; Gerald M. Meier, *International Economics: The Theory of Policy* (New York: Oxford University Press, 1980), pp. 331–34; and Gerald M. Meier, *Leading Issues in Economic Development* (New York: Oxford University Press, 1976), pp. 333–44.

[5] Since the last quarter of 1985, the United States has been the world's largest net debtor. Robert L. Heilbroner and James K. Galbraith, *The Economic Problem* (Englewood Cliffs, N.J.: Prentice-Hall, 1987), pp. 114–15. Economists do not know how to fit this U.S. debt period into a balance of payments stage theory. Because of the widespread use of the dollar for international payments and reserves, global companies and central banks sometimes have accumulated dollar assets even when the United States has a persistent deficit in its balance on goods and services. Foreigners may eventually discontinue providing credit to the United States, which would have to reduce consumption to increase savings and reduce its foreign debt.

importing LDCs had deficits. These deficits continually increased over this period (except for 1976 and 1977), and middle-income LDCs had higher deficits, partly because oil comprised a larger proportion of their total imports than was the case in low-income countries. Middle-income countries' larger deficit was financed disproportionately by commercial loans, with low-income countries receiving primarily aid.[6]

In the 1980s, LDCs had a deficit every year except 1980. The deficit increased during the U. S. and other DCs' recession, 1981-82, but fell from 1983 to 1989. Oil-exporting countries generally had a surplus except for two years at the end of the decade, while oil-importing countries had a deficit for the whole decade. The major sources of financing, loans at bankers' standards, declined over the decade (see Table 16-2), as commercial banks became more cautious with loan write-offs, write-downs, and asset sales by several highly indebted LDCs. Low-income countries received fewer foreign capital resources, as their primary source, aid, as a percentage of GNP declined in the major donor goup, the **Organization for Economic Cooperation and Development** (OECD—the United States, Canada, Western Europe, Japan, Australia, and New Zealand).

Concessional Aid

Aid, or **official development assistance,** includes development grants or loans made at concessional financial terms by official agencies. Military assistance is not considered part of official aid, but technical cooperation is.

The Grant Element of Aid.   Economists distinguish **concessional loans,** which have at least a 25-percent **grant element,** from loans at bankers' standards. In 1986, the average grant component of the member countries of the OECD to *least-developed countries* was 98.9 percent compared to 90 percent for all recipients. Of the $10,900 million the OECD contributed to least-developed countries in 1986, $10,500 million were outright grants. In addition loans totaling $400 million had a grant component of 69 percent, or $276 million. (The grant element of the loan depends on how much the interest rate is below commercial rates, the length of the grace period in which interest charges or repayments of principal is not required, how long the repayment period is, and the extent to which repayment is in local, inconvertible currency.)

Calculating the grant component of OECD aid to the least-developed countries in 1986 is fairly simple. Adding the product of $10,500 million multiplied by 1.00 (the grant component of gifts) to the product of $400 million multiplied by 0.69 (the grant component of loans) equals $10,776 million, the total grant element of aid (grants plus loans). Divide $10,776 million by $10,900 million (total aid) to equal 0.989, the grant component of aid to least-developed countries.[7]

---

[6] World Bank, *World Development Report, 1981* (New York: Oxford University Press, 1981), pp. 49–63.

[7] Sources for the section on concessional aid are Organization for Economic Cooperation and Development (report by John P. Lewis), *Development Cooperation: Efforts and Policies of the Members of the Development Assistance Committee* (Paris, November 1981); OECD (report by Rutherford M. Poats), *Development Cooperation: Efforts and Policies of the Members of the Development Assistance Committee* (Paris, November 1982); OECD, *Resources for Developing Countries, 1980, and Recent*

TABLE 16-2 Developing Countries' Balance on Goods and Services Deficit and Finance Sources, 1980–89 ($ billions)

Item	Year									
	1980	1981	1982	1983	1984	1985	1986	1987	1988	1989
Balance on goods and services deficit	(12.9)[a]	66.5	103.0	83.1	56.0	49.2	70.9	32.9	52.9	64.0
Financed by										
Private transfers	12.3	11.7	8.3	10.2	11.9	11.1	15.2	17.6	18.1	19.7
Official development assistance	5.4	7.0	8.3	9.8	10.8	13.9	15.0	15.6	17.2	18.2
Private direct investment	4.3	18.1	20.3	13.1	14.0	11.2	9.9	13.0	16.6	15.9
Loans (commercial and official) at bankers' standards	99.2	113.3	80.3	52.7	47.6	51.2	38.8	47.7	22.7	45.6
Short-term borrowing	−89.0	−104.0	−75.8	−21.7	−19.3	−16.6	−14.9	−5.4	−6.2	−5.9
Changes in reserves[b]	−45.1	20.4	61.6	19.0	−9.0	−21.6	6.9	−55.6	−15.5	−29.5

[a] () refers to a balance on goods and services surplus.

[b] Minus sign (−) indicates an increase in reserves.

Source: International Monetary Fund, *World Economic Outlook* (Washington, D.C., 1988), pp. 97, 108.

Why Give Aid?   Development assistance is under renewed attack. Traditional critics view it as too softhearted to be hardheaded. Some leftists see aid as imperialist support for repressive LDC regimes, rather than as a way of spurring economic development for the masses. Critics of all persuasions charge that aid is ineffective: It does not do what it sets out to do.

Let us examine this issue more carefully. Foreign aid is usually in the national self-interest. Economic aid, like military assistance, can be used for strategic purposes—to strengthen LDC allies, to shore up the donor's defense installations, to improve donor access to strategic materials, and to keep LDC allies from changing sides in the international political struggle. Assistance can be motivated by political or ideological concerns—to influence behavior in international forums; to strengthen cultural ties; or to propagate democracy, capitalism, socialism, or Islam. (A political and strategic motivation—to promote democracy and private enterprise and minimize Soviet influence in the third world—was important in congressional approval of President Harry Truman's call in 1949 for U.S. "Point Four" economic assistance to LDCs.) Furthermore aid supports economic interests by facilitating private investment abroad, improving access to vital materials, expanding demand for domestic industry, and subsidizing or tying exports. (Tied aid, since it prevents the recipient country from using funds outside the donor country, is worth less than its face value. In some instances, aid may be tied to importing capital-intensive equipment, which may reduce employment in the recipient country.)

Some aid—emergency relief, food aid, assistance for refugees, and grants to least-developed countries—is given for humanitarian reasons. Most OECD countries have a small constituency of interest groups, legislators, and bureaucrats pressing for aid for reasons of social justice.For example, some of the support for Point Four and subsequent aid came from humanitarian groups in the United States.

It is difficult to separate humanitarian motives from the self-interested pursuit of maintaining a stable, global political system. Rich countries have an interest in pursuing a world order that avoids war (especially a nuclear holocaust), acute world population pressures, widespread hunger, resource depletion, environmental degradation, and financial collapse. Economic aid is one aspect of this drama.

How effective has aid been? In some instances, aid has exceeded an LDC's capacity to absorb it. Moreover aid can delay self-reliance, postpone essential internal reform, or support internal interests opposed to income distribution. Specifically food aid can undercut prices for local food producers.

Elliott R. Morss argues that the effectiveness of aid to sub-Saharan Africa declined after 1970, as aid programs placed more burden on scarce local management skills and put less emphasis on recipients' learning by doing. After 1970, donors switched from program support (for example, to infrastructure or agricul-

Trends (Paris, June 1981); Overseas Development Council (Roger D. Hansen and Contributors), *U.S. Foreign Policy and the Third World: Agenda, 1982* (New York: Praeger, 1982), pp. 225–46; Overseas Development Council (John W. Sewell and the Staff), *The United States and World Development: Agenda, 1980* (New York: Praeger, 1980), pp. 215–37; Organization for Economic Cooperation and Development, *Financing and External Debt of Developing Countries: 1987 Survey* (Paris, 1988); Organization for Economic Cooperation and Development, *Financing and External Debt of Developing Countries: 1986 Survey* (Paris, 1987); and Society for International Development, *Survey of International Development* 15 (January/February 1978).

ture) to project assistance, which entailed more specific statements of objectives and means of attaining them, more precise monitoring and evaluation, more foreign control over funds, and more local personnel and resources committed to projects. Furthermore each of the major bilateral, multilateral, and nongovernmental organizations has competing requirements.

When donors underwrite most of the development budget, they insist on continual, extensive project supervision and review, so that recipient government agencies are more answerable to them than to their own senior policy officials. Donors frequently recommend and supervise poorly conceived projects. But even when well conceived, LDC officials fail to learn how to do something until they have the power to make their own decisions. Morss argues that the proliferation of donors and requirements has resulted in weakened institutions and reduced management capacity. For example, in 1981, Malawi, lacking the indigenous capacity to manage 188 projects from fifty different donors, hired donor country personnel (sometimes with donor salary supplements) to take government line positions to manage projects. However, Malawi has not been able to increase its capacity to run its own affairs and establish its own policies.[8]

Nevertheless evidence suggests that aid has been essential to many low-income countries in reducing savings and foreign exchange gaps. Furthermore low-income recipient countries continue to press for more aid from rich countries.

OECD Aid. From 1980 to 1987, OECD countries contributed 78 percent of the world's bilateral (and 56 percent of all) official development assistance to LDCs. The OECD aid increased from $6.9 billion in 1970 to $8.9 billion in 1973 to $13.6 billion in 1975 to $26.8 billion in 1980, but declined to $25.9 billion in 1981 and to $21.8 billion in 1985, before increasing to $30.4 billion in 1987. As a percentage of GNP, it dropped from 0.34 percent of GNP in 1970 to a post-1960s low of 0.30 percent of GNP in 1973. In 1975, this figure increased to 0.33 percent and in 1980 to 0.37 percent before declining to 0.35 percent in 1985, but rebounding to 0.39 percent in 1986, slightly more than half of the 0.70 percent target many OECD accepted a decade before. Only Norway, Netherlands, Sweden, Denmark, and France exceeded this target (see Table 16-3).

Although annual U.S. foreign aid is larger than that of any other country, as a percentage of GNP (0.24 percent), it ranks last among OECD members. The U.S. citizens spend more on participant sporting activities and supplies in a year than their government spends annually on foreign aid. Furthermore aid as a percentage of GNP in the United States declined steadily from 0.50 percent in 1965 to 0.24 in 1985, while other OECD countries maintained a percentage in excess of 0.40 percent, increasing to 0.46 percent in 1985. The real value of U.S. aid dropped from the 1960s to the 1970s, then leveled out in the 1980s, while it increased continually in the rest of the OECD countries.

We can only speculate about why U.S. aid failed to increase. The U.S. political influence has declined dramatically since 1946, when Europe and Japan were war devastated and few LDCs were independent, so U.S. economic aid has come to have less influence too. In any event, the post-1970 U.S. Congress, and at times the

---

[8] Elliot R. Morss, "Institutional Destruction Resulting from Donor and Project Proliferation in sub-Saharan African Countries ," *World Development* 12 (April 1984): 465–70.

TABLE 16-3   Official Development Assistance (ODA) from OECD
Countries (1985)

	ODA ($ million)	ODA as Percent of GNP
U.S.	9,403	0.24
France	3,995	0.78
Japan	3,797	0.29
Germany, Fed. Rep.	2,942	0.47
Canada	1,631	0.49
United Kingdom	1,531	0.34
Netherlands	1,135	0.91
Italy	1,098	0.31
Sweden	840	0.86
Australia	749	0.49
Norway	575	1.03
Denmark	440	0.80
Belgium	438	0.54
Switzerland	303	0.31
Austria	248	0.38
Finland	211	0.40
New Zealand	54	0.25
Ireland	39	0.24
OECD	29,429	0.35

Sources: John W. Sewell, Stuart K. Tucker, and contributors, *Growth, Exports, and Jobs in a Changing World Economy: Agenda, 1988* (New Brunswick, N.J.: Transaction Books, 1988): 240; and Organization for Economic Cooperation and Development, *Financing and External Debt of Developing Countries: 1987 Survey* (Paris, 1988), p. 15.

president, were increasingly skeptical about aid's value in strengthening allies, influencing international behavior, improving U.S. access to markets and raw materials, promoting capitalism, maintaining global stability, and building a world order consistent with U.S. preferences. Even some liberals, churches, and humanitarian organizations traditionally in favor of U.S. economic aid stopped supporting it because they increasingly perceived it as benefiting large U.S. corporations and conservative countries suppressing human rights.

OPEC Aid.   From 1970 to 1987, contributions from member countries of OPEC never comprised more than 18 percent of the world's annual, official aid to LDCs. Yet since 1973, these countries contributed more aid as a percentage of GNP than either the OECD or socialist countries. Between 1975 and 1985, OPEC countries increased foreign aid from $1.3 billion (1.14 percent of GNP) in 1973 to $5.5 billion (2.70 percent of GNP) in 1975 to $7.0 billion (1.35 percent) in 1980 to $3.7 billion (1.05 percent) in 1985. Seven Arab OPEC countries, with a population of about 50 million and a GNP per capita less than half that of the United States, contributed almost as much aid as the United States did in 1985, but primarily to Arab or Muslim countries.

Socialist Country Aid.   Official assistance from the centrally planned economies of the Soviet Union and Eastern Europe, the **Council for Mutual Economic Assistance,** never amounted to more than one-seventh of the world's annual aid from 1970 to 1985.[9]

Aid to Low- and Middle-Income Countries.   Real concessional aid to oil-importing LDCs rose from $9.4 billion in 1973 to $11.6 billion in 1975 to $17.0 billion in 1980 to $17.3 billion in 1985 (in 1978 prices), with low-income countries usually receiving about half the total.

In 1986, 27.3 percent of **bilateral aid** (given directly by one country to another) went to Asia; 26.5 percent to sub-Saharan Africa, the region with the largest number of least-developed countries; 23.6 percent to Latin America, with only one low-income country; and 17.4 percent to the Middle East, with no low-income countries. The top twelve recipients of bilateral aid were Bangladesh (4), Sudan (7), Tanzania (10), and Ethiopia (11)—least developed; India (1), Pakistan (6), and Sri Lanka (12)—low-income; Egypt (3), the Philippines (5), Syria (8), and Indonesia (9)—middle-income; and Israel (2)—high-income.

Ironically middle-income countries received $11.50 official development assistance per capita in 1986 and low-income countries, $6.40. To be sure, donors gave only $1.70 aid per capita to India and China, whose populations comprise almost three-fourths of low–income countries. (Donors defend this small figure on the grounds that these two countries could not be given as much as other low–income countries without destroying the effectiveness of the flows to other recipients.) However even if India and China are excluded from low-income countries, per capita assistance to low-income countries is still only $19.60. (The large amount of aid given to middle-income countries again underscores the importance of donor self-interest.)

Aid to low-income countries (including least developed but not India and China) was 60 percent of their gross investment and 9.0 percent of GNP in 1986. This percentage of GNP is fifteen times as high as India and China and ten times as high as that for middle-income countries. For ministates, Cape Verde and the Maldives, with populations each under 350,000, aid actually exceeded GNP! For Zambia, a country of 7 million, aid was 31.2 percent of GNP, and for Somalia, a country of 6 million located on the strategic horn of Africa, aid was 27.8 percent of GNP. For Bangladesh, with a population of 103 million, aid was 9.5 percent of GNP and four-fifths of gross investment.[10]

Multilateral Aid.   The steady increase in the proportion and real amount of OECD aid channeled through **multilateral agencies** (those involving several donor countries) between 1970 and 1977 was reversed between 1977 and 1988, especially

[9] The last three sections are based on Overseas Development Council, *U.S. Foreign Policy and the Third World: Agenda 1982* (New York: Praeger, 1982), p. 244; Organization for Economic Cooperation and Development, *Financing and External Debt: 1987 Survey,* (Paris, 1988), p. 35; World Bank, *World Development Report, 1988* (New York: Oxford University Press, 1988), pp. 262–63; John W. Sewell, Stuart K. Tucker, and contributors, *Growth, Exports, and Jobs in a Changing World Economy: Agenda, 1988* (New Brunswick, N.J.: Transaction Books, 1988): 235–44; and Table 16-3.

[10] World Bank, *World Development Report, 1988* (New York: Oxford University Press, 1988), pp. 262-65; and Organization for Economic Cooperation and Development, *Financing and External Debt: 1987 Survey,* (Paris, 1988), pp. 25–40.

during U.S. President Ronald Reagan's administration, 1981 to 1988. Some 30.6 percent of OECD development assistance (and 0.11 percent of GNP) went to multilateral agencies in 1980, while 28.1 percent of aid (0.10 percent of GNP) went in 1986. The OECD countries contributed about 90 percent of the concessional resources these agencies received for development programs during the 1970s and 1980s, with OEPC nations the major source for the rest. In the 1980s, the rank order of major multilateral agencies providing concessional aid was the United Nations, the European Community, the **International Development Association (IDA,** an affiliate of the World Bank, which has usually extended credit for 50 years, with a 10-year grace period, no interest charge, and a nominal service charge), and the International Monetary Fund Trust Fund (from the sale of IMF gold in the early 1980s). The IDA gave the largest proportion (80 percent) of aid to low-income countries from 1969 to 1986,[11] with the Asian Development Bank and the African Development Bank and Fund a distant second and third respectively.

One disadvantage of contributions to multilateral agencies is that the donor country loses some control over the aid. For example, in the late 1970s and 1980s, the United States objected to IDA aid to Cuba.

In some instances, donor countries and agencies form consortia (such as the World Bank agencies and OECD countries assisting India, Pakistan, and Bangladesh) to coordinate their aid programs. Multilateral agencies and consortia generally coordinate technical and financial contributions of individual donor countries with one another and with the recipient's economic plan. Aid administered in this way reduces the amount of bidding donor countries make for favors from recipient countries and softens adverse political reactions if a particular project fails.

Food Aid   The economist stressing basic-needs attainment is quite interested in food as foreign aid. As indicated in Chapter 9, there is more than enough food produced each year to feed adequately everyone on earth. However food is so unevenly distributed that malnutrition and hunger exist in the same country or region where food is abundant.

During the 1960s, the United States sold a sizable fraction of its agricultural exports under a concessionary Public Law 480, where LDC recipients could pay for the exports in inconvertible currency over a long period. The U.S. real food aid, as well as food reserves measured in days of world consumption, dropped from the 1960s to the 1970s and 1980s, partly because U.S. farm interests wanted to reduce surplus grain stocks.

Although annual food aid in the later 1970s and 1980s was below that of the 1960s, food and agricultural aid (including that from the United States) increased in real terms from the 1960s to the late 1970s and 1980s. In the late 1970s and 1980s, food and agricultural aid was one-fourth of worldwide economic aid. Although most of this was to increase LDC food and agricultural production, such aid cannot meet the most urgent short-term needs. Direct food aid is essential for meeting these needs.

In the 1980s, about three-quarters of the food aid went to low-income countries; it amounted to about one-third of their cereal imports. Projections in Chap-

---

[11] Sheldon Annis, "The Shifting Grounds of Poverty Lending at the World Bank," in Richard E. Feinberg and contributors, *Between Two Worlds: The World Bank's Next Decade* (New Brunswick, N.J.: Transaction Books, 1986), pp. 96–100.

ters 7 and 9 indicate that food deficits are likely to increase in the 1990s. Yet in the 1980s, the United States, which provides the bulk of total food aid, reduced its food assistance.

Critics of food aid argue that it increases dependence, promotes waste, does not reach the most needy, and dampens local food production. Nevertheless food aid has frequently been highly effective. It plays a vital role in saving human lives during famine or crisis and if distributed selectively, reduces malnutrition. Unfortunately poor transport, storage, administrative services, distribution networks, and overall economic infrastructure hinder the success of food aid programs, but the concept itself is not at fault. Furthermore dependence on emergency food aid is less than that from continuing commercially imported food.

Yet food aid programs need improvement. A World Bank study, which contends that transitory food insecurity is linked to fluctuations in domestic harvests, world prices, and foreign exchange earnings, recommends that international donors emphasize supporting recipient programs safeguarding food security (especially for highly vulnerable people such as lactating women and children under 5 years), investing in projects that promote growth and directly benefit the poorest people, improving the international trade environment (including food price stabilization), and integrating food aid with other aid programs and national institutions and plans, while domestic governments should stress the redistribution of income to relieve afflicted people. The World Bank would not make food self-sufficiency a priority for the recipient LDC but emphasizes preventing substantial food price increases through imports if cheaper.

Moreover recipients should receive food they like. The Bank suggests that recipient governments exchange donated food for cash and buy local foods, thus reducing transport costs and waste.[12]

Workers' Remittances

Remittances from nationals working abroad help finance a LDC's balance on goods and services deficit. These remittances, primarily from migrants to Europe and the oil-affluent Persian Gulf, from Central American migrants to the United States, and from neighboring countries' migrants to South Africa, Ghana, and the Ivory Coast, amounted to $24 billion to oil-importing LDCs in 1980. In 1986, remittances as a percentage of merchandise exports were 2830 percent in the Yemen Arab Republic, 161 percent in Jordan, 78 percent in Pakistan, 57 percent in Morocco, 56 percent in Egypt, 36 percent in Yugoslavia, 21 percent in Turkey, 17 percent in India, 31 percent in Mozambique, 35 percent in Portugal, 67 percent in Bangladesh, and 134 percent in Burkina Faso. Except for the last four countries, this percentage fell during the oil price slump and the European backlash to guest workers in the 1980s. The average propensity to save (saving/income) among Turkish and Pakistani emigrants was several times that of their domestic counterparts. The **average propensity to remit** (remittances/emigrant income) was still 11 percent for Turkish

---

[12] World Bank, *Poverty and Hunger: Issues and Options for Food Security in Developing Countries* (Washington. D.C., 1986); John W. Sewell, Stuart K. Tucker, and contributors, *Growth, Exports, and Jobs in a Changing World Economy* (New Brunswick, N.J.: Transaction Books, 1988), pp. 235–40; and Organization for Economic Cooperation and Development, *Financing and External Debt: 1987 Survey* (Paris, 1988), pp. 7–40.

workers and 50 percent for Pakistanis, and enabled the living standards and invest-ment rates of the emigrants' families to increase substantially.[13] In southern Africa, Mozambique, Botswana, Lesotho, and Swaziland were dependent on South Africa's white-minority government, which could threaten to break migrant worker contracts.

Private Investment and Multinational Corporations

Private foreign investment, a source for financing the balance on goods and services deficit, consists of **portfolio investment,** in which the investor has no control over operations, and **direct investment,** which entails managing the operations. In the nineteenth century, Western European investment in the young growing debtor nations, the United States and Canada, was primaily portfolio investment, such as securities. Today DC investment in LDCs is virtually all private direct investment. **Multinational corporations** (MNCs), business firms with a parent company in one country and subsidiary operations in other countries, are responsible for this direct investment.

In 1971, the United States accounted for 52 percent of the world's stock of foreign direct investment. The remainder was from Western Europe, Japan, and Canada, except for 1.2 percent from South Africa and 2.8 percent from LDCs (whose share increased from 1.1 percent in 1960). By 1983, parent companies from the United States comprised only 39.6 percent of the stock of foreign investment, with the United Kingdom accounting for 16.7 percent; West Germany, 7.0 percent; the Netherlands, 6.4 percent; Japan 5.6, percent; France, 5.2 percent; Canada, 5.1 percent; other DCs, 10.2 percent; South Africa, 1.1 percent; and LDCs, 3.1 percent (including India, South Korea, Hong Kong, Singapore, Brazil, Argentina, Colombia, Peru, the Philippines, Taiwan, and the OPEC countries).[14]

Some LDC governments are ambivalent, or even hostile, toward MNCs. To be sure, these corporations bring in capital, new technology, management skills, new products, and increased efficiency and income; however MNCs seek to maximize the profits of the parent company, rather than the subsidiaries'. It may be in the interest of the parent company to limit the transfer of technology and industrial secrets to local personnel of the subsidiary, to restrict its exports, to force it to purchase intermediate parts and capital goods from the parent, and to set intrafirm (but international) transfer prices to shift taxes from the host country.

Most foreign investment is from large corporations. According to *Fortune,* the total 1977 sales of the largest thirty three MNCs with branches in the third world were $80 billion. The largest MNCs, with hundreds of branches and affiliates

[13] World Bank, *World Development Report, 1981* (New York: Oxford University Press, 1981), p. 51; and World Bank, *World Development Report, 1988* (New York: Oxford University Press, 1988), pp. 242–43, 250–51.

[14] C. Fred Bergsten, Thomas Horst, and Theodore H. Moran, "Home-Country Policy toward Multinationals," in Robert E. Baldwin and J. David Richardson, eds., *International Trade and Finance: Readings* (Boston: Little, Brown, 1981), pp. 267–95; and Paul Streeten, "Multinationals Revisited," in Robert E. Baldwin and J. David Richardson, eds., *International Trade and Finance: Readings* (Boston: Little, Brown, 1981), pp. 308–15; and John H. Dunning, "Transnational Corporations in a Changing World Environment: Are New Theoretical Explanations Required?" in Teng Weizao and N. T. Wang, eds., *Transnational Corporations and China's Open-Door Policy* (Lexington, Mass.: Lexington, 1988), pp. 28–29.

TABLE 16-4 Ranking of Developing Countries and Multinational Corporations according to Production in 1982[a] ($ billions)

1.	China	312.5	20.	Algeria	46.8
2.	Brazil	284.0	21.	*Standard Oil (Cal.)*	45.2
3.	India	186.4	22.	Greece	42.0
4.	Mexico	165.9	23.	Philippines	41.6
5.	Taiwan	165.4	24.	Colombia	39.4
6.	*Exxon*	113.2	25.	Thailand	38.3
7.	Indonesia	88.5	26.	*Ford*	37.1
8.	*Royal Dutch Shell[b]*	82.3	27.	*IBM*	34.4
9.	South Africa	81.2	28.	*Standard Oil (Ind.)*	31.3
10.	Nigeria	77.9	29.	*ENI[b]*	30.9
11.	South Korea	75.1	30.	Egypt	30.6
12.	Argentina	71.6	31.	*Gulf Oil*	30.0
13.	Venezuela	69.1	32.	Hong Kong	27.8
14.	*Mobil*	68.6	33.	Malaysia	27.0
15.	Turkey	63.7	34.	*General Electric*	26.5
16.	Yugoslavia	63.3	35.	Chile	25.4
17.	*General Motors*	60.0	36.	Portugal	24.7
18.	*Texaco*	57.6	37.	*Unilever[b]*	23.1
19.	*British Petroleum*	52.2	38.	All other LDCs less than	23.1

[a]GNP for countries and gross sales for corporations, not strictly comparable, as note 15 in the text indicates.

[b]Corporations based outside the United States—Shell and Unilever (Netherlands/U.K.), and ENI (Italy).

Source: World Bank, *World Development Report, 1984* (New York: Oxford University Press, 1984), pp. 218–19; and Weizao Teng and N. T. Wang, *Transnational Corporations and China's Open Door Policy* (Lexington, Mass.: Lexington, 1988), p. 30. Reprinted by permission of the publisher, from TRANSNATIONAL CORPORATIONS AND CHINA'S OPEN DOOR POLICY by Weizao Teng and N. T. Wang (Lexington, Mass.: Lexington Books, D.C.Heath and Company, copyright 1988, Lexington Books). Author's estimate for Taiwan.

throughout the world, have an output comparable to the LDC with which they bargain. Exxon, Shell, Mobil, General Motors, Texaco, British Petroleum, Standard Oil of California, Ford, and IBM each have an annual output exceeding that of most third-world countries (Table 16-4). Thus for instance, Ford would not negotiate investment in Egypt as an inferior party but as roughly an equal in economic power and size.[15]

MNCs are important actors on the international scene. The UNCTAD estimates that in 1975, MNC foreign production accounted for 20 percent of world output and that their intrafirm trade was 25 percent of international manufacturing trade. Four-fifths of Africa's 1983 commodity trade was handled by MNCs. Thirty-eight percent of total U.S. imports in 1977 consisted of intrafirm transactions by

[15] Strictly speaking one must subtract purchases of inputs from other firms from Ford's production to get its value added, so that the figure is comparable to Egypt's GNP, which does not double count the production of inputs supplied by one firm to another.

MNCs based in the United States. Over one-third of these transactions were from LDCs. Moreover MNCs play an important role in LDC manufacturing exports, responsible for 20 percent of Latin America's manufactured exports. Indeed U.S. affiliates alone accounted for 7.2 percent of 1977 LDC manufacturing exports, 35.7 percent of Mexico's, and 15.2 percent in Brazil, but only 1.5 percent in South Korea.[16]

The markets MNCs operate in are *often* international **oligopolies** with competition among few sellers whose pricing decisions are interdependent. International economists contend that large corporations invest overseas because of international imperfections in the market for goods, resources, or technology. The MNCs benefit from monopoly advantages, such as patents, technical knowledge, superior managerial and marketing skills, better access to capital markets, economies of large-scale production, and economies of **vertical integration** (that is, cost savings from decision coordination at various production stages). An example of vertical integration is from crude petroleum marketing backward to its drilling and forward to consumer markets for its refined products.

Additionally in some industries, control over global marketing and financing still gives MNCs much power in determining the supply and price of LDC primary exports. For example, three conglomerates account for 70–75 percent of the global banana market; six corporations, 70 percent of cocoa trade; and six MNCs, 85–90 percent of leaf tobacco trade.[17]

Yet ironically in some instances, MNCs may increase competition because their intrafirm transactions break down barriers to free trade and factor movement between countries. On the other hand, once MNCs are established in an economy, they may exploit their monopolistic advantages and enhance concentration. Thus MNCs, which accounted for 62 percent of manufacturing's capital stock in Nigeria in 1965, contributed to high rates of industrial concentration. Yet a subsidiary's production that dominates a LDC industry may be only a fraction of the parent company's output and peripheral to the MNC's decision-making process.[18]

You may have already sensed that leaders in LDCs do not agree on whether MNCs are beneficial or not. Some emphasize that MNCs provide scarce capital and advanced technology essential for rapid growth. Others believe such dependence

---

[16] United Nations Conference on Trade and Development Seminar Program, *Intra-firm Transactions and Their Impact on Trade and Development,* May 1978, Report Series no. 2, UNCTAD/OSG/74; Paul Streeten, "Multinationals Revisited," in Robert E. Baldwin and J. David Richardson, eds., *International Trade and Finance: Readings* (Boston: Little, Brown, 1981), pp. 308–15; Economic Commission for Africa (ECA), *Commodity Market Structures, Pricing Policies, and Their Impact on African Trade,* E/ECA/TRADE/3 (Addis Ababa, 1983); Magnus Blomstrom, Irving Kraus, and Robert Lipsey, "Multinational Firms and Manufactured Exports from Developing Countries," National Bureau of Economic Research Working Paper no. 2493, Cambridge, Mass. 1988; and United Nations Center on Transnational Corporations, *Transnational Corporations and International Trade: Selected Issues* (New York, 1985), pp. 3–8.

[17] Economic Commission for Africa, *Commodity Market Structures, Pricing, Policies and Their Impact on African Trade,* E/ECA/TRADE/3 (Addis Ababa, 1983).

[18] Charles P. Kindleberger, "The Theory of Direct Investment," in Robert E. Baldwin and J. David Richardson, eds., *International Trade and Finance: Readings* (Boston: Little, Brown, 1974), pp. 267–85; and E. Wayne Nafziger, *African Capitalism: A Case Study in Nigerian Entrepreneurship* (Stanford: Hoover Institution, 1977), pp. 55–60.

for capital and technology hampers development. In the next two sections, we summarize the benefits and costs of MNCs in less-developed countries.[19]

The Benefits of MNC's   MNCs can help the developing country to

1. Finance a savings gap or balance of payments deficit
2. Acquire a specialized good or service essential for domestic production (for example, an underwater engineering system for offshore oil drilling or computer capability for analyzing the strength and weight of a dam's components)
3. Obtain foreign technology and innovative methods of increasing productivity
4. Generate appropriate technology by adapting existing processes or by means of a new invention
5. Fill part of the shortage in management and entrepreneurship
6. Complement local entrepreneurship by subcontracting to ancillary industries, component makers, or repair shops; or by creating forward and backward linkages
7. Provide contacts with overseas banks, markets, and supply sources that would otherwise remain unknown
8. Train domestic managers and technicians
9. Employ domestic labor, especially in skilled jobs
10. Generate tax revenue from income and corporate profits taxes
11. Enhance efficiency by removing impediments to free trade and factor movement
12. Increase national income through increased specialization and economies of scale

The Costs of MNCs.   In recent years, some radical economists and third-world nationalists have questioned whether MNC benefits exceed costs. These critics charge that MNCs have a negative effect on the developing country because they

1. Increase the LDC's technological dependence on foreign sources, resulting in less technological innovation by local workers.
2. Limit the transfer of patents, industrial secrets, and other technical knowledge to the subsidiary, which may be viewed as a potential rival.[20] For example, Coca-Cola left India in 1977 rather than share its secret formula with local interests (although in 1988–89 it applied to reenter India to forestall dominance by Pepsi Cola's minority-owned joint venture).

---

[19] Sources for these two sections are Ronald Müller, "The Multinational Corporation and the Underdevelopment of the Third World," in Charles K. Wilber, ed., *The Political Economy of Development and Underdevelopment* (New York: Random House, 1979), pp. 151–78; Paul Streeten, "The Multinational Enterprise and the Theory of Development Policy," *World Development* 1 (October 1973): 1–14; and Sanjaya Lall, "Less-Developed Countries and Private Foreign Direct Investment: A Review Article," *World Development* 2 (April–May 1974): 41–48.

[20] Owen T. Adikibi, "The Multinational Corporation and Monopoly of Patents in Nigeria," *World Development* 16 (April 1988): 511–26.

3. Enhance industrial and technological concentration.

4. Hamper local entrepreneurship and investment in infant industries.

5. Introduce inappropriate products, technology, and consumption patterns (see box).

6. Increase unemployment rates from unsuitable technology (see Chapter 10).

7. Exacerbate income inequalities by generating jobs and patronage and producing goods that primarily benefit the richest 20 percent of the population.

8. Restrict subsidiary exports when they undercut the market of the parent company.

9. Understate tax liabilities by overstating investment costs, overpricing inputs transferred from another subsidiary, and underpricing outputs sold within the MNC to another country.

10. Distort intrafirm transfer prices to transfer funds extralegally or to circumvent foreign exchange controls.

11. Require the subsidiary to purchase inputs from the parent company rather than from domestic firms.

12. Repatriate large amounts of funds—profits, royalties, and managerial and service fees—that contribute to balance of payments deficits in the years after the initial capital inflow.

13. Influence government policy in an unfavorable direction (for example, excessive protection, tax concessions, subsidies, infrastructure, and provision of factory sites).

14. Increase foreign intervention in the domestic political process.

15. Divert local, skilled personnel from domestic entrepreneurship or government service.

16. Raise a large percentage of their capital from local funds having a high opportunity cost.

On the last point, Ronald Müller's evidence from Latin America indicates that MNCs contribute only 17 percent, and local sources 83 percent, of the financial capital. However Müller includes as local capital the subsidiary's reinvested earnings and depreciation allowances. If this source is excluded, local financing accounts for 59 percent of total capital. Still if the figure is representative of developing countries as a whole, MNCs contribute less than generally believed. Moreover even if local individuals and financial institutions contribute only 20 to 30 percent, this amount represents substantial funds that invested elsewhere might better meet the country's social priorities.

Southern Africa illustrates MNC cost. Between 1960 and 1985, almost half the Western MNC investment in Africa was in the Republic of South Africa, supporting not only apartheid there but also harming the neighboring countries' development. The MNCs and the Pretoria government viewed South Africa as the core for their expanding activities throughout other parts of southern Africa, which provided labor, a market, and raw materials. The MNCs with subsidiaries also in South Africa's neighboring countries dominated their banking systems, invested much of these countries' financial capital in South Africa, shipped raw materials for processing from them to South Africa, and neglected their manufacturing and (sometimes)

INFANT FEEDING AND THE MULTINATIONALS

Critics charge that multinational corporations introduce inappropriate consumption patterns in LDCs and point to the infant formula industry as a major example.

According to the UN Food and Agriculture Organization (FAO),

> Breast milk is a commodity of very high nutritious value and low production cost which is almost perfectly equitably distributed among the needy—something that . . . cannot be said about supplies of other types of food. . . . In India, a low-paid working woman would have to use her total income in order to purchase formula milk in sufficient quantities.

The World Health Organization contended that major MNCs have used unfair marketing gimmicks to persuade women to buy infant formula for bottle feeding. Labels display bouncing, blue-eyed, white babies, suggesting to poor third-world mothers that their own children can attain robust good health if fed the formula. Some companies have offered scholarships and travel allowances to have rural health officials promote the formulas. Companies often give a new mother free formula as she leaves the hospital. Such a mother may start off her baby on the formula only to discover that when the samples run out, she cannot revert to breast feeding because her milk dries up in about a week if suckling is discontinued.

However to use infant formula effectively, a mother must read the directions on a can, mix the powder with the right amount of purified water, refrigerate the fluid, and feed it to her baby in a sterilized bottle, nearly an impossibility for most poor women in LDCs.

Breast-fed infants are rarely malnourished except when the mother is severely underfed. And bottle feeding infants under such unsanitary circumstances as exist in many LDCs means the infant is subject to diarrhea and gastrointestinal tract infection, which lead to an increased incidence of protein energy malnutrition.

According to FAO, the drastic decline in breast feeding in many urban areas has dramatically increased infant malnutrition in low-income groups. In 1975, in a West African city hospital, 90 percent of the infants below the age of 6 months with diarrhea and dehydration were bottle fed, even though more than three-fourths of urban infants that age were breast fed. In the baby's second year, corresponding to the weaning age, severe cases of malnutrition occur with the highest frequency.

In May 1981, the assembly of the World Health Organization voted over U.S. objection for a voluntary commercial code to ban advertising and restrict marketing practices in the infant formula industry. Some code supporters estimate that implementing it could save the lives of as many as one million infants a year. And while infant formula MNCs, under pressure from consumer groups and other critics, agreed in the early to mid-1980s to restrict LDC marketing practices, in 1988, several consumer lobbyists charged the MNCs with reneging. In response to another incident, a U.S. MNC paid the

Indian government $470 million for a toxic chemical gas leak at a Bhopal pesticide plant that killed 2500 people on December 3, 1984. Although responsibility of the infant feeding and pesticide MNCs may be overstated and not representative of the impact of MNCs in other industries, these cases illustrate why many LDCs want to restrict the flow of foreign investment.

Sources: Food and Agriculture Organization of the United Nations, *The Fourth FAO World Food Survey,* FAO Food and Nutrition Series No. 10 (Rome, 1977), pp. 43–45; *Dollars and Sense* (May–June 1981), pp. 12–14; Ward Morehouse and M. Arun Subramaniam, *The Bhopal Tragedy* (New York: Council on International and Public Affairs, 1986); and "How Union Carbide Fleshed Out its Theory of Sabotage at Bhopal," *Wall Street Journal* (July 7, 1988), p. 1.

mining industries. These neighbors bought capital goods, some consumer goods, and even foodstuffs from South African MNCs. Until the 1980s, the international copper companies in Zambia, Zaïre, Botswana, and Namibia built most fabricating factories in South Africa or the West.[21]

The MNCs and LDC Economic Interests.   The MNC benefits and costs vary among classes and interest groups within a LDC population. Sometimes political elites welcome a MNC because it benefits them through rake-offs on its contract, sales of inputs and services, jobs for clients, and positions on the boards of directors (even though the firm harms the interests of most of the population). However as political power is dispersed, elites may have to represent a more general public interest.

Since the early 1970s, there has been a shift in bargaining power away from the MNCs to third-world governments, which have increased their technical and economic expertise and added alternative sources of capital and technology. An increasing share of MNC investment is in joint ventures with LDC government or business. And LDCs have appropriated more of the monopoly rents from public utilities and mineral production. In the 1970s, the most visible change was the shift in the ownership of OPEC oil concessions from the international oil companies to OPEC member governments (see Chapter 8). Moreover as a result of increasing LDC restrictions, some of the MNC role has shifted from equity investment, capital ownership, and managerial control of overseas facilities to the sale of technology, management services, and marketing. As LDCs become more selective in admitting MNCs, and more effective at bargaining, they increase the benefits and reduce the costs of MNCs.[22]

Alternatives to MNC Technology Transfer.   The LDCs can receive technology from MNCs without their sole ownership. Joint MNC-local country ventures can help LDCs learn by doing. Yet frequent contractual limits on transferring patents, industrial secrets, and other technical knowledge to the subsidiary, which may be viewed as a potential rival, may hamper learning benefits. **Turnkey projects,** where

---

[21] Ann Seidman and Neva Seidman Makgetla, *Outposts of Monopoly Capitalism: Southern Africa in the Changing Global Economy* (Westport, Conn.: Lawrence Hill, 1980).

[22] Paul Streeten, "Multinationals Revisited," in Robert E. Baldwin and J. David Richardson, eds., *International Trade and Finance: Readings* (Boston: Little, Brown, 1981), pp. 308–15.

foreigners for a price provide inputs and technology, build plant and equipment, and assemble the production line so that locals can initiate production at the "turn of a key," are usually more expensive and rarely profitable in LDCs (which usually lack an adequate industrial infrastructure). Other arrangements include management contracts, buying or licensing technology, or (more cheaply) buying machinery in which knowledge is embodied. The late nineteenth-century Japanese government, which received no foreign aid, introduced innovations by buying foreign technology or hiring foreign experts directly. More recently in the 1980s, the Chinese government-owned Jialing Machinery Factory in Chongqing improved the engineering of its motorcycles substantially by buying technical advice, machines, and parts, and licensing technology from Japan's Honda Motor Company. Additionally nonmarket sources of foreign knowledge include imitation, trade journals, and technical and scientific exchange, as well as feedback from foreign buyers or users of exports—all virtually costless.[23]

Sanjaya Lall's conclusion is sensible

> The correct strategy then must be a judicious and careful blend of permitting TNC [MNC] entry, licensing and stimulation of local technological effort. The stress must always be—as it was in Japan—to keep up with the best practice technology and to achieving production efficiency which enables local producers (regardless of their origin) to compete in world markets. This objective will necessitate TNC presence in some cases, but not in others.[24]

Loans at Bankers' Standards

Nonconcessional loans from abroad finance a deficit in the balance on goods and services account. For LDCs the trend of the ratio of official aid to commercial loans was generally declining: from 1.40 in 1970 to 0.66 in 1973 to 0.55 in 1975 to 0.36 in 1978 to 0.23 in 1984, increasing to 0.33 in 1987 mostly because of the fall in private lending discussed below rather than substantial growth in concessional assistance. By the late 1980s, low-income countries received twice the official assistance middle-income countries did, in contrast to the 1970s, when aid was evenly divided among the country categories. However, all but a small fraction of commercial loans (that is, loans at bankers' standards) were to middle-income countries having high credit ratings.[25]

---

[23] Gerald L. Nordquist, "Visit to Jialing Machinery Factory, May 24, 1987," in Louis de Alessi, delegation leader, Report of the May 13–30, 1987 American People to People Economics Delegation to the People's Republic of China, Spokane, Wash., Citizen Ambassador Program, 1987, pp. 66–71; E. Wayne Nafziger, "The Japanese Development Model: Its Implications for Developing Countries," *Bulletin of the Graduate School of International Relations, International University of Japan*, no. 5 (July 1986): 1–26; and Martin Fransman, *Technology and Economic Development* (Boulder, Colo.: Westview, 1986), pp. 11–14, who indicates major modes of transferring knowledge through the market.

[24] Sanjaya Lall, *Multinationals, Technology and Exports: Selected Papers* (New York: St. Martin's Press, 1985), p. 76.

[25] Sources for the section on loans are Organization for Economic Cooperation and Development, *Development Cooperation: Efforts and Policies of the Members of the Development Assistance Committee* (Paris, November 1982); Organization for Economic Cooperation and Development, *Resources for Developing Countries, 1980 and Recent Trends* (Paris, June 1981); Overseas Development Council, *U.S. Foreign Policy and the Third World: Agenda, 1982* (New York: Praeger, 1982), pp. 225–46; Overseas

Two sources of lending fell from 1981 to 1985: (1) private lending as commercial bankers became unwilling to finance in the face of debt rescheduling and default (Chapter 17), recent nonperforming loans, and the change from syndicated to more selective lending by individual banks, and (2) official (or officially supported) export credit finance (a part of short-term borrowing in Table 16-2) as the creditworthiness of oil exporters declined with oil-price reductions, LDC imports decreased (with slower growth and rising debt), and interest rates for bank finance fell.[26]

Bilateral Flows.   OECD official development assistance is only a part of the total net flow of resources to LDCs. As indicated earlier, 0.39 percent of the 1986 GNP of OECD countries was foreign aid. However additional net flows included private capital—0.23 percent of GNP, nonconcessional official flows—0.10 percent of GNP, and private voluntary agencies—0.04 percent of GNP. Thus the total net flow was 0.76 percent of GNP.

The Eurocurrency Market.   **Eurodollars** are dollars deposited in banks outside the United States. More generally **Eurocurrency** deposits are in currencies other than that of the country where the bank (called a Eurobank) is located. The Eurobank system began in the early 1950s when the Soviet Union, using the U.S. dollar for international trade and fearing the U.S. government might block its deposits in U.S. banks, transferred its dollars to English banks. These (and subsequently other European) banks could lend these dollars to MNCs, banks, governments, and other borrowers. Banks increased their profits by avoiding national exchange controls, reserve requirements, and bank interest ceilings, and depositers were attracted by receiving higher interest rates. Dollars comprise three-fourths of the more than $1 trillion deposits in this unregulated financial market, which is located in Europe (Zurich, Paris, Amsterdam, and Luxembourg), Hong Kong, Singapore, Tokyo, Kuwait, Nassau, Panama, Bahrain, and (in 1981 after U.S. banks could accept Eurodeposits) New York City. Eurobanks have played a role in lending to LDCs, including recycling petrodollars to oil-importing LDCs in the mid-1970s. While the absence of reserve requirements provides substantial potential for the multiple expansion of bank deposits (and world inflation), in practice most loan funds are deposited outside Eurobanks, thus leaking out of the system.[27]

Funds from Multilateral Agencies.   In July 1944, at Bretton Woods, New Hampshire, forty four nations established the **World Bank,** envisioned primarily as a source for loans to areas devastated during World War II; and the **IMF,** an agency

---

Development Council, *The United States and World Development; Agenda, 1982* (New York: Praeger, 1982), pp. 215–37; World Bank, *World Development Report, 1981* (New York: Oxford University Press, 1981), pp. 49–63; World Bank, *Annual Report, 1980* (Washington, D.C.: 1980); and International Monetary Fund, *World Economic Outlook* (Washington, D.C., 1988), pp. 96–109.

[26] Organization for Economic Cooperation and Development, *Financing and External Debt of Developing Countries: 1985 Survey* (Paris, 1986), pp. 23–24.

[27] Peter B. Kenen, *The International Economy* (Englewood Cliffs, Prentice–Hall, 1989), pp. 453–54, 468–70; Wilfred J. Ethier, *Modern International Economics* (New York: London, 1988), pp. 498–509; and Daniel R. Fusfeld, *Economics: Principles of Political Economy* (Glenview, Ill.: Scott, Foresman, and Co., 1988), pp. 799–801.

charged with promoting exchange stability to provide short-term credit for international balance of payments deficits. Neither institution was set up to solve the financial problems of developing countries; nevertheless today virtually all financial disbursements from the World Bank are to LDCs, and the IMF is the lender of last resort for LDCs with international payments crises.

The World Bank is a well-established borrower in international capital markets, issuing bonds denominated in U.S. dollars, but guaranteeing a minimal Swiss franc value when the dollar depreciates. In the late 1980s, the Bank, which is the largest source of long-term developmental finance for LDCs, provided about 40 percent of the total net resources to LDCs. It lent more than $30 billion to LDC governments annually, including funds for social investments, such as irrigation and flood control in Indonesia, a hydroelectric plant in Colombia, a mass transit rail system in Brazil, port facilities in Yugoslavia, a water supply system in Thailand, and a college of fisheries in the Philippines. Furthermore the World Bank has used its technical and planning expertise to upgrade projects to meet banking standards. A World Bank affiliate, the International Finance Corporation, has invested almost $1 billion in agencies to stimulate private enterprise, such as the Industrial Credit and Investment Corporation of India, mentioned in Chapter 14. These amounts do not include soft loans (or concessional aid) of more than $3 billion annually made by another World Bank affiliate, the **International Development Association.**

The IMF provides ready credit to a LDC with balance of payments problems equal to the **reserve tranche**—the country's original contribution of gold—or 25 percent of its initial contribution or quota. Beyond that other credit lines include the first credit tranche, with 25 percent of the quota, granted on adoption of a program to overcome international payments difficulties; an **extended facility,** with 150 percent of the quota, based on a detailed medium-term program; a **supplementary financing facility subsidy account,** 140 percent of quota (financed by repayments from trust fund loans and voluntary contributions) to support standby arrangements for eligible low-income LDCs under previous programs; a **compensatory and contingency financing facility (CFF),** 75 percent of quota, to finance a temporary shortfall in export earnings or excess costs of cereal imports beyond the country's control; **buffer stock financing,** 50 percent of the quota, to stabilize export earnings; an **oil facility,** funds borrowed from oil-exporting countries to lend at competitive interest rates to LDCs with balance of payments deficits; and a **subsidy account,** contributed by twenty five DCs and capital surplus oil exporters that makes available interest subsidies to low-income countries.[28] To illustrate, the financial intermediation of the IMF enabled India to borrow $2.85 billion from Saudi Arabia in 1981 at an interest rate of 11 percent, compared to 18 percent in the commercial markets.

Yet between 1983 and 1985, most special funding beyond direct IMF credits dried up, with net lending to LDCs falling from $11.4 billion to $0.2 billion, reducing IMF leverage to persuade LDCs to undertake austerity in the face of internal political opposition. However from 1986 to 1988, the IMF added a **structural adjustment facility (SAF)** which provides concessional assistance for medium-term macroeconomic and adjustment programs to low-income countries facing chronic balance of payments problems; an **enhanced structural adjustment facility** for the poorest IMF members making adjustments; and restored the CFF with an average grant

[28] Herbert G. Grubel, *International Economics* (Homewood, Ill.: Irwin, 1981), pp. 531–33.

element of 20 percent. The first two facilities were financed by recycling the IMF Trust Fund (from the sale of IMF gold) and by Japan and European countries with external surpluses, but not the United States, which had an international deficit and was opposed to IMF long-term concessional aid. As an example of how this aid works, in 1988, the IMF approved $85 million ($35 million as SAF and $18 million as supplementary funding) for Togo, whose export earnings from cocoa, coffee, palm products, and groundnuts had declined from 1985 to 1987.[29]

While the third world's (LDCs and high-income oil-exporters) collective vote in the IMF, based on member quotas, is 40 percent, LDCs often support DCs in laying down conditions for borrowing members in order not to jeopardize the IMF's financial base. In 1988, in exchange for IMF lending, Togo agreed to reduce its fiscal deficit, restrain current expenditures, select investment projects more rigorously, privatize some public enterprises, and liberalize trade. The LDC critics, supported by the Brandt Commission, charge that the IMF presumes that international payments problems can be solved only by reducing social programs, cutting subsidies, depreciating currency, and restructuring similar to Togo's 1988 program. According to the Brandt report, the Fund's insistence on drastic measures in short time periods imposes unnecessary burdens on low-income countries that not only reduce basic-needs attainment, but also occasionally lead to "IMF riots" and even the downfall of governments.[30] Surely the IMF must be satisfied that a borrower can repay a loan. And there may be few alternatives to monetary and fiscal restrictions or exchange-rate devaluation for eliminating a chronic balance of payments deficit. Furthermore as Chapter 17 indicates, the IMF's structural adjustment lending puts more emphasis on growth and efficiency and less on reducing domestic demand and attaining external balance.

Other major multilateral sources of nonconcessional lending in 1988 were the Inter-American Development Bank, the Asian Development Bank, and the European Community.

Private Loans.   In the 1960s, the LDC balance on goods and services deficit was financed primarily by flows from official or semiofficial sources in the form of grants, concessional loans, and market loans. In contrast primarily commercial loans financed deficits in the 1970s. The ratio of private flows to official flows from OECD countries increased from 0.64 in 1964 to 1966 to 0.87 in 1970 to 1.35 in 1975 to 1.95 in 1979, before falling to 1.78 in 1983 and 0.59 in 1987.

In the 1960s, private finance consisted mainly of suppliers' credits and direct foreign investment. Commercial bank lending increased after 1967 but rose even more dramatically in 1973 to 1975. However, the share of commercial bank lending and other private flows declined during the 1980s, because of DC bankers' concerns about the creditworthiness of heavily indebted countries and the LDCs' reluctance to increase their debt burden to private lenders.

---

[29] Richard E. Feinberg, "An Open Letter to the World Bank's New President," in Richard E. Feinberg and contributors, *Between Two Worlds: The World Bank's Next Decade* (New Brunswick, N.J.: Transaction Books, 1986), pp. 14–18; World Bank, *World Development Report, 1988* (New York: Oxford University Press, 1988), p. 141; and *IMF Survey* (February 8, 1988), p. 33, (April 4, 1988), p. 110, (August 19, 1988), p. 273, and (September 26, 1988), p. 302.

[30] International Development Issues, (Brandt report), *North–South: A Program for Survival* (Cambridge, Mass., MIT Press, 1980), pp. 215–16.

SUMMARY

1. Since the 1970s, LDCs have demanded a new international economic order, including changes in all economic relations and institutions linking people from different nations.

2. An independent commission chaired by Willy Brandt contends that the reform of the world economic order is in the mutual interest of both DCs and LDCs. In the 1980s, some DC governments, especially the United States, did not agree that major reform was in their interest.

3. A capital inflow enables a country to invest more than it saves and import more than it exports.

4. A newly industrializing country that effectively uses an inflow of foreign funds should usually be able to pay back its debt from increased output and productivity.

5. Exports minus imports of goods and services equal the international balance on goods and services. Aid, remittances, loans, and investment from abroad finance a balance on goods and services deficit.

6. Countries give concessional aid to LDCs for reasons of national economic and political interest, humanitarianism, and global political maintenance.

7. In 1986, the grant component of concessional aid to LDCs by OECD countries (the West and Japan) was 90 percent.

8. The OECD official aid remained fairly stable as a percentage of GNP through the 1970s and 1980s, changing only from 0.34 percent in 1970 to 0.35 percent in 1985. For the United States, this percentage decreased from 0.32 percent in 1970 to 0.24 percent in 1985. These aid proportions are far below the 0.70 percent aid target set in the 1970s.

9. Middle-income countries received more official aid per capita than low-income countries. However low-income countries (especially the least-developed countries) received more aid, figured as a percentage of GNP, than middle-income countries.

10. The major multilateral agencies providing concessional aid to LDCs were the United Nations, the European Community, and the International Development Association, a World Bank affiliate that was the major aid-giver to low-income countries.

11. Although the United States still accounts for the largest share of the world's foreign, private investment, its share declined between 1971 and 1983.

12. The largest multinational corporations have an economic strength comparable to that of the LDCs with which they bargain. The foreign production of MNCs accounts for about 20 percent of world output and intrafirm trade for about 25 percent of international manufacturing trade.

13. Although MNCs in developing countries provide scarce capital and advanced technology for growth, doing so may increase LDC dependence on foreign capital and technology. The LDCs need a judicious combination of MNCs, joint MNC–local ventures, licensing, and other technological borrowing and adaptation.

14. From the early 1970s to the mid-1980s, developing countries increased their reliance on commercial loans.

TERMS TO REVIEW

- **General Agreements on Tariffs and Trade**
- **capital goods imports**
- **international balance of payments statement**
- **two-gap analysis**
- **investment-limited growth**
- **trade-limited growth**
- **young debtor nation**
- **mature debtor nation**
- **international balance on goods and services**
- **aid (official development assistance)**
- **grant element of aid**
- **concessional loans**
- **Organization for**

- **Economic Cooperation and Development (OECD)**
- **Council for Mutual Economic Assistance (CEMA)**
- **bilateral aid**
- **multilateral agencies**
- **average propensity to remit**
- **portfolio investment**
- **direct investment**
- **multinational corporations**
- **oligopoly**
- **vertical integration**
- **turnkey projects**
- **Eurodollars**
- **Eurocurrency**
- **World Bank**
- **International Development Association (IDA)**

- **International Monetary Fund (IMF)**
- **reserve tranche**
- **IMF extended facility**
- **IMF supplementary financing facility subsidy account**
- **IMF compensatory and contingency financing facility (CFF)**
- **IMF buffer stock financing**
- **IMF oil facility**
- **IMF subsidy account**
- **IMF structural adjustment facility (SAF)**
- **IMF enhanced structural adjustment facility**

QUESTIONS TO DISCUSS

1. To what extent does the Brandt Commission's view of DC and LDC interdependence conflict with Frank's view of LDC dependence?

2. How can foreign aid, capital, and technology stimulate economic growth? How could the roles of foreign aid, capital, and technology vary at different stages of development?

3. What are Chenery's and Strout's two gaps? How do foreign aid and capital reduce these two gaps? What are the strengths and weaknesses of the two-gap analysis?

4. Using national income equations, explain an inflow of capital from abroad in terms of expenditures-income, investment-saving, and import-export relationships. Indicate the relationships between expenditures and income, investment and saving, and imports and exports for a country paying back a foreign loan. Does repaying the loan have to be burdensome?

5. What are sources for financing an international balance on goods and services deficit? Which was the most important source for LDCs in the 1980s?

6. How effective has DC aid been in promoting LDC development? How effective has food aid been?

7. What are the costs and benefits for donor countries giving aid to LDCs? Do the costs outweigh the benefits? Choose one donor country. What are the costs and benefits for this country giving aid? Do the costs outweigh the benefits?

8. What is the trend for OECD aid as a percentage of GNP since 1970?

9. Compare economic aid to low- and middle-income countries in the 1980s. How do you explain the difference?

10. How important was multilateral aid as a percentage of total economic aid during the 1980s?

11. What are the costs and benefits to LDCs of MNC investment? How has the balance between costs and benefits changed in the last decade or so?

12. What was the trend in the ratio of official aid relative to commercial loans to LDCs in the 1970s and 1980s? How important is multilateral lending as a source of nonconcessional loans?

13. How important has the World Bank been as a source of funds for LDCs? How important has the International Monetary Fund (IMF) been as a source of funds for LDCs? Do you think there should be any changes in World Bank and IMF roles in LDC development?

GUIDE TO READINGS

The UN Center on Transnational Corporations (for example, note 16 and subsequent publications in the series); Lall (note 24); John H. Dunning, *International Production and the Multinational Enterprise* (London: Allen and Unwin, 1981); the 1974 and 1981 editions of Baldwin and Richardson (notes 14 and 18) have useful background on the multinational corporation. On Japanese multinationals in LDCs, see Kiyoshi Kojima, *Japanese Direct Foreign Investment: A Model of Multinational Business Operations* (Tokyo: Charles E. Tuttle, 1978). Weizao and Wang (note 14) discuss MNCs in China.

Meier, *International Economics,* pp. 162–64, 331–34, and Chenery and Strout (note 4) analyze the savings and foreign exchange gaps.

Data on aid and loans to LDCs and their balance of payments are in periodic volumes from the IMF (note to Table 16-2), OECD, Overseas Development Council, and World Bank, *World Development Report* (notes 9 and 10). Richard E. Feinberg, Gerald K. Helleiner, Joan M. Nelson, Sheldon Annis, John F. H. Purcell, Michelle B. Miller, Charles R. Blitzer, and Howard Pack contributed essays on the World Bank's contribution to development in Feinberg and contributors (note 11). Vernon W. Rottan discusses "Why Foreign Assistance," in *Economic Development and Cultural Change* 37 (January 1989): 411–24.

Rodney Wilson, *Banking and Finance in the Arab Middle East* (New York: St. Martin's, 1983), discusses Arab OPEC aid and finance.

Chapter Seventeen

THE EXTERNAL DEBT CRISIS

SCOPE OF THE CHAPTER

In Chapter 16, we mentioned the LDCs' persistent balance on goods and services deficit, which together with a decline in loans at bankers's standards after 1983, exacerbated the LDC debt crisis. This chapter discusses the causes, effects, and policy approaches to the debt crisis in more detail, including the U.S. bankers' and LDC governments' perspective, indicators of debt, the major LDC debtors, origins of the debt crisis, how capital flight exacerbates the debt problem, the roles of World Bank and IMF lending, proposals to resolve the debt crisis, and the distributional effects of the debt crisis and relief measures.

THE CRISIS FROM THE U.S. BANKING PERSPECTIVE

During the 1980s, when commercial banks held 72 percent of Latin American debt, U.S. banks (holding 36 percent) and British banks, but few continental European banks, were vulnerable to Latin default. In 1985, Latin American debts to U.S. banks as a percentage of their capital was 69 percent (109 percent for the nine largest U.S. banks), indicating that a complete write-off of these debts would ruin many major U.S. banks. By 1988, Latin American, Philippine, and Polish loans held by U.S. banks sold at a 40–70 percent discount on the second hand market, indicating the market expected at least a partial default. The U.S. bank exposure to LDC foreign debt declined in the 1980s but only as a result of loan write-offs, write-downs, asset sales, and reduced LDC lending. As an example, in May 1987, John S. Reed, chair of the largest U.S. commercial bank, New York's Citicorp, added $3 billion to bank reserves for future LDC loan losses, acknowledging the uncertainty of debt repayment and starting a chain of similar reactions that resulted in losses for Citicorp and several other major banks in 1987. In response to a high percentage of nonperforming LDC loans and shrinking petrodollars from low world oil prices in the 1980s, U.S. banks reduced their loans to non-OPEC developing countries from $120.6 billion in 1982 to $117.6 billion in 1984 to $100.2 billion in 1986, and in 1988 did not plan to resume 1982 lending levels without a major restructuring of their loans. From 1984 to 1988, Japan ranked first in the world in commercial bank lending to LDCs, about double that of the United States, in second place.[1]

THE CRISIS FROM THE LDC PERSPECTIVE

But while DC banks improved their financial position in the late 1980s, living standards of several major LDC debtors declined, especially in Latin America, where external debt totaled $400 million at the end of 1987 (see Figure 17-1). In mid-1985, Peru's President Alan Garcia limited debt payment to 10 percent of exports. Brazil's President Sarney put a moratorium on interest payments for 12 months in February 1987, explaining his country's impatience by indicating that "a debt paid with poverty is an account paid with democracy."[2] Creditors' reactions were to cut Brazil's short-term credits, although the U.S. Federal Reserve and Treasury arranged a short-term debt settlement a year later. At a meeting of leaders of debtor nations in late 1987, Argentine President Raul Alfonsin indicated that the West must recognize how "current economic conditions impede our development and condemn us to backwardness. We cannot accept that the south pay for the disequilibrium of the north."

DEBT INDICATORS

Debt service is the interest and principal payments due in a given year on long-term debt. The **debt-service ratio** is figured by dividing these payments by the year's exports of goods and services. This ratio for LDCs increased from 8.9 percent in 1970 to 12.6 percent in 1979 to 17.8 percent in 1983 to 20.0 percent in 1986. Another indicator of debt burden, debt as a percentage of LDC GNP, increased from 12.3 percent in 1970 to 24.3 percent in 1980 to 33.1 percent in 1984 to 36.6

[1] Rudiger Dornbusch, "International Debt and Economic Instability," in *Debt, Financial Stability, and Public Policy,* proceedings of a Federal Reserve Bank of Kansas City symposium, Jackson Hole, Wyoming, August 27–29, 1986, pp. 63–86; "Debt Breakthrough," *Wall Street Journal* (December 30, 1987): pp. 1, 4; John W. Sewell, Stuart K. Tucker, and contributors, *Growth, Exports, and Jobs in a Changing World Economy: Agenda, 1988* (New Brunswick, N.J.: Transaction Books, 1988), p. 231; Willem H. Buiter and T. N. Srinivasan, "Rewarding the Profligate and Punishing the Prudent and Poor: Some Recent Proposals for Debt Relief," *World Development* 15 (March 1987): 412; and *IMF Survey* (January 25, 1988), p. 17, and (December 12, 1988), p. 385.

[2] Gustav Ranis, "Latin American Debt and Adjustment," *Journal of Development Economics* 27 (October 1987): 189–99; and Guillermo O'Donnell, "Brazil's Failure: What Future for Debtors' Cartels?" *Third-World Quarterly* 9 (October 1987): 1157–66.

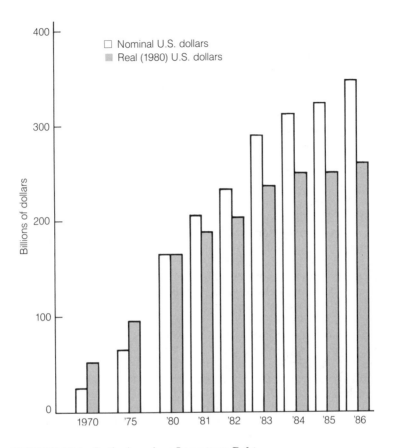

FIGURE 17-1   Latin American Long-term Debt

Source: Mark Drabenstott, Alan Barkema, and David Henneberry, "The Latin American Debt Problem and U.S. Agriculture," *Economic Review: Federal Reserve Bank of Kansas City* 73 (July/August 1988): 42, using data from World Bank, *World Debt Tables: External Debt of Developing Countries,* vol. 1, *Analysis and Summary* (Washington, D.C., 1988): 18–21.

percent in 1988, with debt in Zambia, Madagascar, the Congo, Zaïre, Morocco, Chile, and Nicaragua exceeding 1988 GNP.[3]

MAJOR LDC DEBTORS

Who have been the major LDC debtors? In 1986, the rank order was Brazil ($113 billion), Mexico ($110 billion); South Korea, Argentina, India, Indonesia, Egypt, Venezuela, Turkey, Greece, China, Israel, the Philippines, Nigeria, Chile, Yugosla-

[3] International Monetary Fund, *World Economic Outlook* (Washington, D.C., 1988), pp. 122–32; Jeffrey D. Sachs, "The Debt Crisis at a Turning Point," *Challenge* 31 (May/June 1988): 17–26; and World Bank, *World Development Report, 1988* (New York: Oxford University Press, 1988), pp. 258–59.

via, Malaysia, Algeria (each with over $20 billion of external public debt outstanding); Morocco, Thailand, Portugal, Peru, Pakistan, Saudi Arabia, Colombia, Iraq, Taiwan, and the Ivory Coast (each with over $10 billion of debt). The twenty eight countries indicated accounted for 77 percent of the total LDC debt. Yet none of these countries is least developed, and only two are low-income countries. As a matter of fact, middle-income countries account for 85 percent of the total outstanding debt of all LDCs.[4]

Between January 1980 and September 1987, fifty LDCs renegotiated their foreign debts through multilateral agreements with official creditor groups (the **Paris Club**) or with commercial banks, lengthening or modifying repayment terms. These countries included Brazil, Mexico, Argentina, Egypt, Morocco, the Philippines, Turkey, Chile, Venezuela, Colombia, Peru, Nigeria, Yugoslavia, the Ivory Coast, and low-income Pakistan.[5]

Yet ironically for some countries, a high rank among LDC debtors indicated a high credit rating among commercial banks. South Korea has shown that heavy borrowing can be serviced as long as exports and GNP grow rapidly. Although South Korea's debt rose from $1.8 billion in 1970 to $15 billion in 1979 to $40 billion in 1982 to $54 billion in 1986, its exports grew so rapidly that its debt-servicing capacity improved considerably.[6] A large debt need not be a problem so long as foreign creditors believe an economy can roll over the debt or borrow enough to cover debt service and imports.

While only two major debtors were from sub-Saharan Africa, its external debt ($53 billion, about half Mexico's 1986 figure) was probably as burdensome as any other world region. By the end of 1986, two-thirds of the forty five countries under the IMF African Department had credit outstanding averaging 134 percent of their quotas[7] (compared to only 25 percent unconditional borrowing rights, the reserve tranche). In the 1970s and early to mid-1980s, rulers of Nigeria ($25 billion debt in 1986), Zaïre ($7 billion 1986 debt, most principal and interest from 1971–74 borrowing), and Ghana ($3 billion debt) squandered their loan funds, sometimes expanding patronage for intermediaries and contractors so rapidly that they lost track of millions of dollars borrowed from abroad. During Nigeria's second republic (civilian government), 1979 to 1983, the ports sometimes lacked the capacity for imports like cement going to government agencies controlled by politicians distributing benefits to clients. The countries had to reschedule their debts—Ghana in 1974, after an abrupt decline in the prices of cocoa exports; Zaïre, in 1980 to 1987, after several years of depressed copper export prices; and Nigeria, in 1983 and 1986, after a prolonged oil price slump. Compared to Asian-Latin debtors, the three

[4] Organization for Economic Cooperation and Development, *Financing and External Debt of Developing Countries: 1987 Survey* (Paris, 1988).

[5] World Bank, *World Debt Tables: External Debt of Developing Countries, 1987–88 Edition*, vol. I *Analysis and Summary Tables* (Washington, D.C.: 1988).

[6] Organization for Economic Cooperation and Development, *Financing and External Debt of Developing Countries: 1987 Survey* (Paris, 1988); and World Bank, *World Development Report, 1981* (New York: Oxford University Press, 1981), p. 60.

[7] Organization for Economic Cooperation and Development, *Financing and External Debt of Developing Countries: 1987 Survey* (Paris, 1988), p. 72; and Karamo N. M. Sonko, "The Political Economy of IMF Presence in Africa: An Analysis of the Causes and Consequences," paper presented to the African Studies Association, Chicago, October 27–30, 1988.

African countries have poorer credit ratings among commercial banks because of poor national economic management, as reflected in previous balance of payments crises, and a slow growth in output and exports.

ORIGINS OF THE DEBT CRISIS

The LDC external debt increased from \$49 billion in 1970 to \$157 billion in 1976 to \$816 billion in 1982 to \$908 billion in 1984 to \$1085 billion in 1986[8] for several reasons.

1. The LDC international balance on goods and payments deficit increased from a series of global shocks, including the 1973 to 1974 and 1979 to 1980 oil price rises (which reduced non-oil-producing LDCs' terms of trade) and the 1980 to 1983 OECD recession (with sharply falling commodity prices, slowed export expansion, and increased OECD protectionism).

2. As indicated in Chapter 16, DCs relied more on private bank and other commercial loans, increasing their ratio to official aid from 1970 to the mid-1980s.

3. Like Iowa farmers and Pennsylvania small business people, LDCs reacted to the input price hikes of 1973 to 1975 by increasing their borrowing. The quadrupling of world oil prices in 1973 to 1974 poured tens of billions of petrodollars into the global banking system, which were "recycled" as loans to LDCs and U.S. farmers and business people at low rates of interest. They were lured by **negative world real interest rates,** the nominal rates of interest minus the inflation rate, -7 percent in 1973, -16 percent in 1974, and -5 percent in 1975. Many of these debts came due in the early 1980s when high nominal rates of interest, together with low inflation rates, resulted in high real interest rates (9–12 percent in 1982 to 1985).[9]

   The average interest rate for fixed-interest loans (generally subsidized or long term) rose from 4 percent (1970) to 6 percent (1981) to 7 percent (1986). From 1971 to 1981, interest rates on floating-interest loans (primarily from commercial sources) increased from 8 percent to 18 percent. The decrease in the average loan maturity from 20 years in 1970 to 16 years in 1986, as well as a reduction in the average grace period over the same period from 6 years to 5 years, also aggravated the problem of debt service.[10]

[8] Organization for Economic Cooperation and Development, *Financing and External Debt of Developing Countries: 1987 Survey* (Paris, 1988), p. 218; World Bank, *World Development Report, 1978* (New York: Oxford University Press, 1978), pp. 96–97; and World Bank, *World Development Report, 1988* (New York: Oxford University Press, 1988), pp. 258–59.

[9] Ann O. Krueger, "Origins of the Developing Countries' Debt Crisis," *Journal of Development Economics* 27 (October 1987): 169; Alireza Rahimibrougerdi, "An Empirical Investigation of the Effects of Major Exogenous Shocks on the Growth of Nonoil- and Oil-Exporting Developing Countries from 1965 to 1985" (Ph.D. diss., Kansas State University, 1988), pp. 6, 83; John Cavanagh, Fantu Cheru, Carole Collins, Cameron Duncan, and Dominic Ntube, *From Debt to Development: Alternatives to the International Debt Crisis* (Washington, D.C.: Institute for Policy Studies, 1985), p. 25.

[10] World Bank, *World Development Report, 1988* (New York: Oxford University Press, 1988), pp. 260–61.

4. The inefficiency and poor national economic management indicated before in Nigeria, Zaïre, and Ghana, as well as in Latin American military governments, in the 1970s, meant no increased capacity to facilitate the export surplus to service the foreign debt. Argentina's substantial increase in public spending in the 1970s, financed by borrowing from abroad, increased external debt and reduced export capacity.

5. The adjustment essential to export more than is imported and produce more than is spent requires translating government spending cuts into foreign exchange earnings and competitive gains, usually necessitating reduced demand and wages, real currency depreciation, and increased unemployment. But when many other LDCs go through the same adjustment process, the benefit to any given LDC is less. In 1985, for example, the pressure on debtor countries to increase export revenues contributed to a glut in primary products and a collapse of their prices.

    Mexico reduced real wages 40 percent, increased the unemployment rate, and depreciated the peso from 1980 to 1987 to increase its external competitiveness by 40 percent. Currency depreciation also raised the nominal interest rate essential to spur Mexicans to hold pesos rather than U.S. dollars. Few countries are willing to contract domestic employment and real wages to return the balance on goods and services account to equilibrium.[11]

6. When debts are denominated in U.S. dollars, their **appreciation** (increased value relative to other major currencies) from 1980 to 1984, increased the local and nondollar currency cost of servicing such debts. Or as in 1985 to 1988, nondollar debts increased when measured in dollars that **depreciate** (reduce their value relative to other major currencies). For example, the dollar value of Indonesia's 1985 debt to the Japanese ¥1250 billion) increased from $5 billion to $10 billion in 1988, as the dollar depreciated from ¥250=$1 to ¥125=$1.

7. International lenders require LDC governments to guarantee private debt, increasing public debt service.

8. Overvalued domestic currencies and restrictions on international trade and payments contribute to capital flight from LDCs, exacerbating the current account deficit and external debt problems.

9. The lack of coordination by leading DCs in exchange-rate and financial policies under the world's post-1973 **managed floating exchange-rate system** (one where central banks intervene in the market to influence the price of foreign exchange) results in gyrating exchange rates and interest rates. Efforts to set **target zones** within which key DC exchange rates will float have only increased destabilizing capital movements and unstable exchange-rate changes when inevitably rates approach zone boundaries. This global instability increases external shocks and undermines long-run LDC planning.[12]

[11] World Bank, *World Development Report, 1985* (New York: Oxford University Press, 1985), pp. 62–63; Rudiger Dornbusch, "International Debt and Economic Instability," Proceedings of a Federal Reserve Bank of Kansas City symposium, Jackson Hole, Wyoming, August 27–29, 1986, pp. 71–75; and Jeffrey D. Sachs, "The Debt Crisis at a Turning Point," *Challenge* 31 (May/June 1988), 20.

[12] Deena Khatkhate, "International Monetary System—Which Way?" *World Development* 15 (December 1987): vii–xvi.

CAPITAL FLIGHT

Some economists feel it is futile to lend more funds to LDCs if a large portion flows back through capital flight. John T. Cuddington estimates Mexico's **propensity to flee** from additional external borrowing, 1974 to 1984, was 0.31, meaning that 31 cents from a dollar lent by foreign creditors left the country through capital flight![13] This flight intensifies foreign exchange shortages and damages the collective interest of the wealthy classes that buy foreign assets. Reversing capital flight will not eliminate the debt crisis but can reduce debt burdens and commercial bankers' justification for resisting increased exposure to debtor countries.[14]

Definitions

Which of the domestic holdings of foreign assets (property, equity investment, bonds, deposits, and money) should be classified as domestic capital flight rather than normal capital outflows? Defining **capital flight** as resident capital outflow makes it easier to measure and conceptualize than alternative definitions, such as capital outflows that are illegal, abnormal, undesirable to government or due to overinvoicing imports or underinvoicing exports. Using the World Bank's estimates of capital flight as equal to current account balance, net foreign direct investment, and changes in reserves and debt indicates that the largest capital flights, 1976 to 1984, were from Argentina, Venezuela, and (especially) Mexico, while South Korea's and the Philippines's flights were very small.[15]

Whenever international capital markets are highly integrated and transaction costs are low, private individuals will have strong incentives to circumvent what appears to be arbitrary barriers to capital movements, as even the United States found in the 1960s when interest equalization taxes and foreign credit restraint programs resulted in Eurocurrency and Eurobond market expansion to satisfy the offshore demand for funds.[16]

Causes

Resident capital outflows result from differences in perceived risk-adjusted returns in source and haven countries. We can attribute these differences to slow growth, overvalued domestic currencies, high inflation rates, confiscatory taxation, discriminatory interest ceilings or taxes on residents, financial repression, default on government obligations, expected currency depreciation, limitations on convertibility,

[13] John T. Cuddington, *Capital Flight: Estimates, Issues, and Explanations*, Princeton Studies in International Finance no. 58, Princeton University, 1986.

[14] Donald R. Lessard and John Williamson, eds., *Capital Flight and Third-World Debt* (Washington, D.C.: Institute for International Economics, 1987); and John Williamson and Donald R. Lessard, *Capital Flight: The Problem and Policy Responses* (Washington, D.C.: Institute for International Economics, 1987).

[15] Robert Cumby and Richard Levich, "On the Definition and Magnitude of Recent Capital Flight," in Donald R. Lessard and John Williamson, eds., *Capital Flight and Third-World Debt* (Washington, D.C.: Institute for International Economics, 1987), pp. 27–67.

[16] Donald R. Lessard and John Williamson, eds., *Capital Flight and Third–World Debt* (Washington, D.C.: Institute for International Economics, 1987).

poor investment climate, or political instability in source countries, all exacerbated by the U.S. decision to abandon income taxation on nonresident bank deposit interest and much other investment income, and (in the early 1980s) pay high interest rates. In 1982, Mexico's devaluation and inflation "almost totally wiped out the value of obligations denominated in Mexican pesos." The domestic entrepreneurial energies lost from these policies are substantial.[17]

How to Reduce Flight.   Source countries need robust growth, market-clearing exchange rates and other prices, an outward trade orientation, dependable positive real interest rates, fiscal reform (including lower taxes on capital gains), taxes on foreign assets as high as domestic assets, more efficient state enterprises, other market liberalization, supply-oriented adjustment measures, a resolution of the debt problem, and incorruptable government officials.[18] Haven countries can lower interest rates and cease tax discrimination favoring nonresident investment income, while their banks can refuse to accept funds from major LDC debtor countries.

Just listing policies for source and haven countries suggests how difficult the flight problem is. Rudiger Dornbusch of MIT indicates that capital flight is the caboose, not the locomotive, meaning that flight is symptomatic of the financial repression and economic underdevelopment at the root of the debt crisis, not the cause of it.[19] We have another vicious circle—low growth, capital flight, and foreign exchange restrictions that hamper growth. Ironically John Williamson and Donald R. Lessard, despite recommendation of financial and exchange-rate liberalization, indicate that sometimes LDCs may have to use **exchange controls,** which limit domestic residents' purchase of foreign currency, to limit the exodus of new savings.[20]

WORLD BANK AND IMF LENDING

Throughout most of the post–World War II period, the World Bank emphasized development lending to LDCs, while the IMF lent resources to help DCs and LDCs cope with balance of payments crises. In 1979, the World Bank introduced **structural adjustment loans (SAL),** no longer tied to specific projects, but to support the balance of payments through 15–20 year loans, with 3–5 years' grace, and interest rates only 0.5 percent above the Bank's borrowing costs except for a front-end fee on new commitments. Structural adjustment policies emphasize growth and improved allocative efficiency as well as controlling domestic demand and improving the current account.[21]

---

[17] John Williamson and Donald R. Lessard, *Capital Flight: The Problem and Policy Responses* (Washington, D.C., Institute for International Economics, 1987), with quotation from p. 21.

[18] Ibid., p. 28–58.

[19] Rimmer de Vries, as part of a panel on policy issues in Donald R. Lessard and John Williamson, eds., *Capital Flight and Third–World Debt,* (Washington, D.C., Institute for International Economics, 1987), p. 188.

[20] John Williamson and Donald R. Lessard, *Capital Flight: The Problem and Policy Responses* (Washington, D.C., Institute for International Economics, 1987), p. 57.

[21] Mohsin S. Khan, "Macroeconomic Adjustment in Developing Countries: A Policy Perspective," *The World Bank Research Observer* 2 (January 1987): 26–27.

In the 1980s, the Bank led donor coordination, increasing the power of external leverage. Although IMF direct credits to LDCs fell in the mid-1980s, the IMF retained some influence because of IMF–World Bank cooperation. By 1986 to 1987, the IMF used trust funds and funds from surplus DC countries for SALs to LDCs (especially in Africa) experiencing unanticipated external shocks.[22]

World Bank

In 1975, the World Bank established an interest subsidy account (a "third window") for discount loans for poorest countries facing oil price increases.[23] In 1979 to 1983, SALs accounted for only 9 percent of Bank lending and had little impact on the most highly indebted countries. Although the Bank set up a Special Assistance Program in 1983 to help ease the debt crisis, by the late 1980s, critics, including some U.S. economists and Congress people, voiced their dissatisfaction with the Bank's minimal financial contribution to debt relief arrangements. The leadership of the Bank, while pointing out that 45 percent of its loans were to heavily indebted countries, argues, however, that the Bank's primary role is development lending to poor countries, not financial guarantees for commercial bank loans to middle-income countries.[24]

International Monetary Fund

A **balance of payments equilibrium** refers to an international balance on the goods and services balance over the business cycle, with no undue inflation, unemployment, tariffs, and exchange controls. In practice a member borrowing from the IMF, in excess of the reserve tranche, agrees to certain performance criteria, with emphasis on a long-run international balance and price stability. IMF **conditionality,** a quid pro quo for borrowing, often includes government reducing budget deficits through increased tax revenues and reduced social spending, limiting credit creation, achieving market-clearing prices, liberalizing trade, devaluing currency, eliminating price controls, and restraining public sector employment and wage rates. The Fund monitors domestic credit, the exchange rate, and debt targets closely for compliance. Policies generally shift the internal relative prices away from nontradable goods to tradable goods, promoting exports and "efficient" import substitu-

[22] Richard E. Feinberg, "An Open Letter to the World Bank's New President,"in Richard E. Feinberg and contributors, *Between Two Worlds: The World Bank's Next Decade* (New Brunswick, N.J.: Transaction Books, 1986), pp. 14–18.

[23] Jonathan E. Sanford, "Feasibility of a World Bank Interest Subsidy Account to Supplement the Existing IDA Program," *World Development* (July 1988): 787–96.

[24] "World Bank gives Debtors Condition for More Lending," *Wall Street Journal* (July 1, 1988): p. 19; and Walter S. Mossberg, "World Bank's Conable Runs into Criticism on Poor Nations' Debt," *Wall Street Journal* (June 21, 1988), pp. 1, 24.

An example of skillfully playing the World Bank against the IMF for public relations gains involved President Ibrahim Babangida, who from 1985 to 1986 conducted a year-long dialogue with the Nigerian public, resulting in a rejection of IMF terms for borrowing. Subsequently his Nigerian military government's agreement to impose similar terms "on its own" was approved by the World Bank, which in October 1986 made available (with Western commercial and central banks) a package of $1020 million quickly disbursed loans and $4280 million 3-year project loans.

tion. In effect these policies shift purchasing power from the urban to rural areas, from consumption to investment, and from labor to capital.

John Loxley finds little evidence that IMF programs restore growth and external balance to low-income African countries. In the 1970s, five out of twenty three African countries reached growth targets; thirteen out of eighteen, inflation targets; and eleven out of twenty eight trade targets. Likewise IMF programs have not led to bank credit inflows.[25]

After 1981, the IMF emphasized shock treatment (a 1-year program) for demand restraint in low-income Africa, although rarely providing financing for external adjustments. Demand restrictions, inflation deceleration, and currency depreciation do not switch expenditures to exports and import substitutes rapidly enough to have the desired effect of improving the trade balance. Studies indicate that, even in DCs (for example, the United States, 1985–1988), the current account improvement from devaluation usually takes about 2–5 years, due to lags between changes in relative international prices (from exchange-rate changes) and responses in quantities traded, including recognition, decision (time for assessing the change), delivery, replacement (perhaps waiting until inventories have been depleted and machines wear out), and production (time for increasing output).[26]

Many LDCs feel the IMF focuses only on demand while ignoring productive capacity and long-term structural change. Additionally these governments object to the Fund's market ideology and neglect of external determinants of stagnation and instability. Moreover IMF austerity curtails programs to reduce poverty and stimulate long-run development. Yet while the IMF has perceived its role as providing international monetary stability and liquidity, not development, the concessional component of its structural adjustment loans, which began in 1986 to 1988, emphasized development more. However, in their Declaration of Uruguay, October 27–29, 1988, the seven largest Latin American countries contended that "the conditionality of adjustment programs, sector lending, and restructuring agreements often entails measures that are inadequate and contradictory, making the economic policies more difficult in an extremely harsh economic climate."[27] Economists will be better able to evaluate the IMF's structural adjustment programs in the 1990s.

RESOLVING THE DEBT CRISIS

Although in the 1970s and early 1980s, creditors took a case by case approach to the debt crisis, by the mid to late 1980s, several policymakers had advocated debt relief plans. We focus here on three widely discussed proposals.

Debt Equity Swaps

From 1982 to 1988, the active market for swapping or selling commercial bank claims on LDCs grew rapidly. Debt equity swaps usually conform to the following pattern. A DC commercial bank (Citicorp led here, too) sells an outstanding loan,

---

[25] John Loxley, "The IMF and World Bank Conditionality and sub-Saharan Africa," in Peter Lawrence, ed., *World Recession and the Food Crisis in Africa* (London: James Currey, 1986), pp. 96–103.

[26] Herbert G. Grubel, *International Economics* (Homewood, Ill.: Irwin, 1981), pp. 349–88.

[27] *IMF Survey* (November 14, 1988), p. 354.

made to a debtor country government agency, to a MNC, which presents the loan paper to the debtor's central bank, which redeems all or most of the face value of the loan in *domestic currency* at the market exchange rate. The investor acquires equity interest in a LDC firm. This swap substitutes a repayment stream depending on equity profitability for a fixed external obligation. The U.S. administration proposed that the World Bank promote debt equity swaps, consistent with privatization. As of 1988, Brazil, Mexico, Argentina, Chile, and the Philippines participated in debt equity swaps.[28]

Baker Plan

In the early 1980s, U.S. government strategy was to emphasize debtors paying the full interest due to U.S. banks. However by 1985, Washington realized the constraints the debt crisis placed on Latin American growth and demand for U.S. exports. Peru's President Garcia's 1985 UN speech posing the problem as democracy or honoring debt forced U.S. political leaders to focus on this tradeoff. Later at the September 1985 IMF–World Bank meeting, Secretary of the Treasury James A. Baker, III, unveiled a U.S. proposal, which called for Inter-American Development Bank and IMF credit, World Bank structural adjustment assistance, and contributions from trade surplus countries, such as Japan, as well as additional commercial bank lending, to help the highly indebted middle-income countries. Countries receiving funds were not to sacrifice growth, since the policy of restraining the budget, reforming tax systems, liberalizing trade, and setting public sector prices closer to the market would promote efficiency more than restrain demand. The IMF, under pressure from the U.S. Federal Reserve Board and Treasury and a Mexican threat of debt repudiation, contributed $1.7 billion to a $12 billion "growth-oriented" package of adjustment and structural reform, which included $6 billion from commercial banks. But the Baker approach does not help the poorest countries, and its terms do not take into account past management performance. Moreover Latin American debtors considered the new resources inadequate and asked for a lower interest rate spread over the Eurodollar London rate or London Inter-Bank Offer Rate (LIBOR, virtually a risk-free interest rate) and a ceiling on debt service payments.[29]

Bradley Plan

New Jersey Senator Bill Bradley, concerned about the effect of the debt problem on Latin American demand for U.S. manufacturing exports, linked debt relief (partial write-downs or write-offs of debt principal) to Latin American trade concessions and liberalization and market-oriented reforms. Yet as in the Baker plan, the relief is given independent of debt-servicing efforts and past economic management.[30]

[28] *IMF Survey* (July 11, 1988), p. 226.

[29] Jeffrey D. Sachs, "The Debt Crisis," *Challenge* 31 (May/June 1988): 19; Willem H. Buiter and T. N. Srinivasan, "Rewarding the Profligate," *World Development* 15 (March 1987), 411–13; Gustav Ranis, "Latin American Debt and Adjustment," *Journal of Development Economics* 27 (October 1987): 189–99; and Alireza Rahimibrougerdi, "An Empirical Investigation of the Effects of Major Exogenous Shocks on the Growth of Nonoil- and Oil-Exporting Developing Countries from 1965 to 1985," (Ph. D. diss., Kansas State University, 1988), p. 51.

[30] Willem H. Buiter and T. N. Srinivasan, "Rewarding the Profligate," *World Development* 15 (March 1987), 411–12.

Miyazawa Plan

In June 1988, Japanese Finance Minister Kiichi Miyazawa proposed debtors transfer part of their currency reserves into a special IMF-managed account from which bank loans would be repaid. In return for the assurance of repayment, banks would reschedule debt and negotiate debt equity swaps. Finance ministers of the six other major capitalist DCs were concerned that the debt repayment scheme could evolve into a IMF debt facility.[31]

DISTRIBUTIONAL EFFECTS

The UN Conference on Trade and Development has proposed widespread debt renegotiation to cancel or reschedule debts, especially of the least-developed countries. Since the late 1970s, the Paris Club, comprising of ad hoc meetings of representatives of creditor countries, has increased arrangements to reschedule or consolidate official debts. Sweden, Canada, and the Netherlands have even canceled the debts of some of the poorest countries as a form of development assistance.

Yet these measures affected only a small fraction of total LDC debt, since private creditors hold the majority of the debt. But Jeffrey D. Sachs is critical of such measures as the Baker plan, which saves banks at the expense of the IMF, the World Bank, and Japanese creditors. Moreover both Baker and Bradley proposals emphasize middle-income countries in financial trouble rather than poor countries or more prudent South Korea. Additionally many LDCs adversely affected by external shock or growth deceleration, including India, Bangladesh, and most of low-income sub-Saharan Africa, borrowed less by choice than necessity (low creditworthiness).[32]

Why should DCs or multilateral agencies use concessional aid for debt relief or cancellation? Most of the large debtors are *not* among the poorest countries but are instead middle income. Many countries with debt crises have not managed their economies very well.

Finally Latin America's and sub-Saharan Africa's debt crises have forced many countries to curtail poverty programs, even though few of these programs have been funded by foreign borrowing. In 1985, Tanzanian President Julius K. Nyerere asked, "Must we starve our children to pay our debt?" The UNICEF found that child malnutrition increased and primary school enrollment rates declined in the 1980s in many least-developed countries as external debt constraints cut spending on services most needed by the poor.[33]

[31] "Japanese Proposal on Third-World Debt Disturbs the Peace at Economic Summit," *Wall Street Journal* (June 21, 1988), p. 3.

[32] Jeffrey D. Sachs, "The Debt Crisis," *Challenge* 31 (May/June 1988), 19; and Willem H. Buiter and T. N. Srinivasan, "Rewarding the Profligate," *World Development* 15 (March 1987), 414.

[33] Manuel Pastor, Jr., "The Effects of IMF Programs in the Third World: Debate and Evidence from Latin America," *World Development* 15 (February 1987): 249–62; E. Wayne Nafziger, *Inequality in Africa: Political Elites, Proletariat, Peasants, and the Poor* (Cambridge: Cambridge University Press, 1988), pp. 61–63; UNICEF, *The State of the World's Children, 1989* (New Delhi: 1989); and Jeffrey Sachs and Andrew Berg, "The Debt Crisis: Structural Explanations of Country Performance," *Journal of*

SUMMARY

1. LDCs, especially Latin American, had an increase in their real external debt in the 1970s and 1980s. The LDC debt service ratio more than doubled between 1970 to 1986. The exposure of several major U.S. commercial banks to losses from LDC loan write-offs or write-downs has been substantial.

2. The ratio of debt service to GNP is not always a good indicator of the debt burden. Many large LDC debtors borrowed heavily because of their excellent international credit ratings.

3. Middle-income countries account for 85 percent of the total outstanding debt of all LDCs. Yet the debt burden for low-income countries, such as the majority of sub-Saharan African countries, which have poor credit ratings, may be as heavy as for middle-income countries.

4. In the 1980s, at least fifty LDCs renegotiated their foreign debts through multilateral agreements with official creditor groups.

5. Some of the causes of the debt crisis are global shocks and instability in the 1970s and 1980s, a decline in the ratio of official aid to commercial loans, increased real interest rates from the 1970s to the 1980s, inefficiency, poor economic management, overvalued domestic currencies, and capital flight.

6. Lending to LDCs (especially Latin American) may be undermined by capital flight because perceived risk-adjusted returns are higher in haven countries than in LDCs. Equilibrium exchange rates, fiscal reform, increased efficiency of state enterprises, and nondiscriminatory haven country policies can help reduce flight, but ironically exchange controls may also be necessary sometimes.

7. In the late 1970s, the World Bank began structural adjustment loans, which emphasized growth and improved allocative efficiency, as well as limited aggregate demand. Yet only a small percentage of World Bank lending was for structural adjustment loans.

8. For LDCs borrowing beyond the reserve tranch (25 percent of the quota), the IMF usually requires a quid pro quo, which may include devaluation, reduced government spending, and market liberalization. Critics charge that IMF programs do not restore growth nor external balance to LDCs. Some Latin American countries even contended that the IMF's structural adjustment loans, begun in 1986, made economic policies essential to growth even more difficult.

9. Economists and finance officials have suggested several plans for resolving the debt crisis. Debt equity swaps involve selling an outstanding loan to a private company, which acquires equity interest in a LDC firm. Critics contend that the Baker plan puts too much emphasis on shifting risks from commercial banks to multilateral agencies and surplus countries.

Development Economics 29 (November 1988): 217–306; and Marcelo Selowsky, "Comment on The Debt Crisis: Structural Explanations of Country Performance," *Journal of Development Economics* 29 (November 1988): 307–09.

TERMS TO REVIEW

- debt service
- debt-service ratio
- Paris Club
- negative world real interest rates
- currency appreciation
- currency depreciation

- managed floating exchange-rate system
- target zones
- capital flight
- propensity to flee
- exchange controls
- structural adjustment loans (SAL)

- balance of payments equilibrium
- conditionality
- Baker plan
- Bradley plan
- Miyazawa plan

QUESTIONS TO DISCUSS

1. Discuss the nature and origins of the LDCs' external debt problem. What impact has the debt crisis had on LDC development? On DCs?

2. What is capital flight? What relevance does it have for the debt problem? What can source and haven countries do to reduce capital flight?

3. Analyze the effectiveness of World Bank and IMF approaches to ameliorating LDC external disequilibria and debt problems. What changed roles, if any, would you recommend for the World Bank and IMF in reducing the LDC debt crisis?

4. What plan should the international community adopt to resolve the debt crisis? In your answer, consider debt cancellation as aid, debt rescheduling, debt equity swaps, and the Baker, Bradley, and Miyazawa plans.

5. What impact has incurring major external debt by LDCs had on income distribution? What impact have attempts to reduce the debt crisis had on income distribution?

GUIDE TO READINGS

The OECD (note 4), World Bank (notes 3 and 5), IMF (note 3), and *IMF Survey* (note 27) are major periodic statistical sources on the LDC external debt crisis. You can find useful analyses of the debt problem in Dornbusch, Buiter and Srinivasan (note 1), Ranis (note 2), Sachs (note 3), Kruger (note 9), Loxley (note 25), Pastor (note 33), and Rudiger Dornbusch, "How to Turn Mexico's Debt and Inflation into Growth," *Challenge* 32 (January–February 1989): 4–10.

The Institute of International Economics in Washington, D.C., provides many useful up-to-date monographs on debt problems, including Lessard and Williamson, and Williamson and Lessard (note 14), William R. Cline, *Mobilizing Bank Lending to Debtor Countries* (Washington, D.C.: Institute for International Economics, 1987); and Carol Lancaster and John Williamson, eds., *African Debt and Financing* (Washington, D.C.: Institute for International Economics, 1986). The *International Monetary Fund Staff Papers,* a quarterly journal, frequently has articles discussing LDC debt. The proceedings of the Federal Reserve Bank of Kansas City (note 1) collect analyses of debt policy from Bryon Higgins, Henry Kaufman, Benjamin M. Friedman, Allan H. Meltzer, Rudiger Dornbusch, Rimmer de Vries, A. W. Clausen, Robert A. Eisenbeis, George J. Benston, William Peter Cooke, Lawrence H. Summers, Alan S. Blinder, Phillip Cagan, Stephen H. Axilrod, John G. Heimann, and L. William Seidman.

Chapter Eighteen

INTERNATIONAL TRADE

SCOPE OF THE CHAPTER

A part of LDC demands for a new international economic order include changes in the international trading system. This chapter discusses arguments for and against tariff protection, import substitution and export expansion in industry, DC import policies, expansion of primary export earnings, and foreign exchange-rate policies.

ARGUMENTS FOR AND AGAINST TARIFFS

Argument against Tariffs (Import Duties)

International economists still accept the doctrine of **comparative advantage** formulated by Adam Smith and David Ricardo, English classical economists of the late eighteenth and early nineteenth centuries.

The theory's assumptions include

1. A world of two countries, for example, a LDC like Pakistan and a DC like Japan
2. Two commodities, for example, textiles and steel
3. Given productive resources (land, labor, and capital) that can be combined in only the same fixed proportion in both countries

4. Full employment of productive resources
5. Given technical knowledge
6. Given tastes
7. Pure competition (so the firm is a pricetaker)
8. No movement of labor and capital between countries but free movement of these resources within a country
9. Export value equal to import value for each country
10. No transportation costs

The theory states that world (that is, two-country) welfare is greatest when each country *exports products whose comparative costs are lower at home than abroad* and *imports goods whose* **comparative costs** *are lower abroad than at home.*

International trade and specialization are determined by *comparative costs,* not *absolute costs.* Absolute cost comparisons require some standard unit, such as a common currency (for example, textiles $5 a meter in Pakistan and $10 in Japan). But you cannot compare absolute costs without an exchange rate (such as a Pakistani rupee price of the Japanese yen).

Assume that before international trade, the price of textiles is Rs. 50 per yard in Pakistan and ¥300 in Japan, and the price of steel per ton is Rs. 200 and ¥400 (shown in Table 18-1).

We cannot conclude that both textiles and steel are cheaper in Pakistan simply because it takes fewer rupees than yen to buy them. The two currencies are different units of measuring price, and there is no established relationship between them. If Japan issued a new currency, converting old yen into new ones at a ratio of 100:1, both products would then sell for fewer yen than rupees, even though the real situation had not changed.

It is easy to compare relative prices, however. The ratio of the price of steel to that of textiles is 4:3 in Japan and 4:1 in Pakistan. Hence the relative price of steel is lower in Japan than in Pakistan, and the relative price of textiles is lower in Pakistan than in Japan. Thus Pakistan has a comparative cost advantage in textiles and Japan a comparative cost advantage in steel.

To demonstrate that the LDC (Pakistan) gains when exporting textiles in exchange for Japanese steel, we must use an exchange rate (for example, rupee price of the yen) to convert comparative prices into absolute price differences. Pakistanis will demand Japanese steel if they can buy yen for *less than* half a rupee per 1 yen. Why? Because steel is *absolutely* cheaper in Japan than in Pakistan. If, for example, people purchase 1 yen for one-fourth of a rupee, Japanese steel sells for Rs. 100 (¥400)—cheaper than the Pakistani steel price or Rs. 200. On the other hand, the Japanese will buy Pakistani textiles if they can sell 1 yen for *more than*

TABLE 18-1   Comparative Costs of Textiles and Steel in Pakistan and Japan

	Pakistan	Japan
Textiles (price per meter)	Rs. 50	¥300
Steel (price per ton)	Rs. 200	¥400

one-sixth of a rupee. At an exchange rate of 1 yen per one-fourth of a rupee for example, the Japanese can buy Pakistani textiles for ¥200 (Rs. 50)—cheaper than the Japanese price of ¥300.

International trade takes place at any exchange rate between half a rupee per 1 yen (the maximum rupee price per yen to induce Pakistanis to trade) and one-sixth of a rupee per 1 yen (the minimum rupee price per yen to induce the Japanese to trade). Within this range, the *absolute* price of steel is lower in Japan than in Pakistan, and the *absolute* price of textiles is lower in Pakistan than in Japan, so both countries gain from trade.

This exchange-rate range is not arbitrary. If it is *more than* half a rupee per 1 yen, there is no trade, since Pakistan does not demand any Japanese goods. If it is *less than* one-sixth of a rupee per yen, there is no trade, since Japan demands no Pakistani goods.

Given our assumption, if relative prices are the same in the two countries before trade, there will be no trade. If, for example, the relative prices of steel and textiles are Rs. 200 and Rs. 50 in Pakistan, and ¥1,200 and ¥300 in Japan, there is no exchange rate at which both countries demand a good from the other.

Pakistan gains (or at least does *not* lose) by specializing in and exporting textiles, in which it has a comparative cost advantage, and by importing steel, in which it has a comparative cost disadvantage. Pakistan obtains steel more cheaply by using its productive resources to produce textiles, and trading them at a mutually advantageous rate for steel, rather than by producing steel at home.

Although the theory can be made more realistic by including several countries, several commodities, imperfect competition, variable factor proportions, increasing costs, transport costs, and so on, these changed assumptions complicate the exposition but do *not* invalidate the principle of free trade according to a country's comparative advantage. For example, the **factor proportions theory** or **Heckscher–Ohlin theorem,** introduced by two Swedish economists, shows that a nation gains from trade by exporting the commodity whose production requires the intensive use of the country's relatively abundant (and cheap) factor of production and importing the good whose production requires the intensive use of the relatively scarce factor. International trade is based on differences in factor endowment, such as Pakistani labor abundance and Japanese capital abundance. Pakistan has a comparative advantage in labor-intensive goods (textiles) and Japan a comparative advantage in capital-intensive goods (steel), meaning textile opportunity costs (measured by steel output forgone per textile unit produced) are greater in Japan than in Pakistan.[1]

Does foreign investment in LDCs follow comparative advantage? Japanese economist Kiyoshi Kojima argues that whereas U. S. MNCs invest abroad because of monopoly advantages from patents, technology, management, and marketing (see Chapter 16), Japanese MNCs invest in LDCs to take advantage of their com-

---

[1] Eli F. Heckscher, "The Effect of Foreign Trade on the Distribution of Income," in H. S. Ellis and L. M. Metzler, *Readings in the Theory of International Trade* (Homewood, Ill.: Irwin, 1950), pp. 272–300 (original article published in 1919); and Bertil Ohlin, *Interregional and International Trade* (Cambridge: Harvard University Press, 1933). For an elaboration of the theory of comparative advantage, the Heckscher–Ohlin thesis, and the Leontief paradox contradicting that thesis, see Peter B. Kenen, *The International Economy* (Englewood Cliffs, N. J.: Prentice Hall, 1989), pp. 51–68.

parative advantage in natural resources or in labor-intensive commodities, a pattern that promotes trade and specialization.[2]

Comparative advantage may be based on a **technological advantage** (as in Japan, the United States, and West Germany), perhaps a Schumpeterian innovation like a new product or production process that gives the country a temporary monopoly in the world market until other countries are able to imitate. The **product cycle model** indicates that while a product requires highly skilled labor in the beginning, later as markets grow and techniques become common knowledge, a good becomes standardized, so that less-sophisticated countries can mass produce the item with less skilled labor. Advanced economies have a comparative advantage in nonstandardized goods, while LDCs have a comparative advantage in standardized goods.[3] Product cycle is illustrated by specialization in automobiles shifting from the United States (through the late 1960s) to Japan (the mid-1970s through the late 1980s) to South Korea. Foreign investment and technological transfer by U.S. automobile companies in Japan (for example, General Motors with Isuzu) and Japanese companies in South Korea (Mitsubishi with Hyundai) helped shift comparative advantage. Indeed Japanese economist Miyohei Shinohara speaks of a **boomerang effect,** imports in reverse or intensification of competition in third markets arising from Japanese enterprise expansion in, and technology exports to, other Asian countries.[4]

Contemporary theory implies that (1) less-developed countries gain from free international trade and (2) lose by tariffs (import taxes), subsidies, quotas, administrative controls, and other forms of protection. But theory holds that free trade has benefits other than more efficient resource allocation. It leads to greater productivity because it disperses new ideas. It widens markets, improves division of labor, permits more specialized machinery, overcomes technical indivisibilities, utilizes surplus productive capacity, and stimulates greater managerial effort because of foreign, competitive pressures.[5]

Arguments for Tariffs

Despite their apparent advantage, few newly industrializing countries pursue free trade policies. The rest of this section evaluates some major arguments for tariffs.

The most frequent rationale for tariffs is to protect infant industries. Alexander Hamilton, the first U.S. secretary of the treasury, criticized Adam Smith's doctrine of **laissez-faire** (governmental noninterference) and free trade. Hamilton supported a tariff, passed in 1789, partly designed to protect manufacturing in his young country from foreign competition. **Infant industry arguments** include (1) increasing returns to scale, (2) external economies, and (3) technological borrowing.

[2] Kiyoshi Kojima, *Japanese Direct Foreign Investment: A Model of Multinational Business Operations* (Tokyo: Charles E. Tuttle, 1978), pp. 134–51.

[3] Raymond Vernon, "International Investment and International Trade in the Product Cycle," *Quarterly Journal of Economics* 2 (May 1966): 190–207.

[4] Miyohei Shinohara, *Industrial Growth, Trade, and Dynamic Patterns in the Japanese Economy* (Tokyo: University of Tokyo Press, 1982), pp. 32–33, 72–75, 127–28.

[5] Hla Myint, "The 'Classical Theory' of International Trade and the Underdeveloped Countries," *Economic Journal* 68 (June 1958): 317–37; and Harvey Leibenstein, "Allocative Efficiency vs. 'X-Efficiency'," *American Economic Review* 56 (June 1966): 392–415, discussed in Chapter 13.

Increasing Returns to Scale.   A new firm in a new industry has many disadvantages: It must train specialized management and labor, learn new techniques, create or enter markets, and cope with the diseconomies of small-scale production. Tariff protection gives a new firm time to expand output to the point of lowest long-run average cost.

An argument against this notion is illustrated by a world of two countries, each of which initially produces a different good with decreasing costs at the lowest long-run average cost. Assume that later both countries levy tariffs to start an infant industry in the good produced by the other country, so that the market is divided and both countries produce both goods well below lowest average cost output. In this case, the world loses specialization gains and economies of scale. The world would be better off if each country specialized in one decreasing-cost product, exchanging it for the decreasing-cost product of the other country.

But some may ask if infant industry protection would not be warranted for the firm in a newly industrializing country competing with firms in well-established industrial countries. However in this instance, tariff protection, by distributing income from consumers to producers, amounts to a subsidy to cover the firm's early losses. Why should society subsidize the firm in its early years? If the enterprise is profitable over the long run, losses in the early years can be counted as part of the entrepreneur's capital costs. If the enterprise is not profitable in the long run, however, would not resources be better used for some other investment?

Yet government might still want to protect infant industry. First, government support may cover part of the entrepreneur's risk when average expected returns are positive but vary widely. Second, the state may support local technological learning and knowledge-creating capabilities. Third, government planners may better forecast the future success of the industry than private entrepreneurs but protect or subsidize private investment to avoid direct operation of the industry themselves. Fourth, protecting the new industry may create external economies, or promote technological borrowing, both discussed below.

External Economies.   These are production benefits that do not accrue to the private entrepreneur. They include technological learning, training of skilled labor, and lower input costs to other industries, all of which cannot be appropriated by the investor but may be socially profitable even if a commercial loss occurs. Governments can make a rational case for protecting or subsidizing such investment. The argument can, however, easily be abused by political leaders who discover immeasurable externalities for pet projects.

Technological Borrowing.   Classical economists assumed a given technology open to all countries. In reality much of the world's rapidly improving technology is concentrated in a few countries.

Much international specialization is based on differences in technology rather than resource endowment. Assume both Italy and Indonesia can produce corn, but only Italy has the technical capacity to manufacture transistor radios. Thus Italy trades radios, in which it has a comparative advantage, for Indonesia's corn. Yet Indonesia has the necessary labor and materials, so that if Italy's technology could be acquired, Indonesia's comparative advantage would shift to radios. If Indonesia levies a tariff on transistor radios, Italian companies may transfer capital and technology to produce radios behind Indonesia's tariff wall. Once Indonesia acquires this technology, its average costs will be lower than those in Italy.

Critics raise one question: If Indonesia is open to foreign investment and if foreign technology gives Indonesia a comparative advantage, why is a tariff necessary to induce the foreign entrepreneur to produce radios there? Should not the foreign, radio manufacturer see the opportunity and bring capital and technology to Indonesia?

Tariffs may shelter inefficient technological transfers from abroad. For example, in the 1960s, India used tariffs to protect its automobile manufacturers, who were using European technology. But the foreign exchange cost of inputs alone exceeded the foreign exchange cost of buying automobiles directly from abroad!

Politically it is difficult to end tariff protection for infant industries. When governments feel compelled to protect infant industry, they could instead provide subsidies that are politically easier to remove rather than tariffs.

Changes in Factor Endowment. A government might levy a tariff so that entrepreneurs modify their output mix to match a shifting comparative advantage due perhaps to a change in resource proportions. Thus as its frontier pushed westward and capital expanded, the United States changed from a country rich in natural resources, exporting a wide variety of metals and minerals, to a capital-rich country. Analogously the rapid accumulation of capital and technology may alter comparative advantage from labor-intensive to capital- and technology-intensive goods. Thus in the 1950s and 1960s, Japan's Ministry of International Trade and Industry (MITI) tried to establish capital- and technology-intensive industries, which appeared not to be to Japan's static comparative advantage but offered more long-run growth because of rapid technical change, rapid labor productivity growth, and a high **income elasticity of demand** (percentage change in quantity demanded/percentage change in income).

Yet we must ask why private entrepreneurs would not perceive the changing comparative advantage and plan accordingly. Even in Japan, while MITI facilitated the output of memory chips for semiconductors, it did not encourage electronics production and tried to consolidate Japan's automobile production into a few giant corporations, attempting to prevent Soichiro Honda from producing cars! Indeed while MITI was accommodating and supportive, private entrepreneurs invested and coordinated the essential resources.[6] Government protection (or subsidy) is appropriate only if government forsees these changes better than private entrepreneurs.

Revenue Sources. As indicated in Chapter 15, tariffs are often a major source of revenue, especially in young nations with limited ability to raise direct taxes. In fact U.S. tariffs in 1789, despite Hamilton's intentions, did more to raise revenue than protect domestic industry.

Even for a government unconcerned about the losses a tariff imposes on other people, tariffs have limits. At the extreme, a prohibitive tariff brings no revenue. And a tariff that maximizes revenue in the short run will probably not do so in the long run. In the short run, before domestic production has moved into import-competing industries, demand is often inelastic (that is, the absolute value of the percentage change in quantity is less than the absolute value of the percentage

[6] Charles L. Schultze, "Industrial Policy: A Dissent," *Brookings Review* 2 (Fall 1983): 3–12.

change in price). However once productive resources adjust, demand elasticities increase; and a greater relative quantity decrease—in response to the increased price from the tariff—occurs. Thus a government setting a maximum revenue tariff must take account of the long-run movement of production resources.[7]

Improved Terms of Trade. Some LDCs use tariffs to improve the terms of trade, the ratio of export prices to import prices. One such measure, the **commodity terms of trade,** equals the price index of exports divided by the price index of imports. If export prices increase 10 percent and import prices 21 percent, the commodity terms of trade drop 9 percent, that is, $1.10/1.21 = 0.91$.

Under certain circumstances, a tariff can improve the terms of trade (when the denominator is the index of import prices after tariffs have been substracted) in the short run. A country should levy tariffs only on goods when the increased income from the improved terms of trade exceeds losses from a reduced volume of international trade. These gains are larger the higher the elasticity of demand for imports, so that the foreigner bears the main burden of the tariff. Of course this argument assumes that the countries affected will not retaliate.

Soon after World War II, Raul Prebisch, then Director General of the Economic Commission for Latin America, and Hans Singer, with the UN Department of Economic and Social Affairs, argued that the commodity terms of trade of countries (mainly LDCs) producing primary goods (food, raw materials, minerals, and organic oils and fats) decline in the long run. The trend, taken from a League of Nations statistical series, is inferred from the inverse of the rising terms of trade, 1876-1880 to 1938, of Britain, a manufactures exporter and primary product importer.

The **Prebisch–Singer thesis states** that the terms of trade deteriorated historically because of differences in the growth of demand for, and the market structure in, primary and manufacturing production. **Engel's law** indicates that as income increases, the proportion of income spent on manufactured goods rises and the proportion spent on primary products falls. If resources do not shift from primary to manufacturing output, there will be an excess supply of, and declining relative price in, primary products and an excess demand for, and increasing relative price in, manufactured goods. Moreover primary production is relatively competitive, so that productivity gains result in lower prices, but manufacturing is relatively monopolistic, with productivity gains leading to higher prices.[8]

Is the Prebisch–Singer thesis adequate? Can we arrive at a historical law based on Britain's relatively declining primary product prices for a 7-decade period? If we exclude the depressed prices of the 1930s, the price fall from the 1870s is not really so great. Furthermore the increase in the British commodity terms of

---

[7] Arguments 1–5 are from John Black, "Arguments for Tariffs," *Economic Journal* 69 (June 1959): 191–208; and Charles P. Kindleberger, *International Economics* (Irwin: Homewood, Ill., 1963), pp. 124–34.

[8] United Nations, Department of Economic Affairs, *Relative Prices of Exports and Imports of Underdeveloped Countries* (New York, 1949); Raul Prebisch, "The Economic Development of Latin America and Its Principal Problems," *Economic Bulletin for Latin America* 7, no. 1 (February 1962):1– 22 (first published in 1950); and Hans W. Singer, "The Distribution of Gains between Investing and Borrowing Countries," *American Economic Review* 40, no. 2 (May 1950): 473–85. Ragnar Nurkse's *Patterns of Trade and Development* (New York: Oxford University Press, 1961), contributed to these ideas.

trade shown by the League of Nations data may be partly an artifact of the inadequate measure. The data do not adequately account for qualitative improvements taking place predominantly in manufactured goods. Although there was little difference between a bushel of grain in 1880 and 1938, new and improved manufactured goods were developed during the period. Additionally international shipping costs fell with the opening of the Suez and Panama canals and the development of refrigeration and steamships. Since international transport rates enter only import prices (measured with the cost of insurance and freight, c.i.f.), but not exports, falling rates would reduce import prices more than export prices. The two factors result in an upward bias in the British terms of trade. Yet John Spraos's careful statistical study for the United Nations shows that, when we adjust for the problems mentioned, the League of Nations data would still indicate a deterioration of primary producers' terms of trade, although by a smaller magnitude than Prebisch and Singer thought.

However Spraos's figures for Britain's relative primary prices rose between 1939 and 1973, just after the League's figures. Thus Spraos concludes that while Prebisch and Singer got the direction of changes in the terms of trade from 1876-1880 to 1938 right, if we extend the data to 1973, the falling commodity terms of trade for primary products are open to doubt.[9]

Are other more complex measures more useful than the commodity terms of trade? As illustrated above, if export prices increase 10 percent and import prices 21 percent for a decade, the commodity terms of trade, 1.10/1.21, drop to 0.91. However if the *quantity* of exports expands by 10 percent for the decade, the **income terms of trade** (the value index of exports divided by the price index of imports) are $(1.10 \times 1.10)/1.21 = 1.00$. This figure means the country has the same export purchasing power as it did a decade ago. Although oil-importing, middle-income countries had a decline in commodity terms of trade, from 1970 to 1980, a rapid expansion in export volume enabled them to increase **export purchasing power.**[10] Income terms of trade are also an appropriate measure when the country's export commodities have a large share of the world market (Brazil's coffee and Saudi Arabia's oil), so that export prices depend on export quantum.

The country might be interested in whether it increases the quantity of imports available per factors employed in export production. Assume that output per combined factor inputs increases by 10 percent over the decade. The commodity terms of trade, 0.91, multiplied by 1.10 yields 1.00, the **single factoral terms of trade.** This figure implies that the output of a given amount of the country's productive resources can purchase as many imports as it did a decade ago.

Thus a country's commodity terms of trade may decline at the same time that export purchasing power and single factoral terms of trade increase.

Although the degree of monopoly may differ between DCs and LDCs, the argument for deteriorating terms of trade depends on the change in, *not* the extent of,

[9] W. Arthur Lewis, "World Production, Prices and Trade, 1870–1960," *Manchester School* 20 (May 1952): 105–38; Pan A. Yotopoulos and Jeffrey B. Nugent, *Economics of Development—Empirical Investigations* (New York: Harper & Row, 1976), pp. 342–45; and John Spraos, *Inequalising Trade? A Study of Traditional North/South Specialisation in the Context of Terms of Trade Concepts* (Oxford: Clarendon Press, 1983).

[10] World Bank, *World Development Report, 1981* (New York: Oxford University Press, 1981), p. 21.

TABLE 18-2   Terms of Trade,[a] 1979, 1989 (1970=100)

	1979	1989
Developing countries[b]	150	123
Africa	126	99
Asia	98	90
Latin America	140	113
Middle East	305	233
Less-developed Europe	90	83
Non-oil developing countries	94	82
Oil-exporting countries	357	256
Developed countries	93	100

[a]Commodity terms of trade. A value in excess of 100 in 1979 and an increasing value from 1979 to 1989 indicate increases in the terms of trade, while a value below 100 in 1979 and a declining value from 1979 to 1989 indicate decreases.

[b]Excludes China 1970–79 but includes China 1979–89.

Source: Calculated from International Monetary Fund, *World Economic Outlook: A Survey by the Staff of the International Monetary Fund* (Washington, D.C., 1988), pp. 133, 140.

monopoly power in primary and secondary production. There is no evidence that industrial monopoly power increases more rapidly than agricultural monopoly power.

The view that LDCs export primary products whose terms of trade are declining and DCs export manufacturers with increasing terms of trade is oversimplified in many ways.

Charles Kindleberger's evidence does not support deteriorating long-run terms of trade for *primary product exporters*. He does, however, find the LDCs are especially vulnerable to declining terms of trade because they cannot easily shift resources to accord with shifting patterns of comparative advantage.[11]

Although a larger proportion of exports from developing countries are primary products than from DCs, LDCs still account for less than one-half of the world's primary products (see Chapter 4).

Table 18-2 indicates that major exporters of one primary good, crude petroleum, made extraordinary improvements in their terms of trade in the 1970s. In fact a country's international trade position in oil overwhelmed other factors in determining its direction in the commodity terms of trade. The 1979 terms of trade of petroleum exporters were three to four times 1970 levels and those of petroleum-importing countries decreased over the same period (although slightly less than those of DCs). However, the direction of the terms of trade for oil exporters and oil importers reversed moderately in the 1980s.

For policy what is important is *not* what happened to the terms of trade in the past, but what *will* happen. Although LDCs may want to encourage sectors where relative demand and prices are expected to increase, tariffs levied for terms of trade should be used sparingly.

---

[11] Charles P. Kindleberger, *The Terms of Trade: A European Case Study* (New York: Wiley, 1956).

Improved Employment and the Balance of Payments.   A rise in tariff rates diverts demand from imports to domestic goods, so that the balance on goods and services (exports minus imports), aggregate demand, and employment increase.[12] However the economic injury to other countries may provoke retaliation. Furthermore the effects of import restrictions and increased prices spread throughout the economy, so that domestic- and export-oriented production and employment decline. In fact Lawrence B. Krause's study of the U.S. economy indicates that jobs lost by export contraction exceed jobs created by import replacement.[13] It is probably more effective to use policies discussed in Chapter 10, and when possible, financial policies (Chapter 15) for employment and home currency devaluation to improve employment and the balance of payments.

Reduced Internal Instability.   The sheer economic cost of periodic fluctuations in employment or prices from unstable international suppliers or customers may justify tariffs to reduce dependence on foreign trade. According to the World Bank, commodities accounting for one-third of LDC nonfuel primary exports fluctuated in price by over 10 percent from one year to the next, 1955 to 1976. By encouraging import substitution, tariff protection, can reorient the economy toward more stable domestic production. Losses in allocative efficiency might be outweighed by the greater efficiency implicit in more rational cost calculations and investment decisions. Yet such a policy may be costly. Tariffs on goods with inelastic demand, such as necessities, increase import payments.

Policymakers should compare the costs of alternative ways of stabilizing the internal economy, such as holding reserves. A LDC with adequate foreign exchange reserves can maintain its purchasing power during times of low demand for its exports. Moreover a country can use reserves from import commodities to offset the destabilizing effects of sudden shortages on domestic prices and incomes.[14]

National Defense.   A developing country may want to avoid dependence on foreign sources for essential materials or products that could be cut off in times of war or other conflict. A tariff in such a case is only worthwhile if building capacity to produce these goods takes time. Otherwise the LDC should use cheaper foreign supplies while they are available.

Policymakers will want to examine alternatives to a national defense tariff, such as stockpiling strategic goods or developing facilities to produce import substitutes without using them until the need arises.

In a period of rapid technical change in military and strategic goods, a government must ask whether it is worth increasing costs through tariffs to avoid hypothetical future dangers. Would it not be better to divert these resources to investment, research, and technical education to increase the economy's overall strength and adaptability?

[12] When demand is elastic, the percentage decline in the quantity imported exceeds the percentage increase in price from the tariff, so that import value, price multiplied by quantity, falls. When demand is inelastic, import payments increase, but by less than the government's gain in tariff revenue.

[13] John Black, "Arguments for Tariffs," *Economic Journal* 69 (June 1959): 199–200; and Lawrence B. Krause, *Brookings Papers on Economic Activity* (Washington, D.C.: Brookings Institution, 1971), pp. 421–25.

[14] World Bank, *World Development Report, 1978* (New York: Oxford University Press, 1978), pp. 19–20; and John Black, "Arguments for Tariffs," *Economic Journal* 69 (June 1959): 206–8.

Antidumping. **Dumping** is selling a product cheaper abroad than at home. Why should a country object to it? If a foreign country is supplying cheap imports favorable to consumers, should not such action be considered as a reduction in foreign comparative costs? Yes and no. If the foreign supplier is dumping as a temporary stage in a price war to drive home producers out of business and establish a monopoly, a country may be justified in levying a tariff.[15]

Reduced Luxury Consumption. Government may wish to levy a tariff to curtail the consumption of luxury goods. As indicated in Chapter 14, however, an excise tax is probably preferable to a tariff on luxuries, which would have the unintended effect of stimulating domestic luxury goods production.

Conclusion

From our arguments, it should now be clear that tariff protection need not necessarily be attributed to analytical error or the power of vested interests, but may be based on some genuine exceptions to the case for free trade. Yet many of the most frequent arguments for tariffs, such as protecting infant industry, are more limited than many LDC policymakers suppose. In fact a critical analysis of the arguments for tariffs provides additional support for liberal trade policies.

IMPORT SUBSTITUTION AND EXPORT EXPANSION IN INDUSTRY

Many LDC governments try to industrialize and improve their international balance of payments by import substitution (replacing imports by domestic industry) and export expansion.

The simplest base for early industrial expansion is producing consumer goods for a market previously created by imports. It becomes more difficult, however, to undertake successive import substitution, which usually involves intermediate and capital goods that require more capital-intensive investments with larger import contents.

Import substitution can be justified on many grounds—increasing returns to scale, external economies, technological borrowing, internal stability, and other tariff arguments already presented—but is subject to the same rejoinders. Studies indicate that most LDCs have carried import substitution to the point where gains to local industrialists are less than losses to consumers, merchants, inputs buyers, and taxpayers. Indeed India, which emphasized import substitution, generated self-reliant but socially wasteful technology that would have been written off in a more competitive environment.[16]

A study by the National Bureau of Economic Research (NBER) of ten LDCs indicates that export promotion is generally more effective than import substitution in expanding output and employment. Chile in the 1960s and 1970s provided out-

---

[15] Ibid., 201–4.

[16] Sanjaya Lall, *Multinationals, Technology, and Exports* (New York: St. Martin's Press, 1985), p. 18.

landish incentives for import substitutes and implicitly discouraged export development. South Korea on the other hand provided virtually no incentives for import substitution while heavily encouraging export activity through capital subsidies, depreciation allowances, and import duty exemptions. From 1960 to 1980, Chile's real annual growth rates were 2.5 percent in industry and 1.6 percent overall compared to Korea's 16.3 and 7.0 percents—spurred by scale economies, international competition, price flexibility, and no agricultural and foreign exchange shortages associated with export promotion.[17] Deepak Lal's and Sarath Rajapatirana's later study comparing the four export-promoting NICs (Taiwan, South Korea, Hong Kong, and Singapore) to moderately import-substituting Southern-Cone countries (Argentina, Chile, and Uruguay) and Sri Lanka reinforce the NBER findings not only for the 1970s but for the 1980s, when the NICs not only grew more rapidly but also recovered more quickly from the shock of the world recession in the early 1980s.[18]

Export expansion activities have the following advantages: (1) competitive pressures to improve quality and reduce costs, (2) information provided by DC users can improve export technology and product quality, (3) cost economies from increased market size, and (4) increased imports of productive inputs resulting from the greater availability of foreign exchange earnings.[19]

Still the transition from import replacements to export expansion (and free trade) is difficult. It takes time to expand capacity, reallocate resources, acquire physical inputs, develop skills, upgrade procedures, and learn by doing before new competitive export industries based on comparative advantage can emerge. We can expect export expansion to be slow, since most potential exporters have to produce for a domestic market first.[20]

The LDC manufactured exports grew more rapidly than primary products in the 1980s. Most developing countries with rapid industrial growth emphasized the expansion of manufactured exports. This expansion, however, was concentrated in relatively few LDCs, primarily middle-income countries. Manufactured exports were 52 percent of total merchandise exports in middle-income countries compared to 32 percent for low-income countries other than China and India (see Table 18-3).

Manufactured export volume increased annually by 2.4 percent from 1965 to

[17] Anne O. Krueger, Hal B. Lary, Terry Monson, and Narongchai Akrasanee, eds., *Trade and Employment in Developing Countries*, vol. I, *Individual Studies* (Chicago: University of Chicago Press, 1981); Anne O. Krueger, *Foreign Trade Regimes and Economic Development: Liberalization Attempts and Consequences* (Cambridge: Ballinger, 1978); and World Bank, *World Development Report, 1982* (New York: Oxford University Press, 1982), pp. 111–13.

[18] Deepak Lal and Sarath Rajapatirana, "Foreign Trade Regimes and Economic Growth in Developing Countries," *World Bank Research Observer* 2 (July 1987): 189–217. Peter C. Y. Chow's econometric study demonstrates that export growth promotes both industrial and overall economic growth in the NICs. "Causality between Export Growth and Industrial Development: Empirical Evidence from the NICs," *Journal of Development Economics* 26 (June 1987): 155–63.

[19] Martin Fransman, *Technology and Economic Development* (Boulder, Colo.: Westview, 1986), pp. 75–93.

[20] Heinz Gert Preusse, "The Indirect Approach to Trade Liberalization: Dynamic Consideration on Liberalization-cum-Stabilization Policies in Latin America," *World Development* 16 (August 1988): 883–97; and Staffan B. Linder, *An Essay on Trade and Transformation* (New York: Wiley, 1961).

TABLE 18-3   Structure of Merchandise Exports, 1986 (by country group)

	PERCENTAGE SHARE OF MERCHANDISE EXPORTS				
Country Group	Fuels, Minerals, and Metals	Other Primary Commodities	Textiles and Clothing	Machinery and Transport Equipment	Other Manufactures
Low-income countries (other than China and India)	21	47	17	2	13
China and India	12	22	21	14	31
Middle-income countries	28	20	11	14	27
High-income oil exporters	88	1	0	3	8
High-income, capitalist and mixed countries	8	12	4	42	34

Source: World Bank, *World Development Report, 1988* (New York: Oxford University Press, 1988), pp. 244–45.

1973, and 8.7 percent from 1973 to 1985, in the low-income countries, and by 14.9 percent and 12.9 percent, respectively, in the middle-income countries. In the early period, the most successful LDC expansion was in labor-intensive manufactured exports, such as textiles, clothing, footwear, and simple consumer goods; in the later period, these exports were joined by machinery, transport equipment, and paper manufacturers. Expansion of this kind often means the comparative advantage shifts from the innovating country to a LDC after the technology is disseminated internationally. We must attribute much of this export expansion (except in South Korea) to multinational corporations—sometimes operating in joint ventures with LDCs but most certainly selling technology, subcontracting, making components, breaking down production processes, and providing multinational marketing. These exports tend to be concentrated in a relatively few markets in the West and Japan.

In 1986 Taiwan, South Korea, Hong Kong, and Singapore, comprising less than 2 percent of LDC population, accounted for 65 percent of LDC clothing and textile exports and 54 percent of total LDC manufactured export. If we add the exports of Spain, China, Brazil, Yugoslavia, Poland, India, South Africa, Hungary, Israel, Portugal, and Malaysia, the figure for total LDC manufactured exports reaches 93 percent.

Because of their large populations, China's and India's manufactured output and manufactured exports per capita are below average for LDCs. On the other hand, two other LDCs not on the list of leading manufactures exporters, Mexico and Argentina, oriented primarily toward domestic markets, are relatively advanced industrially.[21]

[21] World Bank, *World Development Report, 1988* (New York: Oxford University Press, 1988), pp. 236–37, 244–45.

DC IMPORT POLICIES

One LDC demand for a new international economic order is that DCs remove or reduce trade barriers against third-world exports, especially manufactured and processed goods. The World Bank estimates the cost of DC protection against LDCs ranges from 2.5 percent to 9 percent of their GNP.[22]

The Tokyo Round tariff cuts negotiated in 1974 to 1979 reduced DC tariffs to an average of 5–6 percent of value. Yet the low rate is misleading. First tariff rates were much higher on labor-intensive goods in which LDCs are more likely to have a comparative advantage. Second the **effective rate of protection,** a measure of protection as a percentage of value added by production factors at each processing stage, is usually higher than the nominal rate for manufactured and processed goods, since DC tariff rates rise as imports change from crude raw materials to semimanufactures to finished goods.

Suppose an industrialized country has no tariff on raw cotton imports but a 5-percent tariff on cotton yarn imports. Assume raw cotton sells for $600 per ton and cotton yarn for $700 a ton, with $100 value added by the cotton yarn industry. The 5-percent nominal cotton yarn tariff (or $35), although only a small fraction of total sales value, is a 35-percent effective tariff rate on the $100 value added. It allows the domestic, DC, cotton yarn producer to be much less efficient than the foreign producer and still retain the home market. World Bank data indicate that although the effective protection rate of post–Tokyo Round tariffs was 2 percent for raw materials, it was 15–20 percent for processed and manufactured products.[23]

Other disturbing developments have been the new trade restrictions—the **Multifiber Arrangement (MFA),** "voluntary" export restraints, trigger price arrangements, antidumping duties, industrial subsidies, and other **nontariff barriers (NTBs)** —introduced in the 1970s and 1980s. In 1987, DC use of NTBs affected about 25 percent of nonfuel imports from LDCs compared to 21 percent of those from other DCs. The MFA, established in 1974 and made increasingly restrictive in 1978, 1982, and 1986, allows bilateral agreements (often arising from economic pressures brought to bear by rich countries) and unilateral ceilings on any product category to limit "disruptive" textile and clothing imports.[24] In 1989, the Super 301 provision of the U.S. Omnibus Trade and Competitiveness Act, which directed the President to identify unfair traders, threatened trade sanctions against Brazil for import licensing and India for foreign investment and insurance company restrictions. **Trigger price mechanisms,** such as the one the United States uses to prevent "unfair" price competition from steel imports, require foreign importers to pay antidumping duties on prices determined to be below domestic production cost. Subsidies, used widely by Norway, Belgium, France, and the United Kingdom, have the same protective effect as tariffs.

Since the late 1960s, the DCs have adopted a **generalized system of tariff**

[22] Ibid., p. 16.

[23] World Bank, *World Development Report, 1987* (New York: Oxford University Press, 1987), p. 136; Gerald M. Meir, *International Economics—The Theory of Policy* (New York: Oxford University Press, 1980), pp. 118–19; and World Bank, *World Development Report, 1981* (New York: Oxford University Press, 1981), pp. 22–34.

[24] *IMF Survey* (December 12, 1988), pp. 386–89; and World Bank, *World Development Report, 1987* (New York: Oxford University Press, 1987), pp. 136–37.

preferences (GSP), by which tariffs on selected imports from LDCs are lower than those offered to other countries. The GSP of the European Community, which agreed in 1975 to accept certain products from fifty one African, Caribbean, and Pacific countries without tariffs, covers 22 percent of the total value of merchandise imports from LDCs; the GSP of the United States is 12 percent (low-income countries accounted for only 0.5 percent of this trade in 1985); and that of all OECD countries is 7 percent from LDCs.[25] Thus far GSP benefits have been modest, but expanding the scheme could make for more rapid LDC industrial export growth. Despite the apparent economic value to LDCs of the Tokyo Round tariff reduction and GSP gains, LDCs were hurt by renewed DC protectionist policies during the 1980 to 1982 international recession and in subsequent years. The increased tariffs and other trade restrictions DCs used to divert demand to domestic production especially hurt LDC primary and light manufacturing export expansion.

EXPANDING PRIMARY EXPORT EARNINGS

The OPEC was fairly successful in the 1970s in maintaining prices and limiting output (Chapter 8). Here we do not concentrate on oil but on other primary products, the major focus of those economists concerned about LDC export expansion.

Staple Theory of Growth

The export of staples, such as primary or primary-product-intensive commodities, is sometimes a major engine of growth. The **staple theory of growth** was first used to explain the association between expanding primary production (wheat) and economic growth in late nineteenth-century Canada.[26] Other examples of staple exports stimulating growth include English textiles (the late eighteenth century); U.S. cotton (the early nineteenth century) and grain (after the Civil War); Colombian coffee (the last half of the nineteenth century); Danish dairy products (the last half of the nineteenth century); Malaysian rubber and Ghanaian cocoa (first half of the twentieth century); and Korean, Taiwanese, and Hong Kong textiles (after 1960). The recent examples of Bangladesh jute, Sri Lankan tea, Zambian copper, and Cuban sugar, however, suggest that staple export expansion does not necessarily trigger rapid economic growth.

Integrated Program for Commodities

Exporters of primary products other than minerals and petroleum frequently face *short-run* demand and supply inelasticities and thus greater price (Chapter 4) and income (price multiplied by quantity) fluctuations than manufactures exporters. In 1976, in the face of OPEC success, low foreign aid, and the perception that commodity markets were biased against LDCs, UNCTAD proposed an **integrated program for commodities**—consisting of output restrictions or export quotas, interna-

[25] World Bank, *World Development Report, 1986* (New York: Oxford University Press, 1986), pp. 142-42; World Bank, *World Development Report, 1981* (New York: Oxford University Press, 1981), pp. 28–30; and Jan S. Hogendorn, *Economic Development* (New York: Harper & Row, 1987), p. 405.

[26] Harold Innis, *Problems of Staple Production in Canada* (Toronto: Ryerson Press, 1933); and Melville H. Watkins, "A Staple Theory of Economic Growth," *Canadian Journal of Economics and Political Science* 29 (May 1963):141–58.

TABLE 18-4   Price Instability of Ten Core Commodities[a]

		Average Percentage Deviation from 7-Year Moving Average, 1960–72 (1974 prices)
Foods		
Cocoa	(2.6)	19.9
Coffee	(6.5)	8.4
Tea	(1.3)	3.1
Sugar	(13.9)	11.5
Fibers		
Cotton	(4.0)	3.9
Jute	(0.2)	12.5
Sisal	(0.2)	18.1
Rubber and metals		
Rubber	(3.5)	11.9
Copper	(5.0)	14.6
Tin	(1.7)	7.7

[a]The figure in parentheses following each commodity indicates its percentage share in total developing-country exports of all primary commodities, excluding fuel, in 1975.

Sources: Karsten Laursen, "The Integrated Program for Commodities," *World Development* 8 (April 1978): 424; and World Bank, *World Development Report, 1978* (New York: Oxford University Press, 1978), pp. 19–20.

tional buffer stocks, a common fund, and compensatory financing—to stabilize and increase primary commodity prices and earnings. Emphasis was on ten **core commodities** (listed in Table 18-4), chosen on the basis of wide price fluctuations, large shares in LDC primary exports, or high export concentration in LDCs.

Cartels.   The number of primary commodities for which collusion would be effective or feasible is small; even the oil cartel was not effective during most of the 1980s. The prime candidates for a successful price-raising cartel appear to be the tropical beverages, coffee, cocoa, and tea, if action were taken to avoid substitution among them. Even though there are competitive threats from coffee grain mixtures and cocoa substitutes, these three beverages have long-run import demand inelasticities. When demand is inelastic, supply reductions increase the price and total revenues. Past efforts suggest that the major difficulty for a beverage cartel controlling supply would be disagreements between traditional and new producers about market shares. Evidence from one study indicates that the major beneficiaries of such a cartel would be middle-income countries.

Danish economist Karsten Laursen argues that sugar, rubber, fiber, and metal cartels are not likely to increase prices because the *long-run* demand elasticity for the *imports* of these goods is high, since potential substitutes are many.[27]

[27]Karsten Laursen, "The Integrated Program for Commodities," *World Development* 8 (April 1978): 423–35.

Buffer Stocks.   Some international agreements among commodity producer governments provide for funds and storage facilities to operate a **buffer stock** to stabilize prices. The buffer stock management buys and accumulates goods when prices are low and sells when prices are high to maintain prices within a certain range.

A 1975 UN General Assembly resolution asks for buffer stocks to secure more "stable, remunerative, and equitable" prices for LDC exports. There are however several major problems with such a program.

First because of overoptimism or pressure from producer interests, buffer stock management often sets prices above long-run equilibrium, and stocks overaccumulate.

Second the costs of storage, interest, and (for some commodities) spoilage are high. Laursen estimates that the annual costs for buffer stocks for the ten core commodities, $900 million, would exceed the gains to producers ($250 million) and consumers ($75 million) by more than $500 million.

Third the objective of commodity stabilization is not clear. Stability may refer to international commodity prices, producers' money income or real income, export earnings, or export purchasing power. Stabilizing one of these variables may sometimes mean destabilizing another. For example, price stability destabilizes earnings if demand is price elastic.

Fourth by reducing risk, price stability may intensify competition and increase investment, decreasing the long-run equilibrium price. On the other hand, price stability, especially in jute, sisal, cotton, and rubber, may prevent consumers from seeking synthetic substitutes.[28]

Common Fund.   The integrating factor in the commodity program is the common fund used to finance international buffer stock agreements. According to UNCTAD, buffer stocks would be cheaper if financed by a common fund than if financed individually, because the fund could (1) take advantage of different phasing of financial flows between stock accounts, (2) obtain better borrowing terms than individual buffer stocks, (3) support new international commodity agreements, and (4) facilitate lending from one commodity agency to another.

Yet the economies attributed to common financing compared to individual financing are relatively small. And the 1983 capital requirements for the ten core commodities, based on Laursen's estimate, are about $12 billion, far in excess of available resources. Furthermore most of the fund's resources might be used by a small number of commodities that loom large in international commodity trade at the expense of the others. The little funding available in 1988 was used for only two commodities, cocoa and rubber.

Compensatory Financing.   Chapter 16 mentioned the IMF's compensatory financing facility, used to finance a temporary shortfall in domestic food supplies (to purchase cereal imports) or in export earnings beyond a country's control. From 1976 to 1986, LDCs borrowed $12 billion from the facility, one-third of total IMF credit. The borrowing limit may be only a drop in the bucket, however, for coun-

---

[28] Ibid., pp. 423–35; World Bank, *World Development Report, 1978* (New York: Oxford University, Press, 1978), p. 19; and Gerald Meier, *International Economics—The Theory of Policy* (New York: Oxford University Press, 1980), p. 312.

tries like copper-exporting Zambia that are so vulnerable to a single commodity's sharply fluctuating price.

Another scheme to stabilize export earnings is the European community's **Stabex,** covering forty eight primary products from fifty eight African, Caribbean, and Pacific countries. To qualify for support, a commodity must have accounted for at least 6.5 percent of a country's total exports in the preceding year, or 2.0 percent for least developed, landlocked, or island countries. Stabex transfers to the thirty five least-developed countries are in the form of grants and to the other countries, interest-free loans to be repaid over 7 years with 2 years grace.[29]

Nevertheless except for compensatory financing, the prospect for these measures improving primary commodity stability or remuneration is limited. Perhaps the most important step countries could take would be to eliminate trade barriers against primary products. Robert McNamara, in his 1976 presidential address to the World Bank's board of governors, estimated that LDC gains from completely free access of their agricultural products to DC markets would be more than $15 billion in 1985. But a simulation by World Bank economists indicates that LDCs, whose trade barriers are biased against other LDCs' agricultural goods, would realize even much larger efficiency gains by free agricultural trade within the developing world.[30]

FOREIGN EXCHANGE RATES

International trade requires one national currency to be exchanged for another. An Indian firm, for example, uses local currency, rupees, to buy the dollars needed to purchase a computer from a U.S. company.

Present Exchange-Rate System

The rules for today's international monetary system tolerate several ways of determining the exchange rate. The world's present managed floating exchange-rate system (mentioned in Chapter 17) is a hybrid of six exchange-rate regimes: (1) the single floats of major international currencies, the U.S. dollar, Canadian dollar, British pound, and Japanese yen; (2) the joint float (with a 2.25-percent spread) of the European Monetary System (West German, French, Danish, Italian, Irish, and Benelux currencies) against the U.S. dollar; (3) the independent (for example Australia, the Philippines, Bolivia, Nigeria, Zaïre, and South Africa) or managed float (for example, Pakistan, India, Indonesia, China, Egypt, Mexico, Argentina, and South Korea) of minor currencies; (4) the frequent adjustment (usually depreciation) of currencies according to an indicator (for example, Brazil, Chile, and Colombia); (5) pegging currencies to a major currency, especially to a dominant

[29] Karsten Laursen, "The Integrated Program for Commodities," *World Development* 8 (April 1978): 423–35; World Bank, *World Development Report, 1980,* (New York: Oxford University Press, 1980), p. 20; and World Bank, *World Development Report, 1986* (New York: Oxford University Press, 1986), pp. 139–42.

[30] Robert S. McNamara, address to the Board of Governors (Washington, D.C.: World Bank, October 1976); World Bank, *World Development Report, 1976* (New York: Oxford University Press, 1976), pp. 122–32, 144.

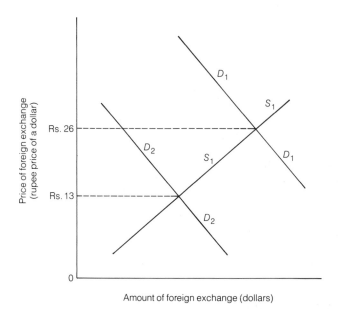

FIGURE 18-1   Determining the Price of Foreign Exchange under the Market and Exchange Controls   If allowed to float freely, the exchange rate will be Rs. 26=\$1, at the intersection of D_1 and S_1. Controls on currency transactions by domestic citizens can repress demand to D_2, which intersects S_1 at a price of foreign exchange Rs. 13=\$1. This rate, however, is likely to discourage exports and encourage attempts to obtain import licenses.

trading partner (thirty eight are pegged to the U.S. dollar, fourteen to the French franc, and five to other currencies); and (6) pegging currencies to a **basket** (composite) **of currencies,** most notably **special drawing rights (SDRs),** bookkeeping entries in the accounts of member countries of the IMF used as an internationalized currency by central banks for official transactions (with the IMF and other central banks).[31]

Domestic Currency Overvaluation

The domestic currency (rupee) price of foreign (U.S. dollar) currency, for example, Rs. 26=\$1, is the **price of foreign exchange.** In a free market, this exchange rate is determined by the intersection of D_1, the demand for foreign currency (depending on the demand for foreign goods, services, and capital); and S_1, the supply of foreign currency (depending on foreign demand for domestic goods, services, and capital). (See Figure 18-1.)

[31] International Monetary Fund, *International Financial Statistics* 41 (October 1988): 22; and Lloyd B. Thomas, Jr., *Money, Banking, and Economic Activity* (Englewood Cliffs, N. J.: Prentice Hall, 1986), pp. 554–63.

India's increased demand for U.S. computers or insurance, *or* a reduced U.S demand for Indian tea or cashews, increases the foreign exchange rate, for example, from Rs. 26=$1 to Rs. 27=$1.

A country's central bank may keep down the price of foreign exchange by using **exchange controls** to limit its citizens' purchase of foreign currency for foreign equipment, materials, consumer goods, and travel. Assume that the market-clearing price of foreign exchange (with no exchange controls) is Rs. 26=$1, determined by D_1 and S_1. To avert a balance of payments crisis and domestic currency devaluation, however, a country may repress demand to D_2 through exchange controls and trade restrictions, so that the actual price of foreign exchange is Rs. 13=$1, at the intersection of D_2 and S_1.

Overvaluing the domestic currency relative to foreign currency, however, may discourage import substitution and exports. At the rate of Rs. 13=$1, the exporter selling tea for $10 a pound earns only Rs. 130, rather than $260 at the market exchange rate. Additionally the domestic steel firm imports a computer whose world price is $5000 at only Rs. 65,000 rather than Rs. 130,000.

Avoiding Bias against Exports

Most LDCs' prices of foreign exchange are lower than market rates (for example, Rs. 13=$1 is lower than Rs. 26=$1), meaning they are biased against exports. Some notable exceptions argue in favor of adjusting exchange rates so they do not discriminate against exports. The yen in rapidly growing, early modern (Meiji) Japan (1868–1912) chronically depreciated vis-à-vis the U.S. dollar, which meant that the real exchange rate (see below) remained virtually unchanged. Fortuitously for Japan, during most of this period, the yen's standard was silver, which declined relative to gold. Moreover Japan's modest trade restrictions (which reduced the demand for dollars and by themselves overvalued the yen) were offset by export promotion schemes (which increased the demand for yen). Doubtlessly, these foreign exchange policies help explain why Japan's annual real average growth rates in exports during the Meiji period were at least twice those of either the United States or Britain. Additionally studies on effective rates of protection and effective subsidies indicate that South Korea, virtually the most rapidly growing LDC after World War II, discriminated *in favor* of exports.[32]

Domestic Currency Devaluation

The country with an overvalued currency could impose compensating duties and surcharges on imported inputs and capital instead of relying on exchange controls, licenses, or quotas that implicitly subsidize the successful applicant. But these duties and surcharges, tax incentives, subsidies, loans, and technical assistance may

---

[32] E. Wayne Nafziger, "The Japanese Development Model: Its Implications for Developing Countries," *Bulletin of the Graduate School of International Relations, I.U.J.* no. 5 (July 1986): 1–26; Martin Fransman, *Technology and Economic Development* (Boulder, Colo.: Westview 1986), pp. 76–85; Larry E. Westphal and K. S. Kim, "Industrial Policy and Development in Korea," Washington, World Bank Staff Working Paper no. 263, 1977; Chong Hyun Nam, "Trade and Industrial Policies and the Structure of Protection in Korea," in W. Hong and C. B. Krause, *Trade and Growth of the Advanced Developing Countries in the Pacific Basin: Papers and Proceedings of the Eleventh Pacific Trade and Development Conference* (Seoul: Korea Development Institute, 1981), pp. 46–73.

stimulate import replacements and exports less than an overvalued domestic currency inhibits these activities. Devaluing the domestic currency to its equilibrium rate in order to ration imports through the market, encourage import substitution, and promote exports may be preferable to inducements under an overvalued currency regime. Additionally domestic currency depreciation would increase labor-intensive production and employment (Chapter 10), improve investment choice (Chapter 12), and reduce structural inflation (Chapter 15).

The Real Exchange Rate

We cannot calculate LDC currency depreciation or appreciation vis-à-vis the dollar over time by looking at changes in the nominal exchange rates. To illustrate, in 1968 (the base year), $1.40=N1 (a Nigerian naira), while the consumer price indices in both the United States and Nigeria were 100. By 1979, $1.78 = N1, while the U.S. consumer price index was 208.5 and Nigeria's was 498.0. The **real exchange rate** (the nominal exchange rate adjusted for relative inflation rates at home and abroad), calculated as

(Nigerian consumer price index/U.S. price index) × dollar price of naira

was $1.40=N1 in 1968, and $4.25=N1, which was an increase of 3.0, meaning the value of the naira vis-à-vis the dollar more than tripled over the 11-year period. With further **real appreciation,** as Nigerian nonoil exports became less competitive and imports more competitive, Nigeria depreciated the naira in 1986 to bring it closer to the 1969 real exchange rate.

Dual Exchange Rates

Currency depreciation can have short-run costs, especially in an economy that adjusts slowly. Inflation and shortages may appear before consumers switch to replacements for foreign food and other consumer goods, before export and import substitution industries expand capacity to take advantage of more favorable prices, and before buyers of imported inputs and capital goods can shift to domestic suppliers. These transitional problems have led some economists to suggest a **dual exchange rate,** with the first a near market rate, used to reduce controls, spur exports and import substitutes, and increase efficiency; and the second, perhaps the old rate overvaluing domestic currency, set to dampen short-run inflationary pressures from price inelastic foreign goods like food, industrial inputs, and capital goods (or their domestic substitutes shifting to exports) or to maintain foreign exchange commitments for foreign corporations repatriating interest and dividends.[33] In 1983, in response to an overvalued cedi, Ghana instituted a dual exchange rate (with a surcharge on nonessential imports and a bonus to exporters), while also increasing farm producer prices, removing price distortions on oil and other goods, and reducing deficit financing. By 1984, inflation fell and growth accelerated. Despite protest from labor unions about its effect on the cost of goods previously consumed, Ghana widened the distance between the two exchange rates in 1985 and 1986. These measures improved the balance on goods and services in

[33] Nicholas Kaldor, "An Exchange-Rate Policy for India," *Economic and Political Weekly* 19 (July 14, 1984): 1093–95.

1986.[34] However dual rates maintain some price distortions, postpone resource adjustments, and spur people to acquire foreign currency cheaply in one market and sell it expensively in the other.

Exchange-Rate Adjustment and Other Prices

Let the student be warned: Market-clearing exchange rates may not provide enough signals for improving the efficiency of resources use if domestic prices of goods and services, wages, interest rates, and other prices are not flexible.[35] The **theory of the second best** states that if economic policy changes cannot satisfy all the conditions necessary for maximizing welfare, then satisfying one or several conditions may not increase welfare (that is, may not lead to a second-best position). This theory indicates that liberalizing one price (for example, the exchange rate) while other prices are still repressed may be worse than having all prices distorted.

Regional Integration in the South

Some LDC economists stress that the fact that in 1984 only 31 percent (or $125 billion) of LDC total exports went to other LDCs (and only 28 percent, or $53 billion, in 1976) indicates the substantial output gain potential from greater *intra-LDC* trade (and factor movements).[36] Many LDC leaders, frustrated by DC protectionism, poor terms of trade, a lack of internal economies of scale, and the slow growth of industrial specialization and exports, have advocated **economic integration,** a grouping of nations that reduces or abolishes barriers to trade and resource movements only among member countries. Integration ranges along a continuum from its loosest form, a preferential trade arrangement, to a free trade area, a customs union, a common market, an economic union, and to the most advanced integration, a complete economic and monetary union.

A **preferential trade arrangement,** illustrated by the Preferential Trade Area for Eastern and Southern African States (PTA), launched in 1984, provides lower tariff and other trade barriers among member countries than between members and nonmembers. A **free trade area** removes trade barriers among members, but each country retains its own barriers against nonmembers. Examples are the Latin American Free Trade Association (LAFTA—Mexico and most of South America, founded in 1960), which stagnated for years and was dissolved in 1980, and the Economic Union of Caribbean Countries (CARIFTA), established as a free trade area in 1968 but coverted into a common market in 1973 before eventually disintegrating. A **customs union,** exemplified by the European Community (EC), 1957 to 1970, goes beyond the free trade area to retain common trade barriers against the rest of the world. A **common market** moves a step beyond a customs union by allowing free labor and capital movement among member states. Examples include

---

[34] E. Wayne Nafziger, *Inequality in Africa: Political Elites, Proletariat, Peasants, and the Poor* (Cambridge: Cambridge University Press, 1988), pp. 153–54.

[35] T. N. Srinivasan, "Economic Liberalization in China and India: Issues and an Analytical Framework," *Journal of Comparative Economics* 11 (September 1987), 427–43.

[36] World Bank, *World Development Report, 1986* (New York: Oxford University Press, 1986), pp. 196–97, 202–03; and World Bank, *World Development Report, 1978* (New York: Oxford University Press, 1978), pp. 86–87, 90–91.

not only the EC since 1970, but also the Central American Common Market (CACM), established in 1960 but paralyzed because of hostilies between some members; the East African Community (EAC), established in 1967 but experiencing tensions until its disintegration in 1977; and the Economic Community of West African States (ECOWAS), created in 1975, whose internal opposition has delayed strides toward trade liberalization and free factor movement. An **economic union** goes further by unifying members' monetary and fiscal policies. The success of the United States, whose 1789 constitution made thirteen states a **complete economic and monetary union,** and that of the EC have partly served as a spur to increased economic integration by LDCs.[37]

There have been numerous attempts by groups of LDC nations to further regional economic cooperation, including the following cases short of economic integration. The Association of South East Asian Nations (ASEAN), formed in 1967, which includes Indonesia, Malaysia, the Philippines, Singapore, Thailand, and six other member states, has a **complementation agreement,** largely unimplemented, under which the organization allocates and shares the costs of starting large-scale infant industries.[38] The Lagos Plan of Action, begun by the Organization of African Unity heads of governments in 1980, aims to speed up regional economic integration and cooperation as necessary instruments for collective self-reliance.

The **Lomé Convention,** the arrangement of the EC with sixty six of its African, Caribbean, and Pacific (ACP) former colonies (omitting several rich or populous Asian members of the British Commonwealth), grants preferences to the EC market for manufactured and primary goods, and special arrangements, such as rights to sell quotas of sugar at a fixed price usually above the world price.[39] Yet the convention may reduce world (and probably LDC) total welfare by **trade diversion** from a ACP beneficiary country displacing imports from a lowest cost third country. (Nevertheless diversion, when compared to separate import substitution policies for each country, may be the lesser of two evils.) However Lomé and LDC regional economic groups are also responsible for some **trade creation,** in which a beneficiary country's firms displace inefficient domestic producers in a member country.

Few LDC attempts at economic integration have succeeded, mainly because less advanced nations are discontented that the most advanced members of the union receive (or are thought to receive) the lion's share of the benefits. In the EAC, the overwhelming amount of new industrial investment went to the relatively developed center, Nairobi, and other cities in Kenya. Working out agreements to compensate members with the smallest shares of gains, or to assign some industries to each member country, is difficult. Moreover the market size of many unions, such as the EAC, CACM, and CARIFTA, is too small to attract industries that require substantial internal economies of scale. A related dilemma is an externally oriented transport system that lacks adequate intraregional transportation facili-

[37] Dominick Salvatore, *International Economics* (New York: Macmillan, 1987), pp. 247–48; and S. K. B. Asante, *The Political Economy of Regionalism in Africa: A Decade of the Economic Community of West African States (ECOWAS)* (New York: Praeger, 1986), pp. 24–28.

[38] Malcolm Gillis, Dwight H. Perkins, Michael Roemer, and Donald R. Snodgrass, *Economics of Development* (New York: Norton, 1987), pp. 471–72.

[39] World Bank, *World Development Report, 1986,* (New York: Oxford University Press, 1986), pp. 140–44.

ties.[40] Furthermore although theory indicates the union gains most from specialization reallocation from less efficient producers exiting the industry and shifting their resources to activities with a greater comparative advantage, most LDCs perceive this "creative destruction" as harmful. Thus while regional integration in the South can reduce dependence on DCs, expand industry, increase efficiency and competition, and improve bargaining power, LDCs are unlikely to use this form of South–South integration for major gains in the last decade of the twentieth century.

We can use some of the same concepts in regional integration to analyze **special** duty free **economic zones (SEZs)** in Puerto Rico, India, Taiwan, the Philippines, the Dominican Republic, Mexico, Panama, Brazil, and (since 1979) coastal cities of China.[41] Indeed although China's SEZs stimulate technological learning and increase domestic incomes from foreign trade and investment, they suffer some backwash effects from outflows of labor, capital, and skills from the rest of China that remind economists of the costs of dualism discussed in Chapter 4.

PROGRESS IN MEETING THE DEMAND FOR A NEW INTERNATIONAL ECONOMIC ORDER (NIEO)

At the beginning of Chapter 16, we mentioned the 1974–1975 LDC demands at the United Nations for a change in the international economic order. In concluding Chapters 16–18, let us indicate major UN recommendations and the progress in implementing them since 1974–1975. The UN recommendations can be divided into the following five categories: (1) transfer of real resources, (2) science and technology, (3) industrialization, (4) food and agriculture, and (5) international trade.[42]

Development Aid and LDC Influence

The UN resolution contains many proposals for increasing the flow of development assistance from developed to developing countries. On the first proposal, for a greater volume and predictability of financial aid, DCs contributed 0.39 percent of GNP in 1986 compared to the 0.70-percent UN target.[43] Contrary to the demand, donors did not increase aid much to least-developed countries, and major creditor countries have devised only limited ways of mitigating LDC debt burdens. International organizations, such as the World Bank Group and the UN Development Program, did enhance the real value of assistance, as the resolution called for.

[40] Mordechai E. Kreinin, *International Economics: A Policy Approach* (San Diego: Harcourt Brace Jovanovich, 1987), pp. 394–96.

[41] Y. C. Jao and C. K. Leung, eds., *China's Special Economic Zones: Policies, Problems, and Prospects* (Hong Kong: Oxford University Press, 1986).

[42] Jan Tinbergen, coordinator, *Reshaping the International Order: A Report to the Club of Rome* (New York: E. P. Dutton, 1976); "Principles for a 'New International Economic Order' Adopted by Sixth Special Session of the United Nations General Assembly," *Survey of International Development* 11 (May–June 1974): 1–4; and "The United Nations Seventh Special Session: A Hopeful Step Forward in the Process of Laying the Foundation for an Alternative World Economic Order," *Survey of International Development,* 12 (September–October 1975): 1–4, summarize these recommendations.

[43] Overseas Development Council, *U.S. Foreign Policy and the Third World: Agenda, 1982* (New York: Praeger, 1982).

The share of SDRs as international reserves increased more slowly than the NIEO resolution envisioned. However when the IMF demonetized gold in the late 1970s, a portion of the proceeds from its gold sales was used to aid LDCs. In a small way, as the UN plan of action asks, international institutions have begun to reflect the greater political, economic, and population weight of Asia, Latin America, and Africa. The IMF, known as the "rich man's club," allotted directorships to Saudi Arabia, China, and the LDCs generally.

From 1974 to 1986, bilateral aid increased slowly, and aid given to multilateral agencies declined if measured in real terms or as a percentage of the donors' GNP. In addition aid volume remained unpredictable. Moreover creditors rescheduled or canceled only a little of the LDC debt.

Science and Technology

While LDC governments have improved their ability to negotiate contracts favorable to transferring science and technology, this transfer has not, as the United Nations requested, increased dramatically. Scientific and technological applications, concentrated largely in the DCs, are bases for their high productivity and the profitability of their large businesses. Contrary to the NIEO statement, DC businesses resist sharing their techniques or devoting their efforts to solving LDC scientific and technological problems when they do not have economic control. Nor have DCs adopted an international code of conduct for transferring technology nor put many resources into strengthening LDC scientific and technological infrastructure, as the UN resolved.

Foreign Investment

The DCs have resisted redeploying most industries that survive only by tariffs and subsidies to LDCs, and where redeployment has been undertaken by MNCs, it has tended to be concentrated in a limited number of countries—most often South Korea, Taiwan, Singapore, Brazil, and Mexico. As LDCs increase their expertise in the economic ministries, many have devised and enforced industrial policies to limit MNCs to participation in investment projects consistent with the laws, regulations, and development programs of the developing countries.

Food and Agricultural Aid

Total food and agricultural aid to LDCs increased between 1974 and 1986, as the NIEO resolution asked, but direct food aid dropped. The DCs did not adopt trade policies more conducive to LDC expansion of export earnings.

International Trade

A limited number of LDCs have been successful in export promotion, stressed by the United Nations. While LDCs made few gains in increasing primary product export price stability, it is doubtful that this NIEO goal should be a LDC priority. Finally LDCs made only modest gains in their goal of improving export income stability.

SUMMARY

1. The LDCs generally gain from a free trade policy wherein they produce goods in which they have a comparative advantage. Factor endowment and technology help determine a country's comparative advantage.

2. Exceptions to the free trade argument include increasing returns to scale, external economies, potential technological borrowing, changes in factor endowment, a revenue tariff, improved terms of trade, increased employment, improved balanced of trade, greater domestic stability, national defense, antidumping, and reduced luxury consumption. Yet most of these tariff arguments are weaker than many LDC economic policymakers think.

3. Export promotion is generally more effective than import substitution in expanding output and employment.

4. Rapid growth in LDC manufactured exports in the 1970s and 1980s was primarily concentrated in middle-income countries, such as Taiwan, South Korea, Hong Kong, Singapore, Spain, Brazil, Yugoslavia, Hungary, Israel, Portugal, and Malaysia.

5. Although the generalized system of tariff preferences and the 1970s' Tokyo Round negotiations reduced DC tariffs on selected LDC imports, these gains may have been outweighed by losses from protectionist policies set up during the 1980s. Additionally DCs increased nontariff trade barriers aginst LDC imports, especially labor-intensive goods, in the late 1970s and 1980s.

6. Expanding primary exports stimulated rapid economic growth in a number of Western countries in the nineteenth century, but this approach has had a more limited impact on growth in today's LDCs.

7. Although the IMF's and European Community's compensatory financing schemes have helped stabilize LDC export earnings, a common fund has not been established, and buffer stock agreements have been of limited value.

8. The LDCs with a foreign exchange price below the market-clearing price can improve import rationing, encourage import substitution, and promote exports by depreciating their currencies. Yet the gains may be limited if domestic prices are still repressed.

TERMS TO REVIEW

- **tariffs**
- **comparative advantage**
- **comparative costs**
- **factor proportions theory**
- **Heckscher–Ohlin theorem**
- **technological advantage**

- **product cycle theory**
- **boomerang effect**
- **income elasticity of demand**
- **laissez-faire**
- **infant industry arguments**
- **commodity terms of trade**

- **Prebisch–Singer thesis**
- **Engel's law**
- **income terms of trade**
- **export purchasing power**
- **single factoral terms of trade**
- **dumping**

- effective rate of protection
- Multifiber Arrangement (MFA)
- trigger price mechanism
- generalized system of tariff preferences (GSP)
- staple theory of growth
- integrated program for commodities
- core commodities
- buffer stocks
- Stabex

- basket of currencies
- special drawing rights (SDRs)
- price of foreign exchange (exchange rate)
- exchange controls
- real exchange rate
- real appreciation
- dual exchange rate
- multiple exchange rate
- theory of the second best
- economic integration

- preferential trade arrangements
- free trade area
- customs union
- common market
- economic union
- complete economic and monetary union
- complementation agreement
- trade diversion
- trade creation
- Lome Convention
- special economic zones (SEZs)
- nontariff barriers (NTBs)

QUESTIONS TO DISCUSS

1. What are the major arguments for and against tariffs in LDCs?

2. Present the four arguments for tariffs you consider strongest and then indicate their weaknesses.

3. Discuss the adequacy of using a model with three factors—land, labor, and capital—in determining comparative advantage. How would we extend the Heckscher–Ohlin model to explain LDC comparative advantage more realistically?

4. Discuss whether a capital poor LDC would better import capital-intensive goods from abroad, subsidize and spur production shifting comparative advantage to these goods, or attract capital from abroad.

5. Do LDCs face historically deteriorating terms of trade?

6. Which is more effective in expanding LDC output and employment: export expansion or import substitution? What policies avoid biases against exports?

7. Name and then characterize those LDCs that were most successful in expanding exports in the 1970s and 1980s.

8. Why is the nominal rate of tariff protection a poor gauge of the effective rate of protection for processed and manufactured goods?

9. Why are nominal exchange-rate changes inadequate when calculating currency depreciation or appreciation? Indicate how to calculate the real exchange rate.

10. What DC changes in tariff policies would aid LDC development?

11. Why has the integrated program for commodities not been more successful in expanding LDC primary product export earnings?

12. Indicate the nature of the present international exchange-rate system and how it affects LDCs.

13. Under what circumstances might a LDC gain from depreciating its currency? What are some of the advantages of depreciation?

14. Discuss the advantages and disadvantages of dual (or other multiple) exchange rates.

15. Why may efforts to achieve a market-clearing exchange rate not improve economic efficiency and growth in a domestic economy that is otherwise not liberalized?

16. Discuss why LDCs have made so few gains in their attempts at regional economic integration.

17. What changes do LDCs want in the international economic order? What progress has been made in implementing these demands? Are any of the demands inconsistent? Are any contrary to LDC interests?

GUIDE TO READINGS

Kenen, pp. 13–68, (note 1) clearly explains the theory of comparative advantage; Black and Kindleberger (note 7) evaluate arguments for tariffs.

Yotopoulos and Nugent, and Spraos (note 9) have good explanations for the concepts and controversies concerning terms of trade. Michael Michaely, *Trade, Income Levels, and Dependence* (Amsterdam: North-Holland, 1984), discusses trade dependence concepts and measurement.

Krueger et al., *Trade and Employment* (note 17), and Lal and Rajapatirana (note 18) have useful analyses of the effect of alternative international trade strategies on output and employment.

The IMF's *World Economic Outlook, International Financial Statistics,* and *IMF Survey,* the World Bank's annual *World Development Report (WDR),* the Bank's and Fund's quarterly *Finance and Development,* and the annual UN *World Economic Survey* have recent information on international trade data and policies.

For an overview of primary commodity problems, see Alfred Maizels, "Commodities in Crisis: An Overview of the Main Issues," *World Development* 15 (May 1987): 537–50. Laursen (note 27) discusses and evaluates the components of UNCTAD's integrated program for commodities. On international comodity agreements, buffer stocks, production and export controls, GSP, the Lomé Convention, the IMF's compensatory financing facility, and Stabex, consult the 1986 *WDR,* pp. 133–44 (note 29). On the last two topics, see Adrian P. Hewitt, "Stabex and Commodity Export Compensation Schemes: Prospects for Globalization," *World Development* 15 (May 1987): 617–32. Naheed Kirmani, "The Uruguay Round: Revitalizing the Global System," *Finance* and *Development* 26 (March 1989): 6–8, discusses the Uruguay Round of multilateral trade negotiations which began in 1986 in Punta del Este, Uruguay.

Economist (October 8, 1988), p. 22, estimates 1984 cocaine (and marijuana) exports as 22–48 percent of legal export earnings in Columbia, 26 percent in Bolivia, and 6–16 percent in Peru. The opium and heroin export percentage in the Golden Triangle (Burma, Thailand, and Laos) and illegal export percentages in some other LDCs are also substantial.

Chapter Nineteen

DEVELOPMENT PLANNING

Most people want to control and plan their economic future. John Kenneth Galbraith points out that today's complex technology and the long time between project conception and completion require planning, either by private firms or government.[1]

Development planning is the government's use of coordinated policies to achieve national economic objectives, such as reduced poverty or accelerated economic growth. A plan encompasses programs discussed previously—antipoverty programs, family planning, agricultural research and extension, employment policies, education, local technology, savings, investment project analysis, monetary and fiscal policies, entrepreneurial development programs, and international trade and capital flows. Planning involves surveying the existing economic situation, setting economic goals, devising economic policies and public expenditures consistent with these goals, developing the administrative capability to implement policies, and (where still feasible) adjusting approaches and programs in response to ongoing evaluation.

Planning takes place in socialist but also in capitalist and mixed, private–public LDCs. Capitalist countries plan in order to correct for externalities, redistribute income, produce public goods (for example, education, police, and fire protection), provide infrastructure and research for directly productive sectors, encourage investment, supply a legal and social framework for markets, maintain competition, and stabilize employment and prices.

[1] John Kenneth Galbraith, *The New Industrial State* (Boston: Houghton Mifflin, 1967).

Usually the country's head of government (prime minister or president) assigns the plan to a planning office that includes politicians, civil servants, economists, mathematicians, statisticians, accountants, engineers, scientists, educators, social scientists, and lawyers, as well as specialists in various industries, technologies, agriculture, international trade, and ethnology.

In the 1950s, economists stressed an expert planning agency independent of political and bureaucratic pressures. After many a sophisticated plan lay on the shelf unused, the emphasis shifted to a planning commission directly responsible to politicians and integrated with government departments of industry, finance, commerce, petroleum, agriculture, health, education, and social welfare, as well as with regional and local government departments and planners.

STATE PLANNING AS IDEOLOGY FOR NEW STATES

Economic planning in LDCs was limited prior to their independence (often gained during the 1950s and 1960s). The British and French used development plans (worked out by territorial governments with help from London and Paris) as a basis for colonial aid after World War II. But the plans, prepared by administrators with little or no planning background, were usually just lists of investment projects. And no attempt was made to integrate the various economic sectors. However, they did have the virtue of being carried out, in contrast to many postindependence plans.

Many intellectuals, nationalist leaders, and politicians believed that laissez-faire capitalism rigidly adhered to during the colonial period was responsible for slow LDC economic growth. So once independence was granted, nationalists and anticolonialists pushed for systematic state economic planning to remove these deep-seated, capitalistic obstacles. Such sentiments were expressed in a statist (usually called socialist) ideology that stressed government's role in assuring minimum economic welfare for all citizens.

Many third-world leaders, even from mixed economies, such as Nigeria, Kenya, India, and Sri Lanka, agreed with Kwame Nkrumah (Ghana's president, 1957–66) who wrote that "the vicious circle of poverty, which keeps us in our rut of impoverishment, can only be broken by a massively planned industrial undertaking." He was skeptical of the market mechanism's effectiveness, argued for the "uncounted advantages of planning," and contended that government interference in the economic growth of developing countries is "universally accepted." Vigorous state planning would remove the distorting effects of colonialism and free a LDC from dependence on primary exports.[2]

And since in many LDCs, the business class was weak at independence, the argument for a major state role in spearheading economic development was strengthened. Yet decisions concerning government size were usually based less on economic reasoning than on ruling elites' interests. Most third-world elites were politicians, professional administrators, and bureaucrats and wanted to protect their interests from business people. Elites perceived anarchy in the market, which reinforced by their lack of control, produced a statist ideology.

[2] Kwame Nkrumah, *Neo-Colonialism: The Last Stages of Imperialism* (London: Nelson, 1965).

AFRO-ASIAN SOCIALISM

African and Asian socialism did not coincide with the Western socialist concept of the ownership of most capital and land by the state (see Chapter 2). Instead the Afro-Asian variety usually included the following: a high-level of state ownership of the **commanding heights** (major sectors of heavy industry, metallurgy, military industries, mining, fuel, transport, banking, and foreign trade), a penchant for public control of resource allocation in key sectors, a deemphasis on foreign trade and investment, a priority on inward-looking production, and a rapid indigenization of high-level jobs.[3]

DIRIGISTE DEBATE

From after World War II to the early 1980s, many development economists favored a major role for the LDC state in promoting macroeconomic stability, national planning, and a sizable public sector. In the early 1980s, a series of World Bank and IMF reports emphasized reversing the LDC government sector's overextension.[4] Indeed World Bank and IMF conditions for balance of payments lending to LDCs sometimes required privatization of LDC state-owned enterprises, a part of policy reforms that stressed state enterprise reform and competition policies in both private and public sectors.[5]

The emphasis on privatization, discussed in Chapter 20, began with the 1981 to 1986 World Bank presidency of former New York bank president A. W. Clausen and continued under former U.S. Congress person Barber B. Conable, appointed in 1986. The emphasis was not just an extension of President Ronald Reagan's and Prime Minister Margaret Thatcher's domestic economics to U.S., British, and Western-dominated multilateral aid and lending programs, but also a LDC response to the failure of public enterprise to match expectations. Frequently LDC governments provided massive subsidies to public enterprises that had been expected to produce an investible surplus.

University of London economist Deepak Lal criticizes development economists' *dirigiste* dogma: a view that standard economic theory does not apply to LDCs, the price mechanism has to be supplanted by direct government controls, and resource allocation is of minor importance in designing public policies. Lal contends that the demise of development economics would be conducive to LDC economics and economies.[6]

Critics charge that Lal does not define development economists to include all authors applying economics to LDCs but only those authors with whom he disagrees. Moreover, Lal's description of their views is a caricature: Dudley Seers, an

---

[3] Shankar N. Acharya, "Perspectives and Problems of Development in sub-Saharan Africa," *World Development* 9 (February 1981): 117–18.

[4] An early report signaling the Bank's emphasis on the private sector was the World Bank, *Accelerated Development in sub-Saharan Africa: An Agenda for Action* (Washington, D.C., 1981).

[5] Paul Mosley, "Privatisation, Policy-based Lending, and World Bank Behaviour," in Paul Cook and Colin Kirkpatrick, eds., *Privatisation in Less-Developed Countries* (Sussex, U.K.: Wheatsheaf, 1988), pp. 125–26.

[6] Deepak Lal, *The Poverty of "Development Economics,"* (London: Institute of Economic Affairs, 1983).

example of Lal's *dirigistes,* rejects a *rigid adherence* to standard economic theory (see Chapter 1), favors income transfers rather than price controls to redistribute income, and criticizes detailed physical planning. Nor is Lal correct in attributing Taiwan's and South Korea's success to little governmental direction, nor the World Bank in linking rapid growth in Malawi in the 1970s to low interference in prices. Taiwan and Korea both promulgated land reform in the late 1940s and early 1950s; provided subsidies for farm products and their inputs beginning in the 1960s; and actively used government incentives, controls, and protection to promote industries for export expansion since World War II. Critics of the World Bank argue that Malawi's agricultural policy in the 1970s had sizable price distortions and the transferring resources from peasant agriculture to commercial agriculture and industry overstated the growth accompanying falling peasant agricultural productivity and declining average real incomes for the population as a whole. The discussion in Chapters 19 and 20 reflects a growing consensus among development economists on planning, the market, and the public sector somewhere between the views of Lal and his straw men and women, the *dirigistes.*[7]

SCOPE OF THE CHAPTER

We look first at state planning as an ideology for nations that have gained independence since World War II. The second section examines Soviet planning and the third Indian planning and their implications for LDCs. The fourth part outlines promarket and proplanning arguments. Fifth, we look at the need for indicative planning in most nonsocialist LDCs. Sections 6–8 analyze planning goals and instruments, plan duration, and the limitations of planning models. In the next part, we examine LDC economic data, emphasizing development of an input-output table. The last two sections deal with public expenditures and private sector policies. Planning state enterprise is discussed in Chapter 20.

SOVIET PLANNING

Many LDCs have turned to the Soviet Union for lessons in state planning. Since 1928, the Soviet **controlling plan,** including Mikhail Gorbachev's economic restructuring (perestroika), has authorized what each key sector enterprise produces and how much it invests. Yet even Soviet planning, probably more comprehensive than that in any other country, has not been so totally planned and rigidly controlled as

[7] Frances Stewart, "The Fragile Foundations of the Neoclassical Approach to Development," *Journal of Development Studies* 21 (January 1985): 282–92; Clive Hamilton, "Class, State, and Industrialisation in South Korea," *IDS Bulletin* 15 (April 1984): 38–43; Martin Fransman, "Explaining the Success of the Asian NICs: Incentives and Technology," *IDS Bulletin* 15 (April 1984): pp. 50–56; Mick Moore, "Agriculture in Taiwan and South Korea: The Minimalist State," *IDS Bulletin* 15 (April 1984): 57–64; Robert Wade, "Dirigisme Taiwan-style," *IDS Bulletin* 15 (April 1984): 65–70; World Bank, *World Development Report, 1983* (New York: Oxford University Press, 1983), pp. 60–63; Jonathan Kydd and Robert Christiansen, "Structural Change in Malawi since Independence: Consequences of a Development Strategy based on Large-Scale Agriculture," *World Development* 10 (May 1982): 355–74; and Jonathan Kydd, "Malawi in the 1970s: Development Policies and Economic Change," paper presented to a Conference on Malawi: An Alternative Pattern of Development, Edinburgh University, Centre of African Studies, May 24–25, 1984.

you might think. Soviet planning began modestly. During the 1918 to 1921 civil war, enterprises ignored planning directives. Not until 1925 to 1926 did **Gosplan,** the State Planning Committee of the USSR, which consults with ministries, republics, and enterprises, have the personnel and authority to plan detailed input-output relationships.

Even today in the centrally planned key sectors (heavy industry, much of light industry, and a small part of agriculture), there is much local, extraplan discretion—government simply cannot control all operations details. For example, bad weather or shortages sometimes prevent delivery of essential materials so that enterprise managers adjust by hoarding, bartering, and other informal arrangements. Presently over half of Soviet GNP remains out of the purview of planners and under the control of local officials, enterprises, and even private markets. These activities however generally depend on state policies for financial controls, purchasing, pricing, wage schedules, labor mobility, education and training, turnover taxes, foreign trade, and so forth.[8]

Leon Trotsky recognized the difficulties of comprehensive Soviet centralized planning early in its history. Trotsky, Communist party leader exiled by Joseph Stalin, criticized Soviet bureaucratic and centralized economic management:

> If there existed the universal mind that projected itself into the scientific fancy of Laplace; a mind that would register simultaneously all the processes of nature and of society, that could measure the dynamics of their motion, that could forecast the results of their interreactions, such a mind, of course, could *a priori* draw up a faultless and exhaustive economic plan, beginning with the number of hectares of wheat and down to the last button for a vest. In truth, the bureaucracy often conceives that just such a mind is at its disposal; that is why it so easily frees itself from the control of the market and of Soviet democracy. . . . The innumerable living participants of the economy, state as well as private, collective as well as individual, must give notice of their needs and of their relative strength not only through the statistical determination of plan commissions but by direct pressure of supply and demand. The plan is checked, and, to a considerable measure, realized through the market. . . . Economic accounting is unthinkable without market relations.[9]

Soviet leader Gorbachev believed that economic restructuring, which relied more on decentralization, was essential in reversing slow USSR growth after 1970.

INDIAN PLANNING

In 1951, India was the first major mixed LDC to have its own planning commission. Decades before he took office, Jawaharlal Nehru, prime minister after India's independence in 1947, had been attracted by English democratic socialism as well as Soviet industrial planning. India's economic policies for its first five-year plans (and several interim plans) through 1978 suffered from the paradox of inadequate attention to programs in the public sector and too much control over the private

[8] Paul R. Gregory and Robert C. Stuart, *Soviet Economic Structure and Performance* (New York: Harper & Row, 1986).

[9] Leon Trotsky, *The Soviet Economy in Danger* (New York: Pioneer Publishers, 1931), pp. 29–30, 33.

sector. Thus we had Indian planners frequently choosing public sector investments on the basis of rough, sketchy, and incomplete reports, with little or no cost-benefit calculations for alternative project locations. And the government, having selected the project, often failed to do the necessary detailed technical preparation and work scheduling related to the project. The bureaucracy was slow and rigid, stifling quick and imaginative action by public sector managers. (Even public firms had to apply for materials and capital import licenses a year or so in advance.) Poorly stated criteria for awarding input licenses and production quotas led to charges of bribery, influence peddling, and ethnic or political prejudice. Key public sector products were often priced lower than scarcity prices, increasing waste and reducing savings. Furthermore political involvement in public enterprises meant unskilled labor overstaffed many projects.

Jagdish N. Bhagwati's and Padma Desai's study shows that such planning problems led to profit rates for public enterprises that were lower than for indigenous, private operations even when adjusted for commercial and social profit discrepancies. This inefficiency explains why the Indian public sector, despite its domination of large industry, contributed only sixteen percent of the country's 1985 total capital formation (Table 14-2).

Indian planners on the other hand tried to influence private investment and production through licensing and other controls. These controls were intended to regulate production according to plan targets, encourage small industry, prevent concentrated ownership, and promote balanced regional economic development.

The Indian government's award of materials and input quotas at below–market prices hampered private industrial efficiency.

1. It subsidized some firms and forced others to buy inputs on the black market or do without.

2. Favoring existing firms discouraged new-firm entry. And inefficient manufacturers sold controlled inputs on the free market for sizable profit.

3. Business people were unproductive, since they were dealing with government agencies and buying and selling controlled materials.

4. Capital was often underutilized, since government encouraged building excess capacity by awarding more materials to firms with greater plant capacity.

5. Entrepreneurs inflated materials requests, expecting allotments to be reduced by a specific percentage.

6. Business people used or sold all materials within the fiscal year to avoid quota cuts the following years.

7. A shortage of controlled inputs could halt production, since the application process took several months.

8. Large companies, which were better organized and informed than small enterprises, took advantage of economies of scale in dealing with the public bureaucracy.

9. Entrepreneurial planning was difficult because of quota delay and uncertainty.[10]

[10] Jagdish N. Bhagwati and Padma Desai, *India: Planning for Industrialization—Industrialization and Trade Policies since 1951* (London: Oxford University Press, 1970); and E. Wayne Nafziger, *Class, Caste, and Entrepreneurship: A Study of Indian Industrialists* (Honolulu: University Press of Hawaii, 1978), pp. 114–19.

India has slowly improved its public sector planning. Indian politicians have increasingly realized the inadequacies of the bureaucracy in controlling private output and prices, and the costs of licensing and quota policies. In the 1980s, the Indian government relaxed production and materials licensing, import restrictions, and other controls on private business, increasing efficiency and savings.

THE MARKET VERSUS DETAILED CENTRALIZED PLANNING

While the Soviet experience indicates how much of an economy remains beyond the control of central planners, the Indian experience suggests the costs of intervention in mixed economies. The inability to work out in-depth programs in the public sector, and excessive private-sector regulation, are endemic in many other mixed economies, including Nigeria, Ghana, and Pakistan.

The plan and the market are separate ways of coordinating transactions. Using the market adds certain costs: discovering relevant prices and negotiating and concluding separate contracts for each exchange transaction. To reduce risks and other costs, managers (together with suppliers and workers) sign long-term contracts rather than making agreements for each separate transaction. Planning and organizing eliminate certain costs of the market system but also increase large-scale diseconomies—diminishing returns to management. A balance between using the market and a planning organization is reached when "the costs of organizing an extra transaction . . . become equal to the costs of carrying out the same transaction by means of an exchange in the open market."[11] In this section, we focus on the free market as an alternative to centralized state planning.

Promarket Arguments

The market efficiently allocates scarce resources among alternative means. First, consumers receive goods for which they are willing to pay. Second, firms produce commodities to maximize profits. If the resulting income distribution is acceptable, consumption and production are socially efficient. Third, production resources hire out to maximize income. Fourth, the market determines available labor and capital. Fifth, the market distributes income among production resources and thus among individuals.

The market provides incentives for economic growth. Consumers try to increase income to acquire more goods. Investors and innovators profit from the market. People invest in human capital and firms in material capital, since such capital earns an income.

The market stimulates growth and efficiency automatically, without a large administration on centralized decision making. Thus, it conserves on skilled personnel, a scarce resource in LDCs. The market needs little policing other than a legal system enforcing contracts. When government abandons the market and starts allocating scarce goods and concessions (for example, foreign currency, licenses,

[11] R. H. Coase, "The Nature of the Firm," in George J. Stigler and Kenneth E. Boulding, eds., *Readings in Price Theory* (Chicago: Irwin, 1952), pp. 331–51 (quote on p. 341); and Oliver E. Williamson, "The Modern Corporation: Origins, Evolution, Attributes," *Journal of Economic Literature* 21 (December 1981): 1537–68.

and materials), corruption, favoritism, bribery, and black markets are more likely to thrive.

Proplanning Arguments

Market decisions do not produce the best results when differences between social and private profitability exist. Social profitability exceeds private profitability when external economies (for example, labor training or measles vaccinations) are rendered free by one firm to a consumer or another producer. External diseconomies (pollution, let us say) mean private profitability exceeds social profitability. (See Chapters 5 and 12.) National planners are more likely to choose investment projects for social profitability rather than for their internal market rates of return.

Social and private profitability also diverge in a market economy when there are monopolistic restraints. A monopolist produces less and charges higher prices than does a competitive firm. National planners reduce a project's monopoly profits but increase social profits by expanding output and lowering prices to the competitive equilibrium. Industry and enterprise managers in a planned economy will however restrict output volume if they are rewarded on the basis of the value of output profits.[12]

The free market may not produce so high a saving rate as is socially desirable. A government generating surplus from its own production, setting low procurement prices for state trading monopsonies, and levying turnover taxes can usually save in excess of households and firms. Centrally planned economies, particularly the Soviet Union, have had higher rates of saving than market economies (Chapter 14).

Relying on the market assumes that people are well informed and want to maximize gains. Should not centralized planning replace the market in LDCs where this assumption is false? The answer is not clearcut. If prospective private entrepreneurs lack information and motivation, the planner's role may be enlarged. On the other hand, the planning agency can ease its task by disseminating information to make the market work more effectively. Although the peasant preoccupied with family survival may not be an income maximizer (Chapter 7), empirical studies demonstrate that the LDC industrialist, trader, and commercial farmer respond to income and price incentives, suggesting that the market works well.

Market Socialism

The income distribution the market produces—partly dependent on the skills and property of the privileged and wealthy (Chapter 12)—may not be just or socially desirable. Yet the greater income inequality of capitalist economies may result less from the market than from unequal holdings of land and capital. Polish economist Oskar Lange's model of decentralized **market socialism** combined the advantages of market allocation with more uniform income distribution by dividing the returns from social ownership of nonhuman, productive resources among the whole population. Lange's approach assumed that individuals allocated their limited income

---

[12] Harry G. Johnson, *Money, Trade, and Economic Growth* (London: George Allen & Unwin, 1962), pp. 152–63; Oskar Lange and Fred M. Taylor, *On the Economic Theory of Socialism,* Benjamin E. Lippincott, ed. (New York: McGraw-Hill, 1965); and Abram Bergson, "Market Socialism Revisited," *Journal of Political Economy* 75, no. 5 (October 1967): 657–65.

among consumer goods and services and provided labor services just as in capitalist economies. Socialist enterprises produced where product price equaled marginal cost (the competitive profit maximization rule), while combining factor inputs to minimize the average cost of production. Industrial authorities chose the rate of expansion or contraction of the industry as a whole. Central planners used trial and error to set prices at equilibrium (where shortages and surpluses disappeared), adjusted prices for externalities through taxes and subsidies, and allocated returns from property owned collectively by society.

Critics argued that pricing consistent with maximum profits would encourage monopolistic behavior by enterprise and industry managers in concentrated industries; planning decisions would not be compatible with political freedom; and central planners would have the impossible task of setting millions of prices for individual products and subproducts.[13] But decentralized enterprises could set prices rather than central planners, who need only intervene to prevent monopoly pricing. One example close to Lange's model, the Soviet New Economic Policy, 1921 to 1927, which enabled the economy to recover rapidly from the chaos and disruption of revolution and civil war, was later replaced because the Communist party bureaucracy lacked control over the economy.

Worker-Managed Socialism: Yugoslavia

Economists in Yugoslavia, the nearest contemporary approximation of Lange's model, argue that socialist planning must be managed by workers to be democratic and must use the market for resource allocation to be efficient. Since 1948 to 1951, each firm elected a workers' council, which hired a professional manager to carry out the council's decision. Workers shared in income from the enterprise, after subtracting material and other costs, based on a democratically agreed-on income distribution determined by the intensity and quality of people's labor. Individuals sought employment anywhere, and firms were free to hire a particular person. Generally the labor-managed firm maximized net income per member.[14]

From 1959, a decade after worker management began, until 1979, Yugoslavia's real GNP grew 6 percent annually, and the labor force was transformed from primarily peasant agriculture into modern sector employment. During the 1980s, however, real GNP per capita declined, the unemployment rate averaged 10–15 percent, strikes were widespread, annual inflation averaged more the 35 percent, and total external debt was the tenth largest in the world ($21 billion in 1988). Workers' councils have been limited by state regulations (including prices) and by political intervention of the League of Communists of Yugoslavia (LCY). Moreover Yugoslavia's 1976 reform established the basic organizations of associated

[13] Oskar Lange and Fred M. Taylor, *On the Economic Theory of Socialism*, Benjamin E. Lippincott, ed., (New York: McGraw-Hill., 1965); and Paul R. Gregory and Robert C. Stuart, *Soviet Economic Structure and Performance* (New York: Harper & Row, 1974), pp. 311–19.

[14] Branko Hôrvat, Mihailo Marković, and Rudi Supek, *Self-Governing Socialism,* 2 vols. (White Plains, N.Y.: International Arts and Sciences Press, 1975); especially Branko Horvat, "An Institutional Model of a Self-Managed Socialist Economy," pp. 307–27, and Jaroslav Vanek, "Identifying the Participatory Economy," pp. 135–40, in Branko Hôrvat, Mihailo Marković, and Rudi Supek, *Sociology and Politics; Economics,* vol. 2 (White Plains, N.Y.: International Arts and Sciences Press, 1975).

labor (BOs), a separate autonomous planning unit for each department in the firm. The BOs, in addition to workers council, trade union, business managers, their administrative and technical staff, the LCY, and the local community, complicated enterprise decision making, introducing multiple checks and balances, so that the firm's hierarchy was ill defined. The need for consensus among so many units gave many people (for example, discontented, even striking work units, such as janitors or carpenters) the capacity to impede and few people the power to implement policies. When coalitions broke down, the state (federation, province, or local community) or LCY bureaucracy could dissolve disruptive workers' councils, recall business managers, or withhold infrastructure or funds.

Other weaknesses of the Yugoslav self-managed socialism have been the lack of participation of rank-and-file employees in important policymaking, the dependence of pay on factors outside BO control (for example, closing down production because suppliers failed to deliver an essential input), the unconcern for long-run performance (considerable turnover of workers, who lack ownership shares in the firm), neglect of externalities, widely varying income among workers doing the same job in different firms, lack of a labor market, the state's **soft budget constraint** (an absence of financial penalties for enterprise failure), restricted entry of new firms to increase competition, collusion between vertically and horizontally linked firms, investment choice based on negotiations not benefit-cost analysis, overborrowing (resulting from no interest charge), disincentives to expand employment, too little investment from current surplus, and too many incentives for highly capital-intensive production (from pressures to distribute higher incomes per member).[15]

Conclusion

Despite Yugoslavia's experience during the 1980s, market socialism's appeal is enhanced by the country's 1948 to 1979 growth and China's post-1978 market-oriented reforms (Chapters 7 and 20), especially in agriculture. Market socialism may appeal to LDCs that oppose private ownership but lack the administrative service and planning capability to run a centralized socialist economy.

INDICATIVE PLANS

The weaknesses of Soviet planning discussed before are minor compared to those of recently established LDC planning agencies that insist that partial planning give way to comprehensive planning. But in economies with a large private sector, government planning can only be partial. Chapter 12 pointed out the difficulty of applying Fel'dman's Soviet planning model to mixed LDCs where planning does not represent a binding commitment by a public department to spend funds. Few third-world planning commissions have the skills and authority needed for Soviet-type planning.

[15] Martin Schrenk, "The Self-Managed Firm in Yugoslavia," in Gene Tidrick and Chen Jiyuan, eds., *China's Industrial Reform* (New York: Oxford University Press, 1987), pp. 339–69; Alec Nove, *The Economics of Feasible Socialism* (London: Allen and Unwin, 1983), pp. 133–41, and Rammath Narayanswamy, "Yugoslavia: Self–Management or Mismanagement?" *Economic and Political Weekly* 23 (October 1, 1988), 2052–54.

Most mixed or capitalist developing countries are limited to an **indicative plan,** which indicates expectations, aspirations, and intentions, but falls short or authorization. Indicative planning may include economic forecasts, helping private decisionmakers, policies favorable to the private sector, ways of raising money and recruiting personnel, and a list of proposed public expenditures—usually not authorized by the plan, but by the annual budget.

PLANNING GOALS AND INSTRUMENTS

Planning sets economic goals. Since government hires the planners, political leaders set the goals, which may or may not reflect the public priorities. Possible planning goals include rapid economic growth, reduced poverty and income inequality, high basic-needs attainment, greater educational attainment, greater employment, price stability, lower international economic dependence, greater regional balance, and adequate environmental quality. Some of the goals, such as reduced poverty and inequality and high basic-needs attainment are complementary rather than independent. Yet where there are conflicts between goals, political leaders must decide what relative weight to give to each goal. In this case, about all planning professionals can do is interpret economic data to identify goals (for example, the need to reduce a region's rural poverty, cope with a balance of payments crisis, or slow down inflation), clearly state them, and formulate the costs of one goal in terms of another.

Planners face such questions as follow: How much real growth should be sacrificed to reduce the rate of inflation by 1 percentage point? How much would increased capital formation lessen low-income consumption? How much GNP would have to be given up to achieve an acceptable level of independence from world markets? How much output should be sacrificed to attain a desired level of environmental quality?

Planners often express goals as **target variables**—for example, annual GNP growth of 6 percent; output growth of manufacturing, 8 percent and of agriculture, 5 percent; poverty reduced by 1 percentage point of the population; and a balance of payments deficit not in excess of $200 million. Goals are achieved through **instrument variables,** such as monetary, fiscal, exchange rate, tariff, tax, subsidy, extension, technology, business incentive, foreign investment, foreign aid, social welfare, transfer, wage, labor training, health, education, economic survey, price control, quota, and capital-rationing policies.[16]

THE DURATION OF PLANS

The availability of instrument variables depends on the length of time in which the goals are to be achieved. To slow down labor force growth takes 15 to 20 years, to build a dam a decade, but to increase free rice allotments per capita may take only a few weeks.

Short-term plans focus on improving economic conditions in the immediate

[16] Hollis B. Chenery, "Development Policies and Programs," *Economic Bulletin for Latin America* 3, no. 1 (March 1958): 55–60.

future (the next calendar or budget year); **medium-term plans,** on the more distant future (say, a five-year plan); and **long-term** (or perspective) **plans,** on the very distant future (15, 20, or more years).

Long-term goals must serve as a background for medium- and short-term plans. Medium-term plans, which often coincide with government office terms, are such that investment returns begin to occur after the first year or so of the plan. These plans can be more precise than long-term plans.

A medium-term plan can be a **rolling plan,** revised at the end of each year. As a planning commission finishes the first year of the plan, it adds estimates, targets, and projects for another year to the last year. Thus planners would revise the five-year plan for 1990 to 1994 at the end of 1990, issuing a new plan for 1991 to 1995. In effect a plan is renewed at the end of each year, but the number of years remains the same as the plan rolls forward in time.

However, a rolling plan involves more than a mechanical extension of an existing plan. It requires rethinking and revising the whole plan each year to set targets for an additional year. Built into the rolling plan are a regular review and revision procedure (in effect needed for all plans, whatever their range). Yet rolling plans have sometimes proved too difficult for most LDCs to manage. A simpler way of bringing a medium-term plan up to date is by implementing part of it through the short-term plan.

Short-term (usually annual) plans carry out government policy in connection with a detailed budget. The size and composition of an annual plan are determined primarily by finances, plan expertise, and the progress made in feasibility studies and projects started in previous periods.[17]

PLANNING MODELS AND THEIR LIMITATIONS

Planners need a bird's eye view of macroeconomic relationships before determining programs, expenditures, and policies, and a simple aggregate model can provide this overall perspective. Most macroeconomic models for the United States are complicated, sometimes consisting of hundreds of variables and equations. But most LDCs cannot afford such complexity. And even if skills, funds, and data were available, the planners' policy control in mixed and capitalist LDCs is too limited for a comprehensive aggregate model to have much practical value.

Nobel laureate W. Arthur Lewis criticizes planning agencies in data-poor, mixed LDCs that hire economists to formulate a complex macroeconomic model. He believes the time spent is not worth the effort. He ironically notes that

> The principal danger of a macroeconomic exercise lies in its propensity to dazzle. The more figures there are in a Plan, produced by an army of professionals who have labored mightily to make them consistent, the more persuasive the Plan becomes. Attention shifts from policy to arithmetic. Consistency can be mistaken for truth. Revision is resisted. Yet the Plan is not necessarily right merely because its figures are mutually consistent. . . . Once the point is grasped that mathematical exercises do not

---

[17] Jan Tinbergen, *Development Planning,* trans. by N. D. Smith (London: World University Library, 1967), pp. 36–38; and Albert Waterston, *Development Planning: Lessons of Experience* (Baltimore: Johns Hopkins University Press, 1969), pp. 120–33.

of themselves produce truth, a Plan with figures is no more dangerous than a Plan without figures.[18]

Many planners still think that planning primarily involves agreeing on macroeconomic targets for investment and output. Lewis notes that when Nigeria's First National Development Plan, 1962 to 1968, was published,

> Argument broke out as to whether the planners had "chosen" the right rate of growth whether they had used the right capital-output ratios, and whether they had determined correctly the amount of capital which private entrepreneurs would be required to invest. All such discussion misconceives what the government can actually do.[19]

For Nigeria, characterized in the 1960s by its Economic Planning Unit head as "planning without facts," Lewis maintains that you can make nearly as good a development plan without national income projections, capital-output ratios, and other such econometric manipulations as with them.[20]

Generally macroeconomic planning models used in LDCs with large private sectors have been ineffective. Actual policies and economic growth in such countries have little relationship to the plan's instrument and target variables. Much of LDC economic growth since the early 1960s has gone in directions unforeseen by the plan or if included in the plan, would have occurred even in the plan's absence![21]

Thus nonsocialist LDC planners should generally not be judged by how well they have reached their target growth rates. The UN Center for Development Planning, Projections, and Policies observed that Nigeria's real growth in gross domestic product from 1970 to 1974, was 12.3 percent per year compared to an annual target of only 6.2.[22]

But this rapid growth had little to do with plan investments. The Nigerian government spent only 63 percent of planned public capital. Planners did not clearly identify feasible industrial projects nor give details of supporting government policies. And poor coordination and personnel shortages resulted in inadequate preparatory work by accountants, economists, engineers, managers, and planners. In reality most Nigerian growth could be explained by factors largely outside the planner's purview—the unexpectedly rapid oil growth and sharply increasing oil prices.

Nonetheless macroeconomic models may be useful in forecasting and projections, enabling decisionmakers to see the economy from a national perspective.

[18] W. Arthur Lewis, *Development Planning: The Essentials of Economic Policy* (London: Allen and Unwin, 1966), pp. 16–17.

[19] W. Arthur Lewis, *Reflections on Nigeria's Economic Growth* (Paris: Development Center of the Organization for Economic Cooperation and Development, 1967), p. 35.

[20] Ibid., 35–36; and Wolfgang F. Stolper, *Planning without Facts: Lessons in Resource Allocation from Nigeria's Development* (Cambridge, Mass.: Harvard University Press, 1966).

[21] Clarence Zuvekas, Jr., *Economic Development: An Introduction* (New York: St. Martin's, 1979), p. 191.

[22] Center for Development Planning, Projections, and Policies, "Implementation of Development Plans: The Experience of Developing Countries in the First Half of the 1970s," *Journal of Development Planning* no. 12 (1977): 1–69.

And if a forecast is based on consultation with the economic ministries and private firms, it may give investors greater confidence in the economy's forward movement. But although planning models have some value, Lewis contends that the most important parts of the plan are the documents showing how to improve data collection, raise revenue, recruit personnel, and select and implement projects—topics discussed below.

Three professionals play an especially important role in planning: (1) the person with treasury experience, used to dealing with government departments and planning public expenditures; (2) the practical economist familiar with the unique problems that emerge in LDCs to help formulate public policies; and (3) the econometrician to construct **input-output tables** to clarify intersectoral economic relations.[23]

ECONOMIC DATA

Economic data in many LDCs are of little value. Since some facts needed for decision making may be unavailable, planners may have to improvise.

Take the case of GNP. In many LDCs, production estimates for domestic food crops, often the largest sector in the economy, are based on informal estimates agricultural officers make about whether output increased or decreased. But even small errors may be of major importance. Assume GNP in 1990 is $10,000 million. If GNP is $10,300 million, with a 5-percent margin of error, the range is between $9785 million (representing a 2.15-percent decrease in GNP) and $10,815 million (an 8.15-percent increase).

Planning in a country with poor economic data should concentrate on organizing an effective census bureau and department of statistics, hiring practical field investigators and data analysts, and taking periodic economic surveys. Sound development planning requires information on national income, population, investment, saving, consumption, government expenditure, taxes, exports, imports, balance of payments, and performance of major industries and sectors, as well as their interrelationships.[24]

The Input-Output Table

The most useful technique for describing these interrelationships is the input-output table, illustrated with interindustry transactions in Papua New Guinea (see Table 19-1). When divided horizontally, the table shows how the output of each industry is distributed among other industries and sectors of the economy. At the same time, when divided vertically, it shows the inputs to each industry from other industries and sectors.

Table 19-1 is more simplified than usually used in planning, but it is realistic in other respects. It consolidates an original forty six productive sectors into eleven.

---

[23] W. Arthur Lewis, *Development Planning: The Essentials of Economic Policy* (London: Allen and Unwin, 1966), pp. 16–17.

[24] Graham Eele, "The Organization and Management of Statistical Services in Africa: Why Do They Fail?" *World Development* 17 (March 1989): 431-38, opposes government departments distinguishing between data collection and policy analysis.

TABLE 19-1 Input-Output Table, Papua New Guinea ($ million; purchasers' values)

| | Purchases by Intermediate Users | | | | | | | | | | | Final Demand Purchases | | Gross Capital | Domestic | | |
Outputs / Inputs	1 Ag	2 Ffm	3 Mfg.	4 Bc	5 Tc	6 Cm	7 Eh	8 Gs	9 Os	10 Be	11 Nmp	Pers. Cons.	Net Current Exp.[a]	Public	Private[b]	Exports	Total Output
Sales of intermediate inputs by processing sectors																	
1 Agriculture	1.89		7.86				0.51	0.35		0.13		17.56			6.20	80.21	114.71
2 Fishing, forestry, mining	0.04		10.53	0.05			0.06	0.04				3.46			0.10	209.80	224.08
3 Manufacturing	9.05	1.66	17.01	40.51	12.21	2.65	2.43	7.04	1.61	2.61		76.52		1.10	2.60	46.78	223.78
4 Building construction	0.48	0.56	0.36	0.61	0.22	0.66	1.15	15.19	1.05	0.08				61.10	57.27		138.73
5 Transport, communication	3.91	0.83	6.32	3.47	3.51	1.51	4.80	14.54	0.21	11.80		16.94		0.40	0.30	13.17	81.71
6 Commerce	6.43	3.00	25.52	7.43	4.11	0.70	0.40	0.24	0.33	1.60		23.99		1.30	8.55	5.41	89.01
7 Education, health												4.70	60.40			0.10	65.36
8 Govt. services, N.E.I.	0.77	0.34	0.22	0.95	0.41	1.59	0.01	0.17	5.51	0.35			106.55	11.60		0.36	128.83
9 Other services			0.03		0.15	8.31	0.19	0.71		9.33		20.71	7.60			7.81	54.84
10 Business expenses	1.45	4.08	6.86	7.25	2.80	13.94	0.52	1.92	4.48							3.87	47.17
11 Nonmarket production												219.00		35.70	4.40		259.10
Payments for Primary Inputs																	
Wages & salaries																	
Indigenes	18.31	8.65	14.54	12.57	9.87	8.19	18.43	23.58	13.05								127.19
Nonindigenes	3.34	9.90	20.66	14.78	15.82	11.69	26.34	46.19	11.11								159.83
Operating surplus[c]	58.03	122.12	44.47	7.76	7.56	31.39	1.84	0.31	12.57		259.10						545.15
Depreciation	2.91	32.52	8.97	5.54	9.89	4.74	0.08	0.25	2.76								67.66
Net indirect tax	0.55	7.22	19.79	1.85	1.46	1.19	0.06	0.04	0.49	1.02		13.16		0.20	3.48	2.34	52.85
Imports, c.i.f.	7.55	33.10	40.64	35.96	13.70	2.45	8.54	18.26	1.61	20.25		96.43		24.60	60.02	9.51	372.62
Sales by final buyers															-0.42	0.42	
Total input	114.71	224.08	223.78	138.73	81.71	89.01	65.36	128.83	54.84	47.17	259.10	492.47	174.55	136.00	142.50	379.78	2,572.62

[a] Net current expenditures of public authorities, missions, and financial enterprises.

[b] Including additions to stocks.

[c] Including indigenous nonmarket income.

Source: M. L. Parker, "An Interindustry Approach to Planning in Papua New Guinea," *Economic Record* 50 (September 1974): 369.

An input-output table used for planning typically includes from forty to two hundred sectors, depending on how much aggregation (or consolidation) is desired.

Even most sectors from a two hundred-row, two hundred-column table require aggregation from several industries. Furthermore sector worksheets may vary widely in detail and quality. The sectoral relationships of inputs to output for a data-poor economy's first table may be based not only on published sources, government department documents, and interviews and surveys, but also on estimates from similar economies or even educated guesses.

Frequently disaggregation may be an advantage, that is, having a detailed breakdown of industries and sectors. If the table is used to forecast, a detailed classification by industry would reveal bottlenecks that might occur during output expansion.[25] Thus the disaggregated input-output table would show how much the electronics and wire industries must be expanded beyond existing capacities for telecommunications to grow.

The upper left-hand quadrant of Table 19-1 records interindustry transactions—the delivery of output from, all sectors (industries) to all other sectors of the economy for production use. In this quadrant, sectoral outputs become inputs in other sectors.

The columns show the structure of inputs for a given sector. Thus the agricultural sector uses $0.04 million of inputs from the fishing, forestry, and mining sector, $9.05 million from the manufacturing sector, $0.48 million from building and construction, $3.91 million from transport and communication, $6.43 million from commerce, $0.77 million from governmental services, and $1.45 million from business expenses. In addition various agricultural units use $1.89 million inputs from other parts of agriculture.

The rows on the other hand show the output distribution of the same sectors. The first row of Table 19-1 shows the output of agriculture to be used in the same sector ($1.89 million), in manufacturing ($7.86 million), in education and health ($0.51 million), in government services ($0.35 million), and business expenses ($0.13 million).

To read the table, remember the following simple rules:

1. To find the amount of purchases from one sector by another, locate the *purchasing industry* at the top of the table, then read *down the column* until you come to the *processing industry*. (For example, the education and health sector purchases $4.80 million of inputs from transport and communication.)

2. To find the amount of sales from one sector to another, locate the *selling industry* along the left side of the table, then read *across the row* until you come to the *buying industry*. (Thus the building construction industry sells $0.36 million of output to the manufacturing industry.)

[25] The treatment here borrows from William H. Miernyk, *The Elements of Input-Output Analysis* (New York: Random House, 1965), pp. 8–57; A. P. Thirlwall, *Growth and Development with Special Reference to Developing Economics* (New York: Wiley, 1977), pp. 219–34; Zoltan Kenessey, *The Process of Economic Planning* (New York: Columbia University Press, 1978), pp. 278–90; W. Duane Evans and Marvin Hoffenberg, "The Interindustry Relations Study for 1947," *Review of Economics and Statistics* 34 (May 1952), pp. 97–142; M. Jarvin Emerson and F. Charles Lamphear, *Urban and Regional Economics: Structure and Change* (Boston: Allyn and Bacon, 1975), pp. 11–24; and Wassily Leontief, *Input-Output Economics* (New York: Oxford University Press, 1966).

While the upper-left quadrant records the sale of intermediate inputs from one sector to another, the major part of the lower-left quadrant gives the payment, by sectors, to foreigners for imports and to production factors for wages, salaries, profits, interest, and rent. In the farthest column right, total factor payments (such as $127.19 million wages and salaries to indigenes) and depreciation all involve payments by intermediate industries. Total imports ($372.62 million) and net indirect taxes ($52.85 million) in the last column however include direct payments by final demand (consumption, investment, and export) purchases, as well as intermediate purchases.

Intermediate inputs from the upper left plus primary inputs from the lower left equal total inputs, for example, $114.71 million for agriculture. This figure equals agriculture's total output, $114.71 million, the sum of intermediate inputs and final demand, which consists of consumption, capital formation, exports, and net current expenditure of public authorities, missions, and financial enterprises. Total input equals total output for all intermediate input sectors.

You would not expect the total of any of the individual rows of the primary inputs to equal the total of any of the final demand columns. But the individual differences must cancel out for the entire economy. As is true of any single processing sector, *total* outlays must equal *total* outputs for the economy as a whole.

The total output in the input-output table for Papua New Guinea, $2,752.62 million, is far in excess of GNP for the same year, $952.68 million, calculated on the income side as factor payments (wages and salaries, and operating surplus), depreciation, and net indirect taxes, or on the expenditures side as final demand purchases minus imports. Every effort is made to eliminate double counting in computing the components of GNP. But since the input-output table measures all *transactions* between sectors of the economy, the value of goods and services produced in a given year is counted more than once. Since some goods will enter into more than one transaction, their value must be counted each time a different transaction takes place. What we have is an accumulation of value added at each stage of the production process until the good is acquired through final demand.

The Input-Output Table's Uses

Analysis based on the input-output table has a number of uses in planning. Data needed to construct the table provide sectoral information that may become invaluable in other aspects of planning. But even more important, if the plan sets a certain level of final demand and indicates which sectors are to produce it, then the detailed interrelationships and deliveries can be well approximated by tracking through the table the direct and indirect purchases needed. Doing this allows the planner to explore the implications of alternative development strategies. Input-output analysis provides a set of consistent projections for an economy. It broadly indicates the economic structure that might emerge given a particular development strategy. Input-output analysis shows the sectoral changes that must occur in the growth process in a way no aggregate macroeconomic model can do.

Assume that planners in Papua New Guinea wish to double building and construction from $138.73 million to $277.46 million. This expansion requires additional fishing, forestry, and mining production of $0.05 million, manufacturing output of $40.51 million, building and construction of $0.61 million, $27.35 million in wages and salaries, and $35.96 million of foreign exchange for imports (to name just a few of the added inputs column 4, Table 19-1, indicates are needed). However, when the manufacturing sector sells more of its output to the building and construction industry, manufacturing industry's demand for the products of agriculture, fishing, forestry, mining, and so on, will likewise increase—the amount of the increase depending on the technical coefficient that relates the amount from an intermediate sector needed for every unit of manufacturing output. (This calculation can be made from information in column 3, Table 19-1.) These effects will spread throughout the processing sector.

Tracing the effects of increased demand throughout the input-output model can provide planners with other valuable estimates. It can help them calculate the effects of intermediate sector expansion on changes in import requirements, balance of payments, employment, investment demand, and national income that go beyond the immediate, direct impact. Rather than using the laborious step-by-step approach, planners can use high-speed electronic calculating equipment to compute a matrix showing the total requirements, direct and indirect, per dollar of demand.

The Input-Output Table's Validity

There are several assumptions underlying input-output analysis that raise questions about its validity. First, the technical coefficients are fixed, which means no substitution between inputs occurs (such as capital for labor, or building and construction for manufacturing inputs). Furthermore input functions are linear, so that output increases by the same multiple as inputs. Production is subject to constant returns to scale. Moreover the marginal input coefficient is equal to the average, implying no internal economies or diseconomies of scale. Second, there are no externalities, so that the total effect of carrying out several activities is the sum of the separate effects. Third, there are no joint products. Each good is produced by only one industry, and each industry produces only one commodity. Fourth, there is no technical change, which rules out the possibility of, say, new, improved agricultural methods reducing the industrial and commercial inputs required per output unit.

Even though we may question the validity of these assumptions, the errors may not be substantial, especially in a period of 5 years or less. For example, there may not be much substitutability between inputs in the short run while relative factor prices and the level of technology are relatively constant. If input coefficients can be derived at regular and frequent intervals, some of these problems can be overcome.

PRIVATE SECTOR TARGETS AND POLICIES

In most LDCs, even many claiming to be socialist, the private sector, comprised, at least, of most of agriculture, is larger than the public sector. Planners may set targets for production, employment, investment, exports, and imports for the private sector but usually have no binding policies to affect the target. Beyond forecasting, the usefulness of target figures for the private sector depends on the reliability of data, the persuasiveness of the planning process, and policy control over the private sector.

Private sector planning means government trying to get people to do what they would otherwise not do—invest more in equipment or improve their job skills, change jobs, switch from one crop to another, adopt new technologies, and so on.

Some policies for the private sector might include the following:

1. Investigating development potential through scientific and market research, and natural resources surveys
2. Providing adequate infrastructure (water, power, transport, and communication) for public and private agencies
3. Providing the necessary skills through general education and specialized training
4. Improving the legal framework related to land tenure, corporations, commercial transactions, and other economic activities
5. Creating markets, including commodity markets, security exchanges, banks, credit facilities, and insurance companies
6. Seeking out and assisting entrepreneurs.
7. Promoting better resource utilization through inducements and controls
8. Promoting private and public saving
9. Reducing monopolies and oligopolies[26]

PUBLIC EXPENDITURES

Planners should ask each government department to submit proposals for expenditures during the plan period. Departments should estimate potential financial (and social) costs and benefits. Each government agency or enterprise should conduct feasibility studies of prospective investment projects in the same detail as would private business. Additionally government must estimate the effect of new capital programs on future, recurrent expenditures. Chapter 20 examines issues associated with public enterprises.

Since the total cost of the various departmental proposals will probably exceed available funds, planners must set priorities. An individual project should be evaluated in relation to other projects, and not in isolation. Wolfgang F. Stolper, University of Michigan professor serving as Nigeria's chief planner in the 1960s, stresses that planning decisions are "more-or-less," not "either-or." Planners should "rarely condemn a project outright but [should] mainly question its size and timing," and make it depend on other decisions simultaneously taken.[27]

A LDC needs government executives, administrators, and technicians experienced in conceiving projects, starting them, keeping them on schedule, amending them, and evaluating them. Without competent government administration, there is no basis for development planning.

---

[26] W. Arthur Lewis, *Development Planning: The Essentials of Economic Policy* (London: Allen and Unwin, 1966), pp. 13–24.

[27] Wolfgang F. Stolper, "Problems of Development Planning," in Gerald M. Meier, *Leading Issues in Economic Development* (New York: Oxford University Press, 1976), p. 822.

SUMMARY

1. Development planning is the government's coordinated policies to achieve national economic goals, such as rapid economic growth. Planning involves surveying the economy, setting goals, devising economic policies, and public spending. It also means implementing and evaluating planning policies.

2. For planning to work, the planning commission must be responsible to political leaders and integrated with government departments and economics ministries.

3. A state planning ideology arose in LDCs as a reaction to nationalist perceptions of slow economic growth under colonial capitalism.

4. Lal argues that development economics is dominated by *dirigiste,* those in favor of government intervention into LDC prices. Critics of Lal respond that while development economists often reject a rigid adherence to Western economic theory, they usually reject price controls, although they put more emphasis on planning than Lal does.

5. Planning in many mixed LDCs has failed because detailed programs for the public sector have not been worked out, and excessive controls are used in the private sector.

6. Even Soviet "controlling" planning, which took years to develop, was still subject to decentralized management discretion, even before the Gorbachev era.

7. Although the market allocates scarce resources efficiently among alternative means, it may not work so well as centralized planning in considering externalities, mobilizing saving, and adjusting for monopolies, and except for market socialism, distributing income.

8. The choice for developing countries is usually not between the plan or the market, but between various combinations of the two.

9. Worker-managed socialism helped contribute to Yugoslavia's rapid economic growth from 1959 to 1979, but 1976 reforms, increasing checks and balances and bureaucraticizing enterprise decision making, hampered policy implementation and increased worker dissatisfaction.

10. Most LDCs with a large private sector are limited to an indicative plan that states expectations, aspirations, and intentions but authorizes little public spending.

11. Planners must usually tell political leaders what the tradeoffs are among multiple economic goals.

12. Most LDCs have too few resources, skills, and data to benefit from complex macroeconomic planning models. Yet a simple aggregate model may be useful as a first step in drawing up policies and projects.

13. In most nonsocialist LDCs, documents showing how to improve data collection, raise revenue, recruit personnel, and select and implement projects are more important for successful planning than planning models.

14. An input-output table is useful for assessing the effects of different development strategies on exports, imports, the balance of payments, employment, national income, and sectoral investment demand and output.

TERMS TO REVIEW

- development plan-
  ning
- commanding
  heights
- *dirigiste*
- controlling plan
- Gosplan
- market socialism
- worker-managed
  socialism
- soft budget con-
  straint
- indicative plan
- target variables
- instrument vari-
  ables
- short-term plans
- medium-term
  plans
- long-term plans
- rolling plans
- input-output table
- intermediate in-
  puts

QUESTIONS TO DISCUSS

1. Why did many political leaders of states gaining independence after World War II emphasize state planning?

2. Why might even a capitalist LDC want to plan?

3. What is the *dirigiste* debate? Indicate Lal's characterization of the *dirigistes* and the response of Lal's critics.

4. Why have so few LDCs been successful at detailed centralized planning?

5. What problems have nonsocialist countries had in using Soviet-type planning?

6. What problems occur when using widespread controls to influence private investment and production in a mixed or capitalist economy?

7. What are the advantages and disadvantages of the market as an alternative to state planning? What economic systems could combine some of the advantages of both planning and the market? How effective are these systems?

8. Indicate the strengths and weaknesses of market socialism and worker-managed socialism in LDCs. How might a LDC avoid Yugoslavia's economic problems of the 1980s?

9. What are the roles of political leaders and planning professionals in formulating an economic plan?

10. What instruments do planners use to achieve goals?

11. Illustrate how the instrument variables used depend on the plan's duration.

12. Why is the use of complex macroeconomic planning models in LDCs limited?

13. What are the most important parts of the plan in a mixed or capitalist LDC?

14. What is an input-output table? Of what value is input-output analysis to a planner? What are some of the weaknesses of the input-output table as a planning tool?

15. What policies can planners undertake to encourage the expansion of private sector production?

16. What advice would you give to the person in charge of development planning in a LDC with a large private sector?

GUIDE TO READINGS

Meier, 1984, 4th ed. (see note 27), has a brief compendium of major views about development planning, including excerpts from Johnson (note 12) and Chenery (note 16).

Lewis (note 18) has useful suggestions for planning in a mixed and capitalist LDC.

Miernyk offers an elementary explanation of input-output analysis (note 25), and Thirwall and Kenessey provide concise applications to LDC planning (note 25).

R. M. Sundrum, *Growth and Income Distribution in India: Policy and Performance since Independence* (Newbury Park, Calif.: Sage Publications, 1987), looks at India's growth and planning; Janos Kornai focuses on Hungary's socialist market economy in "The Dual Dependence of the State-Owned Firm in Hungary," in Tidrick and Jiyuan, eds. (note 15); Schrenk (note 15) examines Yugoslavia's worker-managed socialism; and Gregory and Stuart, 1986, analyze Soviet economic planning (note 8). Lange and Taylor (note 12), Hôrvat, Vanek (note 14), and Nove (note 15) discuss market socialism. The *Journal of Development Studies* 24 (July 1988), devotes a special issues to "Markets within Planning: Socialist Economic Management in the Third World." E. V. K. FitzGerald, M. Wuyts (eds.), Charles Bettelheim, Gary Littlejohn, Max Spoor, David Kaimowitz, Maureen Mackintosh, Gordon White, and Nelson P. Moyo include analyses of China, Vietnam, Nicaragua, Mozambique, Zimbabwe, and more general market socialist models. For an introduction to the economics of socialist planning, see Michael Ellman, *Socialist Planning* (Cambridge: Cambridge University Press, 1989).

Stewart (note 7) responds to Lal's critique of *dirigisme* (note 6).

Coase and Williamson (note 11), though focusing on the firm, have implications for the relative transaction costs of the plan and the market.

In late 1989, Genady Gerisimov, spokesperson for the Soviet Ministry of Foreign Affairs, declared the Sinatra Doctrine, indicating that each socialist economy should go its own way. The *Economist, Problems in Economics*, and *China Business Review* provide current information on socialist economic reform.

Chapter Twenty

PUBLIC ENTERPRISES: SOCIALIZATION, PRIVATIZATION, OR STATUS QUO?

PUBLIC GOODS

Speaking broadly, a public enterprise is a government entity that produces or supplies goods and services for the public. Even in a capitalist country like the United States, government produces **public goods** that the market fails to produce. Public goods like national defense and lighthouses are indivisible, involving large units that cannot be sold to individual buyers. Additionally those who do not pay for the product cannot be excluded from its benefits. On the other hand, **quasi-public goods,** such as education and sewage disposal, while capable of being sold to individual buyers, entail substantial positive spillovers and would thus be underproduced by the market. Government agencies in the United States produce part or all of the following public or quasi-public goods: national defense, flood control, preventive medicine, lighthouses, parks, education, libraries, sewage disposal, postal service, water supplies, gas, electricity, and police and fire protection.[1]

In most countries, however, as the discussion below implies, the government sector supplies more than public and quasi-public goods.

[1] Campbell R. McConnell, *Economics: Principles, Problems, and Policies* (New York: McGraw-Hill, 1987), pp, 93–94.

IMPORTANCE OF THE GOVERNMENT SECTOR

Government employment as a percentage of total nonagricultural employment is 24 percent for OECD countries and 44 percent for LDCs—54 percent in Africa, 36 percent in Asia, and 27 percent in Latin America. In some countries, such as Benin, Ghana, and Zambia, the ratio is more than 70 percent. Peter Heller and Alan Tait indicate that the threshold for public wage awards affecting national wage rate determination is 20–25 percent of nonagricultural employment.

The LDCs rely much less on state and local government than OECD countries. Central government employment constitutes about 85 of total government employment in LDCs and only 42 percent in OECD countries. Central government wages comprise 8 percent of LDC GDP compared to 5 percent for the OECD. Average LDC central government wages are 1.75 times the average wages in manufacturing, compared to only a 1.25 ratio in OECD countries.

Although the mean number of administrators per one hundred population was rather similar for DCs and LDCs, African countries had the highest administrator ratio and Asian countries the lowest.[2]

In Nigeria, government expenditures as a percentage of GDP rose from 9 percent in 1962 to 44 percent in 1979. Nigeria centralized power during its civil war (1967–70) with the breakup of regions and in the 1970s, as the oil boom enhanced the center's fiscal strength and increased political competition for resources. Expansion of the government's share of the economy did not increase political and administrative capacity much, but it did increase incomes and jobs that governing elites could distribute to their clients.[3]

DEFINITION OF STATE-OWNED ENTERPRISES

State-owned enterprises (SOEs), called **public enterprises** or **parastatals,** are common in socialist China and Poland and market-oriented Taiwan, South Korea, and Brazil. Indeed the state sector's share of output is as large in each of these three countries as in India or Bangladesh, which have reputations for state intervention. Most SOEs are in large-scale manufacturing, public utilities (electricity, gas, and water), plantation agriculture, mining, finance, transport, and communication.

For this chapter's discussion, a state enterprise consists of an enterprise (1) where government is the principal (not necessarily majority) owner or where the state can appoint or remove the chief executive officer (president or managing director) and (2) which produces or sells goods or services to the public or other enterprises, where revenues are to bear some relationship to cost. Public enterprises that do not maximize profitability may still qualify if they pursue profit subject to some limitation assigned by the state.[4] This narrow definition of state-owned enterprises differentiates public *enterprises* producing steel, palm products,

[2] Peter Heller and Alan Tait, "Government Employment and Pay: Some International Comparisons," *Finance and Development* 20 (September 1983): 44–47.

[3] E. Wayne Nafziger, *Inequality in Africa: Political Elites, Proletariat, Peasants, and the Poor* (Cambridge: Cambridge University Press, 1988), p. 100.

[4] Malcolm Gillis, Dwight H. Perkins, Michael Roemer, and Donald R. Snodgrass, *Economics of Development* (New York: Norton, 1987), p. 569.

electricity, and telephone, telegraph, banking, and bus services from public *agencies* that run schools, libraries, agricultural extension services, and police departments. The United States, with SOEs that include municipally owned public utilities, intracity transport, the post office, and the Tennessee Valley Authority, has fewer public enterprises than most DCs and LDCs.

SIZE OF THE STATE-OWNED SECTOR

Given this definition, the contribution of state-owned enterprises to GDP in developing countries increased from 7 percent in 1970 to 10 percent in 1980 (the same as in DCs). The 1980 LDC figures varied from a high of 64 percent in Hungary (excluding cooperatives) and 38 percent in Ghana and Zambia to a low of 2–3 percent in the Philippines and Nepal, but most countries ranged from 7–15 percent.[5]

Thirteen percent of LDC nonagricultural employment is in nonfinancial public enterprises compared to 4 percent in the OECD. Public enterprise employees are 1 percent of the total population in LDCs compared to 1.5 percent in the OECD.[6]

ARGUMENTS FOR PUBLIC ENTERPRISES

As argued in Chapter 14, retained earnings from business savings are major sources of capital formation. Advocates of public enterprises argue that private business people, who dissipate a high percentage of earnings in conspicuous consumption or transfers abroad, provide less investable resources than SOEs.[7]

Social profitability in excess of financial profitability (as discussed in Chapter 12) provides additional reasons for public enterprise. Public investment can create external economies, improve integration between sectors, produce social goods for low-income earners, and raise the capital essential for overcoming indivisibilities. Frequently officials indicate that creating new jobs is the rationale for establishing state enterprises. Moreover public firms can rescue bankrupt private firms in key sectors, or state initiative can substitute for private entrepreneurship when risk is high, capital markets are poor, or information is sparse. Finally governments have noneconomic reasons for creating SOEs, including control of key sectors (the commanding heights), wresting control from foreign owners or minority ethnic communities, responding to foreign donor pressure, or to serve other social and political goals, such as avoiding concentration of economic power among private oligopolists.

[5] World Bank, *World Development Report, 1983* (New York: Oxford University Press, 1983), pp. 49–50.

[6] Peter Heller and Alan Tait, "Government Employment and Pay: Some International Comparisons," *Finance and Development* 20 (September 1983), 44–47.

[7] The discussion in this section borrows from *World Development Report, 1983,* pp. 50–51; Paul Cook and Colin Kirkpatrick, eds., *Privatisation in Less-Developed Countries* (Sussex, U.K.: Wheatsheaf, 1988), pp. 5–7; and Malcolm Gillis, Dwight H. Perkins, Michael Roemer, and Donald R. Snodgrass, *Economics of Development* (New York: Norton, 1987), pp. 571–74.

PERFORMANCE OF PRIVATE AND PUBLIC ENTERPRISES

Efficiency

Impressions of the superior performance of private enterprise often originate in anecdotes and informal case studies of Western business people and aid officials. British economist Robert Millward carefully examines studies comparing economic efficiency to test these impressions. Few studies measure precisely the performance of public and private firms of the same size, type, and product mix, and adjust for factor prices across enterprises that management cannot control (for example, the higher wage rates and cheaper capital that public enterprises face).[8]

Studies comparing U.S. and British electricity and transport enterprises in private and public sectors indicate that productivity or cost effectiveness was as high in the public sector as in the private sector. Yet public firms, which charge lower prices, have lower financial profitability than private enterprises.

The following three LDC studies compare public and private firms, while statistically holding other variables equal. W. G. Tyler's analysis of the Brazilian steel industry indicates that if you control for size, whether a firm was privately or publicly owned had no significant impact on technical efficiency. K. S. Kim finds that government ownership had no significant effect on efficiency in Tanzania's food and machinery industries. H. Hill's study of automated weaving in Indonesia indicates that the higher productivity of private firms relative to state firms was explained by diseconomies of scale of the larger state firms.[9]

Thus the Millward survey concludes that the efficiency of public and private enterprises is comparable, given a certain size firm. However, public firms are more likely than private firms to choose an excessive scale of operations. Public firms have easier access to state financing to mute bankruptcy and more pressure to provide jobs and contracts to clients and relatives than private enterprises. As the IMF points out, "Over the years, inefficiency has flourished in many state enterprises, its overt consequences masked by the ready availability of budgetary support."[10]

Employment

Despite political pressures to overstaff LDC state enterprises, most SOEs are more capital-intensive than private firms, which avoid entering capital-intensive sectors because they are characterized by high risk and substantial economies of scale.[11] Also the emphasis of state ownership of the commanding heights—heavy industry,

---

[8] The rest of this section is based largely on Robert Millward, "Measured Sources of Inefficiency in the Performance of Private and Public Enterprises in LDCs," in Paul Cook and Colin Kirkpatrick, eds. *Privatisation in Less–Developed Countries*, (Sussex, U.K.: Wheatsheaf, 1988), pp. 143–61.

[9] Ibid.; W. G. Tyler, "Technical Efficiency in Production in a Developing Country: An Empirical Examination of the Brazilian Plastics and Steel Industries," *Oxford Economic Papers* 31 (November 1979): 477–95; and K. S. Kim, "Enterprise Performance in the Public and Private Sectors: Tanzanian Experience, 1970–5," *Journal of Developing Areas* 15 (April 1981): 471–84; H. Hill, "State Enterprises in a Competitive Industry: An Indonesian Case Study," *World Development* 10 (1982): 1015–23.

[10] International Monetary Fund, *World Economic Outlook* (Washington, D.C., 1986), p. 16.

[11] Malcolm Gillis, Dwight H. Perkins, Michael Roemer, and Donald R. Snodgrass, *Economics of Development*, (New York: Norton, 1987), pp. 581–82.

mining, transport, and banking—means high capital-labor ratios, which, as Chapter 10 indicates, are associated with high unemployment rates, as in Algeria. Brazil's and India's public enterprise sector is several times (and South Korea's nine times) more capital-intensive than the private sector.[12]

Politicians, in both LDCs and rich countries often use employment as a rationale for initiating or rescuing projects with high capital intensity. In the United States, the "bail outs" of Lockheed, Chrysler, and Continental Illinois Bank and bids by governmental units on super accelerators or sports franchises, all capital intensive, were justified by employment effects, despite the high employment opportunity costs of these investments.

Savings

Even Ghana's Nkrumah, Africa's most radical nationalist leader in the 1950s and early 1960s, thinks the SOEs should contribute capital for other public services

> I must make it clear that these state enterprises were not set up to lose money at the expense of the taxpayers. Like all business undertakings, they are expected to maintain themselves efficiently, and to show profits. Such profits should be sufficient to build up capital for further investment as well as to finance a large proportion of the public services which it is the responsibility of the state to provide.[13]

But Table 20-1 indicates that in the late 1970s, SOEs in thirty three of thirty four LDCs incurred overall deficits, which means a deterioration of capital resources (or negative savings). This is despite the fact that SOEs frequently enjoy monopoly privileges, especially in mineral and energy resources.

A separate study on South Korea by Young C. Park indicates that South Korean government-invested enterprises had a 3.7-percent rate of return to capital in 1982, lower than the 10.1 percent figure for Korean industry generally but higher than government enterprises in most other LDCs. However, the government's 1983 comprehensive public enterprise reform program, which eliminated day-to-day interferences by technical ministries, simplified and unified external audits, provided for an objectives-oriented evaluation and incentive system, and gave management greater power over procurement, budgeting, and personnel, improved subsequent performance.[14]

Social and Political Goals

Chapter 12 discusses investment to create integration and externalities, to overcome indivisibilities, and reduce monopolies. Many socialist and mixed LDCs are committed to increasing the socialization of capital and land for political reasons.

[12] John B. Sheahan, "Public Enterprise in Developing Countries," in W. G. Shepherd, ed., *Public Enterprise: Economic Analysis of Theory and Practice* (Lexington, Mass: Lexington Books, 1976), p. 211, on Brazil, India, and Algeria; Leroy P. Jones, *Public Enterprise and Economic Development* (Seoul: Korea Development Institute, 1976), p. 123, on Korea.

[13] Kwame Nkrumah, *Revolutionary Path* (New York: International Publishers, 1973), p. 37, from a 1964 speech.

[14] Young C. Park, "Evaluating the Performance of Korea's Government-invested Enterprises," *Finance and Development* 24 (June 1987): 25–27.

TABLE 20-1   Overall deficits[a] or Surpluses of Public Enterprises as Percent of GDP

	Latest Period of Data	SURPLUS (+) OR DEFICIT (−) AS % OF GDP	
		Latest Period	Next Latest Period
Africa			
Botswana	1978–80	−0.6	−4.7
Guinea	1978–79	−23.4	−8.0
Ivory Coast	1978–79	−8.4	−3.5
Malawi	1978	−3.5	−2.5
Mali	1978	−2.7	−5.9
Senegal	1974	+2.2	
Tanzania	1974–75	−2.8	−2.6
Zambia	1972	−3.4	
Asia			
Burma	1978–80	−10.6	−1.2
India	1978	−6.2	−6.3
Nepal	1974–75	−2.1	−0.5
South Korea	1978–80	−5.2	−5.4
Taiwan	1978–80	−5.5	−7.3
Thailand	1978–79	−2.0	−1.1
Southern Europe			
Greece	1979	−1.6	−1.6
Portugal	1978–80	−8.1	
Turkey	1978–80	−7.5	−7.0
Latin America			
Argentina	1976–77	−3.1	
Bolivia	1974–77	−4.4	−4.5
Brazil	1980	−1.7	
Chile	1978–80	−0.4	−0.2
Colombia	1978–80	−0.1	−0.9
Costa Rica	1977–79	−4.4	
Dominican Rep.	1978–79	−1.6	−0.2
Guatemala	1978–80	−2.1	−1.8
Haiti	1978–80	−0.9	−2.0
Honduras	1978–79	−2.3	
Jamaica	1978–80	−2.3	−4.3
Mexico	1978	−3.7	−3.9
Panama	1978–79	−7.1	−7.1
Paraguay	1978–80	−0.9	−1.6
Peru	1974–77	−1.7	−4.8
Uruguay	1978–80	−0.8	
Venezuela	1978–80	−5.1	−5.2

[a]Revenue plus receipts of current and capital transfers minus (current and capital) expenditures.

Source: R. P. Short, "The Role of Public Enterprises: An International Statistical Comparison," working paper of the International Monetary Fund, Fiscal Affairs Department, Washington, D.C., May 17, 1983, pp. 30–36.

But additionally the fact that DC (even U.S.) banks and aid agencies have found it convenient to hold the LDC government responsible for performance, payments, and debt has encouraged state-controlled enterprise.

Can the state subsidize public enterprises to redistribute goods to the poor? Chapters 6 and 7 indicate the difficulties of using the state to redistribute income.

A SOE should pay for itself in the long run unless the enterprise redistributes income to lower-income recipients (or fulfills some other objective discussed above, such as creating externalities). A public enterprise that does not pay for itself, where the recipient of the service is not charged an economic price, involves a subsidy to him or her. Since the alternative to a subsidy is resource allocation to another project, the burden of proof should fall on the subsidy's advocate.[15] This redistribution policy would be consistent with, for instance, subsidies to goods consumed disproportionately by the poor, such as sorghum (Bangladesh in 1978) and low-quality rice (Sri Lanka, 1968–77), but not with subsidies for fuel (Nigeria, 1980), electricity (most of Africa), or food generally (Poland and Tanzania in the early 1980s) in urban areas with above-average incomes.

DETERMINANTS OF PUBLIC ENTERPRISE PERFORMANCE

Why do some public enterprises perform better than others? Why do SOEs in South Korea and Sweden generally achieve better economic results than those in Ghana? Why is India's Hindustan Machine Tools dynamic when most other Indian public enterprises are far less successful?

1. State enterprises perform better with competition; no investment licensing; no price, entry, nor exit controls; and liberal trade policies (low tariffs, no import quotas, and exchange rates close to market prices). In Pakistan the highly profitable parastatal Heavy Mechanical Complex faces competition from the privatized Ittefaq Foundary in road rollers and sugar mills' output; with imports and another public enterprise (Karachi Shipyard) in constructing cement plants; and with SOE Pakistan Engineering Company in manufacturing electrical towers, boilers, and overhead traveling cranes. Since 1969, India's Hindustan has learned much about remaining competitive from exporting, which has exposed the company to new technologies and management approaches. When economies of scale are not important, breaking up large enterprises, such as the Bolivian Mining Corporation and Sweden's Statsforetag (a holding company), can increase competition.[16]
2. Successful performing SOEs, such as those in Japan, Singapore, Sweden, Brazil, and post-1983 South Korea, have greater managerial autonomy and accountability than others do.[17] Excessive interference in investment, product mix, pricing, hiring and firing workers, setting wages, and procurement by

---

[15] Tariffs have an effect similar to subsidies. Government distorts prices, benefiting special interests by redistributing income from consumers or merchants to industrialists.

[16] This section is based on Mahmood A. Ayub and Sven O. Hegstad, "Determinants of Public Enterprise Performance," *Finance and Development* 24 (December 1987): 26–29.

[17] Harinder S. Kohli and Anil Sood, "Fostering Enterprise Development," *Finance and Development* 24 (March 1987): 34–36.

government suffocates managerial initiative and contributes to operational inefficiencies. Government should demarcate its role (as owner), the board of directors' role (setting broad policy), and the enterprise management role (day-to-day operations). Central or local government rarely has the information or the skills essential for detailed control over parastatal operations. South Korea's 1983 reform is a good example of increasing managerial autonomy and reducing government interference.

Good management usually requires decentralizing power in favor of a professionally skilled board of directors and judging managers by enterprise viability and a limited number of performance indicators. In Sweden the cabinet (the formal owner of the limited liability SOE stock corporation) delegates ownership responsiblity to a staff of eight professionals in the Ministry of Industry, which oversees 90,000 people in state industries. These professionals do not overpower the board with their ownership role except in times of crisis or when state financial support is required. Korea's reforms also increased decentralization and evaluation by enterprise performance.

Until the mid-1980s, managers of SOEs, which comprised 60 percent of Ghana's industrial output, had poor performance and little autonomy. In practice a Ministry of Finance and Economic Planning board set prices and approved wage contracts; the Ministry of Labor authorized worker dismissal; the Ministries of Trade and Finance allocated import licenses; the Bank of Ghana approved import licenses; and the Ghana Investment Center and the Ministry of Interior approved foreign staff quotas.

While many LDCs suffer from the Ghanaian problem of too much interference and unclear, fragmented lines of authority, other LDCs lack any effective control, creating uncertainty, misunderstanding, and distrust, with reactions sometimes swinging to the other pole, excessive control.

Financial autonomy is a major factor contributing to SOE managerial effectiveness. Two French steel parastatals, Usinor and Sacilor, which acquired funds for expansion from their government ministry, have had chronic losses. But public firms scrutinized by independent bankers before getting investment funds usually perform better. Excellent financial management involves specifying financial objectives, monitoring their progress, and holding managers accountable. Government should set SOE noneconomic goals clearly and evaluate whether the firm is using the most cost-effective way of achieving the goal, so that SOE managers do not use these same goals as an excuse for poor performance. In the mid-1980s, Zambia imposed price controls on refined oil and fats use for vegetable oil products and soaps. The controls resulted in large losses and poor staff morale and shifted output away from oil and fats, the opposite of the government's social priorities. Finally government should not allow substantial transfers between SOEs and government to undermine firms ability to acquire "true" financial results.

3. Government reduces (or keeps) the size of the public sector commensurate with technical and managerial skills. Beginning in 1983, South Korea privatized a number of SOEs to improve the effectiveness of government oversight.[18]

---

[18] Young C. Park, "Evaluating the Performance of Korea's Government–invested Enterprises," *Finance and Development* 24 (June 1987), 25–27.

PRIVATIZATION

Privatization refers to a range of policies including (1) changing at least part of an enterprise's ownership from the public to the private sector (through equity sales to the public or sale of the complete enterprise when capital markets are poorly developed), (2) liberalization of entry into activities previously restricted to the public sector, and (3) franchising or contracting public services or leasing public assets to the private sector. Government needs improved competition policy in the private sector if denationalization is to result in gains in allocative efficiency. A government selling a public enterprise faces a tradeoff between the higher sale price when a privatized firm is offered market protection and the greater economic efficiency when the firm operates under competitive market conditions.[19]

PUBLIC ENTERPRISES AND MULTINATIONAL CORPORATIONS

Many LDCs, including much of Latin America as well as South Korea, Taiwan, India, and Indonesia, view SOEs as a counterbalance to the power of MNCs, especially as SOEs began moving into markets previously dominated by MNCs.[20] Yet since the 1970s, joint SOE–MNC ventures and other forms of domestic–foreign tie-ins have become more common and MNC–domestic private firm ventures much less common. At best in these ventures, the LDC government can protect its national interest better, while MNCs can reduce political risks. But for some LDCs, especially in Africa, expanding public enterprises frequently did not reduce dependence much on MNCs, as indicated by our discussion of Nigeria in Chapters 8 and 14. Multinational corporate ownership was replaced by MNC–state joint enterprises, which enriched private middlemen and women and enlarged the patronage base for state officials, but did little to develop Nigerian administrative and technological skills for subsequent industrialization. Kenya, Tanzania, Zäire, Malawi, and the Ivory Coast made even less progress than Nigeria in using public enterprises to reduce dependence on MNCs.[21] Tropical African countries have been less successful than Argentina, Brazil, Mexico, Peru, Venezuela, South Korea, Taiwan, India, and Indonesia in using MNC technology transfer to improve their own industrial capabilities.

CHINA'S STATE INDUSTRIAL ENTERPRISES

In December 1978, two years after Mao Zedong's death, China's Communist party's Eleventh Central Committee, under Deng Xiaoping, committed itself to market socialism within a framework of national economic planning. After 1984,

[19] Paul Cook and Colin Kirkpatrick, eds., *Privatisation in Less Developed Countries* (Sussex, U.K.: Wheatsheaf, 1988), pp. 3–44.

[20] Malcolm Gillis, Dwight H. Perkins, Michael Roemer, and Donald R. Snodgrass, *Economics of Development*, (New York: Norton, 1987), p. 584; Raymond Vernon, "The State-Owned Enterprise in Latin American Export," in Werner Baer and Malcolm Gillis, eds., *Trade Prospects among the Americas* (Urbana.: National Bureau of Economic Research and University of Illinois Press, 1981), pp. 98–114.

[21] E. Wayne Nafziger, *Inequality in Africa: Political Elites, Proletariat, Peasants, and the Poor* (Cambridge: Cambridge University Press, 1988), p. 53.

the state allowed youths, especially the urban unemployed, to start small businesses as individuals or as members of urban collective enterprises; such businesses consisted of small restaurants, repair shops, and retail outlets.[22]

But the key to China's urban reforms is not the informal or services sector, but state-owned enterprises. The reform of these industrial enterprises has not been so successful as China's agricultural reform. Annual gross industrial output growth, 11.4 percent from 1952 to 1978 (9.4 percent, 1965–78), slowed to 7.0 percent from 1978 to 1982, with no substantial improvement in industrial efficiency after 1978.[23] Urban reform entails built-in contradictions, since increased market forces threaten the power and expertise of bureaucrats, who were trained to run a command system.

The reform instituted a **responsibility system,** in which an enterprise manager's task was to be carefully defined and performance was to determine managers' and workers' pay. The initiative and decisions were to be centered in producing units rather than in government administration. Under this system, taxes on enterprise bonuses more than a certain level replaced the profits and losses the state absorbed. But rewarding producers with higher pay for higher productivity requires an increase in consumer goods, especially food. And with reduced investment, growth must rely on technical innovation and increased efficiency. Although the early reform period emphasized worker authority in selecting managers, this selection was deemphasized when it increasingly conflicted with the professionalization and responsibility of managers.[24]

Economists identify several problems with China's industrial reform. A major problem is fragmented administrative control, numerous overlapping authorities for project approval, and multiple levels of controls at different levels of government, what the Chinese call too many mothers-in-law. The Qingdao Forging Machinery Plant, a state enterprise, is responsible to the national Ministry of the Machine Industry, the city materials board, and the county for material supplies, to the municipal machine industry office for plant production, to the county planning agency for output value, to relevant county agencies for supplies from the plant, to two separate county agencies for personnel, and to the county committee for party matters, which is immersed in implementing policies.[25]

Thus planning is not integrated nor coherent, and enterprises are not treated consistently concerning targets. Investment decisions are bureaucratized and politicized. Moreover administrative agencies lack enough information about enterprises and commodities to make good decisions. Despite the management responsibility system, in practice management has still been centralized and rigid, with firm managers having limited control over performance.[26]

[22] Victor D. Lippit, *The Economic Development of China* (Armonk, N.Y.: M. E. Sharpe, 1987), pp. 201–8.

[23] Carl Riskin, *China's Political Economy: The Quest for Development since 1949* (Oxford: Oxford University Press, 1987), pp. 368–72.

[24] Victor D. Lippit, *The Economic Development of China* (Armonk, N. Y.: M. E. Sharpe, 1987), pp. 209–16.

[25] Zheng Guangliang, "The Leadership System," in Gene Tidrick and Chen Jiyuan, eds., *China's Industrial Reform* (New York: Oxford University Press for the World Bank, 1987), pp. 303–4.

[26] This discussion is based on Gene Tidrick and Chen Jiyuan, eds., *China's Industrial Reform* (New York: Oxford University Press, 1987), Peter Nan-shong Lee, "Enterprise Autonomy Policy in

If profits are to guide enterprise behavior, profits must be determined by prices reflecting true relative economic scarcity. If prices are set incorrectly, as in China, they will give the wrong signal, spurring enterprises to produce too little of what is short and too much of what is in surplus.

For the market to have meaning, products of enterprises must be sold on the market rather than delivered to governmental authorities for a fixed price. As of 1988, prices of sixty products subject to mandatory control outside the market include foodstuffs, all energy sources, most metals, basic raw materials for the chemical industry, important machinery and electrical equipment, and several other items.

Prices are arbitrary and distorted and change only incrementally throughout the system. Setting multiple prices by regions does not correspond to the cost of distances traveled. Distorted prices mean that profits are not linked to supply and demand. Enterprises are spurred to produce overpriced goods regardless of the market. Scarce goods that are priced cheaply become even more scarce. Moreover the Chinese, who restrict new firm entry and rarely close down inefficient firms, lack the market's **creative destruction,** in which an industry's old, high-cost producers are replaced by new, low-cost enterprises.[27]

If increasing market forces are to result in higher levels of efficiency, enterprises must compete with each other rather than have monopoly control of particular markets. To be sure, enterprises have more freedom buying and selling, and collective businesses sometimes compete with state enterprises. Yet as long as central planners allocate key inputs administratively, competition is limited, at least for intermediate products.

For the market to have meaning, enterprises must be able to buy productive inputs on the market. But prices usually do not show where resources can best be put to use, thus providing false signals to enterprises. In many instances, enterprises are still not allowed to retain profits for capital; indeed much capital is still allocated administratively rather than by interest payment. Additionally the Chinese lack a labor market, which hampers labor adjustments with changes in demand. Enterprise managers have little control over paying or hiring labor and little discretion in firing unproductive workers. Moreover the variety and amount of supplies available to a firm do not bear much relationship to output targets. Firms have little scope to search the market for the cheapest combination of input costs.

Firms have a soft budget constraint, meaning that though management and worker bonuses are nominally linked to profits and other targets, virtually no enterprise has lost bonuses for not meeting targets, since firms can negotiate during the output year to reduce quotas. Enterprise managers bargain for profit targets, which can often be changed retroactively. Firms may receive inducements for production yet not be able to respond because managers do not have meaningful discretionary authority. Norms for firms are too many, and changes too frequent,

---

Post-Mao China: A Case Study of Policymaking, 1978–83," *China Quarterly,* no. 105 (March 1986): 45–71; Carl Riskin, *China's Political Economy: The Quest for Development since 1949* (Oxford: Oxford University Press, 1987), pp. 352–53; Victor D. Lippit, *The Economic Development of China,* (Armonk, N.Y.: M. E. Sharpe, 1987), pp. 215–16; and A. Doak Barnett and Ralph N. Clough, eds., *Modernizing China: Post-Mao Reform and Development* (Boulder, Colo.: Westview, 1986), pp. 54–57.

[27] Joseph A. Schumpeter, *Capitalism, Socialism, and Democracy* (New York: Harper & Row, 1947), pp. 81–86.

thus making planning difficult. The norms encourage output of high-value commodities that use a high proportion of materials and a delinking of production from marketing.

Chinese industry still suffers from the classic Soviet planning approach—using the preceding year's achievement as the minimum target for the current year, known by the Chinese as "whipping the fast ox." Near the end of the year, enterprises overfulfilling quotas deliberately slow down operations in order not to increase targets too much for the subsequent year. From 1979 to 1980, Beijing instituted profit retention and rewards for fulfilling several performance indicators (including profits) in several pilot firms. But the experiment was suspended, since the growth of profits and other performance indicators slowed down to keep future targets down, and local governments objected to the high administrative costs and reduced control associated with enterprise profit retention.

Moreover most enterprises do not receive their quotas until after the beginning of the planning year. Due to dependence on administrative decisions and the cooperation of other firms in receiving inputs, enterprises keep excessive levels of inventory.

Since the state sets few variety, grade, or style targets, the enterprise has little incentive to produce the variety of goods demanded by the market. Price incentives are also lacking for quality improvement.

The emergence of a buyers' market in 1980, partly a result of substantial increases in the supply of light industry and consumer goods, had more effect, the World Bank and Chinese Academy of Social Sciences point out, than industrial reform in improving industrial performance and quality.

SUMMARY

1. Government employment comprises 44 percent of LDC employment outside agriculture.

2. State-owned enterprises (SOEs) are responsible for 10 percent of the value added to LDC's GDP. The SOEs, common in both socialist and market LDCs, account for a larger share of nonagricultural employment in LDCs than in DCs.

3. Arguments given for public enterprises include higher productive investment, creating external economies and intersectoral integration, improving income distribution, reducing risks, and pursuing national goals.

4. Studies of private and public sectors indicate the two sectors' social cost effectivenes is comparable. However public enterprises can often avoid the creative destruction of bankruptcy to improve efficiency. State firms allowed to incur consistent deficits reduce capital resources.

5. State enterprises in LDCs tend to be more capital-intensive than private enterprises.

6. Public enterprises are rarely effective in redistributing income to the poor.

7. State enterprises perform better with competition, no investment licensing, no entry nor exit controls, liberal domestic and trade policies, managerial autonomy and accountability, and little detailed interference from political

leaders. Government should not expand public enterprises in excess of managerial and technical skills available.

8. Privatization includes changing ownership to the private sector, liberalizing competition with public enterprises, and franchising or contracting public assets to the private sector.

9. Since 1970, tie-ins between SOEs and multinational corporations have increased.

10. China's industrial reform has some built-in inconsistencies, including fragmented administrative control, overlapping authority for project approval, incoherent planning, distorted prices, soft budget constraints, and incentives to limit plan overfulfillment to keep future targets low.

TERMS TO REVIEW

- public goods
- quasi-public goods
- state-owned enterprises (SOEs)
- public enterprises
- parastatals
- privatization
- responsibility system
- creative destruction

QUESTIONS TO DISCUSS

1. Under what conditions, if any, would you advise LDCs to expand the share of their state-owned sector? Under what conditions, if any, would you advise LDCs to reduce SOEs?

2. Compare the performance of private and public sectors in LDCs.

3. Should the state use public enterprises to redistribute income?

4. What can LDCs do to improve the performance of their private sector?

5. What is privatization? How successful have attempts at privatization in LDCs been?

6. Assess the efficacy of MNC–SOE joint ventures in LDCs.

7. Discuss the problems China has had with the reform of its SOEs.

8. Should LDCs put more emphasis on privatization or socialization, or should they continue the status quo?

GUIDE TO READINGS

Heller and Tait (note 2), the World Bank (note 5), and Gillis, Perkins, Roemer, and Snodgrass (note 4) discuss state-owned enterprises. Ayub and Hegsted (note 16), Kohli and Sood (note 17), and Park (note 14) examine the determinants of public enterprise performance.

Cook and Kirkpatrick's contributors (note 7), especially Millward (note 8), have excellent analyses of the issue of privatization. Raymond Vernon, ed., *The Promise of Privatization: A Challenge for American Foreign Policy* (New York: Council on Foreign Relations, 1988), has useful case studies on privatization.

Peter N. S. Lee, *Industrial Management and Economic Reform in China, 1949–1984* (New York: Oxford University Press, 1987), presents a systematic analysis of China's industrial reform. Tidrick and Chen (note 25), Lee (note 26), and Robert F. Dernberger, "Reforms in China: Implications for U. S. Policy," *American Economic Review* 79 (May 1989), 21–25, have thorough discussions of China's difficulties with industrial reform. Riskin (note 23) is a good survey of China's political economy.

NAME AND AUTHOR INDEX

The pages for bibliographical items are in boldface.

SUBJECT INDEX

Highlighted terms are defined or identified on pages designated in boldface.